Introduction to Comp

Northey & Leigh's

Introduction to Company Law

Fourth Edition

L. H. LEIGH BA, LLB, PhD
Professor of Criminal Law at the University of London
(London School of Economics)

V. H. JOFFE MA, LLB
of the Middle Temple, Barrister at Law.
Formerly Lecturer in Law at the London School of Economics

D. GOLDBERG LLM, QC

London
Butterworths
1987

United Kingdom	Butterworth & Co (Publishers) Ltd, 88 Kingsway, LONDON WC2B 6AB and 61A North Castle Street, EDINBURGH EH2 3LJ
Australia	Butterworths Pty Ltd, SYDNEY, MELBOURNE, BRISBANE, ADELAIDE, PERTH, CANBERRA and HOBART
Canada	Butterworths. A division of Reed Inc., TORONTO and VANCOUVER
New Zealand	Butterworths of New Zealand Ltd, WELLINGTON and AUCKLAND
Singapore	Butterworth & Co (Asia) Pte Ltd, SINGAPORE
South Africa	Butterworth Publishers (Pty) Ltd, DURBAN and PRETORIA
USA	Butterworths Legal Publishers, ST PAUL, Minnesota, SEATTLE, Washington, BOSTON, Massachusetts, AUSTIN, Texas and D & S Publishers, CLEARWATER, Florida

© Butterworth & Co (Publishers) Ltd 1987

All rights reserved. No part of this publication may be reproduced or transmitted in any form or by any means, including photocopying and recording, without the written permission of the copyright holder, application for which should be addressed to the publisher. Such written permission must also be obtained before any part of this publication is stored in a retrieval system of any nature.

This book is sold subject to the Standard Conditions of Sale of Net Books and may not be re-sold in the UK below the net price fixed by Butterworths for the book in our current catalogue.

British Library Cataloguing in Publication Data

Northey, J.F.
   Northey & Leigh's introduction to company law.—4th ed.
   1. Corporation law—Great Britain
   I. Title II. Leigh, L.H. III. Joffe, V.H.
   IV. Goldberg, D.
   344.106'66   KD2079

   ISBN Hardcover 0 406 63106 9
         Softcover 0 406 63107 7

Printed and bound in Great Britain by
Biddles Ltd, Guildford and King's Lynn

Preface

Recent years have seen sweeping changes in company law and in related areas of the law about which the student must know something. Companies legislation has been consolidated into a core statute, the Companies Act 1985, and a small constellation of related enactments dealing with insider trading, directors' disqualification, insolvency, and financial services, for the Financial Services Act 1986 touches upon both initial flotation and take-overs. In addition, the courts have been busy, particularly in relation to *ultra vires* and to minority shareholders' rights.

These changes have meant a good deal of re-writing, apart from ensuring that section references are to the appropriate statute. We have rewritten the chapters on insolvency and take-overs, have dealt with developments in *ultra vires,* and have in response to the kindly criticism of colleagues, expanded the treatment of minority shareholders' remedies. In general, we have brought the text up to date as at the end of March 1987, but where possible we have added references to legislation and case law arising after this date.

We hope that this edition, like its predecessors, will be found to be a useful guide to the basic principles of company law. We wish to express our thanks as always to colleagues for their helpful suggestions, to Mrs Susan Hunt for secretarial assistance, and to our publishers for preparing the tables and index, and generally for their assistance in the preparation of this edition.

L. H. Leigh
V. H. Joffe
D. Goldberg

Contents

Preface   v
Table of Statutes   xiii
List of Cases   xxvii

Chapter 1   Introduction   1
History   1

Chapter 2   Incorporation and its Consequences   8
Incorporation   8
The Consequences of Incorporation   18

Chapter 3   Promotions and Formation   30
The Promoter   30
Preliminary Agreements   34
Registration of a Company   36
Certificate of Incorporation   38
Registered Office   38
Certificate re doing Business   38

Chapter 4   Financing the Company   41
Methods of Raising Funds   41
Underwriting   42
Disclosure   44

Chapter 5   Investor Protection   51
Remedies for Mis-statements in or Omissions
    from a Prospectus   51
Restriction on the Sale of Shares and Debentures   59
Criminal Liabilities   60

Chapter 6   Memorandum of Association   70
General   70

viii *Contents*

Contents of Memorandum 70
Alteration of the Memorandum 97

Chapter 7 Articles of Association 101
General 101
Contents of the Articles 102
The Effect of the Memorandum and Articles 105
Alteration of the Articles 110

Chapter 8 Directors and Officers 121
General 121
Appointment 122
Registration, Retirement and Dismissal 123
Disqualification 127
Defective Appointments and Acting after Disqualification 130
Register of Directors and Interests 131
Remuneration 131
Loans and Similar Transactions to or in Favour of Directors 133
Officers 141
The Board of Directors 145
Status and Function of Individual Directors 148

Chapter 9 Accounts, Directors' Report and Audit 162
The Accounts 162
Directors' Report 179
Audit 180

Chapter 10 Directors' Duties 189
The Relationship of Directors to the Company 189
Duties of Care and Skill 189
Duties of Loyalty and Good Faith 191
Competing Directorates 201
Nominee Directors 201
Contracts with the Company 203
Secret Benefits 206
Directors' Contracts of Employment and Substantial Property
    Transactions with Directors 206
Option Dealings 211
Insider Dealing 211

Chapter 11 Enforcement of Directors' Duties 220
Proceedings by the Company 220
Relief from Liability 226
Statutory Protection 227

Contents   ix

Chapter 12   Disclosure of Interests in the Securities of the Company   251
Directors' Interests   251
Other Interests   253
Concert Parties   255
Register of Interests in Shares   257

Chapter 13   Investigations and Inquiries   258
Inspections and Investigations: the Powers   258

Chapter 14   Meetings and Proceedings   271
The Annual General Meeting   273
Extraordinary General Meetings   273
Proxies   276
Proceedings at Meetings   277
Polls   279
Resolutions   280
Minutes   283
Unanimous Acquiescence   283

Chapter 15   Shares   286
Nature of Shares   286
Issue of Shares   286
Members   291
Classes of Shares   293
Variation of Class Rights   305
Calls   308

Chapter 16   Registration, Transfer and Transmission of Shares   310
Register of Members   310
Share Certificates   313
Share Warrants   319
Transfer   319
Transmission   330

Chapter 17   Capital   332
Payment for Share Capital   333
Payment for Assets from Subscribers   336
Relief from Liability   337
Maintenance of Capital   339
Forfeiture and Surrender   340
Lien   341
Variation of Capital   342

x Contents

Issue of Shares at a Premium   343
Reduction of Capital   349
Distribution of Profits and Assets   353
Liability of Directors   358

Chapter 18   Borrowing Powers   359
Provisions of Memorandum   359
Charges   361
Debentures   367
Floating Charges   369
Remedies of Debenture Holders   373

Chapter 19   The Taxation of Companies   379
Corporation Tax   379
Income Tax   389
Set-off of Income Tax Against Corporation Tax   396
Close Companies   396
Capital Gains Tax   400
Groups   403
Inheritance Tax   404
Factors Influencing the Decision Whether or not to Incorporate   405

Chapter 20   Company Reconstruction and Mergers   407
Schemes of Compromise or Arrangement   407
Reconstructions in a Liquidation   415
Take-over Bids   420
Compensation to Directors for Loss of Office   435
Taxation, Reconstructions, Mergers and Take-overs   439

Chapter 21   Winding up and Administration Orders   441
General   441
Winding up by the Court   441
Voluntary Winding up   448
Contributories   451
The Liquidator   452
The Liquidation Committee   458
Proof of Debts   459
Assets of the Company   460
Order of Payment of Debts   460
Transactions at an Undervalue and Preferences   463
Extortionate Credit Transactions   465
Floating Charges   466
Disclaimer of Onerous Property   467

Rights of Execution Creditors   468
Dispositions of Property   469
Stay of Actions   470
Criminal Offences   471
Fraudulent and Wrongful Trading   471
Public Examinations   474
Civil Remedies   475
Commencement of Winding up   475
Dissolution   476
Alternatives to Winding up   478
Voluntary Arrangements   478
Administration Orders   480

Index   487

Table of Statutes

In the following Table references to *Statutes* are to Halsbury's Statutes of England (Fourth Edition) showing the volume and page where the annotated text of the Act will be found.

	PAGE
Air Corporations Act 1967	
Sch 1	201
Air Corporations Act 1969 (4 *Statutes* 58)	
s 4	201
Sch 2	201
Arbitration Act 1950 (2 *Statutes* 535)	
s 31	416
Banking Act 1979 (4 *Statutes* 405)	6
s 1	10
(4)	372
18	442
34	372
36	72
50	442
Banking Act 1987	
s 35	60
Bills of Exchange Act 1908	
s 82	20
Bills of Sale Act (1878) (Amendment) Act 1882 (5 *Statutes* 421)	
s 17	361
Bubble Companies etc. (1825)	4
Business Names Act 1985	
s 1	72
2	72
(2), (3)	73
3, 4	72
5, 7	73
Capital Allowances Act 1968	
s 1–17, 73	389
74	389
(3)	395
Capital Gains Tax Act 1979	
s 4	387
12	402

	PAGE
Capital Gains Tax Act 1979—*contd*	
s 19(3)	401
29	387
29A	400
32	383
35	402
62, 63	400
77	393, 401
78–88	401
123	400
126	400
Chartered Companies Act 1837 (8 *Statutes* 5)	4
Cinematograph Films Act 1938	22
Coal Industry Nationalisation Act 1946	
s 25	298
Companies Act 1862	5, 415
Companies Act 1900	5
Companies Act 1948	6, 37, 333, 347
s 10	118
15	79
27	435
28	10, 328
54	208, 235, 430, 431
98(2)	365
143	118
190	134
191	129, 189
192	130, 424
(1), (2)	423
209	22, 115, 399
Sch 1	37, 71, 100, 102
Table A	146, 148, 277, 283, 284, 321

xiv Table of Statutes

Companies Act 1948—contd
  Sch 1—contd
    Pt I
      art 10 114
        79 123
        130 180
Companies Act 1967 (19 Statutes
  70) 6
  s 2 11
    13(1) 183
    15–24 179
    43 177
Companies Act 1976 .... 6, 7
Companies Act 1980 .... 6, 37
  s 74 195
  Sch 3
    para 38 162
  Sch 4 328
Companies Act 1981 ..... 6, 166, 179
  s 71 .... 243, 259
    (1) 253
  Sch 4 7
Companies Act 1985 (8 Statutes
  107) 461
  s 1(1) 37, 75
    (2)(a), (b) 10
    (3) 36
  2 .... 36, 80
    (1)(a) 70
    (b), (c) 71
    (2) 38, 71
    (3) 71
    (5)(a) 71, 96, 97, 332
    (b), (c) 71
    (6) 71
  4 .... 70, 97, 98, 99, 100
  5 .... 51, 99
    (2)(a), (b) 99
    (3)–(6), (8) 99
  7 102
    (1) 37, 103
    (2) 103
  8 .... 10, 71, 102, 103
    (2) 37, 103
  9 .... 110, 111, 117, 118
  10 .... 37, 38, 105, 143
    (6) 71
  11 37
  12 37
    (3) 37
  13 .... 37, 143
    (1) 38
    (5) 122

Companies Act 1985—contd
  s 13(7) 38
  14 .... 105, 106, 107, 109
  16 111
  17 .... 98, 100
    (9) 354
  19, 20 102
  22 .... 9, 291
    (2) 291
  23 292
    (1)–(4) 435
  24 .... 26, 96, 337
    (6) 336
  25 .... 12, 36, 70
  26 .... 37, 337
    (1) 71
    (d), (e) 71
    (2) 72
  27 .... 70, 74
  28 97
    (1)–(3) 73
  29 72
  30, 31 74
  32 73
  33, 34 70
  35 .... 76, 93, 94, 95, 156, 157,
                              158, 360
    (1), (2) 92
  36 93
    (4) 34, 35, 36
  40 313
  42 .... 38, 98, 105, 123
    (1)(b) 74
  43 .... 11, 451
    (2)(a) 12, 13
    (b) 13
    (c) 12
    (3)(b), (c) 12
  45(2)(a), (b) 13
    (3)–(5) 13
    (6) 14
  46 12
  47 14
    (5) 14
  48 14
  49 .... 17, 18, 141, 451
    (8) 18
  51 .... 17, 451
    (2), (3) 18
  52(2)(b) 140
  53(2) 15
  54 16
    (1) 13

Table of Statutes xv

Companies Act 1985—contd
- s 54(2), (4) 16
- (5)–(7) 17
- 55 .... 15, 16, 57
- 56 33
- 58 54
- 59 303
- 67 .... 57, 58
- 70 60
- 77 18
- 80 305
- (2)–(5), (7), (10), (11) 287
- 81 10
- 84 .... 49, 50
- 85 .... 50, 105, 350, 373
- (2), (3) 50
- 88 .... 33, 293
- (2)(a) 50
- (b) 291
- (3) 50
- 89 289
- (1) 288, 289
- (2)–(4) 288
- 90(1)–(6) 288
- 91(1), (2) 288
- 94 288
- (7) 288
- 95(1), (2) 288, 289
- (3), (4), (6) 289
- 96(1)–(3) 289
- 97 .... 43, 418
- 99(1), (2) 334
- 100 .... 104, 340
- 101 .... 39, 291, 293
- (2) 335
- 102 .... 291, 293
- (1), (3), (5), (6) 335
- 103 .... 291, 293, 337
- (1) 335, 418
- (2) 335
- (3) 335, 418
- (4)–(6) 335
- 104 .... 336, 337
- (1), (3) 336
- (4) 337
- 105 337
- 106 .... 291, 334
- 108(1), (4), (6) 336
- 110 .... 337, 416, 418
- (2), (3) 337
- 111(4) 416
- 112 .... 334, 335
- 113(2)(a), (b) 338
- (4), (5) 338

Companies Act 1985—contd
- s 113(6), (7) 339
- 114, 115 334
- 116 333
- 117 .... 38, 442
- (1) 10
- (3), (4), (6), (7) 39
- (8) 26, 40
- 118 333
- 120 .... 97, 332
- 121 .... 97, 304
- (2)(c) 343
- (d) 342
- 122 304
- 123(1) 343
- 124 97
- (a), (b) 343
- 125 .... 97, 272
- (2) 305, 306
- (3) 306
- (a), (c) 305
- (6) 306
- (7) 305, 306
- 126 97
- 127 111
- (1)–(3) 306
- (4) 307
- 129(1)–(3) 294
- 130 .. 333, 343, 345, 346, 347, 348
- 131 .... 171, 345, 346, 348
- (5), (8) 348
- 132 .... 345, 346, 347, 348
- (7) 347
- 133 .... 345, 346
- 134 .... 345, 346, 349
- 135 .... 97, 305, 340, 349, 407, 409, 415
- 136 ...... 340, 350, 407, 409, 415
- 137 .... 350, 407, 409, 415
- 138 .... 164, 353, 407, 409, 415
- 139 .... 16, 407, 409, 415
- (3) 16
- 140 .... 353, 407, 409, 415
- 141 .... 407, 409, 415
- 142 339
- 143 .... 17, 339, 341, 435
- (3), (4) 340
- 144(1)–(3) 339
- 146 .... 11, 340, 341
- (2) 283, 340
- (4) 340
- 149 340
- (2) 16
- 150 341

xvi Table of Statutes

Companies Act 1985—contd

	PAGE
s 150(1), (3), (4)	341
151	17, 229, 235, 329, 430, 431, 433, 436
(1), (2)	430
152	430
153	430
(1)	430, 431, 432
(2)	430
(3)(a), (b)	431, 432
(4)	432
(5)	433
155(1), (3)	432
(6)	433
156	430
157	430, 433
158	430, 433
159	300, 392, 432
(2)	300
(3)	301
160	432
(1), (4)	301
161	393, 432
162	432
163	432
(2)	301
164	302, 432
(2)–(7)	301
165	301, 432
166	302, 432
(6)	432
168	302, 432
169	432
170	333, 432
171	302, 432
172	432
173	432
(1), (2)	302
174	432
175	302, 432
176	303, 432
177	303, 432
178	432
(4), (5)	303
179–181	432
182(1)	319
183	369
(1)	325
(3)	331
(4)	326
(5)	322
184	330
185	313

Companies Act 1985—contd

	PAGE
s 185(4)	313
186	313
187	330
188	319
191	368
192	372
193	372
194	373
196	372
198	254
(1)(a), (b)	253
(2), (3)	253
(4)	254
199	254
201(2)	253
202(1), (2)–(5)	254
203	254
(2)–(4)	255
204	255
(2)(a)	255, 425
(b)	255
(3), (4)	255
(6)	256
205(1)–(5)	256
206(1), (2)	256
(3)(a), (b)	257
(4)	257
207	257
(2)(a)–(d)	257
208	253
209	253, 268
210	248, 253
211(7), (9)	257
212	264, 268
(4), (5), (6)	268
214	268
215	269
(6)	269
216	269
221	162, 163, 355
(4)	163
222(4)	163
224	163
(4)	163
225, 226	166
227	163, 164, 165, 209, 273
228	165, 166, 167
229	26, 165
230	165, 167
231	26, 170
232	172, 174, 203, 205
234	176

Table of Statutes xvii

Companies Act 1985—contd

s 235	164, 179, 273
(2)	179
(3)	473
236	178, 184
(1)	184
237	176, 184, 185, 187
(4)	185
238(1), (3), (4)	166
240	179
241	164, 178, 184, 273
(4)	96
242	164
(3), (4)	164
246	179
247	176
(2)	176
248	176
(2)	176
249	176
250	176
251	176
252	178, 180
254	178
255	178
(4)	178
256	163, 180
257	165, 167
258	165, 166, 167
259–262	167
263(1)–(3)	354
(5)	356
264	12, 356
(3), (4)	357
265	356
(1)(a), (b)	356
(6)	356
266	356
268	354, 356
269	354
270	357
271	178, 357
275	354
276	355
277	357
(2)	358
281	355
282	10, 122, 123
283	142
(4)	142
284	143
285	130, 158
286	143

Companies Act 1985—contd

s 286(2)	143
287	38
(2)	38
288	131
(2)	123
289	131
290	131, 143
291	130, 131
(2)	319
292	10
293	10, 124, 130, 275
(5)	124
302	123
303	119, 124, 125, 242, 243, 281
(2)	275
(3)	438
(5)	126, 272, 437
304	124
306	451
307	97, 451
309(1)	193
(2)	194
310	142, 188, 202, 236
312	132
313	133
(1), (2)	436
314	133
(1)–(5)	436
315	133, 436
316	133
(1)–(3)	437
317	203, 204, 205
(2)	204
(3)	**204**
(6), (7)	204
(8)	122, 205
318	205, 437
(5)	437
(6)	122, 205
(8), (11)	437
318	131
319	119, 126, 203, 207, 437
(1), (2)	207, 208
(4)–(6)	208
(7)(a), (b)	207
320	203, 210, 211
(1)	208, 209
(2)	209
321	203, 209
(2)	210, 211
(3)	210
322	203, 208

xviii Table of Statutes

Companies Act 1985—contd

s 322(1) 209
 (2), (3) 210
 (5) 211
 (6), (9) 210
323 .... 203, 211
324 .... 251, 252
 (2)(c) 251
 (d) 252
325 131
328 252
 (7) 253
329 252
330 ... **133**, 136, 138, 140, 141, 172,
 203, 204
 (2) 134, 136
 (b), (c) 140
 (3) 135, 136
 (4) 136
 (5) 133
 (6), (7) 136
331 .... 134, 175
 (3) 135
 (5) 137
 (6) 140
 (7) 135
332 139
333, 334 140
335 139
336(a), (b) 140
337 136
 (3) 136, 137
338 137
 (1) 138
 (3), (4), (6) 137, 138
339 .... 137, 138
340 137
 (4) 138
341(1) 140
 (2), (4) 141
342 135
 (5), (6) 177
343 .... 175, 176
344 .... 173, 174
345 .... 137, 138, 139
346 .... 133, 204, 213
 (2) 133, 134
 (3)–(5) 133
348 74
349 74
 (3), (4) 75
350 74
351 75

Companies Act 1985—contd

s 351(3) 38
352, 354–356 310
359 .... 292, 311
360 .... 311, 312, 329
361, 362 312
363 162
 (7) 162
365 145
366 273
 (2) 273
367 .... 271, 273
368 273
369 .... 274, 278
 (1) 278
370 277
 (4) 278
 (5), (6) 279
371 274
372 276
373 280
 (2) 276
374 .... 276, 280
375 292
376 .... 275, 277
377(3) 277
378 .... 111, 281, 415
 (1), (2) 280
379 .... 275, 281
 (1) 280
380 118
 (1), (2) 282
 (4)(e) 74
381 282
382 283
384 .... 181, 273
 (2)–(5) 181
385 .... 180, 181
386 182
387 .... 183, 185
388 .... 182, 183
 (1) 181, 275
389 .... 182, 183
 (2), (6), (7) 183
 (9) 184
390, 391 .... 182, 274
392 185
395 .... 361, 362
396(1)(c), (d) 362
397 364
398 362
400 363
401 364

Companies Act 1985—contd

	PAGE
s 401(2)	365
402, 403	365
404	362, 365, 366
405	365, 374
406–408	367
425	18, 305, 351, 407, 408, 409, 411, 415, 417, 418, 454, 480, 485
(1)	407, 408, 410
(2)	410, 411
(3)	414
(6)	407, 414
426	407, 411
(2)	411
427	97, 407, 414
(3)	414
(e)	414
(6)	414
428	22, 117, 409, 410, 415, 421, 425
(1), (3)–(5), (8)	425
429	22, 409, 410, 415, 420, 421, 427
(1), (2)	425
(3)–(8)	426
430	22, 409, 410, 415, 421
(1), (2)–(6)	425, 426
(7)	425
(8)–(10)	426
430A(1)	426, 427
(2)–(7)	427
430B	427
430C(1)	426, 427
(2), (3)	427
(4)	426, 427
(5)	427
430D(2)–(7)	425
430E	427, 428
(1), (4)–(6), (8)	425
430F	425
431	260, 261, 263, 264
(4)	260
432	260, 261, 266
(1), (2), (3)	261
433	261
(2)	263
434	262
(3), (5)	263
435	262
(2)	262
436	263
437	443

Companies Act 1985—contd

	PAGE
s 437(1)–(3)	263
439	263
(6)	264
440	249, 443
441	263, 267
442	260, 261, 264, 268, 269
(3)	264
443(2)–(4)	264
444	264
445	265
446	260, 261, 269
447	259, 443
(1)	258
(2)–(6), (8)	259
448	443
449	259
450, 451	260
452	260, 265
454	269
(1)–(3)	265
455	269
456	269, 270
(1), (3)	265
457	265, 269
458	473
459	17, 97, 237, 238, 243, 244, 245, 246, 247, 249, 350, 354
(1), (2)	245
460	245
461	97, 247
(2)	247
(c)	223
(d)	245
(3)	111
462	366
582	432
614	377
630	142
651	476, 477
652	476
(1)–(4), (6)	477
653	476
(1), (2)	477
654, 656	478
685, 688	14
705, 711	38
713	162
714	71
719(1)–(4)	194
722	283
723	313
725	124

xx Table of Statutes

Companies Act 1985—contd
s 727 .... 142, 188, 236, 237
735 414
736 .... 26, 165, 166, 435
739 208
741 122
742 354
743 432
744 .... 58, 141, 435, 467, 471
Sch 1 37
Sch 3 32
  para 10 33
Sch 4 ... 164, 165, 166, 167, 171, 179, 180
  Pt I
    Section A
      para 1, 2 167
  Pt II
    Section A (para 9–15) 168
      para 10–15 168
    Section B (para 16-28) 168
    Section C (para 19–34) 168
      para 31, 33, 34 169
  Pt III (para 37–58)
    para 35–40 169
         41 .... 169, 373
         42–51 169
         53–57 170
  Pt V (para 71–74) 169
  Pt VII (para 76–95)
    para 77 355
         90 168
         91 354
Sch 5
  Pt I (para 1–6) 26
    para 4, 6 170
  Pt II (para 7–13)
    para 7, 9–11 171
  Pt IV
    para 20 .... 170, 172
  Pt V 172
Sch 6 .... 173, 174, 205
  Pt I
    para 1 173
         2 .... 172, 173
         3 174
         4 175
         5 .... 173, 174
         9 173
         11 174
  Pt II 174
    para 16 175

Companies Act 1985—contd
Sch 6—contd
  Pt III 175, 176
  Sch 7 .... 179, 184
  Pt I 179
    para 3 .... 3, 180
         5, 7 180
  Pt II 180
Sch 8
  Pt I 11
    para 8 177
Sch 9 ... 165, 166, 167, 171, 179, 180, 184
Sch 13 213
  Pt I
    para 1 252
         3 276
Sch 14 312
Companies Clauses Consolidation
  Act 1845 (8 Statutes 21) 416
Companies (Consolidation) Act
  1908 5
Companies Consolidation (Consequential Provisions) Act 1985
  s 1 .... 36, 442
    2 .... 14, 15, 36, 283
    (1) 14
    (6) 15
    3 .... 14, 15, 36
    4 .... 15, 36
    (4), (5) 15
    5(2) 14
    6 341
    9 333
    12 346
Companies (Floating Charges and
  Receivers) (Scotland) Act
  1972 6
Company Directors' Disqualification Act 1986
  s 1, 2 127
    4–6, 9 128
    10 129
    11 128
Company Securities (Insider Dealing) Act 1985 .... 6, 211, 259, 360
  s 1 .... 212, 213, 216, 217, 218, 219
    (1)–(3) 214
    (4), (6)–(8) 215
    2 .... 212, 217, 218, 219
    (1), (2) 215
    (3) 216
    (4) 215

Table of Statutes xxi

Company Securities (Insider Dealing) Act 1985—*contd*
s 3 .... 217, 219
　(1)(a), (b) 216
　　(c) 217
　4 .... 212, 217, 218, 219
　5 .... 218, 219
　7 216
　8 219
　　(3) 219
　9 213
　10 212
　11 213
　12 .... 213, 217
　13(1) 212
　　(2) 212, 213
　　(4) **217**, 218
　　(5) 218
Employment Protection (Consolidation) Act 1978 (16 *Statutes* 381) 438
Exchange Control Act 1947 259
　s 10 .... 305, 369
Fair Trading Act 1973 6
　s 64 407
Family Law Reform Act 1969 (6 *Statutes* 213)
　s 1 292
Finance Act 1940
　s 44, 56 20
Finance Act 1963
　s 55 440
Finance Act 1965
　s 46 380
　74 397
Finance Act 1969
　s 28 397
　Sch 9 397
Finance Act 1971
　s 40–50 389
　Sch 8 386
Finance Act 1972
　s 84 .... 389, 390
　　(3) 391
　　(4) 389
　86 390
　　(1) 391
　　(3) 394
　87(5) 391
　88 .... 391, 394, 395
　89 .... 391, 395
　　(3) 395
　90 .... 391, 395

Finance Act 1972—*contd*
　s 95(1)–(4) 380
　107(1), (4) 381
　Sch 16
　　para 1 .... 398, 399
　　2, 3, 3A 399
　　4 .... 399, 400
　　5 .... 398, 399
　　8 .... 398, 399
　　9, 10, 12, 12A 398
　　13 399
　Sch 20
　　para 5 396
　Sch 22
　　para 8 392
Finance Act 1973
　s 28 403
　30, 31 .... 389, 403
　32 403
　Sch 12 403
Finance (No. 2) Act 1975
　s 34 394
　43(1) 389
Finance Act 1976
　s 38 385
　72(8) 122
Finance Act 1977
　s 48 385
Finance Act 1978
　s 31 389
Finance Act 1980 .... 398, 399
　s 38, 39, 41 383
Finance Act 1981
　s 36 389
　　(2) 395
　38(2), (4) 385
Finance Act 1982
　s 23 380
　53, 54 393
　60(2) 391
　Sch 9 393
Finance Act 1984
　s 52 390
Finance Act 1985
　s 69 402
　　(5) 402
　Sch 20
　　para 1, 6–71 402
Finance Act 1986
　s 17 389
　64(1), (3) 440
　77 440
　　(3)(a)–(h) 440
Finance Act 1987 ...... 380, 396, 402

xxii Table of Statutes

	PAGE
Financial Services Act 1986	.6, 32, 49, 60, 61, 123
s 6	217
35, 42, 44	421
72, 94, 105	443
Pt IV (ss 142–157)	44
s 142	48
143	44, 48
144, 145	48
146, 147	44, 48
148, 149	48
150	45, 58
151	45, 52, 58
(2)	45
154	52
Pt V (ss 158–171)	42, 44
s 159	45
160	42, 45
161, 162	45
163	45
(1), (3)	46
164	46
166	52, 58
(1)	46
167(1)	46, 58
(2)–(6)	47
170, 171	47
171	52
177	219
196	432
(1)–(5)	432
198	443
212(3)	43
Sch 12	420, 421, 425
Sch 16	
para 16	43
Income and Corporation Taxes Act 1970	
s 53	396
129	382
130	383
177(1)	386, 387
(2)	386, 387, 395
(3)–(5)	386
(6)–(8)	387
178(1), (2)	387
180	389
232	389, 390
233(1)	393
(2)	391, 392, 439
(3)	394
234(1), (2)	392
235	393

	PAGE
Income and Corporation Taxes Act 1970—contd	
s 237(1)	392
238(1), (3), (4)	380
239	394
240(5)	396
243(1)	380
243(3)	380, 382
245(6)	381
247(1)	380, 382
(2), (3)	381
(7)	381
248	395
(1)	439
(2)	385, 391, 439
(3), (4)	384
(5)	385
(6)	385
249	384
250(1)–(3), (6)	382
251(2)	391, 439
254	398
(1), (2)	395
255	396, 398
256	389, 403
(1), (6)	403
257	403
258(5), (8)	403
259–262	403
265(2), (3)	382
267	401
272–274, 278, 278A	404
282(1)	396
283	397
(3)	397
284	397
(2)	397
286(1)–(3), (5), (7)	397
287	398
287A	397
302(2)	396, 397
(6)	396
303(1), (3), (4)	396
304	395
(1), (5)	384
306	395
354–358	466
483	388
(1)	388
484(1)	388
527(1)	382
Income Tax Act 1952	
s 184	391

Table of Statutes xxiii

	PAGE
Inheritance Tax Act 1984	
s 3A, 4, 94–96	404
97, 98	404, 405
103, 161	404
202	405
Insolvency Act 1976 (4 Statutes 653)	
s 9(7)	122
Insolvency Act 1986	123
s 1	408, 432, 478, 480
(1)–(3)	478
2	408, 432, 478, 480
(2)–(4)	479
3	408, 432, 478, 480
(1)–(3)	479
4	408, 432, 478, 480
(1)–(4), (6)	479
5	408, 432, 478, 480
(1)–(4)	480
6	408, 432, 478, 480
(1)–(5), (7)	479
7	408, 432, 451, 478, 480
(2), (3)	480
(4)	480
(b)	442
8	451
(1)–(4)	481
9	478, 480
(1)	481
(2)(a), (b)	481
(3)(b)	481
(5)	481
10	478, 480, 481
11	478, 480
(1)–(3)	481
12	478, 480, 481
13	478, 480
(1)–(3)	482
14	478, 480
(1)–(4)	482
(5), (6)	483
15	478, 480
(1)–(3)	482
(4), (5), (7)	483
16	303, 478, 480
17	478, 480
(1)	482
(2), (3)	483
18	19, 478, 480
(1)–(5)	485
19	478, 480

	PAGE
Insolvency Act 1986—contd	
s 19(1)	482
(2)	485
(3)–(5)	486
20	478, 480
(1)–(3)	486
21	478, 480
(1)–(6)	483
22	478, 480
(1)–(4)	483
23	478, 480
(1)–(3)	484
24	478, 480
(1)–(4)	484
(5)–(7)	485
25	478, 480
(1)–(4), (6)	484
26	478, 480, 484
27	478, 480
(1)–(4), (6)	485
29(2)	481
52–55	367
72(1)	443
73	441
74	293, 296
(1)–(3)	451
(2)(f)	452
75(1)	451
(2)(a), (b)	452
(2)(c)	451
76	442
77	18, 451
79	452
80–82	452
84	281, 283
(1)(a)–(c)	448
(3)	448
85(1), (2)	448
86	475
87(1)	453
88	469
89(1)–(4)	449
90	449
91	454
92	457
93	456
94	457, 476
(1)	476
(3)	457, 476
95(1)–(4)	457
96	457
97(1)	449
98(1)–(3), (6)	449

Table of Statutes

Insolvency Act 1986—contd

	PAGE
s 99(1)(a)–(c)	450
(2)	450
100	454
101	455, 458
102	457
104	457
105	456
106	456, 476
(3)	457, 476
(4)	476
107	450, 454, 463
108(1), (2)	457
109	456
110	415, 416, 417, 418, 419, 454
(1), (2)	415
(3)(b)	415
(4)	415
(6)	419
111	104, 415
(2)	415
112	416, 463, 468, 470, 475
113	455
114	453
116	461
117	441
122	238, 419
(1)	442, 446
(a)	443, 446
(b)–(f)	446
(g)	25, 39, 446
123	419, 442, 466
124	442
(2), (3)	442
(4)	443
(5)	444
125(1)	448
(2)	238, 448
126	468, 470
127	469
(3)	195
128(1)	468
129(1), (2)	475
130(3)	470
132	474
133(1)–(3)	474
(4)	475
134(1)	475
135	453
136(1), (2)	453
(3), (4)	456
137	453
139	453

Insolvency Act 1986—contd

	PAGE
s 141	455, 459
(2), (3)	459
143(1)	454
145	453
146	456
148	452
149	297, 452
152	297
154	463
163	453
165	408, 453, 454, 469
(2), (3)	455
(4)	455
(a)	452
166	408, 453, 454, 469
(2)	449
(3), (4)	450
(5)	449
(7)	450
167	408, 416, 453, 454, 458
(1)(b)	469
(2), (3)	455
168(2), (4)	455
171(1)–(5)	457
172(2)–(6), (8)	456
174(1)–(6)	456
175	461
(2)(a), (b)	462
176	461, 462
(1)	461
178	467
(3)–(5)	467
(6)	468
179	467
181, 182	467
183	469
(1)–(3)	468
184(1), (2)	468
(3)	**330**, 468
(5)	468
187	194
189(1)–(3)	462
(4)	449, 462
195	445, 455
201	441, 476
202–204	441
205	441, 476
209–211	471
212	456, 458, 475
(1), (3)	475
213	129, 452, 471, 472
(2)	26

Table of Statutes xxv

Insolvency Act 1986—contd	
s 214	129, 452, 473
(1)	474
(2)	473
(3), (4)	474
(6), (7)	473
216	104, 129
218	262
(1), (2)	471
(4)	261, 471
235(3)	453
236	416
238	481
(1)	463
(2)	464
(3)	465
(4), (5)	464
239	481
(2)	464
(3)	465
(4)–(7)	464
240	481
(1)	464
(3)	465
241	465
242, 243	481
244(1), (2)	465
(3), (4)	466
245	481
(1), (3)	466
(4)	467
(5), (6)	466
249	464
251	449
386	461, 479
388, 389	454
390(1), (2)	454
391–398	454
435	464
Sch 4	416, 453, 454
Pt I	455
para 2	408
Pt II, Pt III	452, 455
Sch 6	461
Sch 8	
para 12	459
Insurance Companies Act 1982	259, 360

Insurance Companies Act 1982—contd	
s 53–59	442
79	60
Interpretation Act 1978	
s 6	92
Joint Stock Companies (1844)	4, 105
Joint Stock Companies Act 1856	5, 105
Land Charges Act 1972	
s 3	362
Land Compensation Act 1961 (9 Statutes 168)	22
Larceny Act 1861	
s 84	61
Law of Property Act 1925	
s 56	110
74	158
103	373
Limited Partnerships Act 1907	2, 8
Merchant Shipping Act 1894	29
s 502	27, 159
503	161
Misrepresentation Act 1967	
s 1	55
2(1)	33, 56, 57
(2), (3)	56
Partnership Act 1890	8
Prevention of Fraud (Investments) Act 1939	68
Prevention of Fraud (Investments) Act 1958	6, 60
s 14	420, 421
17	421
Registration of Business Names Act 1916	73
Stamp Act 1891	
s 112	440
Statute of Limitations (1623)	459
Stock Transfer Act 1963	6
Theft Act 1968 (12 Statutes 514)	44
s 15(1), (4)	61
19	52, 61
(1)	61
Theft Act 1978 (12 Statutes 780)	44
Trading Stamps Act 1964	
s 1	10

List of Cases

Page references printed in **bold** type indicate where the facts of a case are set out.

A

	PAGE
A and BC Chewing Gum Ltd, Re, Topps Chewing Gum Inc v Coakley (1975)	242, **447**
ABC Coupler and Engineering Co Ltd (No 2), Re (1962)	443
Aaron's Reefs Ltd v Twiss (1896)	54, 55
Abbey Malvern Wells Ltd v Ministry of Local Government and Planning (1951)	25
Aberdeen Rly Co v Blaikie Bros (1854)	**192**
Addlestone Linoleum Co, Re (1887)	55
Aga Estate Agencies Ltd, Re (1986)	**477**
Agra and Masterman's Bank v Leighton (1866)	416
Agriculturist Cattle Insurance Co, Re, Baird's Case (1870)	4
Airedale Co-operative Worsted Manufacturing Society Ltd, Re (1933)	88
Airlines Airspares Ltd v Handley Page Ltd (1970)	**376**
Akerhielm v De Mare (1959)	57
Alabama, New Orleans, Texas and Pacific Junction Rly Co, Re (1891)	412
Alexander v Automatic Telephone Co (1900)	228, 230, **309**
Allen v Gold Reefs of West Africa Ltd (1900)	111, **112**, 117
Allen v Hyatt (1914)	191
Allied Produce Co Ltd, Re (1967)	443
Amalgamated Investment and Property Co Ltd, Re (1985)	460
Amalgamated Syndicate, Re (1897)	446
American Home Assurance Co v Tjmond Properties Ltd (1986)	79
American Pioneer Leather Co, Re (1918)	447
Anchor Insurance Co, Re, ex p Badenoch (1870)	419
Anciens Établissements Panhard et Levassor, SA des v Panhard Levassor Motor Co Ltd (1901)	74
Anderson v James Sutherland (Peterhead) Ltd (1941)	159
Andrews v Gas Meter Co (1897)	101, **104**, 293
Andrews v Mockford (1896)	57
Anglesea Colliery Co, Re (1866)	452
Anglo-Austrian Printing and Publishing Union, Re, Isaacs' Case (1892)	438
Anglo-Continental Supply Co Ltd, Re (1922)	413, 417, 418
Anglo-Greek Steam Co, Re (1866)	446
Anglo-Moravian Hungarian Junction Rly Co, Re, ex p Watkin (1875)	441
Anglo-Overseas Agencies Ltd v Green (1961)	77, 86, 87
Angostura Bitters (Dr J G B Siegert & Sons) Ltd v Kerr (1933)	101

xxviii *List of Cases*

	PAGE
Anns v Merton London Borough Council (1978)	59
Arenson v Casson Beckman Rutley & Co (1977)	59, 325
Argentum Reductions (UK) Ltd, Re (1975)	469
Argy Trading Development Co Ltd v Lapid Developments Ltd (1977)	58
Armstrong v Landmark Corpn (1967)	276
Armstrong Whitworth Securites Co Ltd, Re (1947)	459
Armvent Ltd, Re (1975)	447, 448
Arnison v Smith (1889)	55
Arnold (R M) & Co Ltd, Re (1984)	366
Aro Co Ltd, Re (1980)	468, 470
Art Reproduction Co Ltd, Re (1952)	459
Ashbourne Investments Ltd, Re (1978)	265
Ashburton Oil No Liability v Alpha Minerals No Liability (1971)	290
Ashbury v Watson (1885)	96
Ashbury Railway Carriage and Iron Co Ltd v Riche (1875)	**76**, 84, 104
Ashby, Warner & Co Ltd v Simmons (1936)	362
Ashpurton Estates Ltd, Re (1983)	366
Asiatic Banking Corpn, Re, Symons' Case (1870)	292
A-G v Great Eastern Rly Co (1879)	77
Atwool v Merryweather (1867)	**225**, 227
Automatic Self-Cleansing Filter Syndicate Co Ltd v Cuninghame (1906)	147
Ayerst v C & K (Construction) Ltd (1976)	454

B

	PAGE
B v B (1978)	23
BBH (Middletons) Ltd, Re (1970)	476
Badger, Re, Mansell v Viscount Cobham (1905)	359
Baglan Hall Colliery Co, Re (1870)	291
Bagot Pneumatic Tyre Co v Clipper Pneumatic Tyre Co (1901); affd (1902)	35
Bahia and San Francisco Rly Co, Re (1868)	**315**
Bailey, Hay & Co Ltd, Re (1971)	284
Baillie v Oriental Telephone and Electric Co Ltd (1915)	**275**
Bainbridge v Smith (1889)	130
Baku Consolidated Oilfields Ltd, Re (1944)	446
Balkis Consolidated Co v Tomkinson (1893)	316
Bambi Restaurants Ltd, Re (1965)	442, 447
Bamford v Bamford (1968); affd (1970)	85, 147, 148, 196, 235, 271, 284
Bank of Hindustan, China and Japan, Re, Campbell's Case, Hippisley's Case, Alison's Case (1873)	419
Bank of Hindustan, China and Japan Ltd, Re, Higgs's Case (1865)	418
Bank of South Australia v Abrahams (1875)	359
Banque Industrielle de Moscou, Re (1952)	478
Barclays Bank Ltd v Quistclose Investments Ltd (1970)	460
Barclays Bank Ltd v TOSG Trust Fund Ltd (1984)	94
Baring-Gould v Sharpington Combined Pick and Shovel Syndicate (1899)	416
Barleycorn Enterprises Ltd, Re, Mathias and Davies (a firm) v Down (1970)	467
Barnett v South London Tramways Co (1887)	144
Barnett (Augustus) & Son Ltd, Re (1986)	471
Barron v Potter (1914)	271
Barrow v Paringa Mines (1909) Ltd (1909)	418
Barrow Hæmatite Steel Co, Re (1900); on appeal (1901)	352

List of Cases xxix

	PAGE
Barry and Staines Linoleum Ltd, Re (1934)	237
Barry Artists Ltd, Re (1985)	284, 349
Barton v London and North Western Rly Co (1889)	318
Bayswater Trading Co Ltd, Re (1970)	476
Beattie v E and F Beattie Ltd (1938)	108
Beauforte (Jon) (London) Ltd, Re, Applications of Grainger Smith & Co (Builders) Ltd, John Wright & Son (Veneers) Ltd and Lowell Baldwin Ltd (1953)	85, 86, 90, **91**, 93
Bechuanaland Exploration Co v London Trading Bank Ltd (1898)	319, 369
Bede Steam Shipping Co Ltd, Re (1917)	320, 321
Bell v Lever Bros Ltd (1932)	201
Bell Houses Ltd v City Wall Properties Ltd (1966)	**78**, 86
Bellador Silk Ltd, Re (1965)	238
Bellaglade Ltd, Re (1977)	469
Bellerby v Rowland and Marwood's SS Co Ltd (1902)	341, 349, 451
Belmont Finance Corpn Ltd v Williams Furniture Ltd (1979)	29, 160, 433
Belmont Finance Corpn Ltd v Williams Furniture Ltd (No 2) (1980)	208, 434
Bentley-Stevens v Jones (1974)	233, 243
Berkeley Securities (Property) Ltd, Re (1980)	470
Berry v Tottenham Hotspur Football and Athletic Co Ltd (1936)	321
Berry (L G) Investments Ltd v Attwooll (1964)	384
Bersel Manufacturing Co Ltd v Berry (1968)	125, 126
Beswick v Beswick (1965)	110
Birch v Cropper, Re Bridgewater Navigation Co Ltd (1889)	293, 297
Birch v Sullivan (1958)	225

	PAGE
Bird Precision Bellows Ltd, Re (1986)	244, 249
Bisgood v Henderson's Transvaal Estates Ltd (1908)	**417**, 418, 451
Black v Smallwood (1965)	34
Blair Open Hearth Furnace Co Ltd v Reigart (1913)	292
Blériot Manufacturing Air Craft Co Ltd, Re (1916)	241, 446
Bloomenthal v Ford (1897)	**316**
Boardman v Phipps (1967)	199, 200
Bodega Co Ltd, Re (1904)	130
Bold v Brough, Nicholson and Hall Ltd (1964)	126
Bolton (H L) (Engineering) Co Ltd v T J Graham & Sons Ltd (1957)	28, 160, 331
Borax Co, Re, Foster v Borax Co (1901)	370
Borland's Trustee v Steel Bros & Co Ltd (1901)	109, 286, 322
Boschoek Pty Co Ltd v Fuke (1906)	130
Boston Deep Sea Fishing and Ice Co v Ansell (1888)	205
Bradford Banking Co v Briggs & Co (1886)	107, **342**
Brazilian Rubber Plantations and Estates Ltd, Re (1911)	190
Breckinridge Speedway Ltd v R (1967)	86
Briess v Woolley (1954)	191
Brightlife Ltd, Re (1986)	370
Brinsmead (Thomas Edward) & Sons, Re (1897); on appeal (1897)	446
British Airways Board v Parish (1979)	75
British America Nickel Corpn v M J O'Brien Ltd (1927)	308, 410, 412, 413
British Building Stone Co Ltd, Re (1908)	416
British Eagle International Airlines Ltd v Cie Nationale Air France (1975)	450
British Murac Syndicate Ltd v Alperton Rubber Co Ltd (1915)	119, 120, 438
Briton Medical and General Life Association, Re (1888)	312

xxx List of Cases

	PAGE
Broadcasting Station 2 GB (Proprietary) Ltd, Re (1964)	202
Brown v British Abrasive Wheel Co (1919)	112
Bryanston Finance Ltd v de Vries (No 2) (1976)	444
Bryant Investment Co Ltd, Re (1974)	446
Buchanan (Peter) Ltd and Macharg v McVey (1955)	85
Bugle Press Ltd, Re, Re Houses and Estates Ltd (1961)	22, 117, **428**
Building Estates Brickfields Co, Re, Parbury's Case (1896)	316
Bulawayo Market and Offices Co Ltd, Re (1907)	123
Burdett v Standard Exploration Co Ltd (1899)	106
Burdett-Coutts v True Blue (Hannan's) Gold Mine (1899)	418
Burgess v Purchase & Sons (Farms) Ltd (1983)	325
Burkinshaw v Nicolls (1878)	316
Burland v Earle (1902)	31, 33, 111, 220, 230, 231
Burns v Siemens Bros Dynamo Works (1919)	311
Burrows (J) (Leeds) Ltd, Re (1982)	470
Burston Finance Ltd v Speirway Ltd (1974)	363
Burton v Bevan (1908)	50
Burton and Deakin Ltd, Re (1977)	469, 470
Bushell v Faith (1970)	125, 272

C

Caldwell & Co v Caldwell (1916)	351
Caledonia Community Credit Union Ltd v Haldimand Feed Mill Ltd (1974)	85, 86
Calgary and Edmonton Land Co Ltd, Re (1975)	470
Cambrian Mining Co, Re (1882)	416
Camburn Petroleum Products Ltd, Re (1979)	446
Campbell v Paddington Corpn (1911)	90

	PAGE
Campbell v Rofe (1933)	96
Canadian Aero Service v O'Malley (1974)	199
Candler v Crane Christmas & Co (1951)	58
Cane v Jones (1981)	**117**, 118, 284
Capital Finance Co Ltd v Stokes (1969)	363
Caratal (New) Mines Ltd, Re (1902)	282
Cardiff Savings Bank, Re, Marquis of Bute's Case (1892)	190
Carlen v Drury (1812)	221
Carreras Rothmans Ltd v Freeman Mathews Treasure Ltd (1985)	450, 460
Carrier Australasia Ltd v Hunt (1939)	120
Carrington Viyella, Re (1983)	246, 247
Carruth v ICI Ltd (1937)	412
Castell and Brown Ltd, Re, Roper v Castell and Brown Ltd (1898)	371
Castiglione's Will Trusts, Re, Hunter v Mackenzie (1958)	339, 435
Catalinas Warehouses and Mole Co Ltd, Re (1947)	296, 297
Cawley & Co, Re (1889)	319
Central Rly Co of Venezuela (Directors etc) v Kisch (1867)	51, 54
Centrebind Ltd, Re (1966)	450
Chapel House Colliery Co, Re (1883)	446
Chapleo v Brunswick Permanent Benefit Building Society (1881)	89, 260
Charterbridge Corpn Ltd v Lloyds Bank Ltd (1970)	24, 82, **84**, 85, 193, 361
Charterhouse Investment Trust Ltd v Tempest Diesels Ltd (1986)	431
Charterhouse Oil Co Ltd v Beaumont (1967)	109
Chesterfield Catering Co Ltd, Re (1977)	445
Chida Mines Ltd v Anderson (1905)	144

List of Cases xxxi

Christonette International Ltd, Re (1982)	462
Citizens' Life Assurance Co v Brown (1904)	27
City and County Investment Co, Re (1879)	415, 419
City Equitable Fire Insurance Co Ltd, Re (1925)	189, 190, 236, 438, 475
City of Glasgow Bank, Re, Buchan's Case (1879)	331
City of London Insurance Co Ltd, Re (1925)	237
Civica Investments Ltd, Re (1983)	129
Claridge's Patent Asphalte Co Ltd, Re (1921)	237
Claybridge Shipping Co SA, Re (1981)	442
Cleadon Trust Ltd, Re (1939)	144
Clemens v Clemens Bros Ltd (1976)	115, 231, 243
Clifton Place Garage Ltd, Re (1970)	377, 469
Clinch v Financial Corpn (1868)	419
Coalport China Co, Re (1895)	321
Coltness Iron Co v Black (1881)	383
Coltness Iron Co Ltd, Re (1951)	411
Commerical Bank Corpn of India and the East, Re, Jones's Claim (1868)	419
Compagnie de Mayville v Whitley (1896)	221
Company, a, Re (1980); revsd sub nom Re Racal Communications Ltd (1981)	142
Company, a, Re (1983)	238, 240, 244, 246, 247, 248, 249, 442, 444
Company, a, Re (1984)	442
Company, A, Re (1985)	442
Company, a, Re (1986)	225, 244, 444
Company, A, Re (1986)	442
Connors Bros Ltd v Connors (1940)	20
Consolidated Goldfields of New Zealand Ltd, Re (1953)	452
Consolidated South Rand Mines Deep Ltd, Re (1909)	413, 416
Consort Deep Level Gold Mines Ltd, Re, ex p Stark (1897)	43
Continental Oxygen Co, Re, Elias v Continental Oxygen Co (1897)	372
Conway v Petronius Clothing Co Ltd (1978)	162
Cook v Deeks (1916)	198, 199, 200, 225, 228, 230, 231
Cooper (Cuthbert) & Sons Ltd, Re (1937)	242, 447
Cooper (Gerald) Chemicals Ltd, Re (1978)	472
Copal Varnish Co Ltd, Re (1917)	320, 322
Copeman v William Flood & Sons Ltd (1941)	383
Coregrange Ltd, Re (1984)	470
Cornhill Insurance plc v Improvement Services Ltd (1986)	442
Cornish Manures Ltd, Re (1967)	476
Cotman v Brougham (1918)	75, 78, 81
Cotter v National Union of Seamen (1929)	221
Cousins v International Brick Co Ltd (1931)	276, 277
Coxon v Gorst (1891)	477
Craven-Ellis v Canons Ltd (1936)	108, 132
Crown Bank, Re (1890)	77
Curtis's Furnishing Stores Ltd v Freedman (1966)	435
Customs and Excise Comrs v Hedon Alpha Ltd (1981)	237
Cyclists' Touring Club, Re (1907)	98

D

DHN Food Distributors Ltd v London Borough of Tower Hamlets (1975)	22
Dafen Tinplate Co Ltd v Llanelly Steel Co (1907) Ltd (1920)	113

xxxii List of Cases

	PAGE
Daimler Co Ltd v Continental Tyre and Rubber Co (Great Britain) Ltd (1916)	**21**, 144
Daniels v Daniels (1978)	228, **229**
Danish Mercantile Co Ltd v Beaumont (1951)	148
Darby, Re, ex p Brougham (1911)	31
Davey & Co v Williamson & Sons (1898)	372
Davis and Collett Ltd, Re (1935)	239, 241, 447
Dawson v African Consolidated Land Trading Co (1898)	130
Dean v Prince (1954)	325
De Beers Consolidated Mines Ltd v Howe (1906)	24
de Jong (F) & Co Ltd, Re (1946)	296
De La Rue (Thomas) & Co Ltd and Reduced, Re (1911)	350
Dellow v Busby (1942)	29
Derry v Peek (1889)	57, 58
Devlin v Slough Estates Ltd (1983)	234
Dimbula Valley (Ceylon) Tea Co Ltd v Laurie (1961)	299
Dimond Manufacturing Co Ltd v Hamilton (1969)	59, 187
Dixon v Kennaway & Co (1900)	316
Dixon (C W) Ltd, Re (1947)	478
Doolan v Midland Rly Co (1877)	90
Dorman, Long & Co Ltd, Re, Re South Durham Steel and Iron Co Ltd (1934)	412
Drages Ltd, Re (1942)	98
Duff's Settlement, Re, National Provincial Bank Ltd v Gregson (1951)	**344**
Duncan Sandys (Lord) v House of Fraser plc (1985)	147
Dunford & Elliott Ltd v Johnson & Firth Brown Ltd (1977)	**424**
Dunlop v Higgins (1848)	**48**
Duomatic Ltd, Re (1969)	96, **191**, 237, 284, **291**
Dynamics Corpn of America, Re (1972)	470

E

	PAGE
EBM Co Ltd v Dominion Bank (1937)	284
Eastern Telegraph Co Ltd, Re (1947)	78, 446
Ebrahimi v Westbourne Galleries Ltd (1973)	**239**, 240, 241, 242, 243, 447
Eddystone Marine Insurance Co, Re (1893)	317
Edwards v Halliwell (1950)	222, **224**
Ehrmann Bros Ltd, Re, Albert v Ehrmann Bros Ltd (1906)	366
Eichbaum v City of Chicago Grain Elevators Ltd (1891)	341
El Sombrero Ltd, Re (1958)	274
Elder v Elder and Watson Ltd (1952)	241, 246
Elder's Trustee and Executor Co Ltd v Commonwealth Homes and Investment Co Ltd (1941)	55
Eley v Positive Government Security Life Assurance Co Ltd (1876)	**107**
Ellison v Bignold (1821)	4
Emmadart Ltd, Re (1979)	443
Empire Mining Co, Re (1890)	408
Engineering Industry Training Board v Samuel Talbot (Engineers) Ltd (1969)	468
English and Colonial Produce Co Ltd, Re (1906)	35
English and Scottish Mercantile Investment Trust Ltd v Brunton (1892)	367, 371
English, Scottish and Australian Chartered Bank, Re (1893)	411
Erlanger v New Sombrero Phosphate Co (1878)	31
Ernest v Nicholls (1857)	75, 151
Esparto Trading Co, Re (1879)	341
Estmanco (Kilner House) Ltd v Greater London Council (1982)	223, 226, 227, 230, 231
European Assurance Society, Re, Hort's Case, Grain's Case (1875)	4
Evans v Rival Granite Quarries Ltd (1910)	370

List of Cases xxxiii

	PAGE
Ewing v Buttercup Margarine Co Ltd (1917)	74
Exchange Banking Co, Re, Flitcroft's Case (1882)	358
Exchange Securities and Commodities Ltd, Re (1983)	470
Exchange Securities and Commodities Ltd (No 2), Re (1985)	453
Exchange Securities and Commodities Ltd, Re (1987)	316
Expanded Plugs Ltd, Re (1966)	238, 447
Expo International Pty Ltd v Chant (1979)	378
Express Engineering Works Ltd, Re (1920)	284

F

FG (Films) Ltd, Re (1953)	21
Family Endowment Society, Re (1870)	419
Fargo Ltd v Godfroy (1986)	454
Farrer (T N) Ltd, Re (1937)	132, 438
Fildes Bros Ltd, Re (1970)	243, 244
Findley v Haas (1903)	242
Fir View Furniture Co Ltd, Re (1971)	453
Firbank's Executors v Humphreys (1886)	360
Firestone Tyre and Rubber Co Ltd v Lewellin (1957)	25
First National Reinsurance Co v Greenfield (1921)	309
Fitch Lovell Ltd v IRC (1962)	328
Five Minute Car Wash Service Ltd, Re (1966)	246
Florence Land and Public Works Co, Re, ex p Moor (1878)	370
Florence Land and Public Works Co, Re, Nicol's Case, Tufnell and Ponsonby's Case (1885)	292
Fomento (Sterling Area) Ltd v Selsdon Fountain Pen Co Ltd, Selsdon and Selsdon (1958)	187
Forte (Charles) Investments Ltd v Amanda (1964)	238, 444
Foss v Harbottle (1843)	221

	PAGE
Foster v Coles and M B Foster & Sons Ltd (1906)	295
Foster (W) & Son Ltd, Re (1942)	296
Fowlers Vacola Manufacturing Co Ltd, Re (1916)	353
Freeman and Lockyer (a firm) v Buckhurst Park Properties (Mangal) Ltd (1964)	150, 251

G

Gammack, Petitioner (1983)	238
Garage Door Associates Ltd, Re (1984)	239, 246, 442
Garden Gully United Quartz Mining Co v McLister (1875)	341
Gartside v Silkstone and Dodworth Coal and Iron Co (1882)	368
Gattopardo Ltd, Re (1969)	442
General Auction Estate and Monetary Co v Smith (1891)	77, 359
General Motor Cab Co Ltd, Re (1913)	418
General Rolling Stock Co, Re, Joint Stock Discount Co's Claim (1872)	458
Gerdes v Reynolds (1941)	435
German Date Coffee Co, Re (1882)	77, 80, 241, 446
Gerrard (Thomas) & Son Ltd, Re (1968)	**186**
Gething v Kilner (1972)	**421**
Gibbs v General Mortgage Corpn Ltd (1932)	311
Gilford Motor Co Ltd v Horne (1933)	20, 22
Gilmour (Duncan) & Co Ltd, Re (1952)	101
Gilt Edge Safety Glass Ltd, Re (1940)	237
Glamorganshire Banking Co, Re, Morgan's Case (1884)	416
Glossop v Glossop (1907)	124
Gluckstein v Barnes (1900)	31, 33, 92
Glyncorrwg Colliery Co Ltd, Re, Railway Debenture and General Trust Co v The Company (1926)	377

xxxiv List of Cases

	PAGE
Goodfellow v Nelson Line (Liverpool) Ltd (1912)	413
Government Stock Investment and Other Securities Co v Manila Rly Co (1897)	369, 370
Government of India, Ministry of Finance (Revenue Division) v Taylor (1955)	85, 459
Goy & Co Ltd, Re, Farmer v Goy & Co Ltd (1900)	369
Gramophone and Typewriter Ltd v Stanley (1908)	147
Grant v John Grant & Sons Pty Ltd (1950)	131
Grant v United Kingdom Switchback Railways Co (1888)	148
Gray v New Augarita Porcupine Mines Ltd (1952)	205
Gray's Inn Construction Co Ltd, Re (1980)	469
Great Eastern Electric Co Ltd, Re (1941)	453
Great Munster Rly Co, Re, ex p Inderwick (1850)	445
Great North-West Central Rly Co v Charlebois (1899)	85
Greene, Re, Greene v Greene (1949)	325
Greenhalgh v Arderne Cinemas Ltd (1951)	114, 115, 116, 117
Greenwell v Porter (1902)	107
Greenwood v Algesiras (Gibraltar) Rly Co (1894)	376
Greenwood v Leather Shod Wheel Co (1900)	53
Greymouth-Point Elizabeth Rly and Coal Co Ltd, Re, Yuill v Greymouth-Point Elizabeth Rly and Coal Co Ltd (1904)	146
Grierson Oldham and Adams Ltd, Re (1968)	428
Griffin Hotel Co Ltd, Re, Joshua Tetley & Son Ltd v The Company (1941)	462
Griffith v Paget (1877)	415
Griffiths v Secretary of State for Social Services (1974)	127
Grosvenor Press plc, Re (1985)	351

	PAGE
Grundt v Great Boulder Pty Gold Mines Ltd (1948)	124
Guinness v Land Corpn of Ireland (1882)	101
Guinness (Arthur), Son & Co (Dublin) Ltd v The Freshfield (Owners), The Lady Gwendolen (1965)	29, **160**

H

Haas Timber and Trading Co Pty Ltd v Wade (1954)	54
Hadleigh Castle Gold Mines Ltd, Re (1900)	282
Halt Garage (1964) Ltd, Re (1982)	80, 82, 193
Hampson v Price's Patent Candle Co (1876)	193
Hampstead Garden Suburb Trust Ltd, Re (1962)	99, 100
Hannan's Empress Gold Mining and Development Co, Re, Carmichael's Case (1896)	43
Hansraj Gupta v Asthana (1932)	447
Harlowe's Nominees Pty Ltd v Woodside (Lake Entrance) Oil Co (1968)	196
Harmer (H R) Ltd, Re (1958)	109, 248
Harmony and Montague Tin and Copper Mining Co, Re, Spargo's Case (1873)	49, 293
Hartley Baird Ltd, Re (1955)	271
Haven Gold Mining Co, Re (1882)	446
Hawks v McArthur (1951)	324
Hayes v Bristol Plant Hire Ltd (1957)	234
Head v Gould (1898)	435
Head (Henry) & Co Ltd v Ropner Holdings Ltd (1952)	**345**, 346
Heald v O'Connor (1971)	434
Hector Whaling Ltd, Re (1936)	280
Hedley Byrne & Co Ltd v Heller & Partners Ltd (1964)	58, 187
Helbert v Banner, Re Barned's Bank (1871)	451

	PAGE
Hellenic and General Trust Ltd, Re (1975)	22, 308, 410, 413
Hely-Hutchinson v Brayhead Ltd (1968)	149, 154, 205
Henderson v Bank of Australasia (1888)	193
Henshall (John) (Quarries) Ltd v Harvey (1965)	28
Herbert Berry Associates Ltd v IRC (1977)	462
Heyting v Dupont (1964)	229
Hickman v Kent or Romney Marsh Sheep-Breeders' Association (1915)	438
Highfield Commodities Ltd, Re (1984)	453
Highgrade Traders Ltd, Re (1984)	473
Hilder v Dexter (1902)	343
Hill & Sons (Botley & Denmead) Ltd v Hampshire Chief Constable (1971)	28
Hill's Waterfall Estate and Gold Mining Co, Re (1896)	458
Hivac Ltd v Park Royal Scientific Instruments Ltd (1946)	201
Hoare & Co Ltd, Re (1933)	428
Hodgson v National and Local Government Officers Association (1972)	231
Hogg v Cramphorn Ltd (1967)	85, 196, 235, 291
Holders Investment Trust Ltd, Re (1971)	113, 117, 351, 352, 412
Holdsworth (Harold) & Co (Wakefield) Ltd v Caddies (1955)	126
Holliday (L B) & Co Ltd, Re (1986)	452
Hollman v Pullin (1884)	34
Holmes v Keyes (1959)	102, 123, 130, 280
Holmes (Eric) (Property) Ltd, Re (1965)	364
Holt v IRC (1953)	325
Holt Southey Ltd v Catnic Components Ltd (1978)	446
Hong Kong and China Gas Co Ltd v Glen (1914)	293

List of Cases xxxv

	PAGE
Hop and Malt Exchange and Warehouse Co, Re, ex p Briggs (1866)	54
Horne and Hellard, Re (1885)	371
Horsley and Weight Ltd, Re (1982)	80, **82**, 193
Houghton & Co v Nothard, Lowe and Wills (1927); affd (1928)	144, **154**
Houldsworth v City of Glasgow Bank and Liquidators (1880)	27, 55, 56
House Property and Investment Co Ltd, Re (1954)	459
House of Fraser plc, Petitioners (1983)	269
Household Fire and Carriage Accident Insurance Co v Grant (1879)	49
Howard v Patent Ivory Manufacturing Co, Re Patent Ivory Manufacturing Co (1888)	35, 155
Howard Marine and Dredging Co Ltd v A Ogden & Sons (Excavations) Ltd (1978)	56
Hubbard & Co Ltd, Re, Hubbard v Hubbard & Co Ltd (1898)	372
Huckerby v Elliott (1970)	191
Hull and County Bank, Re, Burgess's Case (1880)	452
Hunter v Hunter (1936)	320, 324
Hutton v West Cork Rly Co (1883)	77, 131, 193

I

Imperial Bank of China, India and Japan v Bank of Hindustan, China and Japan (1868)	419
Imperial Chemical Industries Ltd, Re (1936)	311
Imperial Mercantile Credit Association, Re (1871)	416
Imperial Mercantile Credit Association v Coleman (1873)	203
Industrial Development Consultants Ltd v Cooley (1972)	**198**, 199, 200

xxxvi List of Cases

	PAGE
Ingram (J G) & Son Ltd v Callaghan (Inspector of Taxes) (1968)	388
IRC v Goldblatt (1972)	378
IRC v Olive Mill Ltd (1963)	458
IRC v Reid's Trustees (1949)	391
IRC v Ufitec Group Ltd (1977)	150
Insuranshares Corpn of Delaware v Northern Fiscal Corpn Ltd (1940)	435
International Cable Co Ltd, Re, ex p Official Liquidator (1892)	438
International Life Assurance Society and Hercules Insurance Co, Re, ex p Blood (1870)	419
International Sales and Agencies Ltd v Marcus (1982)	84, 93, 95, 157, 192
International Securities Corpn Ltd, Re (1908)	446
Introductions Ltd (No 2), Re (1969)	455
Introductions Ltd, Re, Introductions Ltd v National Provincial Bank Ltd (1970)	80, 86
Irvine v Union Bank of Australia (1877)	**153**
Isle of Thanet Electric Supply Co Ltd, Re (1950)	295, **298**
Isle of Wight Rly Co v Tahourdin (1883)	222

J

JEB Fasteners Ltd v Marks, Bloom & Co (a firm) (1983)	188
JN2 Ltd, Re (1977)	443
Jarvis Motors (Harrow) Ltd v Carabott (1964)	96, 274, 322
Jermyn Street Turkish Baths Ltd, Re (1970); revsd (1971)	247, 331
Jessel Trust Ltd, Re (1985)	411
John v Rees (1970)	278
Johnson (B) & Co (Builders) Ltd, Re (1955)	378
Jones v Bellgrove Properties Ltd (1949)	145

	PAGE
Jones (M) v Jones (R R) (1971)	325
Jones v Lipman (1962)	22
Jones (William) & Sons Ltd, Re (1969)	**352**
Josephs v Pebrer (1825)	4
Jubilee Cotton Mills Ltd (official receiver and liquidator) v Lewis (1924)	38
Jupiter House Investments (Cambridge) Ltd, Re (1985)	351

K

K/9 Meat Supplies (Guildford) Ltd, Re (1966)	238, 241, 447
Kelner v Baxter (1866)	34, 35
Kenyon (Donald) Ltd, Re (1956)	477
Kerr v John Mottram Ltd (1940)	110, 283
Kingston Cotton Mill Co (No 2), Re (1896)	185
Kingston Cotton Mill Co, Re (1896)	187
Kirby v Wilkins (1929)	339
Kitson & Co Ltd, Re (1946)	78, 446
Knightsbridge Estates Trust Ltd v Byrne (1940)	367, 373
Knowles v Scott (1891)	458
Koscot Interplanetary (UK) Ltd, Re, Re Koscot AG (1972)	448
Krasnapolsky Restaurant and Winter Garden Co, Re (1892)	446
Kraus v J G Lloyd Pty Ltd (1965)	109
Kreglinger v New Patagonia Meat and Cold Storage Co Ltd (1914)	373
Kris Cruisers Ltd, Re (1949)	366
Kuenigl v Donnersmarck (1955)	21

L

L Hotel Co Ltd and Langham Hotel Co Ltd, Re (1946)	414
La Caisse Populaire Notre Dame Ltée v Moyen (1967)	86

List of Cases xxxvii

Lady Gwendolen, The. See
 Guinness (Arthur), Son & Co
 (Dublin) Ltd v The Freshfield
 (Owners), The Lady
 Gwendolen
Lagunas Nitrate Co v Lagunas
 Syndicate (1899) . . . 31, 32
Land Mortgage Bank of
 Florida, Re (1896) . . . 413
Lands Allotment Co, Re
 (1894) 192
Langen and Wind Ltd v Bell
 (1972) 322
Langley Constructions
 (Brixham) Ltd v Wells
 (1969) 470
Larocque v Beauchemin
 (1897) 293
Latchford v Beirne (1981) . . 378
Latchford Premier Cinema Ltd
 v Ennion (1931) 124
Leadenhall General Hardware
 Stores Ltd, Re (1971) . . . 240
Lee v Chou Wen Hsien (1984) . **125**
Lee v Lee's Air Farming Ltd
 (1961) 20, 159, 438
Lee v Neuchatel Asphalte Co
 (1889) 355
Lee, Behrens & Co Ltd, Re
 (1932) 82, 158, 193
Leigh v English Property Corpn
 Ltd (1976) 325
Leitch (William C) Bros Ltd,
 Re (1932) 473
Lennard's Carrying Co Ltd v
 Asiatic Petroleum Co Ltd
 (1915) 27, 92, **159**
Leon v York-O-Matic Ltd
 (1966) 455
Leslie (J) Engineers Co Ltd, Re
 (1976) 470
Levin v Clarke (1962) . . . 202
Levy (A I) (Holdings) Ltd, Re
 (1964) 469
Lewis and Smart Ltd, Re
 (1954) 477
Licensed Victuallers' Mutual
 Trading Association, Re, ex p
 Audain (1889) 43
Liggett (B) (Liverpool) Ltd v
 Barclays Bank Ltd (1928) . 155

Lindgren v L and P Estates Ltd
 (1968) 202, 203, 302
Lines Bros Ltd, Re (1983) . . 460
Linz v Electric Wire Co of
 Palestine Ltd (1948) **87**
Liverpool and District Hospital
 for Diseases of the Heart v
 A-G (1981) 463
Lloyd (F H) Holdings plc, Re
 (1985) 269
Loch v John Blackwood Ltd
 (1924) 241, 447
Logan (Thomas) Ltd v Davis
 (1911) 147
London and County Coal Co,
 Re (1866) 446
London and County Securities
 Ltd v Nicholson (1980) . . 263
London and General Bank, Re
 (1895) 184, 185
London and Mashonaland
 Exploration Co Ltd v New
 Mashonaland Exploration Co
 Ltd (1891) 201
London Flats Ltd, Re (1969) . 271,
  457
London Sack and Bag Co Ltd v
 Dixon and Lugton Ltd
 (1943) 110
London School of Electronics
 Ltd, Re (1986) 249
London Suburban Bank, Re
 (1871) 445, 446
Lonrho Ltd v Shell Petroleum
 Co Ltd (1980) 23
Lowerstoft Traffic Services Ltd,
 Re (1986) 443
Lubin, Rosen and Associates
 Ltd, Re (1975) 445
Lundie Bros Ltd, Re (1965) . 246,
  447
Lundy Granite Co Ltd, Re,
 Lewis's Case (1872) . . . 132
Lyle and Scott Ltd v Scott's
 Trustees and British
 Investment Trust Ltd (1958) . **323**
Lympne Investments Ltd, Re
 (1972) 446
Lynall v IRC (1970) . . . 325
Lynde v Anglo-Italian Hemp
 Spinning Co (1896) 54

M

	PAGE
McCabe v Andrew Middleton (Enterprises) (1969)	453
MacConnell v E Prill & Co Ltd (1916)	281
MacDougall v Gardiner (1875)	107, 109, 233, 234
Mace Builders (Glasgow) Ltd v Lunn (1986)	467
Mackenzie & Co Ltd, Re (1916)	307
McMahon v North Kent Ironworks Co (1891)	376
McNeil v McNeil's Sheepfarming Co Ltd (1955)	103
Magna Plant v Mitchell (1966)	29
Mahesan S/O Thambiah v Malaysia Government Officers' Co-operative Housing Society Ltd (1979)	206
Mahony v East Holyford Mining Co Ltd (1875)	131, 151, 152
Maidstone Buildings Provisions Ltd, Re (1971)	472
Malyon v Plummer (1964)	25
Manchester Diocesan Council for Education v Commercial and General Investments Ltd (1969)	49
Manurewa Transport Ltd, Re (1971)	371
Marshall Hus & Partners Ltd v Bolton (Inspector of Taxes) (1981)	382
Marshall (Thomas) (Exports) Ltd v Guinle (1979)	200
Marx v Estates and General Investments Ltd (1975)	276
Mason v Harris (1879)	203
Mason v Motor Traction Co Ltd (1905)	418
Mawcon Ltd, Re (1969)	453
Maxform SpA v Mariani & Goodville Ltd (1979)	75
Maxwell v Department of Trade and Industry (1974)	267
Mechanisations (Eaglescliffe) Ltd, Re (1966)	364
Medical Invalid and General Life Assurance Society, Re, Griffith's Case (1871)	419
Medical Invalid and General Life Assurance Society, Re, Spencer's Case (1871)	419
Medisco Equipment Ltd, Re (1983)	443
Memco Engineering Ltd, Re (1986)	469
Menier v Hooper's Telegraph Works (1874)	228
Mesco Properties Ltd, Re (1980)	461
Metcalfe (William) & Sons Ltd, Re (1933)	298
Metropolitan Coal Consumers' Association, Re, Karberg's Case (1892)	54
Midland Bank Trust Co Ltd v Green (1981)	94
Midland Express Ltd, Re, Pearson v Midland Express Ltd (1914)	368
Milroy v Lord (1862)	327
Minster Assets plc, Re (1985)	411, 414
Molton Finance Ltd, Re (1968)	363
Monarch Insurance Co, Re, Gorrissen's Case (1873)	292
Monolithic Building Co, Re, Tacon v Monolithic Building Co (1915)	371
Moore v I Bresler Ltd (1944)	29
Moore v North Western Bank (1891)	326
Moore v Northwood (1960)	341
Moorgate Mercantile Holdings Ltd, Re (1980)	281
Morel (E J) (1934) Ltd, Re (1962)	461
Morgan v Gray (1953)	331
Morrice v Aylmer (1874)	404
Morris v Harris (1927)	477
Morris v Kanssen (1946)	130, 153, 158
Mortgage Insurance Corpn, Re (1896)	413
Mosely v Koffyfontein Mines Ltd (1911)	224
Mulligan v Lancaster (1937)	142

List of Cases xxxix

	PAGE
Multinational Gas and Petrochemical Co v Multinational Gas and Petrochemical Services Ltd (1983)	84
Musson v Howard Glasgow Associates Ltd (1960)	426
Mutual Life and Citizens' Assurance Co Ltd v Evatt (1971)	58

N

NFU (or National Farmers' Union) Development Trust Ltd, Re (1972)	408
Nadler Enterprises Ltd, Re (1980)	461
Natal Land and Colonization Co Ltd v Pauline Colliery and Development Syndicate (1904)	35, 36
Natal Co Ltd, Re (1863)	445
National Bank Ltd, Re (1966)	410
National Bank of Wales Ltd, Re (1901)	190
National Drive-in Theatres Ltd, Re (1954)	447
National Dwellings Society v Sykes (1894)	278
National Dwellings Society Ltd, Re (1898)	305
National Equitable Provident Society, Re, Wood's Case (1873)	49
National Telephone Co, Re (1914)	297, 298
National Telephone Co v St Peter Port Constables (1900)	87
Nelson Guarantee Corpn Ltd v Hodgson (1958)	186
New British Iron Co, Re, ex p Beckwith (1898)	108, 438, 452
New Brunswick and Canada Rly and Land Co v Muggeridge (1860)	51
New Finance and Mortgage Co Ltd (in liquidation), Re (1975)	79
New Timbiqui Gold Mines Ltd, Re (1961)	477
New Transvaal Co, Re (1896)	298

	PAGE
New York Taxicab Co Ltd, Re, Sequin v New York Taxicab Co Ltd (1913)	413
New Zealand Gold Extraction Co (Newbery-Vautin Process) v Peacock (1894)	419
Newborne v Sensolid (GB) Ltd (1954)	34
Newhart Developments Ltd v Co-operative Commercial Bank Ltd (1978)	377
Newman (George) & Co, Re (1895)	284
Newman and Howard Ltd, Re (1962)	445
Newspaper Pty Syndicate Ltd, Re, Hopkinson v Newspaper Pty Syndicate Ltd (1900)	158
Newton v Anglo-Australian Investment Co's Debenture-holders (1895)	361
Nissan v A-G (1970)	88
Noble (R A) & Sons (Clothing) Ltd, Re (1983)	247
Nokes v Doncaster Amalgamated Collieries Ltd (1940)	414
Normandy v Ind, Coope & Co Ltd (1908)	275
North-West Transportation Co Ltd and Beatty v Beatty (1887)	111, 230
Northern Publishing Co Ltd v White (1940)	27
Northumberland Avenue Hotel Co Ltd, Re, Sully's Case (1886)	35
Norton v Yates (1906)	372
Norwest Holst Ltd v Secretary of State for Trade (1978)	266
Nurcombe v Nurcombe (1985)	25, 226

O

OC (Transport) Services Ltd, Re (1984)	248
Oakes v Turquand and Harding, Peek v Turquand and Harding, Re Overend, Gurney & Co (1867)	55, 311
Oceanic Steam Navigation Co Ltd, Re (1939)	409

xl *List of Cases*

	PAGE
O'Duffy v Jaffe (1904)	75
Old Silkstone Collieries Ltd, Re (1954)	352
Oliver v Dalgleish (1963)	276
Omnium Electric Palaces Ltd v Baines (1914)	33
Ooregum Gold Mining Co of India v Roper (1892)	44
Oriental Inland Steam Co, Re, ex p Scinde Rly Co (1874)	458
Osborne v Steel Barrel Co Ltd (1942)	293
Othery Construction Ltd, Re (1966)	238
Ottos Kopje Diamond Mines Ltd, Re (1893)	314

P

Pacific Coast Coal Mines Ltd v Arbuthnot (1917)	275
Page v International Agency and Industrial Trust Ltd (1893)	332
Palmer Marine Surveys Ltd, Re (1986)	443
Panorama Developments (Guildford) Ltd v Fidelis Furnishing Fabrics Ltd (1971)	144
Paradise Motor Co Ltd, Re (1968)	325, 327
Paraguassu Steam Tramroad Co, Re, Black & Co's Case (1872)	458
Parke v Daily News Ltd (1962)	193, 195
Parker and Cooper Ltd v Reading (1926)	118
Parsons v Albert J Parsons & Sons Ltd (1978)	159
Patent Invert Sugar Co, Re (1885)	349
Patrick and Lyon Ltd, Re (1933)	473
Paul (H R) & Son Ltd, Re (1973)	274
Pavlides v Jensen (1956)	226, **229**
Payne v Cork Co Ltd (1900)	104, 417
Payne (David) & Co Ltd, Re, Young v David Payne & Co Ltd (1904)	84, 86, 361

	PAGE
Pearce, Duff & Co Ltd, Re (1960)	280
Peat v Clayton (1906)	326
Pedley v Inland Waterways Association Ltd (1977)	275
Peek v Gurney (1871)	52, **57**
Peel v London and North Western Rly Co (1907)	429
Penang Foundry Co Ltd v Gardiner (1913)	316
Pender v Lushington (1877)	107, 230, **233**
Percival v Wright (1902)	89, **192**
Performing Right Society Ltd, Re, Lyttleton v Performing Right Society Ltd (1978)	310
Pergamon Press Ltd, Re (1970); on appeal (1970)	263, 267
Pergamon Press Ltd v Maxwell (1970)	278
Peruvian Amazon Co Ltd, Re (1913)	447
Peso-Silver Mines Ltd v Cropper (1966)	199
Peter's American Delicacy Co Ltd v Heath (1939)	117
Phillips v Manufacturers' Securities Ltd (1917)	230
Phœnix Bessemer Steel Co, Re (1875)	376
Phoenix Oil and Transport Co Ltd, Re (1958)	452
Phonogram Ltd v Lane (1982)	34, 35, 93
Piercy v S Mills & Co (1920)	195
Pilkington v United Railways of the Havana and Regla Warehouses Ltd (1930)	405
Pitman (Harold M) & Co v Top Business Systems (Nottingham) Ltd (1984)	455
Poole v National Bank of China Ltd (1907)	350
Potters Oils Ltd, Re (1985)	467
Pound (Henry) Son and Hutchins, Re (1889)	375
Powell v Kempton Park Racecourse Co Ltd (1899)	224
Practice Note [1934] WN 142	410
Press Caps Ltd, Re (1949)	428
Primrose (Builders) Ltd, Re (1950)	461

List of Cases xli

	PAGE
Property Discount Corpn Ltd v Lyon Group Ltd (1981)	362
Prudential Assurance Co Ltd v Chatterley-Whitfield Collieries Ltd (1949)	352
Prudential Assurance Co Ltd v Newman Industries Ltd (No 2) (1981); on appeal (1982)	221, 223, **226**, 228, 229, 230, 231, 232, 233
Puddephatt v Leith (1916)	107
Pulbrook v Richmond Consolidated Mining Co (1878)	234
Pulsford v Devenish (1903)	419, 458
Punt v Symons & Co Ltd (1903)	118, 195
Pyle Works, Re (1890)	332

Q

Quin and Axtens Ltd v Salmon (1909)	109, 147

R

R v Andrews Weatherfoil Ltd (1972)	28, 160
R v Austen (1985)	129
R v Bishirgian (1936)	61
R v Board of Trade, ex p St Martin Preserving Co Ltd (1965)	378
R v Campbell (1984)	129
R v Corbin (1984)	129
R v Grantham (1984)	473
R v Harris (1970)	267
R v Huggins (1730)	27
R v King (1983)	129
R v Lord Kylsant (1932)	53, 55, 61
R v Murray Wright Ltd (1970)	29
R v Ovenell (1969)	90
R v Panel on Takeovers and Mergers (1987)	424
R v Registrar of Companies, ex p Central Bank of India (1986)	14, 367
R v Secretary of State for Trade, ex p Perestrello (1981)	259
R v Shacter (1960)	142, 184
R v Sorsky (1944)	29

	PAGE
R-R Realisations Ltd (formerly Rolls-Royce Ltd), Re (1980)	463
Radio Chain Stores Ltd, Re (1932)	49
Rama Corpn Ltd v Proved Tin and General Investments Ltd (1952)	152, **154**, 156
Ramel Syndicate Ltd, Re (1911)	298
Rampgill Mill Ltd, Re (1967)	461
Ramsgate Victoria Hotel Co v Montefiore (1866)	49
Rankin and Blackmore Ltd, Re (1950)	411
Rayfield v Hands (1960)	105, 110, 324
Read v Astoria Garage (Streatham) Ltd (1952)	439
Red Rock Gold Mining Co Ltd, Re (1889)	446
Regal (Hastings) Ltd v Gulliver (1942)	**197**, 199, 200, 232
Resinoid and Mica Products Ltd, Re (1983)	366
Richards v Kidderminster Overseers (1896)	462
Richards & Co, Re (1879)	414
Richmond Gate Property Co Ltd, Re (1964)	108, 132
Richmond Hill Hotel Co, Re, Elkington's Case (1867)	49
Ridge Nominees Ltd v IRC (1962)	420
Ridge Securities Ltd v IRC (1964)	85, 193
Rights and Issues Investment Trust Ltd v Stylo Shoes Ltd (1965)	116
Rita Joan Dairies Ltd v Thomson (1974)	36
Road Transport Industry Training Board v Readers Garage Ltd (1969)	159
Roberts Petroleum Ltd v Bernard Kenny Ltd (1983)	468
Robson v Smith (1895)	372
Roith (W & M) Ltd, Re (1967)	193
Rolled Steel Products (Holdings) Ltd v British Steel Corpn (1986)	82, 83, 84, 118, 285

xlii List of Cases

	PAGE
Rose, Re, Midland Bank Executor and Trustee Co Ltd v Rose (1949)	328
Rose, Re, Rose v IRC (1952)	328, 329
Roundwood Colliery Co, Re, Lee v Roundwood Colliery Co (1897)	371
Row Dal Constructions Pty Ltd, Re (1966)	363
Rowell v John Rowell & Sons Ltd (1912)	341, 349
Royal British Bank v Turquand (1856)	**151**, 360
Ruben v Great Fingall Consolidated (1906)	314
Russell v Wakefield Waterworks Co (1875)	231
Russell (J) Electronics Ltd, Re (1968)	444
Russian Spratts Patent Ltd, Re, Johnson v Russian Spratts Patent Ltd (1898)	361
Rutherford (James R) & Sons Ltd, Re (1964)	461

S

S v Shaban (1965)	24, 237
SBA Properties Ltd, Re (1967)	443
Sadler v Worley (1894)	374
Safeguard Industrial Investments Ltd v National Westminster Bank Ltd (1980); affd (1982)	**323**
St James' Court Estate Ltd, Re (1944)	349, 409
St Piran Ltd, Re (1981)	268
Salisbury Gold Mining Co v Hathorn (1897)	278
Salisbury Railway and Market House Co Ltd, Re (1969)	455
Salmon v Quin and Axtens Ltd (1909)	234
Salomon v A Salomon & Co Ltd (1897)	**19**, 20, 21, 29, 31, 32
Saltdean Estate Co Ltd, Re (1968)	299
Sandwell Park Colliery Co Ltd, Re (1914)	418
Sarflax Ltd, Re (1979)	472, 473

	PAGE
Savings and Investment Bank Ltd v Gasco Investments (Netherlands) BV (1984)	268
Savory (E W) Ltd, Re (1951)	296, 297
Savoy Hotel Ltd, Re (1981)	408, 410
Scholey v Central Rly Co of Venezuela (1868)	54
Scott v Frank F Scott (London) Ltd (1940)	105
Scott v Scott (1943)	354
Scott (Peter) & Co Ltd, Re (1950)	411
Scott Group Ltd v McFarlane (1978)	187
Scottish Co-operative Wholesale Society Ltd v Meyer (1959)	24, 203, 247
Scottish Insurance Corpn v Wilsons and Clyde Coal Co (1949)	**298**, 352
Scottish Petroleum Co, Re (1883)	54, 55
Sea and River Marine Insurance Co, Re (1866)	445
Second Consolidated Trust Ltd v Ceylon Amalgamated Tea and Rubber Estates Ltd (1943)	276
Second Scottish Investment Trust Ltd, Re (1962)	411
Secretary of State for Trade and Industry v Hart (1982)	183
Selangor United Rubber Estates Ltd v Cradock (a bankrupt) (No 3) (1968)	24, 189, 191, 201, 429, 433, 434
Servers of Blind League, Re (1960)	476, 477
Sharpe, Re, Re Bennett, Masonic and General Life Assurance Co v Sharpe (1892)	358
Sharpley v Louth and East Coast Rly Co (1876)	54
Shaw (John) & Sons (Salford) Ltd v Shaw (1935)	147
Shearer (Inspector of Taxes) v Bercain Ltd (1980)	345, 346
Sheffield Corpn v Barclay (1905)	**318**

List of Cases xliii

	PAGE
Shindler v Northern Raincoat Co Ltd (1960)	126, 159, 272, 438
Shuttleworth v Cox Bros & Co (Maidenhead) Ltd (1927)	114
Sidebottom v Kershaw, Leese & Co (1920)	105, 116
Signland Ltd, Re (1982)	444
Simm v Anglo-American Telegraph Co (1879)	317
Simmonds v Heffer (1983)	75
Simpson v Molson's Bank (1895)	312
Simpson v Westminster Palace Hotel Co (1860)	224
Sinclair v Brougham (1914)	87
Skinner, Re (1958)	414
Slavenburg's Bank NV v Intercontinental Natural Resources Ltd (1980)	364
Smith v Anderson (1880)	8
Smith v Incorporated Council of Law Reporting for England and Wales (1914)	436
Smith and Fawcett Ltd, Re (1942)	192, 320, 321
Smith Knight & Co, Re, ex p Gibson (1869)	419
Smith, Knight & Co, Re, Weston's Case (1868)	319
Smith (Howard) Ltd v Ampol Petroleum Ltd (1974)	195, 196, 290
Smith, Stone & Knight Ltd v Birmingham Corpn (1939)	23
Smith's (John) Tadcaster Brewery Co Ltd, Re, The Company v Gresham Life Assurance Society Ltd (1953)	307, 352
Société Générale de Paris v Tramways Union Co (1884)	312
Société Générale de Paris v Walker (1885)	329
South Australian Barytes Ltd v Wood (1975)	344, 359
South London Greyhound Racecourses Ltd v Wake (1931)	314
South Western Mineral Water Co Ltd v Ashmore (1967)	434
Southard & Co Ltd, Re (1979)	445

	PAGE
Southern Foundries (1926) Ltd v Shirlaw (1940)	118, **119**, 120, 438
Sovereign Life Assurance Co v Dodd (1892)	410, 411
Sovfracht (V/O) v Van Udens Scheepvaart en Agentuur Maatschapij (NV Gebr) (1943)	21
Sowman v David Samuel Trust Ltd (1978)	375
Spackman v Evans (1868)	184
Spencer v Kennedy (1926)	130
Spink (Bournemouth) Ltd v Spink (1936)	434
Spottiswoode, Dixon and Hunting Ltd, Re (1912)	477
Staines UDC's Agreement, Re, Triggs v Staines UDC (1969)	87
Standard Chartered Bank Ltd v Walker (1982)	378
Standard Manufacturing Co, Re (1891)	361
Stanley, Re, Tennant v Stanley (1906)	1
Staples v Eastman Photographic Materials Co (1896)	295
State of Wyoming Syndicate, Re (1901)	144
Steen v Law (1964)	192, 433, 434
Stephen (Robert) Holdings Ltd, Re (1968)	351
Stockton Malleable Iron Co, Re (1875)	319, 320
Stonegate Securities v Gregory (1980)	442, 446
Stoneleigh Finance Ltd v Phillips (1965)	361
Straw Products Pty Ltd, Re (1942)	241
Strong v Carlyle Press (1893)	375
Stubbs (Joshua) Ltd, Re, Barney v Joshua Stubbs Ltd (1891)	375
Suburban Hotel Co, Re (1867)	446
Sullivan v Henderson (1973)	469
Surplus Properties (Huddersfield) Ltd, Re (1984)	443
Sussex Brick Co Ltd, Re (1961)	428

xliv List of Cases

	PAGE
Sutherland (Duke) v British Dominions Land Settlement Corpn Ltd (1926)	321
Swabey v Port Darwin Gold Mining Co (1889)	438
Swaledale Cleaners Ltd, Re (1968)	322
Symons (Walter) Ltd, Re (1934)	294, 296

T

Taff Vale Rly Co v Amalgamated Society of Railway Servants (1901)	90
Taupo Totara Timber Co Ltd v Rowe (1978)	133
Tea Corpn Ltd, Re, Sorsbie v Tea Corpn Ltd (1904)	411
Teague, Petitioner (1985)	238, 240
Tesco Supermarkets Ltd v Nattrass (1972)	28, 29, 160
Tett v Phoenix Property and Investment Co Ltd (1984)	107, 321, 324
Thompson v J Barke & Co (Caterers) Ltd (1975)	82, 84, 86
Thompson and Riches Ltd, Re (1981)	476
Tomkinson v South-Eastern Rly Co (1887)	80
Touche v Metropolitan Railway Warehousing Co (1871)	33
Towers v African Tug Co (1904)	358
Tracy v Mandalay Pty (1952)	31
Transatlantic Life Assurance Co Ltd, Re (1979)	311
Transplanters (Holding Co) Ltd, Re (1958)	142, 145, 184
Transvaal Lands Co v New Belgium (Transvaal) Land and Development Co (1914)	203
Travel and Holiday Clubs Ltd, Re (1967)	250, 443
Trevor v Whitworth (1887)	340
Trix Ltd, Re, Re Ewart Holdings Ltd (1970)	454
Trussed Steel Concrete Co Ltd v Green (1946)	159
Tunstall v Steigmann (1962)	23
Twycross v Grant (1877)	31

U

	PAGE
Underwood (A L) Ltd v Bank of Liverpool and Martins (1924)	20, 155
Unit Construction Co Ltd v Bullock (1960)	**25**
United States v Harry L Young Inc (1975)	29
Uxbridge Permanent Benefit Building Society v Pickard (1939)	156

V

Valletort Sanitary Steam Laundry Co Ltd, Re, Ward v Valletort Sanitary Steam Laundry Co Ltd (1903)	370, 371
Vandervell's Trusts (No 2), Re, White v Vandervell (1974)	328
Vane v Yiannopoullos (1965)	27
Victor Battery Co Ltd v Curry's Ltd (1946)	433
Victoria Steamboats Ltd, Re, Smith v Wilkinson (1897)	376, 377
Victors Ltd v Lingard (1927)	204

W

Wakley, Re, Wakley v Vachell (1920)	295
Wallace v Evershed (1899)	370
Wallersteiner v Moir (1974)	23, 134, 229, 433
Wallersteiner v Moir (No 2) (1975)	223, 229, 232
Wallis and Simmonds (Builders) Ltd, Re (1974)	363
Ward (Alexander) & Co Ltd v Samyang Navigation Ltd (1975)	148, 454
Watson v Duff Morgan and Vermont (Holdings) Ltd (1974)	366
Webb v Earle (1875)	295
Wedgwood Coal and Iron Co, Re (1877)	413
Wedgwood Coal and Iron Co, Re, Anderson's Case (1877)	101
Weeks v Propert (1873)	360
Wellington Publishing Co Ltd, Re (1973)	431

	PAGE		PAGE
Welsbach Incandescent Gas Light Co Ltd, Re (1904)	101, **104**	Wolverhampton Steel and Iron Co Ltd, Re (1977)	452
Welton v Saffery (1897)	109, 324	Wondoflex Textiles Pty Ltd, Re (1951)	241
Westbourne Grove Drapery Co Ltd, Re (1878)	477	Wood v Odessa Waterworks Co (1889)	106
Westburn Sugar Refineries Ltd, ex p (1951)	353	Wood, Skinner & Co Ltd, Re (1944)	296
Western Manufacturing (Reading) Ltd, Re (1956)	426	Woodroffes (Musical Instruments) Ltd, Re (1986)	370
Western of Canada Oil, Lands and Works Co, Re (1873)	446	Woolfson v Strathclyde Regional Council (1978)	23
Westminster Bank Ltd v Osler (1933)	440	Wragg Ltd, Re (1897)	293
Westminster Corpn v Haste (1950)	372	Wrexham, Mold and Connah's Quay Rly Co, Re (1899)	88
Whaley Bridge Calico Printing Co v Green (1879)	31	**Y**	
White v Bristol Aeroplane Co Ltd (1953)	307, 352	Yenidje Tobacco Co Ltd, Re (1916)	**240**, 241, 447
White, Petitioner (1984)	246	Yeovil Glove Co Ltd, Re (1965)	466
White Star Line Ltd, Re (1938)	293	Yetton v Eastwoods Froy Ltd (1966)	126
Whyte (G T) & Co Ltd (1983)	466	Yorkshire Miners' Association v Howden (1905)	224
Willcocks (W R) & Co Ltd, Re (1974)	445	Yorkshire Woolcombers' Association Ltd, Re, Houldsworth v Yorkshire Woolcombers' Association Ltd (1903)	369
Wilson and Garden Ltd v IRC (1982)	398		
Windsor Steam Coal Co (1901) Ltd, Re (1929)	458		
Windward Islands Enterprises (UK) Ltd, Re (1983)	273		

Chapter 1

Introduction

This book is concerned primarily with companies as defined in the Companies Act 1985, that is, those companies which are formed and registered under that Act or were incorporated under an earlier Companies Act.[1] There are of course companies incorporated otherwise than under the Companies Act 1985 or its predecessors. The famous Hudson's Bay Company was, for example, formed under Royal Charter. Some companies were formed under private Act of Parliament. The nationalised industries were created by public general statutes as bodies corporate. Numerically, however, most companies derive their existence from registration under the Companies Acts. The company is, of course, only one form of business association.[2] Others include partnerships, clubs, building and friendly societies and unit trusts. In this book we deal primarily with registered companies. Comparisons are, from time to time, made with partnerships and other unincorporated bodies where a similarity or difference provides a useful illustration of the history or present content of company law. We do not, however, discuss other forms of business association as such.[3]

HISTORY [4]

Bodies enjoying corporate status have existed since medieval times.

---

1   CA 1985, s 735.
2   The word company is sometimes used as part of a firm name, and it has no precise connotation. All companies formed under the Companies Act enjoy corporate status. *Re Stanley, Tennant v Stanley* [1906] 1 Ch 131, 134, per Buckley J.
3   The partnership is of course a common form of organisation. See *Underhill's Law of Partnership* (12th edn, 1986). On clubs and other unincorporated bodies the most useful source is H. A. J. Ford, *Unincorporated Non-Profit Associations* (1959).
4   For an ampler account of the history, see *Gower's Principles of Modern Company Law* (4th edn, 1979) chapters 2 and 3.

Early corporations owing their existence to royal charter or deemed by prescription to have received such a charter were primarily ecclesiastical or public bodies such as chapters, monasteries or boroughs. The trading company as such was a later development. Trading on joint account was accomplished through forms of partnership known as the *commenda*, and the *societas*, and later, through the company, the first form of which was the regulated company. Dr C. A. Cooke describes *commenda* and *societas* thus:[5]

> The *commenda* ... was a partnership in which one of the partners supplied the capital (in money or goods) without personally taking part in the management of the venture ... *commenda* was, by the fifteenth century, a partnership which avoided the usury laws and which contained the essential elements of limited liability and the modern sleeping partnership.[6]
> ... Though there may have been exceptions, the general technique of business in England was necessarily limited to simple division of profits and simple participation in the business. To this *societas* was suited; by the sixteenth century it had firmly established features of common responsibilities and common privileges among all partners ... This solidarity, coupled with a higher degree of permanence, marked *societas* from *commenda*.

Societas was the typical English partnership and it profoundly influenced the law of partnership and, ultimately, company law.

Trading companies enjoying corporate status began to appear in the sixteenth century. These were the regulated companies, in form rather like the medieval guilds, in which each member traded on his own stock and on his own account, subject to obeying the rules of the company. Charters of incorporation were sought in order to give the members a monopoly over the trading and to give the company governmental powers over foreign stations. The Crown, too, benefited. Through its power to grant charters it could regulate and control foreign trade and colonisation. In turn, the joint stock company developed.[7] In this form of organisation the proprietors pooled their stock and traded on the basis of the joint stock. Thus, in the East India Company, a permanent joint stock became the rule by 1653, and by 1692 private trading was disallowed.

By the end of the seventeenth century, charters of incorporation became particularly prized. Such a charter conferred certain

---

5   *Corporation, Trust & Company* (1950), pp 45–47.
6   The limited partnership was not however given legislative recognition until the Limited Partnership Act 1907 (c 24).
7   See Carr, *Select Charters of English Trading Companies,* Selden Society (1913).

advantages. The company could have a perpetual existence, it could sue in its own name, a distinction was drawn between the company's acts and those of its members, and its shares could be readily transferred. While companies formed for foreign trade declined, companies formed for internal trading increased.

Early in 1720 there was a boom in share prices of which the increasing of premiums in the stock of the South Sea Company were the most spectacular. Many joint stock ventures had no charter or had obtained a charter for a quite different purpose. In April 1720, a committee of the House of Commons which had been appointed to investigate 'bubbles' reported, recommending legislation to prevent the misuse of charters and to restrain the rush of highly speculative undertakings. This led to the passage of the famous Bubble Act[8] which, Maitland says, 'even when we now read it, seems to scream at us from the statute book'.[9] It prohibited unincorporated trading companies from acting or purporting to act as corporations. It further prohibited the use of charters for purposes other than those for which they were granted.

Proceedings by *scire facias* were started under the Bubble Act against four chartered companies. A restrictive policy was commenced in relation to the granting of charters. While no proceedings by *scire facias* were taken against the South Sea Company, its shares fell dramatically in the general atmosphere of panic which ensued.[10] Ultimately the company was propped up by the government, but the damage was done and joint stock companies fell under a cloud of suspicion for the next century.

The Bubble Act, notwithstanding, there remained a need for large aggregations of capital. This need was met by a marriage of the partnership and the trust. Rather than incur the delay and expense of securing a Royal Charter or private Act of Parliament, the members executed an instrument called a deed of settlement. The rights and obligations of the members were settled in the deed. Trustees, who could be persons other than the directors,[11] were appointed to hold the property of those who were parties to the deed, while the business was managed by directors. The prohibition in the Bubble Act against bodies presuming to act as corporations

---

8   6 Geo I c 18.
9   F. W. Maitland, 'Trust and Corporation' in Maitland, *Selected Essays* (1936, ed Hazeltine, Lapsley and Winfield), p 208.
10 Much of this account derives from L. C. B. Gower, 'A South Sea Heresy' (1952), 68 LQR 214. See also, A. B. duBois, *The English Business Company after the Bubble Act* (1938).
11 L. S. Sealey, 'The Director as Trustee' (1967) Camb LJ 83.

was seen ultimately as primarily directed against the creation of a freely transferable stock.[12] Deeds of settlement normally therefore contained restrictions on transfer. Again, only corporations could make byelaws.[13] The deed of settlement therefore contained detailed rules concerning the management of the company. Deed of settlement companies were recognised by the Court of Chancery as possessing most of the characteristics of companies.[14] Whether such companies could limit the liability of their members was a matter of doubt. The fact that it was difficult for such companies to be sued was not seen by the members as a serious defect; but it was a circumstance leading to Parliamentary action.[15]

In the nineteenth century, the difficulties, obscurities and deficiencies of the law led to Parliamentary action. The Bubble Act was repealed in 1825.[16] In 1837 statutory authority was conferred on the Crown to grant letters patent to persons who wished to associate for trading purposes and to limit their liability.[17] Then, in 1844, the Companies Act[18] recognised for the first time the need for facilitating the incorporation of trading companies. Incorporation was allowed by registration. Two stages were involved; provisional registration with limited powers, followed by full registration on filing the deed of settlement. Limited liability was not yet introduced, but the liability of a member ceased after three years from the time at which he disposed of his shares. The 1844 Act adopted also the principle of full publicity as the best means of protection for the investing public.

The next step was the attainment of limited liability for registration companies.[19] Persons investing in such companies did so at the risk of their fortunes. The result was at least a partial divorce between capital and enterprise. By 1854 the debate was turning on fundamental issues. Some companies enjoyed limited liability under private Acts of Parliament or charters; others were denied it. The safe investment for small capitalists was canals and railways.

12 *Ellison v Bignold* (1821) 2 Jac & W 503. And see CA 1948, Table A, arts 24 and 25 which still restrict transferability.
13 *Josephs v Pebrer* (1825) 3 B & C 639.
14 See the remarks of James L. J. in *Re Agriculturist Cattle Insurance Co (Baird's Case)* (1870) 5 Ch App 725, 734, and in *Re European Assurance Society (Grain's Case)* (1875) 1 ChD 307, 320.
15 See generally, Holdsworth, *History of English Law,* Vol xv, pp 47–48.
16 Bubble Companies Act 1825 (6 Geo IV c 91).
17 Chartered Companies Act 1837 (7 Will 4 & 1 Vict c 73).
18 Joint Stock Companies Act 1844 (7 & 8 Vict cc 110 and 111).
19 See generally, B. C. Hunt, *The Development of the Business Corporation in England 1800–1867* (1936).

The former were almost completed. Limited liability would open fresh fields to private investment. After considerable parliamentary opposition in 1854, the Government in 1855 rushed through a bill for limited liability despite a protest from the Lords. This was followed by the first of the modern Companies Acts, that of 1856,[20] which was followed in turn by a consolidating Act, the Companies Act 1862.[1] Provisional registration was abolished. The deed of settlement was superseded by the modern memorandum and articles. A company could, on registration, enjoy limited liability. Provision for winding up was made. On the other hand, the surprisingly modern looking accounting provisions in the 1844 Act were abolished, and it was not until 1900 that all companies were required to submit to an annual audit.[2] While the basic structure of the company as we now know it had taken shape, some of the implications of incorporation with limited liability were not immediately perceived. Thus commercial and industrial circles, imbued with the ideas of personal participation and unlimited liability which prevailed in the law of partnership, issued partly-paid shares of high denomination. Company liquidity crises were met by successive calls on shares.[3] It was not until a number of company crashes had demonstrated the vulnerable position of shareholders holding partly-paid shares of high par value that companies began to issue shares of low par value, on a fully paid-up basis. In practical terms, this marks the completion of the process of public acceptance of limited liability.

By the end of nineteenth century, the Board of Trade had established the practice, since followed, of securing an expert committee to review company law at intervals of about 20 years and of carrying out some of the recommended amendments by statute. The enhanced accounting requirements introduced in 1900 were followed by the exemption from them of the private company, which did not issue any invitation to the public to subscribe for its securities.[4] But the thrust of company law reform has changed. Its primary goals have been to ensure that shareholders, creditors and the public shall have as much information concerning corporate affairs as they reasonably require, and to find means for making it easier for shareholders to exercise a more effective general control

20 Joint Stock Companies Act 1856 (19 & 20 Vict c 47).
1 25 & 26 Vict c 89.
2 Companies Act 1900 (63 & 64 Vict c 48).
3 See Jeffrey, 'The Denomination and Character of Shares' in *Essays in Economic History*, Vol I (ed Carus-Wilson, 1954).
4 Companies (Consolidation) Act 1908 (8 Edw 7 c 69).

6 *Chapter 1 Introduction*

over the management of their companies.[5] At the same time, committees have considered such related areas as unit trusts[6] and share-pushing.[7] The Companies Act 1948 which followed the report of a committee under Lord Cohen was successively amended by the Companies Acts 1967, the Companies Act 1976, and extended by the Companies Act 1980 and the Companies Act 1981. Then in 1985 company law was consolidated into the Companies Act 1985, the Companies Consolidation (Consequential Provisions) Act 1985, and the Company Securities (Insider Dealing) Act 1985. These, with certain later amendments, are the statutes in force. In addition there are a number of other statutes which apply to corporate affairs.[8]

In any event, it is certain that the main emphasis of company law reform has changed with the accession to the European Economic Community. The main impetus for reform has come (and is indeed likely in future years to continue to come) from the move towards harmonisation of company law within the Community. The full implications of this shift of emphasis have yet to be felt. Prior to the accession, the trend in British company law was towards assimilation of the treatment of public and private companies, as is evident from the Companies Act 1967. However, the principal concern of the Directives on harmonisation of company law is the public company; private companies remain relatively untouched. This separation between public and private companies was reflected in the Companies Acts of 1980 and 1981.[9] It is doubtful whether future committees appointed to consider company law reform will be able or will wish to adhere to the useful, but conservative, statement of aims formulated in 1947.[10] For example, the provisions of what is now Sch 7, Part I, para 3 of the Companies Act 1985 concerning particulars of political contributions, cannot be attributed solely to

---

5 Report of the Company Law Committee Cmnd 6659 (1945), para 5.
6 Cmnd 5259 (1936).
7 Cmnd 5539 (1937).
8 Eg Stock Transfer Act 1963; Financial Services Act 1986; Companies (Floating Charges and Receivers) (Scotland) Act 1972; Banking Act 1979; Insolvency Act 1986; and, more generally, such statutes as the Fair Trading Act 1973 obviously affect corporate affairs.
9 Which implement the Second and Fourth Directives on the Harmonisation of Company Law. See also 'Company Accounting and Disclosure' Cmnd 7654 (1979).
10 See further Nock 'The Ford Foundation Workshop on Company Law' (1970) 11 JSPTL 1; Atiyah, 'Thoughts on Company Philosophy' (1964) 8 The Lawyer 19.

History 7

the traditional policy of informing shareholders.[11] The question of workers' control has already been the subject of discussion.[12] It is in particular doubtful whether one Act can adequately cater for the divergent problems of the small family concern and the giant company.[13] It may be necessary to ask whether our law makes provision for enough types of organisation, particularly in view of membership of the Common Market.[14] Finally, and ultimately, it has been doubted whether the modern company is the best form of organisation which can be devised for carrying on large businesses.[15] Certainly it is unrealistic, at least in the case of large public companies, to regard shareholders as having much greater control over the affairs of the company than debenture holders. The latter are merely lenders of money and are not members of the company. Shareholders and debenture holders alike are suppliers of funds who look to the company for a satisfactory return on their investment.[16]

Doubts of this cataclysmic character seem, at all events, not to trouble the investing public. The company continues to be a popular form of business organisation. Even after the Companies Act 1967 which required disclosure as the price of limited liability, substantial numbers of new companies were registered. In 1968, 20,654 new companies were registered.[17] But in 1977, after the coming into operation of the Companies Act 1976 (which strengthened provisions relating to company accounts and auditing) the number of new registrations was 63,566.[18] This trend continues, and incorporations in 1985 stood at 102,549 companies with a nominal capital of £6,318,098, but alas the current economic climate is responsible for an increasing number of liquidations as well.[19]

11 Formerly CA 1967, s 20 required disclosure of exports, but that provision was repealed (with savings) by CA 1981, s 16(2) and Sch 4.
12 Report of the Commission of Inquiry on Industrial Democracy Cmnd 6706 (1977); 'Industrial Democracy' Cmnd 7231 (1978).
13 See further M. Chesterman, *Small Businesses* (1977).
14 A brief outline of some of the principal types of association in French law can be found in Vuillermet, *Droit des Sociétés Commerciales* (1969) Vol 1, pp 48–55. On Germany see articles by Vagts (1966) 80 Harv LR 23 and on the multinational corporation, Vagts in (1970) 83 Harv LR 739. See also Pennington, *Companies in the Common Market* (2nd edn, 1970).
15 K. W. Wedderburn *Company Law Reform* (1963).
16 Pickering 'The Problems of the Preference Share' (1963) 26 Mod LR 499.
17 Board of Trade, Companies in 1968, p 5.
18 Department of Trade, Companies in 1978, p 9.
19 Department of Trade, Companies in 1981.

Chapter 2

Incorporation and its Consequences

INCORPORATION

Incorporation is a means to an end. Companies are formed for a number of specific reasons, and the function of a company will depend upon the objects to be achieved by those who are responsible for its formation. Some companies, relatively few in number, are non-profit-making. Social or charitable companies are of this type. Other companies are formed to take over an existing business. An individual or firm may decide that it would be preferable if a company (often a private company) were formed to take over the business. After incorporation of the company as a private company, there will probably be little internal structural change in the business; the company will own it, but the former owners will probably be its directors and majority shareholders. Public companies today often represent a conversion from the private form, rather than an initial incorporation as a public company. The most important reason for going public is the wish to secure additional capital by the issue of shares or debentures to the public at large. The Stock Exchange Rules really militate against this in the case of untried companies.[1] Most companies which solicit funds from the public have a considerable business history.

The company is, of course, only one mode of organisation for the conduct of business. A trading business can be carried on as a sole proprietorship or as a partnership,[2] or limited partnership.[3] Persons can invest in an organisation created for the purpose of holding securities as a unit trust, though an aggregation of persons holding an interest in a fund the assets of which are shares and debentures, is neither a company nor a partnership.[4] Persons organising for social

---

1 Chap 4, post.
2 Partnership Act 1890 (c 39).
3 Limited Partnerships Act 1907 (c 24).
4 *Smith v Anderson* (1880) 15 ChD 247.

Incorporation 9

or charitable purposes may do so in a club or other unincorporated association or through the medium of a trust.[5] The decision whether to incorporate or to adopt one of these other modes of organisation may be influenced by a number of factors. Of these the desire for privacy is perhaps the most significant. Companies having limited liability must file accounts which may be inspected by the public.[6] If persons wish privacy and do not wish to form a company with unlimited liability, they may decide to carry on business in partnership. The impact of taxation may be a critical factor. In some cases it will be advantageous for individuals to incorporate, in others not. While incorporation does not minimise liability to capital tax, it may enable a business to survive notwithstanding the effect of death duties. If the business is carried on by individuals its assets may have to be sold to meet a capital transfer tax liability.[7] But if the business has been incorporated, shares in the business may be sold instead of assets. In this way the business is enabled to continue, although generally the purchaser of the shares will require some share in the control of the company. Among the other positive advantages of incorporation may be limited liability, greater ease in raising money for the business and in giving security therefor,[8] freedom for the incorporators in disposing of their shares, at any rate if the company is public, and the ability of the incorporators to dispose of their interests in part at least, while retaining control over their investment from which their income derives.

TYPES OF COMPANY

The Companies Acts make provision for private and public companies. These may or may not have a share capital, and may or may not have limited liability. The Acts confer a wide range of options upon the incorporators. The would-be incorporator must decide not only whether to incorporate, but also what attributes to choose for his company.

The differences between private and public companies are not fundamental. As a matter of convenience, the company will usually

---

5 See F. W. Maitland, 'The Unincorporated Body', *Selected Essays* (1936) pp 28 et seq, and 'Trust and Corporation', ibid, pp 140 et seq. The leading modern text is H. A. J. Ford, *Unincorporated Non-Profit Making Associations* (OUP, 1959).
6 CA 1985, s 221. The requirements are modified in relation to small and medium-sized companies: see Chap 9, post.
7 See Chap 17 generally on taxation aspects.
8 The reference here is to raising money by a floating charge. See Chap 16, post.

10 Chapter 2 Incorporation and its Consequences

be incorporated as a private company. There will be no need to obtain a certificate that the company is entitled to do business.[9] Only one director is required.[10] The requirements of the Acts concerning the election and tenure of directors are less stringent in the case of a private company.[11] The most significant difference between the private and the public company is that the minimum capital requirements apply only to the public company. Section 81 of the CA 1985 provides that a private limited company commits an offence if it offers to the public (whether for cash or otherwise) any shares in or debentures of the company or allots or agrees to allot any shares or debentures of the company with a view to all or any of those shares or debentures being offered for sale to the public. An allotment made in contravention of the section is, however, valid.[12]

An unauthorised company must not engage in advertising for deposits[13] and a private company must not conduct trading stamp schemes.[14]

The company whether public or private may be limited by shares, or by guarantee, or be an unlimited company. A company limited by shares is one which the liability of the shareholders to contribute to the company's assets is limited by the memorandum of association to the amount, if any, unpaid on their shares.[15] A guarantee company is one in which the liability of the members is limited by the memorandum to such amount as the guarantors agree to contribute to the assets of the company in the event of its being wound up.[16] In an unlimited company the shareholders are fully liable for the debts incurred by the company.[17].

Undoubtedly, the most significant decision to be taken by the incorporators will be whether to register in the limited or unlimited

---

9   CA 1985, s 117(1).
10 Ibid, s 282.
11 Ibid, ss 292, 293. Note that the latter provision assimilates the position of the director of a private company subsidiary of a public company to that of a director of a public company.
12 Formerly under s 28 of the CA 1948 (repealed) private companies could not have more than 50 members. This irksome restriction has been removed.
13 Banking Act 1979, s 1.
14 Trading Stamps Act 1964, s 1.
15 CA 1985, s 1(2)(a).
16 CA 1985, s 1(2)(b). A guarantee company may also have a share capital in which case the members are liable to pay the amount, if any, unpaid on their shares in addition to the amount unpaid under the guarantee. Section 8 and Table D; no new companies of this type may be formed.
17 CA 1985, s 1(2)(c).

form.[18] Put briefly, all limited companies must file accounts.[19] Unlimited companies which are fully independent, however, enjoy the privilege of privacy.[20] This position reflects the view taken both in the Report of the Company Law Committee[1] and by the Government that the privilege of limited liability ought to bear with it an obligation to make financial disclosures in the interests both of creditors and the public generally. Deference was at one time paid to the desire of family concerns to retain privacy in order to avoid disclosing their affairs to competitors. In 1948 exceptions to disclosure were conferred upon the 'exempt private company'. These exceptions to disclosure were however relied on by companies for which they were never intended.[2] Furthermore, the Schedules to the Act which had to be complied with were difficult to apply.[3] In the result, the Companies Act 1985 requires disclosure from all limited companies. A company which desires complete privacy must register as unlimited. Unfortunately perhaps, the need to make the correct decision on incorporation is enhanced by the difficulties of converting, in particular from the limited to the unlimited form.

CHANGES IN FORM

Private companies may be re-registered as public companies and vice versa. In some circumstances a company is obliged by the Companies Act 1985 to re-register from public to private.[4]

A private company may re-register as a public company. In order to do so a special resolution must be passed, an application in the prescribed form and signed by a director or secretary of the company delivered to the Registrar together with certain supporting documents, and certain statutory conditions satisfied.[5]

The special resolution must alter the company's memorandum so

18 For conversion, see p 18, post.
19 CA 1967, s 2, which abolished the 'exempt private company'; but see now CA 1985, Sch 8, Pt I.
20 Ibid, s 241(4), which stipulates that the unlimited company must not be the subsidiary or holding company of a limited company.
1 Cmnd 1749 (1962), paras 55–63.
2 The Report of the Company Law Committee Cmnd 1749 (1962), para 57, noted for example that at 31 December 1961, of 387,000 private companies on the Register, some 269,000 or 70% had claimed status. Some of these companies were not small.
3 Ibid, para 57.
4 CA 1985, s 146.
5 CA 1985, s 43; this provision represents the normal mode of alteration.

Chapter 2 Incorporation and its Consequences

that it states that the company is to be a public company.[6] Alterations in the memorandum are to be made such as are necessary to bring it in substance and in form into conformity with the requirements of the Companies Act 1985 with respect to the memorandum of a public company.[7] It must make such alterations in and additions to the company's articles as are requisite in the circumstances.[8]

An application must be submitted to the Registrar signed by a director or secretary of the company[9] and including:

(1) copies of the altered memorandum and articles;
(2) a copy of a written statement by the auditors that a balance sheet prepared not more than seven months before the application shows that at the date of the balance sheet the amount of the company's net assets was not less than the aggregate of its called-up share capital and undistributable reserves;[10]
(3) a copy of that balance sheet together with a copy of an unqualified report by the company's auditors in relation to that balance sheet;[11]
(4) a copy of any report concerning the valuation of non-cash assets accepted between the date of the balance sheet and the special resolution in payment or part payment for any shares of the company;[12]
(5) a statutory declaration by a director or secretary that the conditions concerning valuation of non-cash assets or undertakings, and conditions concerning nominal capital have been satisfied,[13] and that between the balance sheet date and the application of the company for re-registration there has been no change in the financial position of the company that has resulted in the company's net assets becoming less than the aggregate of its called-up share capital and undistributable reserves.[14]

---

6 CA 1985, s 43(2)(a) and note that by s 25 the company will be known as a public limited company or its equivalent in Welsh.
7 Ibid, s 43(2)(b).
8 Ibid, s 43(2)(c).
9 Ibid, s 43(3).
10 Ibid, s 43(3)(b) for the meaning of 'undistributable reserves' see s 264.
11 Ibid, s 43(3)(c) and s 46 which defines 'unqualified report' as one which states that the balance sheet has been properly prepared in accordance with the Companies Acts and which gives a true and fair view of the company's affairs as at the date of the balance sheet.
12 Ibid, s 43(3)(d).
13 Ibid, s 43(3)(e).
14 Ibid, s 43(3)(e)(ii).

There are mandatory requirements as to the share capital of a private company applying to re-register as public. At the time when the special resolution was passed:[15]

(1) the nominal value of the company's issued share capital must be not less than the authorised minimum;[16]
(2) each of its allotted shares must be paid up to at least one-quarter of the nominal value of that share and the whole of any premium on it;[17]
(3) where any shares have been allotted as fully or partly paid up for work or services the undertaking must have been performed or otherwise discharged;[18]
(4) where shares have been allotted as fully or partly paid up, as to their nominal value on any non-cash premium payable upon them, with an undertaking to transfer a non-cash asset to the company, then that undertaking must either have been performed or otherwise discharged, or it must be subject to a contract providing for transfer within five years from its date.[19]

Shares issued before 22 June 1982 or shares allotted in pursuance of an employees' share scheme and by reason of which the company would, but for the provisions of CA 1985, s 43(2)(b), be precluded from being re-registered as a public company, may be disregarded for the purposes of determining whether conditions (2) to (4) above have been complied with.[1] Thus, shares so allotted do not bar re-registration of the company because cash or other consideration has not been received for them, or services performed in relation to them, or an undertaking discharged or contracted for in respect of them. Such disregarded shares are treated for the purposes of the minimum value requirement as though they did not form part of the issued share capital of the company.[2]

Shares issued before 22 June 1982 are not to be disregarded if the aggregate value of shares which it is proposed to disregard is more than one-tenth of the nominal value of the company's issued share

15 CA 1985, s 54(1).
16 Ibid, s 45(2)(a).
17 Ibid, s 45(2)(b).
18 Ibid, s 45(3).
19 Ibid, s 45(4).
20 Ibid, s 45(5).
1 Ibid, s 45(5).
2 Ibid.

capital. This latter figure is computed without regard to shares allotted under employees' share schemes and thus disregarded.[3] In other words, if shares issued during the transitional period equal one-tenth or more of the nominal value of the issued share capital less shares allotted pursuant to employees' share schemes, the shares issued during the transitional period must be taken into account.

Where the Registrar is satisfied that the Act has been complied with, he issues a certificate of incorporation stating that the company is a public company.[4] A certificate so issued is conclusive as to compliance with the requirements of the Act and the status of the company.[5] Such a certificate of registration cannot be challenged on an application for judicial review.[6]

Provision is also made for the registration of unlimited companies and joint stock companies as public companies.[7] In the case of unlimited companies the above procedure applies with minor modifications. The provisions relating to joint stock companies are more elaborate but again are directed towards maintaining the integrity of the capital rules.

Old public companies are required to opt for public company or private company status under the Companies Consolidation (Consequential Provisions) Act 1985. Failure to deliver the appropriate declaration to the Registrar renders the company and any officer thereof who is in default guilty of an offence.[8]

Briefly, where it is desired to convert an old public company to a public company, the machinery is as follows:[9]

(1) the directors must pass a resolution to that effect (ie a resolution of shareholders is not required); and
(2) an application signed by a director or secretary of the company has been delivered to the Registrar together with a printed copy of the memorandum as altered pursuant to the resolution and statutory declaration evidencing compliance with the statutory requirements including the minimum capital requirements;[10]

3 Ibid, s 45(6).
4 Ibid, s 47.
5 Ibid, s 47(5).
6 *R v Registrar of Companies, ex p Central Bank of India* [1986] QB 1114, [1986] 1 All ER 105, CA.
7 Ibid, ss 48, 685 and 688.
8 Companies Consolidation (Consequential Provisions) Act 1985, s 5(2).
9 Companies Consolidation (Consequential Provisions) Act 1985, s 2(1).
10 Ibid, ss 2 and 3.

Incorporation 15

The formal provisions noted above concerning the issue and status of the certificate of incorporation apply.[11] Where it is desired to convert an old public company to a private company it may proceed by a special resolution of the shareholders.[12] If such a special resolution is passed and either no application to cancel it is made within 28 days from its passing, or proceedings pursuant to an application for cancellation are concluded without the Court making an order for cancellation, the Registrar must issue the company with a certificate that it is a private company. Again, such a certificate is conclusive as to the status of the company and the fact of compliance with the provisions of the Act.[13]

An old public company also acquires private company status if it delivers to the Registrar a statutory declaration signed by not less than two directors of the company either that the nominal value of the company's issued share capital is less than the authorised minimum or that its issued share capital does not satisfy the requisite conditions concerning the consideration for which it was issued, or concerning the performance of work or services or the transfer of assets for which the shares were issued.[14]

This procedure is obviously useful when the company does not satisfy the minimum capital requirements. A company which does not satisfy those requirements could, none the less, register as a public company by meeting the minimum capital requirements and passing a resolution to convert.[15]

A public company[16] may re-register as private.[17] A special resolution is required, and this must not have been cancelled by the Court.

The application for re-registration must be delivered to the Registrar. Where an application for cancellation is made and the Court confirms the resolution or the application is withdrawn, the company must deliver an office copy of the order to the Registrar.[18]

The resolution must alter the company's memorandum so that it no longer states that the company is to be a public company and deletes the appelation 'public limited company' from its name.[19]

11 Ibid, s 2(6).
12 Ibid, s 4.
13 Ibid, s 4(5).
14 Ibid, s 4(4).
15 Ibid, ss 2 and 3.
16 Not an old public company.
17 CA 1985, s 53.
18 Ibid, s 55.
19 Ibid, s 53(2).

16 Chapter 2 Incorporation and its Consequences

The Registrar, if satisfied that the statutory conditions have been complied with, must issue a certificate of incorporation having the usual effect concerning the status of the company and compliance with the requirements of the section.[20]

A company may be re-registered as a private company by order of the Court without the necessity of passing a special resolution in that behalf. This procedure refers to an order confirming the reduction of a company's capital below the authorised minimum for a public company.[1] In such case the order for reduction may not be registered unless the company first re-registers as a private company. The Court may authorise such a re-registration without the necessity for a special resolution, and where it does so must specify in the order the alterations in the company's memorandum and the alterations and additions to the company's articles to be made in consequence.[2] A company may also be re-registered as a private company where the effect of a forfeiture or surrender of shares would be to reduce the nominal value of the allotted capital below that required for a public company.[3] A company is obliged to pass a resolution altering its status. Failure to do so involves a default fine upon the company and every officer in default.[4]

There is a procedure, available in the case of special resolutions by an old public company not to be re-registered as a public company or to a like resolution by a public company to be re-registered as a private company, to apply to the Court for cancellation of that resolution.[5] Such an application may be made by the holders of not less in aggregate than 5% in nominal value of the company's issued share capital or any class thereof, or, if the company is not limited by shares, by not less than 5% of the company's members or by not less than 50 of the company's members.[6] No such application may be made by any person who consented to or voted in favour of the resolution.[7]

Any such application must be made within 28 days of the resolution and may be made by a representative of the members appointed by them in writing.[8] The Court must make an order either

---

20 Ibid, s 55.
1 Ibid, s 139.
2 Ibid, s 139(3).
3 Ibid, s 146(2)(b).
4 Ibid, s 149(2).
5 Ibid, s 54.
6 Ibid, s 54(2).
7 Ibid.
8 Ibid, s 54(4).

cancelling or confirming the resolution.[9] Its powers are wide. It may make the order on such terms and conditions as it thinks fit. It may adjourn the proceedings in order that an arrangement may be made to its satisfaction for the purchase of shares of dissentient members and it may make such orders as it thinks fit for facilitating or carrying into effect any such arrangement.[10]

It is interesting that the section empowers the Court to provide for the purchase by the company of the shares of any members of the company and for the reduction accordingly of the company's capital, and to make any consequential alterations in and additions to the memorandum and articles of the company.[11] The Court may also require the company to refrain from making any, or any specified, alterations in the memorandum and articles.[12]

While the discretion of the Court is large and the Court is not given explicit guidance concerning the principles to be applied, it would seem that its discretion ought primarily to be exercised in order to prevent members from being locked into a situation in which their shares would become less readily alienable and in which their interests might well diverge from those of a controlling group. The intention must be to avoid oppression of such members in the future and understandings concerning rights of management of the newly private company, the terms of proposed pre-emption clauses and understandings concerning the distribution of profits as dividends would no doubt be treated as material on an application to cancel such a resolution.[13]

It is possible to re-register from the limited to the unlimited form and vice versa. The relevant sections conspicuously lack the virtue of ready comprehensibility. Their effect is as follows. No public company may apply to be re-registered as an unlimited company.[14]

An unlimited company may (provided that it has not previously converted from the limited to the unlimited form pursuant to s 43 of the Companies Act 1967 or s 49 of the Companies Act 1985) convert

---

9 Ibid, s 54(5).
10 Ibid.
11 CA 1985, s 54(6); in general, a company may neither purchase its own shares ibid, s 143, nor provide financial assistance to another person to purchase its shares, as to which see CA 1985, s 151.
12 CA 1985, s 54(8).
13 These are matters which are considered relevant in an application to end unfairly prejudical conduct under either IA 1986, s 122(g) or s 459 of the CA 1985.
14 CA 1985, s 51.

to the limited form.[15] A special resolution is required which, if the company is to be limited by shares, states what the share capital is to be, and provides for the making of such alterations to the memorandum as are necessary to bring it into conformity with the requirements concerning companies limited by shares or guarantee.[16] The personal liability of members of the company continues in the event of winding up, for a period after re-registration of the company as a limited company.[17] A limited company may convert to the unlimited form.[18] The principal difficulty here is that the members must unanimously agree to the change.[19] It is probable that this requirement will prove to be a substantial impediment to such conversions.[20]

THE CONSEQUENCES OF INCORPORATION

On incorporation, the company becomes a body corporate, a legal person enjoying the historic attributes of corporate status. These include the power to sue and be sued in its own name, the right to hold and alienate its own property, and perpetual succession.[1] It may or may not enjoy limited liability. Whether it does so will, as we have explained, depend upon the form of incorporation chosen by its promoters. As a general rule, a company is governed by directors who are chosen by the members. The directors are vested with the executive government of the company while the shareholders enjoy a residual power. But, although the shareholders are members of the company, having an ultimate power of control, and although the directors manage it, the company is a legal entity separate and distinct from its members and directors. The company holds property and enters into contractual relations with outsiders. In relation to such activities it is the company which will primarily be liable and not the members or directors. This fundamental principle was firmly established by:

---

15 Ibid, s 51(2); a company which has previously converted from limited to unlimited and which wishes to change again may have to resort to a scheme of arrangement order. CA 1985, s 425.
16 Ibid, s 51(3).
17 IA 1986, s 77; the period is three years from the date of re-registration.
18 CA 1985, s 49.
19 Ibid, s 49(8).
20 See Morley, 'The Companies Act 1967' (1967) 69 LS Gazette 536.
1   Blackstone, *Commentaries*, Book IV, pp 475–476.

Salomon v Salomon & Co Ltd [1897] AC 22.

The appellant, Salomon, had for many years prior to the formation of the respondent company carried on business as a leather merchant and wholesale boot manufacturer. The business was transferred to the company, a company with liability limited by shares. The purchase price agreed to be paid by the company for the business was slightly less than £39,000. The nominal capital of the company was £40,000 divided into 40,000 £1 shares. Salomon applied £20,000 of the purchase moneys received from the company in the purchase of 20,000 fully paid £1 shares. At the time of the proceedings 20,001 shares were held by the appellant and his wife, daughter and four sons had one share each. No other shares were issued. The company had issued debentures for £10,000 to the appellant in part payment of the purchase moneys.[2] The company failed and, after applying the assets to repayment of the debentures held by the appellant, there was nothing for distribution to unsecured creditors. Salomon himself was not fully paid off. In addition to the debt to Salomon, about £7,800 was owing to trade creditors who asserted that the company was no more than the agent or alias of the appellant, that the issue of debentures to him was merely a scheme to defeat the creditors, and that as the company was no more than Salomon's agent, he as principal should indemnify the company and pay its creditors. These arguments were effectively disposed of by the House of Lords, who were satisfied that the motive in forming a company was merely to give a share in the business to his family. Their share in the business was, of course, purely nominal; they had only six £1 shares between them. Lord Macnaghten stated at p 51:

When the memorandum is duly signed and registered, though there be only seven shares taken, the subscribers are a body corporate 'capable forthwith', to use the words of the enactment, 'of exercising all the functions of an incorporated company'. Those are strong words. The company attains maturity on its birth. There is no period of minority— no interval of incapacity. I cannot understand how a body corporate thus made 'capable' by statute can lose individuality by issuing the bulk of its capital to one person, whether he be a subscriber to the memorandum or not. *The company is at law a different person altogether from the subscribers to the memorandum:* (italics inserted) and, though it may be that after the incorporation the business is precisely the same as it was before, the same persons are managers and the same hands receive the profits, the company is not in law the agent of the subscribers or trustee for them. Nor are the subscribers as members liable, in any shape or form, except to the extent and in the manner provided by the Act. That is, I think, the declared intention of the enactment. If the view of the

---

2 IA 1986, s 18, which renders invalid floating charges created within six months of the commencement of winding up.

learned Judge were sound, it would follow that no common law partnership could register as a company limited by shares without remaining subject to unlimited liability.

The House of Lords decided that the company was not Salomon's agent, that Salomon was not, therefore, liable to indemnify the company against the claims of creditors, and that Salomon was entitled to retain the monies paid to him as debenture holder.

Salomon's case established beyond doubt that in law a registered company is an entity distinct from its members, even if one person holds almost all of the shares in the company. There is no difference in principle between a company consisting of only two or even one beneficial shareholder and a company consisting of 200 members. In each case the company is a separate legal entity and the same principles apply to both.[3] Common lawyers have not engaged in much philosophical speculation about the nature of corporate personality. Our law with its immensely fertile concept of the trust and the well developed doctrines of agency and vicarious responsibility has not needed to do more than treat the corporation as far as possible as if it were a natural person. The law has developed according to the needs and public policy of the day.[4] Whenever, in the view of the courts, justice demands a different result from what would follow from a rigid application of the principle of the separate corporate existence of the company apart from its members and officers, they have not hesitated to take a decision which seems fair even if it means lifting or piercing the veil of incorporation and having regard to the realities behind the façade of separate corporate identity.[5] The courts have determined, case by case, whether and to what extent the rules of law governing the legal relations of natural persons should also apply to artificial persons.[6]

---

3 *Lee v Lee's Air Farming Ltd* [1961] AC 12, [1960] 3 All ER 420.
4 W. S. Holdsworth, *History of English Law* (3rd edn, 1944), Vol IX, 70 and H. L. A. Hart, 'Theory and Definition in Jurisprudence' (1959) 70 LQR 37. Reference should also be made to *Gilford Motor Co Ltd v Horne* [1933] Ch 935, [1933] All ER Rep 109, where the Court treated the company as a mere sham for enabling Horne to evade his contractual obligations. Cf *Connors Bros Ltd v Connors* [1940] 4 All ER 179.
5 See *Gower's Principles of Modern Company Law* (4th edn, 1979) pp 112–138, and see also E. J. Cohn and C. Simitis, 'Lifting the Veil in the Company Laws of the European Continent' (1963) 12 Int & Comp LQ 189.
6 The courts have not been alone in lifting the veil of incorporation. The legislature, too, has played its part, especially in relation to taxation, eg Finance Act 1940, ss 44 and 56. See also *A. L. Underwood Ltd v Bank of Liverpool* [1924] 1 KB 775, in relation to the scope of the Bills of Exchange Act 1908, s 82.

These decisions must, however, be treated as exceptional and in no way seriously limiting the generality of the principle embodied in *Salomon's* case. It is not possible to offer a principle under which these cases can be subsumed; they can be said merely to be examples of situations where it was decided that to treat the company as a distinct entity from its members and its directors would not have been justified.

Although no general principle can be advanced which embraces all the cases in which the separate legal entity rule has been disregarded, it can be said by way of summary (which is not intended to be exhaustive) that the principle has frequently been ignored (or modified):

(1) in time of war to determine enemy character.[7]

Daimler Co Ltd v Continental Tyre and Rubber Co (Great Britain) Ltd [1916] 2 AC 307.

C, a private company incorporated in England, had a capital of 25,000 £1 shares. The members of the company were a company incorporated in Germany holding 23,398 shares and five individuals who held the remainder. Four of these individuals were German subjects. The other, the secretary, a British subject, resident in England, held one share. The House of Lords held that the company was an enemy company for the purpose of trading with the enemy legislation because its effective control was in enemy hands. *Salomon's* case did not cover such questions as the determination of enemy character; the character of the members of the company was crucial in determining whether the company had enemy character.

(2) in cases where the company was formed for a fraudulent purpose.

Re F. G. Films Ltd [1953] 1 All ER 615, [1953] 1 WLR 483.

The company was incorporated in England. Its capital was £100 in £1 shares, 90 of which were held by J, the president of a United States film

---

7 See also *V/O Sovfracht v Van Udens Scheepvaart En Agentuur Maatschappij (N V Gebr)* [1943] AC 203, [1943] 1 All ER 76, where the 'control' test was applied, and the remarks of McNair J in *Kuenigl v Donnersmarck* [1955] 1 QB 515, 535, [1955] 1 All ER 46, 52, where the learned Judge was of the opinion that a company might have enemy character and yet remain subject to obligations to the Crown under the Companies Acts.

company, and 10 were held by another director, a British subject. The company contended that it was the 'maker' of a film which should therefore be registered as a British film under the Cinematograph Films Act 1938. The Court refused to agree that the film was made by the British company, whose participation in it was so small as to be practically negligible; the company was merely the nominee or agent of the United States company which had provided £80,000 for the making of the film and which had brought the British company into existence for the sole purpose of enabling the film to qualify as a British film. The modest capital of the British company and its shareholding were treated by the Court as evidence that the British company had been formed with a view to evading the legislation.

Similarly, the separate legal entity principle was ignored in *Gilford Motor Co Ltd v Horne*[8] where the company was formed to avoid the burden of a covenant restricting the business which could be carried on by the company's former managing director in competition with it. And there are other reported examples of the disregard of the separate legal entity principle in cases of fraud and sharp practice.[9]

(3) as between a holding company and its subsidiary. Here, the problems are often complex. One group of cases concerns when a subsidiary may be said to hold its property as an emanation of its parent.

D. H. N. Food Distributors Ltd v London Borough of Tower Hamlets [1976] 3 All ER 462.

The issue concerned compensation under the Land Compensation Act 1961 which is to be made for the value of the land and also for disturbance to the business. The land compulsorily purchased was owned by B Ltd which at all material times was a wholly-owned subsidiary of D.H.N. Ltd and was a mere holding company without trading or business activities. There was also another wholly-owned subsidiary which operated delivery vehicles in conjunction with the business. The local authority paid B Ltd for the land but denied that B Ltd was entitled to

8 [1933] Ch 935.
9 Eg *Jones v Lipman* [1962] 1 All ER 442, [1962] 1 WLR 832 (where the company was acquired by the defendant and the land transferred to it in order to defeat a claim, for the specific performance of a contract for the sale of land); *Re Bugle Press Ltd* [1961] Ch 270, [1960] 3 All ER 791 (where the company was formed in order, fraudulently, to invoke the compulsory acquisition powers in CA 1948, s 209 now CA 1985, ss 428–430 as substituted by FSA 1986); *Re Hellenic and General Trust Ltd* [1975] 3 All ER 382, [1976] 1 WLR 123 decided under similar circumstances.

compensation for disturbance because they did not actually occupy the land. D.H.N. Ltd was refused compensation it being alleged that it had neither a legal nor an equitable interest in the land but was at best a mere licensee of B Ltd on a year to year basis to whom minimal compensation need only be paid. The Court of Appeal, however, held that having regard to the pattern of control, B Ltd could not determine D.H.N. Ltd's licence which was irrevocable. More broadly, where companies form part of a group one can look to the economic entity of the whole group, especially where the subsidiaries are wholly-owned.

How far the group principle is to be taken is obscure; in the above case Lord Denning MR took an expansive view of the matter while Goff and Shaw LJJ based themselves firmly on the facts of the case and in particular the wholly-owned character of the subsidiaries. Earlier, in *Wallersteiner v Moir*[10] Lord Denning MR suggested that a loan is made by a company to a person who is its director if it is made to another company which is wholly owned by him and is otherwise his creature.

However, each case seems to depend very much on its own facts. For example, in *Lonrho Ltd v Shell Petroleum Co Ltd*[11], documents which it was claimed were relevant to an arbitration in London were held by certain of the defendant's subsidiaries in Rhodesia and South Africa, some of which were wholly-owned. The local directors of the subsidiaries refused to disclose the documents and the plaintiff sought an order for their disclosure on the ground that the documents were in the defendant's 'power' for the purposes of order 24 of the Rules of the Supreme Court 1965. It was held that the question whether a parent company had power over documents in the possession of its subsidiaries depended on the facts of each case and since in the present case the local directors had a considerable degree of autonomy, the documents were not in the defendant's 'power' for the purposes of order 24, even though it effectively held all of the shares in some of the subsidiaries. The 'group' cases generally do not seem to go beyond the area of wholly owned subsidiaries;[12] they may be contrasted with *Tunstall v Steigmann*,[13] where the Court declined to treat a proposed occupation of

---

10 [1974] 3 All ER 217, [1974] 1 WLR 991.
11 [1980] QB 358, [1980] 2 WLR 367; aff'd [1980] 1 WLR 627. The case concerned questions of discovery under Order 24 of the Rules of the Supreme Court 1965. See also *B v B (matrimonial proceedings: discovery)* [1978] Fam 181, [1979] 1 All ER 801.
12 *Smith, Stone and Knight v Birmingham Corpn* [1939] 4 All ER 116.
13 [1962] 2 QB 593, [1962] 2 All ER 417; *Woolfson v Strathclyde Regional Council* (1978) 38 P & CR 521, HL.

premises by a company wholly owned by the plaintiff as an occupation by the plaintiff herself, even though she had formed the company to carry on an existing business. In the result an application by the defendant, a tenant of the premises, for a new tenancy, prevailed. It is true that the case does not involve the parent-subsidiary relationship. It none the less asserts the general rule, which seemingly ought to prevail in such cases, that the company is not to be identified with its controllers.

Certainly, where the company is not wholly controlled by its parent, the separate legal entity principle will be applied. In *Scottish Co-operative Wholesale Society Ltd v Meyer*,[14] the Society which had formed a subsidiary to participate in the manufacture of rayon materials determined to kill it off. This course of action was at variance with the interest of the minority shareholders. The House of Lords held that the companies were distinct and that the interests in them conflicted. The directors nominated by the parent owed their duties to the subsidiary as well as to the parent. 'By subordinating the interests of the textile company to those of the co-operative society, they conducted the affairs of the textile company in a manner oppressive to the other shareholders.'[15]

It cannot be said that the law in this area is clear, at any rate in relation to directors' duties in the parent-subsidiary context. It is probable that English law will not permit a director placed on the board of a company by a parent to act as a mere puppet.[16] At the other extreme, he is not bound to ignore the interests of the parent of a group when engaged in decision-making on the board of a subsidiary.[17] In between there is a grey area, at present largely uncharted.[18]

(4) in some revenue cases. The courts for example commonly investigate the control structures of companies in order to determine questions of residence. The residence of a company for tax purposes is said to be the place where its real business is carried on, and the real business is carried on where central management and control actually abides.[19] On

---

14 [1959] AC 324, [1958] 3 All ER 66.
15 [1959] AC 324, 367 per Lord Denning.
16 *Selangor United Rubber Estates Ltd v Cradock* (No 3) [1968] 2 All ER 1073, [1968] 1 WLR 1555; *S v Shaban* 1956 (4) SA 646 (W).
17 *Charterbridge Corpn v Lloyds Bank* [1970] Ch 62, [1969] 2 All ER 1185.
18 See discussion in connection with directors' duties Chap 10, post.
19 *De Beers Consolidated Mines Ltd v Howe* [1906] AC 455.

occasions, this task involves the court in an inquiry which, by stressing functional rather than formal considerations, does not give full effect to the separate legal entity principle.

Unit Construction Co Ltd v Bullock [1960] AC 351.

A United Kingdom company had three wholly-owned subsidiaries which were formed and registered in Kenya. Each had a board of directors distinct from that of the parent company. Under their articles, board meetings could not be held in the United Kingdom. The board of the parent company (which conducted its business in the United Kingdom) in fact controlled the operation of the Kenya subsidiaries although it had no constitutional authority to do so. The House of Lords held that for tax purposes the Kenya subsidiaries were resident in the United Kingdom where central management and control was in fact located.

Another, and different tax case in which the separate legal entity principle was departed from is *Firestone Tyre and Rubber Co Ltd v Llewellin*,[20] where an English subsidiary was treated as holding its property as an emanation of its parent.

(5) in a miscellaneous group of cases. These cannot be fitted into a pattern. In some cases, judicial benevolence appears to have played a substantial role.[1] One could perhaps also cite cases where, though the separate legal entity principle was not formally departed from, the fact that the company was held by few shareholders produced a result which depended upon there being no true corporate interest in the case.

Nurcombe v Nurcombe [1985] 1 All ER 65, [1985] 1 WLR 370, CA.

Husband and wife were the majority and minority shareholders in a company. As part of an order in matrimonial proceedings, the wife was compensated for financial loss arising in respect of her shareholding, the value of which was diminished by the husband's action in diverting a corporate opportunity from the company to another company. The wife later sought to commence a derivative action on behalf of the company

---

20 [1957] 1 All ER 561, [1957] 1 WLR 464.
1 Eg *Malyon v Plummer* [1963] 1 QB 419, [1962] 3 All ER 884 (where the effect of ignoring the company was to give the widow of its controller a direct benefit under an insurance policy taken out by the company on her husband's life); *Abbey Malvern Wells Ltd v Ministry of Local Government* [1951] Ch 728, [1951] 2 All ER 154, and see also the cases on winding up under IA 1986, s 122(g).

in respect of the diversion. Held: that the right to bring such an action is in the discretion of the court, that all personal objections to the plaintiff must be considered, and that to allow her to bring an action here would benefit her inequitably, through her shareholding, given the order for compensation already made.

This decision does not deny the separate legal entity principle, but it does recognise the realities of the position of the company and its two shareholders. If the shareholding had been more widely dispersed, it is difficult to believe that the original order for compensation would have been made, but if it had, doubtless another shareholder would have been allowed to sue.

In addition, the Companies Act in a number of instances disregards the separate legal entity principle.[2] This is particularly marked in connection with group enterprises where there is no obligation to present group accounts[3] and to give detailed information in a holding company's accounts concerning its subsidiaries.[4] There is also provision whereby, if a company carries on business without having at least two members and does so for more than six months, a person who is a member of the company (for the whole or any part of the period that it so carries on business after those six months) and knows that it is carrying on business with only one member, may be jointly and severally liable with the company for debts contracted by the company during such part of that period as he was a member of the company.[5] If a company engages in fraudulent trading, any persons who were knowingly parties to the fraud are liable to make such contribution to the company's assets as the court thinks proper.[6] If a public company enters into a transaction to allot shares in contravention of the provisions which require it to obtain a certificate before doing business, the directors of the company are jointly and severally liable to any third party injured in consequence of such breach.[7]

Exceptional cases apart, the general recognition of the company as a separate legal entity has meant that the company is competent in matters of property and contract. Companies are also liable in tort and crime.

---

2   For a full discussion see *Gower's Principles of Modern Company Law,* (4th edn, 1979) pp 113–123.
3   CA 1985, s 229. For the definition of holding and subsidiary companies, see s 736.
4   Ibid, s 231 and Sch 5, Pt I.
5   Ibid, s 24.
6   IA 1986, s 213(2).
7   CA 1985, s 117(8).

A company, like any other employer, is liable for torts committed by its servants in the course of their employment. Thus companies have been held liable for negligence, fraud and even libel.[8] It has never been finally determined whether companies are liable for the torts of their servants where the servants are engaged in activities *ultra vires* the company. There are conflicting *dicta* both for and against liability.[9] In New Zealand it has been held that a company is liable for the torts of its servants committed within the scope of their employment even though the activity in which they were engaged was *ultra vires* the company.[10]

Some tort liability as for example the liability of the owner of a British ship for loss under s 502 of the Merchant Shipping Act 1894, requires the tortfeasor to be personally at fault before liability can be imposed. To such situations the concept of vicarious liability cannot apply; the master cannot be made liable simply for the acts of his servants. This poses particular difficulties in the case of the company which can only act through its directors, officers and agents. In order to meet this type of case, the courts have fashioned a basis upon which personal liability may be ascribed to the company. The basis so devised has served also as a basis for the imposition of criminal liability upon corporations.[11] Such a basis was required (a) because much crime requires the accused to have formed a guilty intent and it is accordingly necessary to impute a mind to the company, and (b) because there is, in general, no vicarious criminal liability for crimes of intent.[12]

The basis of personal corporate liability was provided in *Lennard's Carrying Co Ltd v Asiatic Petroleum Co Ltd*.[13]

> A corporation is an abstraction. It has no mind of its own any more than it has a body of its own; its active and directing will must consequently be sought in the person of somebody who for some purposes may be called an agent, but who is really the directing mind and will of the corporation, the very ego and centre of the personality of the corporation. That person may be under the direction of the shareholders in general

---

8 *Citizen's Life Assurance Co v Brown* [1904] AC 423; *Houldsworth v City of Glasgow Bank* (1880) 5 App Cas 317.
9 See Chap 6, post.
10 *Northern Publishing Co v White* [1940] NZLR 75.
11 See further Leigh, *The Criminal Liability of Corporation in English Law* (1969), esp chapter 5.
12 *R v Huggins* (1730) 2 Ld Raym 1547. For vicarious liability in licensing cases see *Vane v Yiannopoullos* [1965] AC 486, [1964] 3 All ER 820, and in general Leigh, op cit, chapter 6.
13 [1915] AC 705.

meeting; that person may be the board of directors itself, or it may be, and in some companies it is so, that that person has an authority co-ordinate with the board of directors given to him under the articles of association, and is appointed by the general meeting of the company . . . The fault or privity is the fault or privity of somebody who is not merely a servant or agent for whom the company is liable upon the footing respondent superior, but somebody for whom the company is liable because his action is the very action of the company itself.

No difficulty was experienced in rendering a company liable for nonfeasance or for those crimes, such as nuisance and criminal libel, where *mens rea* was not an essential ingredient in the crime.

The detailed rules pertaining to the criminal liability of bodies corporate can be found elsewhere.[14] In summary, the rules appear to be the following:

(1) a company is to be treated as having a mind capable of entertaining *mens rea*. For this purpose the mental state of persons occupying a superior situation in its managerial structure are to be so treated. The test is partly formal and partly functional; it includes the board of directors, the managing director, and other directors and officers provided that these persons enjoy autonomous management powers over a significant aspect of the company's activities.[15] It is impossible to be more definite than this. Courts are inclined to express themselves metaphorically if not anthropomorphically, distinguishing between brains and hands;[16]

(2) it follows that the company is thus generally identified with the mental states and even the actions of its controller. The point is not that these persons are the mind of the company, in some ultimate metaphysical sense, but rather that for the purposes of imposing criminal liability their mental state is imputed to the company. However, in certain cases the mental state of the controllers of the company will not be attributed to it, for example, where the controllers conspire

---

14 L. H. Leigh, *The Criminal Liability of Corporations in English Law* (1969); 'The Criminal Liability of Corporations and Other Groups' (1977) 9 Ottawa L Rev 247, J. C. Smith and B. Hogan, *Criminal Law* (5th edn, 1983) pp 155–160.
15 *Tesco Supermarkets Ltd v Nattrass* [1972] AC 153, [1971] 2 All ER 127; *R v Andrews-Weatherfoil Ltd* [1972] 1 All ER 65, [1972] 1 WLR 118.
16 *H L Bolton (Engineering) Co Ltd v T J Graham & Sons Ltd* [1957] 1 QB 159 at pp 172–173; *Hill & Sons (Botley and Denmead) Ltd v Hampshire Chief Constable* [1972] RTR 29; *John Henshall (Quarries) Ltd v Harvey* [1965] 2 QB 233, [1965] 1 All ER 725.

to act in breach of statutory provisions designed to protect the company;[17]
(3) the company is generally criminally responsible. In some exceptional cases where the offence as a matter of statutory interpretation must be regarded as incapable of attribution to the company, for example bigamy, the company will not be liable;[18]
(4) the company may be criminally liable even though the officer in question acted without intent to benefit the company and even in fraud of it.[19] This principle has not however been recently assessed;[20]
(5) the fact that a company is liable in respect of the *mens rea* and acts of its officers does not mean that those persons are not also criminally liable for the same offences; on the contrary, corporate criminal liability is cumulative rather than substitutionary.[1]

By way of summary, it may be said that there have been a number of instances where the courts have, because of practical or other considerations, disregarded the principle of the separate corporate personality of the company as established by *Salomon's* case or at any rate have examined questions of corporate control. The decisions in relation to tortious liability show that the theoretical limitations on the capacity of the company have in some cases been ignored; in the criminal cases the courts have held the company liable where it has been possible to impute to the company the acts and intentions of its officers. In so doing the courts have looked to see whether the acts in question were performed or commanded by persons having a primary managerial responsibility over the company's affairs or some relevant facet of them.[2]

17 *Belmont Finance Corpn Ltd v Williams Furniture Ltd* [1979] Ch 250, [1979] All ER 118.
18 For a rare example, see *R v Murray Wright Ltd* [1970] NZLR 476.
19 *Moore v I Bresler Ltd* [1944] 2 All ER 515.
20 The American rule, which seems preferable, rejects liability where the servant acts with intent to benefit some person or body other than the corporation which he serves. See *United States v Harry L Young Inc* 464 F 2d 1295 (1975).
1 *Dellow v Busby* [1942] 2 All ER 439; *R v Sorsky* [1944] 2 All ER 333.
2 *Magna Plant Ltd v Mitchell* [1966] Crim LR 394. The same tendency is evident in cases arising under the Merchant Shipping Act 1894. See *The Lady Gwendolen* [1965] P 294, [1965] 2 All ER 283, and Leigh (1965) 28 Mod LR 584. In *Tesco Supermarkets Ltd v Nattrass* [1972] AC 153, [1971] 2 All ER 127 *dicta* by Lords Reid and Dilhorne support this view. Lord Diplock, however, would restrict the doctrine to persons entitled by the articles of association or under a power of delegation in them, to act for the company. Lords Morris and Pearson do not consider the matter at large.

Chapter 3

Promotions and Formation

THE PROMOTER

It should not be assumed that all promoters are professional company promoters who, for a relatively high return for their labours, bring a company into existence and then abandon it to its fate. In most cases, the promoters will be persons who have an established business and who have decided to gain the benefits of incorporation and limited liability. Such persons, who intend to hold most of the shares in the company, or at any rate to retain control of it, have a real interest in the success of the legal entity they propose to create.

The promoters of a company are those responsible for its formation. They decide the scope of its business activities; they negotiate, if necessary, for the purchase of an existing business; they instruct solicitors to prepare the necessary documents; they secure the services of directors; they provide the registration fees and carry out the other duties involved in the formation of a company. They will also take responsibility, in the case of a company in respect of which a prospectus is to be issued before its incorporation, for the preparation of the prospectus and the employment of those whose reports must accompany the prospectus.

As was explained by Bowen J in *Whaley Bridge Calico Printing Co v Green and Smith*,[1] 'the term promoter is a term not of law, but of business, usefully summing up in a single word the number of business operations familiar to the commercial world by which a company is generally brought into existence'. The term includes those who assist in the promotion, those who secure the services of directors, those who negotiate the preliminary agreements, if any, and those who arrange the underwriting. Those who act in a purely professional capacity, eg solicitors and accountants, will not be treated as having taken part as promoters of the company.

---

[1] (1879) 5 QBD 109, 111.

It is a question of fact, determined by the Court in each case, when promotion began and when it can be said to have ended and the company's officers to have assumed responsibility for the company's affairs. If, for instance, the promoters have purchased property which is later sold to the company, they will be treated as having purchased it as promoters if it can be established that the purchase and formation of a company were part of the one scheme.[2] Moreover, a promoter cannot escape liability by having others act under his directions;[3] the Court will inquire who was the guiding spirit and, even if the directors have been appointed, will hold the promoters liable for acts done thereafter if the directors allowed the promoters to continue with the work of promotion.[4]

Although they may not be in the strict sense agents or trustees for the company, promoters stand in a fiduciary relation to it. They must disclose the nature and extent of the profits taken from the promotion, otherwise such profits may be recovered by the company. It is contrary to the good faith required of promoters that they should derive a secret profit from the promotion.[5]

Where the promoter wishes to sell his own property to the company, he must, if he wishes to retain the profits, take steps to see that the interests of the company are protected. In *Erlanger v New Sombrero Phosphate Co* (1878) 3 App Cas 1218, Lord Cairns said that a promoter must take care that he sells his property to the company through the medium of a board of directors who can and do exercise an independent and intelligent judgment on the transaction. The decision in that case was given before *Salomon's* case was decided. In *Lagunas Nitrate Co v Lagunas Syndicate* [1899] 2 Ch 392, 426, Lindley MR was of the opinion that since *Salomon's* case, it was impossible to hold that a promoter must provide the company with an independent board of directors. Salomon certainly had not done so. The learned Master of the Rolls considered that a promoter had discharged his responsibility to the company if the real truth of the transaction was disclosed to those who had been

---

2 Cf *Burland v Earle* [1902] AC 83, and *Gluckstein v Barnes* [1900] AC 240.
3 *Re Darby, ex p Brougham* [1911] 1 KB 95, where the Court treated the promoter company as merely the 'alias' of its two directors who had established the company for the purpose of concealing the profit they were making by selling their property through the promoter company to the purchaser company.
4 *Tracy v Mandalay Pty Ltd* (1952) 88 CLR 215, and *Twycross v Grant* (1877) 2 CPD 469, 541, per Cockburn CJ.
5 *Whaley Bridge Calico Printing Co v Green* (1879) 5 QBD 109, 113. See also *Gluckstein v Barnes* [1900] AC 240; *Mann v Edinburgh Northern Tramways Co* [1893] AC 69.

induced by the promoter to join the company.[6] In those cases where disclosure to an independent board of directors is not possible, disclosure to the existing or potential shareholders must be made if the promoter wishes to retain the profit on the sale to the company.

The facts of the *Lagunas Nitrate* case supra were unusual. The Lagunas Syndicate Ltd was incorporated to acquire nitrate deposits and re-sell them to companies to be formed to exploit the deposits. The Syndicate promoted a company to purchase part of the deposits it had acquired. The price paid by the company was much higher than that paid by the Syndicate. The first directors of the company were all members of the Syndicate. A prospectus was issued disclosing that the directors of the company were directors of the Syndicate and the price being paid for the land by the company to the Syndicate (but not the price paid by the Syndicate). Applications for shares exceeded the number allotted. The company worked the deposits and while it was making substantial profits, the Syndicate sold at a premium the shares it had received as part of the purchase price. When the company was later wound up, the shareholders contended that an exorbitant price had been paid for the deposits. Proceedings were brought against the Syndicate claiming, inter alia, rescission of the contract with the Syndicate or an account of all profits made by it. Fraud was not alleged. The Court of Appeal recognised that the business was of a highly speculative nature and that the shareholders could not be said to have been ignorant of the position of the directors, which had been disclosed in the memorandum and articles[7] and in the prospectus issued by the company. Rescission of the contract was not available because of the actions of the company in working the deposits. Non-disclosure of the profit made by the Syndicate was said to be not fatal to the validity of the sale. Furthermore, knowledge of the directors of the Syndicate could not be imputed to them in their capacity as directors of the company. The question was whether they as directors had failed to discharge their duties. They were certainly not independent, but since *Salomon's* case that could not be insisted upon. On the facts, they were held to have made adequate disclosure to prospective shareholders and had taken decisions bona fide in the interests of the company with that degree of care demanded of them.

6 Where a prospectus is issued and until the Financial Services Act 1986 comes into force, compliance is required with the Third Schedule to the Companies Act 1985.
7 Note, however, that in the view of Rigby LJ, who dissented, disclosure in the memorandum and articles (and the operation of the doctrine of constructive notice of their contents) did not relieve promoters of their responsibilities; p 449.

A promoter who discloses his dealings with the company must make full disclosure. Thus, if he understates the profit which he is making on the transaction, the company will be entitled to rescind the contract.[8]

If the promoter fails to discharge the obligations demanded of his fiduciary position, the company may rescind the contract,[9] and thus deprive the promoter of his profits. Because such situations involve a misrepresentation, the company may in the alternative choose to take advantage of the contract and sue the promoter for damages for breach of his duty to the company.[10] Either way, the dishonest promoter is deprived of his advantage. Secret profits on the sale of property can be recovered from a promoter only where the property was bought and sold to the company while he was acting as promoter: *Burland v Earle*.[11]

Promoters may also be liable for untrue or misleading statements in a prospectus. The promoter cannot protect himself by provisions in the articles relieving him of liability.[12]

The nature of the promoter's assistance in the formation of a company calls for considerable skill for which he should be adequately remunerated. Lord Hatherley said in *Touche v Metropolitan Railway Warehousing Co* (1871) 6 Ch App 671, 676:

> The services of a promoter are very peculiar; great skill, energy and ingenuity may be employed in constructing a plan and in bringing it out to the best advantage.

His remuneration may take the form of a fee, the issue of shares,[13] or he may be remunerated in other ways, but the remuneration paid must be disclosed in the prospectus.[14] The liability of the company to pay promoter's expenses under a preliminary agreement is discussed below.[15]

---

8   *Gluckstein v Barnes* [1900] AC 240.
9   The usual contractual principles apply to the right to rescind. If the company has affirmed the contract after becoming aware of the true facts or if *restitutio in integrum* is not possible, the right to rescind is lost.
10 Misrepresentation Act 1967, s 2(1).
11 [1902] AC 83. The remedies available to the company will depend upon the circumstances of the case; see Chap 10, post. See also *Gluckstein v Barnes* [1900] AC 240.
12 *Omnium Electric Palaces v Baines* [1914] 1 Ch 332.
13 CA 1985, s 88 requires that the contract evidencing the title of the allottee must be filed with the Registrar.
14 CA 1985, s 56 and para 10, Sch 3.
15 See pp 34–36, infra.

PRELIMINARY AGREEMENTS

Agreements affecting a company about to be formed are commonly made before its incorporation. The agreements may relate to property which the promoters wish to secure for the company or they may be made with persons whose 'know how' is vital to the success of the company and whose services it is essential to secure. The promoters may perhaps have arranged for the company to take over an existing business and therefore need to make an agreement with the vendor for its sale and purchase. In other cases, their object may be to ensure that the company is obliged to reimburse them for promotion or other expenses they have incurred.

The difficulty with preliminary agreements is that, as a company does not possess the capacity to make contracts until it is incorporated, they cannot be made with the proposed company. Thus, where the wording of the contract shows that the company is purporting to contract, the third party cannot enforce it against the company after incorporation or against the 'agent' signing the contract purportedly in the company's name because there is no contract capable of enforcement;[16] however, where an agent purports to contract for and on behalf of a non-existent company, the third party may enforce the contract against the agent where the form of wording used shows that the agent is contracting personally.[17] Section 36(4) of the Companies Act 1985[18] provides a partial remedy. It specifies:

> 36(4) Where a contract purports to be made by a company, or by a person as agent for a company, at a time when the company has not been formed, then subject to any agreement to the contrary the contract shall have effect as a contract entered into by the person purporting to act for the company or as agent for it, and he shall be personally liable on the contract accordingly.

The difficult and illogical[19] distinction at common law between the case where the wording shows that it is the company which is contracting and the case where the wording shows that the agent is contracting personally has been rendered irrelevant by s 36(4)

---

16 *Hollman v Pullin* (1884) Cab & El 254; *Newborne v Sensolid (Great Britain) Ltd* [1954] 1 QB 45, [1953] 1 All ER 708.
17 *Kelner v Baxter* (1866) LR 2 CP 174.
18 EEC Council Directive 68/151, which led to the introduction of s 36(4) is binding only in spirit and intention. Since s 36(4) is in accordance with such spirit and intention, it falls to be construed according to its own terms without reference to the Directive: *Phonogram Ltd v Lane* [1982] QB 938, [1981] 3 All ER 182.
19 *Black v Smallwood* (1965) 117 CLR 52.

which applies whether the contract is made with the company or an agent of the company.[20] Section 36(4) applies to a contract purporting to be made by a person or agent for a company which is about to be formed even though it is not in the course of formation at the time when the contract is made, and moreover, for the purposes of the section, a contract can purport to be made by or on behalf of a company notwithstanding that both contracting parties know that the company is not formed and that it is only about to be formed; there is no need for the person purporting to act for the company to represent that the company is in existence.[1]

Seemingly, despite the explicit reference in the concluding words of the section to the liability of the agent, it is intended that he shall be able to enforce the contract as against the other party to the contract.[2] This if correct would overcome one of the significant disadvantages of the common law rule preventing enforcement on the basis that no contract came into existence; for, in such cases, just as there was no contract capable of enforcement against the purported agent or non-existent principal, there was no contract which the agent or company when formed could enforce against the third party.[3]

It is unclear how much farther the section extends. At common law a company would not be bound by such a pre-incorporation agreement and there appears to be nothing in the section which alters that rule.[4] Again, at common law a company could not ratify or otherwise enforce a preliminary agreement.[5] It is submitted that this rule has been affected by statute; that the effect of s 36(4) is to recognise a contract which takes effect as one between the agent acting personally and the third party so that the benefit of it can be assigned to the company on formation. Enforceability should

---

20 *Phonogram Ltd v Lane* [1982] QB 938, [1981] 3 All ER 182.
1 Ibid.
2 So argued by J. G. Collier and L. Sealey (1973) 32 CLJ 1.
3 *Newborne v Sensolid (Great Britain) Ltd,* supra, *semble,* despite *dicta* in that case the agent could always have been held liable in breach of warranty of authority, *Black v Smallwood,* supra and see a note in (1967) 30 Mod LR 328.
4 *Kelner v Baxter* (1866) LR 2 CP 174.
5 *Re English and Colonial Produce Co Ltd* [1906] 2 Ch 435; the Courts thereupon created a confusing body of case law the essence of which was the drawing of a distinction between acts pursuant to the original contract by which it could not be ratified, and acts which might be referable to a new contract (in similar terms) by the company which could be enforced. See *Re Northumberland Avenue Hotel Co* (1886) 33 ChD 16; *Howard v Patent Ivory Manufacturing Co* (1888) 38 ChD 156, 164, 168 per Kay J; *Bagot Pneumatic Tyre Co v Clipper Pneumatic Tyre Co* [1901] 1 Ch 196, 201–202, per Kekewich J; and *Natal Land and Colonisation Co Ltd v Pauline Colliery Syndicate Ltd* [1904] AC 120.

36   Chapter 3 Promotions and Formation

in that event pose no problem as the agent is treated as a full contracting party. But it is not clear what view the Courts will ultimately take of the matter; the only safe rule is that the company can sue and be sued if there is a novation.[6] It seems a pity that the statute did not provide in plain terms for adoption by the company of pre-incorporation contracts unilaterally upon formation.

Section 36(4) only applies 'Subject to any agreement to the contrary'. These words mean 'unless otherwise agreed' and there must be a clear, express exclusion of the agent's personal liability to prevent the application of the section. An 'agreement to the contrary' will not be inferred merely by the fact that the contract is signed by a party acting 'as agent'.[7]

REGISTRATION OF A COMPANY

The Companies Act provides for both private and public companies. The differences between the two forms are not of fundamental significance, but a minimum capital provision applies, together with other restrictions, to public companies.

Apart from important transitional provisions dealing with old public companies,[8] that is, companies registered as public companies under former legislation, companies are classified as either public or private companies and in the former case bear the designation public limited company or its Welsh equivalent.[9] A public company formed after the coming into force of the Act must be limited by shares or by guarantee.[10] Its memorandum must state that the company is to be a public company and the appropriate registration provisions must have been complied with.[11] 'Private company' simply means a company that is not a public company.[12]

Any two persons may form a company, whether it be a public or a

---

6   *Natal Land Co and Colonisation Ltd v Pauline Colliery Syndicate Ltd* [1904] AC 120; in a previous edition of this book we suggested that one solution might be for the promoter to enter into an agreement as trustee for an unformed company. For the manifold deficiencies of this approach, see *Rita Joan Dairies Ltd v Thomson* [1974] 1 NZLR 285, discussed in [1974] ASCL 579–580.
7   *Phonogram Ltd v Lane,* supra.
8   Companies Consolidation (Consequential Provisions) Act 1985, ss 1–4.
9   CA 1985, s 25.
10 Under the Companies Act 1948 it was possible to incorporate a company limited by guarantee and having a share capital. By CA 1985, s 1(4), no company limited by guarantee shall have a share capital unless it had one immediately before 22 December 1980.
11 CA 1985, s 2.
12 Ibid, s 1(3).

private company.[13] The procedure involves two stages, the first of which is the delivery of a memorandum for registration.

A memorandum of association must be registered in respect of every company, but it is not necessary for all companies to register articles of association.[14] A company limited by shares need not register articles, but if it does not register them the regulations contained in Table A[15] become the articles of the company.[16] Companies limited by guarantee and unlimited companies must register articles signed by the subscribers to the memorandum.[17]

The memorandum and articles (where necessary) are delivered to the Registrar, who registers[18] them when he is satisfied that all relevant provisions of the Act have been complied with;[19] and that the name of the company is acceptable.[20]

In addition, where the proposed company is a public company the amount of the share capital stated in the memorandum to be that with which the company proposes to be registered must not be less than the authorised minimum, at present £50,000.[1]

In addition to the memorandum and articles (if any) the following particulars must be delivered to the Registrar:

(1) a statement containing the names and relevant particulars of the person who is or the persons who are to be the first director or directors of the company and the first secretary or joint secretaries of the company;[2]
(2) a statutory declaration in the prescribed form by a solicitor engaged in the formation of a company or by a person named as a director or secretary of the company in the statement of first directors and secretary that the requirements of the Companies Acts 1985 have been complied with. The Registrar may accept such a declaration as sufficient evidence of compliance.[3]

---

13 Ibid, s 1(1).
14 Ibid, s 13.
15 Table A is set out in the Companies (Tables A–F) Regulations (SI 1985/1208).
16 Ibid, s 8(2).
17 Ibid, s 7(1).
18 Ibid, s 12.
19 Ibid.
20 CA 1985, s 26.
 1 CA 1985, s 11. Note that the Secretary of State can raise the authorised minimum by statutory instrument.
 2 CA 1985, s 10 and Sch 1. These include such matters as name, address, nationality and other directorships.
 3 CA 1985, s 12(3).

CERTIFICATE OF INCORPORATION

This certificate is issued by the Registrar. It is conclusive evidence that the statutory requirements concerning registration and matters precedent and incidental thereto have been complied with, that the company is authorised to be registered and is duly registered and if the certificate contains a statement that the company is a public company, that it is such a company.[4] It certifies also whether the company is a limited liability company.[5] The Registrar also allocates to the company a registered number.[6]

REGISTERED OFFICE

Every company must have a registered office, the location of which must be notified to the Registrar before incorporation.[7] The memorandum must state whether the registered office is to be in England or Scotland, but it may specify Wales instead.[8] Notice of a change in the company's registered office must be furnished to the Registrar within 14 days of the proposed change.[9] Unless such change is registered, the company cannot rely on it in legal proceedings.[10]

CERTIFICATE RE DOING BUSINESS

The second stage is the obtaining of a certificate that the company may do business and may exercise borrowing powers. A company registered as a public company on its original incorporation shall not do business or exercise any borrowing powers unless the Registrar of companies has issued it with a certificate enabling it to do so or the company is re-registered as a private company.[11]

The Registrar must be satisfied that the nominal value of the

---

4 Ibid, s 13(7).
5 Ibid, s 13(1); the certificate is also evidence that the company came into existence on that date, *Jubilee Cotton Mills v Lewis* [1924] AC 958.
6 Ibid, s 705.
7 Ibid, s 10. See also ss 287 and 711.
8 CA 1985, s 2(2); in such case the Welsh equivalent of 'Limited', viz, 'cyfyngeding' shall appear as the last word of its name, but the company's documents must state clearly in English that its liability is limited; and see ibid, s 351(3).
9 CA 1985, s 287(2).
10 Ibid, s 42.
11 Ibid, s 117.

public company's issued share capital is not less than the authorised minimum, presently £50,000.[12]

A statutory declaration must be delivered to the Registrar, signed by a director or secretary of the company, and must state:[13]

(a) that the nominal value of the company's allotted share capital is not less than the authorised minimum;
(b) the amount paid up, at the time of the application, on the allotted share capital of the company;
(c) the amount, actual or estimated, of the preliminary expenses of the company and the persons by whom they have been paid or are payable; and
(d) benefits given or intended to be paid or given to any promoter of the company, and the consideration therefor.

A share allotted pursuant to an employee's share scheme may be taken into account in determining the nominal value of the company's allotted share capital, if it is paid up at least as to one-quarter of the nominal value of the share and the whole of any premium on it.[14]

The importance of the certificate is that it is conclusive evidence that the company is entitled to do business.[15] If a company does business or exercises borrowing powers without such a certificate the company and any officer in default is guilty of an offence.[16] Furthermore, the Secretary of State may present a petition to wind up a public company which has not been issued with a certificate if more than a year has elapsed since that company's registration as a public company. The Court may grant such a petition on the ground that it is just and equitable to do so.[17]

These provisions do not affect the validity of transactions entered into by a company. Third parties dealing with the company are therefore protected. On the other hand, if a company being required to meet its obligations under such a transaction fails within 21 days to do so, the directors of the company are personally jointly and severally liable to the third party in respect of loss or damage

---

[12] Ibid, s 117, and see s 101 by which a public company shall not allot a share except as paid up at least as to one-quarter of the nominal value of the share and the whole of any premium on it.
[13] Ibid, s 117(3).
[14] Ibid, s 117(4).
[15] Ibid, s 117(6).
[16] Ibid, s 117(7).
[17] IA 1986, s 122(1)(g).

suffered by him.[18] The statute does not specify what the position is where the third party is aware that the company lacks a certificate; seemingly, as against the company, recovery in these circumstances could be refused on the ground that the knowledge of the third party renders any contract void for illegality and invalid on that ground.[19]

---

[18] CA 1985, s 117(8).
[19] See *Chitty on Contracts* (24th edn, 1977) paras 908–909.

Chapter 4

Financing the Company

In this chapter we consider the raising of capital for the purposes of the company. We are, perforce, waiting in the shade of the Financial Services Act 1986, the disclosure provisions of which relating to unlisted securities will soon be brought into effect. We have keyed our discussion to the future law, as best we can, rather than to prospectus provisions which will soon be replaced. The reader will obviously have to check commencement orders with care.

Only public companies can raise money from the public by the sale of their shares. The private company is, essentially, restricted to sources such as banks and other institutions such as assurance companies since it cannot offer its shares to the public. Furthermore, public companies seeking to raise money from the public will have a considerable business history since only where the shares are likely to be readily marketable will the company or its agents be able to arrange an underwriting. An underwriting, as will be seen, is an essential form of insurance against a failure by the public to subscribe for securities in adequate amounts. An underwriter who thus ensures an issue will not wish to assume responsibility where there is a high risk of the issue failing to reach its target.

METHODS OF RAISING FUNDS

Because few companies are able to secure from their own funds or from the resources of members the moneys necessary for expansion or to cover the cost of large capital works, it is common for the public to be invited to subscribe for shares or debentures in the company. Essentially, there are three basic methods of raising capital.[1] These are:

---

1 See the Jenkins Report, Cmnd 1749 (1962) paras 235–252. See further *Gower's Principles of Modern Company Law* (4th edn, 1979) pp 339–345.

(1) direct offers to the public, now used only in the case of issues for which it is certain the public will subscribe. For, if the company makes a public issue, it bears the risk and will have to arrange its own underwriting.
(2) an offer for sale. In this case the company sells the issue to an issuing house. The issuing house then prepares a prospectus offering the security at a higher price. It bears the risk and will normally arrange an underwriting at its own risk.
(3) a placing, in which case the issuing house undertakes to place the securities with or without purchasing them itself.[2] No invitation is made to the public generally. The issuing house will attempt to induce its clients, for example institutional investors, to purchase the securities. Whether a prospectus is legally required depends on whether the issuing house issues an advertisement offering securities.[3]

An additional method of raising funds is by a rights issue. In such an issue, the invitation is made to the company's existing shareholders. The invitation enables the shareholder to subscribe for additional shares in proportion to his original holding, or may take the form of a provisional letter of allotment, allotting to the shareholder the number of shares which he is entitled to take up. This letter of allotment is usually renounceable. By signing the renunciation and handing the letter to a purchaser, the shareholder can sell his right to subscribe.[4]

A bonus issue is not used to raise fresh capital. Bonus shares are provided out of profits or reserves. Their purpose is to capitalise profits which are available for distribution. The shareholder does not pay for bonus shares. Letters of allotment of such shares may, however, be dealt with on a stock exchange if the shares are quoted.

UNDERWRITING

When a company is being formed, the promoter will, if necessary, see that the shares offered to the public are underwritten. This duty

---

[2] In general, see Financial Services Act 1986, Part V.
[3] Ibid, s 160.
[4] The machinery is described in Pennington, *The Investor and the Law* (1966) pp 133–135. In some cases rights issues will be subjected to the prospectus requirements of the Act. The Stock Exchange will only allow a placing of listed securities where the issue is so small that any other method would be impractical.

falls on the directors if new shares are issued by an existing company that wishes to increase its capital. The purpose of underwriting is to ensure the success of an issue of shares. Companies will seldom be confident that all, or even the major part, of an issue of shares will be taken up by the public. Market conditions may not be favourable and underwriting is a form of insurance against a poor reception by the public. Cotton LJ in *Re Licensed Victuallers' Mutual Trading Association*[5] said that 'an "underwriting" agreement means an agreement entered into before the shares are brought before the public, that in the event of the public not taking up the whole of them, or the number mentioned in the agreement, the underwriter will, for an agreed commission, take an allotment of such part of the shares as the public had not applied for'.

The essence of underwriting is, therefore, that by paying a commission, the company can be confident that, failing the desired response from the public, the shares will be taken up by the underwriter. Underwriting commissions are to be distinguished from brokerage, ie the sums payable to a share broker who agrees to *place* shares, not to *take* shares. Subject to the statutory maximum provided by any rules made under the FSA 1986,[6] the amount of commission payable to an underwriter will depend upon market conditions and the attractiveness of the investment to the public.

Those arranging underwriting agreements must in practice ensure that the underwriter has sufficient funds to meet the possible liability under the agreement.

The underwriting agreement may be a formal agreement signed by both parties, or be concluded by an exchange of letters.[7]

Underwriting commission may only be paid in accordance with s 97 of the Companies Act 1985 which enables a company to pay a commission to any person in consideration of his subscribing or agreeing to subscribe for shares, or procuring or agreeing to procure subscriptions for any shares in the company (eg a placing). Commission may be paid only if the following conditions are satisfied:[8]

(1) the payment of the commission must be authorised by the articles; and

---

5 (1889) 42 ChD 1, 6.
6 CA 1985, s 97(2) as amended by FSA 1986, s 212(2), Sch 16, para 16; the maximum is 10% unless the rules provide otherwise.
7 *Re Consort Deep Level Gold Mines Ltd* [1897] 1 Ch 575; *Re Hannan's Empress Gold Mining and Development Co* [1896] 2 Ch 643.
8 CA 1985, s 97 as amended by FSA 1986.

(2) the commission must not exceed the maximum provided by any rules made under the FSA 1986, or otherwise exceed 10% of the price at which the shares are issued or the amount or rate authorised by the articles, whichever is the less.

The Act then forbids any commissions or discounts save as above permitted, in consideration for subscribing or agreeing to subscribe for shares, or for procuring subscriptions.

This section does not affect the power of any company to pay brokerage charges which are fair and necessary. No commission which is not authorised by the Act may be paid since this would amount to an unauthorised reduction of capital.[9]

DISCLOSURE

Legal controls relating to statements made in connection with the advertisement of securities for purchase and sale are directed towards ensuring that full disclosure of the company's affairs will be made to the investing public or its advisers. These controls are contained in Parts IV and V of the Financial Services Act 1986.

LISTED SECURITIES

Application for listing is made to the Stock Exchange. This requires that the listing rules be complied with.[10] These particulars contain a general duty of disclosure.[11] Specifically, the listing particulars must contain all such information as investors and their professional advisers would reasonably require and reasonably expect to find there, for the purpose of making an informed assessment of assets and liabilities, financial position, profits and losses and prospects of the issuer of the securities, and the rights attaching to those securities. Significant changes in respect of matters contained in the listing particulars or the emergence of new matters will require the filing of supplementary listing particulars.[12]

The person or persons responsible for listing particulars are liable to pay compensation to any person who acquired the securities in question and who suffered loss as a result of any untrue statement in

---

9 *Ooregum Gold Mining Co of India Ltd v Roper* [1892] AC 125, HL.
10 Financial Services Act 1986, s 143.
11 Ibid, s 146.
12 Ibid, s 147.

or omission from the listing particulars.[13] A person who satisfies a court that he believed on reasonable grounds that the statements made were true and not misleading or that an omission was justified, may be exempt from liability.[14] In particular, he is entitled to rely on the opinion of a person whom he reasonably believes was entitled to hold himself out as an expert and who consented to the making of the statement.[15]

There are, furthermore, important provisions concerning, especially, advertisements for listed securities, and the content of listing particulars. No account is taken of them here.

UNLISTED SECURITIES

At the time of writing, the provisions of the Financial Services Act 1986 relating to unlisted securities have not been brought into effect. It is expected that this will happen late in 1987. What follows is an outline of the statutory scheme which will apply to such securities, but it should be noted that the Act's provisions will be supplemented by rules concerning the contents of prospectuses made under its authority, and the student will want to consult these when they are available.

In the case of an offer of securities expressed to be on admission to an approved exchange, a prospectus must be submitted to and approved by the exchange and delivered to the Registrar of companies.[16] In the case of other offers of securities, that is, for example, offers to subscribe for or underwrite securities, no advertisement may be issued until the issuer has delivered a prospectus relating to the securities to the Registrar of companies.[17]

A prospectus must comply with any requirements imposed by rules made by the Department of Trade.[18] In addition, it attracts a general duty of disclosure.[19] A prospectus must contain such information as investors and their professional advisers would reasonably require and reasonably expect to find there for the purpose of

13 Ibid, s 150; liability can also be based on failure to comply with the obligation to provide supplementary listing particulars.
14 Ibid, s 151.
15 Ibid, s 151(2), and note the following subsections which ensure that the defendant's belief continued either to the time of acquisition of the securities or beyond the time when it was practicable to warn persons likely to acquire the securities.
16 Ibid, s 159; note that neither this nor the next section applies to an advertisement offering securities conditional on their being listed, ibid, s 161.
17 Ibid, s 160.
18 Ibid, s 162.
19 Ibid, s 163.

making an informed assessment of assets and liabilities, financial position, profits and losses, and prospects of the issuer of the securities and the rights attaching to them.[20] In determining what information is to be included, regard is to be had to the nature of the securities and the issuer, to the nature of persons likely to consider their acquisition, to the fact that certain matters may reasonably be expected to be within the knowledge of professional advisers which such persons may reasonably be expected to consult, and to information available to investors and investment advisers by virtue of requirements imposed by statute or a recognised exchange.[1] A supplementary prospectus may be required in certain cases; the criteria are akin to those which apply in the case of listed securities.[2]

As with listed securities, the persons responsible for a prospectus or supplementary prospectus are, unless exempted by the court, liable to pay compensation to any person who has acquired shares to which the prospectus relates and who has suffered loss in respect of them by reason of any untrue or misleading statement in the prospectus.[3] The persons responsible are the issuer, each director of a corporate issuer, each person who, in the case of a corporate issuer has authorised himself to be named in the prospectus or supplementary prospectus, and generally, each person who has authorised the issue of a prospectus or supplementary prospectus.[4] The provision concerning liability implies not only that the prospectus was misleading, but also that the person dealt in reliance upon representations made in it. Exemption is premised upon the person responsible satisfying the court of the like matters which apply in the case of listed securities, viz, reasonable belief based on reasonable inquiries that the statement was true and not misleading, or that an omission which caused loss was properly omitted, and that he continued in that belief until the securities were acquired or until it was no longer practicable to bring a correction to the notice of the person damnified, or that he took all reasonable steps to correct the impression before acquisition, or that the securities were acquired after such a lapse of time that he ought reasonably to be excused.[5]

---

20 Ibid, s 163(1).
1 Ibid, s 163(3).
2 Ibid, s 164.
3 Ibid, s 166(1); the omission of relevant information is, by sub-s (2), treated as a statement that matter required to be disclosed does not exist.
4 Ibid, s 168. Note the provisions concerning issue by subsidiaries.
5 Ibid, s 167(1). Note that this paragraph does not apply where the securities are dealt with on a recognised exchange unless the person responsible satisfies the court that he continued to believe the statement to be true until after the commencement of dealings on the exchange.

Such a situation could arise where the person damnified took securities so long after the issue of a prospectus that it could not reasonably be supposed that any prospective purchaser would have been influenced by the prospectus. As with listed securities, the issuer is entitled to rely on an expert's report. Again, he must continue in the belief that the report was one which the person was entitled to make as an expert until acquisition of the securities, or until there was no longer time to bring to the attention of others that the expert was not competent or had not consented to the inclusion of his report, or that before acquisition he had taken all reasonable steps to ensure that that fact was brought to the attention of prospective customers, or that the securities were acquired after such a lapse of time he ought reasonably to be excused.[6] A person may, furthermore, be excused if he satisfies the court that he published a timely correction, or that the expert was not competent or had not consented to the publication of his report, or that he took all reasonable steps to secure such publication and reasonably believed that such publication had taken place.[7]

Exemption from liability is further provided for a person who relied on a public official document which is published in the prospectus,[8] or who satisfies the court that the person suffering the loss was aware of the false or misleading nature of a statement, omission, change or new matter.[9]

No private company and no old public company may issue or cause to be issued any advertisement offering securities to be issued by that company unless authorised to do so by the Department of Trade and Industry.[10]

An authorised person who contravenes the unlisted securities provisions will be treated as having breached the conduct of business rules of his regulatory organisation or body; an unauthorised person will commit a criminal offence punishable on conviction for imprisonment for up to two years or a fine or both.[11]

---

6 Ibid, s 167(2); sub-s (3) makes the same provision concerning securities dealt with on an exchange as apply to statements of belief in the matters specified in the prospectus.
7 Ibid, s 167(3).
8 Ibid, s 167(4).
9 Ibid, s 167(5). By sub-s (6) he does not incur liability if he satisfies the court that he reasonably believed that the change or new matter was not such as to call for a supplementary prospectus.
10 Ibid, s 170.
11 Ibid, s 171.

STOCK EXCHANGE REQUIREMENTS

In order to secure a listing, securities will have to comply with the listing requirements of the Stock Exchange.[12] The Stock Exchange, in relation to a full listing, has initial listing requirements which militate against the listing of very speculative securities. The companies securities must have a minimum market value of £700,000 in the case of shares and £200,000 in the case of debt securities other than tap issues. The Committee of the Stock Exchange may admit securities of lower value to listing provided that they are satisfied that adequate marketability can be expected. Further issues of shares of a class already listed are not subject to these limits.

Whilst it is not possible in a book of this size and format to deal extensively with the requirements of the Stock Exchange and the relevant statutory instruments, it should be noted that these have a considerable impact on the structure and internal government of the company.[13] Listing carries with it the acceptance of continuing obligations, for example in respect of precautions to prevent insider trading, in respect of accounts including departure from accepted conventions, in respect of the notification of changes in the directorate, and concerning adherence to a model code for securities transactions. The influence of the listing agreement is thus wide.

ALLOTMENT

The ordinary principles of contract apply to a contract to take shares from a company. There must be an offer, an acceptance and communication of the acceptance. In the normal course of events, a person wishing to secure shares applies to the company for them; this is an offer. The directors resolve to allot shares to the applicant; this is an acceptance. When the acceptance is communicated to the applicant a binding contract is made. Formal written notice of allotment is unnecessary; so long as the company indicates that shares have been allotted, eg by a letter demanding payment of a call, this will be sufficient:

Dunlop v Higgins (1848) 1 HL Cas 381.

> The letter advising the applicant that shares had been allotted to him was delayed. It was held that a binding contract was made when the letter was posted.

---

12 See generally Financial Services Act 1986, ss 142–149 and SI 1986/2246.
13 *Admission of Securities to Listing* (1984) and in particular s 5.

This accords with the ordinary principles of contract, and even if the allotment letter were lost the contract would be binding when the letter was posted: *Household Fire and Carriage Accident Insurance Co Ltd v Grant*.[14] Where a company offers shares to an existing member, the contract is made when the member's acceptance is posted.

Ramsgate Victoria Hotel Co Ltd v Montefiore (1866) LR 1 Exch 109.

> The company did not allot shares until five months after application. It was held that the company had been unduly dilatory and that the applicant's offer had lapsed before allotment. He was entitled to refuse to take the shares.

This rule is said to be based on the view that if an offeree has not accepted the offer within a reasonable time, he is to be treated as having refused it. Thus, if between the time of the offer and the acceptance the conduct of the parties shows that the offeree did not intend to refuse the offer it will not be treated as having lapsed.[15]

An application for shares may be conditional. Where the condition is a condition precedent, eg where the applicant is to receive an appointment with the company, the condition must be satisfied before the allotment will be binding.[16] But where the condition is a condition subsequent, eg a collateral agreement to be performed at a later date, the allotment will be binding and the member must be content with an action for damages under the collateral agreement.[17]

If there is some element in the contract to take shares that would vitiate an ordinary contract, eg mistake, fraud or illegality, the contract will not be binding.

EFFECT OF IRREGULAR ALLOTMENT

If (until the coming into force of the FSA 1986) an allotment contravenes CA 1985, s 84, it is voidable by the applicant. Section

---

14 (1879) 4 Ex D 216, CA.
15 *Manchester Diocesan Council for Education v Commercial and General Investments Ltd* [1969] 3 All ER 1593, [1970] 1 WLR 241.
16 *Woods Case* (1873) LR 15 Eq 236; *Re Radio Chain Stores Ltd* [1932] NZLR 1048.
17 *Elkingtons' Case* (1867) 2 Ch App 511, and see *Re Harmony and Montague Tin and Copper Mining Co Ltd, Spargo's Case* (1873) 8 Ch App 407.

84 prohibits allotment unless either the share capital of the company is subscribed in full, or the offer states that even if full subscription does not occur, shares may be allotted either under conditions or in any event. If the former applies, the conditions specified must be satisfied. It should further be noted that this provision applies both to cases where shares are subscribed for cash or for a wholly or partly non-cash construction. In this context, therefore, 'subscription' differs from its ordinary meaning which is that of subscription for cash. The allotment is voidable within one month of allotment.[18] The allotment may be avoided although the company is being wound up. If a director knowingly contravenes the provisions as to allotment he is liable to compensate the company and the allottee for any loss or damage suffered thereby. Proceedings against a director must be commenced within two years of allotment.[19]

A member entitled to avoid an irregular allotment of shares will lose his rights if, after becoming aware of the irregularity, he exercises any rights of a member.[20]

RETURN OF ALLOTMENTS

A company limited by shares, or by guarantee and having a share capital, must make a return of shares allotted within one month of allotment.[1] The return must state the number and nominal amount of shares allotted, the names, addresses and descriptions of the allottees and the amount, if any, paid or payable on each share. Where shares are allotted as fully or partly paid up, otherwise than in cash, a contract in writing constituting the title of the allottee, together with any contract of sale or for services or other consideration for the allotment must be registered. If the contract is not reduced to writing, particulars of it must be registered.[2]

---

18 Ibid, s 85.
19 Ibid, s 85(2) and (3).
20 *Burton v Bevan* [1908] 2 Ch 240.
1   CA 1985, s 88(2)(a).
2   Ibid, s 88(3).

Chapter 5

Investor Protection

In the previous chapter we discussed the provisions relating to disclosure where the company or an issuing house on its behalf has issued an invitation to the public to subscribe for shares and debentures. In this chapter we discuss, somewhat more widely, the remedies available to persons who have suffered loss as a result of a misleading inducement to deal in securities. We are also concerned with the criminal penalties available in such cases.

REMEDIES FOR MIS-STATEMENTS IN OR OMISSIONS FROM A PROSPECTUS

The responsibility of those issuing a prospectus was discussed by Kindersley V-C in *New Brunswick and Canada Rly and Land Co v Muggeridge*.[1]

> ... those who issue a prospectus holding out to the public the great advantages which will accrue to persons who take shares in a proposed undertaking, and inviting them to take shares on the faith of the representations therein contained, are bound to state everything with strict and scrupulous accuracy, and ... to abstain from stating as facts that which is not so ... and ... they have no right to turn round upon those who refuse to fulfil their contracts to take shares and say to them, 'You ought to have been more prudent, more circumspect, more cautious, more vigilant; you ought, by applying your reasoning powers, to have concluded that our representations could not be true in the sense in which the language we used in the prospectus naturally and fairly imports ...'

If those who issue a prospectus fail to meet these standards or omit statements that must under the Act appear in a prospectus, or

---

1 (1860) 1 Drew & Sm 363, 381–382, cited with approval by Lord Chelmsford LC in *Central Rly Co of Venezuela v Kisch* (1867) LR 2 HL 99.

make omissions which render what is stated false, they will be liable to compensate those who suffer injury thereby. The person who has purchased shares or debentures on the faith of a prospectus that fails to comply with the statute or which contains false or untrue statements may in appropriate cases pursue one of the following civil remedies:[2]

(1) he may repudiate the contract and sue the company for the return of moneys paid to it, or
(2) he may bring an action for misrepresentation, or
(3) he may sue for compensation under CA 1985, s 67 (for the future ss 151 or 166 of the FSA 1986).

Criminal proceedings may be taken under s 70 of the CA 1985 (for the future ss 154 and 171 of the FSA 1986) and s 19 of the Theft Act 1968. In order to avoid criminal liability under s 70, those persons who authorised the issue of the prospectus including an untrue statement must prove either that the statement was immaterial, or that they had reasonable grounds for believing, and did up to the time of the issue of the prospectus, believe, that the statement was true. The onus of proof lies on the accused.

RESCISSION OF THE CONTRACT

Where a person has subscribed for shares in or debentures of a company on the faith of a prospectus which contained an untrue or misleading, but not necessarily fraudulent, statement he should seek rescission of the contract, and the rectification of the register of members or debenture holders. This remedy is merely an ordinary contractual remedy available to any person who has been induced by a misrepresentation to enter into a contract. It is not open as against the company to a person who purchases shares on the market; but only to one who subscribes for shares from the company on the faith of the prospectus.[3] The shareholder or debenture holder should commence his action against the company for rescission and rectification immediately he becomes aware of the misrepresentation. If he succeeds in his action, he will secure the return

---

2 In appropriate cases, the plaintiff may combine in the same action a claim for rescission, damages for fraud and compensation, but in no case will the amount recovered exceed the loss suffered. See Cmnd 6659 (1945) paras 41–46, for the recommendations of the Cohen Committee in respect of liability for statements in a prospectus.
3 *Peek v Gurney* (1873) LR 6 HL 377.

of the purchase money paid to the company. In order to succeed, the shareholder or debenture holder must prove:

(1) that the prospectus included an untrue or misleading statement or misrepresentation.

Greenwood v Leather Shod Wheel Co [1900] 1 Ch 421.

> The prospectus of the company stated that 'orders have already been received from the House of Commons' and that 'wheels for the trolleys in the House of Commons have been ordered, and are now in use'. These statements were incorrect; the person supplying refreshments to the House of Commons had one trolley with these wheels but orders had not been placed by the House of Commons. The statement was held to be misleading and untrue.

(2) That the untrue or misleading statement or misrepresentation was in respect of a material matter and was one of the inducements to apply for shares or debentures.

R v Kylsant [1932] 1 KB 442, [1931] All ER Rep 179.

> The prospectus stated 'after providing for all taxation, depreciation of the fleet, etc, adding to the reserves and payment of dividends on the preference stocks, the dividends on the ordinary stock during the last 17 years have been as follows:'
> A table was set out showing that, between 1911 and 1927, the company had paid dividends varying from 5% to 8%, except in 1914, when no dividend was paid, and in 1926 when a dividend of 4% was paid. This statement was true, but the effect of the prospectus was to mislead, as it did not state that in the years 1921–27 inclusive trading losses had been made and dividends were paid from accumulated profits in the boom years 1918–20. Avory J stated at pp 448–449:
>
> > In the opinion of this Court there was ample evidence on which the jury could come to the conclusion that this prospectus was false in a material particular in that it conveyed a false impression. The falsehood in this case consisted in putting before intending investors, as material on which they could exercise their judgment as to the position of the company, figures which apparently disclosed the existing position, but in fact hid it. In other words, the prospectus implied that the company was in a sound financial position and that the prudent investor could safely invest his money in its debentures. This inference would be drawn particularly from the statement that dividends had been regularly paid over a term of years, although times

had been bad—a statement which was utterly misleading when the fact that those dividends had been paid, not out of current earnings, but out of funds which had been earned during the abnormal period of the war, was omitted.

Although this case concerns a prosecution under the Larceny Act 1861, the principle stated applies also to actions for rescission of a contract to take shares or debentures.[4]

(3) That the company was answerable for the statement or misrepresentation: *Lynde v Anglo-Italian Hemp Spinning Co*.[5] The company is responsible for misrepresentations or statements made by its directors and servants within their authority.[6] It will also be responsible for the contents of a prospectus issued before it was incorporated where the shares or debentures were subscribed for and allotted on the basis of such a prospectus.

(4) That he has taken action promptly to rescind the contract.[7] The delay that will preclude a shareholder or debenture holder from rescinding varies according to the circumstances. But the investor need not act on rumour. He is entitled to wait until he has sufficient knowledge. Furthermore, he is not deemed to have knowledge of the falsity of a prospectus merely because the prospectus refers to sources from which its accuracy could be verified.[8]

If a shareholder, after becoming aware of the misrepresentation, or mis-statement, does any act inconsistent with his right to rescind, eg by attending meetings, by paying a call, or accepting dividends,[9] or by attempting to sell the shares,[10] he will lose his right to

---

4 *Aaron's Reefs Ltd v Twiss* [1896] AC 273.
5 [1896] 1 Ch 178.
6 If the statement or misrepresentation was made by an unauthorised person, the company is not responsible for it. But where a prospectus is issued by promoters prior to the incorporation of the company, the statements are treated as if they were made by the company if the allotment is made on the basis of the prospectus. *Re Metropolitan Coal Consumers' Association* [1892] 3 Ch 1. Reference should also be made to CA 1985, s 58.
7 In *Re Scottish Petroleum Co* (1883) 23 ChD 413; *Sharpley v Louth and East Coast Rly Co* (1876) 2 ChD 663, p 685.
8 *Central Rly Co of Venezuela v Kisch* (1867) LR 2 HL 99.
9 *Scholey v Central Rly Co of Venezuela* (1869) LR 9 Eq 266n.
10 Other circumstances showing an intention to accept the shares were dealt with in *Re Hop and Malt Exchange and Warehouse Co, ex p Briggs* (1866) LR 1 Eq 483, where the allottee had attempted to sell the shares. See also *Haas Timber and Trading Co Pty Ltd v Wade* (1954) 94 CLR 593.

rescind.[11] A shareholder who has repudiated the contract to take shares must also take action to have the register of members rectified. The right to rescind must be exercised before the commencement of winding up: *Oakes v Turquand and Harding*.[12]

The right to rescind is subject to ordinary contractual principles. By s 1 of the Misrepresentation Act 1967 the contract may be rescinded whether or not it has been executed. If the shareholder delays bringing his action after becoming aware of his right to rescind, the lapse of time may be sufficient to deprive him of his remedy. The presence of his name on the register of members may have induced other persons to give credit to the company or to become members of it: *Aaron's Reefs Ltd v Twiss*.[13] It is not enough merely to serve on the company notice of repudiation. Steps must be taken to have the shareholder's name removed from the register: *Re Scottish Petroleum Co*.[14] A successful plaintiff will secure the repayment of moneys paid to the company (normally with interest).

If the shareholder has lost his right to rescind, by reason of delay or otherwise, he cannot secure damages for misrepresentation *from the company*.[15] This was established by *Houldsdworth v City of Glasgow Bank*[16] and is based on the principle that a shareholder, being an integral part of the company, may not recover damages from himself or his fellow shareholders. But such a shareholder can, without rescinding, sue the directors or other persons responsible for the issue of the prospectus.[17]

If the effect of the suppression of information is to make what has been stated misleading, the contract will be set aside and an order for the repayment of moneys will be made. In *Aaron's Reefs Ltd v Twiss*[18] Lord Halsbury LC said that the whole prospectus should be

11 If a shareholder who has independent grounds for rescission loses his right to rescind on one ground, he may not be precluded from rescinding on another ground. *Elder's Trustee and Executor Co Ltd v Commonwealth Homes and Investment Co Ltd* (1941) 65 CLR 603.
12 (1867) LR 2 HL 325.
13 [1896] AC 273, 294 per Lord Davey.
14 (1883) 23 ChD 413, 439 per Fry LJ.
15 This rule does not, however, apply to debenture holders; a debenture holder does not stand in the same relationship to the company as does a shareholder.
16 (1880) 5 App Cas 317. It was applied to a limited company in *Re Addlestone Linoleum Co* (1887) 37 ChD 191. These decisions were given before *Salomon's* case and may require reconsideration in the light of the principle there established: see pp 19–20 supra. The decision can be justified on the principle that share capital is a guarantee fund for creditors and should not be diminished by a shareholder's claim. See J. A. Hornby in 19 Mod LR 54 and the reply by L. C. B. Gower, ibid, p 185.
17 *Arnison v Smith* (1889) 41 ChD 348.
18 [1896] AC 273, 281. See also *R v Lord Kylsant* [1932] 1 KB 442.

taken together to determine whether a false representation has been made.

> I do not care by what means it is conveyed—by what trick or device or ambiguous language: all those are expedients by which fraudulent people seem to think they can escape from the real substance of the transaction. If by a number of statements you intentionally give a false impression and induce a person to act upon it, it is not the less false, although if one takes each statement by itself there may be a difficulty in shewing that any specific statement is untrue.

DAMAGES FOR MISREPRESENTATION

If the statement which induced the investor to subscribe contains a material misrepresentation, the investor has an action for damages provided also that he rescinded his contract in time.[19] Where the misrepresentation was made innocently, the person making it has a defence to the action provided he can show that he had reasonable ground to believe and did believe up to the time that the contract was made that the facts represented were true.[20] In *Howard Marine and Dredging Co Ltd v A Ogden & Sons (Excavations) Ltd*[1] Bridge LJ described the operation of the section thus: 'If the representee proves a misrepresentation which, if fraudulent, would have sounded in damages, the onus passes immediately to the representor to prove that he had reasonable ground to believe the facts represented. In other words the liability of the representor does not depend upon his being under a duty of care the extent of which may vary according to the circumstances in which the representation is made. In the course of negotiations leading to a contract the statute imposes an absolute obligation not to state facts which the representor cannot prove he had reasonable ground to believe.'

Unless the shareholder (but not of course a debenture holder) has rescinded he will be unable to sue the company for damages:[2] he

---

19 Misrepresentation Act 1967, s 2(1), as affected by *Houldsworth v City of Glasgow Bank* (1880) 5 App Cas 317. It is unlikely that such an action will be very useful since the plaintiff will recover the moneys paid for the shares on rescission. By s 2(2) where rescission is claimed, the Court could award damages in lieu. This seems anomalous in the light of the *Houldsworth* case.
20 Misrepresentation Act 1967, s 2(3).
1 [1978] QB 574, [1978] 2 All ER 1134.
2 This follows from the provision of s 2(1) of the Misrepresentation Act 1967 that an action for damages in innocent misrepresentation only lies where the misrepresentation, if made fraudulently, would give rise to a right of action in damages.

will be obliged to sue the directors and other persons who were responsible for the issue of the prospectus.[3] If the investor has rescinded, but has been unable to recover the moneys from an insolvent company, an action against the directors and others for misrepresentation is a valuable additional remedy. Such an action may be either a common law action for deceit or a statutory action for innocent misrepresentation based upon s 67 of the Companies Act 1985.[4] To succeed in an action for fraud the plaintiff must prove that a statement of fact was made 'to be acted upon by others, which is false, and which is known to be false or is made by him recklessly or without care whether it be true or false': *Derry v Peek*.[5] Mere negligence or want of reasonable ground for belief does not amount to fraud. In *Derry v Peek* the director honestly believed that the statement was true, although he had no reasonable ground for his belief; he was not liable for fraud. The question is whether the defendant '. . . honestly believed the representation to be true in the sense in which he understood it albeit erroneously when it was made'.[6]

Only the persons to whom the prospectus was directed, ie those who were intended to act upon it, can sue for fraud.

Peek v Gurney (1873) LR 6 HL 377.

> The person alleging fraud was not an allottee but a person who purchased shares on the market. It was held that he could not succeed as the prospectus was not addressed to him.[7]

DAMAGES OR COMPENSATION UNDER THE FINANCIAL SERVICES ACT

As indicated in the previous chapter, a person responsible for particulars may, both in the case of listed and unlisted securities, be made liable to pay compensation in respect of loss caused through dealings by persons damnified as the result of false or misleading

---

3   In deceit, or under CA 1985, s 67. There will be no action against the *agent* for damages under s 2(1) of the Misrepresentation Act 1967 because the Act seems intended only to affect the position of parties to the contract.
4   There may be an action for statutory fraud under CA 1985, s 56.
5   (1889) 14 App Cas 337, 350 per Lord Bramwell.
6   *Akerhielm v De Mare* [1959] AC 789, at 805.
7   Cf *Andrews v Mockford* [1896] 1 QB 372, where *Peek v Gurney* was distinguished. The prospectus was issued not only to induce applicants for shares but also to induce persons to buy shares on the market. The defendants were guilty of 'continuous fraud' and liable to the plaintiff.

particulars.⁸ As noted, the court may exempt such persons from liability provided that they acted without fault as specified in the exempting sections.⁹

ACTIONS FOR NEGLIGENCE AT COMMON LAW

Historically, at common law, no action for damages could lie in respect of damages caused by merely negligent misrepresentations.[10] It was to remedy this deficiency that s 67 of the CA 1985 was first passed. Section 67, however, deals only with prospectuses inviting the public to subscribe for shares and debentures of the company. It does not apply to documents which, because they offer shares for purchase or sale, or because they offer shares for other than a cash consideration, are not prospectuses within the meaning of the Companies Acts.[11] In 1964, in *Hedley Byrne & Co v Heller & Partners Ltd*,[12] the House of Lords held that an action in tort lay against a person negligently making a false statement in circumstances where, as a reasonable man, he ought to have foreseen that a person or class of persons would rely on the statement to his or their detriment. In Lord Morris' judgment the following passage, which seems particularly relevant to this discussion, appears:[13]

> ... if in a sphere in which a person is so placed that others would reasonably rely on his judgment or his skill or upon his ability to make careful inquiry, a person takes it on himself to give information or advice to, or allows his information or advice to be passed on to another person whom he knows or should know, will place reliance on it, then a duty of care will arise.

The earlier cases stress that liability depends on the plaintiff being able to show that the defendant stood in a special relationship to him, either by holding himself out as possessing a special skill, or by having a financial interest in a transaction in which he acts as adviser.[14] This view has, however, been strongly challenged. In the

---

8 Financial Services Act 1986, ss 150 and 166.
9 Ibid, ss 151 and 167.
10 *Derry v Peek* (1889) 14 App Cas 337. See also *Candler v Crane, Christmas & Co* [1951] 2 KB 164, [1951] 1 All ER 426.
11 CA 1985, s 744.
12 [1964] AC 465, [1963] 2 All ER 575.
13 Ibid, p 503.
14 *Mutual Life and Citizens' Assurance Co Ltd v Evatt* [1971] AC 793, [1971] 1 All ER 150; *Argy Trading Development Co Ltd v Lapid Developments Ltd* [1977] 3 All ER 785, [1977] 1 WLR 444.

Howard Marine case noted above,[15] Lord Denning MR states that there is a duty of care where the representation concerns a business or professional transaction whose nature makes clear the gravity of the inquiry and the importance attached to the answer. This obligation extends beyond an obligation to the initial inquirer and attaches in respect of those to whom it is reasonably foreseeable it will be furnished and by whom it will be acted upon.

This formulation reflects the neighbour principle generally invoked in tort cases.[16] It is consistent with the general modern trend of development, summed up by Lord Simon of Glaisdale as one in which the general and overriding principle of public policy is that where there is a duty to act with care with regard to another person and there is a breach of such duty causing damage to the other person, public policy demands in general that such damage should be made good to the party to whom the duty is owed by the person owing the duty. There may be a secondary public policy which demands immunity from suit, but such immunities are exceptional.[17]

It is probable that an action will lie for mis-statements of the sort under discussion.

Most circulars of this character will contain opinion as well as fact and will be intended to be acted upon. The issuers will have, in addition, a financial interest in the transaction. There seems no reason, therefore, to assume an overriding public interest in favour of no liability. This conclusion is reinforced by the New Zealand decision in *Dimond Manufacturing Co Ltd v Hamilton*[18] where Turner J was prepared to hold that purchasers of a company's shares could maintain an action against the company's auditors where the auditor handed a copy of the audited balance sheet to the purchaser's agent for use in the negotiations. This amounted to an implied representation as to the correctness of the balance sheet to purchasers who, it could be foreseen, would act on it.

RESTRICTION ON THE SALE OF SHARES AND DEBENTURES

Share-pushing, essentially the sale of securities by manipulative means, generally by high-pressure selling and often from abroad

---

15 At p 63, ante.
16 *Anns v Merton London Borough Council* [1978] AC 728, [1977] 2 All ER 492.
17 *Arenson v Casson Beckman Rutley & Co* [1977] AC 405, [1975] 3 All ER 901.
18 [1969] NZLR 609.

into the United Kingdom, is dealt with by the Financial Services Act 1986. Selling on fraudulent forecasts, cold-calling and other practices are struck at by both criminal and non-criminal sanctions, and references may be made to specialist studies of the topic.

Investor protection is further extended by the Banking Act 1987. The Prevention of Fraud (Investments) Act 1958, formerly in force but now superseded by the Financial Services Act 1986, and the prospectus provisions of the Companies Acts had been evaded by companies which instead of offering securities, advertised for short term loans. Accordingly, s 35 of the Banking Act 1987 makes provisions concerning statements inducing persons to invest money on deposit. Deposit business is now basically the province of recognised banks and licensed institutions. Section 79 of the Insurance Companies Act 1982 makes a similar provision against wrongful inducements to purchase equity linked insurance policies, thus closing a loophole which became prominent in recent years.

CRIMINAL LIABILITIES

UNDER THE COMPANIES ACTS

Under CA 1985, s 70, a person who authorises the issue of a prospectus containing any untrue statement is liable on conviction to a term of imprisonment or to a fine or both.

UNDER THE THEFT ACT

Under the Theft Act 1968 there are provisions which penalise persons who make false statements with respect to the affairs of companies.

By s 19(1) thereof, where an officer of a company with intent to deceive members or creditors of the company about its affairs publishes or concurs in publishing a written statement or account which to his knowledge is or may be misleading, false or deceptive in a material particular, he may be liable to conviction on indictment for a term not exceeding seven years. A person who has entered into a security for the benefit of the company is to be treated as a creditor of it. It should be noted that the officer will be liable even though neither he nor the company obtained property as a result of the false statement. It would, it is submitted, be enough if the officer by means of a false written statement induced members to retain their shares as a result of the false impression engendered. Nor need the document be a prospectus: any written statement will suffice.

Much of the former law under s 84 of the Larceny Act 1861 is applicable; a statement may be false as much by reason of what it conceals as what it contains. The falsity or otherwise of a prospectus is to be gauged by reading it as a whole.[19]

Unlike the former law, a company and an officer or person who aids it in publishing a false or deceptive prospectus with intent to induce some person to subscribe for securities of the company, whether shares or debentures, also commits the offence of obtaining property by deception.[20] Deception can include a fraudulent forecast concerning the company's future potential.[1] There is therefore a considerable overlap between the offences of obtaining property by deception, and making a false written statement contrary to s 19 of the Theft Act. Similarly, there is a partial, but not a total overlap, with the provisions of the Financial Services Act 1986.

---

19 *R v Lord Kylsant* [1932] 1 KB 442 and see *R v Bishirgian* [1936] 1 All ER 586.
20 Theft Act 1969, s 15(1).
1 Ibid, s 15(4).

Chapter 6

Memorandum of Association

GENERAL

A company's memorandum of association is its most important document because it is the memorandum that determines the powers of the company. A company may pursue only such objects and exercise only such powers as are conferred expressly in the memorandum or by implication therefrom; that is, in the latter case, such powers as are reasonably incidental to the attainment of the objects. All other activities are *ultra vires* and void. It is, therefore, important that special care be taken in the drafting of the memorandum. Although the Act provides for the alteration of the memorandum,[1] the process is not without difficulty and it is better to ensure prior to incorporation that all the activities in which the company is likely to wish to engage are authorised by the memorandum.

CONTENTS OF MEMORANDUM

The memorandum of a company limited by shares[2] must state:

(1) the name of the company with 'Limited' or if it is a public company the words 'public limited company' or their equivalent in Welsh, as the last word of the name;[3]

---

1 CA 1985, s 4 and see the discussion at pp 97–100, post.
2 The requirements as to the memorandum of an unlimited company and a company limited by guarantee are slightly different as is shown in the footnotes appearing below.
3 CA 1985, ss 2(1)(a) and 25 and note that it is an offence by s 33 for a company which is not a public company to trade under the guise of a public company. Similarly, a public company cannot trade under the guise of a private company. For the appropriate abbreviations see ibid, s 27. An unlimited company does not have 'Limited' as part of its name. Ibid, s 34 provides a penalty for the improper use of the word 'Limited'.

(2) whether the registered office of the company is to be in England, Wales or Scotland;[4]
(3) the objects of the company;[5]
(4) that the liability of the members is limited;[6]
(5) the amount of share capital with which the company is to be registered and its division into shares of a fixed amount;[7]
(6) that the subscribers to the memorandum desire to form a company and agree to take the shares set opposite their respective names. This is the association clause.

Each subscriber must take at least one share[8] and write opposite his name the number of shares he takes.[9] The memorandum must be signed by each subscriber or his agent authorised in writing, and the signature must be witnessed.[10] The witness must not be a subscriber and must add to his signature his description and address.

The form of memorandum of a company must be in accordance with the forms specified in regulations made by the DTI or as near thereto as circumstances permit.[11]

THE NAME OF THE COMPANY

The name of the company is selected by the promoters. There are considerable limitations upon the name which may be used. A company may not be registered by a name which includes 'limited' or any abbreviation thereof, save where it is placed at the end of the name.[12] A name may not be used which already appears on the register,[13] nor may a name be used which, in the opinion of the Secretary of State would constitute a criminal offence or be offensive.[14] Approval of the Secretary of State is required to register or re-register a company by a name which, in his opinion, would be

4 CA 1985, s 2(1)(b) and (2); by, ibid, s 10(6) the intended location of the office must be notified when the memorandum is delivered for registration.
5 Ibid, s 2(1)(c).
6 Ibid, s 2(3).
7 Ibid, s 2(5)(a), this applies to companies having a share capital, but not to unlimited companies.
8 Ibid, s 2(5)(b).
9 Ibid, s 2(5)(c).
10 Ibid, s 2(6).
11 Ibid, s 8. See Companies (Tables A to F) Regulations 1985 (SI 1985/805) Tables B–F.
12 CA 1985, s 26(1).
13 For details of the register of company names, see ibid, s 714.
14 Ibid, s 26(1)(d) and (e).

likely to give the impression that the company is connected with central or local government, or which contains words or expressions specified in regulations as words or expressions for which the Secretary of State's approval is considered desirable.[15]

A company which seeks to use such a word or expression in its name must secure approval, requesting the government department or other relevant body to specify whether it has objections to the proposal.[16]

The words and expressions for which approval is required are set out in the Company and Business Names Regulations 1981, which also indicates the bodies whose approval is required. They are rather a mixed bag; alphabetically they range from 'abortion' to 'United Kingdom'. 'Duke' is stringently protected by the Home Office! In general, names suggestive of the monarchy are safeguarded.[17] By s 36 of the Banking Act 1979 there are stringent restrictions against the unauthorised use of a name indicating that a company is conducting a banking business. The word 'British' is not allowed in a name unless the undertaking is British controlled and entirely or almost wholly British owned; nor will it be allowed where the name of the company taken as a whole would give the unjustified impression that the company was pre-eminent in its field of activity. In practice, the promoters often consult the Registrar of Companies before incurring the expense of printing the memorandum and articles. This does not bind the DTI, but it is a useful precaution for the promoter.

A company (or any other form of business enterprise) may carry on business by a name other than the name by which it is registered.[18] Two matters are of importance in respect of companies. A company may not, without the written approval of the Secretary of State carry on business in Great Britain under a name which would be likely to give the impression that the company is connected with central or local government, or under a name for which approval would be required if it were sought to use that name as the name of the company on registration.[19] Secondly, a wide range of business documents and communications must disclose the corporate name of the enterprise.[20] These provisions do not, however, affect the

---

15 Ibid, s 26(2).
16 Ibid, s 29; Business Names Act 1985, s 3. For details of the procedure, see L. H. Leigh and H. C. Edey, *Companies Act 1981, Text and Commentary* (1981) para 185.
17 SI 1981/1685; SI 1982/1653.
18 BNA 1985, ss 1 and 4.
19 Ibid, s 2.
20 Ibid, s 4.

continued use of a name which did not contravene the Registration of Business Names Act 1916 (since repealed).[1] Where the business is transferred to another, the transferee has a period of 12 months within which to seek the Secretary of State's approval for the continued use of the name.[2]

Failure to comply with these provisions entails criminal and civil consequences. Apart from being a criminal offence, non-compliance may also result in a claim under contract by the business being defeated, provided that the defendant to proceedings can show either that he has been unable to pursue a claim against the plaintiff by reason of the plaintiff's failure to disclose required information, or that he has suffered some financial loss as a result thereof. The Court may, none the less, allow proceedings to continue if it thinks it just and equitable to do so.[3]

CHANGE OF NAME

A company may change its name by special resolution.[4] It takes effect from the date when an altered certificate of registration is issued. The Secretary of State may within 12 months of the time of registration direct a company to change its name where, in his opinion, it is the same as or too like that of any name which either appears on the register or should have appeared on the register when the name was registered.[5] He has similar powers, valid for five years, where a company has provided misleading information for the purposes of its registration by a particular name, or has given unfulfilled undertakings or assurances.[6] In addition, it may at any time direct a company to change the name by which it is registered, if that name gives so misleading an indication of the nature of its activities as to be liable to cause harm to the public.[7] Seemingly, this power cannot be used simply because the name under which the company is registered is similar to that of an existing company. The problem of a company which passes itself off as another must either be dealt with administratively by the DTI within 12 months after the date of registration, or thereafter by an injunction at the suit of the person aggrieved. The Court will grant an injunction in a passing-off action even though the plaintiff company does not, at the time of

1   Ibid, s 2(3).
2   Ibid, s 2(2).
3   Ibid, ss 5 and 7.
4   CA 1985, s 28(1).
5   Ibid, s 28(2).
6   Ibid, s 28(3).
7   Ibid, s 32.

suit, carry on business in England.[8] A person or company is not entitled to profit from the goodwill of a business carried on by another.[9] An injunction may in such cases be granted, even though the offending name was innocently selected.

A change of name does not affect existing rights or obligations of the company.[10]

POWER TO DISPENSE WITH 'LIMITED' AS PART OF THE NAME

A private company limited by guarantee, or a company which immediately before the coming into force of the CA 1981 was a private company limited by shares and licensed under s 19 of the CA 1948 is exempt from the requirements to use limited as part of its name, to publish its name and to send lists of members to the Registrar of Companies. The objects of such a company must be the promotion of commerce, art, science, education, religion, charity or any profession, and anything incidental or conducive to any of those objects. The memorandum or articles must require the company's profits or income to be applied in promoting its objects, they must prohibit the payment of dividends to its members, and require that the assets be transferred on winding up to another body with similar or charitable objects. A company which is in breach of the relevant requirements, for example by engaging in profit-making activities, may be directed by the Secretary of State to change its name by resolution so that it ends in 'limited'.[11]

PUBLICATION OF NAME

Every company is required to publish its name outside its registered office, to have its name engraved or permanently marked in legible characters on its seal, and to have its name on all business letters, notices and other official publications of the company.[12] The abbreviations 'Co.', 'Coy.' are recognised as lawful[13] as are, by virtue of CA 1985, s 27, 'PLC' and 'Ltd.'.

If any officer of the company uses a seal on which the company's name is not engraved or issues a business letter or bill of exchange,

---

8 *La Societé etc Panhard et Levassor v Panhard Levassor Motor Co Ltd* [1901] 2 Ch 513.
9 *Ewing v Buttercup Margarine Co Ltd* [1917] 2 Ch 1.
10 A company cannot, however, rely on a change of name against other persons until it has been registered and published in the Gazette: CA 1985, s 42(1)(b).
11 CA 1985, ss 30, 31, 380(4)(e).
12 Ibid, ss 348–350.
13 *Banque de l'Indochine et de Suez SA v Euroseas Group Finance Co Ltd,* supra.

promissory note, cheque or order for money or goods on which the company's name is not mentioned, he is liable to criminal penalties and (perhaps more seriously in financial terms) personally liable on the bill of exchange, note, cheque or order if the company does not pay.[14] The company must print on its business letters and order forms its place of registration, the address of its registered office, and where it is a limited company exempt from the obligation to use 'limited' as part of its name, the fact that it is a limited company. If in the case of a company with a share capital there is on its stationery or order forms a reference to the amount of any share capital, the reference must be to paid-up share capital.[15]

THE OBJECTS CLAUSE

The Companies Act requires that the memorandum of every company shall state the objects of the company. The objects must be lawful and include all the activities in which the company is likely to engage.[16] The objects clause, it has been said, 'must delimit and identify the objects in such plain and unambiguous manner as that the reader can identify the field of industry within which corporate activities are to be confined'.[17] The objects expressed or powers implied in the memorandum determine what the company may do. The source of a company's powers is to be found in its memorandum or by implication from the terms thereof. Any activities not expressly or impliedly authorised by the memorandum are *ultra vires* the company.[18]

The *ultra vires* rule, first formulated in connection with statutory companies, was intended to control the directors by preventing them from departing from the objects for which the company was formed. The rule was justified as being in the interests of all the members.[19] By it, members could in theory be assured that their investment would not be frittered away on activities which they did not have in contemplation when they invested their moneys in the

---

14 CA 1985, s 349(3) and (4); *British Airways Board v Parish* [1979] 2 Lloyd's Rep 361; *Maxform SA v Mariani & Goodville Ltd* [1979] 2 Lloyd's Rep 385.
15 CA 1985, s 351.
16 CA 1985, s 1(1). Courts have held that although objects were not illegal, the activity was none the less such as should not be carried on by a company and have therefore prevented companies from carrying it on, eg the practice of a learned profession. See *O'Duffy v Jaffe* [1904] 2 IR 27.
17 *Cotman v Brougham* [1918] AC 514, 522 per Lord Wrenbury.
18 See, eg *Simmonds v Heffer* [1983] BCLC 298. However, the *ultra vires* doctrine does not apply to chartered companies.
19 *Ernest v Nicholls* (1857) 6 HL Cas 401.

company. It could also be justified as safeguard for creditors who would be protected from seeing the property of the company diverted to uncontemplated objects. The rule has been almost universally criticised. Its abolition was proposed by the Cohen Committee in 1945 on the grounds that it served no useful purpose but was merely a source of prolixity and vexation.[20] The Jenkins Committee proposed sweeping changes to it while retaining limitations to the agency powers delegated to directors.[1] Unhappily, while the *ultra vires* rule has, as will be seen, been limited in application by CA 1985, s 35, it has not been abolished. Hence it is not only necessary to consider that statute, but all the former law as well.

The rule was put in its strict modern form in:

Ashbury Railway Carriage and Iron Co v Riche (1875) LR 7 HL 653.

> The company was incorporated for a number of objects but went beyond them by contracting to finance the construction of a railway in Belgium. The company, acting under a provision in the articles adopted a resolution confirming the actions of the directors. Later, the company repudiated the agreement and was sued for breach of contract. The company set up its lack of capacity under the *ultra vires* doctrine as a defence. The House of Lords held unanimously that the agreement was *ultra vires* and that not even the unanimous agreement of the members could validate it. Lord Cairns LC said at p 672: '... it is not a question whether the contract ever was ratified or was not ratified. If it was a contract void at its beginning, it was void because the company could not make the contract.'

The limitation on the company's powers was inferred from the enumeration of objects in the incorporating statute. If ratification were allowed then Lord Cairns stated:

> The shareholders would thereby, by unanimous consent, have been attempting to do the very thing which, by the Act of Parliament, they were prohibited from doing.

The *ultra vires* rule was thereafter applied to registered companies as well. The courts stressed that the rule was to be applied reasonably, so that whatever was fairly incidental to the objects set out in the memorandum would be *intra vires* unless expressly

---

20 Cmnd 6659 (1945) para 12.
1 Cmnd 1749 (1962) para 39.

prohibited.[2] Thus powers required to enable a company to pursue its objects would be implied. It was for example held that a trading company has an implied power to borrow money for the purposes of its business, and therefore no such power need be set out in the memorandum or articles.[3] There were, however, uncertainties surrounding the doctrine, particularly in connection with the remuneration of directors and the making of gifts.[4]

The uncertainties surrounding the *ultra vires* rule, and the desire not to preclude diversification of corporate activities soon led to attempts to evade it. Powers, instead of being left to implication, were set out in the objects clause. That clause also began to enumerate all the different businesses into which the company might at some future date wish to venture. The courts tried to maintain control by recourse to principles of construction. Thus the *ejusdem generis* rule was employed by which if the main objects of the company were followed by wide general powers, these would be construed as covering their exercise only for the purposes of the main objects. It was further held that words enabling a company to carry on any lawful business whatever would not be a sufficient compliance with the Companies Acts. In some limited cases, the name of the company might be prayed in aid of a restrictive interpretation.[5] The courts also sought to rely on the substratum rule. Where the company had a main object and that object failed, it could be wound up on the petition of a shareholder. In *Re German Date Coffee Co*[6] the Court stated that where the company was formed for a primary purpose:

> ... then, although the memorandum may contain other general words, which include the doing of other objects, those general words must be read as being ancillary to that which the memorandum shows to be the main purpose and if the main purpose fails and fails altogether, then ... the substratum of the association fails.

The substratum rule is a narrow and unsatisfactory method of control. The question whether the substratum of a company has gone is distinct from the question whether the activity is *intra vires* the company. If the activity in which the company engages is authorised by the objects clause, the activity will be *intra vires*.[7] The

2 *A-G v Great Eastern Rly Co* (1880) 5 App Cas 473.
3 *General Auction Estate and Monetary Co Ltd v Smith* [1891] 3 Ch 432.
4 *Hutton v West Cork Rly Co* (1883) 23 ChD 654.
5 *Re Crown Bank* (1890) 44 ChD 634.
6 (1882) 20 ChD 169, p 177 per Kay J.
7 *Anglo-Overseas Agencies Ltd v Green* [1961] 1 QB 1, [1960] 3 All ER 244.

company's substratum may have vanished, but the Court will not order a winding up unless a member applies for an order.[8] Furthermore, the company may have more than one main object. If that is the case, the failure of one such object will not suffice to found a petition.[9] In fact it became apparent at an early stage that by careful drafting of the objects clause both the *ejusdem generis* and substratum rules of construction could be excluded. The leading authority on these aspects of the construction of the objects clause is:

Cotman v Brougham [1918] AC 514.

> The company was formed to acquire certain rubber and tobacco estates. The objects clause contained clause (8) giving the power to promote and form companies and deal in the stocks and shares of such companies, clause (12) giving a general power to deal in stocks and shares, and clause (30) which provided (a) that the objects specified in any clause were not to be restrictively construed by reference to the contents of any other sub-clause, and (b) that no object should be construed as subsidiary or auxiliary to any other entry in the objects clause. The company underwrote shares in another company which went into liquidation, and was placed on the list of contributories. It applied to be struck off that list on the ground that the entire transaction was *ultra vires*. The House of Lords concluded however that the underwriting transactions were authorised by clauses (8) and (12) which, by clause (30), had to be given primary effect as separate and independent objects. The result was the '... modern memorandum of association with its multifarious list of objects and powers specified as objects and its clauses designed to prevent any specified object being read as ancillary to some other object.' Per Lord Parker.

The *ultra vires* doctrine has also been eroded by judicial acceptance of subjectively worded objects clauses.

Bell Houses Ltd v City Wall Properties Ltd [1966] 2 QB 656, [1966] 2 All ER 674.

> The main business of the plaintiff company was the development of housing estates. The chairman of the board of directors to whom the board had delegated the management of the company acquired knowledge of and skill in securing finance for the company's operations. A contract was made between the plaintiff and defendant companies for

---

8 *Re Eastern Telegraph Co Ltd* [1947] 2 All ER 104, p 109 per Jenkins J.
9 *Re Kitson & Co Ltd* [1946] 1 All ER 435.

the payment of a fee for arranging finance for one of the defendant company's schemes of development. When the plaintiff company brought action for its fee, the defendant alleged that the making of the agreement was *ultra vires* the plaintiff company. Mortgage broking was not a stated object in the plaintiff company's memorandum. Clause 3(c) thereof however, authorised the company to carry on any trade or business whatever which could *in the opinion of the directors* be advantageously carried on by the company in connection with or ancillary to any of the businesses specified in the objects clause. The Court of Appeal held that the memorandum, once registered, is deemed to have complied with the provisions of the Companies Acts,[10] that the question was one of construction, and that the bona fide opinion of the board expressed through the chairman to whom management had been delegated determined whether the activity was *intra vires*. The plaintiff company thus succeeded in its action.[11]

The Courts will, however, seek to evade the rule where that is possible and there are striking instances of judicial constructions the result of which was to benefit persons dealing honestly with the company.

Re New Finance and Mortgage Co Ltd (in Liquidation) [1975] Ch 420, [1975] 1 All ER 684.

The company was empowered to carry on business as financiers, capitalists, concessionaires, bankers, commercial agents, mortgage brokers, financial agents, and advisers, exporters, importers and merchants generally. There was the usual clause specifying that each head of the objects clause was to be read independently of the others. The company operated a petrol station and became indebted to its supplier of motor fuel. The liquidator rejected the supplier's proof of claim on the grounds that the debt had been incurred for *ultra vires* trading. The Court held that the business was *intra vires,* not as that of a concessionaire because in context that word was not intended to refer to a retail venture, but as a merchant which, in common usage and context referred to wholesalers and retailers and to all purely commercial occupations.

It is, however, clear that the *ultra vires* rule lives on and that not even modern drafting techniques necessarily enable the company or the person dealing with it entirely to surmount its rigours.

---

10 Formerly CA 1948, s 15, now repealed.
11 See also *American Home Assurance Co v Tjmond Properties Ltd* [1986] BCLC 181.

POWERS AND *ULTRA VIRES*

It has been pointed out that notwithstanding that they are not expressly included in the memorandum, certain powers will be implied in order to enable a company to pursue its objects. A modern authoritative statement of the rule is contained in the judgment of Buckley LJ in *Re Horsley and Weight Ltd*.[12]

> 'The Companies Act 19[85], s 2, requires the memorandum of association of a company incorporated under the Act to state the objects of the company. A company has no capacity to pursue any objects outside those which are so stated. It does not follow, however, that any act which is not expressly authorised by the memorandum is *ultra vires* the company. Anything reasonably incidental to the attainment or pursuit of any of the express objects of the company will, unless expressly prohibited, be within the implied powers of the company.'

However the Court will not imply a power, even if potentially beneficial to the company, if it is not reasonably incidental to the company's business.[13]

Normally the company will set out in its memorandum the powers which it is to have. Such powers may be expressed as objects. The practice and its effect were explained thus in *Re Horsley and Weight Ltd*.[14]

> 'It has now long been a commercial practice to set out in memoranda of association a great number and variety of "objects", so called, some of which (for example, to borrow money, to promote the company's interests by advertising its products or services, or to do acts or things conducive or incidental to the company's objects) are by their very nature incapable of standing as independent objects which can be pursued in isolation as the sole activity of the company. Such "objects" must, by reason of their very nature, be interpreted merely as powers incidental to the ture objects of the company and must be so treated notwithstanding the presence of a separate objects clause: *Introductions Ltd v National Provincial Bank Ltd* [1970] Ch 199. Where there is no separate objects clause, some of the express "objects" may upon construction fall to be treated as no more than powers which are ancillary to the dominant or main objects of the company: see, for example, *Re German Date Coffee Co* (1882) 20 ChD 169.'

---

12 [1982] 3 WLR 431, 436/7.
13 *Tomkinson v South-Eastern Rly Co* (1887) 35 ChD 675; *Re Halt Garage (1964) Ltd* [1982] 3 All ER 1016.
14 Supra.

The distinction between objects and powers is well demonstrated by:

Introductions Ltd v National Provincial Bank Ltd [1969] 2 WLR 791, CA.

> The company was created with objects enabling it to provide services and accommodation for overseas visitors. It later carried on the business of letting deck-chairs. Some years later, after a change in management, it began pig-farming. The objects did not include power to carry on pig-farming but they did enable the company to borrow money, contained a subjective ancillary clause enabling the company to carry on any trade or business which, in the opinion of the directors could be advantageously carried on in connection with or as ancillary to the business of the company, and provided that all the items in the objects clause were to be construed as separate and independent objects. The bank, knowing that the company was engaging in pig-farming (and knowing of the objects clause) advanced money to the company on the security of a debenture. A claim on the debenture was resisted by the liquidator. It was held that notwithstanding the ancillary clause, and the clause requiring each item to be read as an independent object, the entry relating to borrowing was a power rather than an object, that borrowing for any purpose not warranted by the objects clause was *ultra vires,* and that the bank could not rely on the debenture.

The Court treated the clause requiring each sub-clause of the objects clause to be treated independently of the others as limited in application to the interpretation of those clauses which could properly be read as objects in the sense that they authorised the company to undertake some activity as a business activity. Given the context, this could not be said of the borrowing power. That power, enabling the company to borrow money on security could not be construed as a business object. Nor could it be converted into an object by the ancillary clause enabling the directors to carry on any business which in their opinion could advantageously be carried on in connection with the general business of the company. By contrast, in *Cotman v Brougham* [1918] AC 514 the underwriting clauses could be construed as objects. They specified businesses in which a company could engage as its primary activity.

The fundamental point is that the question whether a stated 'object' is truly an independent object or purpose is always a question of construction of the memorandum. Indeed, even borrowing or lending money are objects capable of being independent objects (eg in the case of a bank) notwithstanding that, in the case of the vast majority of companies, they would not.[15]

In order to validate the disposition of corporate property, it must be shown that the company had the power to make the disposition. The doing of an act which is expressed to be, and is capable of being, an independent object of the company cannot be *ultra vires,* for it is by definition something the company is formed to do and necessarily *intra vires.*[16] For example

Re Horsley and Weight Ltd [1982] 3 WLR 431.

> The objects of the company included a power to grant pensions to its past and present directors and employees. The company purchased a pension policy for a director and employee, who were about to retire. It was held that the power to grant pensions was a substantive object of the company and not merely a power and therefore the purchase of the policy was valid.

There is no necessity in the case of the performance of an act or disposition within the express objects of a company for it to be shown that the act or disposition will benefit or promote the prosperity of the company, unless the memorandum expressly or impliedly provides that an express object only extends to acts or dispositions which do so, for a company's objects need not be commercial and may be charitable or philanthropic.[17]

Where the act or disposition is not expressly authorised, it will be necessary, in order to establish that it is *intra vires,* to show that the transaction is reasonably incidental to the carrying on of the company's business, but this is no more than a specific instance of the general proposition that anything reasonably incidental to the attainment or pursuit of the company's express objects will, unless prohibited, be within the company's implied powers.

Formerly it was thought that, in addition to the requirements that it be reasonably incidental to the carrying on of the company's business, in order to be valid a disposition of corporate property pursuant to an implied power had to be (i) bona fide and (ii) for the

---

15 *Rolled Steel Products (Holdings) Ltd v British Steel Corpn* [1986] Ch 246, [1985] 3 All ER 52, CA.
16 *Re Horsley & Weight Ltd* [1982] 3 WLR 431 at 437.
17 *Charterbridge Corpn v Lloyds Bank Ltd* [1970] Ch 62, [1969] 2 All ER 1185; *Re Horsley & Weight Ltd* [1982] 3 WLR 431 at 440; *Rolled Steel Products (Holdings) Ltd v British Steel Corpn* (supra).

Contents of Memorandum 83

benefit and to promote the prosperity of the company.[18] It is now clear that this is not the case, and that the questions of bona fides and benefit to the company relate solely to the directors' exercise of their powers.[19]

Even though an act or disposition may otherwise be *intra vires* the company, is the act or disposition open to challenge on the grounds that the directors, when causing the company to perform the act or make the disposition in question, acted in breach of their fiduciary duties or have abused their powers? In other words, are questions of the capacity of the company, and the proper exercise of the director's powers, wholly separate?[20]

If a particular act is of a type which, on the true construction of the memorandum, is capable of being performed as reasonably incidental to the attainment or pursuit of its objects, the act will not be rendered *ultra vires* the company merely because in a particular instance its directors, in performing the act in its name, are doing so for purposes other than those set out in the memorandum; the directors' state of mind is irrelevant when considering whether an act is *ultra vires* the company, although possibly relevant to questions of breach of directors' duties.[1] In this connection, if the power is expressed to be exercisable 'for the purposes of the company', the Court will not construe the statement as a limitation on the company's powers but on those of the directors.[2]

Confusion may arise from the fact that the phrase '*ultra vires*' is frequently used in two senses in relation to the capacity of a company to enter into a transaction. When used in the 'narrow' sense, it describes a transaction outside the scope of the objects expressed in the memorandum or which cannot be implied as reasonably incidental to the attainment of those objects. A transaction '*ultra vires*' in this sense is as we have seen beyond the company's powers. The phrase is also used in a 'wide' sense to describe a transaction which, although falling within the scope of the company's powers express or implied is entered into for unauthorised purposes and in breach

---

18 *Re Lee, Behrens & Co Ltd* [1932] 2 Ch 46.
19 *Re Halt Garage (1964) Ltd* [1982] 3 All ER 1016; *Re Horsley & Weight Ltd* [1982] 3 WLR 431. See also *Charterbridge Corpn v Lloyds Bank Ltd* [1970] Ch 62, [1969] 2 All ER 1185; and *Thompson v Barke & Co (Caterers) Ltd* 1975 SLT 67.
20 See the discussion in *Re Halt Garage Ltd, supra; Rolled Steel Products (Holdings) Ltd v British Steel Corpn* [1986] Ch 246, [1985] 3 All ER 52, CA.
1   *Rolled Steel Products (Holdings) Ltd v British Steel Corpn* [1986] Ch 246, [1985] 3 All ER 52.
2   Ibid.

of the directors' duties accordingly.³ The vital distinction is that a transaction which is *ultra vires* in the narrow sense is void and cannot, as we have seen, be adopted or ratified even by a unanimous general meeting;⁴ one which is *ultra vires* in the wider sense is merely voidable and may confer rights on third parties who can show that they dealt with the company in good faith and for valuable consideration without notice of the unauthorised purpose of the transaction.⁵ Such a transaction may be adopted by the shareholders, at any rate where there is no fraud on the creditors and the company is solvent.⁶

A leading case is:

Charterbridge Corporation v Lloyds Bank Ltd [1970] Ch 62, [1969] 2 All ER 1185.⁷

> Castleford, a company in a group of companies, executed first and second mortgages on its freehold property in order to guarantee the indebtedness of other companies in the group of which it was a member. A second mortgage was executed in favour of the bank. Castleford had express power to mortgage its properties to secure the obligations of any other person or company with whom it had dealings or in whose business it was concerned. Ultimately Castleford sold the mortgaged property to the plaintiff company, but failed to pay off the mortgage to the bank. The bank threatened to realise its security, and the plaintiff company thereupon brought action for a declaration that the mortgage in favour of the bank was *ultra vires*. The ground upon which the plaintiff company relied was that the directors of Castleford, in granting the mortgage, acted *ultra vires* in not considering whether the granting of the mortgage was for the benefit of the Castleford company alone. The action was dismissed. Pennycuick J held (1) that the directors in considering the transaction could have regard not only to the affairs of the company considered in isolation but also to its affairs as a member of the group. He held further (2) that where the directors act under an express

---

3 *Rolled Steel Products (Holdings) Ltd v British Steel Corpn* [1982] 3 WLR 715 at p 733 and [1986] Ch 246, [1985] 3 All ER 52, CA. In *Re Halt Garage,* [supra] Oliver J doubted whether *'ultra vires'* in the wider sense was not more properly a question of abuse of directors' powers. Cf *International Sales and Agencies Ltd v Marcus* supra at p 556.
4 *Ashbury Railway Carriage and Iron Co v Riche* (1875) LR 7 HL 653.
5 *Re David Payne & Co Ltd* [1904] 2 Ch 608; *Rolled Steel Products (Holdings) Ltd v British Steel Corpn,* supra.
6 *Rolled Steel (Holdings) Ltd v British Steel Corpn* (supra); *Multinational Gas and Petrochemical Co v Multinational Gas and Petrochemical Services Ltd* [1983] Ch 258, [1983] 2 All ER 563.
7 See also *Thompson v J Barke & Co (Caterers) Ltd* 1975 SLT 67 and (1970) 33 Mod LR 81; *International Sales and Agencies Ltd v Marcus* [1982] 3 All ER 551.

power, the disposition cannot be *ultra vires,* but it may be voidable where, in so acting, the directors base themselves upon considerations which they are not entitled to take into account when determining whether the transaction is for the benefit of the company.

It appears therefore that where express powers are purportedly exercised in the pursuit of the company's objects, the transaction is *intra vires,*[8] but if the directors in exercising the power take into account circumstances which they are not allowed to take into account, the transaction may well be voidable against the third party at the option of the company.[9] If the transaction involves implied powers then, unless the suggested power is one which would be reasonably incidental to the carrying out of the company's business objects, no such power will be implied and the transaction will be *intra vires.* Finally, in the case of express powers the power, unless it is drafted in unqualified terms, will be restrictively construed, as a power, eg to make gifts which are potentially of benefit to the company, rather than an unqualified power to make any gifts which the directors wish to make.[10]

ULTRA VIRES CONTRACTS

Because a company has no power to enter into obligations directed towards the pursuit of activities other than those specified in the objects clause, an *ultra vires* contract should be a nullity. In this respect the knowledge of the third party should be immaterial. Furthermore neither side should be capable of enforcing the contract against the other. This is of course the orthodox position.[11] In fact, however, the position is more obscure.

All persons who deal with the company are deemed to have knowledge of the contents of the memorandum. The fact therefore that a person who enters into a contact with the company does not know of the contents of the memorandum and does not know that

8 *Charterbridge Corpn v Lloyds Bank Ltd* [1970] Ch 62, [1969] 2 All ER 1185.
9 As in the share allotment cases. See *Hogg v Cramphorn Ltd* [1967] Ch 254, [1966] 3 All ER 420; *Bamford v Bamford* [1970] Ch 212, [1969] 1 All ER 969.
10 Thus express powers are restrictively construed so as not to warrant an illegality. See *Ridge Securities Ltd v IRC* [1964] 1 All ER 275, [1964] 1 WLR 479; *Peter Buchanan Ltd and Macharg v McVey* (1950–1951), [1955] AC 516n, cited with approval in *Government of India v Taylor* [1955] AC 491, 510.
11 *Re Jon Beauforte Ltd* [1953] Ch 131, [1953] 1 All ER 634; *Great North-West Central Rly Co v Charlebois* [1899] AC 114; cf *Caledonia Community Credit Union Ltd v Haldimand Feed Mill Ltd* (1974) 45 DLR (3d) 676 which holds on a basis of unjust enrichment that a person who has borrowed money from a company cannot set up want of capacity against the lender.

86 Chapter 6 Memorandum of Association

the contract is *ultra vires* the company will not assist him. The contract is a nullity and he cannot enforce it.[12] There has been an exception in the case of loan transactions. Where the lender lends money to a company which has power to borrow, the lender is treated as entitled to assume that the money will be expended on objects competent to the company. The lending contract is therefore treated as *intra vires*[13] but this principle will not avail the recipient of a payment in circumstances where it is clear that the payment has not been made for the purposes of the company which made it. This principle may extend beyond loan contracts to contracts for goods and materials provided that these are such as might be used in the legitimate business of the company. It would seem that where the contract is not one for goods and services supplied in the ordinary course of trade, and the contract relates to an *ultra vires* purpose, lack of knowledge that the activity is not authorised by the company's objects clause will not avail the third party. Where the third party knows of the purpose for which a loan is required[14] or for which goods are required[15] and that purpose is not authorised by the objects, the transaction will be treated as *ultra vires* and incapable of conferring rights.[16]

It has been suggested, notwithstanding the doctrine that an *ultra vires* contract is a nullity, that in cases where a company has performed its side of the bargain, the third party contracting with the company should not be permitted to set the company's lack of capacity up as a defence to an action brought by the company upon the contract.[17] It has been suggested that the *ultra vires* rule exists primarily for the benefit of shareholders, and that to refuse the company the right to bring an action in such cases would be to allow the rule to be employed in a manner adverse to the right of shareholders. This view enjoys some support in *dicta* here and in the Commonwealth.[18] None the less, there are decisions which treat

---

12 *Anglo-Overseas Agencies v Green* [1961] 1 QB 1, [1960] 3 All ER 244.
13 *Re David Payne & Co* [1904] 2 Ch 608; cf *Thompson v J Barke Co (Caterers) Ltd* 1975 SLT 67.
14 *Re Introductions Ltd, Introductions Ltd v National Provincial Bank* [1970] Ch 199, [1969] 1 All ER 887.
15 *Re Jon Beauforte Ltd* [1953] Ch 131, [1953] 1 All ER 634.
16 At least so long as the contract remains executory.
17 *Bell Houses Ltd v City Wall Properties Ltd* [1966] 2 QB 656 at p 690 per Salmon LJ.
18 *Re K L Tractors Ltd* (1960) 106 CLR 318 at pp 335, 337–338 and *Breckinridge Speedway Ltd v R* (1967) 64 DLR (2d) 488; *Caledonia Community Credit Union Ltd v Haldimand Feed Mill Ltd* (1974) 45 DLR (3d) 676; *La Caisse Populaire Notre Dame Ltée v Moyer* (1967) 61 DLR (2d) 118, 147–48 followed.

such contracts as nullities,[19] and it must be remembered that in the *Ashbury* case itself, it was held that unanimous ratification by the shareholders was not enough to invest such a contract with legal effect. Admittedly there it was the company which set up its own lack of capacity as a defence. If, however, the Court had taken the view that the purpose of the rule was to protect shareholders, and that shareholders could determine to waive that protection by validating transactions, a strict rule of nullity would not have been required. It is doubtful, in our submission, whether a third party can be prevented from raising the company's lack of capacity as a defence to an action brought by it on an *ultra vires* contract, recent *dicta* to the contrary notwithstanding.[20]

It is doubtful whether an *ultra vires* contract can properly be treated as passing property. It is sometimes asserted, on the authority of a decision on appeal from the Channel Islands, that property can pass under such a contract.[1] This seems to be incorrect. All that the decision holds is that a company may protect its possession of property. But possession may be protected by the possessor against any person not having a superior title. The true rule appears to be that the contract does not pass property, but that a property right which founds originally on an *ultra vires* transaction may be asserted provided that in order to do so it is not necessary to rely on the contract as such.[2]

Linz v Electric Wire Co of Palestine Ltd [1948] AC 371, [1948] 1 All ER 604, PC.

> In 1935 the appellant was allotted 775 preference shares which she later transferred to third parties, the transferees being placed on the register of members of the company in her place. In 1943 she began proceedings against the company alleging that the resolution whereby she was allotted shares was invalid, that the allotment to her was void, and claiming the return of the money paid by her for the shares. It was held that while in general subscribers who have paid money for an allotment of shares which is *ultra vires* the company can recover their money, the plaintiff after selling her shares was estopped from alleging either that they had not been lawfully issued, or that there had been a total failure of consideration.

---

19 *Anglo-Overseas Agencies v Green* [1961] 1 QB 1, [1960] 3 All ER 244.
20 No such suggestion has been made in relation to an executory contract. *Triaas v Stains UDC* [1969] 1 Ch 10, [1968] 2 All ER 1.
1 *National Telephone Co v St Peter Port Constables* [1900] AC 317.
2 *Sinclair v Brougham* [1914] AC 398, pp 418, 426, 441, 458.

Chapter 6 Memorandum of Association

It would seem to follow that the transferee could estop the transferor from denying the validity of his title.

OTHER REMEDIES

The fact that the *ultra vires* character of the contract prevents an action being brought upon it does not debar a third party who has dealt with the company under such a transaction from all remedy.

(1) He may be able to assert a claim to 'subrogation'. If the company had borrowed money from a third party on an *ultra vires* contract and money has been used either in whole or in part in the payment of *intra vires* debts of the company, the lender is entitled to claim as an ordinary creditor in respect of moneys so paid. The lender is not however entitled to the benefit of any security held by the creditor who was paid off.[3] The lender's right is to rank as an unsecured creditor in respect of the sums paid. This right of subrogation applies even where the *intra vires* indebtedness which has been repaid out of the borrowing arose after the borrowing. The lender will still be treated as a creditor to the extent to which the money borrowed from him is used to pay off an *intra vires* debt.[4]

(2) A claim may be possible in quasi-contract. In *Bell Houses Ltd v City Wall Properties Ltd* at trial[5] Mocatta J suggests that while an *ultra vires* contract is a nullity, and therefore the company could validly be met by the plea that the contract was invalid, the company might none the less be able to claim for money had and received. The difficulty here is that historically, such actions were treated as *quasi ex contractu,* depending upon an implied promise to pay. In *Sinclair v Brougham*[6] it was held that because in a case of *ultra vires* no express promise to pay could validly be made, no action based on implied promise would lie either. While modern statements cast doubt upon whether actions for money had and received rest upon implied promise,[7] the accepted position has not as yet been reversed.

(3) A proprietary tracing remedy may be asserted. The leading case is:

---

3 *Re Wrexham, Mold and Connah's Quay Rly Co* [1899] 1 Ch 440.
4 *Re Airedale Co-operative Worsted Manufacturing Society Ltd* [1933] Ch 639.
5 [1966] 1 QB 207; revsd [1966] 2 QB 656.
6 [1914] AC 398.
7 See eg *A-G v Nissan* [1970] AC 179 at p 228 per Lord Pearce, and generally Goff and Jones, *The Law of Restitution* (3rd edn, 1986) at pp 5–12. See also *International Sales and Agencies Ltd v Marcus* [1982] 3 All ER 551.

Sinclair v Brougham [1914] AC 398.

A Building Society developed an *ultra vires* banking business and borrowed large sums of money. On the winding up of the Society three classes of persons made claims against its assets; (1) outside creditors, (2) shareholders of the Building Society, and (3) bank customers on current and deposit account. By consent, the outside creditors were paid out in full. The House of Lords held that the customers who had lent money to the Building Society on an *ultra vires* contract could not sue on the contract to recover it. Nor could they (as we have noted) bring an action in quasi-contract. They were allowed to assert a proprietary remedy and to trace their funds into the moneys of the Society. The relationship between the directors and the lenders is said to be a fiduciary relationship,[8] the money in the hands of the directors was for all practical purposes trust money, and the beneficiaries, the lenders, could trace the sums lent into the assets of the Society. As between themselves and the shareholders, the equities were treated as equal. Neither had a better right to the money. Each could therefore claim *pari passu* in the fund.

But of course the right to trace is a limited remedy. It will lie only against a fund or asset which represents the proceeds of the *ultra vires* borrowing, and it cannot be asserted against a person who has taken bona fide for value and without notice of the equities.[9]

(4) Proceedings against officers may be possible. If the officers or agents of a company persuade a third party to enter into a transaction which is *ultra vires* the company, an action may lie against them in breach of warranty of authority.[10] The action lies as a result of the erroneous assertion that the agent has been empowered by his principal, the company, to enter into contractual relations with the third party. The fact that the company cannot be made liable as a result of the *ultra vires* rule does not militate against allowing an action against the company's agent. Certainly there can be no valid reason in public policy for denying such a right of action to the third party.

ULTRA VIRES IN TORT AND CRIME

The orthodox view is that the rule of *ultra vires* is a rule of nullity. Any activity which is not authorised by the objects clause is, on this

---

8   This is the explanation suggested in *Re Diplock, Diplock v Wintle* [1948] Ch 465, [1948] 2 All ER 318, but it accords ill with the accepted dogma that the directors of a company owe fiduciary duties to the company and not to any individual member of it. See *Percival v Wright* [1902] 2 Ch 421.
9   See in general Snell's *Principles of Equity* (28th edn) pp 295–303.
10 *Chapleo v Brunswick Permanent Building Society* (1881) 6 QBD 696.

Chapter 6 Memorandum of Association

view, not treated as an act of the company.[11] It would follow from a strict application of this rule that a tort or crime committed in the course of an activity which was not warranted by the objects clause would be considered to be *ultra vires* and the company would not be liable in respect of it. It is also the view which is most consistent with the decided cases. In *Mill v Hawker*[12] the Court recognised that where the activity was *ultra vires,* an act committed during the course of it is not a corporate act for which the company can be held liable. There are *dicta* to the same effect in the *Taff Vale* case[13] and in some Commonwealth decisions.[14] There is one English decision which appears to suggest that a company is always liable in tort in respect of *ultra vires* activities, but that decision is really based on illegality rather than *ultra vires*.[15] There is a *dictum* suggesting that this is the appropriate result as well,[16] but, although followed in New Zealand, it has not been followed elsewhere, either in England or the Commonwealth.[17] It is thought that the correct rule is that a company will be liable for torts or crimes committed in the pursuit of its stated objects, but not otherwise. In any event, whether the company is liable for torts or crimes committed *ultra vires* or not, the officer, agent or servant who commits the act is personally liable.[18]

REFORM OF THE RULE

The *ultra vires* rule has long since outlived any utility which it might have had. As the Cohen Committee noted, the practice of drafting long and prolix objects clauses is an illusory protection for the shareholders and yet may be a pitfall for their parties dealing with the company.[19] The case of *Re Jon Beauforte Ltd*[20] affords a graphic example of this.

---

11 *Ashbury Railway Carriage and Iron Co v Riche* (1875) LR 7 HL 653.
12 (1874) LR 9 Exch 309.
13 *Taff Vale Rly Co v Amalgamated Society of Railway Servants* [1901] AC 426, at p 433 per Farwell J.
14 *Tunney v Orchard* [1957] SCR 436 at p 446 per Rand J; *Williams v Hursey* (1960–61) 103 CLR at pp 128, 129 per Menzies J.
15 *Campbell v Paddington Corpn* [1911] 1 KB 869.
16 *Doolan v Midland Rly Co* (1877) 2 App Cas 792 at p 806 per Lord Blackburn.
17 See further, Leigh, *The Criminal Liability of Corporations in English Law* (1969) at pp 48–50.
18 This is clear in tort, and as to crime see *R v Ovenell* [1969] 1 QB 17, [1968] 1 All ER 933.
19 Cmnd 6659 (1945) para 11.
20 See also Chap 2, ante.

Re Jon Beauforte Ltd [1953] Ch 131, [1953] 1 All ER 634.

> The company was empowered to carry on business as manufacturers of women's clothing. Later it began to manufacture veneer plywood panelling. The company later went into liquidation. A supplier of coke claimed inter alia, on the ground that the fuel supplied by him could have been used for an *intra vires* purpose and that he ought therefore to recover. Unfortunately, the company's letterhead disclosed that the company was carrying on the business of plywood manufacturers. It was held that the supplier was fixed with knowledge of the memorandum which did not empower the company to carry on the plywood business, and had actual knowledge that the company was carrying on a business which was *ultra vires*. Although the supplier could have recovered had he had no notice of the purpose for which the coke was being used, he could not, having such knowledge from the letterhead, prove for the debt which was incurred on an *ultra vires* contract.

The extreme technicality of this result is further illustrated by *Re New Finance and Mortgage Co Ltd (in Liquidation)*, noted above, where the transaction was held valid because the activities in which the company engaged were in fact *intra vires*, but on a basis different from that which the company itself supposed.[1]

STATUTE AND THE *ULTRA VIRES* RULE

The *ultra vires* rule was amended not as a result of the urging of company law committees nor in the ways which they suggested, but by the European Communities Act 1972 in such a way as to comply with European Economic Community Council Directive 68/151 of 9 March 1968 relating to the protection of third parties dealing with companies.[2] There have been happier measures of reform.

In its relation to *ultra vires,* CA 1985, s 35, effectively re-enacting s 9(1) of the European Communities Act 1972, provides:

> (1) In favour of a person dealing with a company in good faith, any transaction decided on by the directors shall be deemed to be one which it is within the capacity of the company to enter into, and the power of the directors to bind the company shall be deemed to be free of any limitation under the memorandum or articles.
> (2) A party to a transaction so decided on is not bound to enquire as to the capacity of the company to enter into it or as to any such limitation to the powers of the directors, and is presumed to have acted in good faith unless the contrary is proved.

---

1 Page 79, ante.
2 Already referred to in connection with preliminary contracts: see Chap 3.

92 *Chapter 6 Memorandum of Association*

This is certainly obscure. It does not abolish the *ultra vires* rule; the principal questions concern those aspects of the rule which it has restricted in operation and the extent to which they have been restricted. It does not prevent a member from restraining a proposed transaction on the grounds of *ultra vires,* neither does it preclude making the directors responsible for the misapplication of corporate property disposed of by an *ultra vires* transaction.[3]

A third party will only be protected if the transaction is one decided upon by the directors. This should be apt to cover both an initial authorisation and ratification. The question concerns what is meant by the word 'directors', whether it refers to the board of directors, any committee of directors, a managing director, or, by virtue of the Interpretation Act 1978, s 6 which provides that save where the context otherwise requires the singular is included in the plural, any director.

There is much to be said in favour of the submission that the word 'directors' refers to the board of directors only and that, accordingly, the only occasion on which a decision by one director will constitute the transaction as decided upon by the 'directors' is when, in the case of a private company, that director is the sole director and thus constitutes 'the board'. In English law the primary organs of the company are the board of directors and the general meeting.[4] The managing director enjoys this status only by derivation from the articles of association if these are appropriately worded and if they have been exercised in fact.[5] Individual directors have never been considered to be organs and whether or not they can act as agents of the company depends on their having been appointed or held out as such.[6] The use of 'the directors' seems in context to be an attempt to refer to a collegiate decision but without the use of the relatively unfamiliar word 'organ' the term used in the Directive leading to the implementation of s 9(1) (subsequently CA 1985, s 35(1) and (2)). This usage can be seen under, for example, in art 70 of Table A which uses the term in a collegiate sense in conferring managerial powers on the directors.[7] If the section were

---

3 See pp 88–89, ante.
4 See further, L.H. Leigh, *The Criminal Liability of Corporations in English Law* (1969) chapter 7; for explicit use of the term see *Gluckstein v Barnes* [1900] AC 240.
5 The point is recognised by Lord Haldane and Lord Dunedin in *Lennard's Carrying Co Ltd v Asiatic Petroleum Co Ltd* [1915] AC 705.
6 Chap 8, post.
7 (SI 1985/805). A similar argument is advanced by N. Spinks (1972) 122 NLJ 1145.

read as referring to any director, whether or not he enjoyed delegated managerial or agency powers, it would not only abridge the *ultra vires* rule but also subvert primary limitations upon the exercise of agency powers by individual directors.

However, in *International Sales and Agencies Ltd v Marcus*[8] it was held obiter that where dealings were decided upon by M, a sole effective director to whom all actual authority to act for the plaintiff's directors had been effectively delegated, the dealings had been decided upon by the plaintiff's directors for the purposes of s 35. If followed, this dictum will clearly considerably broaden the scope of the phrase 'decided on by the directors'.

The section protects a third party dealing with the company; it does not expressly deal with the problem which arises where the third party wishes to set up a want of capacity against a company which seeks to enforce an *ultra vires* agreement against him. This is one of the inequitable aspects of the present law; it may ultimately be altered by judicial creativity, but the section does not touch the problem.[9]

The reference in the section to limitations under the articles of association underlines the point, again deriving from the Directive, that s 35 goes beyond classical *ultra vires* and also cures defects stemming from managerial limitations placed upon the directions in the articles of association. This enables the third party to rely on dealings with the directors; it supports the inference that 'the directors' is being used in a collegiate sense. The third party is protected from particular provisions which companies may adopt from time to time in their own articles.

The plaintiff must deal with the company 'in good faith'. This phrase is again obscure. If the Directive is taken as a guide, it seems intended to remove from the ambit of protection persons who knew that the activities in question were outside the objects of the company. Indeed, if interpretation followed the Directive slavishly the worst aspects of *Re Jon Beauforte Ltd*[10] would be perpetuated; for the Directive also enables national legislatures to deny protection to persons who in the circumstances could not have been unaware

---

8 [1982] 3 All ER 551.
9 See discussion at pp 88–89, ante.
10 [1953] Ch 131, [1953] 1 All ER 634. But see *Phonogram Ltd v Lane* [1981] 3 All ER 182 as to the extent to which resort may (or rather may not) be had to the Directive in construing CA 1985, s 36. Presumably the same principles apply to s 35. Cf, however, *International Sales and Agencies Ltd v Marcus* [1982] 3 All ER 551 at p 559, which suggests (probably incorrectly in the light of *Phonogram Ltd v Lane,* supra) otherwise.

of the *ultra vires* character of the act. It does proceed to provide that mere proof that the third party read the statutes does not establish the latter point and the third party would be protected where *ultra vires* could only be discerned by a process of interpretation.

Useful guidance was given on the meaning of good faith by Nourse J in *Barclays Bank Ltd v TOSG Trust Fund Ltd:*[11]

> My view of that question is this. In the case of a transaction decided on by the directors s 35 has abolished the rule that a person who deals with a company is automatically affected with constructive notice of its objects clause. But, by retaining the requirement of good faith, it nevertheless ensures that a defence based on absence of notice shall not be available to someone who has not acted genuinely and honestly in his dealings with the company. Notice and good faith, although two separate beings, are often inseparable. There is a most valuable account of their liaison in the speech of Lord Wilberforce in the recent case of *Midland Bank Trust Co Ltd v Green* [1981] AC 513 at 528, 529. What it comes to is that a person who deals with a company in circumstances where he ought anyway to know that the company has no power to enter into the transaction will not necessarily act in good faith. Sometimes, perhaps often, he will not. And a fortiori where he actually knows. Next, a person who acts in good faith will sometimes, perhaps often, act in a manner which can also be described as being reasonable. But I emphatically refute the suggestion, if such it is, that reasonableness is a necessary ingredient of good faith. That would require the introduction of an objective standard into a subjective concept and it would be contrary to everything which the law has always understood of that concept. In my judgment a person acts in good faith if he acts genuinely and honestly in the circumstances of the case. Beyond that it is neither possible nor desirable to attempt an examination of the circumstances in which s 35 may or may not apply ...

In *International Sales and Agencies Ltd v Marcus* (supra) it was also held that the test of lack of good faith in somebody entering into obligations with a company is to be found either in proof of his actual knowledge that the transaction was *ultra vires* the company or where it can be shown that such a person could not in view of all the circumstances have been unaware that he was a party to an *ultra vires* transaction. It would seem however that a person who has read the memorandum but has honestly misconstrued its terms is protected by the section, but the position of a third party who deliberately does not consult the memorandum in order not to discover limitations which he believes may well not be present is obscure.

11 [1984] BCLC 1, 18.

The section refers to a person 'dealing' with a company; this appears to go beyond contract but does not affect the principles of constructive trust in relation to the recipients of companies' money knowingly paid in breach of trust.[12] It does not restrict the protection of the section to outsiders.[13] It would seem therefore that insiders of a company who contract with it in ignorance of the memorandum or articles (a not impossible but, one may hope, an unusual situation) would be protected.

The section refers not to an activity of the company, but to a transaction; it would therefore seem that the third party would not be protected where the directors did not decide on a particular *ultra vires* activity but had committed the company to an *ultra vires* course of business, a natural consequence of which was the transaction in question.

The section does not refer to the operation of the *ultra vires* rule in tort; this is certainly a blemish.

It has been suggested that s 35 will provide adequate scope for 'pernickety liquidators, clever counsel and pedantic judges'.[14] Prince Metternich disliked both the use of a babel of languages in international affairs and the creation of Customs Unions. However sympathetic one may be towards the new European order instituted by the European Economic Communities, it is difficult not to have sympathy for both propositions.

THE LIABILITY OF MEMBERS

The memorandum of a company limited by shares or by guarantee must state that the liability of members is limited. In the case of a company limited by shares, the liability of a member is the amount, if any, unpaid on his shares. The liability of a member of a company limited by guarantee is limited to the amount he undertook to contribute to the assets of the company in the event of winding up. If a company limited by guarantee has a share capital the member will also be liable to pay the amount, if any, unpaid on his shares.

It is possible for a company to be registered where no limit is set to the liability of its members.[15] The members of an unlimited company are obliged in effect to act as guarantors of the company's

---

12 *International Sales and Agencies Ltd v Marcus* [1982] 3 All ER 551. See further on these points J. G. Collier and L. S. Sealey, 'European Communities Act 1972–Company Law' (1973) 32 CLJ 1.
13 Ibid, p 4.
14 Ibid.
15 See Chap 2, ante.

obligations. A creditor does not, of course, have a right of action against the member himself; his action is against the company, which will look to the members to provide sufficient funds to discharge its debts. The unlimited company does, however, possess an advantage which for some family firms may be substantial; it can ensure privacy for its accounts.[16]

However, if a company carries on business for more than six months while the number of members is less than two, a member aware of this fact is liable for all of the debts contracted by the company after the period of six months has elapsed.[17] Where this provision applies, the creditor has a right of action in respect of his debt against members jointly and severally with the company. Normally, the separate legal personality of the company protects the member from an action by a creditor in respect of obligations undertaken by the company.

A 'one-man' company is legally possible; the reduction in members below that which is required for incorporation does not of itself terminate the legal existence of the company.[18] But the effect of the above provision would be to make such a company for practical purposes an unlimited company.

CAPITAL[19]

The memorandum of all companies having a share capital must, unless the company is an unlimited company, state the amount of share capital with which the company is to be registered. It must also state that the capital is divided into shares of a fixed amount.[20]

The amount of capital with which a company is to be registered and the amounts into which it is to be divided are matters for the judgment of the promoters. It may be divided into shares of £1,000, £5, £1 or even 5p. The amount of the capital will be determined by the needs of the company and the availability of finance. Moneys borrowed on debentures do not form part of the capital of a company.[1] The word 'capital' is used here in the sense demanded by CA

16 CA 1985, s 241(4).
17 Ibid, s 24.
18 *Jarvis Motors (Harrow) Ltd v Carrabott* [1964] 3 All ER 89, [1964] 1 WLR 1101. *Re Duomatic Ltd* [1969] 2 Ch 365, [1969] 1 All ER 161.
19 See Chap 17, post, for a discussion of the various classes of capital. In yet another sense 'capital' denotes the excess in the value of assets over liabilities.
20 CA 1985, s 2(5)(a). It is thus not possible to issue no par value shares.
1 It is unwise to state in the memorandum the classes of shares into which the capital is divided and the rights attached to those classes: *Ashbury v Watson* (1885) 30 ChD 376, and *Campbell v Rofe* [1933] AC 91.

1985, s 2(5)(a). Other meanings are given to the word 'capital' according to the context in which it appears.

ALTERATION OF THE MEMORANDUM

Unless the object of including a provision in the memorandum is to make it difficult or impossible to change, it is unwise to include in the memorandum any provisions other than those which must be placed therein. If the memorandum contains provisions for which the Act makes no provisions for alteration, those provisions are unalterable. This may prove acutely embarrassing at a later date. The Act states that a company may alter its memorandum only in the cases, in the manner and to the extent for which express provision is made by the Act.[2] The following sections provide for the alteration of a company's memorandum, but only CA 1985, s 4 as to alteration of the objects clause will be dealt with here.

(1) CA 1985, s 28 as to change of name;[3]
(2) CA 1985, s 121 as to alteration of capital;[4]
(3) CA 1985, ss 120 and 124 as to the creation of reserve capital;[5]
(4) CA 1985, s 135 as to reduction of capital;[6]
(5) CA 1985, s 307 under which the liability of directors may be made unlimited;
(6) CA 1985, s 427 as to arrangements and reconstructions;[7]
(7) CA 1985, ss 125 and 126 as to the alteration of class rights.[8]

The Court is empowered by CA 1985, ss 459 and 461 to make such order as it thinks fit to end the unfairly prejudical treatment of minority shareholders. The section provides for an order which might involve an alteration in the company's memorandum. If such an order is made, the company cannot, without leave of the Court, alter its memorandum in a manner inconsistent with the order.

A company may by special resolution alter the provisions in its memorandum with respect to the objects of the company to enable it:

---

2 CA 1985, s 2(7).
3 See pp 79–80, supra.
4 See pp 342–343, post.
5 See ibid.
6 See Chap 20.
7 See pp 349–353, post.
8 See Chap 11.

(1) to carry on its business more economically or more efficiently; or
(2) to attain its main purpose by new or improved means; or
(3) to enlarge or change the local area of its operations; or
(4) to carry on some business which under existing circumstances may conveniently or advantageously be combined with the business of the company; or
(5) to restrict or abandon any of the objects specified in the memorandum; or
(6) to sell or dispose of the whole or any part of the undertaking of the company; or
(7) to amalgamate with any other company or body of persons.

In order for a company to rely against other persons on an alteration of the memorandum or articles (in this connection the powers conferred by s 17 of the Companies Act 1985 are relevant), the alteration must have been officially notified at the relevant time to the Registrar of Companies.[9]

A company cannot rely on head (4) where the change is of a fundamental character which alters the basic business of the company.[10] Nor can the alteration be incompatible with or opposed to the existing objects.

Re Cyclists Touring Club [1907] 1 Ch 269.

> The memorandum of the club stated that its objects were to promote, assist and protect the use of bicycles and other similar vehicles on public roads, and to give legal assistance in the enforcement of members' rights to use the roads. The club wished to alter its memorandum to permit all tourists, including motorists, to join the club. The Court refused to sanction the alteration, because (1) the change would have altered fundamentally the character of the club's activities; the new activities would have swamped the old, and (2) because the protection of members against motorists was one of its original objects. The new activity would have been inconsistent with the original purpose of the club.

Under head (5) the alteration of a provision of the objects clause which raised a secondary beneficiary to the position of a primary beneficiary on a winding up was held not to be an alteration

---

9 CA 1985, ss 4, 42.
10 And a fortiori no alteration can be made where the company has abandoned the pursuit of its original objects: *Re Drages* [1942] 1 All ER 194.

enabling the company to restrict or abandon any of its objects. The alteration was, therefore, not allowed.[11] The heads of s 4 are wide, but they are not unlimited, and a good deal of case law is available to guide the Court.[12]

An alteration may be objected to and an application made to the Court for its cancellation, in which case it will not take effect except in so far as it is confirmed by the Court.[13] An application may be made by the holders in aggregate if not less than 15% in value of the company's issued share capital or any class thereof (or the like percentage of its members if the company is not limited by shares)[14] or by the holders of not less than 15% of the company's debentures entitling the holders to object to alterations of its objects.[15] No application may be made by any person who consented to or voted in favour of the alteration.[16] The application must be made within 21 days after the date upon which the resolution altering the articles was passed. After this time limit has expired, the alteration cannot be challenged on the basis that it was not authorised by the section.[17]

The Court, on an application made under the section, may make an order confirming the alteration either wholly or in part and on such terms and conditions as it thinks fit. The Court may order that the company purchase the shares of any of its members and may provide accordingly for the reduction of the company's capital. It may also order alterations and additions to the memorandum and articles and these cannot be varied without leave of the Court.[18]

---

11 *Re Hampstead Garden Suburb Trust Ltd* [1962] Ch 806, [1962] 2 All ER 879.
12 See Report of the Company Law Committee Cmnd 1749 (1962) para 48 which recommends that there should be a general power to alter the objects, and which also recommends that an objection to an alteration should only require the support of 5% of shareholders; and see B. Davies (1974) 90 LQR 79.
13 CA 1985, s 5.
14 Ibid, s 5(2)(a). In *Re Hampstead Garden Suburb Trusts Ltd,* supra, the applicants were 15% of the holders of deferred shares.
15 Ibid, s 5(2)(b). By sub-s 8 debentures entitling the holders to object are those same series as debentures so issued. The holders are entitled to the same notice as are members.
16 Ibid, s 5(2) Proviso.
17 Ibid, s 5(3).
18 Ibid, s 5(4)–(6). It has been suggested that the above requirements do not apply where the alteration is blatantly outside the ambit of the section, and that therefore any individual member may object, presumably by an application for injunction or for a declaration; see further B. Davies (1974) 90 LQR 79; it is difficult to conceive of fact situations which could be so characterised but the procedure contained in the section does seem to be premised on a valid alteration.

One finds from time to time that an item in the objects clause is of a character which could have been placed in the articles. In such a case the item may be altered by special resolution, but the procedure stipulated for the alteration of objects including the right of a dissentient minority to protest will apply.[19] A company cannot argue that an item in the objects clause which is expressed as an object is merely a condition which could have been placed in the articles and so alterable in the same manner as the articles.[20]

---

[19] CA 1985, s 17. It follows that the alteration need not be for any of the purposes specified in s 4 so that the scope of alteration may be much wider.
[20] *Re Hampstead Garden Suburb Trust Ltd* supra. As to problems which could arise on a variation of rights if for example rights attaching to particular classes of shares were inserted in the memorandum, see discussion in Chap 11, post.

Chapter 7

Articles of Association

GENERAL

The articles of association are the company's regulations; they spell out in some detail the manner in which the company's business shall be conducted. The articles are subject to the memorandum and cannot confer wider powers on the company than those given in the memorandum. If there is a conflict between the memorandum and articles, the provisions of the former must prevail. However, if the memorandum is ambiguous or contains no provision on the question, there are certain cases where it will be permissible to refer to the articles to resolve the difficulty or to supplement the memorandum.[1] Jessel MR stated in *Re Wedgwood Coal and Iron Co* (1877) 7 ChD 75, p 99:

> Where there are two contemporaneous documents executed and assented to by the same persons at the same time ... it appears to me that the ordinary rule applies according to which contemporaneous documents are to be read together, so that if there is an ambiguity in one it may be explained by the other.

If, however, the ambiguity relates to some matter required by statute to appear in the memorandum, the articles cannot be looked at to modify the memorandum. Bowen LJ in *Guinness v Land Corporation of Ireland* (1882) 22 ChD 349, p 381, explained the relationship between the memorandum and articles in these words:

> The memorandum contains the fundamental conditions upon which alone the company is allowed to be incorporated. They are conditions

---

1 *Angostura Bitters Ltd v Kerr* [1933] AC 550. This question was before the courts in *Re Duncan Gilmour & Co Ltd* [1952] 2 All ER 871, where Wynn-Parry J examined the earlier authorities; also *Andrews v Gas Meter Co* [1897] 1 Ch 361, and *Re Welsbach Incandescent Gas Light Co Ltd* [1904] 1 Ch 87.

introduced for the benefit of the creditors and the outside public, as well as of the shareholders. The articles of association are the internal regulations of the company. How can it be said that in all cases the fundamental conditions of the charter of incorporation, and the internal regulations of the company are to be construed together?

... In any case it is, as it seems to me, certain that for anything which the Act of Parliament says shall be in the memorandum, you must look to the memorandum alone. If the Legislature has said one instrument is to be dominant you cannot turn to another instrument and read it in order to modify the provisions of the dominant instrument.

The articles of association are to be regarded as a business document and should be so construed where possible as to give them reasonable business efficacy.[2]

Copies of the memorandum and articles are to be made available to members,[3] and every copy issued after they have been altered must embody the alterations.[4]

The contents of articles of listed companies are influenced by the requirements of the Stock Exchange, whose rules governing stock exchange listings extend to matters included in the articles of association of companies, in particular in connection with the voting rights of preference shares and equity shares. For instance, the Stock Exchange disapproves of non-voting equity shares.

CONTENTS OF THE ARTICLES

The CA 1985 requires that, except in the case of a company limited by shares, the articles of association shall be in accordance with the forms set out in the Tables approved in regulations made by the Secretary of State or as near thereto as circumstances permit.[5] This suggests that only modest departures from those Tables are permissible, but in practice the words of the section are not treated as imposing serious restraints on company draftsmen.

All companies, other than companies limited by shares, must register articles of association together with the memorandum of association.[6] The articles must be signed by the subscribers to the memorandum.[7] A company limited by shares *may* register articles,

---

2 *Holmes v Keyes* [1959] Ch 199, 215, [1958] 2 All ER 129, p 138, per Jenkins LJ.
3 CA 1985, s 19.
4 Ibid, s 20.
5 Ibid, s 8 and see Companies (Tables A–F) Regulations 1985 (SI 1985/805).
6 Ibid, s 7.
7 Ibid.

but if it does not do so, the provisions of Table A[8] apply as the company's regulations.[9] Moreover, the appropriate portions of Table A will apply where articles are registered which do not exclude or modify the provisions of Table A. As a rule, it will be found that some modification of Table A is necessary. For example, the provisions as to quorums, rights attaching to different classes of shares, the number of directors and the rotation of directors are commonly modified. Table A is normally excluded altogether and the articles set out in full, even if this does mean adopting and thereby duplicating most of Table A, because where Table A is permitted to apply, it is the Table A that was in force at the time of the registration of the company that governs the affairs of the company. In the case of companies that were incorporated under previous Companies Acts, this could lead to inconvenience and confusion.

If there is an inconsistency between different parts of the articles of association, the courts are bound to consider the whole of the articles in construing a particular article and where possible to bring it into harmony with the other provisions of the articles. In *McNeil v McNeil's Sheepfarming Co Ltd*[10] the New Zealand Court of Appeal was asked to interpret the meaning of inconsistent articles as to voting rights. Article 5 gave each member of the company one vote, but art 65 of Table A made a different provision. It was decided that as there was an inconsistency between the two articles, art 65 of Table A was inapplicable to the company even though the article was not expressly declared not to apply to the company.

The articles of an unlimited company which has a share capital must state the amount of share capital with which the company proposes to be registered.[11] The articles of an unlimited company and of a company limited by guarantee which do not have a share capital must state the number of members with which the company proposes to be registered.[12] The form of articles must, except in the case of a company limited by shares, so far as circumstances permit, follow the appropriate Table.[13] Subject to this provision, and the qualifications set out below, the articles of any company may contain whatever rules the members decide should regulate the business of the company.

8   Table A is set out in SI 1985/805.
9   Ibid, s 8(2).
10 [1955] NZLR 15.
11 CA 1985, s 7(2).
12 Ibid, s 7(1) and (2).
13 Ibid, s 8.

(1) The articles may not contain anything illegal.
(2) The articles may not authorise anything expressly or impliedly forbidden by the Act, eg the issue of shares at a discount, a practice forbidden by s 100 of the CA 1985.
(3) The articles may not extend or modify the memorandum. Lord Cairns LC in *Ashbury Railway Carriage and Iron Co Ltd v Riche*[14] stated:

> The memorandum is, as it were, the area beyond which the action of the company cannot go; inside that area the shareholders may make such regulations for their own government as they think fit.

But the articles may permit something which is not expressly or impliedly forbidden by the memorandum.

Andrews v Gas Meter Co [1897] 1 Ch 361.[15]

> There was no power in the memorandum or articles, as registered, to issue preference shares. The articles were altered by special resolution to authorise the issue of such shares. On an increase of capital, preference shares were issued. That issue was held to be valid. The Court of Appeal expressed the opinion that so long as there was no provision to the contrary in the memorandum, the rights of shareholders were matters for regulation by the articles. The articles could, in such circumstances, be altered to authorise preference shares.

This case should not be regarded as establishing that the objects clause can be extended by amendment of the articles. Only when what is contemplated is not inconsistent with the memorandum can the change be made.

(4) The articles may not deprive members of the rights conferred on them by the Act, eg their right conferred by IA 1986, s 111 to be paid out in cash where they dissent from a scheme of reconstruction under that section.[16]
(5) The articles many stipulate conditions upon which a person may continue to remain a shareholder in the company. Thus a company may provide in its articles that any member who is engaged in competition with the company shall be required to transfer his shares (subject to payment) to a nominee of

---

14 (1875) LR 7 HL 653, 671.
15 Cf *Re Welsbach Incandescent Gas Light Co Ltd* [1904] 1 Ch 87.
16 *Payne v Cork Co Ltd* [1900] 1 Ch 308.

the directors.[17] A company may alter its articles to give itself this power.

The articles must be printed, divided into paragraphs numbered consecutively, and signed by each subscriber to the memorandum, the signature being properly attested.[18] By s 42 of the CA 1985 a company may not rely against other persons on any alteration in its articles of association unless these have been officially notified in the Gazette.

THE EFFECT OF THE MEMORANDUM AND ARTICLES

Section 14 of the Companies Act 1985 provides that the memorandum and articles shall, when registered,[19] bind the company and the members thereof to the same extent as if they respectively had been executed as a deed by each member and contained covenants on the part of each member to observe all the provisions of the memorandum and of the articles.

The precise effect of s 14 cannot yet be said to have been finally determined by the courts.[20] A provision similar to s 14 was enacted in the 1844 Act, but at that time the deed of settlement companies were flourishing.[1] The 1856 Act, which provided for incorporation on registration of the memorandum and articles of association, did not take into account, when the provision was re-enacted, the essential difference between the two kinds of company. There is no doubt that the memorandum and articles are given contractual effect, but though the courts speak the language of contract, they are in some respects treated more as an instrument of government.[2]

A point not to be overlooked is that the memorandum and articles may contain provisions for the benefit or protection of

---

17 *Sidebottom v Kershaw, Leese & Co Ltd* [1920] 1 Ch 154.
18 CA 1985, s 7(3).
19 It will be noted that the section refers to the memorandum and articles 'when registered'. The same principles govern companies which in fact register articles and those which do not; CA 1985, ss 10 and 14.
20 *Rayfield v Hands* [1960] 1 Ch 1, [1958] 2 All ER 194, which raises a number of interesting points, discussed at p 110, post.
 1 For the history and a criticism of this section, see Gower's *Pinciples of Modern Company Law* (4th edn, 1979) p 315.
 2 All of the ordinary contractual rules do not apply to this contract. Rectification is not available, *Scott v Frank Scott (London) Ltd* [1940] Ch 794, [1940] 3 All ER 508, and it is to be noted that this contract, unlike other contracts, can be varied without the consent of all parties.

members, eg as to the acquisition of shares, which they, and not the company, are interested in enforcing against other members.

RIGHTS OF MEMBERSHIP

Section 14 binds members to act in accordance with the articles in relation to matters falling within them. This rule is illustrated by

Hickman v Kent or Romney Marsh Sheep Breeders Association [1915] 1 Ch 881.

> A dispute arose between the plaintiff, a shareholder and the company as a result of which the plaintiff brought an action for an injunction and other equitable relief. One of the articles required that disputes concerning rights under the articles be submitted to arbitration. The company moved successfully to stay the suit, urging that the article constituted a sufficient submission to arbitration. Astbury J enumerated the following three propositions (at p 900):
> ... I think this much is clear: first, that no article can constitute a contract between the company and a third person; secondly, that no right merely purporting to be given by an article to a person, whether a member or not, in a capacity other than that of a member, as, for instance, as solicitor, promoter, director, can be enforced against the company and thirdly, that articles regulating the rights and obligations of the members generally as such do create rights and obligations between them and the company respectively.

The Court thus concluded that the articles are intended to bind the member as a member. They do not bind him in any other capacity. Here the plaintiff was bound, since to allow him to sue in the courts to enforce rights under the articles would have involved a breach of his obligation to take such disputes to arbitration.

Where the articles provided that a dividend, if declared, should be paid in a given fashion, an individual shareholder was entitled to require that dividends be so paid, and could not be forced by a majority to accept payment otherwise.[3]

A member is entitled to enforce compliance with a clause in the articles giving him a right to a share certificate.[4]

The right to vote is also safeguarded as a proprietary right enuring to the benefit of the member. Thus where the articles of a company provided that a member should have one vote per ten

---

3 *Wood v Odessa Waterworks Co* (1889) 42 ChD 636.
4 *Burdett v Standard Exploration Co* (1899) 16 TLR 112.

shares subject to a maximum of 100 votes, the Court held that the chairman of a meeting was bound to receive the votes of registered holders without regard to whether the registered owners were only trustees for another who was using the device of multiplying legal ownership to increase his voting power.⁵ Similarly, a member may bind himself to vote in a given fashion by a voting agreement. The company will still be obliged to receive his vote in accordance with the articles, and such a shareholders' voting agreement can be enforced by a mandatory injunction.⁶ It should also be noted that the articles may create a lien on shares in respect of amounts due by members to the company.⁷

RIGHTS OTHER THAN RIGHTS OF MEMBERSHIP

The s 14 contract concerns rights of membership. It is a basic rule that the articles do not confer rights upon an outsider or upon a member who claims rights in a capacity other than member, eg as a director.

Eley v Positive Government Security Life Assurance Co Ltd (1876) 1 Ex D 88.

> The articles provided that the plaintiff should be the company's solicitor for life, removable only for misconduct. He became the solicitor and a member. Later, the company terminated his employment. The plaintiff sued the company for breach of the contract contained in the articles. It was held that the articles could function as an agreement between the members to appoint the plaintiff, or a direction to the directors to appoint him, but the articles did not, of themselves, constitute a contract between the plaintiff in his capacity as solicitor, and the company.

Again, in *Tett v Phoenix Property and Investment Co Ltd*⁸ which dealt with a claim by beneficiaries who took shares on the death of a member, the court held that such persons can accept an offer to purchase made by members of the company, but cannot enforce a

---

5 *Pender v Lushington* (1877) 6 ChD 70; but see *MacDougall v Gardiner* (1875) 1 ChD 13 and the discussion in Chap 11 in connection with the protection of minority shareholders' rights.
6 *Puddephat v Leith* [1916] 1 Ch 200; *Greenwell v Porter* [1902] 1 Ch 530. It has been said that this rule and others like it permit a shareholder to act in a wholly egoistic way in the protection of his interest: Giguère, 'Contrôle de la gestion par l'assemblée générale' in *Studies in Canadian Company Law* (1967) p 403.
7 *Bradford Banking Co v Briggs* (1886) 12 App Cas 29.
8 [1984] BCLC 599.

right of pre-emption contained in the articles against the members. The contract is only as between members of the company. Similarly, an arbitration provision in the articles does not bind a member in his capacity as director. Thus a dispute between the company and a director is not referable to arbitration under the article.[9]

It should be noted that in some cases an article, while not a contract between the company and an outsider, or a person acting in a capacity other than member, may be embodied in and form part of the contract with the company, eg as director.[10] This proposition does not detract from the authority of the cases noted above. *Re Richmond Gate Property Co Ltd*[11] which concerned the remuneration of a managing director appears however to do so. The relevant article provided that the managing director should receive such remuneration as the directors might determine. The managing director at a pre-incorporation meeting agreed with the other promoters that no remuneration would be paid to himself until the company was on its feet.

Plowman J held that the articles, coupled with the fact that the managing director was a member of the company, constituted a contract between the company and the managing director. Because the directors had not determined a salary and the articles were an express contract, no question of remuneration on the basis of a *quantum meruit* could arise.[12] The best explanation of this case, perhaps, is that the managing director by undertaking that he would not receive remuneration until the company got firmly on its feet barred himself from recovery in contract or quasi-contract.[13] It has also been suggested that this case recognises the rights of shareholders to have the business of the company conducted in accordance with the articles. This, if correct, would lead to the conclusion that a member, by suing to enforce the articles, could vindicate without limitation rights which he enjoys in another capacity. These issues were not placed before the Court in *Re Richmond Gate Property Co Ltd* and the explanations are, perhaps, overambitious.[13]

There is also authority for the proposition that because each member has a contractual right to have the business of the company managed in accordance with the provisions of the articles, a

---

9 *Beattie v E and F Beattie Ltd* [1938] Ch 708, [1938] 3 All ER 214.
10 *Re New British Iron Co, ex p Beckwith* [1898] 1 Ch 324.
11 [1964] 3 All ER 936, [1965] 1 WLR 335.
12 *Craven-Ellis v Canons Ltd* [1936] 2 KB 403, [1936] 2 All ER 1066 was distinguished.
13 D. M. Evans (1966) 29 Mod LR 608, founding on a passage in [1965] 1 WLR 335, 338; cf K. W. Wedderburn (1965) 28 Mod LR 347.

member may sue to enforce the allocation of powers under the articles even though the effect of the suit is, for example, to vindicate the rights of the plaintiff *qua* director as well as *qua* member.[14] These cases also need to be reconciled with the proposition that an individual member cannot complain of a mere internal irregularity.[15] It is suggested, with deference, that cases such as the *Eley* case do not apply to bar a suit brought ostensibly to force management to conform with the basic constitutional allocation of powers, or the consitutional conditions upon which a given person may exercise powers, even though the effect of the suit is to enforce an 'outsider right'.[16]

RIGHTS BETWEEN THE MEMBERS *INTER SE*

Section 14 also purports to be a contract between the members *inter se*. Thus, where the articles provided that a certain class of shareholder might be required to transfer her shares to existing members at a price (not to exceed par value), it was held that a bankrupt member and his trustees were bound to transfer the shares on requisition, notwithstanding that the par value of the shares was well below their true value.[17] Similarly, an article which makes the minutes of a meeting, once signed, conclusive evidence of the facts therein is conclusive in the absence of fraud.[18] In these cases, the provisions of the articles were used as a defence against a member's action.

It is a vexed question whether one member can sue another member directly on the contract. In *Welton v Saffery* Lord Herschell states that:[19]

> ... there is no contract in terms between the individual members of the company; but the articles do not any the less, in my opinion, regulate their rights *inter se*. Such rights can only be enforced by or against a member through the company, or through the liquidator representing the company; but I think that no member has, as between himself and another member, any right beyond that which the contract with the company gives.

---

14 *Quin and Axtens Ltd v Salmon* [1909] AC 442, and see *Re H R Harmer Ltd* [1958] 3 All ER 689, [1959] 1 WLR 62.
15 *MacDougall v Gardiner* (1875) 1 ChD 13.
16 See also *Kraus v F G Lloyd Pty Ltd* [1965] VR 232, Hahlo 465; *Charter Oil Co Ltd v Beaumont* (1967) 65 DLR (2d) 112.
17 *Borland's Trustee v Steel Bros & Co Ltd* [1901] 1 Ch 279.
18 *Kerr v John Mottram Ltd* [1940] Ch 657, [1940] 2 All ER 629.
19 [1897] AC 299, at p 315.

110 *Chapter 7 Articles of Association*

The inference is that while each shareholder is deemed to be in privity with the company, he is not deemed to be in privity with any other individual member.[20] This statement, though approved in a later case,[1] is inconsistent with the *Eley* case and others.[2] In one case at least, in connection with pre-emptive rights, a direct action by one member against another on the contract was allowed. In *Rayfield v Hands*[3] a member of a company in an action against the directors sought to compel the directors to purchase his shares in terms of the articles. The company was not joined as a party. Vaisey J was satisfied that the articles formed a contract between the member and the defendants as members rather than as directors. The directors, as members, were obliged under the articles to purchase the plaintiff's shares. Vaisey J's reasoning is in part tortuous, and in part now unsustainable.[4] None the less, there seems no very good reason, in cases of this sort, involving pre-emptive rights, why the company should be joined in the action.[5]

Finally, it should be noted that the articles have no application to disputes between members entirely outside the company relationship such as outside trading relationships between persons who happen to be members.[6]

ALTERATION OF THE ARTICLES

BY SPECIAL RESOLUTION

Subject to the provisions of the Act and to the conditions contained in its memorandum, a company may by special resolution alter its articles.[7] A special resolution is a resolution passed by a majority of not less than three-quarters of such members as, being entitled to

---

20 Despite the seemingly clear words of s 14 which, it may be thought, are apt to put the parties statutorily in privity.
1 *London Sack and Bag Co Ltd v Dixon and Lugton Ltd* [1943] 2 All ER 763.
2 See also *Borland's Trustee v Steel Bros & Co Ltd* [1901] 1 Ch 279 at 290; *Kerr v John Mottram Ltd* [1940] Ch 657 at 660.
3 [1960] Ch 1, [1958] 2 All ER 194.
4 See the comments in (1958) 21 Mod LR 401 and (1958) Camb LJ 148. Vaisey J assumed that the members were not in privity. He relied on s 56 of the Law of Property Act 1925 to allow the plaintiff to take the benefit of a contract which, on this view, existed between the company and the members and not the members *inter se*. But, in *Beswick v Beswick* [1968] AC 58, [1967] 2 All ER 1197, it was held that s 56 could not be relied on to overcome the normal rules relating to privity.
5 See Gower's *Principles of Modern Company Law* (4th edn, 1979) pp 316–317.
6 *London Sack and Bag Co Ltd v Dixon and Lugton Ltd* (supra).
7 CA 1985, s 9.

do so, vote in person, or, where proxies are allowed, by proxy at a general meeting of which not less than 21 days' notice specifying the intention to propose the resolution as a special resolution, has been given.[8] An alteration made in the articles by special resolution is valid, unless it falls within one of the following qualifications:

(1) the alteration must not contain anything illegal;

(2) the alteration must not authorise anything expressly or impliedly forbidden by the Companies Act 1985. It is necessary to emphasise the phrase 'subject to the conditions stated in its memorandum' appearing in CA 1985, s 9, because it would seem that a company could, if it decided to do so, 'entrench' certain of its articles. If, for example, the memorandum provided that those articles dealing with the rights of certain shareholders or the tenure and powers of its directors could not be changed, those articles would be unalterable in terms of s 9. If the proposed alteration is inconsistent with the conditions stated in the memorandum, the alteration is one which is not authorised by the Act;

(3) the alteration must not extend or modify the memorandum;[9]

(4) the alteration must not deprive members of rights conferred on them by the CA 1985, s 127 which deals with class rights or by the Court under s 461(3);[10]

(5) the alteration must not, without the consent in writing of a member, require him to take or subscribe for more shares or increase his liability to contribute to the company;[11]

(6) the alteration must not amount to a fraud on a minority, but if the alteration is bona fide for the benefit of the company as a whole the interests of a minority may be sacrificed.

The doctrine of fraud on the minority raises vexed problems. The courts have, of recent years, adhered markedly to a *laissez-faire* attitude to the principle that the regulation of the company's affairs is a matter for the members. Members are expected to wield proprietary rights, with regard to this self-interest, but subject to an ill-defined obligation not to oppress the minority.[12]

The Court intervenes to hold the ring as little as possible. The result is a body of principle which is, in part, ill-defined and in general ungenerous to the minority shareholder.

---

8 Ibid, s 378. Under this section, a resolution may be adopted as a special resolution with shorter notice if the majorities therein specified agree.
9 *Andrews v Gas Meter Co* [1897] 1 Ch 361.
10 See Chap 11, post.
11 CA 1985, s 16.
12 *North-West Transportation Co v Beatty* (1887) 12 App Cas 589, PC; *Burland v Earle* [1902] AC 83, PC.

The early, but important case of *Allen v Gold Reefs of West Africa Ltd*[13] suggested a test which was in part objective and therefore potentially interventionist. The case involved an alteration of the company's articles in order to give it a lien over fully-paid shares. The only holder of such shares was in fact one Zuccani whose executors sought to impeach the alteration. Lord Lindley MR stated:[14]

> The power thus conferred on companies to alter the regulations contained in their articles is limited only by the provisions contained in the statute and the conditions in the company's memorandum of association.... It must, like all other powers, be exercised subject to those general principles of law and equity which are applicable to all powers conferred on majorities and enabling them to bind minorities. It must be exercised, not only in the manner required by law, but also bona fide for the benefit of the company as a whole, and it must not be exceeded. These conditions are always implied, and are seldom, if ever, expressed. But if they are complied with I can discover no ground for judicially putting any other restrictions on the power conferred by the section than those contained in it.

The case is an authority for the proposition that an alteration may alter members' rights to their prejudice, and retrospectively, so far as such rights are founded upon alterable articles. In this case the alteration was valid. The altered article applied to all fully-paid shares and so was not formally discriminatory.[15] The alteration was made bona fide and for the benefit of the company.

After this decision, some decisions sought to breathe life into the supposed general principles of law and equity referred to by the Court. In *Brown v British Abrasive Wheel Co*[16] Astbury J was faced with a proposed alteration which would have permitted the expropriation of the shares of a minority. It was not shown that the alteration was necessary to benefit the company, or that it had a tendency to do so, or that it was likely to do more than further the interests of the majority alone. Adverting approvingly to the existence of a governing body of general principles of law and equity, Astbury J struck down the alteration. Even if the existence of such principles be not conceded, however, the decision might be rested on the existence of overt discrimination in circumstances where the majority would appear not to have had regard to the interests of the

---

13 [1900] 1 Ch 656, CA.
14 At pp 671–672.
15 Vaughan Williams LJ dissented on this point.
16 [1919] 1 Ch 290.

company as a whole, meaning by that phrase, the interests of the general body of shareholders taken as a whole.[17]

Dafen Tinplate Co Ltd v Llanelly Steel Co (1907) Ltd [1920] 2 Ch 124.

> The company was controlled by directors appointed by a number of steel firms which were among its shareholders. Fearing that some members might deal with other companies and use their inside information of the defendant company's affairs to its detriment, the company sought to alter its articles to enable the shares of existing shareholders to be bought out at a fair price to be settled by the company's board. The alteration would also have had the effect of requiring the members to take steel bars from the defendant company at its price. The original understanding had been that members would voluntarily purchase supplies from the company. Peterson J held the proposed alteration to be improper because (1) it enabled any shareholder to be bought out whatever his conduct and thereby conferred an unrestricted power on the majority to expropriate the minority and (2) it placed one member (to whom the alteration would not have applied) in an uniquely privileged position.

The decision turns on the proposition that the alteration went beyond what might be required for the benefit of the company as a whole. The discriminatory provision in favour of one member also could not be supported on accepted criteria.

The case proceeded on an application of objective standards. These have since been departed from in most cases but, in relation to alterations having an expropriatory effect, such standards may still operate.

The applicability of overriding objective standards was, however, denied in *Sidebottom v Kershaw, Leese & Co Ltd*.[18] There the company passed a resolution to alter its articles by providing that the directors (who were majority shareholders) should have the power to require shareholders who carried on a business in competition with the company to transfer their shares at a fair value to the directors. The Court, in upholding the alteration, doubted whether any objective standards were applicable. The test is whether the majority in voting for the alteration did so on their view of benefit to the company. The issue of *mala fides* might be raised if an alteration were aimed at a particular member, but the only effect

---

17 See also *Re Holders Investment Trust Ltd* [1971] 2 All ER 289, [1971] 1 WLR 583.
18 [1920] 1 Ch 154.

of such particularity was to raise the general issue. The subjective approach became dominant. In *Shuttleworth v Cox Bros & Co (Maidenhead) Ltd*[19] articles conferring life tenure on the directors were altered so as to give the directors power to declare a vacancy in the office. The alteration was aimed at a particular director who had been dismissed from a secure position because of irregularities in his accounts, but who had refused to resign as director. The Court, in upholding the alteration, held that the test is whether the majority voted in good faith in what they believed to be the best interests of the company. Unless the alteration were so oppressive as to raise the issue of *mala fides* or so extravagant that no reasonable man could consider it to be for the benefit of the company, the Court would accept the view of the majority. This is the view now followed. The leading case is:

Greenhalgh v Arderne Cinemas Ltd [1951] Ch 286, [1950] 2 All ER 1120.[20]

Article 10 of the articles of the A company provided that a member could sell his shares to another member by private arrangement, but otherwise the shares must first be offered to other members, *pro rata* at a price fixed by the auditors. In order to effect a sale of 135,815 of the 205,000 ordinary shares to S, who was not a shareholder, the majority shareholders called an extraordinary general meeting which passed a resolution altering art 10 by adding the following words:

> Notwithstanding the foregoing provisions of this article, any member may with the sanction of an ordinary resolution passed at any general meeting of the company transfer his shares or any of them to any person named in such resolution as the proposed transferee, and the directors shall be bound to register any transfer which has been so sanctioned.

An ordinary resolution was later passed approving the sale to S. A minority shareholder sought to impeach the alteration on the ground that the interests of the minority had been sacrified without any reasonable prospect of advantage to the company, thereby committing a fraud on the minority. The alteration was upheld. After examining the authorities Evershed MR stated:[1]

19 [1927] 2 KB 9.
20 See the articles on this case, (1951) 101 LJ 173 and (1955) Camb LJ 37.
1 At p 291.

Certain principles, I think, can be safely stated as emerging from those authorities. In the first place, I think it is now plain that 'bona fide for the benefit of the company as a whole' means not two things but one thing. It means that the shareholder must proceed upon what, in his honest opinion, is for the benefit of the company as a whole. The second thing is that the phrase, 'the company as a whole', does not (at any rate in such a case as the present) mean the company as a commercial entity, distinct from the corporators: it means the corporators as a general body. That is to say, the case may be taken of an individual hypothetical member and it may be asked whether what is proposed is, in the honest opinion of those who voted in its favour, for that person's benefit.

I think that the matter can, in practice, be more accurately and precisely stated by looking at the converse and by saying that a special resolution of this kind would be liable to be impeached if the effect of it were to discriminate between the majority shareholders and the minority shareholders, so as to give to the former an advantage of which the latter were deprived. When the cases are examined in which the resolution has been successfully attacked, it is on that ground. It is therefore not necessary to require that persons voting for a special resolution should, so to speak, dissociate themselves altogether from their own prospects and consider whether what is thought to be for the benefit of the company as a going concern. If, as commonly happens, an outside person makes an offer to buy all the shares, prima facie, if the corporators think it a fair offer and vote in favour of the resolution, it is no ground for impeaching the resolution that they are considering their own position as individuals.[2]

Greenhalgh v Arderne Cinemas Ltd was followed in a case which did not concern an alteration of the articles.

Clemens v Clemens Bros Ltd [1976] 2 All ER 268.[3]

The plaintiff held 45% of the issued shares in the defendant company, whilst her aunt held the remaining 55%. There were five directors, of whom the aunt was one. At an extraordinary general meeting, the board put forward proposals to issue further shares to the non-shareholding directors and to a trust for the company's employees. The proposals, if implemented, would have reduced the plaintiff's shareholding to less than 25% thereby depriving her of the power to block special resolutions. Although the plaintiff voted against the proposed issues of shares, the aunt's majority shareholding ensured that the extraordinary general meeting approved the scheme. The court set aside the resolutions.

---

2 The passage in [1950] 2 All ER 1120, 1126, is differently reported.
3 See D. Prentice (1976) 92 LQR 502 and V. Joffe (1977) 40 Mod LR 71.

Foster J, referring to *Greenhalgh v Arderne Cinemas Ltd* posed the question: 'did the aunt honestly believe that the scheme would be for the benefit of the plaintiff?' It is submitted that this is too wide an interpretation of the principles expounded in the earlier cases, which do not permit the court to invalidate a resolution merely because the majority did not honestly believe that the resolution would be for the benefit of those opposing it. On the contrary, the position reached by these cases appears to be this: a shareholder is not expected to ignore the effect of a resolution on him personally, but he must also consider whether it is for the benefit of the company. The Court can invalidate a decision if it is shown to be so unreasonable that a hypothetical fair-minded shareholder would not have voted for it. Where an independent majority agrees to an alteration of the articles the Court will be inclined to treat this as conclusive that the alteration was considered to be for the benefit of the company. In *Rights and Issues Investment Trust Ltd v Stylo Shoes Ltd*[4] a minority of management shares had nearly half the voting rights. The company proposed to acquire the capital of B company in exchange for shares. The controllers in order to keep the proportion of management shares constant, proposed an alteration to the articles to increase their voting rights. The management shares did not vote on the alteration. The alteration was passed by a large independent majority. It was held that so large a vote by persons who had nothing to gain personally from the alteration was an indication that the alteration was resolved on bona fide for the benefit of the company as a whole. The alteration of voting rights was not, as such, oppressive.

When, therefore, will an alteration be held invalid? An alteration may be unreasonable where it formally discriminates between shareholders in circumstances raising the issue of *mala fides*.[5] It must however be stressed that an alteration will only be struck down where it formally discriminates between shareholders. In *Greenhalgh v Arderne Cinemas Ltd* the alteration could have had the effect of enabling a majority shareholder to buy up a minority interest by blocking a sale to anyone else. The Court none the less held that this functional discrimination did not vitiate the alteration provided that it was passed bona fide and in the best interests of the company. And it will not be struck down simply because it discriminates, as the *Shuttleworth* case discloses. The discrimination must be such as does not benefit the company or goes far beyond what its interests require.

4 [1965] Ch 250, [1964] 3 All ER 628.
5 *Sidebottom v Kershaw, Leese & Co Ltd* [1920] 1 Ch 154.

These decisions reflect a value judgment on the part of the courts; the view that the conduct of the company's affairs is primarily a matter for the members. The content is invariably one of conflicting interests, and '... the adjustment is left by law to the determination of those whose interests conflict'.[6] None the less, in *Greenhalgh v Arderne Cinemas Ltd*[7] the Court stressed that the case was not one of the class where shareholder interests were being expropriated as the result of a discriminatory article which was wider than was required for the protection of the company's business. It is also perhaps worth noting that the courts, in considering the effect of CA 1985, s 428 which enables a take-over bidder who secures at least 90% of the equity shares to buy out the dissentient minority compulsorily, have stressed the necessity for strict compliance with the section.[8] It may be, therefore, that the courts will adopt a stricter attitude towards alterations which give the power to expropriate shares than towards other forms of alteration however onerous their effect in fact.[9] Thus, an expropriatory alteration which goes further than is needed to protect the company may still be struck down, no doubt on the footing that the majority failed to consider the relevant factors sufficiently closely.

BY AGREEMENT BETWEEN THE SHAREHOLDERS

Provided that the shareholders of a company are unanimous, the company's articles may be altered or overridden by agreement between them notwithstanding the absence of a resolution under CA 1985, s 9.

Cane v Jones [1981] 1 All ER 533, [1980] 1 WLR 1451.

> KPS Ltd was incorporated by P and H who were its only directors. The articles of KPS provided inter alia that P and H should be life directors, that the directors should elect the chairman of the board and that the chairman should have a casting vote at board and general meetings. In 1967, all of the then shareholders entered into an agreement—which

---

6 Per Dixon J in *Peters American Delicacy Co Ltd v Heath* (1939) 61 CLR 457, p 512.
7 [1951] Ch 286, [1950] 2 All ER 1120.
8 *Re Bugle Press Ltd* [1961] Ch 270, [1960] 3 All ER 791.
9 See on an analogous point, *Re Holders Investment Trust Ltd* [1971] 2 All ER 289, [1971] 1 WLR 583. But of course in some cases an alteration giving a power to expropriate will be upheld as perfectly proper. *Allen v Gold Reefs of West Africa Ltd* [1900] 1 Ch 656.

they did not meet to sign—providing inter alia that the chairman should not exercise a casting vote and if an equality of votes occurred an independent chairman would be appointed. Subsequently, at a time when some of the shares had changed hands, a dispute arose as to whether P was chairman and, if so, whether he had a casting vote. R (a joint owner of some of the shares in KPS) and P argued that the articles could only be altered by resolution under CA 1948, s 10 (now CA 1985, s 9) and that the agreement did not alter the articles.

It was held (i) P was not the chairman and (ii) the agreement was effective to override the articles with regard to the chairman's casting vote and accordingly any chairman of the company would have no such vote.

In *Cane v Jones*,[10] the argument that the articles could only be altered by special resolution was decisively rejected. The Court held that s 9 merely laid down a procedure whereby some only of the shareholders can validly alter the articles, for it is a basic principle of company law that all of the corporators of a company acting together (whether they act simultaneously or at different times[11]) can do anything which is *intra vires* the company, and s 9 does not affect this principle.[12]

The fact that a shareholder's agreement is drafted only as an agreement and not as a resolution does not prevent it overriding the articles, and the agreement does not (like a special resolution altering the articles) require registration under CA 1985, s 380.[13] Furthermore, the position appears to be that even if the agreement does not state expressly that it amends or overrides the articles it will validly do so provided that that is its effect.[14]

ARTICLES AND BREACH OF CONTRACT

A company cannot, by a provision in its articles, deprive itself of its power to alter its articles, and a contract that it will not alter them is probably invalid.[15] But a company which, acting under its altered

10 Supra.
11 Ibid, p 539; *Parker and Cooper Ltd v Reading* [1926] Ch 975, [1926] All ER Rep 323; *Rolled Steel Products (Holdings) Ltd v British Steel Corpn* [1986] Ch 246, [1985] 3 All ER 52, CA.
12 *Cane v Jones* supra p 539.
13 Ibid, p 540.
14 Ibid, p 541.
15 *Punt v Symons & Co Ltd* [1903] 2 Ch 506. It is not altogether clear to what extent this decision represents good law in view of the later decision in *Southern Foundries (1926) Ltd v Shirlaw* [1940] AC 701, [1940] 2 All ER 445. It would seem that a provision in the articles to the effect that the articles will not be altered could not be specifically enforced.

articles, commits a breach of contract entered into before the alteration was made cannot plead its altered articles as a defence in an action for breach of contract.

Southern Foundries (1926) Ltd v Shirlaw [1940] AC 701, [1940] 2 All ER 445.

By a contract, S was appointed managing director of the appellant company for ten years from 1933. The articles gave power to remove directors 'subject to the provisions of any contract between him and the company'. In April 1936 new articles were adopted because another company (the F.F. Co) had acquired control of the company. These articles gave power to the F.F. Co to remove any director. S was removed in 1937 and he sued for breach of contract. It was held by the House of Lords (Viscount Maugham and Lord Romer dissenting),[16] that there was an implied term in the agreement of 1933 that the appellant company would not remove S from his directorate during the term of ten years. Lord Porter stated respectively at pp 740–1, 469:

> The general principle therefore may, I think, be thus stated. A company cannot be precluded from altering its articles thereby giving itself power to act upon the provisions of the altered articles—but so to act may nevertheless be a breach of contract if it is contrary to a stipulation in a contract validly made before the alteration.
>
> Nor can an injunction be granted to prevent the adoption of the new articles and in that sense they are binding on all and sundry, but for the company to act upon them will none the less render it liable in damages if such action is contrary to the previous engagements of the company. If, therefore, the altered articles had provided for the dismissal without notice of a managing director previously appointed, the dismissal would be *intra vires* the company but would nevertheless expose the company to an action for damages if the appointment had been for a term of (say) ten years and he were dismissed in less.

In an earlier case, *British Murac Syndicate v Alperton Rubber Co Ltd* [1915] 2 Ch 186, the Court issued an injunction restraining the company from altering its articles for the purpose of committing a breach of contract. The effect of the decision of the House of Lords in the *Shirlaw* case on the *British Murac Syndicate* case is not

---

16 It is significant that the division of judicial opinion in the House of Lords placed the common lawyers on one side and the equity lawyers on the other. See also CA 1985, ss 303 and 319 and Chap 8, post, as to removal of directors.

perfectly clear.[17] The earlier decision is not mentioned in any of the judgments but it appears that all members of the House of Lords treated the decision in *Punt v Symons* as correct and *British Murac Syndicate* as wrongly decided. Because Shirlaw sought damages and not an injunction restraining the alteration of the articles, the issue before the Court in *British Murac Syndicate* did not arise. It must be noted also that in the *Shirlaw* case there was no suggestion that the articles had been altered with the intention of enabling the company to commit a breach of contract.[18] It is at least implicit in the judgments of all members of the House of Lords that the alteration of the articles was valid. It is submitted, therefore, that Shirlaw could not have obtained an injunction restraining the company from altering its articles. It follows from that submission that, whatever the motives of the company might have been in altering its articles, an injunction restraining the alteration will not be issued. There is more explicit Australian authority to the like effect as well.[19] *British Murac Syndicate* should therefore be treated as overruled by *Shirlaw*.[20] That case establishes that, provided a director or other officer of a company can prove that he has a binding contract[1] for a fixed term he will, if dismissed prematurely, succeed in an action for breach of that contract, despite the fact that the company may have had the power under the articles to terminate his employment as it did. Notwithstanding this decision it is possible for directors to entrench themselves, as, for example, by having the articles accord extra voting rights to their shares on a motion for dismissal.

---

17 None of the decisions discussed was concerned with an alteration of the articles which was inconsistent with a prior contract (as distinct from the articles themselves) defining the rights of members. Probably, such a case would be governed by the principles already discussed, but it is not free from doubt; see D. G. Rice (1958) 22 Conv (NS) 282, 289–290.
18 Shirlaw was not removed until the year after the articles were amended. See the statement of Lord Romer at p 731, where he speaks of the removal of Shirlaw as an indirect and unintended consequence of the alteration of the articles.
19 *Carrier Australasia Ltd v Hunt* (1939) 61 CLR 534, where the alteration was made in order to enable an employment to be terminated.
20 Cf Gower's *Principles of Modern Company Law* (4th edn, 1979) pp 558–559.
 1 As has already been stated, the articles do not constitute a contract with a director.

Chapter 8

Directors and Officers

GENERAL

Control over the modern registered company is distributed among its organs; the board of directors, the managing director if any, and the general body of shareholders. The Companies Act 1985 does not impose any particular managerial structure upon companies. In some smaller companies the board will exercise a close control over the company's affairs. In the case of many large companies, the board of directors exercises only a general control leaving the task of management including the implementation of policy to the managing director. A large company could be, and some are, governed by a two-tier board in which one tier may have ultimate guidance over finance and policy while the 'lower' tier (or full board) concerns itself with the discussion and resolution of more detailed managerial problems.[1] In the case of large companies having a widely diffused shareholding, the general body of shareholders exercises essentially an approval function. The company may in fact be governed by a self-perpetuating managerial oligarchy.[2]

Modern articles of association normally confer executive powers on the board of directors and a managing director.[3] An individual director will exercise executive powers including the power to enter into valid contracts on behalf of the company only where he

---

1 See Betts, 'Characteristics of British Company Directors', 4 Journal of Management Studies 71 (1967). These issues were adumbrated by Lord Aldington in a paper given before the Ford Foundation Workshop on Company Law in July 1969. Management structures are also discussed in *Report of the Committee of Inquiry on Industrial Democracy* (Chairman, Lord Bullock) Cmnd 6706.
2 P. S. Florence, *Ownership, Control and Success of Large Companies* (1961) pp 184–193. The classic study in this field is Berle and Means, *The Modern Corporation and Private Property* (1932).
3 Table A, arts 70 and 88–98.

occupies a service position to which such powers attach, or where the board has delegated such powers to him.[4]

The word 'director' is partially defined by s 741 of the Companies Act 1985, to include any person occupying the position of director, by whatever name he may be called. In a number of statutes, particularly those which deal with what might be called economic crimes, the definition is extended to include any person purporting to act in such a capacity or any person in accordance with whose instructions the directors of any company act.[5]

It should also be noted that any person in accordance with whose directions or instructions the directors of a company are accustomed to act is by the same provision termed a 'shadow director' and treated for the purposes of CA 1985, s 317(8), s 318(6), and the provisions relating to unauthorised distributions as a director of the company. However, a person is not a shadow director if the directors of the company are merely acting on his advice given in a professional capacity.[6] This provision prevents a person giving advice solely as, for example, solicitor to a company, from becoming a shadow director by reason of the fact that the company's directors are accustomed to act in accordance with his advice.

APPOINTMENT

Every company, except a private company, must have at least two directors.[7] The persons named as directors in the statement of first directors and secretary[8] are deemed on the incorporation of the company to have been appointed as the first directors of the company.[9] Any purported appointment of the first directors by the articles is void, unless the persons named in the articles are also those named in the statement. The appointment of subsequent directors is governed by the articles, or, if there is no provision therein, and Table A does not apply, by general meeting. In order to increase shareholders' control over the directors, it is provided that resolutions for the election of directors of a public company shall be submitted in respect of each director separately unless the

---

4 Table A, art 72.
5 Eg Insolvency Act 1976, s 9(7); Finance Act 1976, s 72(8).
6 CA 1985, s 741.
7 Ibid, s 282.
8 See pp 141–145, post.
9 CA 1985, s 13(5).

general meeting by resolution without dissent resolves otherwise.[10]

A company must notify the Registrar of Companies of any change amongst its directors or secretary, and the notification must contain a consent signed by the new director or secretary, to act in that capacity.[11] Unless it has complied with the requirement of notification, the company may not rely, as against any other person who is unaware of the change, on any change amongst its directors.[12]

Unless the articles contain provisions to the contrary, those holding a majority of the shares with voting rights will be able to appoint an entire board of directors of their choosing.

Any person (and apparently a corporation as such is not disqualified)[13] may be appointed a director:

(1) unless he is an undischarged bankrupt, but the Court may give him leave to act,[14] or
(2) unless he is disqualified by the Court which has power to restrain fraudulent persons, persons who have persistently defaulted in complying with the provisions of the Companies Act 1985 and the Insolvency Act 1986, and persons who are unfit to act in the management of companies from managing companies for up to 15 years without the leave of the Court.[15]

Where qualification shares are required by the articles, a director must obtain these within two months of his appointment.[16] If a director fails to secure his qualification shares within this period, or any shorter period fixed by the articles, he vacates office.[17]

RESIGNATION, RETIREMENT AND DISMISSAL

RESIGNATION

A director may resign his office at any time. Provision for resignation is usually made in the articles. Thus art 81(d) of Table A provides that the office of director shall be vacated if the director

---

10 CA 1985, s 282.
11 Ibid, s 288(2).
12 Ibid, s 42.
13 See *Re Bulawayo Market and Offices Co Ltd* [1907] 2 Ch 458.
14 Ibid, s 302.
15 See pp 127–130, post.
16 See *Holmes v Keyes* [1959] Ch 199, [1958] 2 All ER 129.
17 See p 130, post.

resigns his office by notice in writing to the company. A director who has given notice of resignation to the company in terms of such an article cannot withdraw such notice without the concurrence of the remaining directors.[18] Even though the articles require resignations to be in writing, a resignation made orally before a general meeting of the company is effective.[19]

RETIREMENT

The articles normally make provision for the retirement of directors by rotation. Article 73 of Table A, for example, provides that one-third of the directors shall retire by rotation in each year. Retiring directors, are, generally speaking, eligible for re-election.[20] If Table A is followed, the articles will provide that a retiring director who offers himself for re-election will be deemed to be re-elected unless at such meeting it is expressly resolved not to fill the vacated office, or a resolution for the re-election of such director has been put to the meeting and lost.[1]

Under CA 1985, s 293, a director of a public company or a private company which is a subsidiary of a public company must vacate office at the conclusion of the next annual general meeting commencing after he attains the age of 70. This provision can be waived by a resolution, of which special notice was given to the general meeting.[2]

DISMISSAL

Under ss 303–304 of the CA 1985 a company may, by ordinary resolution, remove a director before the expiration of his period of office notwithstanding anything in its articles or any term of any contract between the company and the director. Special notice is required of any resolution to remove a director under this section, or to appoint any person in his place. The director may require the company to circulate to members before the meeting any representations (of reasonable length) which he may wish to make. If time does not permit this, the chairman may be required to read the

---

18 *Glossop v Glossop* [1907] 2 Ch 370. For the formalities of service see CA 1985, s 725.
19 *Latchford Premier Cinema Ltd v Ennion* [1931] 2 Ch 409.
20 Table A, arts 75–77.
1 Table A, art 75. For the problem which this article seeks to surmount, see *Grundt v Great Boulder Pty Gold Mines Ltd* [1948] Ch 145, [1948] 1 All ER 21.
2 CA 1985, s 293(5).

representations out at the meeting. The company may, however, apply to the Court for an order that it be not obliged to follow this procedure on the grounds that the rights conferred by the section are being abused to secure needless publicity for defamatory matter.

The power to remove a director is a fiduciary power, but its misuse does not deprive the removal of effect.

Lee v Chou Wen Hsien [1984] 1 WLR 1202, [1985] BCLC 45.

> The articles of the O company provided that the office of director 'shall be vacated' if a director was requested by all his co-directors to resign. Following upon differences of policy, the plaintiff, an original director of the company, was requested to resign. He moved for a declaration that because the directors had misused their powers, he remained a director of the company. HELD: that the removal was valid. Allegations of bad faith do not leave the expelled director a director; that would be to introduce too much uncertainty into management. The office was vacated.

The director may still, as will be seen, be able to claim in breach of contract if he has a service contract with the company. In some circumstances he may be able to move for a winding up or for relief against oppressive conduct.

A vacancy created by the removal of a director under this section may be filled at the meeting at which he is removed, or, if not, may be filled as a casual vacancy.

Unfortunately perhaps, s 303 can be circumvented. In addition, it may prove a costly device for a company to invoke. The problems posed by circumvention disclose that while s 303 may be wholly beneficial in the case of a public company, a strict and invariable application of it might be disadvantageous to the proprietors of certain private companies.

As to the manner of circumvention, it should be noted that the articles can create an office of permanent life director with special powers including the power to remove other directors.[3] This, together with the power to fill up the positions of dismissed directors, may be sufficient to quell any attempted coup. Secondly, the articles could weight the directors' voting rights as members sufficiently to prevent his removal from office under s 303. In *Bushell v Faith*[4] a majority of the House of Lords held that while a

---

3 *Bersel Manufacturing Co Ltd v Berry* [1968] 2 All ER 552, HL.
4 [1970] AC 1099, [1970] 1 All ER 53.

company could not deprive itself of the benefit of s 303 by requiring the concurrence of particular shareholders to a resolution to dismiss directors, it could lawfully attain the same ends by weighting the voting right attaching to certain shares. This view of public policy has been criticised.[5] In relation to private companies there is, perhaps, much to be said for the sorts of device which have been adopted, as was pointed out in an earlier decision.[6] By enabling managerial power to be partially divorced from shareholding, founding members are enabled to divest themselves of shares in favour of the next generation without relinquishing control of the business or risking the loss of benefits from it.

Section 303 may prove costly to invoke in the light of sub-s (5) which preserves any right of compensation which a director may have under the terms of any contract between him and the company relating to his dismissal.[7] If the contract is to employ the director in a service position for a fixed term, the company will be taken to have engaged impliedly not to put an end to 'that state of affairs under which alone the arrangement can be operative', the continuance of the service director in his directorship. Consequently, it will have to pay compensation if it exercises its power under the section.[8] However, the impact of s 303(5), is in many cases substantially reduced by s 319 which, in the absence of approval by the general meeting, prohibits directors' service contracts from exceeding five years in duration. Compensation may include not only losses of salary, and where applicable commission, but also diminution in pension and loss of life insurance cover under the company's pension and assurance scheme, and the amount of premiums under such scheme which the company had contracted to pay.[9] A dismissed service director is bound to mitigate his damages. He does not unreasonably refuse to do so by refusing to accept alternative employment at a significant reduction in status.[10]

Quite apart from s 303, a company may dismiss a director in

---

5 D. Prentice (1969) 32 Mod LR 693.
6 *Bersel Manufacturing Co v Berry* [1968] 2 All ER 552, HL.
7 The principles applied by the courts are analogous to those applied where a director's position is adversely affected by an alteration in the articles. See Chap 7, ante.
8 *Shindler v Northern Raincoat Co Ltd* [1960] 2 All ER 239, [1960] 1 WLR 1038.
9 *Bold v Brough, Nicholson and Hall Ltd* [1964] 3 All ER 849, [1964] 1 WLR 201.
10 *Yetton v Eastwoods Froy Ltd* [1966] 3 All ER 353, [1967] 1 WLR 104. But a managing director may be required to restrict his activities to the management of a subsidiary and this will not be regarded as a breach of his agreement: *H Holdsworth & Co (Wakefield) Ltd v Caddies* [1955] 1 All ER 725, [1955] 1 WLR 352, HL.

accordance with the terms of any contract between the company and the director. In such a case, the director will have no claim for compensation against the company.

In *Griffiths v Secretary of State for Social Services*[11] it was argued that the appointment of a receiver by debenture holders automatically terminated the service contract of the company's managing director. The Court held that, provided that where, as in that case, the continuation of the managing director's employment was not inconsistent with the receiver's role, the receivership would not automatically terminate the service contract. Presumably, if the continuation of the service contract was inconsistent with the receiver's status and terminated accordingly, the director would, unless the service contract (or articles incorporated therein) otherwise provided, be entitled to damages for breach of contract.

DISQUALIFICATION

Disqualifications from acting or continuing to act as a director are contained in the Company Directors Disqualification Act 1986 and in company articles. Such orders may disqualify a person not only from acting as a director, but also from being a liquidator or administrator of a company, or a receiver or manager of its property, or from being concerned in any way, whether directly or indirectly, with the promotion, formation or management of a company.[12]

The first group of disqualifications comprise disqualifications in the case of a conviction for an indictable offence, for persistent default under the Companies Acts, for fraud in a winding up, and for conviction for certain summary offences.

Section 2 of the Company Directors Disqualification Act 1986 provides that where a person is convicted of an indictable offence (whether on indictment or summarily) for an offence in connection with the promotion, formation, management or liquidation of a company or with the receivership or management of a company's property, he may be disqualified for a maximum period of 15 years if the case were tried on indictment, or five years if it were tried summarily.

---

11 [1974] QB 468.
12 Company Directors Disqualification Act 1986, s 1; for a more elaborate account see L. H. Leigh 'Disqualification Orders in Company and Insolvency Law' (1986) 7 Co Lawyer 179.

A disqualification order for a maximum period of five years may be made for persistent default in relation to the reporting requirements of companies legislation. This may be conclusively proved by showing that in the five years preceding the date of the application, the person concerned has been adjudged guilty of three or more defaults in relation to those provisions. He can of course be proved by other evidence to have been in default, but the inference raised by such other evidence is rebuttable.

Disqualification orders may also be made, under s 4, where there has been fraud in a winding up. The company must actually be in winding up for this power to apply. If it appears that a person, not necessarily a director, has committed an offence of fraudulent trading (for which he need not actually have been convicted) or has otherwise been guilty while an officer, or liquidator of the company or receiver or manager of its property, of any fraud or breach of duty in relation to it, he may be disqualified for a maximum period of 15 years.

A person may, furthermore, be disqualified under s 5 after being convicted of a summary conviction offence provided that it is the result of a contravention of or failure to comply with requirements of companies legislation requiring accounts, etc, to be delivered to the Registrar.

In addition, s 11 renders liable to a fine an undischarged bankrupt who acts as a director or liquidator of a company without leave of the court. The Official Receiver must be notified of any application for leave and is to oppose it if he considers that to allow the bankrupt so to act would be contrary to the public interest.

A further group of powers relates to unfit directors of insolvent companies. First, under s 6, a court must make a disqualification order against a person who is or has been a director of a company which has at any time become insolvent (whether while he was a director or subsequently). His conduct as director of that company must be such as to make him unfit to be concerned in the management of a company. In assessing this, the court may have regard to his record as a director of other companies. No maximum period of disqualification is imposed, but a two year mimumum period is specified. Application for an order may be made by the Secretary of State or, if he so directs, by the Official Receiver. No application may be made after two years from the date of the insolvency unless the leave of the court is obtained. The Official Receiver, a liquidator, administrator or administrative receiver is under a duty to report cases of unfitness to the Secretary of State.

The above power is mandatory. In addition, under s 9, the Secretary of State may bring proceedings for disqualifcation where, following an investigation of the company, he deems disqualification to be expedient in the public interest. In such case the court may make such an order, for a maximum period of 15 years.

The court is furthermore empowered under s 10 to disqualify a person against whom it has made a declaration under ss 213 or 214 of the Insolvency Act 1986 requiring him to contribute to the company's assets.

In addition there is, under s 216 of the Insolvency Act 1986, an interesting disqualification, or perhaps preclusion, which should help to combat the phenomenon often encountered in long-term fraud, of a person successively setting up businesses under similar names, and even in the same location, and so operating them as to defraud creditors. Where a company has gone into insolvent liquidation, then a person who was a director or shadow director of the company within a period of 12 months before it went into liquidation may not, without the leave of the court, use the name of the company or one so similar to it as to suggest an association with the insolvent company. This ban lasts for five years from the date of insolvency.

The Company Directors Disqualification Act 1986 specifies in great detail what matters the court must take into account in deciding whether to make a disqualification order. They include misapplication of the company's money, misfeasance or breach of statutory duty in relation to the company, the director's responsibility for transactions at an undervalue, failures to comply with accounting and reporting obligations, the responsiblity of the director for giving preferences (where the company is in winding up), etc.

There is a growing body of case law on the principles which ought to govern the disqualification of directors and the length of time for which such orders may be made. In particular, on the former point courts have stressed the breadth of the phrase 'being concerned in the management'. Such activities as advising directors concerning financial management may fall within the ban,[13] so too will such activities as negotiating sales financing.[14] In the latter case, the periods specified by the statutes are, as has been noted, maximum periods.[15] The presence or absence of dishonesty is relevant as is a record showing a person to be quite unfit to manage a company.[16]

If Table A articles are employed, art 81 will apply. Apart from

---

13 *R v Campbell* [1984] BCLC 83, CA.
14 *R v Corbin* (1984) 6 Cr App Rep (S) 17; *R v Austen* [1985] LS Gaz R 2499.
15 *Re Civica Investments Ltd* [1983] BCLC 456.
16 *R v King* [1983] 1 All ER 929, [1983] 1 WLR 411, CA.

the disqualification noted above, art 81 further provides that the office of director shall be vacated if he ceases to be a director by virtue of s 291 or s 293 of the CA 1985. Section 293 refers to age limits. Section 291 refers to share qualifications. A director who is required by the articles to obtain qualifying shares within a given time and who does not (or who sells all the qualifying shares which he is required to hold), vacates office on the expiration of the period allowed.[17] A director is taken to hold shares within the meaning of the section if he is actually on the register with power to vote.[18] No account is taken of any beneficial interests which others may have in the shares.[19]

Other grounds included in the articles upon which the office is vacated include unsoundness of mind, and absence without permission from meetings of the directors for a period of more than six months.

The effect of the words in art 81, 'the office of director shall be vacated...' is that the director automatically vacates his office on the occurrence of the disqualifying event. If the directors wish him to continue to act, they must procure his re-election or the casual vacancy has to be filled up under an article to that effect.[20]

DEFECTIVE APPOINTMENTS AND ACTING AFTER DISQUALIFICATION

Section 285 of the CA 1985 provides that the acts of a director are valid notwithstanding any defect that may afterwards be discovered in his appointment or qualification. The section does not apply where there never was an appointment at all.[1] The sort of defect in qualification with which the section deals is illustrated by *Dawson v African Consolidated Land and Trading Co.*[2] There it was held that the section validated the actions of a duly appointed director who at the time of the transaction had ceased to hold qualification shares but had later re-acquired them. Technically, he vacated office on parting with the shares but the disqualification raised no disability to his re-appointment and he was treated as a director by the other

---

17 *Holmes v Keyes* [1959] Ch 199, [1958] 2 All ER 129.
18 *Spencer v Kennedy* [1926] Ch 125.
19 *Boschoek Pty Co Ltd v Fuke* [1906] 1 Ch 148; *Bainbridge v Smith* (1889) 41 ChD 462.
20 *Re Bodega Co Ltd* [1904] 1 Ch 276.
1   *Morris v Kanssen* [1946] AC 459, [1946] 1 All ER 586.
2   [1898] 1 Ch 6, CA.

directors who could have done so. A person, whether a member or an outsider, may be able to rely on the section to validate a transaction or proceeding if he were unaware of the irregularity or were not put on inquiry.[3]

REGISTER OF DIRECTORS AND INTERESTS

Every company must keep a register of its directors and secretaries at its registered office. This register must disclose the name, address, business occupation of any other directorships held by each director. The Registrar must be notified of these particulars.[4] It must also contain particulars of past directorships held by the company's directors, within the preceding five years.

In addition to the register of directors, s 325 of the Companies Act 1985 provides that the company must keep a register disclosing the interest of directors in the shares or debentures of the company or its associated companies. These matters are dealt with in Chapter 12.

Disclosure is further advanced by requiring that copies of directors' service contracts be kept by the company at its registered office, or at the place where the register of members is kept, or at its principal place of business.[5] In addition, there are further provisions relating to matters to be disclosed in the accounts and directors' report, and these are discussed in connection with company accounts.[6]

REMUNERATION

Because directors are not servants but rather controllers of the company, they will have no claim to the payment of any fees unless the articles make provision to this effect.[7] Modern articles such as art 82 of Table A provide that the directors shall be entitled to such remuneration as shall be voted in general meeting. A resolution for remuneration authorises the directors to pay it. A director can sue for remuneration which the company has agreed to pay him, and he

---

3 *Mahony v East Holyford Mining Co* (1875) LR 7 HL 869, and see also *Grant v John Grant & Sons Pty Ltd* (1950) 82 CLR 1.
4 CA 1985, ss 288–290.
5 CA 1985, s 318.
6 See the discussion in Chap 9, post.
7 *Hutton v West Cork Rly Co* (1883) 23 ChD 654.

may prove for it in a winding up.[8] The articles may stipulate that the directors are to be paid a fixed sum per annum. This notwithstanding, directors cannot sue for such remuneration unless they can prove a contract with the company and a provision in the articles is insufficient.[9] However, Wright J in *Re New British Iron Co* stated that an implied contract might be created on the basis of the articles.[10]

> That article (providing for the payment to directors of £1,000 per annum) is not in itself a contract between the company and the directors; it is only a part of the contract constituted by the articles of association between the members of the company *inter se*. But where on the footing of that article the directors are employed by the company and accept office the terms of (the article) are embodied in and form part of a contract between the company and the directors. Under the articles as thus embodied the directors obtain a contractual right to an annual sum of £1,000 as remuneration.

In the absence of a valid agreement, a director who also holds a service position, as for example that of managing director, may recover for his services under a *quantum meruit*. In such cases the Court will hold that there is an implied promise to pay for services rendered on behalf of and accepted by the company.[11]

Certain information concerning the remuneration of directors and officers must be stated in any accounts of the company laid before it in general meeting or in a statement annexed thereto. These matters are dealt with in the chapter on accounts.[12]

By virtue of CA 1985, s 312, it is unlawful for a company to pay a director any sum as compensation for the loss of office or in consideration of his retirement, unless particulars have been disclosed to members and the payment approved by them in general meeting. However, this provision only applies to uncovenanted payments. It does not apply where the payment is made in connection with the director's employment or to payments which the company is contractually bound to make: accordingly if the director's service

---

8 Cf *Re Richmond Gate Property Co Ltd* [1964] 3 All ER 936, discussed in Chap 7, ante.
9 *Re Lundy Granite Co Ltd, Lewis's Case* (1872) 26 LT 673.
10 [1898] 1 Ch 324 at 326; see also *Re T. N. Farrer Ltd* [1937] Ch 352, [1937] 2 All ER 505.
11 *Craven-Ellis v Canons Ltd* [1936] 2 KB 103, [1936] 2 All ER 1066, where however the plaintiff was not a director.
12 Chap 9, post.

contract provides for compensation on termination of his office, no general meeting approval is required for the payment.[13]

It is also unlawful for a company to pay a director in connection with a take-over, any sum as compensation for loss of office or in consideration of his retirement without disclosure to the general meeting and approval of the payment by it.[14]

LOANS AND SIMILAR TRANSACTIONS TO OR IN FAVOUR OF DIRECTORS

The Companies Act 1985, s 330 prohibits companies from making loans and similar transactions to or in favour of directors and, in some cases, persons connected with them. It will be recalled that the term 'director' includes, for the purposes of s 330, a shadow director.[15]

CONNECTED PERSONS

Four classes of person are connected with a director for the purposes of s 330:[16]

(1) the director's spouse, or his infant child or step-child;[17]
(2) a company with which the director is associated.[18] A director is associated with a company if he satisfies one of two complicated tests. Broadly speaking, a director is associated with any company in which he and persons connected with him (i) are interested in at least one-fifth of the nominal value of the equity share capital, or (ii) are entitled to exercise or control more than one-fifth of the voting power at a company's general meeting.[19] A body corporate with which a director is associated is regarded as not connected with that director for these purposes unless it is also connected with

---

13 *Taupo Totara Timber Co Ltd v Rowe* [1978] AC 537, [1977] 3 All ER 123.
14 CA 1985, ss 313–316.
15 Ibid, s 330(5).
16 And for the purposes of this part of the Act generally: ibid, s 346. It should be noted that the definition of 'connected' here differs substantially from the definition of 'connected' for the purposes of insider trading.
17 CA 1985, s 346(2). Illegitimate children and step-children are included: ibid, s 346(3).
18 Ibid, s 346(4).
19 Ibid, s 364(4). For further details see Joffe, *The Companies Act 1980*, paras 8.204–207.

him in its capacity as a trustee for the purposes of classes (3) and (4) below, and a trustee of a trust the beneficiaries of which include or may include a body corporate with which the director is associated shall not be treated as connected with a director only by reason of that fact;[20]
(3) a trustee of any fixed or discretionary trust whose beneficiaries include the director, his spouse, any of his children or step-children, or a company with which he is associated;[1]
(4) a partner of the director or any person connected with the director by reason of the fact that he falls within categories (1)–(3) above.[2]

There is one exception to these rules. A person falling within any of the categories of connected persons cannot be connected with the director of a company if he is also a director of the same company.[3] However, this exception does not exempt persons who are otherwise connected from being treated as such in relation to every company of which either is a director, but only from being so treated in relation to companies of which they are co-directors.

PROHIBITED TRANSACTIONS

A company may not make a loan to a director of the company or of its holding company, nor may it enter into any guarantee[4] or provide any security in connection with a loan made by any other person to such a director.[5]

A public company (or a company which is a member of a group including a public company) may not:

(1) make a quasi-loan to a director of the company or of its holding company;
(2) make a loan or quasi-loan to a person connected with such a director;

---

20 CA 1985, s 346(5).
1 Ibid, s 346(2)(c). Trustees of employees' share schemes or pension schemes are excluded.
2 Ibid, s 346(2)(d).
3 Ibid, s 346(2).
4 For the purposes of CA 1985, s 330, guarantee includes indemnity: ibid, s 331.
5 Ibid, s 330(2). A loan contravened the similarly worded predecessor (CA 1948, s 190) if made to a company wholly-owned or controlled by the director: *Wallersteiner v Moir* [1974] 3 All ER 217, 239.

(3) enter into a guarantee or provide any security in connection with a loan or quasi-loan made by any other person for such a director or connected person;
(4) enter into a credit transaction as creditor for such a director or connected person; or
(5) enter into any guarantee or provide any security in connection with a credit transaction made by any other person for such a director or connected person.[6]

A quasi-loan is defined as a transaction under which one party ('the creditor') agrees to pay, or pays otherwise than in pursuance of an agreement, a sum for another ('the borrower'), or agrees to reimburse, or reimburses otherwise than in pursuance of an agreement, expenditure incurred by another party for another ('the borrower') either (i) on terms that the borrower (or a person on his behalf) will reimburse the creditor; or (ii) in circumstances giving rise to a liability on the borrower to reimburse the creditor.[7]

This definition is obscure and it is not easy to ascertain its limits. Nevertheless, for example, any agreement or arrangement whereby a company pays private health insurance premiums for a director, or provides him with a credit card in the company's name, on the condition or understanding that the director will reimburse the company for sums paid by it to the insurance company or operator of the credit card, is a quasi-loan.

A credit transaction is defined as a transaction under which one party ('the creditor'):

(1) supplies any goods or sells any land under a hire-purchase or conditional sale agreement;
(2) leases or hires any land or goods in return for periodical payments; or
(3) otherwise disposes of land or supplies goods or services on the understanding that payment is to be deferred.[8]

Companies are prohibited from entering into two further types of arrangement.

---

6 CA 1985, s 330(3). Contravention of this section may involve criminal sanctions being imposed upon a public company (or a company which is a member of a group including a public company) or upon its directors: ibid, s 342.
7 Ibid, s 331(3).
8 Ibid, s 331(7).

(1) A company may not arrange for the assignment to it or assumption by it of any rights, obligations or liabilities under a transaction to which the company is not a party but which, if it had originally been entered into by the company, would have contravened s 330(2), (3) or (4).[9] This provision prevents a company from, for example, taking an assignment of the rights of a creditor who had previously made a loan to one of the company's directors.

(2) A company may not take part in any arrangement with another person whereby, in return for some benefit from the company or its holding company or a subsidiary of the company or its holding company, the other person enters into a transaction which, if entered into by the company, would have contravened s 330(2), (3), (4) or (6).[10] This provision prevents, for example, a company from making a special payment to a bank in return for the making by the bank of a loan to a director of the company.

EXCEPTIONS

The Act provides for a number of exceptions to s 330.

(1) General Exceptions
A company may provide any of its directors with funds to meet expenditure incurred or to be incurred by him for the purposes of the company or of enabling him properly to perform his duties as an officer of the company, or to enable any of its directors to avoid incurring such expenditure.[11] Such funds may only be provided with the prior approval of the general meeting, at which there must be disclosed the purpose of the expenditure, the amount of the funds to be provided by the company and the extent of its liability under any connected transaction. If such prior approval is not obtained, the funds must be advanced on the condition that, if the company's approval is not given before or at the next general meeting, the loan will be repaid and any other liability under any connected transaction will be discharged within six months from the conclusion of the meeting.[12] The maximum net amount which may be advanced

---

9 Ibid, s 330(6). For ease of reference, this type of arrangement is called a 'prohibited assignment arrangement'.
10 Ibid, s 330(7). For ease of reference, this type of arrangement is called a 'back-to-back' arrangement.
11 Ibid, s 337.
12 Ibid, s 337(3).

by a public company (or a company which is a member of a group including a public company) pursuant to this exception is £10,000.[13]

Furthermore, a money-lending company may make a loan or quasi-loan to any person or enter into a guarantee in connection with any other loan or quasi-loan.[14] Advantages may be taken of this exception only if (i) the loan or quasi-loan is made or the guarantee entered into in the ordinary course of the company's business; and (ii) the person to whom the loan or quasi-loan is made or in whose favour the guarantee is given does not receive more favourable treatment (whether in respect of the amount of the loan or quasi-loan, or amount guaranteed, or in respect of the terms of the loan, quasi-loan or guarantee) than that which would be afforded to a person of the same financial standing but unconnected with the company.[15]

The maximum amount which may be advanced pursuant to this exception by a public company (or by a company which is a member of a group including a public company) is £50,000. This limitation does not apply to recognised banks.[16]

However, provided that the loan or quasi-loan is made or the guarantee entered into the ordinary course of the company's business, and provided that such loans are ordinarily made by the company to its employees on no less favourable terms, a money-lending company may make a loan to one of its directors or a director of its holding company for the purpose of purchasing or improving a dwellinghouse for use as the director's only or main residence, even though the terms of the loan are more favourable than those which would be offered to a person of the same financial standing as the director but unconnected with the company.[17] The

---

13 Ibid, s 337(3). The specified sum of £10,000 may be raised by statutory instrument: ibid, s 345. In calculating the amount advanced, account must be taken not only of the value of all transactions already made pursuant to this exception in favour of the director or any person connected with him (less any amount by which the value of the transaction has been reduced), but also of the value of the proposed transaction or arrangement: ibid, s 339. For the 'value' of a transaction, see s 340.
14 Ibid, s 338. A money-lending company is a company whose ordinary business includes the making of loans or quasi-loans or the giving of guarantees in connection with loans or quasi-loans: ibid, s 338(2).
15 Ibid, s 338(3).
16 Ibid, s 338(4). A recognised bank is a company which is recognised as a bank for the purposes of the Banking Act 1979: ibid, s 331(5).
17 CA, ibid, s 338(6). The loan may be made either for the purchase or improvement of a house or a flat, together with any land to be occupied and enjoyed therewith. A loan in substitution for a loan previously made by some other person for such purpose is also permissible.

maximum amount which may be advanced pursuant to this exception is, in the case of all companies, £50,000.[18]

In determining whether the £50,000 ceiling has been exceeded, special rules apply to banks. Where it is a bank which proposes to make a housing loan to a director, any other transaction which would not be taken into account, because for example it was a loan made in the ordinary course of business on commercial terms, to its directors, shall not count in terms of the s 330 prohibition unless it too was made for housing loan purposes. If it were, it will have to be aggregated with the later transaction and the £50,000 limit will apply.[19]

In calculating, in relation to one of its directors, whether it may make a proposed loan or quasi-loan or enter into a proposed guarantee pursuant to the exception contained in s 338(1), a company must aggregate:

(1) the value of the proposed transaction or arrangement; and
(2) the value of any prohibited assignment or back-to-back arrangement or any other transaction made pursuant to that exception for the director or any person connected with him (or if the proposed transaction or arrangement is to be made for a person connected with a director of the company, for that director or any person connected with him) by the company or any subsidiary or, if the proposed transaction or arrangement is to be made for a director of its holding company or a person connected with such a director, by a subsidiary of its holding company.[20]

The company cannot enter into the proposed transaction or arrangement if the aggregate of these values exceeds £50,000.[1]

---

[18] Ibid, s 338(4). The specified sum of £50,000 may be raised by statutory instrument: ibid, s 345. It should not be forgotten that s 338(6) merely constitutes an exception to the provisions of s 338(3). Therefore, the maximum amount which may be advanced or guaranteed by a public company or by a company which is a member of a group including a public company is £50,000, and in calculating whether a public company may make a loan, such a company must take account of any other transactions entered into pursuant to ibid, s 338(1)(a) and (3).
[19] CA 1985, s 339.
[20] Ibid, s 339. The value of a loan is the principal advanced; the value of a quasi-loan is the liability or maximum liability of the borrower. In the case of a guarantee, the value is the amount guaranteed: ibid, s 340(4).
[1] This sum may be raised by statutory instrument: ibid, s 345.

(2) Transactions of Low Value or made in the Ordinary Course of Business

A quasi-loan may be made by a public company (or a company which is a member of a group including a public company) to one of its directors or a director of its holding company, provided that the terms of the quasi-loan require the creditor company to be reimbursed within two months of its incurring expenditure pursuant to the quasi-loan.[2] A quasi-loan may only be made in accordance with s 332 if the aggregate amount of the quasi-loan and any outstanding liabilities of the director under any other quasi-loans made to the director by virtue of that exception by the creditor company or its subsidiary (or, if the director is a director of the creditor company's holding company, any other subsidiary of the latter) does not exceed £1,000.[3]

In addition, a public company (or a company which is a member of a group including the public company) may enter into a credit transaction or guarantee or provide security in connection with such a transaction for any person either:

(1) if the aggregate amount of the proposed transaction and the net amount outstanding under any other transactions entered into by virtue of this exception for the director in question and persons connected with him (or, if the transaction is to be made for a person connected with a director of a company, for that director or any person connected with him) does not exceed £5,000; or
(2) if the company enters into the transaction in the ordinary course of its business and the person for whom the transaction is made does not receive more favourable treatment (whether in respect of the value of the transaction or in respect of its terms) than that which would have been afforded to a person of the same financial standing as the person for whom the transaction was made, but unconnected with the company.[4]

In addition, a loan may be made to the director of a company or its holding company, where the aggregate of the relevant amount does not exceed £2,500. Where a small loan of this sort is made,

---

2 CA 1985, s 332.
3 The sum of £1,000 may be raised by statutory instrument: ibid, s 345.
4 Ibid, s 335.

other loans to connected persons are disregarded for the purpose of determining whether the relevant amounts do in aggregate exceed £2,500.[5]

(3) Intra Group Transactions

Notwithstanding CA 1985, s 330(2) (b) and (c), where a public company or other relevant company[6] is a member of a group it is not prevented from making a loan or quasi-loan to another member of the group, or guaranteeing or securing a loan or quasi-loan by a third party to another member of the group by reason only that a director of one member of the group is associated with another.[7]

Conversely, a loan or quasi-loan by a company to its holding company or the entering by a company into a guarantee or providing security in connection with a loan or quasi-loan made by any person to its holding company is not prohibited by s 330.[8] And a company may also enter into a credit transaction as creditor for its holding company or enter into a guarantee or provide security in connection with a credit transaction made by any other person for its holding company.[9]

CONTRAVENTION OF s 330

A transaction or arrangement entered into by a company in contravention of s 330 is voidable at the instance of the company (although not, apparently, at the instance of the other party to the transaction).[10]

The company's right to avoid the transaction is lost if:

(1) restitution of any money or any other asset which is the subject matter of the arrangement or transaction is no longer possible;
(2) the company has been indemnified (pursuant to s 52(2) (b)) for any loss or damage suffered by it; or
(3) any rights acquired bona fide for value and without actual notice of the contravention by any person other than the person for whom the transaction or arrangement was made would be affected by its avoidance.

5 Ibid, s 334.
6 Ibid, s 331(6).
7 Ibid, s 333.
8 Ibid, s 336(a).
9 Ibid, s 336(b).
10 Ibid, s 341(1).

In addition, the company is granted statutory rights to recover improper gains and receive monetary compensation. Whether or not the transaction or arrangement entered into by the company in contravention of s 49 has been avoided, any director of the company or of its holding company or any person connected with such a director for whom the transaction or arrangement was made, and any other director of the company who authorised the transaction or arrangement is liable:

(1) to account to the company for any gain which he has made directly or indirectly by the arrangement or transaction; and
(2) (jointly and severally with any other person liable under these provisions) to indemnify the company for any loss or damage resulting from the arrangement or transaction.[11]

Certain defences are available to a person against whom the company raises a claim pursuant to these provisions. Where an arrangement or transaction is entered into by a company and a person connected with a director of the company or of its holding company in contravention of s 330, the director in question is not liable to account for gains or compensate the company if he is able to show that he took all reasonable steps to secure the company's compliance with s 330. Furthermore, a person connected with the director of the company or of its holding company, and any director (other than a director of the company or of its holding company for whom the transaction or arrangement contravening s 330 was entered into) who authorised the transaction or arrangement may escape liability if he shows that, at the same time when the arrangement or transaction was entered into, he did not know the circumstances constituting the contravention.[12]

OFFICERS

The company is managed by its officers as well as its directors. A director who occupies a service position will also fill the position of officer. The term 'officer' is partially defined in the Companies Act 1985 to include a director, manager or secretary.[13] The expression 'manager' is not equated with the managing or other director or a general manager. Any person who in the affairs of the company

11 Ibid, s 341(2).
12 Ibid, s 341(4).
13 Ibid, s 744.

exercises a supervisory control which reflects a general policy of the company for the time being or which is related to the general administration of the company is in the sphere of management. Therefore, the manager need not be a member of the board of directors (whether as managing or other director) or subject to specific instructions from the board. A person is an officer or manager of the company if he fulfils a function which touches the central administration of the company.[14] The term 'officer' includes the accountant[15] and, for some purposes, the auditor.[16] It may also include departmental heads. The test is essentially a functional one, depending on the status and functions of the individual concerned.[17] The powers and functions of the particular officers will depend upon the authority vested in them by the company under the articles or by contract or commercial usage. The powers of officers to act as agents of the company may also depend on doctrines of holding out. These are discussed more fully below.

The liabilities of officers are in part determined by contract. It should be noted that certain statutory provisions affecting liability apply to officers as well as directors. Thus CA 1985, s 310 applies and renders invalid any provision in the articles or in a contract purporting to relieve the officer from liability for negligence, breach of duty or breach of trust. Similarly, s 727 applies to enable the Court to relieve against liability. There are special provisions relating to proceedings against directors and officers for misfeasance or breach of trust discovered in the course of winding up.[18]

THE SECRETARY

Every company must have a secretary and a sole director may not also be secretary.[19] A company may have another company as its secretary. No company, however, may have as secretary a corporation the sole director of which is a sole director of the company, nor may it have as sole director of the company a corporation the sole director of which is secretary to the company.[20] The Companies Act

---

14 *Re a Company* [1980] Ch 138, [1980] 1 All ER 284 (a case on CA 1948, s 441). Reversed on other grounds sub-nom *Re Racal Communications Ltd* [1981] AC 374, [1980] 2 All ER 634, HL.
15 *Re Transplanters (Holding Co) Ltd* [1958] 2 All ER 711, [1958] 1 WLR 822.
16 *R v Shacter* [1960] 2 QB 252, [1960] 1 All ER 61, but he is not an agent of the company.
17 See *Mulligan v Lancaster* [1937] 1 DLR 414.
18 CA 1985, ss 630 and 631.
19 Ibid, s 283.
20 Ibid, s 283(4).

1985 provides that where a thing must be done by or to a director and the secretary, the provision is not satisfied by the action being taken by the same person acting in a dual capacity as director and secretary.[1] The register of directors includes particulars of the secretaries.[2]

It is normal for the directors to be empowered to appoint the secretary and to fix his term of office and the conditions upon which he is to hold office.[3] However, the person named as secretary in the statement of first directors and secretary is deemed to have been appointed as the first secretary of the company; and any purported appointment of the first secretary by the articles (or by the directors) is void, unless the person so appointed is also the person named in the statement.[4]

It is unnecessary for the secretary of a private company to be qualified in any way to hold office. The directors of a public company are, however, under a duty imposed by CA 1985, s 286 to ensure both that the company's secretary appears to them to have the requisite knowledge and experience to discharge the functions of secretary of the company and that he:

(1) held the office of secretary or assistant or deputy secretary on 22 December 1980; or
(2) held the office of secretary of a public company for at least three of the five years immediately preceding his appointment as secretary of the company;
(3) is a member of a specified body of accountants or secretaries;[5]
(4) is a barrister, advocate or solicitor called or admitted in the UK; or
(5) is a person who, by virtue of his holding or having held any other position or his being a member of any other body appears to the directors to be capable of discharging the functions of secretary of the company.

---

1 Ibid, s 284.
2 Ibid, s 290.
3 Table A, art 99.
4 CA 1985, ss 10 and 13.
5 The specified bodies are (CA 1985, s 286(2)): The Institute of Chartered Accountants in England and Wales; The Institute of Chartered Accountants of Scotland; The Association of Certified Accountants; The Institute of Chartered Accountants in Ireland; The Institute of Chartered Secretaries and Administrators; The Institute of Cost and Management Accountants; and The Chartered Institute of Public Finance and Accountancy.

The duty of the directors of a public company to ensure the appointment of a duly qualified secretary is a duty enforceable by the company alone.[6]

The secretary is a servant of the company.[7] The legal rules relating to the functions of a secretary describe the powers which it is assumed that a secretary enjoys in right of his office. It was once thought that in law, the secretary was to be regarded as a mere servant employed to do what he was told, and devoid of agency powers.[8] A leading text on company secretaries points out that while in some companies the secretary's duties are strictly secretarial in character, in others his work is in reality that of an office manager or one of the chief executives of the company. In many companies the secretary, in addition to doing normal secretarial work pertaining to the office, is responsible for the organisation of the office, the control of office staff and the keeping of the accounts.[9]

The courts now recognise these aspects of the secretary's position. The modern secretary is an important official who enjoys the power to contract on behalf of the company within a considerable part of the company's administration. He can sign contracts in the administrative operations of a company, including the hiring of office staff and the management of the office, and can hire cars to meet customers.[10] His authority is not unlimited. He cannot, without authority, borrow money on behalf of a company.[11] He cannot without authority commence litigation on the company's behalf.[12] He cannot summon a general meeting himself[13] nor register a transfer without the board's approval,[14] nor may he without approval strike a name off the register.[15] These are powers which are vested in the directors.

The secretary's duties, as we have indicated, vary to some extent from company to company. Certain duties are, however, directly

---

6 The enforcement of the directors' duties is discussed in Chap 11.
7 See cases cited at note 10 below.
8 *Barnett v South London Tramways Co* (1887) 18 QBD 815.
9 A. Palmer, *Company Secretarial Practice* (10th edn, 1966) p 10.
10 *Panorama Developments (Guildford) Ltd v Fidelis Furnishing Fabrics Ltd* [1971] 2 QB 711, [1971] 3 All ER 16, CA. He has not, however, a general authority to contract over the whole range of the company's activities. See *Houghton & Co v Nothard, Lowe and Wills* [1928] AC 1.
11 *Re Cleadon Trust Ltd* [1939] Ch 286, [1938] 4 All ER 518.
12 *Daimler Co Ltd v Continental Tyre and Rubber Co Ltd* [1916] 2 AC 307.
13 *Re State of Wyoming Syndicate* [1901] 2 Ch 431.
14 *Chida Mines Ltd v Anderson* (1905) 22 TLR 27.
15 *Re Indo-China Steam Navigation Co* [1917] 2 Ch 100.

imposed upon him by statute. These are secretarial in character and include the submission of the annual return,[16] the verification of certain statements and applications and the keeping of minutes.[17]

THE ACCOUNTANT

The accountant is regarded as an officer of the company. He owes a contractual duty to the company to prepare the accounts properly and, like the auditor, may in some cases owe a duty of care to third persons who act in reliance on his skill in their preparation.[18] Seemingly, the accountant can acknowledge a debt on behalf of the company.[19]

THE AUDITOR

The position of the auditor is considered in Chapter 9. It may suffice here to point out that while for certain purposes the auditor is an officer of the company, he is independent of the directors and owes his duty directly to the general meeting. In this he is unique.

THE BOARD OF DIRECTORS

The Board of Directors, as we have seen, constitutes the governing or executive organ of most commercial companies. Directors exercise their executive powers as members of the board, at board meetings.

Meetings of the board are held as decided by the directors and in terms of the articles.[20]

The business of the directors is conducted at meetings at which a quorum must be present. If there is not a quorum, decisions taken are invalid. The quorum and the manner of dispatch of business and the keeping of minutes are usually governed by the articles.[1] If the articles provide that a director interested in a question shall not vote

---

[16] CA 1985, s 365.
[17] See Table A, art 99 for appointment and remuneration of the secretary.
[18] See Chap 9, post.
[19] *Jones v Bellgrove Properties* [1949] 2 KB 700, [1949] 1 All ER 498, and see *Re Transplanters (Holding Co) Ltd* [1958] 2 All ER 711, [1958] 1 WLR 822.
[20] Table A, arts 88–98.
[1] Table A, art 94.

on that question, he cannot be counted in determining whether a quorum is present.[2]

In terms of Table A, art 94, a director who is interested in a matter, including a contract or arrangement which is before the board shall not vote on it or be counted in the quorum, but this prohibition is subject to qualifications and may be suspended or relaxed by the general meeting. This matter is further discussed in connection with directors' duties.[3]

POWERS OF THE BOARD OF DIRECTORS

Where the articles of a company follow the most recent form of Table A (art 70), the business of the company is to be managed by the directors, subject to the provisions of the Companies Act, the memorandum and articles, and any directions given by special resolution. This means, although the details of management powers under such an article have not yet been worked out by the courts, that the autonomy of directors in respect of matters vested in them may be curtailed by the general meeting, and that, indeed, they may be forced to exercise powers in a way which is uncongenial to them, or to resign. The board of directors may pay all promotional expenses. It may exercise all such powers of the company as are not required by the articles to be exercised by the company in general meeting.[4] Among the powers reserved to the general meeting are changes to the memorandum and articles of association and the appointment and dismissal of directors. The board is given power to appoint a managing director who, while he retains office, may exercise powers conferred upon him either collaterally with or to the exclusion of the board's powers.[5] His status is therefore different to that of the ordinary director, and he may exercise a wide range of executive functions. In practice, he is said to be the most important single figure in company management.[6]

The form of articles under Table A to the 1948 Act is, however, the most likely to be encountered in practice. The relevant article made no reference to the directors being subject to directions given by special resolution. The effect of such provisions is to render management, in the exercise of its powers, independent of the general meeting. The directors are not agents of the general

---

2 *Re Greymouth-Point Elizabeth Railway and Coal Co Ltd* [1904] 1 Ch 32.
3 See Chap 10.
4 CA 1985, table A, art 70.
5 CA 1985, table A, art 72.
6 P. S. Florence, op cit, at pp 79–80.

meeting; they enjoy an authority constitutionally independent of it. It follows that the general meeting cannot dictate to the directors the manner in which their executive authority is to be employed. In this respect, the articles of the company will be decisive, both as to the grant of authority and the rights of the members.[7]

The position where the articles confer an explicit power on the directors is illustrated by *John Shaw & Sons (Salford) Ltd v Shaw*. The articles gave to certain of the directors the power to commence litigation on behalf of the company. The defendants, former directors who were sued in respect of a settlement which they had made with the company, sought an order to the effect that the action could not be brought without the approval of a general meeting, and that it had, therefore, been brought without authority. The Court, however, held that the director's action in commencing litigation could not be impeached either by the former directors or the general meeting. Greer LJ stated:[8]

> If powers of management are vested in the directors, they and they alone can exercise these powers. The only way in which the general body of shareholders can control the exercise of the powers vested by the articles in the directors is by altering their articles, or by refusing to re-elect the directors of whose action they disapprove. They cannot themselves usurp the powers which by the articles are vested in the directors any more than the directors can usurp the powers vested in the articles in the general body of shareholders.

The powers of the board are accordingly limited only by the Companies Acts, the articles of association and resolutions altering the articles.[9] Thus a resolution requiring the directors to exercise their powers in a particular fashion will be inconsistent with the article conferring the power and hence inoperative.[10]

It has been suggested that the general meeting has a residual executive power greater than the powers conferred upon directors, since the exercise of powers by directors is dependent upon their acting in good faith for the benefit of the general body of shareholders as a whole.[11] It is submitted that this proposition cannnot be sustained under the 1948 form of articles, though it probably

---

7 *Quin and Axtens Ltd v Salmon* [1909] AC 442; *Gramophone and Typewriter Co v Stanley* [1908] 2 KB 89; *Automatic Self-Cleansing Filter Syndicate v Cuninghame* [1906] 2 Ch 34.
8 [1935] 2 KB 113, 134.
9 See also *Lord Duncan Sandys v House of Fraser plc* 1985 SLT 200 (OH).
10 *T Logan Ltd v Davis* (1911) 104 LT 914.
11 *Bamford v Bamford* [1968] 2 All ER 655, [1968] 3 WLR 317, affd on other grounds [1970] Ch 212, [1969] 1 All ER 969.

represents the correct analysis under the 1985 form. Under the 1948 Table A form of articles, the grant of powers to the directors is, it is submitted, exhaustive of executive powers (save in such exceptional cases as a breakdown of the board). While acts done outside the powers of directors, but *intra vires* the company, may be ratified by the shareholders, the shareholders do not retain executive powers over the matters allocated to the directors.[12]

Nevertheless, even under the 1948 Table A, the general meeting does have a residuary executive power in cases where the board of directors is unable to act by reason of deadlock,[13] or in cases where the company is without directors.[14]

STATUS AND FUNCTION OF INDIVIDUAL DIRECTORS

AS AGENTS

The individual director is not, as such, an agent of the company. The managing director normally is. An individual director will, however, be able to bind the company in contract with outsiders where some competent organ of the company has conferred agency powers upon him, or has allowed him to represent himself to outsiders as the company's agent. In general, the competent organ will be the board of directors. Where a person who is duly appointed as an agent of the company acts within the scope of the authority conferred upon him, the company will be liable, even though the third party was unaware that the agent had authority. The actual authority of an agent may be express, or it may be implied from the position of the agent and the nature of the business which he undertook. In order to show that an agent had actual authority, it must be shown that a competent organ of the company conferred powers upon him. Such powers are often conferred explicitly. In some cases, however, an actual conferring of powers may be proven by showing that, for example, the board placed a director in such a position that he could hold himself out as the company's agent and acquiesced in his doing so.

---

12 See *Grant v United Kingdom Switchback Railways Co* (1888) 40 ChD 135, and in particular *Bamford v Bamford* [1969] 2 WLR 1107, 1113 per Harman LJ, p 1114 per Russell LJ.
13 *Danish Mercantile Co Ltd v Beaumont* [1951] Ch 680, [1951] 1 All ER 925.
14 *Alexander Ward Co v Samyang Navigation Co Ltd* [1975] 2 All ER 424, [1975] 1 WLR 673.

Hely-Hutchinson v Brayhead Ltd [1968] 1 QB 549, [1967] 3 All ER 98.

R was chairman of Brayhead and acted as its *de facto* managing director. He was the chief executive who made any final decision on financial matters and was entrusted with authority over take-overs. He often entered into large transactions on behalf of the company, sometimes merely reporting the transaction to the board without seeking prior authority or subsequent confirmation. The board acquiesced in this course of conduct. In connection with the take-over of Perdio, R purported on behalf of the company to guarantee moneys advanced to Perdio by H, and to guarantee H against a claim by the bank on a prior personal guarantee given by H to the bank in respect of Perdio's debts. Perdio became a subsidiary of Brayhead and H went on the board of Brayhead, but at the time R purported to give the guarantee H had attended only one board meeting of Brayhead. Perdio later went into liquidation. H sought to enforce the undertaking given by R against Brayhead which resisted the claim on the ground inter alia, that R had no authority to give such an undertaking.

It was held that Brayhead was liable. While R had no actual authority arising from his position as chairman, he had authority from the board to act as the company's chief executive, and the transaction fell within the authority which would normally attach to such a positon.

The representation that a purported agent has authority will normally come from the agent. It must also be shown that the making of the representation was authorised by the board. In the above case this was shown by inference from the board's conduct in placing R in a position where he could hold himself out as agent and in acquiescing in his conduct '. . . so that it can be said that they have in effect caused the representation to be made'.[15]

The company may also be liable on the ground of apparent authority. Whereas actual authority depends on a consensual agreement between principal and agent (in these cases between an organ of the company and a director acting as its agent), apparent authority is based on estoppel by representation.[16] In cases of apparent authority, the purported agent has not been given the power to enter into transactions by the company.

---

15 *Hely-Hutchinson v Brayhead Ltd* [1968] 1 QB 549, p 593, per Lord Pearson.
16 See further, Montrose, 'The Apparent Authority of an Agent of a Company' in *Precedent in English Law* (ed, Hanbury, 1968) pp 244 ff.

Chapter 8 Directors and Officers

Apparent authority:[17]

> ...is a legal relationship between the principal and the contractor created by a representation made by the principal to the contractor intended to be and in fact acted on by the contractor, that the agent has authority to enter on behalf of the principal into a contract of a kind within the scope of the apparent authority so as to render the principal liable to perform any obligations imposed on him by such a contract.

The leading decision is:

Freeman and Lockyer v Buckhurst Park Properties (Mangal) Ltd [1964] 2 QB 480, [1964] 1 All ER 630.[18]

> K, a property developer who wished to purchase certain land for a development, but who had insufficient resources to do so, formed with H, the defendant private company. H invested the necessary money and the estate was conveyed to the company. The directors were K, H, and two nominees. H went abroad and left the management of the estate and the planning of the develoment and sale to K. No properly convened board meetings were held, and K was never authorised by resolution to act for the company. The directors were, however, aware that K was managing the estate. K employed the plaintiffs (architects) to draw up the necessary plans for development and to apply for planning permission. The plans for development proved abortive, K disappeared, and the plaintiffs sued the company for their fees. It was held that while K had never been appointed managing director or agent of the company, his actions were within his apparent authority. The apparent authority derived from the board's knowledge that K was purporting to act as an agent of the company, and their acquiescence in his doing so.

It is of course necessary to show that the representation of authority was made by the board to the third party, and that the company was not precluded from entering into the type of contract in question or from conferring the type of authority in question on an agent. A representation of authority is made by the board when it, with knowledge of the purported agent's activities, allows him to act as such. In such a case, the representation of authority is a representation by conduct.

It is confusing that acquiescence can found both actual authority and liability based on estoppel. In *Hely-Hutchinson v Brayhead Ltd*

---

[17] *Freeman and Lockyer v Buckhurst Park Properties (Mangal) Ltd* [1964] 2 QB 480, p 503 per Diplock LJ.
[18] Applied in *IRC v Ufitec Group Ltd* [1977] 3 All ER 924.

(supra) there was, perhaps, more than simple acquiescence. The director not only acted as an agent to the company's knowledge, he also at times reported transactions to the board. Its knowledge was therefore more comprehensive and detailed than that of the board in *Freeman and Lockyer v Buckhurst Park Properties (Mangal) Ltd* (supra), where, in any event, no actual authority point was taken.

In order for a company to be bound by such a representation, the representation must not be inconsistent with the memorandum and articles of association. If, for example, the representation is made in respect of a transaction which is *ultra vires* the company, the company will not be bound. It cannot in any event, confer upon an agent powers greater than those which it possesses.[19] Similarly, if the articles restrict the class of persons who may enter into contracts on behalf of the company, a representation of authority which is inconsistent with the articles may not be relied upon against the company.[20] This forms part of the doctrine of constructive notice. Persons dealing with the company are deemed to have notice of the memorandum, articles and other public documents of the company. If persons:[1]

> do not choose to acquaint themselves with the powers of the directors, it is their own fault, and if they give credit to any authorised persons they must be contented to look to them only, and not to the company at large.

The doctrine of constructive notice is, however, subject to an important qualification known as the rule in *Turquand's* case. It is also known as the rule of indoor management.

Royal British Bank v Turquand (1856) 6 E & B 327.

> The directors of the bank were authorised by the registered deed of settlement to issue bonds pursuant to a resolution adopted by a general meeting of the company. A bond was issued to T. It was claimed that the necessary resolution had not been passed and that the bond was invalid. It was held that the bond was valid and that T was entitled to assume that the resolution had been passed. Persons dealing with a company are bound with knowledge of the registered documents, but they are entitled to assume that the internal proceedings of the company, including in this case a preliminary authorisation, have been regularly performed.

---

19 *Mahoney v East Holyford Mining Co Ltd* (1875) LR 7 HL 869.
20 *Ernest v Nicholls* (1857) 6 HL Cas 401, and see *Freeman and Lockyer v Buckhurst Park Properties (Mangal) Ltd* [1964] 2 QB 480, [1964] 1 All ER 630.
1   *Ernest v Nicholls* (supra) p 419 per Lord Wensleydale.

Thus persons transacting business with the company are deemed to have notice of what they would have discovered by making a search at the office of the Registrar of Companies, and they will be estopped from asserting that they had not read the documents and were not aware that the documents were inconsistent with the representation of authority.[2] But such persons are not deemed to have notice of, nor are they under a duty to inquire into, the internal proceedings of a company.

The doctrine of constructive notice is a negative doctrine. A third party is bound by the registered documents if they are adverse to his claim. If, however, the registered documents are not inconsistent with the representation of authority made by the company, the third party will be able to rely on the representation. He is not under an obligation to have read the documents before relying on the representation. In *Freeman and Lockyer v Buckhurst Park Properties (Mangal) Ltd*[3] the company argued that the plaintiffs could not rely on apparent authority because they had no actual knowledge of the company's articles and could not therefore rely on any power of delegation contained in them. This contention was rejected. Where the claim rests on apparent authority and the circumstances are such that the third party could reasonably infer that the purported agent had authority, the third party need not rely on the articles at all. If of course the third party relies on a power of delegation in the articles as an element in the appearance of authority, he must have read them at the time of the transaction.[4] It will, however, be seldom that an outsider will be able to found part of his case of apparent authority from a perusal of the articles. In most cases, the articles are equivocal; while permitting the company to delegate agency powers to a managing director, or to a director, they will not name any individual as the recipient of such powers or establish that the company has in fact made such a delegation.

The company will therefore not be bound by the acts of its agent or purported agents in the following circumstances:

(1) where the company, because it lacks power to enter into a particular transaction could not confer power upon its agent to do so on its behalf;[5]

---

2 *Mahony v East Holyford Mining Co Ltd* (1875) LR 7 HL 869.
3 [1964] 2 QB 460, [1964] 1 All ER 630.
4 *Rama Corpn Ltd v Proved Tin and General Investments Ltd* [1952] 2 QB 147, [1952] 1 All ER 554.
5 *Mahony v East Holyford Mining Co Ltd* (1875) LR 7 HL 869.

(2) where the public documents of the company preclude the conferring of the purported authority upon which the third party relies.[6] This goes beyond the memorandum and articles and related to other public documents as well.

Irvine v Union Bank of Australia (1877) 2 App Cas 366, PC.

> The registered articles of a company gave the directors power to borrow any sums not exceeding in aggregate one half the paid-up capital. The articles could be altered by simple majority, but, under the Companies Act 1862, s 53, such an alteration would be registered. The directors borrowed moneys from the bank in excess of their borrowing powers, giving the bank the deeds to certain property as security. The articles were never altered, not did the shareholders ratify the directors' actions. The bank sought an order for sale of the properties to satisfy the full value of the loan. It was held that, as there was no ratification, the bank could claim only up to the limit of the borrowing authorised by the articles. The bank could see from the articles that the borrowing powers of the directors were limited. Any extension of such powers by a resolution of the general meeting was required by statute to be registered. Therefore, the transaction was not saved by the rule in *Royal British Bank v Turquand*.

In addition, a third person cannot rely on an appearance of authority where:

(1) he is an insider of the company, such as a director. Such a person is under a duty to inform himself of the company's activities. An insider cannot rely on the rule in *Turquand's* case. That rule is designed for:[7]

> the protection of those who are entitled to assume just because they cannot know, that the person with whom they deal has the authority which he claims.

This proposition applies to a person who purports to act as a director even though he has never validly been appointed as such. In *Hely-Hutchinson v Brayhead Ltd* at trial, it was suggested that a director who contracts in his private capacity with his company acting by another director is not automatically to be taken to have notice of any defects in the other director's power to bind the

---

6 If, for example, Table A articles are employed, only the directors will have power to borrow money on behalf of the company or charge its property.
7 *Morris v Kanssen* [1946] AC 459, 475.

company.[8] That case was of course exceptional in that the plaintiff had only recently been appointed to the board of the company and the transaction was entered into after the first board meeting which he attended. The point was not decided on appeal because the Court of Appeal found that the director with whom the plaintiff dealt had actual authority to bind the company;

(2) the company had done nothing to hold out the director as having authority.

Rama Corporation Ltd v Proved Tin and General Investments Ltd [1952] 2 QB 147, [1952] 1 All ER 554.

> The plaintiffs purported to enter into an oral contract with the defendant company whom a director, Titley, purported to represent as agent. Titley had no authority and had never been held out by the defendant company as its agent. Plaintiffs paid over certain sums to Titley pursuant to the alleged agreement. Titley defalcated, leaving a balance of £1,000 owing to plaintiffs. It was held that the plaintiffs could not recover against the defendant company because it had never held Titley out as having authority. Furthermore, the plaintiffs could not rely on a power of delegation in the articles as the foundation of a representation of authority because they had not read the articles at the time when they entered into the transaction.

(3) the transaction is of an unusual character. In such a case the third party is put on inquiry whether the purported agent has the powers which he represents himself as having.

Houghton & Co v Nothard, Lowe and Wills Ltd [1927] 1 KB 246.

> Plaintiffs, fruit brokers, advanced money to P Co. P Co and the defendant company were both engaged in the fruit trade. Lowe was a director of both P Co and the defendant company. The advance was made in consideration of a promise by Lowe on behalf of both P Co and the defendant that H Co should have the right to sell all the fruit of both companies and should be entitled to keep the purchase moneys as security for the loan. H Co, concerned about Lowe's authority, contacted the defendant company. Prescott, its secretary, informed the plaintiffs that Lowe's action was authorised. Prescott had not authority to make such a representation. The defendant company's articles contained a power of delegation, but plaintiffs had not read the articles at

---

8 *Hely-Hutchinson v Brayhead* Ltd [1968] 1 QB 549, at 567 per Roskill J.

the time of the transaction. The plaintiffs ultimately sought to enforce the agreement against the defendant company. It was held that it could not do so. Neither Lowe nor the secretary had authority to make the representations in question. The transaction was, furthermore, of an unusual character, and it was incumbent upon the plaintiffs to ensure that power to enter into such a contract had actually been conferred upon the purported agent.

Similarly, it has been held that the drawing of bills of exchange by a branch manager upon his company is an unusual transaction, and therefore a third party should be put on inquiry concerning his authority to do so.[9] A bank where a director keeps his private account is put on inquiry if a director pays cheques made in favour of his company into it.[10] Similarly, a bank is put on inquiry where a cheque which it is asked to pay out is not signed by the proper signing authority;[11]

(4) in cases where the third party knows that matters relating to internal management have not been complied with. Thus, where the directors are given limited borrowing powers under the articles, a third party who knows that this limit has been exceeded and who knows that the consent of a general meeting has not been obtained in respect of the excess borrowing, cannot rely upon the action of the directors and cannot enforce any security purportedly given in respect of the excessive borrowing;[12]

(5) in cases where the document is a forgery. The extent of this rule is uncertain. It has been held in several cases that a forgery is a nullity. Even though the transaction appears to be regular, and despite the general rule that a third party is not bound to inquire into details of internal management, it is generally said that the company will not be liable on a forgery and that the internal management rule has no application.

The leading cases tend to state in categorical terms that a forgery is a simple nullity. They can, however, be explained also on the basis that the documents were not put forward as genuine by a person empowered to bind the company, or acting within the scope of apparent authority, and therefore the company would not in any event be estopped from denying liability on them.[13]

---

9 *Kreditbank Cassel GmbH v Schenkers Ltd* [1927] 1 KB 826.
10 *A L Underwood Ltd v Bank of Liverpool* [1924] 1 KB 775.
11 *B Liggett (Liverpool) Ltd v Barclays Bank Ltd* [1928] 1 KB 48.
12 *Howard v Patent Ivory Manufacturing Co* (1888) 38 ChD 156; *Irvine v Union Bank of Australia* (1877) 2 App Cas 336, PC.
13 See Gower's *Principles of Modern Company Law* (4th edn, 1979) pp 203–205.

Ruben v Great Fingall Consolidated [1906] AC 439.

Plaintiff lent money to the secretary of defendant company, receiving a certificate to certain shares as security for the transaction. The certificate appeared to be in proper form, but the secretary had in fact forged the directors' signatures and affixed the corporate seal without authority. Plaintiff brought action against the company claiming damages for its refusal to register him as a shareholder. The company was held not liable. Lord Loreburn held (a) that the share certificate was a nullity to which the rule of indoor management did not apply. '... this doctrine applies only to irregularities that otherwise might affect a genuine transaction. It cannot apply to a forgery,' and (b) the secretary had not authority express or implied from his office to give any warranty that the share certificate was genuine. Nor was he held out as having any such authority.

Similarly, in *Kreditbank Cassel GmbH v Schenkers Ltd*,[14] where a branch manager purported to draw bills of exchange upon his company, the company was held not liable both on the ground of lack of authority and upon the ground of forgery. It may be significant that in recent cases courts have tended to explain the case on the former ground.[15] Under the general principles of agency a principal would be liable on a forgery where that forgery has been put forward as genuine in circumstances where the agent acted within the scope of his actual authority or within the scope of an apparent authority.[16] It may be that a future Court will hold that a company will be liable on a forgery where it emanates from an official acting within the scope of actual or apparent authority, and where there are no circumstances apt to put the third party on inquiry.

Apart from the rules of internal management, a third party dealing with the company may also be able to rely for protection upon s 35 of the Companies Act 1985. The problems of the interpretation of this section, which applies both to cases falling within the *ultra vires* rule and to cases where it is alleged that the company's agent had no authority to enter into the transaction in question, have already been referred to.[17] In either type of case, the sub-

14 [1927] 1 KB 826.
15 *Rama Corpn Ltd v Proved Tin and General Investments Ltd* [1952] 2 QB 147, pp 156 ff; *Freeman and Lockyer v Buckhurst Park Properties (Mangal) Ltd* [1964] 2 QB 480, pp 507–508 per Diplock LJ.
16 *Uxbridge Permanent Benefit Building Benefit Society v Pickard* [1939] 2 KB 248, [1939] 2 All ER 344 (where, however, the company cases were explained as depending on principles other than those of agency).
17 See discussion in Chapter 6.

section raises identical difficulties. However, in agency cases, the protection afforded by s 35 is in one respect particularly narrowly circumscribed, in so far as transactions concluded by or on the initiative of a single director are generally not comprehended within its ambit. The only exceptions are where a private company has only one director, for such a director must, on his own, constitute the board, and, *semble*, if there are several directors of a company where the director in question is the sole effective director to whom all actual authority to act for the board has been effectively delegated.[18] In these cases it seems that any transaction decided upon by a sole or 'sole effective' director is capable of falling within s 35.

In a case otherwise falling within s 35, mere failure to consult the company's public documents cannot, without more, prejudice the third party's position as against the company. Indeed, it is expressly provided by s 35 that where the directors have decided upon the transaction, the third party is not bound to inquire either into the company's capacity or the director's authority to enter into the transaction in question. To this extent, the constructive notice rule is abrogated by s 35. As emerged from the earlier discussion, the third party cannot in any event take advantage of s 35 unless he has dealt with the company in 'good faith', although he is presumed to have done so unless the contrary is proven. The requirement of 'good faith' is not defined by s 35. Certainly the third party could not claim to have acted in good faith if circumstances showed that he had been guilty of a lack of probity, and it is unlikely that the Court would regard a third party as acting in good faith if he knew of the unusual character of the transaction or if he knew that matters relating to internal management had not been complied with. Furthermore, it would appear that the third party could not claim to be acting in good faith if, with reasonable grounds for suspicion, he nevertheless avoided consulting the public documents.

The statutory protection is co-extensive with that afforded by the rule in *Turquand's* case, except in two respects. In the first place, under the rule in *Turquand's* case, the company is not bound by the acts of its agent or purported agents (i) where the company, because it lacks power to enter into a particular transaction, cannot confer power upon its agent to do so on its behalf or (ii) where the public documents of the company preclude the conferring of the purported authority upon which the third party relies. However, both these sets of circumstances fall within the ambit of s 35 and, where

---

18 *International Sales and Agencies Ltd v Marcus* [1982] 3 All ER 551, [1982] 2 CMLR 46.

the subsection is applicable, the third party will be entitled to hold the company bound to the agreement made by its agent or purported agents, despite any lack of power on the part of the company to enter into the transaction in question or to confer such power on its agent, or despite any prohibition in the company's public documents preventing the conferring of the purported authority on which the third party relies.

In the second place, s 35 provides wider protection than the rule in *Turquand's* case. The latter is clearly limited to the protection of outsiders, but as previously stated, the statutory protection is not subject to a similar limitation. Accordingly any 'insider', be he a director or other officer of the company, or a member, may take advantage of s 35, provided that he can otherwise meet its requirements. However, in so far as an insider will usually have a far greater opportunity to acquaint himself with the internal management of the company and hence to become aware of irregularities, it may prove extremely difficult for him to establish that those requirements have been met.

A third party dealing with the company may also be able to rely upon s 285 of the Companies Act 1985 which provides that the acts of director or manager shall be valid notwithstanding any defect that may afterwards be discovered in his appointment or qualification. That section will apply to protect a person where there has been purported appointment which is invalid because of some technical defect. It does not apply where there has been no appointment at all; that is, where there has been a simple usurpation of power.[19]

Special statutory rules govern deeds and other instruments executed by companies. A deed is deemed to have been duly executed if the seal of the company is affixed in the presence of and is attested by its clerk, secretary, or other permanent officer or his deputy, and a member of the board of directors.[20]

AS SERVANTS

A director may be regarded as an officer or servant of the company. It was at one time thought that a director, and even a managing director, could not be regarded as a servant of the company.[1] Modern cases recognise, however, that a managing director who is

---

19 *Morris v Kanssen* [1946] AC 459, [1946] 1 All ER 586.
20 Law of Property Act 1925, s 74.
 1 *Re Lee, Behrens & Co Ltd* [1932] 2 Ch 46; *Re Newspaper Proprietary Syndicate Ltd* [1900] 2 Ch 349.

bound to devote his full time to the company may be regarded as employed by it.[2] Furthermore, the Privy Council has recognised that a director may also occupy another status in relation to the company. In *Lee v Lee's Air Farming Ltd*[3] the Privy Council thus held that the widow of a man who was at once the sole beneficial shareholder, managing director and pilot of a small company engaged in aerial topdressing could recover under the Workmen's Compensation Acts on the footing that in one capacity he was a servant of the company.[4] As will be seen, the fact that a director having a service contract is a servant of the company can have a stultifying effect on the power of the general meeting to remove him by ordinary resolution since, if the power to remove him is exercised, a breach of contract in respect of which damages may be payable, will result.[5]

AS ALTER EGO

In general, English law treats the directors of a company as its agents, or, in another capacity, as its servants. Most practical problems relating to liability in tort, for example, do not require any other analysis because a company is generally liable for the torts of its servants or agents which are committed in the course of their employment.[6] There are, however, cases in which if a company is to be held liable, or fully liable, it must be shown that the company was personally at fault. Liability, in such cases, cannot be predicated on the fault of some person who is regarded simply as a servant or agent. The solution is to treat the mental state and acts of the board of directors, the managing director, and in some cases individual directors and officers as the acts of the company itself.

Lennard's Carrying Company v Asiatic Petroleum Company Ltd [1915] AC 705.

Asiatic sued Lennard's for the loss by fire of a marine cargo of benzine. Lennard's sought to evade liability by relying on s 502 of the Merchant

---

2   *Road Transport Industry Training Board v Readers Garage Ltd* (1969) 4 ITR 195 QBD; *Trussed Steel Concrete Co Ltd v Green* [1946] Ch 115, 121; but see *Parsons v Albert J Parsons & Sons Ltd* [1978] ICR 456.
3   [1961] AC 12, [1960] 3 All ER 420.
4   See also *Anderson v James Sutherland (Peterhead) Ltd* 1941 SC 230.
5   *Shindler v Northern Raincoat Co Ltd* [1960] 2 All ER 239, [1960] 1 WLR 1038.
6   A full history of this development is contained in Leigh, *The Criminal Liability of Corporations* (1969) Chap 7.

160 *Chapter 8 Directors and Officers*

Shipping Act 1894 which provides that the owner of a British ship shall not be liable for losses arising without his actual fault or privity. It was held that personal fault could be ascribed to a company where the fault was that of an organ such as the board of directors or the managing director which enjoyed primary managerial powers over the company, per Lord Haldane LC: the directing will of a corporation which, being an abstraction has no mind of its own, must be sought in the person of somebody who though called an agent for some purposes, is really the directing mind and will of the corporation.

The distinction drawn is between persons who are mere servants and agents of the company, and others such as '... directors and managers who represent the mind and will of the company, and control what it does.'[7] The distinction is not an easy one to draw. For example, in *Tesco Supermarkets Ltd v Nattrass*[8] it was held that the manager of a supermarket, which comprised part of a large chain of supermarkets, could not be identified with the company, even though he apparently had a considerable degree of autonomy and responsibility. However, the board of the defendant did not delegate any of its managerial functions to the manager.

While some cases ascribe personal liablity in respect of the acts and mental states of persons who are constitutionally invested with primary powers of control, the rule is not so restrictive as this. In both civil and criminal law, the question asked by the courts is, essentially, whether the function is a primary managerial one, and whether the person to whom it is entrusted enjoys primary control.[9]

The Lady Gwendolen [1965] P 294 (CA).

A collision in fog occurred between a vessel, 'The Lady Gwendolen' owned by Arthur Guinness Son & Co (Dublin) Ltd and another vessel, 'The Freshfield'. The crucial issue was whether Guinness's had adequately warned the master of Ministry of Transport instructions concerning navigation in fog, and had supervised the master sufficiently to ensure that he was using radar properly, and conducting his vessel with due circumspection in fog conditions. The master habitually navigated

---

7 Per Denning LJ in *H L Bolton Engineering Co Ltd v T J Graham & Sons Ltd* [1957] 1 QB 159, 172.
8 [1972] AC 153, [1971] 2 All ER 127; see also *R v Andrews Weatherfoil Ltd* [1972] 1 All ER 65, [1972] 1 WLR 118.
9 However, even if the person whose mental state is sought to be attributed to the company is entrusted with primary control of the company, his mental state will not always be so attributed: *Belmont Finance Corpn Ltd v Williams Furniture Ltd* [1979] Ch 250, [1979] 1 All ER 118; and see Chap 2, ante.

at excessive speeds in fog. He had not adequately been informed of Ministry of Transport directives about navigation in fog and no steps had been taken to ensure that he was using radar properly. An assistant managing director had been informally entrusted with supervision over shipping, but he left this matter to a traffic manager and a marine superintendent. The traffic manager never sought to interfere with and displayed no interest in navigational problems. The marine superintendent never discovered the master's propensity to navigate at high speed in fog. It was held that the failure to supervise and warn the master was personal to the company. The person whose fault is to be taken as that of the company need not have been formally invested with powers over the area, and indeed need not be a director at all: per Winn LJ '... wherever the fault either occurs in a function or sphere of action which the owner has retained for himself or is that of a manager independent of the owner to whom the owner has surrendered all relevant powers of control, it is actual fault within the meaning of the section' (in this case s 503 of the Merchant Shipping Act 1894).

This analysis is generally employed. It enables personal liability to be imposed in tort under the Merchant Shipping Act and, as we have seen, enables companies to be held generally liable in crime.

Chapter 9

Accounts, Directors' Report and Audit

Every company having a share capital must, at least once in every year, make a return to the Registrar containing details of the registered office of the company, registers of members and debenture holders, indebtedness, members and directors.[1] A fine is provided in case of default, against the company and any officer responsible therefor.[2] The Registrar may also require the company, by notice, to file a return.[3]

Every company must prepare and keep two types of accounts. First, it must keep accounting records of its day to day transactions. These records reflect the continuous history of the company's dealings. Secondly, the company must prepare regular annual accounts, namely the profit and loss account and the balance sheet, which together give an overall view of its financial performance. The principal responsibility for preparing and keeping both types of accounts is placed on the directors.[4]

THE ACCOUNTS

Every company is required to keep proper accounting records. The records must be such as (i) shall be sufficient to show and explain the company's transactions, (ii) to disclose the company's financial position at any time, and (iii) to enable the directors to ensure that any balance sheet or profit and loss account prepared by them complies with the requirements of the Act as to form and content.[5]

---

1   CA 1985, s 363. For the form of the return, Companies (Annual Return) Regulations 1977 (SI 1977/1368) as amended by CA 1980, Sch 3, para 38.
2   CA 1985, s 363(7).
3   Ibid, s 713.
4   Ibid, s 221.
5   CA 1985, s 221. The books are to be kept at the registered office of the company, and must be open to inspection by the officers of the company at all times: *Conway v Petronius Clothing Co Ltd* [1978] 1 All ER 185, [1978] 1 WLR 72.

The company is obliged to maintain daily records of sums received and expended by it, and the matters to which those items of receipt and expenditure relate; and in addition, it must maintain a record of its assets and liabilities. In the case of a company which deals in goods, the accounting records must contain a statement of the company's stock, its stocktaking statements, and, except where its goods have been sold in the ordinary course of the retail trade, statements of all goods purchased and sold, and the buyers and sellers of the goods.[6] The Department of Trade has power to alter or add to the accounting requirements, and in particular the Accounting Schedules, subject to Parliamentary approval if the addition is onerous.[7]

The directors of every company must prepare a profit and loss account in respect of each of the company's accounting reference periods, and they must also prepare a balance sheet as at the date to which the profit and loss account is made up. The accounting reference period must coincide with the company's financial year.[8]

The provisions relating to the accounting reference period are complex. A company is entitled to give notice to the Registrar of Companies within six months of its incorporation of the date on which in each successive year its accounting reference period is to be treated as coming to an end. The date specified in the notice is the company's accounting reference date, but the accounting reference date for any company which fails to notify the Registrar of Companies that it has selected an alternative date is 31 March.[9]

The company's first accounting reference period commences on the date of incorporation and ends on the company's accounting reference date. However, the first accounting reference period may, as long as it does not exceed 18 months, be any period longer than 6 months.[10] The subsequent accounting reference periods of the company are those successive periods of 12 months commencing on the day after the company's accounting reference date and ending on the company's next following accounting reference date.[11]

---

6   Ibid, s 221(4). The records must be kept for six years from the date on which they were made, although a private company is obliged to keep the records for three years only: ibid, s 222(4).
7   CA 1985, s 256. See, eg, Companies (Accounts and Audit) Regulations 1982 (SI 1982/1092) the provision does not enable alterations to be made to the requirements of s 221.
8   CA 1985, s 227.
9   Ibid, s 224.
10 Ibid, s 224(4).
11 Ibid.

The company may alter its accounting reference date by giving notice of its new accounting reference date to the Registrar of Companies. It must state in its notice whether its current or previous accounting reference period is to be treated as shortened or extended by reason of the change in the accounting reference date, and it must draw up accounts for that shortened or extended period, whichever is appropriate. After notice of change has been given to the Registrar of Companies, accounting reference periods subsequent to the shortened or extended period commence on the day after, and with, the new accounting reference date.[12]

The profit and loss account in respect of the company's first accounting reference period must commence on the first day of that period and end either on the date on which the period ends (that is, on the company's accounting reference date) or within seven days of that date. Each subsequent profit and loss account must commence on the day after the date to which the previous profit and loss account was made up and end either on the date on which the accounting reference period in respect of which it is drawn up ends, or within seven days of that date.[13]

The directors of the company are required within seven months or, in the case of a private company, ten months, after the end of each accounting reference period to lay before the general meeting and to deliver to the Registrar of Companies copies of the profit and loss account and balance sheet (together with copies of the auditors' and directors' reports required by CA 1985, ss 235 and 238 to be attached thereto) relating to that accounting reference period.[14] Where the company's first accounting period commences on its date of incorporation and exceeds 12 months, the time for laying and delivering the accounts and reports is reduced by the amount of time by which the accounting reference period exceeds 12 months. However, the period cannot be reduced to less than 3 months after the end of the accounting reference period.[15]

The financial documents must give a true and fair view of the state of affairs of the company at the end of its financial year, that is, at the end of its accounting reference period. This requirement overrides the requirements of Sch 4 and all other requirements of the

---

12   Ibid, ss 225–226.
13   Ibid, s 227.
14   Ibid, ss 239, 241 and 242; certain unlimited companies (broadly those which are independent of any limited company) are exempt from delivering copies of the profit and loss account, balance sheet and auditors' and directors' reports to the Registrar of Companies.
15   CA 1985, s 242(4). For companies with overseas interests, the time may be extended, s 242(3).

Companies Acts as to matters to be included in a company's accounts and notes to the accounts.[16] The accounts are required to set out the matters contained in Sch 4 or 9 to the Act.[17] Where at the end of a financial year a company has subsidiaries, copies of the group accounts as well as the parent company's own accounts are to be laid before the general meeting and delivered to the Registrar of Companies.[18] The group accounts of a holding company are to be consolidated accounts comprising a consolidated balance sheet and profit and loss statement.[19] The contents of such accounts are required to give a true and fair view of the state of affairs and profit or loss of the company and its subsidiaries dealt with thereby as a whole.[20]

The meaning of 'holding company' and 'subsidiary' is dealt with in s 736 of the Companies Act 1985.[1]

A company is deemed to be a subsidiary company of another company if:

(1) that other company either:
  (a) is a member of it and controls the composition of its board of directors; or
  (b) holds more than half in nominal value of its equity share capital; or
(2) the first-mentioned company is a subsidiary of any company which is that other company's subsidiary.

Equity share capital means its issued share capital excluding any part thereof which, neither as respects dividends nor as respects capital, carries any right to participate beyond a specified amount in a distribution.

A company is deemed to be another company's holding company if, but only if, that other company is its subsidiary.

This definition is basically predicated on control. The section continues to provide a test for determining when the composition of the company's board of directors shall be deemed to be controlled by another company. If, but only if, the other company can by the

---

16 CA 1985, s 228.
17 Ibid, ss 227, 228, 257, 258.
18 Ibid, s 229.
19 Ibid, s 229.
20 Ibid, s 230.
1 For further details, see Gower's *Principles of Modern Company Law* (4th edn, 1979) pp 118–120.

Chapter 9 Accounts, Directors' Report and Audit

exercise of its independent power appoint or remove all or a majority of directors, the company's board of directors shall be deemed to be controlled by it. The 'parent' company is deemed to have power to appoint to a directorship where a person cannot be appointed without its consent, or where a person's appointment to a directorship in the company follows necessarily from his appointment as a director of the 'parent' or the directorship is held by the parent or by another subsidiary of the parent.[2]

The profit and loss account of a company and any group accounts of a holding company are to be annexed to the balance sheet (which must be signed by two directors or if there is only one director by that director)[3] and the auditors' report is to be attached thereto.[4]

FORM AND CONTENTS OF THE ACCOUNTS

The details of presentation of the accounts are dealt with in CA 1985, s 228 and 258 relating to individual company accounts, and s 230 and 259 relating to group accounts, and in Sch 4 and 9 to the CA 1985.[5] The combined effect of these provisions is to require the accounts of most companies to comply with Sch 4. CA 1985 incorporates the provisions of the EEC Fourth Directive concerning company accounts.[6] For the first time in English law, specific formats for balance sheets and profit and loss statements are required, and principles and rules are laid down for the valuation of assets and calculation of profits.

The basic accounting requirements with which, subject to certain exceptions noted below, all companies must comply[7] are set out in Sch 4 of the CA 1985. By way of exception to this general rule, accounts prepared by any company in respect of any financial year beginning before the appointed day[8] and in respect of any financial year by any banking, insurance and shipping company may be governed by the individual and group accounting requirements of

---

2 CA 1985, s 736.
3 Ibid, s 238(1).
4 Ibid, s 238(3) and (4).
5 As originally substituted by the CA 1981; only a brief account of these Schs can be given here; for a fuller treatment, see L. H. Leigh and H. C. Edey, *The Companies Act*, 1981.
6 Fourth Council Directive of 25 July 1978, OJ L222/11.
7 CA 1985, s 225.
8 That is, 15 June 1982: Companies Act 1981 (Commencement No 4) Order 1982 (SI 1982/672).

Sch 9.[9] The basic accounting requirements of Sch 4 are substantially relaxed in favour of small and medium-sized private companies. Group accounts must comply with s 230 of the CA 1985 and Sch 4, save that a similar dispensation to that which applies in the case of individual companies permits holding companies with banking, insurance or shipping subsidiaries to follow Sch 9.[10]

We have noted that the requirement that the accounting documents give a true and fair view is an overriding requirement. If, therefore, the financial documents drawn up in accordance with Sch 4 and the other requirements of the Companies Act 1985 would not suffice to present a true and fair view, the information necessary to do so must be included in the balance sheet or profit and loss account or in a note to the accounts.[11] A company which is affected by special circumstances such that adherence to the requirements of form in the Acts would prevent the accounts showing a true and fair view shall, so far as it is necessary to do so, depart from the requirements of the Acts and the departure must be particularised and explained in a note to the accounts.[12]

GENERAL RULES

Every balance sheet must show the items listed in one or other of the two balance sheet formats, and every profit and loss account must show the items listed in one or other of the four profit and loss formats.[13] Companies must adhere to the same formats from financial year to year unless, in the directors' opinion, there are special reasons for change. In that case, particulars of the change must be disclosed and the reasons explained in a note to the accounts in the new format.[14]

Apart from matters of form, the Sch also deals with the accounting principles and rules that are to be used in determining the amounts to be included in respect of the items shown. These are to apply unless it appears to the directors that there are reasons for departing from them in any financial year, in which case particulars

---

9 CA 1985, ss 257–262. For the definition of banking, insurance and shipping companies, see s 257. The auditors of such companies taking advantage of CA 1985, Sch 9, Pt III, must state in their reports whether or not the accounts have been properly prepared in accordance with the Companies Acts 1948–1981: Companies (Accounts and Audit) Regulations 1982 (SI 1982/1092).
10 Ibid, s 259.
11 Ibid, s 228.
12 Ibid.
13 Ibid, Sch 4, para 1.
14 Ibid, para 2.

of the departure, the reason for it and its effect is to be given in a note to the accounts.[15]

The principles, contained in section A of Pt II of Sch 4, specify that the company is presumed to carry on business as a going concern; accounting policies are to be applied consistently from year to year; the amount of any item is to be determined on a prudent basis; and in particular only realised profits are to be included in the profit and loss account, and all liabilities and losses which have arisen or are likely to arise in relation to the financial year or any preceding year are to be taken into account; income and charges are to be included without regard to the date of receipt or payment, that is, on an accrual basis; and the amount of each individual asset or liability forming part of an item is to be determined separately.[16] Whether profits are realised is to be determined by the application of generally accepted accounting principles.[17]

Section B of Pt II of Sch 4 contains the basic rules which are known as the historical cost accounting rules. These apply subject to section C which allows a company to make use of the alternative accounting rules permitting the revaluation of assets.

The historical cost rules for fixed assets provide that they are to be shown at purchase price or production cost, less depreciation where appropriate.[18] Fixed assets with a limited economic life are to be reduced by systematic provisions for depreciation. Where an asset has diminished permanently in value the amount shown must be reduced by a provision for diminution. There are special provisions for goodwill and development costs.[19]

The historical cost rules for current assets provide that these are to be included at their purchase price or production cost, unless their net realisable value is lower, in which case the lower figure is to be used.[20]

Section C of Pt II contains the alternative accounting rules. Their effect is to permit the use of current cost accounting in a company's main accounts, but they also permit the selective revaluation of fixed assets and indeed of stocks and current asset investments as well.[1] The broad effect is to replace the purchase price or production cost bases by current cost, or in some cases market value.

15 Ibid, paras 9 and 15.
16 Ibid, Sch 4, paras 10–14.
17 Ibid, para 90.
18 Ibid, paras 17–19.
19 Ibid, paras 20 and 21.
20 Ibid, paras 22 and 23.
 1 These provisions take advantage of art 33 of the EEC Fourth Directive which was concerned particularly with the question of accounting under inflation.

Where the rules are used, the items affected, and the basis of valuation of each, are to be disclosed in a note to the accounts.[2] Furthermore, subject to an exception for stocks, the comparable historical cost amounts, or the differences between these amounts and those shown in the balance sheet, must be disclosed.[3] The differences in book values arising on the revaluation are to be transferred to a revaluation reserve. There are restrictions on the amounts that may be transferred from the reserve to profit and loss account.[4]

NOTES TO ACCOUNTS

Part III of the Sch specifies information that, if not given in the accounts, is to be given by way of note to them. The accounting policies used are to be stated.[5] Among the further information required is particulars of the authorised share capital and of any redeemable shares; details of shares allotted and reasons for allotments during the financial year; information on contingent rights to the allotment of shares; particulars of debentures issued; amounts of, and changes in, fixed assets before and after depreciation, and details of any revaluations; particulars of interests in land and buildings; details of investments and values thereof; changes in reserves and provisions for taxation (other than deferred taxation, which however is included in the formats); particulars of amounts due to creditors, distinguishing those of greater than five years maturity, and of terms of payment and security; arrears of fixed cumulative dividends; charges on the company's assets to secure the liabilities of others; details of contingent liability, of financial commitments not provided for which are relevant in assessing the company's state of affairs, and of capital expenditure contracted for or authorised but not provided for; pension commitments; loans for the acquisition of shares in the company; and the aggregate amount recommended for dividend.[6]

Information required to supplement the profit and loss account includes particulars of interest on loans to the company; amounts set aside to redeem shares or loans; income from listed investments; rents from land, where substantial; hire of plant and machinery; and remuneration of auditors. Details of taxation are to be given, including particulars of any special circumstances affecting the

2 CA 1985, Sch 4, paras 31 and 33.
3 Ibid, para 33.
4 Ibid, para 34, but see paras 71–74 concerning investment companies.
5 Ibid, Sch 4, paras 35 and 36.
6 Ibid, paras 37–51.

company's liability. An analysis of turnover by different classes of business and by different geographical markets is required, where appropriate, but there is a saving where the directors consider that disclosure would be seriously prejudicial to the interests of the company. Information is to be given of the average number of employees and, so far as not stated in the profit and loss account, of wages and salaries, social security costs and other pension costs. Details are to be given of amounts in the profit and loss account relating to preceding financial years and of extraordinary and exceptional items during the financial year.[7]

Sundry other matters to be specified in the accounts or the notes thereto may be mentioned. One group of sections relates to details to be given, in the holding company's accounts, of the identities and places of incorporation of subsidiaries and of particulars of the parent company's shareholdings therein. Exemption from disclosure is provided for where the subsidiary is incorporated outside the United Kingdom or carries on business outside the United Kingdom if the disclosure would, in the opinion of the directors of the parent, be harmful to the business of the parent or other companies in the group and the Department of Trade agrees.[8] Similarly, if the company has a large number of subsidiaries, and disclosure would result in particulars of excessive length being given, disclosure need only be made of those subsidiaries the results of whose activities principally affected the fortunes of the group.[9] The fact that this course is being adopted must be disclosed in the accounts.[10]

Similarly, the accounts of a subsidiary must disclose the identity of any company regarded by its directors as its ultimate holding company. An exemption from disclosure similar to that indicated above for subsidiaries, where disclosure might be harmful, is provided where the company carried on business outside the United Kingdom.[11]

The company's accounts or a note attached thereto must also disclose the identities and places of incorporation of companies, not being subsidiaries, whose shares it holds and particulars of these shares. The obligation to disclose arises:

7 Ibid, paras 53–57.
8 Ibid, s 231 and Sch 5.
9 Ibid, Sch 5, Pt 1, para 4.
10 Ibid, Sch 5, para 6.
11 Ibid, Sch 5, Pt IV, paras 20–21.

(1) where the company holds shares exceeding one-tenth of the nominal value of the issued shares of any class of equity share capital of another company;[12] or
(2) where shares which it holds in another company exceed one-tenth of the assets which it holds;[13] or
(3) in the case of Sch 4, but not Sch 9 accounts, where, at the end of its financial year, a company holds shares comprised in the share capital of another body corporate which is not its subsidiary, exceeding in nominal value one-tenth of the allotted share capital of that body.[14]

Head (3) requires disclosure whatever the nature of the shares in question, whether ordinary voting shares or preference shares. Furthermore, in respect of all three heads above, where the shares held by the reporting company exceed in nominal value one-fifth of the allotted share capital of that body, then information concerning the capital, reserves and profit and loss of that body corporate must be disclosed.[15]

A company which enters into an arrangement for the acquisition of shares in another company to which s 131 applies must disclose particulars of the transaction and of the profits and losses of the other company in the accounts of the company for the financial year in which the transaction occurred.[16]

Again there is an exemption where the other company carries on business outside the United Kingdom and the directors are of opinion (and the Department of Trade agrees) that such disclosure might prove harmful.[17] If the company has a greater than 10% shareholding in more than one company, and the number of such companies is such that in the opinion of the directors, disclosure would result in particulars of excessive length being given, disclosure need only be given of shareholdings in those bodies whose results principally affected the amount of profit or loss of the company or the amount of its assets.[18] Provisions of this character go some distance towards recognising that companies may be regarded as within a group, even though legally they are not under the same control.

---

12 Ibid, Sch 5, Pt II, para 7.
13 Ibid, para 9.
14 Ibid, s 260.
15 For details of the disclosures to be made, see ibid, Sch 5, Pt II.
16 Companies (Accounts and Audit) Regulations 1982 (SI 1982/1902).
17 CA 1985, Sch 5, Pt II, para 10.
18 Ibid, para 11.

The following must be disclosed in a note to the accounts:[19]

(1) the emoluments of the company's chairman during the financial year;
(2) the number of directors (employed wholly or mainly inside the United Kingdom) who had no emoluments, or whose several emoluments amounted to not more than £5,000 and thereafter the number enjoying emoluments falling with successive bands of £5,000;
(3) the emoluments of any director enjoying emoluments greater than those of the chairman, or, if more than one earns emoluments greater than the chairman, then disclosure of the emoluments of the highest paid director;
(4) the number of directors who had waived emoluments which, but for the waiver, would have had to be disclosed in the accounts as part of the aggregate amount of the directors' emoluments, and the aggregate amount so waived;
(5) the number of employees working wholly or mainly within the United Kingdom enjoying emoluments of more than £10,000 in successive bands of £5,000.

In the case of directors, the term 'emoluments' includes fees and percentages, any sums paid by way of expenses allowances so far as these are chargeable to United Kingdom income tax, and the estimated money value of any other benefits received by him otherwise than in cash.[19] In the case of officers, the term includes in addition payments made or payable in respect of his services by the company or a subsidiary, or in respect of his services as a director of a subsidiary.[20]

The CA 1985 makes detailed provision for disclosure of a range of transactions involving directors and other officers. Section 232 requires disclosure by way of notes to a company's accounts of (i) transactions or arrangements of a kind described in CA 1985, s 330 (that is, principally, loans, quasi-loans, credit transactions, prohibited assignment and back-to-back arrangements; (ii) agreements to enter into any such transactions or arrangements; and (iii) any other transactions or arrangements with the company or with a subsidiary in which a director of the company has, directly or indirectly, a 'material interest'. A transaction or arrangement prohibited by s 330 is not exempt from disclosure.[1]

19 Ibid, Sch 5, Pt V.
20 Ibid, para 20.
1 Ibid, Sch 6, Pt I, para 2.

Every company must disclose by way of notes to its accounts or, if it is a holding company, to its group accounts, particulars of transactions or arrangements of the kind described in s 330, and agreements to enter into such transactions or arrangements, entered into by the company for any person who was during the financial year in respect of which the accounts were prepared a director of the company or of its holding company or connected with such a director.[2] Holding companies must also in their group accounts disclose any such transactions, arrangements or agreements entered into by each of their subsidiaries for any director of the subsidiary or of its holding company or persons connected with such a director, and subsidiary companies must also disclose in their accounts any such transactions, arrangements or agreements which they have entered into for persons who were at any time during the financial year directors of their holding companies or persons, companies or persons connected with such directors.[3]

Similarly, every company must disclose in notes to its accounts or, if it is a holding company, to its group accounts, particulars of transactions or arrangements with the company in which a person, who was at any time during the financial year in respect of which the accounts were prepared a director of the company or its holding company, had a direct or indirect material interest.[4] There is, however, an exemption for small transactions or arrangements which do not exceed in aggregate £1,000 in the relevant accounting period or which, if greater in amount, do not exceed the lesser of £5,000 or 1% of the value of the net assets of the company.[5] A holding company must also in notes to its group accounts disclose any transactions or arrangements made with subsidiary companies in which any of the directors of the subsidiary or of the holding company are directly or indirectly materially interested,[6] and subsidiary companies must also disclose any transactions or arrangements made by them in which a director of their holding company has a direct or indirect material interest.[7]

The term 'material interest' is not defined by the CA 1985, but any transaction or arrangement between a company and a director of the company or of its holding company (or a person connected with such a director) is treated as a transaction, arrangement or

---

2 Ibid.
3 Ibid, paras 1, 5, 9.
4 Ibid, para 2.
5 Ibid, s 344 and Sch 6, Pt I.
6 Ibid, para 1.
7 Ibid, para 2.

174 *Chapter 9 Accounts, Directors' Report and Audit*

agreement in which the director is interested.[8] However, an interest is not material if a majority of the directors (other than the interested director) are of the opinion that it is not material.[9]

The obligation to make disclosure of transactions or arrangements in which a director has a material interest requires the company to include in the notes to its accounts details of contracts for services, but no disclosure need be made of any contract of service between a company and one of its directors or a director of its holding company, or between a director of a company and any of that company's subsidiaries.[10]

The accounts must contain the principal terms of any transaction, arrangement or agreement of which disclosure is required and, in addition, certain specified details must be given, for example, the name of the person for whom the transaction, arrangement or agreement was made.[11]

Certain transactions are exempt from the disclosure requirements imposed by s 232 and Sch 6. In the case of credit transactions,[12] disclosure need only be made where the aggregate values of each transaction, arrangement or agreement made for the director or connected person in question, less any amount by which the liabilities of the person for whom the transaction or arrangement was made has been reduced, exceeded £5,000 during the financial year in respect of which the accounts were prepared.[13] Similarly, there is an exemption from disclosure in the company's accounts of particulars of certain minor transactions or arrangements with a company or any of its subsidiaries in which a director of the company or of its holding company had, directly of indirectly, a material interest. The conditions are that the value of each such transaction or arrangement by which the liabilities of the person for whom the transaction or arrangement was made have been reduced, did not at any time during the relevant period exceed in the aggregate £1,000 or, if more, did not exceed £5,000 or 1% of the value of the net assets of the company preparing the accounts as at the end of the relevant period for those accounts, whichever is the less.[14]

In the case of the accounts of a company which is a recognised

---

8 Ibid, para 3.
9 Ibid.
10 Ibid, para 5.
11 Ibid, Sch 6, Pt II.
12 And related transactions: ibid, s 344 and Sch 6, Pt I.
13 Ibid, para 11.
14 Ibid, para 11(2).

bank[15] or the group accounts of a holding company of such a bank, any transaction or arrangement of a kind described in s 330 (or an agreement to enter into such a transaction or arrangement) to which the recognised bank is a party is exempt from disclosure in the accounts.[16] However, a company which is, or which is the holding company of, a recognised bank is required to maintain a register containing particulars of every transaction, arrangement or agreement which would otherwise fall to be disclosed in accordance with Sch 6 and, except in the case of a wholly-owned subsidiary of a UK company, to make available for inspection by members before the company's annual general meeting a statement of such particulars.[17]

A company is also subject to disclose requirements in respect of loans, quasi-loans and credit transactions, and guarantees and securities and prohibited assignment and back-to-back arrangements relating thereto, where any such transactions, arrangements or agreements are made for officers of the company other than directors. Notes to the accounts of a company or, if it is a holding company, its group accounts must contain, in relation to such transactions, arrangements or agreements made by the company (and, if it is a holding company, by a subsidiary of the company) for the company's officers, a statement of the net aggregate amounts outstanding under those transactions, arrangements or agreements, and the numbers of officers for whom they were made.[18] Transactions, arrangements and agreements made by the company or any of its subsidiaries for any officer of the company are exempt if the aggregate amount outstanding at the end of the period, for the officer, does not exceed £2,500.[19] Transactions, arrangements or agreements made by recognised banks for their officers or officers of their holding companies are exempt from this requirement.[20] However, the accounts of a company which is a recognised bank, or the group accounts of a company which is the holding company of a recognised bank, must contain a statement of transactions, arrangements or agreements made by the company and, in the case of a holding company, by any of its subsidiaries which is a recognised bank, for persons who were at any time during the financial year in

---

15 Ibid, s 331.
16 Ibid, Sch 6, Pt I, para 4.
17 Ibid, s 343.
18 Ibid, Sch 6, Pts II and III.
19 Ibid, Sch 6, Pt II, para 16.
20 Ibid, s 233(3).

Chapter 9 Accounts, Directors' Report and Audit

respect of which the accounts were prepared directors of the company or connected with such a director.[1]

If the directors fail to comply with the accounting requirements, the auditors must include in their report, so far as they are reasonably able to do so, a statement of the required particulars.[2]

THE ACCOUNTING EXEMPTIONS

The accounting exemptions apply both to small and medium-sized companies, and to groups which meet the qualifying tests.[3] They relate only to the accounts delivered to the Registrar. Certain classes of companies may not benefit from the accounting exemptions. These include public companies, banking, insurance or shipping companies, and any company which is a member of an ineligible group.[4]

Status as a small or medium-sized company depends on turnover, balance sheet total, and the number of people whom it employs. To qualify as a small company, a company must, in respect of the instant and the immediately preceding financial year, satisfy at least two of the following conditions: its turnover must not exceed £1,400,000, its balance sheet total must not exceed £700,000 and the average number of persons employed by the company in the financial year in question (determined on a weekly basis) must not exceed 50.[5] The conditions for a medium-sized company are similar, but the amounts are higher, turnover not in excess of £5,750,000, a balance sheet total not in excess of £2,800,000, and an average weekly employment total not exceeding 250 persons.[6]

A company does not cease to qualify for small or medium-sized status simply because it fails to meet the qualifying conditions in any one year. If, having met the conditions, it has an unusual year, it may continue to claim the status for that year and, if it again meets the qualifying conditions, for the next succeeding year.[7]

The accounting exemptions also apply to group accounts of a holding company where the group would meet the qualifications for small or medium-sized company status if it were an actual company.[8] Where the group would qualify to be treated as a medium-

---

1 Ibid, s 234 and Sch 6, Pt III.
2 Ibid, s 237. A similar duty is imposed on auditors in respect of breaches of requirements relating to banks, etc; see s 343.
3 Ibid, ss 247–251.
4 Ibid, s 247(2).
5 Ibid, s 248.
6 Ibid, s 248(2).
7 Ibid, s 249.
8 Ibid, s 250.

sized company, then the holding company is to be so treated even though it would by itself meet the small company requirements. In determining questions of group status, aggregate figures for the group apply.[9]

A small company may deliver to the Registrar a modified balance sheet instead of the full balance sheet which would otherwise be required. It need not deliver a profit and loss statement to him, nor need it deliver a directors' report to the Registrar.[10] The modified balance sheet is an abbreviated version of the full document required under Sch 4; in particular, it allows for the disclosure of aggregated figures for assets, investments and the like. Only some parts of the information normally required to be given by way of notes to the accounts need be given. The company need not disclose aggregate amounts of directors' salaries, etc, nor give detailed particulars of salaries of directors, or employees earning more than £20,000 per annum.

A medium-sized company must comply with the balance sheet requirements of the Companies Acts. It may, however, deliver a modified profit and loss account to the Registrar, and it is not required to give particulars of turnover in relation to classes of business and markets.[11] A directors' report is required. A modified profit and loss statement may combine certain entries according to the format chosen.

Certain procedural formalities apply to the submission of a modified balance sheet (employed in the case of small companies). In addition to the normal formalities of signature, the directors must submit a signed statement that they have relied on the exemptions on the ground that the company was entitled to them, and must submit either a special auditors' report, or a statement that the company was a dormant company throughout the financial year. The full significance of dormant company status is dealt with below.

OTHER ACCOUNTING MATTERS

A company may publish accounts otherwise than by delivery to the registrar. Publication is defined basically as circulating or making matter available for public inspection in a manner calculated to invite members of the public generally, or any class, to read it.[12]

---

9 Ibid.
10 What follows is an abbreviation of CA 1985, Sch 8.
11 Ibid, Sch 8, Pt I, para 8; one of the basic formats must of course be followed.
12 Ibid, ss 342(5) and (6).

Where a company publishes full individual accounts, that is, either accounts in the ordinary form or accounts as modified for small or medium-sized companies, it must publish the relevant auditors' report with them. Similar provisions apply to full group accounts.[13]

A company may publish abridged accounts.[14] If it does so, it must publish a statement indicating that the accounts are not full accounts, whether accounts have been delivered to the Registrar, or whether the company is exempt from doing so as an unlimited company,[15] whether the auditors have made a report in respect of the accounts of the company,[16] and whether the report was an unqualified report.[17] A company may not publish a statutory auditors' report with abridged accounts.[18]

DORMANT COMPANIES

Certain dormant companies may, upon passing a special resolution, be exempted from appointing auditors.[19] Two cases are envisaged; the first is where an active small company has become dormant, and the second is where a company has been dormant from the time of its formation until the necessary resolution has been passed. The facility does not apply to a company which is obliged to file group accounts for the accounting reference period in respect of which accounts are laid before the meeting. However, a dormant company which would have been entitled to small company status but for its membership of an ineligible group may take advantage of it.

A company is regarded as dormant during any period in which no significant accounting transaction for the company has occurred. If such a transaction occurs, the company is no longer regarded as dormant. A significant accounting transaction is defined in terms of the matters required to be entered in a company's accounting records, and includes such matters as moneys received and expended, and purchases and sales of goods. A transaction arising from the taking of shares in the company by a subscriber to the memorandum of the company in pursuance of any undertaking of his contained in it is, however, not so regarded.

---

13 Ibid, s 254.
14 Ibid, s 255.
15 Ibid, s 241.
16 Ibid, s 236.
17 Ibid, s 271.
18 Ibid, s 255(4).
19 Ibid, s 252.

DIRECTORS' REPORT

A directors' report must be attached to every balance sheet. In what follows, we consider the report which must accompany Sch 4 accounts only; the requirements for Sch 9 accounts are somewhat different, but they affect only a minority of companies.

The directors' report must contain a fair review of the development of the business of the company and its subsidiaries during the relevant financial period and of their position at the end of it, the amount (if any) which the directors recommend should be paid as dividend, and the amount (if any) which they propose to carry to reserves. Members of the company, debenture holders and any other persons entitled to receive notices of meetings and copies of the accounts have a right to receive such report.[20] The particulars required to be inserted in the directors' report have rightly been said to be extraordinarily diverse.[1] The report now gives much information derived from the accounts, but, also, much matter which could not conveniently be contained in the accounts.

The content of the directors' report has been steadily expanded over the years.[2] The directors' report must in addition to other matters state the names of the persons who were directors of the company during the financial year, and the principal activities of the company and of its subsidiaries during that year, and any significant change in these activities during that year.[3]

Disclosure must be made of any significant changes in fixed assets during the year. If the balance sheet value of land differs substantially from the market value, the difference must be indicated with such degree of precision as is practicable.[4]

There must be stated, either in the directors' report or in a note to the accounts, whether or not, in respect of each person who was a director of the company at the relevant year end, the company's register shows that he was interested in shares of the company or its subsidiary or holding company, and the nature and extent of such interests.[5]

The directors' report must contain particulars of important events affecting the company or any of its subsidiaries since the end

---

20 CA 1985, s 235 and Sch 7, and an entitlement to see the report, ss 240 and 246.
1   Palmer's *Company Law* (22nd edn, 1976) p 752.
2   For the statutory history, see CA 1967, ss 15–24, as amended, especially by the CA 1981.
3   CA 1985, s 235 and Sch 7.
4   Ibid, s 235(2).
5   Ibid, Sch 7, Pt I.

of the relevant financial year, an indication of likely future developments in the business of the company and its subsidiaries, and an indication of the activities, if any, of the group in the field of research and development.[6]

The directors' report must now give particulars of acquisition of the company's own shares.[7] Disclosure is required when shares are purchased by the company, or acquired by forfeiture or surrender in lieu of forfeiture, or pursuant to the power enabling a company limited by shares to acquire its own fully paid shares otherwise than for valuable consideration or on a reduction of capital,[8] where shares are acquired by the company's nominee or other person with its financial assistance,[9] or are made subject to a permitted lien or charge by the company.[10]

The directors' report must contain particulars of contributions—if over £200—for political or charitable purposes. The amount must be disclosed, and in the case of political contributions, the identity of the recipient or the political party.[11] Political contribution is widely defined to include a contribution to any political party or to a person whose activities are likely to affect public support for any political party.[12]

The Secretary of State is given wide powers, by CA 1985, s 256 as amended, to alter the requirements relating to the accounts, and he may alter or add to the requirements both of Sch 4 and 9.

AUDIT

The articles of a company normally make provision for the appointment, remuneration and duties of auditors.[13] In addition to whatever provisions are made in the articles, there are statutory provisions as to those questions. Subject to the provisions of s 252 of the CA 1985, which permits certain dormant companies to avoid the obligation to appoint auditors, every company must at each general meeting appoint an auditor or auditors to hold office until

---

6 Ibid, Sch 7, Pt II.
7 Ibid, Sch 7, Pt II.
8 Ibid, para 7.
9 Ibid.
10 Ibid.
11 Ibid, Sch 7, Pt I, para 3.
12 Ibid, para 5(2).
13 CA 1985, s 385.

the conclusion of the general meeting before which the accounts for the next following accounting reference period are laid.[14]

The first auditors may be appointed by the directors at any time prior to the first general meeting before which accounts are laid, and auditors so appointed shall hold office until the conclusion of that meeting.[15]

However, if the directors fail to exercise their powers to appoint the first auditors, the company in general meeting may appoint them.[16]

The retiring auditor or auditors may, if willing, be re-appointed at the general meeting by ordinary resolution. It is not necessary for special notice to be given of such a resolution, unless the retiring auditor was appointed by the directors to fill a casual vacancy.[17]

The directors or a general meeting may fill any casual vacancy in the office of auditor, but while any such vacancy continues, the surviving or continuing auditor or auditors, if any, may act.[18]

Where at a general meeting before which accounts are laid no auditors are appointed or reappointed the Department of Trade may appoint a person to fill the vacancy. The company is required to notify the Department of Trade within one week of the occurrence of the failure to appoint.[19]

The remuneration of the auditors is fixed by the company in general meeting or in such manner as the company in general meeting may determine, but if an auditor is appointed by the directors or the Department of Trade, his remuneration is fixed by them or the Department.[20]

The auditor may resign at any time during the currency of his office by depositing a written notice of resignation at the company's registered office. The notice is ineffective unless it contains either a statement to the effect that there are no circumstances connected with his resignation which the auditor considers should be brought to the notice of the members or creditors of the company, or a statement of any circumstances there may be. The company must within 14 days of the receipt of the notice send copies thereof to the

---

14 CA 1985, s 384.
15 Ibid, s 384(2).
16 Ibid, s 384(3).
17 Ibid, s 388(1).
18 Ibid, s 384(4). Special notice is required for a resolution at a general meeting: ibid, s 388(1).
19 Ibid, s 384(5).
20 Ibid, s 385.

Registrar of Companies and to every person who is entitled to receive copies of the company's accounts.[1]

If the notice of resignation contains a statement of circumstances which he considers should be brought to the notice of the members or creditors, the auditor is entitled to require the directors to convene an extraordinary general meeting in order that he may place an explanation of the circumstances connected with his resignation before the meeting. He is also entitled to require the company to send to members with the notice of the meeting (or with the notice of any general meeting at which his term of office would otherwise have expired or at which it is proposed to fill a vacancy caused by his resignation) a statement relating to those circumstances. The resigning auditor is entitled to attend any such meeting and be heard on any business concerning him as the former auditor of the company.[2]

The Court has power to order on the application of the company or any aggrieved person that copies of the notice or of the statement need not be sent out if it is satisfied that the auditor is using the notice or the statement to secure needless publicity for defamatory matter.[3]

The company may by ordinary resolution remove an auditor at any time prior to the expiration of his term of office, and its right to do so cannot be excluded by any agreement between the company and the auditor. Nevertheless, the removal of the auditor before the expiry of his office may, if without good cause, prove an expensive exercise, for the auditor's right to compensation or damages for termination of his appointment is not affected by his removal.[4]

Special notice is required for a resolution at a company's general meeting (i) appointing as auditor a person other than a retiring auditor, or (ii) filling a casual vacancy in the office of auditor, or (iii) reappointing as auditor a retiring auditor who was appointed by the directors to fill a casual vacancy, or (iv) removing an auditor before the expiry of his term of office. The company must send a copy of the notice of resolution to the person proposed to be appointed or removed or (as the case may be) to the auditor who is retiring or has resigned.[5]

Where the resolution seeks to appoint as auditor a person other than a retiring auditor or seeks to remove an auditor before the

[1] Ibid, s 390.
[2] Ibid, s 391.
[3] Ibid, ss 389–390.
[4] Ibid, s 386.
[5] Ibid, s 388.

expiry of his term of office, the retiring auditor or auditor whose removal is proposed is entitled to require the company to send to members with the notice of the meeting a copy of any representations that the auditor may wish to make. An auditor who has been removed is entitled to attend the general meeting at which his term of office would have expired or at which it is proposed to fill the vacancy caused by his removal and be heard on any business concerning him as the former auditor of the company.[6]

The provisions of the Acts relating to qualification for appointment as an auditor are complicated. A person is not qualified for appointment unless he is a member of the United Kingdom body of accountants which is recognised for the purpose by the Department of Trade, or is specially authorised by the Department of Trade as having comparable qualifications.[7] However, there are certain transitional provisions enuring to the benefit of persons who, formerly, were auditors of exempt private companies. Such persons may, if specially authorised by the Department of Trade prior to 10 April 1978, continue to act provided that the company concerned is unquoted and is not the subsidiary of a quoted company.[8]

It is crucial that the auditor be independent of the company which he serves. Therefore, the following persons are not qualified to act as auditor.[9]

(1) an officer or servant of the company;
(2) a person who is a partner of or in the employment of an officer or servant of the company;
(3) a body corporate.

It is an offence for any person to act as the auditor of a company at a time when he knows that he is disqualified.[10] This offence is not one of strict liability and the requisite knowledge on the part of the person charged must be proved.[11] An auditor who becomes

---

6 Ibid, ss 387 and 388.
7 Ibid, s 389. The bodies of accountants which are recognised are: The Institute of Chartered Accountants in England and Wales; The Institute of Chartered Accountants of Scotland; The Association of Certified Accountants; The Institute of Chartered Accountants in Ireland. The list may be amended by the Secretary of State.
8 CA 1967, s 13(1) as continued by CA 1985, s 389(2).
9 CA 1985, s 389(6).
10 Ibid, s 389(7) and on the construction of this provision see *Secretary of State for Trade and Industry v Hart* [1982] 1 All ER 817, [1982] 1 WLR 481.
11 *Secretary of State for Trade and Industry v Hart* [1982] 1 All ER 817, [1982] 1 WLR 481.

184 Chapter 9 Accounts, Directors' Report and Audit

disqualified during his term of office must resign forthwith and commits an offence if he does not do so.[12]

The duties and powers of auditors are dealt with in ss 236 and 237 of the Companies Act 1985. Section 236(1) provides that the auditors shall make a report to the members on the accounts examined by them, and on every balance sheet, every profit and loss account and all group accounts of which a copy is laid before the company in general meeting during their tenure of office.[13]

The auditors are under a duty, in preparing their report on the company's accounts to consider whether the information given in the directors' report is consistent with the accounts. If they consider that it is inconsistent with the accounts, they must state that fact in their report.[14] The auditors' duty is owed, therefore, not to the directors but to the members in general meeting.[15] While for some purposes an officer of the company,[16] the auditor is not an agent of the shareholders,[17] nor is he an agent of the company for the purpose of making acknowledgements of debt.[18]

The auditors' report is to be read before the company in general meeting. It is open to inspection by any member.[19]

Except in the case of companies group accounts under Sch 9,[20] the auditors' report must state whether the accounts of the company (and if it is a holding company submitting group accounts the group accounts) have been properly prepared in accordance with the Companies Act 1985 and whether they give a true and fair view of the financial affairs of the company or group financial year.[1]

In preparing their report, the auditors are under a duty to carry out such investigations as will enable them to form an opinion whether proper books of account have been kept and proper returns adequate for their audit have been received from branches not visited by them. They must also carry out investigations requisite to enable them to judge whether the balance sheet and profit and loss account are in agreement with the accounting records and returns.[2] If the auditors are not satisfied of these matters they are required to

---

12 CA 1985, s 389(9).
13 Ibid, Sch 7.
14 Ibid, s 237; the requirement does not apply to Sch 9 accounts.
15 *Re London and General Bank (No 2)* [1895] 2 Ch 673.
16 *R v Shacter* [1960] 2 QB 252, [1960] 1 All ER 61.
17 *Spackman v Evans* (1868) LR 3 HL 171, 196.
18 *Re Transplanters (Holding Co) Ltd* [1958] 2 All ER 711, [1958] 1 WLR 822.
19 CA 1985, s 241.
20 Ibid, Sch 9.
 1 Ibid, s 236.
 2 Ibid, s 237.

state that fact in their report.³ Similarly, the auditors have a right of access at all times to the books of account and vouchers of the company. The auditors are entitled to require from the officers of the company such explanations and information as they require for the audit.⁴ If the company has a subsidiary incorporated in Great Britain, the subsidiary company and its auditors are under a duty to give to the auditors of the holding company such information as the auditors of the holding company may reasonably require for their purposes as such auditors; and if the subsidiary is incorporated outside Great Britain, there is imposed upon the holding company itself a duty to take such steps as are reasonably open to it to obtain such information.⁵ If they fail to obtain the information and explanations which they believe to be requisite, the auditors are to state that fact in their report.⁶

The auditors are entitled to receive notices of, to attend and, in relation to matters concerning the audit, to speak at any general meeting.⁷

It is unclear what standards are today expected of auditors.⁸ Professional standards have become more rigorous since the late nineteenth century when most cases dealing with the question were decided. Furthermore, the statutory duties of auditors have become more explicit and, it may be, more onerous. The principal difficulties concern the standards of care required of the auditor in checking for errors, fraud and other discrepancies. His duty is to use reasonable care and skill in making inquiries and investigations. And he must be honest.⁹ But, in the words of Lopes LJ in *Re Kingston Cotton Mills (No 2)*.¹⁰

> An auditor is not bound to be a detective, or, as was said, to approach his work with suspicion or with a foregone conclusion that there is

---

3 Ibid. See also *Re London and General Bank (No 2)* [1895] 2 Ch 673, 684. An author should not qualify his report where the discrepancy is insignificant. See Palmer's *Company Law* (22nd edn, 1976) p 767.
4 CA 1985, s 237.
5 Ibid, s 392.
6 Ibid, s 237(4).
7 Ibid, s 387.
8 The subject is dealt with in detail by R. Baxt, 'The Modern Company Auditor—A Nineteenth Century Watchdog' (1970) 33 Mod LR 413. While English courts generally accept as reasonable accounting practice those which the profession regards as reasonable, American courts give such practices weight but do not treat them as conclusive. See Isbell, 'The Continental Vending Case' (1970) Canadian Chartered Accountant 247.
9 *Re London and General Bank* [1895] 2 Ch 673.
10 [1896] 2 Ch 279.

something wrong. He is a watch-dog, but not a bloodhound. He is justified in believing the servants of the company in whom confidence is placed by the company. He is entitled to assume that they are honest, and to rely upon their representations provided he takes reasonable care. If there is anything calculated to excite suspicion he should probe it to the bottom; but in the absence of anything of that kind he is only bound to be reasonably cautious and careful.

The problem, in evaluating this test, is that it is keyed to the standards of the reasonably careful and skilful auditor. Accounting practices change. The reported cases do not necessarily throw much light on what standards are now regarded as reasonable by auditors. Thus, for example, it has been held that the auditor who undertakes an annual audit need not make test checks during the currency of the financial year so as to be able with greater certainty later to certify the accounts for the year, and to detect current mistakes or misappropriations. This is based on the Court's findings concerning the practice of auditors (and of course a judgment that such standards are reasonable).[11] On the other hand, it may well be that an auditor is not entitled wholly to rely on the word of the company's officers in stock taking.[12] Current auditing practice is to verify part of the stock-in-trade and, if found correct, to accept the assurances of the officers of the company as to the balance. If of course there are circumstances of suspicion, these must be probed.

Re Thomas Gerrard & Son Ltd [1968] Ch 455, [1967] 2 All ER 525.

> C, the managing director of the company, falsified the accounts between 1957 and 1962, thereby concealing both the modest 1956–57 profit and subsequent losses. Dividends were paid either wholly or in part out of capital from 1957. The auditors accepted C's explanation for alterations in the stock figures and did not pursue the matter further. It was held that the discovery of altered invoices put the auditors on inquiry and that they had failed to perform their duties in not making further investigations. The auditors were liable to compensate the company for the losses caused by their breach of duty. Though the principle stated in the *Kingston Cotton Mills* cases was adopted, Pennycuick J observed that the actual decision in that case was capable of being distinguished on the grounds that 'the standards of reasonable care and skill are, on the expert evidence, more exacting today than those which prevailed in

11 *Nelson Guarantee Corpn Ltd v Hodgson* [1958] NZLR 609.
12 Even if as Pennycuick J suggests in *Re Thomas Gerrard & Sons Ltd*, post, the auditors' duties remain unchanged, reliance on the word of others alone in stock-verification may not be 'reasonably careful'.

1896' (p 536). The auditors were not entitled, once having discovered alterations, to rest content with the assurances of the officers of the company. Their suspicions should have been aroused and inquiries should have been made from suppliers to verify those assurances.

The most striking modern statement of the standards expected of auditors are to be found in *dicta* of Lord Denning in *Fomento (Sterling Area) Ltd v Selsdon Fountain Pen Co Ltd*.[13] There, Lord Denning rejected the argument that the functions of auditors were essentially mechanical; those of a professional 'adder-upper and subtractor'. Lord Denning states:

> His vital task is to take care to see that errors are not made, be they errors of computation, or errors of commission or downright untruths. To perform this task properly, he must come to it with an inquiring mind—not suspicious of dishonesty I agree—but suspecting that someone may have made a mistake somewhere and that a check must be made to ensure that there has been none.

His Lordship remarked that *Re Kingston Cotton Mills (No 2)*[14] did not relieve the auditor of the duty of making a proper check. Indeed, such a duty is explicitly provided for by s 237 of the CA 1985.

LIABILITY OF AUDITORS

If auditors fail to perform their duties, they will be liable to the company for the loss resulting from their negligence or default.[15] However, their duty goes further than this. The auditors are under a duty of care to any person—for example, a person considering the purchase of the share capital of the company—who they know or reasonably should have foreseen at the time when they audited the accounts in question might rely on those accounts and could suffer loss if they were inaccurate. The plaintiff must prove the reliance and the necessary actual or constructive notice on the auditors' part. Conversely, if the situation is one where it is not reasonable

---

13 [1958] 1 All ER 11, [1958] 1 WLR 45.
14 Supra.
15 See eg *Re Kingston Cotton Mills Co (No 2)* [1896] 2 Ch 279. In some cases a wider liability may arise to third parties if the auditor knows that, for example, audited accounts are being prepared with a view to the third party acting upon them. See *Hedley Byrne & Co Ltd v Heller & Partners Ltd* [1964] AC 465, [1963] 2 All ER 575, esp per Lord Reid; *Dimond Manufacturing Co Ltd v Hamilton* [1969] NZLR 609, Hahlo 669; *Scott Group Ltd v McFarlane* [1978] 1 NZLR 553.

for the accounts to be relied upon, the auditors will not be liable or under any duty to any third party in the absence of express knowledge.[16] Any provision in the articles or in any contract with the company exempting them from liability or indemnifying them against liability is void.[17] The Court can grant relief against liability in proceedings brought against an auditor for negligence, default, breach of duty or trust. The auditor must show that he has acted honestly and reasonably and that he ought fairly to be excused.[18]

---

[16] *JEB Fasteners v Marks, Bloom & Co* [1981] 3 All ER 289. The judge restricted his statement of principle to the facts of the case but there appears no good reason so to restrict his statement and analysis of authority.
[17] CA 1985, s 310.
[18] Ibid, s 727.

Chapter 10

Directors' Duties

THE RELATIONSHIP OF DIRECTORS TO THE COMPANY

At one time directors were sometimes spoken of as trustees. The directors of deed of settlement companies were sometimes also the trustees of the property of the company in terms of the trust deed. Such directors were primarily fiduciary agents of the company. Nowadays, while as we have seen it is still often appropriate to refer to the directors as agents of the company, it is misleading to refer to them as trustees. There is, however, no doubt that they stand in a fiduciary relationship to the company. They are agents standing in a fiduciary relationship to the company which is their principal.[1]

The duties of director are:

(1) common law duties of care and skill,
(2) fiduciary duties of loyalty and good faith,
(3) statutory duties of disclosure, most of which relate to the fiduciary position of directors.

These, especially in relation to share dealings and to remuneration, are discussed in the chapter dealing with the registration of shares and the directors' report respectively.

DUTIES OF CARE AND SKILL

Directors' common law duties of care and skill are not unduly onerous. The difficulties encountered in attempting to set a high standard derive from the very broad nature of directoral responsibilities and powers, and from the reluctance of the Court to intervene in matters of essentially business judgment. Directors

---

1 *Re City Equitable Fire Insurance Co Ltd* [1925] Ch 407; *Selangor United Rubber Estates Ltd v Cradock (No 3)* [1968] 2 All ER 1073, [1968] 1 WLR 1555.

must exercise ordinary care and skill, and if possessed of special knowledge or experience they must use it in the affairs of the company.[2] They will be liable for negligence in the carrying out of their duties, but will escape liability if damage results to the company from their reliance on officers whom they believed to be reliable and competent.[3]

The nature of a director's responsibilities to the company were discussed by Romer J in *Re City Equitable Fire Insurance Co Ltd*.[4] Romer J states that, as a general proposition, a director will not be held liable for negligence unless guilty of '... gross or culpable negligence in a business sense'. He then stated three propositions which still prevail and which form the core of the law relating to duties of care and skill.

(1) A director need not exhibit in the performance of his duties a greater degree of skill than may reasonably be expected from a person of his knowledge and experience. '... a director of a life insurance company for instance, does not guarantee that he has the skill of an actuary or a physician'.

(2) A director is not bound to give continuous attention to the affairs of the company. His duties are of an intermittent nature to be performed at periodic board meetings.

(3) In respect of all duties that, having regard to the exigencies of business, and the articles of association, may properly be left to some other official, a director is, in the absence of grounds for suspicion, justified in trusting that official to perform such duties honestly.

The proposition that a director need not attend all meetings of the board and is not obliged to devote his full time to the affairs of the company requires qualification in the case of a director occupying a full-time service position. Such a director will be required to devote such time to the affairs of the company as his contract stipulates. In the case of an ordinary director, it has been held that while liable for a negligent decision to which he was a party, he will not be liable in respect of a decision taken at a meeting at which he was not present.[5] It is doubtful how far this rule applies. It may well not apply in cases where the director had knowledge or notice that a duty which ought to have been performed at the meeting was not being performed. However it is not generally the duty of each director to exercise control over the daily running of the business,

2 *Re Brazilian Rubber Plantations and Estates Ltd* [1911] 1 Ch 425.
3 *Dovey v Cory* [1901] AC 477.
4 [1925] Ch 407.
5 *Marquis of Bute's Case* [1892] 2 Ch 100.

nor to supervise the activities of other directors or officials of the company unless the transaction presents circumstances apt to arouse his suspicion.[6]

A director must, in exercising his powers, bring an independent judgment to bear. He will be liable in damages for loss caused to the company where he simply acts under the direction of another person, at least where the other person is perpetrating a fraud. The requirement of independence of approach may be modified as respects nominee directors appointed by a parent company or by an outsider with a genuine interest in the company to protect.[7]

In some circumstances directors will be expected to seek specialist advice and will be held liable for loss occasioned by their failure to do so.

Re Duomatic Ltd [1969] 2 Ch 365.

> The directors made a payment to a former director as compensation for loss of office without notifying the shareholders as required by s 191 of the CA 1948, and without considering whether the director's conduct warranted a payment being made and if so in what amount. The directors failed to take legal advice on the point. It was held that they acted unreasonably in failing to take advice and were therefore liable to make good the moneys to the company. Nor, having acted unreasonably, were they entitled to be indemnified under CA 1948, s 448.

DUTIES OF LOYALTY AND GOOD FAITH

The courts have stated on numerous occasions that the directors occupy a fiduciary position and must therefore exercise their powers in good faith and for the benefit of the company as a whole. The fiduciary duty so owed is owed to the company as a whole and not to any individual member of it.[8]

---

6 *Huckerby v Elliott* [1970] 1 All ER 189.
7 *Selangor United Rubber Estates Ltd v Cradock (No 3)* [1968] 1 WLR 1555, at p 1578 per Ungoed Thomas J.
8 But a director will owe fiduciary duties to a shareholder as where for example shareholders constitute the directors as agents for the sale of their shares. *Allen v Hyatt* (1914) 30 TLR 444; *Briess v Woolley* [1954] AC 333, [1954] 1 All ER 909.

Percival v Wright [1902] 2 Ch 421.

> The plaintiff, a shareholder of a company the shares in which were not quoted on a stock exchange and which were transferable only with the consent of the board, wrote to the company secretary to inquire whether the secretary knew of anyone who might be prepared to purchase his shares. Ultimately, the plaintiff sold his shares to the chairman and two other directors at an agreed price. He later discovered that at the same time the directors had been approached by a third party with a view to that person's purchasing the shares of the company at a higher price. These negotiations proved abortive. The plaintiff however brought action to set aside his sale to the directors. He alleged that they were in breach of duty to him in not informing him of the negotiations. It was held that his action failed. The directors do not owe fiduciary duties to any individual shareholder. Accordingly they were not under a duty to inform the plaintiff of the negotiations.

Because the directors stand in a fiduciary relationship to the company, they are not allowed to enter into engagements in which there is a possibility that the director's personal interests could conflict with those of the company which he is bound to protect.[9] In consequence, directors are for example bound to repay, as trustees, moneys belonging to the company which they have misapplied.[10]

DUTY TO ACT IN BEST INTERESTS OF COMPANY

There is clear authority for the proposition that the directors of a company are under a duty to act in what they consider to be the 'best interests of the company as a whole'.[11] Unfortunately however the meaning to be attributed to this phrase is not altogether clear. The difficulty in determining the exact meaning of 'the best interests of the company' stems from the fact that this or a similar phrase 'the benefit of the company' is used, with different meanings in other contexts—such as the alteration of articles by a majority—and a sharp distinction has not always been drawn between the differing meanings.

---

9 *Aberdeen Rly Co v Blaikie Bros* (1854) 2 Eq Rep 1281, 1 Macq 461.
10 *Re Lands Allotment Co* [1894] 1 Ch 616 at 631 per Lindley J; *Steen v Law* [1964] AC 287, [1963] 3 All ER 770; *International Sales and Agencies Ltd v Marcus* [1982] 3 All ER 551 see at 556 per Lawson J 'It is ... unarguable that a director who gives away his company's money without the consent of the shareholders is not in breach of his fiduciary duty as constructive trustee of the money in the banking accounts of the companies over which he has control.'
11 *Re Smith and Fawcett* [1942] Ch 304, [1942] 1 All ER 542.

In cases where the question is whether an exercise of powers by the directors is effective,[12] the phrase 'best interests of the company' refers to the company as a corporate entity and it appears that the content of the directors' duties in this regard is to act so as to promote the prosperity of the corporate entity.[13] The directors are obliged to balance a long-term view against short-term interests, but it is not certain how far this principle extends.[14]

In cases more properly classified as dealing with the question of how far a majority in general meeting can force a particular measure on a dissentient minority,[15] the phrase is used in the same sense as that in which it is used in the cases dealing with the power of the majority to alter the articles:[16] that is, 'the company', in those circumstances, means 'the members'.[17]

The distinction between cases where the question is whether the exercise of powers by directors is effective and those where the question was how far a majority can force a measure on a minority was not taken in CA 1985, s 309(1). That section provides that the directors must, in the performance of their functions, have regard to the interests of the general body of the company's employees as well as having regard to the interests of the members. It is presumably open to the Courts to construe the phrase 'the interest of the members' in this context very widely so as to include the prosperity of the latter and (since its prosperity affects that of the members) of the company. It is in any event clear from that section that the director's duty to act in the best interests of the company requires him to have regard to the interests of the company's employees, although he may not advance the latters' interests to the exclusion of all else.

The duty to have regard to the interests of the employees is, in common with other fiduciary duties, owed to the company alone and is enforceable in the same way as any other fiduciary duty owed

---

12 *Re Lee, Behrens & Co Ltd* [1932] 2 Ch 46; *Ridge Securities Ltd v IRC* [1964] 1 All ER 275, [1964] 1 WLR 479; *Re W & Roith Ltd* [1967] 1 All ER 427, [1967] 1 WLR 432; *Charterbridge Corpn v Lloyds Bank Ltd* [1970] Ch 62, [1969] 2 All ER 1185. As to the first and third of these see *Re Horsley and Weight Ltd* [1982] Ch 442, [1982] 3 All ER 1045.
13 *Re Halt Garage Ltd* (1978) 25 May (unreported) cited in [1982] 3 WLR at p 726.
14 See L.C.B. Gower in 68 Harv LR 1176 (1956).
15 *Hampson v Price's Patent Candle Co* (1876) 45 LJ Ch 437; *Hutton v West Cork Rly Co* (1883) 23 ChD 654; *Henderson v Bank of Australasia* (1888) 40 ChD 170; *Parke v Daily News Ltd* [1962] Ch 927, [1962] 2 All ER 929.
16 *Re Halt Garage Ltd* (supra).
17 See especially *Hutton v West Cork Rly Co* (supra).

to a company by its directors.[18] The company's employees have no direct right of enforcement.[19] In connection with the directors' duty to act in the best interests of the company, it should be noted that there is a major statutory exception to the general rule in that a company is empowered to make provision for employees and former employees when it closes or transfers the whole, or part, of its business and provision may also be made for employees and former employees of a subsidiary of the company where the whole or part of the subsidiary's business is closed or transferred,[20] and this power may be exercised even if the making of such provision is not in the best interests of the company.[1]

The making of provision for employees in accordance with this power must be sanctioned by ordinary resolution of the general meeting or (if the memorandum or articles so provide) by a resolution (such as a special resolution) requiring more than a simple majority of members voting.[2] However, if empowered to do so by the memorandum or articles, the board may sanction the making of provision for employees.[3] In addition, in any case where the company makes such provision, any conditions specified by the memorandum or articles with regard to its power to do so must be complied with.[4] Creditors of the company are protected; provision for employees may only be made out of profits of the company available for dividend.[5]

Where a company which has validly decided to make provision for its employees under the statutory power passes into liquidation before it is able to act on its decision, the provision may be made by the liquidator.[6] Furthermore, a company which is in liquidation may also make provision for employees if, after the company's liabilities have been met and the costs of the winding up provided for, the making of such provision is sanctioned by an ordinary resolution or (if the memorandum or articles so provide) by a resolution requiring more than a simple majority of members

---

18 CA 1985, s 309(2). It is uncertain whether a derivative action (see Chap 11) would lie for breach of this duty.
19 And, presumably, the general meeting could ratify any breach of ibid, s 309(1) committed by the directors in perfecting the interests of the members to those of the employees.
20 CA 1985, s 719(1) and (2).
1 Ibid, s 719(3).
2 Ibid.
3 Ibid, s 719(3)(b).
4 Ibid, s 719.
5 Ibid, s 719(4).
6 IA 1986, s 187.

voting.⁷ After the commencement of the winding up of the company, however, provision may only be made out of assets of the company available to members on its winding up⁸ and it is accordingly unlikely that a company in insolvent liquidation will be able to take advantage of the statutory power to provide for its employees.

DUTY TO EXERCISE POWERS FOR PROPER PURPOSES

The powers conferred upon directors may only be exercised for the benefit of the company, and must not be exercised for the directors' own benefit, or for that of any person other than the company.⁹ The directors may only exercise a power for the purpose for which that power has been given to them, although a subsidiary purpose, albeit improper, will not invalidate the exercise of the power, as long as the main purpose for which the power has been exercised is a proper one. When the directors' exercise of a power is challenged, the Court must ascertain the nature of the power and the limits within which it can be exercised. After doing so, the Court must identify and examine the substantial purpose for which the power was exercised and reach a conclusion as to whether that purpose was proper or not.¹⁰ If satisfied that the directors have acted improperly, the Court will set aside the exercise of the power.

Problems of this nature frequently arise in cases dealing with the improper allotment of shares. The power to allot shares is given to directors in order to enable them to raise money or to secure other advantages for the company. It is clear that the directors may not issue fresh shares to themselves simply in order to establish or maintain their own control. Such an issue may be set aside even though full value is paid for the shares.¹¹ Similarly, although the directors are entitled to exercise their powers even though their decision to do so runs contrary to the wishes of the majority of the shareholders, the directors are not entitled to use their powers to issue shares to change the balance of power within the company, by destroying an existing majority or by creating a majority which did not exist before. Absence of self-interest on the part of the directors

---

7   Ibid, s 187(2). Any other requirement applicable to the exercise by the company of its statutory power must also be met.
8   Ibid, s 187(3).
9   *Parke v Daily News Ltd* [1962] Ch 927, [1962] 2 All ER 929 (reserved on its facts by CA 1980, s 74).
10 *Howard Smith Ltd v Ampol Petroleum Ltd* [1974] AC 821, [1974] 1 All ER 1126.
11 *Punt v Symons* [1903] 2 Ch 506; *Piercy v S Mills & Co Ltd* [1920] 1 Ch 77.

will not suffice to validate the issue in such a case.[12] Furthermore, an issue of shares may not be made to a third party in order to forestall a take-over, even though the motives of the board were laudable.

Hogg v Cramphorn Ltd [1967] Ch 254, [1966] 3 All ER 420.

> Under the articles of the company the directors had power to issue unallotted shares. The directors, acting to forestall a take-over bid which they genuinely believed not to be in the best interests of the company, allotted 5,707 shares to trustees for the employees and purported to attach 10 votes to each share. Among the matters which the directors took into account in deciding that the take-over bid would be detrimental to the company was the unsettling effect the bid was having on employees, possible prejudice to customers, and a judgment that the existing board would be better for the company than one responsive to the take-over bidder. It was held, in part, that the allotment was voidable as against the company, but could be ratified by a majority of the members existing before the allotment was made.

An issue of shares which is made in excess of power is therefore voidable at the option of the company. A general meeting can ratify the improper actions of the directors in issuing the shares.[13] It will follow that in such a case, a third party who purchases shares from an allottee in good faith will obtain a valid title to them.[14]

SECRET PROFITS

The consequences of the fiduciary position of directors can be seen in connection with secret profits. The director must account to the company for any profits he may make by placing himself in a position where his personal interests conflict with his duty to the company.

A director is not entitled to keep profits which he makes by reason of opportunities acquired as a result of his position unless these profits are disclosed to and approved by the company.

---

12 *Howard Smith Ltd v Ampol Petroleum Ltd* [1974] AC 821, [1974] 1 All ER 1126. But see also *Harlowe's Nominees Pty Ltd v Woodside (Lakes Entrance) Oil Co* (1968) 42 ALJR 123 and *Macanie (London) Ltd v Cook and Watts* [1967] CLY 482 which make it clear that where an allotment serves a valid purpose, it will not be set aside simply because it had the incidental effect of blocking a take-over bid.
13 *Bamford v Bamford* [1970] Ch 212, [1969] 1 All ER 969, CA.
14 *Bamford v Bamford* [1970] Ch 212, [1969] 1 All ER 969, CA; *Harlowe's Nominees Pty Ltd v Woodside (Lakes Entrance) Oil Co* (1968) 42 ALJR 123.

Regal (Hastings) Ltd v Gulliver [1942] 1 All ER 378.

R was a company operating a cinema. It wished to acquire two other cinemas and then sell the property of the company as a going concern. It was decided that these cinemas should be purchased by a subsidiary company, H, in which R was to take 2,000 £1 shares, the balance of 3,000 to be taken by the directors and R's solicitors. This arrangement was made at board meetings of R and H which were held at the same time and place. Ultimately, it was decided not to sell the property of the company, but to sell the shares in R and H. The shares of the H company which the directors had purchased were issued at par, but on their sale a profit of £2 16 1d per share was made. The new controllers of the R company sought to recover this profit. The Court was satisfied that the transactions were bona fide but the directors were nevertheless ordered to account to the company for the profits made. Viscount Sankey stated at pp 381–382:

> In my view, the respondents were in a fiduciary position, and their liability to account does not depend on proof of *mala fides*. The general rule of equity is that no one who has duties of a fiduciary nature to perform is allowed to enter into engagements in which he has or can have a personal interest conflicting with the interests of those whom he is bound to protect. If he holds any property so acquired as trustee, he is bound to account for it ...
>
> At all material times, they were directors and in a fiduciary position, and they used and acted upon their exclusive knowledge acquired as such directors. They framed resolutions by which they made a profit for themselves. They sought no authority from the company to do so, and by reason of their position and actions, they made large profits for which, in my view, they are bound to account to the company.

Lord Russell of Killowen stated at p 389:

> ... I am of opinion that the directors standing in a fiduciary relationship to Regal in regard to the exercise of their powers as directors, and having obtained these shares by reason and only by reason of the fact that they were directors of Regal and in the course of the execution of their office, are accountable for the profits which they have made out of them.

It is necessary that the two elements mentioned by Lord Russell should co-exist before the company can recover the profits secured by the directors. There must be an acquisition of the property by reason of the office held and in the course of the execution of that office.[15]

Similarly, the director will be liable to disgorge in favour of the company any profits he has made by misappropriating an opportunity which it was his duty to acquire on behalf of the company.

---

15 See Lord Porter's speech at p 395.

Cook v Deeks [1916] 1 AC 554, PC.

> A railway company invited the T company, on the basis of its past good performance, to tender for a particular contract. Two of its directors who were at odds with the third diverted the contract to a new company which they had formed. They also procured a resolution of the T company ratifying their conduct. On an action brought by the plaintiff shareholder, the Privy Council held first, that the directors were in breach of duty, secondly that the benefit of the contract belonged in equity to the company and they were bound to account to the company for it, and thirdly that they could not use their voting power to expropriate the property of the company.

The directors will also be liable to account to the company where he has made profits by using information which has come to him whilst he is a director or which he has acquired in the course of his duties, and which is of concern to the company.

Industrial Development Consultants Ltd v Cooley [1972] 2 All ER 162, [1972] 1 WLR 443.

> IDC was engaged in the business of providing services, including architectural and project management services, to industrial concerns. C was appointed as managing director of IDC. Shortly after C's appointment, IDC attempted unsuccessfully to procure work from the Eastern Gas Board in relation to four depots which the Board wished to construct. The Board did not desire to place the work with IDC, but indicated to C that they would be prepared to engage him personally. C failed to inform IDC of his negotiations with the Board. Subsequently, C, by falsely representing that he was in poor health, induced IDC to agree to release him forthwith from his employment as managing director. Within a few days of the termination of his employment with IDC, C was engaged by the Board to execute work relating to the depots. This work was substantially similar to that which IDC desired to secure for itself. IDC sought to recover from C all profits due to him under his contract with the Board.
>
> Roskill J held inter alia (i) that C was in breach of his fiduciary duty to IDC in failing to pass to IDC all the relevant information received in the course of his dealings with the Board and (ii) that because of his breach of duty he was liable to account to IDC for all the profits he had received or would receive under his contract with the Board.

However, it should be noted that the director is liable to account for any profits he has made by use of such information not only in cases where the company is ignorant of the content of the

Duties of Loyalty and Good Faith 199

information, but also in cases where it has become apprised of the information (through the director or otherwise).[16]

A difficult question arises whether, when information has first come to a director in the course of his duty, he can in any circumstances utilise that information in order to make an undisclosed profit. It has been suggested in Canada that where an offer, made to a company, is bona fide rejected by the board as an investment which the company should not make, a director may thereafter, at least if subsequently approached personally by the offeror, make use of the opportunity and retain any profit so made without making disclosure to the company.[17] This result has been justified on the footing that the director does not, in such circumstances, make the profit by reason of his personal position or by the use of confidential information. It is doubtful whether an English Court would reach the same conclusion. The rejection of the opportunity by the company does not wholly deny any possibility of a conflict of duty and interest. The decision to reject the opportunity deprives the company of the benefit of it and, at the same time, may be a circumstance facilitating its exploitation by a director for private profit. Historically, English courts have refused to extend their inquiry further than to ask the question whether the situation presented a possible conflict of duty and interest. For this purpose, the possibility of conflict need only be a slight one.[18]

A director otherwise liable to account for profits made in breach of his fiduciary duty cannot escape liability by proving that the company could not, in any event, have reaped the benefit which he has obtained. It is no defence to the company's claim if the director shows, for example, that the company possessed insufficient funds to take advantage of the opportunity which has resulted in the receipt of profits by the director.[19] Such matters do not excuse the director or otherwise relieve him of the liability to account.

In some cases the courts will go further than simply imposing a duty to account and will impose a trust upon property acquired by a director.[20] It is difficult to determine when a Court will impose such

---

16 *Industrial Development Consultants Ltd v Cooley* [1972] 2 All ER 162, [1972] 1 WLR 443; *Canadian Aero Service Ltd v O'Malley* (1974) 40 DLR (3d) 371. The former is noted by Collier in [1972A] CLJ 222 and Rajak in (1972) 35 Mod LR 655 and the latter by Prentice in (1974) 37 Mod LR 464.
17 *Peso-Silver Mines Ltd v Cropper* (1966) 58 DLR (2d) 1 (SC), noted by Prentice in (1967) 30 Mod LR 450.
18 *Boardman v Phipps* [1967] 2 AC 46, [1966] 3 All ER 721.
19 *Regal (Hastings) Ltd v Gulliver* [1942] 1 All ER 378; *Industrial Development Consultants v Cooley* [1972] 2 All ER 162, [1972] 1 WLR 443.
20 See, eg *Cook v Deeks* [1916] 1 AC 554, PC.

a trust. It may be possible to assert that a trust will only be imposed where the director, being under a duty to acquire property or an opportunity for his company, wrongly diverts the property or opportunity to himself. This was certainly the case in *Cook v Deeks*[1] whereas in *Regal (Hastings) Ltd v Gulliver*[2] the directors were under no obligation to acquire the cinemas for the company. This argument cannot be reconciled with *Boardman v Phipps*[3] where such a trust was imposed upon a fiduciary in spite of the fact that the fiduciary was under no obligation to deal on the trust's behalf in certain shares. As a result of such dealings he obtained a considerable benefit from a personal acquisition of shares and was held to hold them on trust for the beneficiary. It may be that the rules apply less harshly in the field of company law than in the law of trusts generally.[4]

It should be noted that where a director makes a secret profit he may keep the benefit provided that he discloses the transaction either before or after he embarks on it, and obtains the approval of the shareholders.[5]

However, in such a case, the directors cannot use their voting power to ratify the transaction against the wishes of the dissentient minority shareholders.[6]

A director's duties may continue to bind him, even after he has ceased to hold office. This will be so where the director has during his term of office committed acts amounting to breach of duty and either (i) resigns or secures his release in order to reap the benefit of his breach of duty,[7] or (ii) after his resignation or release, commits similar acts which, if he were still a director, would amount to a breach of duty on his part.[8] In either case, the former director will be held to be in breach of fiduciary duty and liable to account to the company for any profits made by reason thereof, even if those profits arise after the termination of the directorship.[9]

1 [1916] 1 AC 554.
2 [1942] 1 All ER 378.
3 [1967] 2 AC 46, [1966] 3 All ER 721.
4 A Court might in this respect be disposed to rely on the statement of Romer J in *Re City Equitable Fire Insurance Co Ltd* [1925] Ch 407 at 426 that while directors are fiduciaries, their duties cannot be described by analogy to the duties of trustees.
5 *Regal (Hastings) Ltd v Gulliver* [1942] 1 All ER 378, p 389 per Lord Russell.
6 *Cook v Deeks* [1916] 1 AC 554, PC.
7 *Industrial Development Consultants Ltd v Cooley* [1972] 2 All ER 162, [1972] 1 WLR 443.
8 *Thomas Marshall (Exporters) v Guinle* [1979] Ch 227, [1978] 3 All ER 193.
9 *Industrial Development Consultants Ltd v Cooley* (supra).

COMPETING DIRECTORATES

One curious exception to the rigid rules governing the duties of fiduciaries is that, in the absence of a provision to the contrary in his contract or in the articles, a director may accept a directorship in another company which is in direct competition with his own. He may not, however, use any confidential information which he obtains as the result of his office in the one company for the benefit of the other company unless the former company agrees to this.[10] In the nationalised industries, by contrast, competing directorships are usually forbidden by the applicable statutes.[11]

NOMINEE DIRECTORS

Nothing precludes the election to the board directors who are essentially nominated in order to further the particular interests of a person or group having an interest in the company. Such a person or group may, for example, have lent money to the company and may seek representation on the board in order better to protect his or its interests. Again, where a company becomes a subsidiary of another, whether partly or wholly-owned, the parent will wish to be represented on and indeed control the board. Whilst the practice of having nominee directors on boards is well established, the rules regulating their conduct have not been fully worked out.

Whether, and if so the extent to which the nominee director is entitled to regard himself as owing duties primarily to those whom he represents rather than to the company, is unclear. The nominee may not use his position in order to perpetrate a fraud on the company.[12] On the other hand it can be argued that the shareholders, by accepting as a director a person whom they knew to be the nominee of another interest, intend to waive, in some measure, the rigour of the fiduciary duties which would otherwise be imposed on the director and enure to the benefit of the company. This

---

10 *London and Mashonaland Exploration Co Ltd v New Mashonaland Exploration Co Ltd* [1891] WN 165, approved by Lord Blanesburg in *Bell v Lever Bros Ltd* [1932] AC 161. See also *Hivac v Park Royal Scientific Instruments Ltd* [1946] Ch 169, [1946] 1 All ER 350, which illustrates that the rules governing employees and, presumably, directors with service contracts such as managing directors, are much stricter.
11 Eg now repealed Air Corporations Act 1967, Sch 1, para 6A (added by Air Corporations Act 1969, s 4 and Sch 2).
12 *Selangor United Rubber Estates Ltd v Cradock (No 3)* [1968] 2 All ER 1073, [1968] 1 WLR 1555.

solution has been hinted at in England[13] and actively asserted in *dicta* in Australia.[14] The Australian cases suggest on this basis that a nominee director may have regard, explicitly, to the interests of his principal, in taking decisions as a director of the company. On the other hand, the directors must address their minds to the question whether the proposed transaction is positively detrimental to the company, and, if it is, oppose their principal's wishes. It has been pointed out that this test does not resolve all the difficulties:[15]

> It would not solve the nominee director's dilemma in the event of a major conflict of interest between the holding company and the subsidiary over such issues, for example, as whether the subsidiary should be allowed to export its products to the detriment of the parent's international organisation. On the other hand it would allow him to act without pretence in relying upon the holding company's instructions in the ordinary course of affairs.

Nor, at all events, is it necessary to go so far as to agree that the members, by agreeing to the election of nominee directors, waive the company's right to require the director to have regard to the best interests of the company. It is not necessary to regard them as estopped from complaining if the nominee director in taking a decision has regard only to the interests of his principal. The implied agreement, if such there be, may in some cases amount to no more than by allowing the principal to choose a director, to give him an additional forum in which to express his interests. There are intermediate positions on the one hand requiring a nominee director to have regard to the interests of the company on whose board he is, and on the other, permitting him to consider the interests of his principal exclusively.

The English cases establish that a nominee director in a group situation must consider the interests of his own company. He may, in deciding upon a course of action, have regard to the interests of the group as a whole.[16] It would seem that in a case of conflict between the interests of his company and the group, the nominee

---

13 *Lindgren v L and P Estates Ltd* [1968] Ch 572, at 594 per Harman LJ.
14 *Levin v Clark* [1962] NSWR 686, 700–701 per Jacobs J; *Re Broadcasting Station of GB Pty Ltd* [1964–1965] NSWR 1648.
15 A.B. Afterman, 'Directors' Duties in Joint-Venture and Parent Subsidiary Companies' (1968) 42 ALJ 168, at p 169. It is doubtful whether the articles could wholly absolve nominee directors of their obligation to have regard to the interests of their company. See CA 1985, s 310.
16 *Charterbridge Corpn Ltd v Lloyds Bank* [1970] Ch 62, [1969] 2 All ER 1185; *Lindgren v L and P Estates Ltd* [1968] Ch 572, [1968] 1 All ER 917.

director must protect the legitimate interests of his company. He may not sacrifice the interests of his company to those of his principal, especially where the rights of minority shareholders are concerned.[17] The director of a parent company seems not to be under any fiduciary duty towards a subsidiary, at least where the subsidiary has an independent board.[18] In effect, this seems to mean that while a director of a company in a group can have regard to the interests of the group or the parent when taking decisions, the director owes no fiduciary duties to any other member of the group.[19]

CONTRACTS WITH THE COMPANY

The effect of contracts made by a director with a company of which he is director presents considerable difficulty. At common law, and in the absence of a liberating provision in the articles, a director could not safely contract with his company unless a general meeting, after full disclosure, approved the contract.[20] The director could use his voting power to cause the company to ratify or adopt the contract, provided that to do so was not fraudulent or oppressive to the members.[1] Where the articles of association required that a director before contracting with the company should declare his interests, the nature of the interest and not a mere declaration that the director was interested was required.[2]

In time, the requirement that full disclosure be made to a general meeting was thought by directors to be unduly onerous. As a result, exemption clauses were commonly resorted to in the articles which provided for disclosure to a meeting of the directors. The matter is now regulated by s 317 of the Companies Act 1985 as amended, to which art 85 of Table A responds.

A director who is directly or indirectly interested in a contract or proposed contract, or any transaction or arrangement (whether or

---

17 *Scottish Co-operative Wholesale Society Ltd v Meyer* [1959] AC 324, [1958] 3 All ER 66.
18 *Lindgren v L and P Estates Ltd* [1968] Ch 572, [1968] 1 All ER 917.
19 The group analysis is much more explicitly recognised in s 323 of the CA 1985, preventing dealings by directors in options to buy and sell listed securities of the director's company or group. See also CA 1985, ss 232, 319–322, 330.
20 *Transvaal Lands Co v New Belgium (Transvaal) Land and Development Co* [1914] 2 Ch 488.
1 *North-West Transportation Co Ltd v Beatty* (1887) 12 App Cas 589. For an example of fraud and oppression, see *Mason v Harris* (1879) 11 ChD 97.
2 *Imperial Mercantile Credit Association v Coleman* (1873) LR 6 HL 189.

not constituting a contract) with the company is under a duty to declare the nature of his interest at a meeting of the directors.[3] For the purposes of s 317, a transaction or arrangement of a kind described in the Companies Act 1985, s 330[4] made by a company for a director of the company or a person connected with such a director is treated as a transaction or arrangement in which the director in question is interested.[5]

Section 317(2) requires that the declaration be made at the meeting of the directors when the question of entering into a contract (or transaction or arrangement) is first taken into consideration, or if the director was not then so interested, at the first meeting after he becomes so interested. This is a substitute for disclosure to the general meeting.

Section 317(3)[6] provides that a general notice given to the directors by a director to the effect that

(1) he is a member of a specified company or firm and is to be regarded as interested in any contract which may, after the date of the notice, be made with that company or firm; or
(2) he is to be regarded as interested in any contract which may after the date of the notice be made with a specified person who is connected with him (within the meaning of CA 1985, s 346)

shall be deemed to be a sufficient declaration of interest in relation to any such contract. Section 317(3) (in common with the remainder of s 317) applies to any transaction or arrangement, whether or not constituting a contract.[7]

Section 317 applies with equal force to a shadow director.[8] However, a shadow director must declare his interest not at a director's meeting, but by a written notice to the company's directors. The shadow director's notice must either be a specific notice given before the date of the directors' meeting at which, if he had been a director, he would have been required to make a declaration in accordance with s 317(2), or a general notice under s 317(3). The

---

3 CA 1985, s 317.
4 See Chap 8.
5 Ibid, s 317(6).
6 For 'connected person', see s 346.
7 Ibid, s 317(7), provides criminal penalties for breach of the section but does not thereby render a contract entered into in breach of its provisions a nullity: *Victors Ltd v Lingard* [1927] 1 Ch 323.
8 See Chap 8.

shadow director's notice must be recorded in the minutes of a directors' meeting.[9]

The provisions of s 317 are further reinforced by:

(1) CA 1985, s 318, requiring that a copy of a director's contract of service with the company of which he is a director or with a subsidiary of that company be kept at the registered office of the company, or the place where the register of members is kept, or its principal place of business;[10]
(2) CA 1985, s 232 and Sch 6, requiring the directors to disclose in notes to the accounts of a company transactions or arrangements with the company in which a director of the company or of its holding company has a material interest and in the group accounts of a holding company transactions or arrangements with the company or with any of its subsidiaries in which a director of the company has such an interest.

If articles in the form of Table A are employed, a director will be permitted to contract with the company provided that he makes disclosure complying with s 317. Subject to certain exceptions relating to contracts indemnifying a director against loss in connection with obligations assumed by him in favour of the company, or to underwrite securities of the company, a director may not vote in respect of any contract in which he is interested, nor shall he be counted towards a quorum at the director's meeting at which such contract is considered.[11]

A contract which has been entered into by the company and in respect of which a director's interest has not been disclosed is not a nullity. It is, however, voidable at the option of the company.[12] Disclosure, to validate the contract, must not simply be of the director's interest. The nature of that interest must be specified, and if the contract is later impeached, it is incumbent upon the director to show that full and adequate disclosure was made. As Lord Radcliffe stated in *Gray v New Augarita Porcupine Mines Ltd* [1952] 3 DLR 1, PC:

> There is no precise formula that will determine the extent of detail that is called for when a director declares his interest or the nature of his

---

9 Ibid, s 317(8).
10 A shadow director is treated as a director: ibid, s 318(6). Accordingly, a shadow director's service contract must be available for inspection.
11 Table A, art 85.
12 *Hely-Hutchinson v Brayhead Ltd* [1968] 1 QB 549, [1967] 3 All ER 98.

interest . . . If it is material to their (the directors') judgment that they should know not merely that he has an interest, but what it is and how far it goes, then he must see to it that they are informed.

SECRET BENEFITS

The rule relating to the taking of secret benefits by a director is the same as that which is applied to all other fiduciaries. A director who takes a bribe or a concealed benefit is liable to account therefor. In *Boston Deep Sea Fishing and Ice Co v Ansell,* Bowen LJ states:[13]

> There can be no question that an agent employed by a principal or master to do business with another, who, unknown to that principal or master, takes from that other person a profit arising out of the business which he is employed to transact, is doing a wrongful act inconsistent with his duty towards his master, and the continuance of confidence between them . . . if it is a profit which arises out of the transaction, it belongs to his master, and the agent or servant has no right to take it, or keep it, or bargain for it, or receive it without bargain, unless his master knows it.

A director who has placed himself in this position must therefore account for any secret profit which he has made.

DIRECTORS' CONTRACTS OF EMPLOYMENT AND SUBSTANTIAL PROPERTY TRANSACTIONS WITH DIRECTORS

Two types of contract between companies and their directors and directors of their holding companies are afforded special treatment by the Companies Act 1985. These are (i) directors' contracts of employment and (ii) substantial property transactions involving directors.

DIRECTORS' CONTRACTS OF EMPLOYMENT

Without the prior approval of its general meeting, a company may not incorporate in any agreement a term which provides:

---

13 (1888) 39 ChD 339; on the remedies available, see *Mahesan s/o Thambiah v Malaysian Government Officers' Co-operative Housing Society Ltd* [1979] AC 374, [1978] 2 All ER 405.

(1) that a director's employment[14] with the company of which he is the director or, if he is the director of a holding company, his employment within the group[15] is to continue, or may be continued, otherwise than at the instance of the company (whether under the original agreement or under a new agreement entered into in pursuance of the original agreement) for a period exceeding five years; and
(2) that during the period for which the director is employed, the company cannot terminate the employment by notice, or can only terminate it by notice in specified circumstances.[16]

The application of these provisions is not avoided if the director enters into a series of contracts of employment (under which the company has no or only a restricted right of termination) of less than five years' duration. Special provisions apply where a person is or is to be employed with a company under an agreement which cannot be terminated by the company by notice or can be so terminated only in specified circumstances, and more than six months before the expiration of the period for which he is or is to be so employed, the company enters into a further agreement[17] under which he is to be employed with the company (or, where he is a director of a holding company, within the group). In such a case, a period equal to the unexpired period of the original agreement is added to the period for which the director is to be employed under the further agreement and, if the total of these periods exceeds five years, prior approval of the company's general meeting is required if the further agreement provides that the director's employment cannot be terminated by the company by notice or can be so terminated only in specified circumstances.[18]

A term falling within the ambit of s 319 may, as indicated, be incorporated by a company in any agreement, provided that the term has first been approved by resolution of the company's general meeting. In the case of the employment of a director of a holding

---

14 For the purposes of CA 1985, s 319 the term 'employment' includes employment under a contract for services: ibid, s 319(7)(a) and see further Joffe, *The Companies Act 1980*, paras 9.103, 10.501.
15 In relation to the director of a holding company, the term 'group' means the holding company and its subsidiaries: CA 1985, s 317(7)(b).
16 CA 1985, s 319(1) and (2).
17 These provisions are inapplicable where the further agreement is entered into by the company pursuant to a right conferred on the other party by the original agreement: ibid, s 319(1)(b). Such a case would in any event fall within ibid, s 319(1).
18 Ibid, s 319(2).

company within the group, the term in question must also first be approved by resolution of the holding company in general meeting.[19] A resolution approving such a term may not be passed at a general meeting of a holding or any other company unless a written memorandum setting out the proposed agreement (incorporating the term in question) is available for inspection by members of the company both at the company's registered office for a period of at least 15 days immediately preceding the meeting, and at the meeting itself.[20]

A term incorporated into an agreement in contravention of these provisions is void to the extent of the contravention.[1] However, the agreement is otherwise unaffected and its remaining express or implied terms continue in force and bind the contracting parties. If an agreement does incorporate a term which is avoided by reason of such a contravention, the agreement (and, where CA 1985, s 319(2) applies, the original agreement) is deemed to contain a term enabling the company to terminate it at any time by reasonable notice.[2]

SUBSTANTIAL PROPERTY TRANSACTIONS

The provisions of CA 1985, s 320 protect companies in two types of case. These provisions apply to arrangements[3] whereby:

(1) a director of the company or of its holding company or a person connected with such a director is to acquire one or more non-cash assets of the 'requisite value' from the company; or
(2) the company acquires one or more non-cash assets of the 'requisite value' from such a director or connected person.[4]

A non-cash asset[5] is of the requisite value if its value at the time

---

19 Ibid, s 319(1). No approval is required where the contract is between a director and a wholly-owned subsidiary of a holding company, ibid, s 319(4).
20 Ibid, s 319(5).
1 Ibid, s 319(6).
2 Ibid, s 319(6).
3 A term wider than 'contract'. Section 322 draws a distinction between 'arrangements' whereby it is agreed that a result shall be brought about, and 'transactions' whereby the result is actually brought about. For an example (in the context of the now repealed CA 1948, s 54) of the distinction between an arrangement and a transaction, see *Belmont Finance Corpn v Williams Furniture Ltd (No 2)* [1980] 1 All ER 393.
4 CA 1985, s 320(1).
5 Any property or proprietary interest other than cash: CA 1985, s 739.

the arrangement is entered into exceeds either £50,000, or 10% of the amount of the company's net assets as determined by reference to the most recent accounts prepared and laid by the company.[6]

A company is prohibited from entering into any such arrangement unless the arrangement in question is first approved by a resolution of the company in general meeting.[7] In the case of a proposed arrangement with a director of the company's holding company or a person connected with such a director, prior approval for the arrangement must also be secured by a resolution of the holding company in general meeting.[8]

An arrangement entered into by a company in contravention of these provisions is voidable at the instance of the company (although not, apparently, at the instance of the other party), as is any transaction entered into pursuant to the arrangement.[9] It is important to note that, provided that the company is a party to the arrangement in question, such a transaction may be avoided at the company's instance, whether or not the company is a party to the transaction itself.[10] However, in four sets of circumstances, the company loses its right to avoid arrangements contravening s 320 and transactions entered into in pursuance of such arrangements.

The company's right of avoidance is lost when:

(1) restitution of any money or any other asset which is the subject matter of the arrangement or transaction is no longer possible;
(2) the company has been indemnified pursuant to s 322 by any other person for the loss or damage which it has suffered;[11]
(3) any right acquired bona fide for value and without actual notice of the contravention by any person who is not a party

---

6 CA 1985, s 320(2). Where no accounts have been prepared and laid under CA 1985, s 227, a non-cash asset is of the requisite value if its value exceeds either £50,000 or 10% of the amount of a company's called-up share capital. Note also that a non-cash asset can only be of the requisite value if its value is not less than £1,000: ibid.
7 Ibid, s 320(1).
8 Ibid. No approval is required where the arrangement is between a director or connected person and a wholly-owned subsidiary of a holding company: ibid, s 321.
9 Ibid, s 322(1).
10 Ibid.
11 Ibid, (a) refers to the company losing its right of avoidance where the company 'or the person nominated by it' has been indemnified. These words were apparently overlooked when the subsection was redrafted during the passage of the Companies Bill 1980 through Parliament, from whence the present provision derives, and are virtually incapable of any rational interpretation.

to the arrangement or transaction would be affected by its avoidance; or

(4) the arrangement is affirmed by the company in general meeting within a reasonable period. Where the arrangement is for the transfer of an asset to or by a director of the company's holding company or a person who is connected with such a director, the company's right of avoidance is only lost by affirmation if the company affirms with the approval of the holding company given by a resolution in general meeting.[12]

In addition to its right to avoid the arrangement or transaction, a company enjoys specific monetary remedies where the provisions of s 320 have been contravened. The section provides that where the company has entered into an arrangement with a director of the company or of its holding company or a person connected with such a director in contravention of those provisions, the director in question, the connected person and any other director of the company who authorised the arrangement or any transaction entered into in pursuance of the arrangement are each liable to account to the company for any gain made directly or indirectly by the arrangement or transaction. Furthermore, any person liable under this provision is liable jointly and severally with any other person liable under the subsection to indemnify the company for any loss or damage resulting from the arrangement or transaction.[13] A company is entitled to exercise these monetary remedies whether or not the arrangement or transaction has been avoided.[14] The formalities required by s 320 are not required in order to validate the transaction where a non-cash asset is to be acquired by a holding company from any of its wholly-owned subsidiaries, or by one wholly-owned subsidiary from another such subsidiary in the same group, or if the arrangement is entered into by a company which is being wound up, unless the winding up is a members' voluntary winding up.[15] In the former case, there is no conflict of interest between the various parties; in the latter the winding up procedure is subject to a declaration of solvency. Similarly, no such formalities are required where there is an arrangement by which a person is to acquire an asset from a company of which he is a member if the arrangement is made with that person in his character as a member.[16] This latter

12 Ibid, s 322(2).
13 Ibid, s 322(3)(b).
14 Ibid, s 322(9).
15 Ibid, s 321(2).
16 Ibid, s 321(3).

exception is intended to cover, for example, distribution *in specie* or bonus issues but it would not it is thought enable a director/member to claim exemption from s 320 merely on the grounds that he was a member of the company. It would seem that the burden of proving that the arrangement comes within s 321(2) falls on the member alleging that such is the case.

Where the company enters with a person connected with a director of the company or of its holding company into an arrangement contravening s 320, the director will not be liable to account to the company or indemnify it if he can show that he took all reasonable steps to secure the company's compliance with the section.[17] It should also be noted that a person connected with a director of the company or of its holding company, and any director of the company who authorised the arrangement or transaction (other than the director with whom or with whose connected person it was made) may escape liability if he can show that, at the time the arrangement was entered into, he did not know the circumstances constituting the contravention.[18]

OPTION DEALINGS

The Companies Act 1985[19] prohibits purchase and sale of options in the listed securities of the director's company or group. This prohibition is intended to further the interests of fairness by denying to directors an opportunity to use inside information which the ordinary members do not possess. It can also be justified as a means of preventing insiders from manipulating the stockmarkets.[20] The primary aim of this section is to protect members and not the company. In this respect it is, like certain provisions of the Company Securities (Insider Dealing) Act 1985, a departure from the rule in *Percival v Wright* (supra).

INSIDER DEALING

An 'insider dealer' is a person who has, by reason of his connection with a company, acquired in confidence a particular piece of information materially affecting the value of the securities of the

---

17 Ibid, s 322(5).
18 Ibid.
19 Ibid, s 323.
20 Loss, *Securities Regulation* (1961) Vol I p 486.

company (or any company in the same group) and who buys or sells such securities without disclosing that piece of information.[1]

Prohibitions on insider dealing are imposed by the Company Securities (Insider Dealing) Act 1985 (hereinafter ID 1985). However, these prohibitions do not apply to companies, and are expressed to be applicable to 'individuals' only. Nevertheless, an individual is treated as dealing in securities for the purposes of ID 1985, ss 1, 2, and 4 whether he deals as principal or agent.[2] It follows that although a company cannot contravene the provisions of those sections, an individual connected with the company who deals in securities on its behalf is capable of such contravention, even though he has no personal interest in the transaction in question.

The prohibitions in ID 1985 against insider dealing are stated by reference to the use or possession of 'unpublished price sensitive information', that is, information which

(1) relates to specific matters relating or of concern (directly or indirectly) to the company in question, that is to say, is not of a general nature relating or of concern to that company; and
(2) is not generally known to those persons who are accustomed or who would be likely to deal in the securities to which the information relates, but which would, if it were generally known to them, be likely materially to affect the price of those securities.[3]

Unfortunately, the Act does not lay down any test for determining whether a particular piece of information relates to 'specific matters' concerning the company, or whether it is merely of a 'general nature' relating or of concern to the company. The categorisation of particular pieces of information is therefore a question of fact to be determined in each individual case.

Sections 1 and 2 apply primarily to the dealing in securities on a 'recognised stock exchange'.[4] However, those sections are also applicable to dealing in securities through an investment exchange.[5] An investment exchange is an organisation maintaining a system whereby an offer to deal in securities made by a subscriber to the organisation is communicated, without his identity being revealed,

---

1 Report of the Company Law Committee, Cmnd 1749, para 89.
2 ID 1985, s 13(1).
3 Ibid, s 10.
4 The only stock exchange currently so recognised is the Stock Exchange.
5 Ibid, s 13(1).

to other subscribers to the organisation, and whereby any acceptance of the offer by any such subscriber is recorded and confirmed.[6] Prohibitions on 'off-market' dealing are imposed by ss 4 and 5.[7]

Section 1 deals with the position of individuals who are 'knowingly connected' with a company. An individual is connected with a company for these purposes only if:

(1) he is a director of the company in question or a related company (that is, a subsidiary or holding company of the company in question, or a company in the same group as the latter[8]); or
(2) he occupies a position
   (a) as an officer (other than director) or employee of the company or a related company; or
   (b) involving a professional or business relationship between him and the company in question or a related company. The position must be reasonably expected to give him access to unpublished price sensitive information in relation to securities of either company, which it would be reasonable to expect him not to disclose except for the proper performance of his functions.[9]

In accordance with this definition, a company's secretary or its auditors, for example, would, on the basis that they would reasonably be expected to have access to unpublished price sensitive information relating to the company's securities, be connected with the company.

An individual who is (or who at any time in the preceding six months has been) knowingly connected with a company may not deal in securities[10] of that company if he has information which:

(1) he holds by virtue of being connected with the company;
(2) it would be reasonable to expect a person so connected and in the position by virtue of which he is so connected not to disclose except for the proper performance of the functions attaching to that position; and

---

6 Ibid, s 13(2).
7 See infra.
8 Ibid, s 11.
9 Ibid, s 9. This definition of 'connected' differs substantially from the definition of 'connected' in CA 1985, s 346 and Sch 13.
10 'Securities' means both securities of the company listed on the Stock Exchange and (even if not listed) shares, debentures and any right to subscribe for, call for or make a delivery of a share or debenture: ID 1985, s 12.

(3) he knows is unpublished price sensitive information in relation to those securities.[11]

In addition such an individual may not deal in the securities of any other company if he has information which satisfies conditions (1) and (2) above, and which

(4) he knows is unpublished price sensitive information in relation to the securities of the other company; and
(5) relates to any transaction (actual or contemplated) involving both the company with which he is connected and the other company, or involving one of them and the securities of the other, or to the fact that any such transaction is no longer contemplated.[12]

ID 1985 also prevents individuals who receive unpublished price sensitive information from dealing in securities to which that information relates. Where an individual obtains information (either directly or indirectly) from another individual who is or was, at any time within the period of six months preceding the obtaining of the information, connected with a particular company, and where the recipient of the information either knows or has reasonable cause to believe that:

(1) the individual connected with the company in question held that information by virtue of being so connected; and
(2) because of the latter's position, it would be reasonable to expect him not to disclose the information except for the proper performance of the functions attaching to his position,

the recipient of the information may not himself deal in securities of that company, if he knows that the information is unpublished price sensitive information in relation to those securities.[13] Furthermore, he may not deal in securities of any other company, if he knows that the information is unpublished price sensitive information in relation to those securities, and that it relates to any transaction (actual or contemplated) involving the company with which the individual providing the information is connected and the other company, or

---

11 ID 1985, s 1(1).
12 Ibid, s 1(2).
13 Ibid, s 1(3).

involving one of them in the securities of the other, or to the fact that any such transaction is no longer contemplated.[14]

An individual contemplating a take-over offer for a company in one capacity (for example, as trustee of a trust) may not deal in securities of that company in any other capacity (for example, for himself personally) if he knows that information that the offer is contemplated or no longer contemplated is unpublished price sensitive information in relation to those securities.[15] If such an individual communicates (directly or indirectly) to another individual information that such a take-over offer is being or is no longer contemplated, the recipient of the information is prohibited from dealing in the securities of the company, if he knows that the information is unpublished price sensitive information in relation to those securities.[16]

Any individual who is prohibited from dealing in the securities of a company may not counsel or procure any other person to deal in the securities in question if he knows or has reasonable cause to believe that the latter would deal in those securities.[17] In addition, if the individual is prohibited from dealing by reason of the fact that he holds information, he may not communicate that information if he knows or has reasonable cause to believe that some other person will make use of the information for the purpose of dealing, or counselling or procuring any other person to deal, in the securities in question.[18]

Similar prohibitions are also imposed on a public servant[19] who holds unpublished price sensitive information in relation to the securities of a particular company which it would be reasonable to expect him not to disclose except for the proper performance of his functions, and also on an individual who knowingly obtains such information from a public servant, knowing or believing the public servant to hold information in question by virtue of his position.[20]

---

14 Ibid.
15 Ibid, s 1(4).
16 Ibid, s 1(6).
17 Ibid, s 1(7).
18 Ibid, s 1(8).
19 An individual who holds office under, or who is employed by, the Crown, and a member, officer or servant of a designated agency, competent authority or transferee within the meaning of the Financial Services Act 1986, an officer or servant of a self-regulating organisation, recognised investment exchange or recognised clearing house, or a person declared by order to be a public servant for the purposes of that Act: ID 1985, s 2(4); the list may be extended by statutory instrument.
20 Ibid, s 2(1) and (2).

These prohibitions prevent the public servant or recipient of the information from:

(1) dealing in securities of the company in question;
(2) counselling or procuring any other person to deal in such securities, knowing or having reasonable cause to believe that the other person would deal therein; and
(3) communicating to any other person the information held or obtained, if he knows or has reasonable cause to believe that that person or any other person, will use the information for the purpose of dealing, or counselling or procuring any other person to deal, in those securities.[1]

There are a number of exceptions to s 1:

(1) an individual may deal in securities where he does not do so with a view to the making of a profit or the avoidance of a loss, whether for himself or for another (for example, where he is obliged to sell securities in order to repay a debt which has fallen due).[2] A trustee or personal representative who would otherwise be prevented from dealing in securities or from counselling or procuring any other person to deal in securities is, if he deals in those securities or counsels or procures any other person to deal in them, presumed to have acted otherwise than with a view to the making of a profit or the avoidance of a loss provided that he acts on the advice of a person who appears to him to be an appropriate person from whom to seek such advice, and who did not appear to him to be prohibited by s 1 from dealing in the securities in question;[3]
(2) an individual may enter into a transaction in the course of the exercise in good faith of his functions as liquidator, receiver of trustee in bankruptcy;[4]
(3) an individual is not precluded from doing any particular thing in relation to any particular securities if he obtained the information in the course of his business as a market maker in those securities in which he was engaged or employed, and it was of a description which it would be reasonable to expect him to obtain in the ordinary course of his business, and he

---

1 Ibid, s 2(3).
2 Ibid, s 3(1)(a).
3 Ibid, s 7.
4 Ibid, s 3(1)(b).

acts in good faith in the course of that business.⁵ The definition of market maker is technical, but the essence of it is that the person holds himself out in compliance with the rules of a recognised stock exchange as willing at all normal times to buy and sell securities at a price specified by him;⁶

(4) an individual who holds information relating to a particular transaction may do anything necessary solely to facilitate the completion or carrying out the transaction;⁷

(5) off-market dealings in advertised securities and off-market dealings abroad are not prohibited by s 1 of the ID 1985 if the dealing is done by or on behalf of a person who is an authorised person in respect of that dealing under the Financial Services Act 1986.⁸ He must act in conformity with rules made under the Financial Services Act 1986.⁹

By virtue of s 4, the provisions of ss 1 to 3 prevent an individual from dealing in the advertised securities[10] of any company:

(1) through an off-market dealer who is making a market[11] in the securities in question, in the knowledge that:
  (a) he is an off-market dealer;
  (b) he is making a market in those securities; and
  (c) the securities are advertised securities; or
(2) as an off-market dealer who is making a market in those securities or as an officer, employee or agent of an off-market dealer acting in the ordinary course of the dealer's business.

Furthermore, the provision of ss 1 and 2 prohibit an individual from:

---

5 Ibid, s 3(1)(c).
6 Ibid.
7 Ibid, s 3(2); a similar exception applies to s 2.
8 Ibid, s 6.
9 Ibid, s 6(b).
10 Listed securities or securities in respect of which not more than six months before the transaction in question information indicating the prices at which persons have dealt, or were willing to deal, in those securities have been published for the purpose of facilitating deals in those securities: ibid, s 12(c).
11 An off-market dealer makes a market in securities if in the course of his business as an off-market dealer he holds himself out to both prospective buyers and to prospective sellers of those securities (other than particular buyers or sellers) as willing to deal in them otherwise than on a recognised stock exchange: ibid, s 13(4).

(1) counselling or procuring any person to deal in advertised securities in the knoweldge or with reasonable cause to believe that he will deal in them in a manner prohibited by s 4; and
(2) communicating any information in the knowledge or with reasonable cause to believe that it will be used for such dealing or counselling or procuring.[12]

An 'off-market dealer' is a person who is an authorised person under the Financial Services Act 1986.[13]

An individual is taken to deal in advertised securities *as* an off-market dealer if he deals in such securities or acts as an intermediary in connection with deals made by other persons in such securities.[14] Conversely, an individual is taken to be dealing *through* an off-market dealer if the off-market dealer is:

(1) a party to the transaction in question; or
(2) an agent for either party to that transaction; or
(3) acting as an intermediary in connection with the transaction.[15]

The insider dealing provisions of the ID 1985 also apply to foreign stock exchanges. An individual prohibited by ss 1 and 2 from dealing in securities because he holds any information may not:

(1) counsel or procure any other person to deal in the knowledge or with reasonable cause to believe that the other person will deal in the securities in question outside Great Britain on any stock exchange;
(2) communicate the information which he holds to any other person in the knowledge or with reasonable cause to believe that the other person (or some third party) will make use of the information for the purpose of dealing, or counselling or procuring any other person to deal, in the securities in question outside Great Britain on any stock exchange.[16]

---

12 Ibid, s 4(c).
13 No account can be given here of this aspect of the Financial Services Act 1986; see for a fuller account A. Wedgwood, G. Pell, L.H. Leigh and C. Ryan, *the Financial Services Act 1986* (FTS).
14 Ibid, s 13(4).
15 Ibid, s 13(5).
16 Ibid, s 5.

These provisions prevent an individual from dealing not only in the securities of British companies, but also from dealing in the securities of foreign companies.[17]

Section 177 of the Financial Services Act enables the Secretary of State to appoint inspectors to determine whether there have been contraventions of the insider dealing provisions. The powers of such investigators are similar to those of inspectors under the Companies Act 1985. Refusal by a person required to appear before the inspectors and to produce documents may result in his being punished as for a contempt of court.

An individual who contravenes the provisions of ss 1, 2, 4 or 5 renders himself liable to criminal sanctions.[18] However, the ID 1985 provides for no civil remedies for an injured party: a transaction contravening these provisions is not void or voidable.[19]

---

[17] Ibid, s 16.
[18] Ibid, s 8. Leave is required for a prosecution.
[19] Ibid, s 8(3). Cf Report of the Company Law Committee, Cmnd 1749, paras 89 and 99(b).

Chapter 11

Enforcement of Directors' Duties

Directors' duties may be enforced by proceedings at common law and under certain statutory provisions.

PROCEEDINGS BY THE COMPANY

In *Burland v Earle*[1] Lord Davey stated:

> It is an elementary principle of the law relating to joint stock companies that the Court will not interfere with the internal management of companies acting within their powers, and in fact have no jurisdiction to do so. Again, it is clear law that in order to redress a wrong done to the company or to recover moneys or damages alleged to be due to the company, the action should prima facie be brought by the company itself.

The rule has been stated to depend on two distinct principles; the corporation principle and the partnership principle.[2] The former, which proceeds from the separate corporate identity of the company, naturally requires that it is for the company, not the members, to bring an action to redress wrongs done to the company. The latter principle was formulated in relation to partnerships (and in 1843, when the rule was stated, deed of settlement companies were akin to partnerships) and under it the Court refused to interfere in matters which were matters of internal management. If what was complained of was an irregularity (as opposed to an illegality) in the conduct of the affairs of the company, the courts would not intervene at the instance of a shareholder. The courts thus recognised a

1 [1902] AC 83.
2 K. W. Wedderburn, 'Shareholders Rights and the Rule in *Foss v Harbottle*' (1957) Camb LJ 194 and (1958) Camb LJ 93.

right of the majority of members to bar a minority action whenever the majority might lawfully ratify the wrong complained of.[3]

These rules were stated in the form which applies today in *Foss v Harbottle*.[4] Two members of a company brought an action against the directors to compel them to make good losses sustained by the company as the result of fraudulent acts of the directors who had allegedly misapplied the company's assets. The wrong alleged was done to the company, and it was prima facie the proper plaintiff. The Court, holding that the acts might be ratified by a majority of the members, refused to intervene in what it perceived to be a matter of internal management. While the Court recognised that certain exceptions to the rule had to be made, as where the directors' action was *ultra vires* and therefore a nullity, it held that, where a general meeting could confirm the action taken, the minority could not be permitted to bring an action which might nullify the wishes of the majority of shareholders. Later courts advanced additional reasons for the rule; that it was necessary to inhibit futile litigation,[5] or to prevent a company from tearing itself to pieces. It must be borne in mind that an unwanted action may, even though resulting in an award of damages to the company, also subject it to disproportionate harm.[6] The courts stressed the principle of majority rule. There was much judicial unwillingness to intervene in matters of business judgement,[7] and the courts had in mind a particular model of the company as a city-state or corporate democracy. While some writers of the period recognised that in the corporation or the large deed of settlement company, the members were often passive recipients of income who did not interest themselves closely in the conduct of the companies of which they were members,[8] the view taken in this area reflected the notion that the ultimate power of control over the company rested with the general meeting which could dictate to the directors in matters of policy.

---

3 See generally, A. J. Boyle, 'The Minority Shareholder in the Nineteenth Century' (1965) 28 Mod LR 317.
4 (1843) 2 Hare 461.
5 *Cotter v National Union of Seamen* [1929] 2 Ch 58.
6 *La Compagnie de Mayville v Whitley* [1896] 1 Ch 788 at p 807; remarks of the Court of Appeal in *Prudential Assurance Co Ltd v Newman Industries Ltd (No 2)* [1982] 1 All ER 354 at 364.
7 The most celebrated example is probably the statement of Lord Eldon LC in *Carlen v Drury* (1812) 1 Ves & B 154 to the effect that the Court would not undertake the management of every brewhouse and playhouse in the kingdom.
8 See Collyer, *The Law of Partnership* (1839); Adam Smith, *The Wealth of Nations* (Modern Library Edn 1937) pp 699–700.

222 Chapter 11 Enforcement of Directors' Duties

While supported by certain decisions,[9] this mode of thought has now, as we have seen, become outmoded.[10]

None the less, the rule barring minority actions could not be given an inflexible application. Certain matters, because *ultra vires*, could not be ratified by a general meeting. Matters requiring a special resolution could not be made subject to ratification by an ordinary majority since this would subvert the protection accorded by the requirement. Certain rights were personal to shareholders and could not be stultified by a majority. Finally, and most troublesome, were cases in which the controllers of a company diverted corporate assets to their own pockets. As a result, a number of exceptions to the rule in *Foss v Harbottle* were recognised. In the leading modern case, *Edwards v Halliwell*,[11] the rule and its exceptions were compendiously stated. The rule, according to Jenkins LJ is:

> First, the proper plaintiff in an action in respect of a wrong alleged to be done to a company or association of persons is prima facie the company or association of persons itself. Secondly, where the alleged wrong is a transaction which might be made binding on the company or association and on all its members by a simple majority of the members, no individual member of the company is allowed to maintain an action in respect of that matter for the simple reason that, if a mere majority of the members of the company or association is in favour of what has been done, then *cadit questio* . . . . If, on the other hand, a simple majority of the company or association is against what has been done, then there is no valid reason why the company or association itself should not sue.

To this rule, there are the following exceptions:

(1) where the activity is *ultra vires* any individual member may sue because the matter is one which the members cannot ratify;
(2) where the matter is one which must be decided by a special resolution, an action is not barred by majority ratification since, if the rule in *Foss v Harbottle* applied, a company could by refusing to initiate an action do indirectly what it could not do directly;

---

9 *Isle of Wight Rly Co v Tahourdin* (1883) 25 ChD 320.
10 See Chap 8 ante, dealing with the division of powers between the board of directors and the general meeting.
11 [1950] 2 All ER 1064 at pp 1066–1067.

(3) where the action represents an infringment of the personal rights of shareholders. In such a case any individual shareholder affected by it may sue;
(4) where the activity falls within that class of cases which are compendiously termed a fraud on the minority;
(5) where, in a case where the interests of some part of the members have been unfairly prejudiced, the Court makes an order pursuant to CA 1985, s 461(2)(c)[12] authorising civil proceedings to be brought in the name and on behalf of the company by such person or persons and on such terms as the Court may direct. This provision effectively gives the Court an important discretion, where an application based on unfair prejudice is well-founded, to waive the rule in *Foss v Harbottle*.

It may be that this list is not closed in the sense that there are cases which do not fall within these categories of exceptions, but to which the rule in *Foss v Harbottle* is inapplicable. However no accepted test has been formulated for such cases.[13]

Where the action is brought by a shareholder in respect of an *ultra vires* act or an infringement of his personal rights, the shareholder may sue in his personal capacity. Where the action is brought by a shareholder not only in respect of his own personal rights, but in respect of the personal rights of a group of members (such as a class of shareholders), the shareholder may sue in a representative capacity on behalf of himself and all other shareholders whose rights are the same as his own, and the controllers are made defendants.[14] However, where the action is brought essentially to vindicate the company's rights, the action is derivative in character and may be brought by the shareholder in a representative capacity on behalf of himself and all other shareholders except the controllers, who are made defendants, or in his own name. In the latter case also, the controllers are made defendants. Although it is the company's right which is being vindicated, it is, because the directors will not allow litigation to be brought in its name, not formally made a plaintiff in the action. It is instead joined as a party defendant.[15] By this means, the interests of the company are protected and it is bound by the judgment.

---

12 Discussed at pp 244–250, post.
13 *Prudential Assurance Co Ltd v Newman Industries Ltd (No 2)* [1982] Ch 204, [1982] 1 All ER 354; *Estmanco (Kilner House) Ltd v Greater London Council* [1982] 1 All ER 437, [1982] 1 WLR 2.
14 See RSC 1965, O 15, r 12.
15 *Wallersteiner v Moir (No 2)* [1975] QB 373, [1975] 1 All ER 849.

We may now consider the exceptions to the rule. The exception based on *ultra vires* reflects the fact that the activity cannot be ratified by the company. Furthermore, each member has the right to ensure that the funds of the company are applied to its proper objects.[16] In such a case, the court has regard only to the issue whether the activity is *ultra vires*, and not to the character of the activity, whether meritorious or otherwise.[17] An individual shareholder may also maintain a personal action where the activity is illegal.[18] And he may sue to restrain the company from performing *ultra vires* or illegal acts even though he has in the past been a party to the type of misconduct complained of.[19]

The exception based upon special resolutions is neatly illustrated by:

Edwards v Halliwell [1950] 2 All ER 1064.

> The constitution of a trade union provided that contributions were not to be altered until a ballot vote of the members had been taken and a two-thirds majority obtained. A delegate meeting of the union, without taking any ballot, passed a resolution increasing the contributions of members. The plaintiffs, two members of the union, sued two members of the executive committee of the union and the union itself for a declaration that the resolution was invalid. It was held that the resolution was invalid. Jenkins LJ stated that if the company alone were allowed to sue in cases of this character, a company which had broken its own rules by doing something without a special resolution which could only be done validly by a special resolution, would in effect be allowed to do by ordinary resolution that which, according to its own regulations, could only be done by special resolution.

In addition, the matter was classified as an invasion of the personal rights of members.

The principal difficulties are associated with exceptions (3) and (4) to the rule; actions based on an infringement of the personal rights of shareholders, and actions based on fraud on the minority. Because it has been suggested that many of the restrictions which exist in connection with the action based on fraud can, and are, being overcome by extensions of the personal action, we deal first with fraud on the minority.

16 *Simpson v Westminster Palace Hotel Co* (1860) 8 HL Cas 712.
17 *Yorkshire Miners Association v Howden* [1905] AC 256.
18 *Powell v Kempton Park Racecourse Co Ltd* [1899] AC 143.
19 *Mosely v Koffyfontein Mines Ltd* [1911] 1 Ch 73.

FRAUD ON THE MINORITY

Actions based on fraud on the minority are derivative in character. The wrong is esentially one which has been caused to the company, and the action is brought by minority shareholders to vindicate corporate rights. The basic rule is that a resolution of the general meeting cannot authorise or validate a fraud upon the company.

Atwool v Merryweather (1867) LR 5 Eq 464.

> The case involved the sale of a worthless mine by a promoter to the company. He took shares in part payment and cash was paid on subscription for the shares for the balance. The promoter and another sold the mine at an overvalue, and split the profit. One of them in addition received a commission for assisting the company in the purchase of the mine. The agreement was concealed from the other directors and shareholders. Ultimately, this action was brought by a shareholder, on behalf of himself and all other shareholders except the defendants, for the purpose of setting aside the contract for the purchase of the mine and an order for the repayment of the sums paid to them, and for a return of the shares allotted as part of the consideration for the purchase. It was held by Page Wood VC that the shareholders could maintain the action, notwithstanding the rule in *Foss v Harbottle*. Were such an action as this not possible, '... it would be simply impossible to set aside a fraud committed by a director under such circumstances, as the director obtaining so many shares by fraud would always be able to outvote everybody else.'

Similarly, the general meeting cannot ratify a breach of the director's duties where the Court imposes a trust on property received by the directors in breach of their duties, or where they have misappropriated the company's property. This is especially so where the ratification is only secured with the assistance of the director's voting powers.[20]

In order to maintain an action under this head, the minority shareholder must allege and prove:[1]

(1) that a fraud (in the sense of a 'fraud on the minority') was perpetrated on the company, and
(2) that the wrongdoers are in control and will not lend the name of the company to the proceedings.

---

20 *Cook v Deeks* [1916] 1 AC 554; *Re a Company* [1986] 2 All ER 253, [1986] 1 WLR 281.
1 *Birch v Sullivan* [1958] 1 All ER 56, [1957] 1 WLR 1247.

However, as a rule of practice, it should be decided as a preliminary point whether the minority shareholder is entitled to take advantage of an exception to the rule in *Foss v Harbottle*: that question should not be left until the trial.[2] For the purposes of the preliminary point, the shareholder must establish a prima facie case (i) that the company is entitled to the relief claimed and (ii) that the action falls within the proper boundaries to the exception to the rule in *Foss v Harbottle*.[3] The plaintiff must also show that he or she is a proper person to bring the action. Even though a wrong has been done to the company, the Court may refuse to allow a plaintiff who has already substantially recovered directly what he or she could recover indirectly through a derivative action to bring that action.[4] The meaning to be attributed to control is not altogether clear. Where the wrongdoers hold a majority of shares either personally or through nominees, the task of establishing control is reasonably easy. The Courts have indicated a willingness in a proper case to go behind the apparent ownership of shares to determine whether they are held by nominees in favour of the alleged wrongdoer.[5] This task should in future be facilitated by the disclosure provisions of the Companies Act 1985 relating to directors' and members' interests.

It is uncertain whether a derivative action may be brought if the defendants do not have voting control of the company on whose behalf the derivative claim is brought. The leading case is:

Prudential Assurance Co Ltd v Newman Industries Ltd [1982] 1 All ER 354.

> B and L were directors of two companies, N and TPG. B and TPG were shareholders in N but did not hold a majority of its shares. B and L held 35 of TPG's shares through their wholly-owned company.
>
> By the beginning of 1975, TPG was in severe financial difficulties and B and L decided without the authority or knowledge of B's board, that N would purchase some of TPG's assets. Subsequently, B conceived a plan to sell TPG's remaining assets (other than its shares in N) to N and drew up a document for N's board explaining the plan, but a valuation on

---

2 *Prudential Assurance Co Ltd v Newman Industries Ltd (No 2)* [1982] Ch 204, [1982] 1 All ER 354; *Estmanco (Kilner House) Ltd v Greater London Council* [1982] 1 All ER 437, [1982] 1 WLR 2.
3 *Prudential Assurance Co Ltd v Newman Industries Ltd (No 2)* (supra) 366. It would appear that this principle of the preliminary point applies to all of the exceptions to the rule.
4 *Nurcombe v Nurcombe* [1985] 1 All ER 65, [1985] 1 WLR 370.
5 *Pavlides v Jensen* [1956] Ch 565, [1956] 2 All ER 518.

which the proposed purchase was based was made on the basis of misleading information given by B and L, who used deceit to induce the majority of N's board to accept the transaction as being in N's interests. N entered into the agreement conditionally upon the approval of its general meeting and a circular, drafted with the assistance of B and L, was sent to all of the members of N, recommending approval of the agreement. The matter was put to the vote at general meeting before an independent report on the transaction was completed, and passed by a small majority.

P, which held 3.2% of N's shares, brought proceedings against (inter alia) BL and TPG seeking (inter alia) (i) damages against B and L for N for breach of fiduciary duty; (ii) on its own behalf, damages for conspiracy; (iii) on behalf of N's shareholders a declaration that the circular was misleading and tricky and damages for conspiracy. At first instance, Vinelott J held that, on the authority of *Atwood v Merryweather*,[6] the fraud on the minority exception applied wherever the persons against whom the action is sought to be brought on behalf of the company are shown to be able 'by any means of manipulation of their position in the company' to ensure that the action is not brought by the company: in other words, that that exception applied in cases of *de facto*, as well as *de jure*, control.

The Court of Appeal did not dissent from this. It noted that control embraces a broad spectrum extending from an overall absolute majority of votes at one end, to a minority of votes at the other end, made up of those likely to be cast by the delinquent himself, plus those voting with him as a result of ignorance and apathy.

It seems clear that there is no inflexible standard of control, and that the inquiry is largely factual. The Courts will it is submitted, treat a shareholding less than a clear majority in some cases as a controlling block for the purposes of a minority action. It has been demonstrated that a company can, if its shareholding is diffused, be controlled by persons having comparatively small shareholdings.[7]

Apart from control, the plaintiff must show that the action amounted to a fraud on the company. It is unclear precisely what is meant by 'fraud' in this context. It is wider than fraud at common law, and comprises fraud in the wider equitable sense of that term,[8]

---

6 (1868) LR 5 Eq 464.
7 Pickering 'Shareholder Voting Rights and Company Control' (1965) 81 LQR 278; Beck, 'An Analysis of *Foss v Harbottle*' in Ziegel (ed) *Studies in Canadian Company Law* (1967), and of course the modern classic, Berle and Means, *The Modern Corporation and Private Property* (1932).
8 *Estmanco (Kilner House) Ltd v Greater London Council* [1982] 1 All ER 437, [1982] 1 WLR 2.

embracing even cases where the directors negligently (but not fraudulently) confer benefits on themselves at their company's expense.[9] In *Prudential Assurance Co Ltd v Newman Industries Ltd (No 2)*[10] Vinelott J summarised the position thus:

> '... the authorities show that the exception applies not only where the allegation is that directors who control a company have improperly appropriated to themselves money, property or advantages which belong to the company or, in breach of their duty to the company, have diverted business to themselves which ought to have been given to the company, but more generally where it is alleged that directors though acting "in the belief that they were doing nothing wrong" (per Lindley MR in *Alexander v Automatic Telephone Co* [1900] 2 Ch 56, 65) are guilty of a breach of duty to the company, including their duty to exercise proper care, and as a result of that breach obtain some benefit. In the latter case it must be unnecessary to allege and prove that the directors in breaking their duty to the company acted with a view to benefiting themselves at the expense of the company; for such an allegation would be an allegation of misappropriation of the company's property. On the other hand, the exception does not apply if all that is alleged is that directors who control a company are liable to the company for damages for negligence it not being shown that the transaction was one in which they were interested or that they have in fact obtained any benefit from it.' ...[11]

It has been trenchantly observed that '[a]part from the benefit to themselves at the company's expense, the essence of the matter seems to be an abuse or misuse of power.' Fraud on the minority, can fairly readily be established if the action of the controllers amounts to the wrongful expropriation of corporate assets or opportunities for their own benefit. *Cook v Deeks*[12] is of course a classic example of the expropriation of corporate benefits. The leading cases on the expropriation of corporate property also make it clear that:[13]

> ... although it may be quite true that the shareholders of a company may vote as they please, and for the purpose of their own interests, yet that

---

9 *Daniels v Daniels* [1978] Ch 406, [1978] 2 All ER 89.
10 [1981] Ch 257, [1980] 2 All ER 841.
11 *Estmanco (Kilner House) Ltd v Greater London Council* (supra) at p 12; echoing *Prudential Assurance Co Ltd v Newman Industries Ltd (No 2)*, (supra) at p 568.
12 [1916] 1 AC 554.
13 *Menier v Hoopers Telegraph Works* (1874) 9 Ch App 350, at 354, per James LJ.

the majority of shareholders cannot sell the assets of the company and keep the consideration, but must allow the minority to have their share of any consideration which may come to them.

Similarly, the minority shareholder is entitled to bring proceedings where the controllers have wrongfully used the company's money for their own purposes, for example, in breach of CA 1985, s 151.[14] A minority shareholder's derivative action will also lie where the claim is founded upon the tort of conspiracy[15] or, it seems, deceit.

But, although an exception is made to the rule in *Foss v Harbottle* in cases of fraud, or cases where some property or advantage is monopolised by the majority to the exclusion of the minority,[16] no exception is made in cases where the allegation is one of negligence without fraud. In such a case, a general meeting can validly determine not to take proceedings against the directors whose alleged negligence caused damage to the company.

Pavlides v Jensen [1956] Ch 565, [1956] 2 All ER 518.

> The pleadings alleged that the directors of the company sold a mine belonging to it at a considerable undervalue and that they were therefore grossly negligent. It was held that the company could validly resolve not to take proceedings against the directors and that the action was therefore not maintainable.

However, even in a case where there is no question of fraud, the minority shareholders are entitled to bring proceedings, if the director's negligence not only harms the company, but also confers benefits upon the directors:

Daniels v Daniels [1978] Ch 406, [1978] 2 All ER 89.[17]

> It was alleged by the minority shareholders that the defendants, who were the directors and majority shareholders of the company, had caused the company to sell to the second defendant at a gross

---

14 *Wallersteiner v Moir* [1974] 3 All ER 217, [1974] 1 WLR 991; *Wallersteiner v Moir (No 2)* [1975] QB 373, [1975] 1 All ER 849 decided under CA 1948, s 54, the basic prohibition of which is continued by CA 1985, s 151.
15 *Prudential Assurance Co Ltd v Newman Industries Ltd (No 2)* [1981] Ch 257, [1980] 2 All ER 841, apparently not questioned on appeal.
16 *Heyting v Dupont* [1964] 2 All ER 273, [1964] 1 WLR 843, CA.
17 See (1978) 41 Mod LR 569.

undervalue land belonging to the company. The second defendant had made a large profit on the re-sale of the land. The plaintiffs did not allege fraud on the part of the defendants. Templeman J held that minority shareholders were entitled to bring an action where directors negligently, although without fraud, conferred a benefit upon themselves at the company's expense.

It has further been suggested that an action ought to lie where the result of the director's actions is not to benefit themselves, but some associated person, for example the wife of an associate.[18] It is, however, far from clear how far the *Daniels v Daniels* principle extends. A learned author submits, understandably but, it is submitted, wrongly, that the *ratio* of the case turns on the point that the benefit obtained by the directors was an appropriation and disposal of the company's assets and therefore a misappropriation of advantages, and that the action was derivative though not cast in representative form.[19] It is apparent that the authorities upon which Templeman J relies do concern breaches of fiduciary duty where fraud need not be alleged in order to obtain rcovery.[20] It is also probable that the principle in *Daniels v Daniels* is most likely to apply in the context of acquisitions and dispositions of corporate property. Furthermore, the case has been cited in a later judgment as an example of a fraud upon a power.[1] None the less, no court has sought to characterise the case definitively as pertaining to breaches of fiduciary duty. The ambit of fraud is thus uncertain, and is likely to remain so as the courts strive to bring an increasing number of difficult cases within it.

It should be noted, however, that shareholders voting at the general meeting are not subject to fiduciary duties when exercising their voting rights, and they are entitled to vote in their own interests, whilst disregarding competing interests of other shareholders.[2] The shareholder who is also a director is treated simply as

---

18 *Prudential Assurance Co Ltd v Newman Industries Ltd (No 2)* [1980] 2 All ER 841 at 864 per Vinelott J; the issues are not discussed in the Court of Appeal.
19 Lord Wedderburn in (1978) 41 MLR 569.
20 *Alexander v Automatic Telephone Co* [1900] 2 Ch 56; *Cook v Deeks* [1916] 1 AC 554.
1 *Estmanco (Kilner House) Ltd v Greater London Council* [1982] 1 All ER 437, [1982] 1 WLR 2.
2 *North-West Transportation Co v Beatty* (1887) 12 App Cas 589; *Burland v Earle* [1902] AC 83; *Pender v Lushington* (1877) 6 ChD 70, 75, 76; *Philips v Manufacturers Securities Ltd* (1917) 116 LT 290, 296; *Prudential Assurance Co Ltd v Newman Industries Ltd (No 2)* [1982] Ch 204, [1982] 1 All ER 354; but see *Estmanco (Kilner House) Ltd v Greater London Council* [1982] 1 All ER 437, [1982] 1 WLR 2.

a shareholder when voting at a general meeting and is not subject to extra fiduciary duties on account of his directorship.[3] Nevertheless, he cannot use his votes to commit or ratify a fraud on the company.[4] Furthermore, a majority shareholder is not permitted to vote in his own selfish interests so as to injure voteless fellow shareholders by preventing them from obtaining voting rights, depriving the company of a cause of action and stultifying the purpose for which the company was formed.[5]

There may also exist a further exception to the rule in *Foss v Harbottle*. Dicta in a number of cases have suggested that such an exception exists where the interests of justice so require.[6] However, this formulation of the exception has been decisively rejected as an impractical test,[7] although no satisfactory alternative has been suggested. Instead of elaborating this residual head, courts tend to widen the concept of fraud. In *Estmanco (Kilner House) Ltd v Greater London Council*[8] Megarry V-C held that injustice is a reason for making an exception to the rule in *Foss v Harbottle*, but it is not the rule itself. It is too variable to be so. The jurisprudence of exceptions continues to develop, however. His Lordship suggests, tentatively, that:[9]

'It may be that the test may come to be whether an ordinary resolution of the shareholders could validly carry out or ratify the act in question.'

---

3 *North-West Transportation Co v Beatty* (supra), *Burland v Earle* (supra). So far as *Clemens v Clemens Bros* [1976] 2 All ER 268 suggests the contrary, it would appear to be incorrect.
4 *Cook v Deeks* [1916] 1 AC 554. But see *Prudential Assurance Co Ltd v Newman Industries Ltd* [1980] 3 WLR 543 at p 568.
5 *Estmanco Ltd v Greater London Council* [1982] 1 All ER 437, [1982] 1 WLR 2.
6 *Heyting v Dupont,* supra, *Wallersteiner v Moir (No 2),* supra, and see *Russell v Wakefield Waterworks Co* (1875) LR 20 Eq 474 at p 480; and see *Prudential Assurance Co Ltd v Newman Industries Ltd (No 2)* [1981] Ch 257, [1980] 2 All ER 841. However, in *Hodgson v National Local Government Officers Association* [1972] 1 All ER 15, [1972] 1 WLR 130 Goulding J held that the rule in *Foss v Harbottle* should not be applied if the result would be to deprive the majority of an opportunity of carrying out their will, eg where a general meeting could not be convened in time to be of practical effect in relation to the matter in respect of which the minority were suing (in effect, the position in *Hodgson v National Association Local Government Officers* (supra)). See D. Prentice (1972) 35 Mod LR 318.
7 *Prudential Assurance Co Ltd v Newman Industries Ltd (No 2)* [1982] 1 All ER 354 at p 366; *Estmanco Ltd v Greater London Council* [1982] 1 WLR 2 at p 10.
8 [1982] 1 All ER 437.
9 Ibid, at 444.

This formula is, however, circular.[10] Nor is it helpful to explain recent decisions on the footing simply of fraud on a power, for that would render inexplicable cases like *Regal (Hastings) Ltd v Gulliver*[11] where the misuse of power was treated as ratifiable. In the *Prudential Assurance* case, Vinelott J strove to find an intermediate category between fraud and simple negligence such as would justify an action but, references to *Daniels v Daniels* apart, it cannot be said to have resulted in any settled principle and the boundaries of the fraud exception to *Foss v Harbottle* remain ill-defined. At the same time, the existence and extent of the residual exception in the interests of justice remain doubtful.

One of the principal obstacles in the path of the minority shareholder who wishes to bring proceedings in respect of a wrong done to the company (in a case where he may properly do so) is the cost of the litigation. The size of this obstacle has been considerably diminished, in that the Court of Appeal has held that the Court has power to order the company to indemnify the plaintiff against his costs, for it is the company which will ultimately benefit from the proceedings.[12]

THE PERSONAL ACTION

It has, however, been suggested that the exception in favour of a shareholder who is asserting a right personal to himself, may confer a wider right of action to enforce adherence by management to the provisions of the articles. This general right postulated in a shareholder to have the company managed in accordance with the articles would obviously considerably enhance shareholder protection.[13] It is therefore necessary to determine how extensive this right of action is.

Shareholders to a point have and can exercise personal rights against the company and the directors. Thus a shareholder has a right to exercise the rights which appertain to his shareholding. If the shareholder's individual rights are infringed on a matter of substance, he has an unqualified right of action in order to vindicate them.[14] The leading case is:

---

10 See per Vinelott J in *Prudential Assurance Co Ltd v Newman Industries Ltd (No 2)* [1980] 2 All ER 841 at 859–60.
11 [1967] 2 AC 134n, [1942] 1 All ER 378.
12 *Wallersteiner v Moir (No 2)* [1975] QB 373, [1975] 1 All ER 849.
13 Wedderburn (1968) 31 Mod LR 668.
14 *Edwards v Halliwell* [1950] 2 All ER 1064.

Pender v Lushington (1877) 6 ChD 70.

Under the articles, each member was entitled to one vote for every ten shares which he held subject to a maximum of 100 votes. No member was allowed to vote until he had held his shares for at least three months. A member who had a large number of shares transferred part of his holding to P, P to vote at his direction. The member thereby sought to overcome the limitation on the maximum number of votes exercisable in right of his shareholding. P had held his shares for more than three months when his votes at a meeting were disallowed, and an amendment to a resolution thereby carried. P brought action for an injunction restraining L and other directors from disallowing his votes and from acting on the amendment. It was held, per Jessel MR, the plaintiff as a registered shareholder had an unqualified right to vote his shares, and that this right was a right of property. The company could not under the articles inquire into the beneficial ownership of shares, or refuse to allow the shareholder to exercise his proprietary right to vote.

However, where the shareholder's only complaint is that damage has been done to the company, no personal action will lie, even if the damage to the company causes a diminution in the value of his shares.[15]

On the other hand, even though the action is personal, it may in some cases be defeated by ratification. Where for example, the complaint refers to a mere matter of procedure, the Courts will hold that the irregularity in question is one which could be ratified or excused by a majority. Thus in *MacDougall v Gardiner*[16] the formal issue was whether the plaintiff could bring an action founded on the action of the chairman of a meeting in carrying an adjournment and refusing a poll on the matter. The Court there held that the matter was an internal dispute, and could not be made the subject of an action unless there were something illegal, oppressive or fraudulent in the case.[19] Thus, for example, while the Courts will intervene to prevent the dissipation of the company's funds by payments made on the basis of inaccurate accounts, they will not allow a

---

15 *Prudential Assurance Co Ltd v Newman Industries Ltd (No 2)* [1982] Ch 204, [1982] 1 All ER 354. Although a derivative action might lie.
16 (1875) 1 ChD 13. See also *Bentley-Stevens v Jones* [1974] 2 All ER 653, [1974] 1 WLR 638.
17 But for the view that (except in cases of *ultra vires* or illegallity) the general meeting is competent, if its interests do not conflict with that of the company, to ratify any act or transaction whatever its character, that is whether it is fraudulent or not. see *Prudential Assurance Co Ltd v Newman Industries Ltd (No 2)* [1980] 3 WLR 543 at p 568 per Vinelott J.

shareholder to complain of the manner in which the company's accounts were prepared, this being a matter of business judgment.[18]

One problem therefore is that of ratification; when will it be allowed to defeat or preclude an action? The other problem, raised by recent decisions, is whether a personal action is defeated by the possibility of ratification where that is applicable, or only by the fact of ratification itself.

Ratification, in connection with the personal action, is not substantially different in its sweep from ratification where the cause of action is corporate. As we have seen, the shareholder's proprietary right to vote cannot be defeated by a majority. Furthermore, it appears that the unqualified right of a shareholder to insist on the articles being observed extends to cases where directors seek to subvert provisions in the articles which require the concurrence of all directors in certain types of activity,[19] or which restrict the class of persons who may be appointed and act as directors.[20] Similarly, a shareholder has a right to require the directors not to exclude one of their number from board meetings.[1] These are, of course, matters of fundamental significance. On the other hand, shareholders can ratify actions of the directors which, while in excess of their powers, are *intra vires* the company and which do not subvert the basic constitutional framework of the company. These issues arise in the share allotment cases which are discussed in connection with the second point relating to ratification.

The second point is whether a personal action can be defeated by the mere possibility of ratification. Prima facie, the answer ought to be in the affirmative, for, in *MacDougall v Gardiner*[2] the Court states that:

> Nothing connected with internal disputes between the shareholders is to be made the subject of a bill by some one shareholder on behalf of himself and others, unless there be something illegal, oppressive or fraudulent.

---

18 *Devlin v Slough Estates Ltd* [1983] BCLC 497; no question of formats or qualification by the auditors was involved.
19 *Salmon v Quin and Axtens Ltd* [1909] 1 Ch 311.
20 *Kraus v J G Lloyd Pty Ltd* [1965] VR 232, noted in [1966] Ann Survey of Comm Law 454.
1   *Pulbrook v Richmond Consolidated Mining Co* (1878) 9 ChD 610. Note that a director has a right of action *qua* director, even where he holds no shares, to prevent his unlawful exclusion from the board; *Hayes v Bristol Plant Hire Ltd* [1957] 1 All ER 685, [1957] 1 WLR 499, where, however, the director was also a shareholder.
2   (1875) 1 ChD 13.

None the less, it has been suggested that recent cases have altered this rule in connection with personal actions.[3] This view is founded on an interpretation of two decisions, *Hogg v Cramphorn, Ltd*[4] and *Bamford*.[5] In *Hogg v Cramphorn Ltd,* as we have seen, an action was brought in respect of the alleged improper allotment of shares to trustees for employees. It was alleged that the allotment was made in order to block a take-over bid, and was therefore not made in good faith and for the best interests of the company. It is true that the action proceeded even though the allotment was ultimately held to be ratifiable by the shareholders. The action does not, however, break new ground in respect of the operation of ratification as a bar to such an action.[6] Two of the allegations in the pleadings were of unratifiable breaches, namely a breach of s 54 of the Companies Act 1948 (now s 151 of the Companies Act 1985) which if made out was illegal, and of attaching to the shares more votes than were permitted by the articles. The third allegation, that the allotment was improper, was ultimately held to involve a ratifiable breach, but it must be appreciated that before this case, it was doubtful whether such an excess of powers was ratifiable at all. The facts in *Bamford v Bamford* were not dissimilar. Again, the form which the action took is important. It went to the Court on a preliminary point of law; whether the director's actions in making the allotment could be and had been validly ratified by a resolution of the general meeting. While the trial judge did express himself in terms wide enough to justify the view that a shareholder has an indefeasible right to bring a personal action notwithstanding the possibility of ratification, the Court of Appeal dealt with the matter more narrowly. The allotment was, it held, ratifiable. Provided that the directors do not act fraudulently or dishonestly, their actions can be ratified by a general meeting, and if there has been ratification, the matter cannot be made the subject of an action.

The whole problem is further exacerbated by a question of classification; when should a wrong be treated as one done to a shareholder and when as one done to the company in respect of which it

---

3 Wedderburn (1968) 31 Mod LR 668. See also generally Smith (1978) 41 Mod LR 147.
4 [1967] Ch 254, [1966] 3 All ER 420. The question whether the issue should be ratified was remitted by the Court to a general meeting which duly ratified it, the Court directing that the newly allotted shareholders should not vote.
5 [1970] Ch 212, [1969] 1 All ER 969.
6 See further Atiyah in [1967] Ann Survey of Comm Law at p 478. Atiyah altered his view in [1968] Ann Survey of Comm Law at p 546 in the light of the decision at trial in *Bamford v Bamford* [1968] 2 All ER 655 now affd by the CA in [1970] Ch 212, [1969] 1 All ER 969.

alone can complain. In *Hogg v Cramphorn Ltd* the wrong is treated as one done to the shareholder; an infringement of his rights to have the articles observed. In *Bamford v Bamford* in the Court of Appeal the wrong is treated as one done to the company in that it is a breach by the directors of their duty to the company. Either or both classifications are attractive and probably right. The question in such cases as these is not one concerning the head under which the action is founded; it is one concerning the permissible limits of ratification. And here, unless a proprietary right attaching to a share is being denied to the member, or there is an attempt fundamentally to subvert the company's constitution, the principle of ratification will operate. The personal action is, in an unqualified form, relatively narrow in scope. Even were it wider, many of the problems would remain unsolved. Simple negligence by the directors would still not be actionable, unless one could point to some article which had been infringed. The most significant problem is that of ratification. The doctrine which permits ratification unless the case is one of fraud or oppression is simply too wide.[7]

RELIEF FROM LIABILITY

Prior to 1929, a director could shield himself from liability by an indemnity clause in the articles.[8] But under s 310 of the CA 1985 any provision in the articles or in a contract exempting a director or other officer, including an auditor, from, or indemnifying him against a liability that would otherwise attach to him in respect of any negligence, breach of duty, or breach of trust of which he is guilty is void. There is a proviso to the section permitting the company to honour an indemnity given by the company where the officer is successful in defending proceedings or is given relief under s 727.[9]

The Court has power under s 727 to grant relief to any officer of a company, including an auditor, who is charged with negligence, default, breach of duty or breach of trust. If the Court is satisfied that the officer has acted honestly, and reasonably and ought fairly to be excused, the Court may relieve him in whole or in part from his liability. The obligation to act reasonably can be discharged by showing that the director had done everything which a normal man

---

7 See Report of the Company Law Committee Cmnd 1749 (1962) paras 206–207.
8 *Re City Equitable Fire Insurance Co Ltd* [1925] Ch 407.
9 Eg Table A, art 118.

would do in the conduct of his own affairs.[10] This may in some cases include the obligation to take professional advice such as that of a solicitor before committing the company to a particular course of action.[11] The section applies to enable the Court to grant relief even where the activity complained of was *ultra vires*. In one such case the Court relieved against liability where it was shown that the directors had adverted to the *ultra vires* issue and had proceeded in accordance with counsel's advice.[12] The Court will not relieve against liability where directors fail to exercise a discretion of their own and simply follow the instructions of the person who secured their election to the board. Directors who act as puppets do so at their own risk.[13]

The Court's powers can be exercised to grant relief either in connection with proceedings which have commenced or which the director believes may be commenced. In determining whether to grant relief the Court will have regard to the view which the shareholders take of the matter, but their view is not decisive.[14]

There is an important limit on the ambit of s 727. Although the section is expressed in wide language, the only proceedings where relief can be claimed under it are those brought against the director for breach of his duties towards the company or its shareholders or for breach of his duties under the Companies Acts, and even then it is only applicable where the company, as opposed to a third party, brings the proceedings in question.[15]

STATUTORY PROTECTION

The restrictive character of the rule in *Foss v Harbottle* has led to the creation of statutory remedies for minority shareholders. The most impressive of these is the power conferred on the Court by CA 1985, s 459 to make orders remedying a situation in which the members or some part of them have been unfairly prejudiced. An

10 *Re City of London Insurance Co Ltd* (1925) 41 TLR 521.
11 *Re Duomatic Ltd* [1969] 2 Ch 365, [1969] 1 All ER 161.
12 *Re Claridge's Patent Asphalte Co Ltd* [1921] 1 Ch 543.
13 *Selangor United Rubber Estates Ltd v Cradock (No 3)* [1968] 2 All ER 1073, [1968] 1 WLR 1555 and see *S v Shaban* 1965 (4) SA 646, Hahlo 430.
14 *Re Gilt Edge Safety Glass Ltd* [1940] Ch 495, [1940] 2 All ER 237, qualifying the remarks of Maugham J in *Re Barry and Staines Linoleum Ltd* [1934] Ch 227.
15 *Customs and Excise Comrs v Hedon Alpha Ltd* [1981] QB 818, [1981] 2 All ER 697. Presumably the same principle applies where the director seeks relief under s 727, ie he can only claim relief if he has been guilty of breach of duty to the company or its shareholders or under the Companies Acts in circumstances where the company might seek redress from him.

aggrieved member may also have recourse to another, quite independent remedy, the winding up on the just and equitable ground. These remedies are to a point, related in scope, and are therefore considered together.[16]

WINDING UP

Under s 122(g) of the Insolvency Act 1986 a Court may grant an application to wind up a company if it is of opinion that it is just and equitable to do so. The Court is obliged to grant the order if it is of opinion that the petitioners are entitled to relief either by winding up or by some other means, and that in the absence of any other remedy it would be just and equitable to order winding up unless it is also of the opinion both that some other remedy is available to the petitioners and that they are acting unreasonably in seeking to have the company wound up rather than pursuing that other remedy.[17] The conditions are thus conjunctive. On the hearing of such a petition, the petitioner must show that the continuance of the company would be unjust to the petitioner and that that injustice cannot be remedied by any other step reasonably open to him.[18] The remedy under CA 1985, s 459 is in many instances an alternative to that contained in IA 1986, s 122(g), and the reasonableness of the petitioner in seeking a winding up rather than the alternative remedy is a relevant matter for the Court to take into consideration.[19]

In order to obtain the remedy, a shareholder (or his personal representative) must show that he has a tangible interest in a winding up; that is, that there would be assets available for distribution if a winding up were ordered.[20] He may not bring the petition for an ulterior purpose such as that of forcing the repayment of a loan[1] or attempting to force the directors to register a transfer of shares which it is within their powers to refuse.[2] On the other hand,

---

16 In the New Zealand edition of this book, these topics are considered under winding up. Their essential thrust is however in the direction of minority rights and hence we have altered the order and some of the substance of the treatment (ed).
17 IA 1986, s 125(2).
18 *Re a Company* [1983] 2 All ER 854, [1983] 1 WLR 927.
19 *Gammack, Petitioner* 1983 SLT 246; *Teague, Petitioner* 1985 SLT 469.
20 *Re Expanded Plugs Ltd* [1966] 1 All ER 877, [1966] 1 WLR 514; *Re Othery Construction Ltd* [1966] 1 All ER 145, [1966] 1 WLR 69.
1 *Re Bellador Silk Ltd* [1965] 1 All ER 667.
2 *Charles Forte Investments Ltd v Amanda* [1964] Ch 240, [1963] 2 All ER 940. But note that where grounds for a winding up order exist, a bankrupt member may petition as a contributory at the instance of his trustee in bankruptcy: *Re K/9 Meat Supplies (Guildford) Ltd* [1966] 3 All ER 320, [1966] 1 WLR 1112.

where the petitioner relies on oppressive conduct, he need not show that he is being oppressed *qua* member; it is enough if he is a member and the oppression relates to him in some other corporate capacity such as that of director.[3] His status as a shareholder must, however, be clear; where it is not and that issue is disputed, the petition will be dismissed and the parties left to proceed by writ to have the matter cleared up.[4]

The principles upon which the Courts will grant a winding up order on the just and equitable ground were considered by the House of Lords in:

Ebrahimi v Westbourne Galleries Ltd [1972] 2 All ER 492.

N, his son and the petitioner formed the company to take over an existing rug business run by N and the petitioner as partners. N and the petitioner were each allotted 400 shares and N's son was allotted 200 shares. All were directors. All the profits were taken as director's fees (but it was intimated at the hearing of the petition that this, in the light of the petitioner's exclusion, would be changed). Friction developed, the petitioner alleging in effect that N and his son were milking the company for their own benefit. The petitioner was ultimately voted off the board and brought this petition for a winding up order. His allegations that the respondents were milking the company were found not to be proven. He maintained his complaint on the further ground that exclusion from office afforded a ground for a winding up order. The House of Lords held that since it could be inferred that the petitioner had, after a long period in equal partnership with N, agreed to the formation of the company on the basis that the character of the association would remain the same, in view the petitioner's exclusion by N and his son, it was just and equitable that the company should be wound up.

Lord Wilberforce stated at p 500:
'The "just and equitable" provision . . . enable[s] the court to subject the exercise of legal rights to equitable considerations; considerations, that is, of a personal character arising between one individual and another, which may make it unjust, or inequitable, to insist on legal rights, or to exercise them in a particular way.

It would be impossible, and wholly undesirable, to define the circumstances in which these considerations may arise. Certainly the fact that a company is a small one, or a private company, is not enough. There are very many of these where the association is a purely commercial one, of which it can safely be said that the basis of association is adequately and

---

3 *Ebrahimi v Westbourne Galleries Ltd* [1973] AC 360, [1972] 2 All ER 492; *Re Davis and Collett Ltd* [1935] Ch 693.
4 *Re Garage Door Associates Ltd* [1984] 1 All ER 434, [1984] 1 WLR 35.

exhaustively laid down in the articles. The super-imposition of equitable considerations requires something more, which typically may include one, or probably more, of the following elements: (i) an association formed or continued on the basis of a personal relationship, involving mutual confidence—this element will often be found where a pre-existing partnership had been converted into a limited company: (ii) an agreement, or understanding, that all, or some (for there may be "sleeping" members), of the shareholders shall participate in the conduct of the business: (iii) restriction on the transfer of the member's interest in the company—so that if confidence is lost, or one member is removed from management, he cannot take out his stake and go elsewhere.'

The Courts will order a winding up on the just and equitable ground in a number of varied circumstances. The petitioner does not have to show that his claim for relief falls within any special category, and it is important to observe that the petitioner does not have to show that the acts which he alleges constitute grounds for the winding up of the company were not carried out bona fide in the interests of the company or that they were carried out *mala fides*.[5] On the other hand, the remedy will not avail a member whose exclusion is attributable to his own fault.[6] Furthermore, as we have seen, the equities may well favour some remedy other than a winding up. In such a case the Court may prefer to proceed under some other provision, perhaps the oppression remedy under s 459, or stand the petition over.[7]

The remedy will be awarded where the substratum of the company has failed; nowadays a rather rare occurrence.[8] It is also a remedy used in cases of deadlock, particularly where the company is controlled by a small number of persons.

Re Yenidje Tobacco Co Ltd [1916] 2 Ch 426.

W and R formed a private company of which they were the only shareholders and directors. Hostility arose leading to a deadlock in

---

5 *Ebrahimi v Westbourne Galleries Ltd* [1973] AC 360, [1972] 2 All ER 492. See generally L. H. Leigh (1972) 88 LQR 468 and M. R. Chesterman (1973) 36 Mod LR 127.
6 *Re Leadenhall General Hardware Stores Ltd* (1971) 115 Sol Jo 202.
7 *Re a Company* [1983] 2 All ER 854, [1983] 1 WLR 927; *Gammack, Petitioner* 1983 SLT 246; *Teague, Petitioner* 1985 SLT 469.
8 *Re Bleriot Manufacturing Aircraft Co Ltd* (1916) 32 TLR 253; *Re German Date Coffee Co* (1882) 20 ChD 169.

management, although the company was still making profits. It was held that, though a company, the business was structurally akin to a partnership and that, in a case where the only members were at odds, and there was no separate general meeting which might settle the difficulty, the company ought to be wound up.

In such a case the remedy is granted because it is no longer possible to carry on the affairs of the company harmoniously.

In a number of cases, where grounds exist which, if the company were a partnership, would justify a dissolution, the Court has ordered that the company should be wound up on the basis that it is a quasi-partnership, that is, a company structurally similar to a partnership.[9] However, the Court may not order that a company be wound up merely because of the existence of grounds which would justify a winding up in the case of partnership. In each case, the Court must examine the relationship between the members and their rights and obligations towards each other in order to ascertain whether, in all circumstances, grounds exist which make it just and equitable that the company should be wound up.[10]

The most important ground for intervention relates to oppressive conduct on the part of the controller against the petitioner. In order to succeed, the petitioner must show that there has been at the least an unfair use of powers and an impairment of confidence in the probity with which the affairs of the company are being conducted. It is not enough that a minority feels aggrieved at being outvoted on a mere matter of domestic policy.[11] A wrongful course of conduct must be alleged.

Where the petitioner can show that the affairs of the company have been so conducted as to cause a justified lack of confidence in the controller's probity in the general conduct of the business, a petition will lie. Thus in *Loch v John Blackwood*[12] relief was granted where the directors failed to hold general meetings, render accounts and recommend a dividend in circumstances which

---

9 *Re Yenidje Tobacco Co Ltd* [1916] 2 Ch 426; *Re Davis and Collett Ltd* [1935] Ch 693. See also *Re Straw Products Pty Ltd* [1942] VLR 222, 223; *Re Wondoflex Textiles Pty Ltd* [1951] VLR 458.
10 *Re K/9 Meat Supplies (Guildford) Ltd* [1966] 3 All ER 320, [1966] 1 WLR 1112. *Ebrahimi v Westbourne Galleries Ltd* [1972] 2 All ER 492 at 500, per Lord Wilberforce.
11 *Elder v Elder and Watson* 1952 SC 49.
12 [1924] AC 783, PC.

indicated that this conduct was deliberate and calculated to enable them to purchase the petitioners' shares at an undervalue.

Similarly, relief will be given where the controllers unjustifiably seek to 'freeze out' the petitioner from his rightful share in the management of the company. Exclusion *per se* is not, however, a ground for the making of a winding up order.

Where there are valid business reasons for such exclusion and there is no other element of unfairness, the petition is unlikely to succeed.[13] The petitioner must show that his exclusion was unjustified, for example where he has been excluded from management in contravention of the company's articles or in contravention of the express terms of an agreement between him and his co-members.[14]

The petitioner's exclusion may be unjustified even in cases where his co-members or the directors have proceeded strictly in accordance with the company's articles or the Companies Acts. The question the Court must decide is whether it is equitable in the circumstances to allow one or more of the members to make use of his legal rights, for example those of removing a director under CA 1985, s 303, to the prejudice of his co-member or members. Accordingly, the petitioner may be able to show that his exclusion is unjustified by establishing that the underlying basis of the relationship between him and his co-members is that during the continuance of the business, each should be entitled to participate in management. In such a case, the exclusion of the petitioner constitutes so serious a breach of fundamental obligations of the relationship that the Court is entitled to conclude that the company should be wound up.[15]

Furthermore, where the directors, pursuant to powers contained in the articles, refuse to register as members persons to whom shares have been bequeathed or sold, the Court may, if the directors' refusal is unjustified or arbitrary, hold that the directors have acted inequitably and order that the company be wound up.[16] However, whereas a member can undoubtedly complain of any

---

13 *Lewis v Haas* 1970 SLT (Notes) 67.
14 *Re A and BC Chewing Gum Ltd, Topps Chewing Gum Inc v Coakley* [1975] 1 All ER 1017, [1975] 1 WLR 579.
15 *Ebrahimi Westbourne Galleries Ltd* [1973] AC 360, [1972] 2 All ER 492. It is likely that in cases of exclusion from management, such further matters as informal understandings concerning the conduct of the business and voting agreements will prove to be important.
16 *Ebrahimi v Westbourne Galleries Ltd* [1973] AC 360, [1972] 2 All ER 492, disapproving of *Re Cuthbert Cooper & Sons Ltd* [1937] Ch 392, [1937] 2 All ER 466, a decision to contrary effect.

attempt to exclude him from the benefits of a membership, a petition will not succeed when the petitioner's complaint is that an understanding upon which a business was carried on should be and is not being altered to provide for his inclusion. The petitioner cannot complain where the controllers do no more than act in accordance with what was the settled practice between them.[17]

Nevertheless, the principles expounded in *Ebrahimi v Westbourne Galleries Ltd*[18] do not permit the Court to grant an injunction preventing the expulsion or preventing the company from exercising its legal rights. In particular, the Court cannot prevent the company from exercising its right to remove a director under CA 1985, s 303.[19] *Ebrahimi v Westbourne Galleries Ltd*[20] merely establishes that 'if the plaintiff is removed under a power valid in law then he may, in appropriate circumstances, be entitled to a winding up order on the just and equitable ground.'[1]

In *Clemens v Clemens Bros Ltd*[2] it was suggested by the Court, in reliance upon *Ebrahimi v Westbourne Galleries Ltd*,[3] that equitable considerations could prevent a shareholder from exercising a vote in a particular way. Taken to its logical conclusion, this line of argument would in effect enable the Court to prevent the company or the shareholder from exercising its or his legal rights. It is submitted that the correct interpretation is that stated in *Bentley-Stevens v Jones*,[4] and not that stated in *Clemens v Clemens Bros Ltd*.[5]

A further point in connection with winding up should be mentioned. The petitioner may bring such a petition simply in order to provoke a settlement on more equitable terms. While the oppression remedy under s 459 may be more appropriate where the petitioner claims in respect of an injury to him as member, it may well not apply where his complaint is that of exclusion from management.[6] The Courts have sometimes asserted a broad equitable jurisdiction to deal with such matters.

An example of the discretion claimed is provided by a case

---

17 *Re Fildes Bros Ltd* [1970] 1 All ER 923, [1970] 1 WLR 592.
18 [1973] AC 360, [1972] 2 All ER 492.
19 *Bentley-Stevens v Jones* [1974] 2 All ER 653, [1974] 1 WLR 638.
20 [1973] AC 360, [1972] 2 All ER 492.
1 *Bentley-Stevens v Jones* supra at 655 per Plowman J.
2 [1976] 2 All ER 268.
3 [1973] AC 360, [1972] 2 All ER 492.
4 [1974] 2 All ER 653, [1974] 1 WLR 638.
5 [1976] 2 All ER 268.
6 But this would form a basis for a petition under s 459.

involving a freeze out from management.⁷ The petitioners had been given adequate financial information by the controllers to enable them to assess accurately the fairness of offers made for their shares and the Court accepted that the petitioner acted unreasonably in not accepting the offer. Vinelott J pointed out that a minority shareholder, unlike a partner, has no right to have the assets of a company sold in the open market so that he can be sure that a fair value is obtained for them, nor can he insist that the directors buy the shares at his own valuation or face a winding up. None the less, rather than dismiss the petition which a strict application of principle would seem to have required, His Lordship stood the petition over pending a settlement and further intimated that the shares should be valued at the current, lower valuation, because the petitioners acted unreasonably in refusing the former offer. The petitioner furthermore suffered in costs.

It is, however, submitted that the course of action taken by the Court, though convenient, cannot be justified by the statute because the Court is required to determine whether the petitioner is entitled to relief by way of winding up, a point which goes directly to jurisdiction.⁸ It should be noted that the petitioner is limited in arguing his petition to the heads of complaint set forth in it. He cannot refer to any new head not fairly covered by it. The Court, in deciding whether or not to grant a petition, has regard to the facts subsisting at the time of hearing. Past abuses, if amended, will not found an order.⁹

THE REMEDY UNDER SECTION 459

An alternative remedy, wholly independent of the just and equitable winding up, is available under the provisions of s 459 of the Companies Act 1985. It is no objection to a petition under s 459 that similar relief could also be given by a derivative action. In such a case, the petitioner is entitled to choose that procedure which is convenient to him.¹⁰. Section 459 provides that (where) the affairs of the company are being or have been conducted in a manner which is unfairly prejudicial to the interests of some part of the members or (where) any actual or proposed act or omission of the company (including an act or omission on its behalf) is or would be

7   *Re a Company* [1983] 2 All ER 854, [1983] 1 WLR 927.
8   See under s 459, on a similar point, *Re Bird Precision Bellows Ltd* [1986] Ch 658, [1985] 3 All ER 523.
9   *Re Fildes Bros Ltd* [1970] 1 All ER 923, [1970] 1 WLR 592.
10 *Re a Company* [1986] 2 All ER 253, [1986] 1 WLR 281.

prejudicial, the Court may, if satisfied that the application is well-founded, make such order as it thinks fit for giving relief in respect of the matters complained of. The Court may give relief against even a former member, for example an order that the former member buy out shares.[11] The Court may, in particular, make an order:

(1) regulating the conduct of the company's affairs in the future;
(2) requiring the company to refrain from doing or continuing an act complained of by the applicant or to do an act which the applicant has complained it has omitted to do;
(3) authorising civil proceedings to be brought in the name and on behalf of the company by such person or persons and on such terms as the Court may direct; or
(4) provide for the purchase of the shares of any members of the company by other members or by the company itself, and in the case of a purchase by the company, for the reduction of the company's capital.[12]

Clearly, the power to authorise civil proceedings to be brought in the company's name and on its behalf may, in an appropriate case, be exercised in favour of a minority shareholder. Any such proceedings brought by a minority shareholder pursuant to an order of the Court will not be subject to the restrictions imposed on minority shareholders' actions by the rule in *Foss v Harbottle*.[13] This statutory exception to the rule in *Foss v Harbottle*[14] may well, in time, prove to be the most important of the exceptions to that rule.

A petition may be brought by a member or any person to whom shares in the company have been transferred or transmitted by operation of law,[15] for example, the personal representative of a deceased member. A petition may also be brought by the Department of Trade.[16]

It is not clear whether a member who petitions under CA 1985, s 459 must allege unfair prejudice to his interests as member, or whether he may, as in the case of a just and equitable winding up, allege unfair prejudice to a wider range of interests, as for example those arising under any understandings concerning the right to

---

11 Ibid.
12 CA 1985, s 461(2)(d).
13 (1843) 2 Hare 461.
14 Ibid.
15 CA 1985, s 459(1) and (2).
16 Ibid, s 460.

manage. Under this provision's predecessor, s 210 of the CA 1948, the petitioner was obliged to allege conduct which injured him as a member. The present provision speaks, not as its predecessor did of injury to some part of the members, but of unfair prejudice to their interests.[17] Commentators assume that in this respect the law remains unchanged[18] and that view has been upheld in at least one reported case.[19] On the other hand, Vinelott J has suggested that the change in wording was intended to bring a case such as *Ebrahimi's* case within the section.[20] So too has Nourse J.[1] The matter remains doubtful; the wording may have been altered simply in the interests of elegance; after all, it was the interests of the members which were being injured before, as now but the better view seems to be that the wider connotation was intended.

Section 459 requires that the conduct complained of was unfairly prejudicial to some part of the members. Thus in *White, Petitioner*[2] where a majority of shareholders wished to replace directors who had determined to cause the company to bring an action against another company in which the majority was interested, the Court held that this could found an application under s 459. The replacement of directors would be unfairly prejudicial because a majority of the new directors would have an interest in the outcome of the action which would not coincide with the interests of the company. This, in turn, would be unfairly prejudicial to the interests of the plaintiff directors as shareholders. At least one decision seems to suggest that where the conduct adversely affects the interests of all shareholders alike, it may not be made the subject of a s 459 petition.[3] This, if so, looks decidedly odd, but it may be premised on the view that the normal machinery of the general meeting affords a sufficient vehicle of redress and, with respect to contrary views, the conclusion is consonant with the principles of majority rule and judicial abstention from interference with the internal affairs of companies, which s 459 may not have been intended to disturb. Its

---

17 *Re Five Minute Car Wash Services Ltd* [1966] 1 All ER 242, [1966] 1 WLR 745; *Re Lundie Bros Ltd* [1965] 2 All ER 692, [1965] 1 WLR 1051; *Elder v Elder & Watson Ltd* 1952 SC 49, 1952 SLT 112; as to cases where the status of petitioner as shareholders is concerned, see *Re Garage Door Associates Ltd* [1984] 1 All ER 434, [1984] 1 WLR 35.
18 Eg V. Joffe and A. Hochhauser, *The Companies Act 1980: A Practical Guide* (1980) para 12.203.
19 *Re a Company* [1983] Ch 178, [1983] 2 All ER 36.
20 *Re a Company* [1983] 2 All ER 854, [1983] 1 WLR 927.
1 *Re a Company* (1983) Times, 4 November.
2 1984 SLT 30.
3 *Re Carrington Viyella plc* (1983) 4 Co Law 164 and note by Sealey.

function may be to provide a wider range of procedures and ampler remedies.

Section 459 is cast in terms of unfairly prejudicial conduct. This must refer to a subsisting interest. A member cannot, for example, complain of the directors' refusal to propound a scheme of arrangement or purchase which might benefit him.[4] Otherwise, the phrase is a wide one, presumably much wider than the test which formerly applied (under CA 1948) of burdensome, harsh or wrongful.[5] A shareholder can bring himself within the provision by showing that the value of his shareholdings has been seriously diminished or jeopardised by the unfair conduct of the company's controller. The reach of the section is, however, wider, and extends to cases where the reasonable bystander would regard the petitioner as having been unfairly prejudiced. The petitioner need not show that the controller acted in bad faith or with a conscious intent to prejudice him.[6] It seems clear that at least some invasions of the shareholders' right to have the constitution observed will not be taken as unfairly prejudicial.[7] A member must, however, show not only prejudice, but also an element of unfairness. He cannot, therefore, complain of prejudicial conduct where the company can show that it acted fairly in the interests of the general body of shareholders.[8] Nor can he complain of exclusion from management where his own conduct is the substantial cause of the destruction of mutual competence between the parties in a company which is a quasi-partnership.[9]

Under s 459 the Court may make an order where the act or omission complained of or anticipated is a single instance; the Court's powers are not restricted to the case where there has been an unfairly prejudicial course of conduct.

As noted, the Court may, on a petition under s 459, make any order it thinks fit. Section 461 lists by the way of example, the following types of orders:[10]

(a) regulating the conduct of the company's affairs in future;
(b) requiring the company to refrain from doing or continuing to do an act complained of or to do an act which it has failed to do;

---

4 *Re a Company* [1983] 2 All ER 854, [1983] 1 WLR 927.
5 *Scottish Co-operative Wholesale Society v Meyer* [1959] AC 324, [1958] 3 All ER 66.
6 *Re R A Noble & Sons (Clothing) Ltd* [1983] BCLC 273.
7 *Re Carrington Viyella plc* (1983) 4 Co Law 164.
8 *Re Jermyn Street Turkish Baths Ltd* [1971] 3 All ER 184, [1971] 1 WLR 1042.
9 *Re R A Noble & Sons (Clothing) Ltd*, supra.
10 CA 1985, s 461(2).

(c) authorising civil proceedings to be brought in the name and on behalf of the company; and
(d) providing for the purchase of the petitioner's and other shares in the company by other members or by the company, and in the latter case making provision for the reduction of capital accordingly.

While there has as yet been little case law on these provisions, an example of the first type of order can be seen in *Re HR Harmer Ltd*,[11] a case under the former s 210 where a tyrannical father who held a majority of votes in the company by virtue of a weighted shareholding, exercised his control irregularly without regard to the wishes of the board. The Court upheld an order that the father be retained as a consultant, but that he not further interfere with the management of the company, but enjoy the office of life president without duties, rights or powers. In short, the power is a wide one, to restructure management.

The order most commonly applied for is one which directs the majority of the company to purchase the petitioner's shares. Here, there have been helpful statements on the issue of share valuations, always a difficult problem where the shares are not listed on the Stock Exchange or commonly dealt with. There is no categoric rule concerning the time at which shares are to be valued. If, for example, the petitioner acted unreasonably in refusing offers made for his shares, and the company's business deteriorates in the period preceding the petition, the shares may be properly valued in accordance with the company's state of affairs at the time of hearing.[12] This may well not apply, however, where the respondent's misconduct, rather than general economic conditions, caused the diminution in value. Where the respondents refuse to make a fair offer and the company's business declines, the fair rule may be to order a valuation at the date of the matters complained of. Again, where share values might have suffered a change by reason of the manner in which business was carried on or assets used over a period during which negotiations were taking place, it may be that valuation should relate to a date prior to the petition.[13] In some cases it may, in valuing shares, be right to take into account the fact that the petitioner was frozen out of all benefits in the company.[14]

---

11 [1958] 3 All ER 689, [1959] 1 WLR 62.
12 *Re a Company* [1983] 2 All ER 854, [1983] 1 WLR 927.
13 *Re OC (Transport) Services Ltd* [1984] LS Gaz R 1044.
14 *Re a Company* [1983] 2 All ER 854, [1983] 1 WLR 927.

In several recent cases the Courts have ventured some general guidance in matters of share valuation. The existence of any general rule concerning valuation has been denied.[15] The Court has a wide discretion to do whatever is fair and right in the circumstances. Where the petitioner acquired shares on the formation of a company formed to take over an existing business or to start a new one on what was essentially a quasi-partnership basis, the valuation adopted cannot properly be discounted on the footing that the shares represent a minority holding. The petitioner, after all, seeks an order because of unfair prejudice by the controllers making it intolerable for him to remain a member. His shares should be valued pro rata according to the value of the company's shares as a whole. If the order provides for the purchase of a delinquent majority, it would not be fair to give them a price which involved an element of premium. A discounted valuation might be proper where the petitioner deserved to be excluded. Such a basis might well be proper also where the petitioner acquired his shares originally on a discounted basis. A shareholder who acquired shares from another at a discounted price because they were a minority shareholding, cannot expect to be bought out at a price which is more favourable than his predecessor would have received. In general, however, the pro rata basis for valuation appears to be that which the Courts favour in the absence of circumstances pointing to another basis as more just in the given case. Prima facie, an interest in a going concern ought to be valued as at the date of the order for purchase.[16] As in the normal s 459 case where there will have been no agreement for the purchase of shares, there can be no power in the Court to award interest on the purchase price in respect of any period before judgment.[17]

The Department of Trade also has powers which it can exercise for the benefit of the company. It has the right to institute proceedings for a civil remedy in certain cases, and it has wide powers of investigation. The Department can, for example, if it determines that it is expedient in the public interest that a company be wound up, apply to the Court for a winding up order on the just and equitable ground.[18] The report of an inspector appointed by the Department may afford sufficient evidence upon which the Court

---

15 *Re Bird Precision Bellows Ltd* [1986] Ch 658, [1985] 3 All ER 523; *Re a Company* (1983) Times, 4 November; *Re London School of Electronics* [1986] Ch 211, [1985] 3 WLR 474.
16 *Re London School of Electronics* [1986] Ch 211, [1985] 3 WLR 474.
17 *Re Bird Precision Bellows Ltd*, supra.
18 CA 1985, s 440.

can act, at least if the petition is not challenged.[19] The Department may, in addition to or instead of seeking a winding up order, petition under CA 1985, s 459 where the interests of some part of the company's members have been unfairly prejudiced. The Department, furthermore, has power to bring civil proceedings on behalf of the company, and in this respect is not limited by the rule in *Foss v Harbottle*.[20] The Department may, in particular, exercise its powers as the result of a preliminary investigation or full inspection, a topic dealt with in Chapter 13.

---

19 *Re Travel and Holiday Clubs Ltd* [1967] 2 All ER 606, [1967] 1 WLR 711.
20 CA 1985, s 438.

Chapter 12

Disclosure of Interests in the Securities of the Company

Every company must keep a register of the interests of directors in the shares and debentures of the company.[1] It is not only directors who must disclose; similar provisions apply to persons holding individually or in concert a 5% interest in the voting shares of the company. The purposes of disclosure are to enable members and others to determine what interests its controllers have in the company, and to enable members, and others, to determine who controls or may be in a position to obtain control of, the company.

DIRECTORS' INTERESTS

Disclosure of interests in the shares or debentures of the company or its associated company must be made to the company by existing directors and by persons who, having such interests, subsequently become directors. In addition, a director is obliged to notify the company in writing of the occurrence, while he is a director, of any of the following events:[2]

(1) any event in consequence of which he becomes or ceases to be interested in such shares or debentures;
(2) the entering into by him of a contract to sell any such shares or debentures;
(3) the assignment by him of a right granted to him by the company to subscribe for shares or debentures of the company;[3]
(4) the grant to him, or the assignment or exercise of a right granted to him by a subsidiary of the company, or by the company's holding company, or by a subsidiary of the

---

1 See Chap 8.
2 CA 1985, s 324.
3 Ibid, s 324(2)(c).

company's holding company of a right to subscribe for shares or debentures of the other company. Failure to comply with these provisions may subject the director to criminal penalties.[4]

These provisions are extended to the interests of spouses and infant children of directors, which must also be disclosed and registered.[5] Additional provisions for disclosure apply where the shares or debentures of the company are listed on a recognised Stock Exchange. In such a case, the company is obliged to notify the Stock Exchange of any matter which the director has notified to it pursuant to his obligations of disclosure[6] and which affects the listed securities.[7] The Stock Exchange is entitled to publish the information if it sees fit.

Schedule 13, Pt I of the Companies Act 1985 contains detailed rules to determine when a director is interested in securities. An interest of any kind suffices.[8] Briefly, a director is deemed to be so interested where:

(1) he is a beneficiary of a trust of any property which comprises any interest in shares or debentures;
(2) he enters into a contract to purchase shares (for cash or other consideration) or not being the registered holder he is entitled to exercise or to control the exercise of any right conferred by the holding of the shares, eg voting rights. This latter provision does not include a right to vote at any specified meeting of the company or class meeting which has been conferred by proxy;
(3) he can control one-third of the voting power in a company which is interested in the securities (or of that in a company which can control any of the voting power at general meetings of another company so interested) or if the directors of such a company are accustomed to act in accordance with his directions or instructions;
(4) otherwise than by virtue of an interest in a trust he has the right to call for or direct the delivery of the shares or debentures or to acquire an interest in shares or debentures or is under an obligation to take an interest in shares or

---

4 Ibid, s 324(2)(d).
5 Ibid, s 328.
6 Imposed by ibid, ss 324 and 328.
7 Ibid, s 329.
8 Ibid, Sch 13, Pt I, para 1.

debentures. This provision does not include rights or obligations to subscribe for shares or debentures.

These rules also apply to the determination of whether the spouse or infant children of a director are interested.[9] In the result, a wide range of personal and family interests of directors are subject to disclosure and registration.

OTHER INTERESTS[10]

A person who acquires a 5% interest[11] in voting shares of a public company, whether or not it is listed on a stock exchange, or who, having acquired such an interest ceases to have it, is obliged to inform the company of that fact and of any significant change in the number of shares in which he is interested above the 5% level.[12] An obligation to disclose is capable of arising in two circumstances. The first is where the person to his knowledge acquires any notifiable interest in the voting capital of the company or ceases to be interested in such shares (whether or not he retains an interest in other such shares). The second circumstance is where he becomes aware that he has acquired any notifiable interest in such shares, or that he has ceased to be interested in such shares in which he was previously interested.[13] Failure to fulfil the reporting requirements is made a criminal offence.[14]

The obligation to disclose arises; first, where the person becomes aware that he has a notifiable interest in the voting capital which he did not previously have; secondly, where he had such an interest but becomes aware that he no longer has such an interest; or, thirdly, where both before and after the event he had such an interest but becomes aware that the percentage levels of his interest immediately before and after the event are not the same.[15] Whether a

9 CA 1985, s 328(7).
10 For more detailed discussion, see L. H. Leigh and H. Edey, *The Companies Act, 1981* from which this account draws freely.
11 The 5% level may be altered by Statutory Instrument, and that may affect the duty to report: CA 1985, s 201(2).
12 'Voting share' means an issued share carrying rights to vote in all circumstances at general meetings of the company and includes a share the voting rights of which are temporarily suspended; CA 1985, s 198(2).
13 CA 1985, s 198(1)(a) and (b). Interest is defined in s 208, including certain interests arising under proxies or options, while s 209 indicates which interests may be disregarded, including certain interests held as security only. See also Public Companies (Disclosure of Interests in Shares) (Exclusions) Regulations 1982 (SI 1982/677) made under CA 1981, s 71(1)(j).
14 CA 1985, s 210.
15 Ibid, s 198(3).

person has a notifiable interest depends upon whether he knows facts which would render his interest notifiable; he comes under a duty to notify when he becomes aware of the relevant facts, not on the happening of an event of which he may be unaware.[16]

A person's interest may be affected simply by a change in the amount of the company's share capital of the relevant voting class. In such a case, a person who is aware of the change in circumstances, comes under a duty to report.[17] In effect, where there is an increase in share capital, no reporting or further reporting will be required. Where share capital is reduced, a person whose interest rises to the notifiable level as a result of the reduction, will be required to report.[18] A person who is required to report must do so in writing within five days of becoming aware of the relevant circumstances.[19]

Interests in shares may arise otherwise than through holding them as registered owner. Consequently, a notification of a person's interest must disclose the identity of each registered holder to which the notification relates, and the number of shares held by each registered holder, so far as known to the person making the notification. Once again, the obligation to notify depends upon awareness by the reporter of relevant facts.[20] Within five days of acquiring knowledge, the reporter must notify the company in writing concerning changes in registered holders or the number of shares held by each registered holder in which he is interested, even though there has been no such change in his aggregate shareholding as would require a fresh notification under the preceding section.[1]

Certain family and corporate interests must be disclosed. A person is taken to be interested in any shares in which his spouse or infant child or stepchild is interested.[2] A person is taken to be interested in shares if a body corporate is interested in them and either of two conditions concerning control is met. The first is that that body corporate or its directors are accustomed to act in accordance with his directions or instructions. The second is where he is entitled to exercise or control the exercise of one-third or more of

---

16 Ibid, s 198(4).
17 Ibid, s 198.
18 Ibid.
19 Ibid, s 199.
20 Ibid, s 202(1).
1 Ibid, s 202(2), (3) and (4); note that by s 202(5) a person interested in shares continues to be so regarded until he becomes subject to an obligation to make a notification that he no longer has a reporting interest in those shares.
2 Ibid, s 203.

the voting power at general meetings of that body corporate.³ Furthermore, a person who is entitled to exercise or control one-third of the voting power at general meetings of the body corporate is treated, for the purposes of attribution of interest, to be entitled to control the exercise of any of the voting power at general meetings of any other corporation which the first corporation is entitled to exercise.⁴

CONCERT PARTIES

The disclosure provisions apply to interests arising under concert parties. Here, a word of explanation is necessary. The purpose of the concert party provisions is to give companies early warning of combinations to acquire shares which could be as significant as the build up of shares in the hands of individuals, and to prevent avoidance of the disclosure provisions by the use of nominee companies to amass significant holdings without falling under any obligation to notify the company involved.

The basic approach adopted is to identify a relationship between different persons and to provide for the mutual attribution of interests to each. Subject to an exception in favour of underwriting agreements, agreements between two or more persons for the acquisition of interests in a target company are brought under a reporting requirement, provided that certain conditions are met.⁵ The conditions are, first, that provisions exist in the agreement imposing obligations or restrictions on any one or more of the parties with respect to their use,⁶ retention or disposal of interests in that company's shares, whether or not together with any other interests of theirs in the target company's shares is in fact acquired by any of the parties pursuant to the agreement.⁷

Agreements are excluded which do not have as their object the acquisition of an interest, or which do not contain an element of mutual understanding concerning the way in which the interest acquired under the agreement is to be used.

The obligation to report may arise even though the agreement is not legally binding. A non-legally binding requirement is only

3   Ibid, s 203(2)(a) and (b).
4   Ibid, s 203(3); for circumstances in which a person is entitled to exercise control, see s 203(4).
5   Ibid, s 204.
6   For the definition of use, see s 204(3).
7   Ibid, s 204(2)(a) and (b); once such an interest is acquired, the agreement remains subject to the section even though no further shares are acquired under it, the parties to it change, or its terms are varied, or it is an agreement substituted for the original: ibid, s 204(4).

256 *Chapter 12 Disclosure of Interests in the Securities of the Company*

comprehended where there is mutuality in the undertakings, expectations or understandings of the parties to it.[8] This curious, and probably redundant stipulation, is intended to exclude, inter alia, the case where one person agrees with another that he will buy shares and simply hold them.

Because the object of the reporting provisions is to notify the company of the totality of share interests of reporting persons, since otherwise the provisions would not give adequate warning, the whole of each party's interests is attributed to the other party or parties to the agreement.[9] An interested person who is required to report must notify the company of the whole of his interests, including those which arise otherwise than under the agreement, together with the totality of the interests of other parties to the agreement. If a party to an agreement is party to another, separate agreement in respect of shares of the same target company—a spider's web of agreements—all the interests which he has under such agreements will be attributable to him.[10]

The obligation to report lies upon each party to the agreement, but the members can nominate one of their number to act for all. That would not, of course, absolve the other members from liability in the event of the nominee's failure to report.

A notification made by a member of a concert party shall state that the reporter is a party to a relevant agreement, shall state who are the members of it, and shall contain particulars of the interests arising under it.[11] A person is also to give notice when he ceases to be a member of such an agreement.[12]

Members of concert parties are required to keep each other informed of all relevant facts. A party to such an agreement must notify his fellows in writing of particulars of any interest of his arising otherwise than under the agreement, where the company concerned is a public company, the shares in question are or include voting capital of the company, and he knows the facts which make the agreement subject to the reporting requirements, and the facts specified above concerning the company and its shares.[13] A reporter must, therefore, not only disclose to his fellows interests arising under the agreement, but also interests in such shares arising from notifiable family or corporate interests, or under other

8 Ibid, s 204(6), for further explanation see L. H. Leigh and H. C. Edey, op cit, p 302.
9 Ibid, s 205(1).
10 Ibid, s 205(2) and (3).
11 Ibid, s 205(4).
12 Ibid, s 205(5).
13 Ibid, s 206(1) and (2).

agreements.[14] He must also notify his fellows of particulars of the registered ownership of other voting shares of the company in which he is interested apart from the agreement.[15]

A member of an active concert party, or a person to whom family or corporate interests are attributed as a result, must notify the company as soon as his interest passes the 5% limit, or such other limit as may be set, or where the person ceases to be interested in such shares.[16] Three circumstances are specified when a person becomes or ceases to be interested in shares by virtue of another person's interest: where the relationship comes into being or ceases; where the relationship exists when such a related person acquires or disposes of an interest; or because the person in question joins a concert party or leaves one. The same principle applies where the agreement ceases to amount to a concert party.[17] The requirement of knowledge is satisfied when the person knows both the relevant facts with respect to that other person's interest in those shares, and the relevant facts by virtue of which he himself has become or ceased to be interested in the shares in accordance with the provisions of the CA 1985, discussed above.

REGISTER OF INTERESTS IN SHARES

Every public company is obliged to maintain a properly indexed register of interests in shares, for the purpose of recording the required notifications.[18] A company which ceases to be a public company must continue to keep the register and associated index for a period of six years from the date upon which it ceases to be a public company.[19] While in principle the register is open to inspection, confidentiality is provided for so far as it contains information respecting a company which is entitled to exemption from disclosure in the accounts of particulars of shareholders in subsidiaries or other bodies corporate carrying on business outside the United Kingdom in circumstances where disclosure would be harmful to business.[20] Enforcement of the reporting requirements is facilitated by the grant of powers to the company to investigate interests held in its securities. These are dealt with in Chapter 13.

14 Ibid, s 206(3)(a) and (b).
15 Ibid, s 206(4).
16 Ibid, s 207.
17 Ibid, s 207(2)(a)–(d).
18 Ibid, s 211; full details of the register requirements are contained in s 211, including the criminal penalties for failure to keep it.
19 Ibid, s 211(7).
20 Ibid, s 211(9).

Chapter 13

Investigations and Inquiries

This chapter deals with investigations and inquiries into aspects of company affairs, both by the Department of Trade either at its own instance or that of others, and by the company itself. In the latter case we are concerned with inquiries into share ownership. The purpose of Departmental inquiries is to establish the facts where prima facie some irregularity has been shown in the way a company has been run and to report those facts to the Department. The inspector's report may lead to prosecution, or it may be published to inform investors, employees and creditors with information about how a company has been run, leading perhaps to civil proceedings, or it may found a winding up order. Over and above these uses, it may also provide a basis for public discussion, and action by governmental or professional bodies, on aspects of the law and administration which the facts show to be in need of improvement or reform.[1]

INSPECTIONS AND INVESTIGATIONS: THE POWERS

The Department of Trade has powers to call for an inspection of the company's books and papers, a step which falls short of a formal investigation, or it may decide to mount a formal investigation. Most formal investigations are preceded by Departmental inspection.

PRELIMINARY INSPECTIONS

In respect of the designated classes of bodies corporate, which includes all companies registered under the Companies Acts,[2] the

---

1 Department of Trade, *Handbook of the Companies Investigation System* (1980).
2 CA 1985, s 447(1).

Department may direct the body corporate to produce specified books and papers, or authorise any officer of the Department to specify books and documents which the company must produce to him.[3] Similarly, any person who appears to be in possession of such books or papers may be required to produce them.[4] Copies may be taken of papers when produced.[5] It is an offence to fail to comply with such directions.[6] The person who is required to produce books and papers, or any other person who is a present or past officer of the relevant body corporate may be required to provide an explanation of any of them.[7] A statement so made may be used in evidence in civil or criminal proceedings against its maker.[8] Such an inspection is a policing measure. The Department's officers are expected to act fairly, but a company or individual cannot decline to produce material on the ground that the inspector is biased against him or it.[9]

In addition to demanding production, the Department may obtain a warrant from a justice of the peace empowering a constable to enter premises and search for and seize books and documents of the company under inspection.[10]

Material obtained either as a result of a Departmental direction or under a search warrant is protected from disclosure unless the company under inspection consents in writing to its disclosure.[11] There are, however, exceptions to confidentiality where disclosure is required:[12]

(a) in respect of a prosecution under or arising out of the Companies Act 1985, the Insider Dealing Act 1985, the Insurance Companies Act 1982, or any criminal proceedings for an offence entailing misconduct in connection with the management of the body's affairs or misapplication or wrongful retainer of its property;

(b) in respect of criminal proceedings arising out of the Exchange Control Act 1947 (the operation of which is currently suspended);

---

3 Ibid.
4 Ibid, s 447(4).
5 Ibid, s 447(5).
6 Ibid, s 447(6).
7 Ibid, s 447(5) (2).
8 Ibid, s 447(8).
9 *R v Secretary of State for Trade, ex p Perestrello* [1980] 1 QB 19, [1980] 3 All ER 28.
10 Ibid, s 447.
11 Ibid, s 449.
12 Ibid, s 449.

(c) for the purposes of the examination of any person by an inspector appointed under ss 431, 432, 442 or 446 of the CA 1985;
(d) for the purpose of enabling the Secretary of State to exercise his functions, in relation to the corporation under inspection or any other body, of any of his functions under the Companies Act 1985, the Financial Services Act 1986, the Insider Dealing Act 1985, the Insurance Companies Act 1982; and
(e) for the purposes of proceedings in respect of obstructing a search warrant.

Ancillary provisions make it an offence to destroy, mutilate or falsify records, or[13] to knowingly or recklessly make false explanations or statements.[14] There is a saving from disclosure on grounds of legal professional privilege, and a limited protection for bankers in respect of customers' records.[15]

FORMAL INVESTIGATIONS

The Department of Trade has discretionary powers to appoint inspectors either on the motion of the company or a specified proportion of its members, or on its own motion. It may, in addition, be required by the court to appoint inspectors.

In cases where members or the company wish to requisition an investigation, the following powers apply. The Department may appoint inspectors to inspect and report:[16]

(1) in the case of a company having a share capital, on the application either of not less than 200 members or of members holding not less than one-tenth of the shares issued;
(2) in the case of a company not having a share capital, on the application of not less than one-fifth of the company's registered shareholders; and
(3) in any case, on the application of the company. The application must be supported by evidence showing good reason for requesting the investigation. The applicants may be required to furnish security for costs of the investigation not exceeding £5,000 or such other sum as the Secretary of State may specify by order.[17]

13 CA 1985, s 450.
14 Ibid, s 451.
15 Ibid, s 452.
16 Ibid, s 431.
17 Ibid, s 431(4).

The court may by order require the Department to appoint inspectors.[18] In addition, the Department may appoint inspectors on its own motion where it appears to the Department that there are circumstances suggesting that the affairs of the company have been conducted for fraudulent or unlawful purposes, or in a manner which is unfairly prejudicial to some part of its members, or that any actual or proposed act or omission of the company or on its behalf is or would be so prejudicial, or that it was formed for any fraudulent or unlawful purpose; or that persons concerned with its formation or the management of its affairs have been guilty in connection therewith of fraud, misfeasance or other misconduct towards it or towards its members; or that its members have not been given all the information with respect to its affairs that they might reasonably expect.[19] The Department of Trade may order an inspection on the above grounds even though the company is being voluntarily wound up.[20]

Inspectors appointed under these provisions who think it necessary to do so, have the power to investigate and report on the affairs of related companies.[1] These are defined as any company which is or has at any relevant time been the company's subsidiary or holding company or a holding company of its subsidiary.

In addition to the above powers, the Department of Trade is empowered to appoint inspectors to investigate and report on the membership of any company, and otherwise with respect to the company for the purpose of determining the true persons who are or have been financially interested in the real or apparent failure of the company, or able to control or materially influence its policy.[2] It may order an investigation into share dealings in order to determine whether contraventions of the disclosing provisions of the CA 1985 have occurred.[3] Furthermore, where a liquidator of a company in voluntary winding up reports to the DPP or Lord Advocate that any present or past officer of a company has committed a criminal offence in relation to its affairs, the DPP or Lord Advocate may refer the report to the Department of Trade for further inquiry. In such case, the Department may exercise all the powers available to inspectors under ss 431 and 432 of the CA 1985.[4]

---

18 Ibid, s 432(1).
19 Ibid, s 432(2).
20 Ibid, s 432(3).
1 Ibid, s 433.
2 Ibid, s 442.
3 Ibid, s 446.
4 IA 1986, s 218(4).

Inspectors, and the Department, enjoy wide powers to compel the production of documents, and evidence, on investigation. Officers and agents of the company and of any other body corporate whose affairs are being investigated are under a duty to produce books and documents relating to those bodies which are in their custody or power, to attend before the inspectors when required to do so, and otherwise to give to the inspectors all assistance in connection with the investigation which they are reasonably able to give.[5] Persons not formally connected with any company under investigation who the inspectors consider to have relevant information may also be placed under similar obligations.[6] This provision will, it is submitted, enable inspectors to require an officer of a body corporate which, while not a subsidiary or holding company of the company under investigation, was used in a suspect transaction involving the investigated company, to give information concerning its affairs. It also would make officers of the Take-Over Panel and presumably the Stock Exchange, compellable witnesses in an investigation. It is likely that in practice the Department will continue to emphasise that inspectors should approach these bodies with some circumspection.[7]

Inspectors may in certain circumstances require a director or past director of the company or other body corporate under investigation to produce documents relating to a bank account maintained by him jointly, or with another person, provided certain statutory conditions are met.[8] These are, briefly, that the following categories of payments have been paid into it, namely, undisclosed directors' emoluments, or moneys relating to certain undisclosed contracts and transactions between the director and his company,[9] or any money which has been connected in any way with any act or omission or series thereof which constituted misconduct by that director towards the company or its members. Such misconduct need not have been fraudulent. There seems no reason why negligent misconduct would not suffice, but some element of turpitude at least in that latter sense is, we submit, required.

Inspectors may examine any person required to give evidence

---

5   CA 1985, s 434; note that similar obligations are imposed on officers by IA 1986, s 218 in respect of prosecutions following liquidators' reports.
6   Ibid, s 434.
7   Department of Trade, *Handbook of the Companies Inspection System* (1980), Appendix C.
8   Ibid, s 435.
9   Note in particular the provisions of s 435(2) concerning transactions involving banks and their directors.

under the above provisions, on oath.[10] Where such a person refuses to produce books and documents or answer questions, the inspectors may refer the matter to the court which may punish the offender as if he had been guilty of contempt of court.[11] Furthermore, no claim for privilege on the grounds of self-incrimination applies to the proceedings; officers may be required to give evidence notwithstanding that their evidence may tend to incriminate them.[12]

In this connection it should be observed that generally all evidence given by a person to an inspector, whether sworn or unsworn, is admissible in subsequent proceedings, whether criminal or civil, brought against him by the company or its liquidator. Accordingly, the transcripts of the witness's evidence—and if his evidence is subsequently amplified in correspondence, the latter—are, unless excluded from disclosure by reason of the fact that they are confidential documents which the public interest requires to be so excluded, admissible.[13]

In addition to their final report, inspectors may make and may be required to make, interim reports to the Department.[14] An inspector may, indeed, inform the Department of Trade at any time of circumstances tending to show that an offence has been committed, without making an interim report.[15] This is intended to militate against delay in the mounting of prosecutions.

The expenses of an investigation under the preceding sections are met in the first instance by the Department of Trade.[16] The Department may, however, recoup its costs from certain categories of persons specified in s 439 of the CA 1985. These include persons convicted on a prosecution brought as a result of such an investigation or ordered to pay damages or restore property as a result; a company which has recovered money or property as a result of such proceedings; any body corporate dealt with by the report when the inspector was appointed otherwise than by the Department's own motion and the applicant or applicants for the investigation where the inspector was appointed under s 431 of the CA 1985, that is, on

10 CA 1985, s 434(3).
11 Ibid, s 436.
12 Ibid, s 434(5). Even before the amendments, incriminating statements were admissible; *Re Pergamon Press* [1970] 2 All ER 449, affd [1970] 3 All ER 535.
13 *London and County Securities Ltd v Nicholson* [1980] 3 All ER 861, [1980] 1 WLR 948.
14 CA 1985, s 437(1); for provisions relating to publication of the report, see s 437(2) (3): for its status as evidence, see s 441.
15 Ibid, s 433(2).
16 Ibid, s 439.

264　*Chapter 13 Investigations and Inquiries*

the motion of the company or a percentage of its members. A person made liable under these provisions is not necessarily made liable for the full costs of the investigation; the court or the Department may require him to pay a lesser amount.[17]

The Department of Trade may, in its discretion and of its own motion, appoint inspectors to investigate and report on the membership of any company.[18] It is under a duty to do so where a sufficient number of shareholders so require, unless the Department is satisfied that the application is vexatious.[19] A comparison of these powers with those under s 431 where the application may also be made by the company suggests that, save in cases of clear public interest where the Department may wish to act on its own motion, a company which wishes to have its share ownership investigated will be expected to proceed under the powers conferred on it by s 212, discussed below. The powers under s 442 are apparently intended to enable minority shareholders to determine who really is responsible for the financial affairs of and policies followed by the company.

The powers which apply to investigations into the company apply, with modifications, into investigations into share ownership. Their effect is that inspectors may require information not only from persons believed to be financially interested in the company's real or apparent success or failure, and persons able to control or materially influence policy, but also from any other person whom the inspector has reasonable cause to believe possesses relevant information.[20] The Secretary of State may, for good reason, keep certain parts of a report confidential.[1] Expenses of such an investigation are met by the Department of Trade.[2]

In addition, the Department may, where it thinks that there is good reason to investigate the ownership of a company's securities, but that it is unnecessary to appoint inspectors, require any person whom they have reasonable cause to believe to have or to be able to obtain information concerning present or past share ownership, to give information to the Secretary of State.[3]

The Department of Trade may impose substantial restrictions in respect of shares and debentures whose ownership is under

---

17　Ibid, note that by s 439(6) the inspectors may make recommendations concerning who should defray costs and to what extent.
18　Ibid, s 442.
19　Ibid, s 442(3).
20　Ibid, s 443(2).
 1　Ibid, s 443(3).
 2　Ibid, s 443(4).
 3　Ibid, s 444.

investigation.[4] These render transfers of the shares void, provide that no voting rights shall be exercisable in respect of them, prevent rights issues or issues made pursuant to an offer to the holder of the shares, and prevent any payment being made by the company in respect of those shares, whether in respect of capital or otherwise, except in a liquidation.[5] Furthermore, save in respect of an approved sale, any agreement to transfer shares or the right to be issued with unissued shares, is void.[6] Where the restrictions on issuing shares or making payments on shares apply, any agreement to transfer any right to be issued with the shares or to receive any payment on them, except in a liquidation, is also void. Again this is subject to agreements made subject to the approval of the court or the Secretary of State.[7]

An aggrieved person may apply to the court for an order directing that the restrictions be lifted.[8] The court, or the Secretary of State, may make an order lifting such restrictions only if it or he is satisfied that the relevant facts have been disclosed to the company and that no unfair advantage accrued to any person as a result of the failure to disclose, or the shares are to be sold and the court or the Secretary of State approves the sale.[9] Where any shares in a company are made subject to restrictions under s 445, the court may direct that they be sold, subject to its approval of the terms of sale, and restrictions imposed upon them may be lifted in consequence.[10]

As with preliminary inspections, provision is made for legal professional privilege, and in favour of the company's bankers who need not disclose information about the affairs of any of their other customers.[11]

THE PROCEDURES[12]

Investigations into the affairs of private companies are usually carried out by Departmental personnel; in the case of large public

4 Ibid, s 445.
5 Ibid, s 454(1).
6 Ibid, s 454(2).
7 Ibid, ss 454(3) and 456(3)(b).
8 Ibid, s 456(1).
9 Ibid, s 456(3).
10 Ibid; for consequential provisions, and in particular concerning the payment of proceeds to persons beneficially interested, see ibid, s 457, and *Re Ashbourne Investments Ltd* [1978] 2 All ER 418, [1978] 1 WLR 1346.
11 Ibid, s 452.
12 Much of the ensuing discussion relies upon Department of Trade, *Handbook of the Companies Inspection System* (1980), and L. H. Leigh, *The Control of Commercial Fraud* (1982) chap 11.

companies a Queen's Counsel and an eminent accountant are appointed. It is considered desirable that investigations be completed within 12 months, and the Department may indicate to inspectors those aspects of the company's affairs which it considers warrant particular attention.

Most investigations are commenced by the Department under its own powers in s 432 of the CA 1985. The Department considers that its powers are for use principally in cases of fraud, misfeasance or other misconduct, including conduct unfairly prejudicial to members. An important ground invoked in some of the leading investigations has been a failure to keep members informed of the affairs of the company. The Department's powers are not, however, intended for use in cases of simple insolvency, or as a substitute for civil remedies available through the courts, or in cases of simple mismanagement.

When exercising its powers, the Department of Trade must act in good faith, but as long as it does so, it is not obliged to disclose the material in its possession which has induced it to appoint inspectors, or to give reasons for the inquiry. The company is not entitled to be informed in advance that the Department proposes to appoint inspectors and the Department does not need to give the company an opportunity to state its case or to submit its comments before the appointment is made. It is for the Secretary of State to weigh the need for an investigation against any possible prejudice to the company.[13]

In conducting an investigation, inspectors are under a duty to act fairly. Their inquisitorial procedures have been described thus:[14]

'The powers and procedures of company inspectors are exceptional in English jurisprudence. They sit in private. As the case develops they must devise and frame their own provisional charges and accusations and then proceed to test them. Everyone may become a "defendant" to a possible criticism but he is not able to cross-examine his accusers. Even mild criticism of professional men can be extremely damaging. Unless inspectors are very careful a witness may not be aware of the strength of the evidence against him in time to make his answers.'

Lurid comment upon persons under investigation should be eschewed.

---

13 *Norwest Holst Ltd v Secretary of State for Trade* [1978] Ch 201, [1978] 3 All ER 280.
14 Department of Trade, *Peachey Property Corporation Limited*, Report (1979) at p 4.

The Courts have declined to lay down hard and fast rules concerning the conduct of investigations. Persons giving evidence may not require the inspector to adopt a particular procedure or refuse to answer questions because he will not do so. The inspector is under a duty to act fairly, but not to adopt any particular procedure.[15] The inspector should put to a witness any points that he proposes to consider which may involve criticism of the witness but he is not obliged to put every matter of detail to him. Furthermore, the inspector is under no obligation, once he has heard all the evidence and reached his conclusions, to put to the witness any conclusion he has reached which is critical of him.[16]

In practice, inspectors adopt elaborate procedures in the interests of fairness, and these can result in protracted investigations.[17] Witnesses are supplied with transcripts of their own evidence. They are given full opportunity to develop their version of the case, are informed of criticisms to be made of their conduct, and are invited to comment upon them. Legal representation is permitted. Witnesses may be given the opportunity to comment on draft conclusions. They have not, however, been allowed to examine other witnesses or to have transcripts of the evidence of other witnesses. On the whole, it is fanciful to liken the procedures followed by inspectors to Star Chamber tactics.[18]

THE RESULT OF INVESTIGATIONS

As we have noted, investigations may lead to criminal prosecution or civil redress, at the suit either of the company or the Department of Trade. In this latter aspect it is important to note the status of the report as evidence. A certified copy of any inspector's report is admissible in any legal proceedings as evidence of the opinion of the inspectors in relation to any matter contained in the report.[19] More significantly, it has now been held that a contributory who moves to wind up a company may rely on the report of Departmental inspectors to the same extent as the Secretary of State could on a petition presented by him. Such a report is not mere hearsay because inspectors act in a statutory fact-finding capacity. The court may

---

15 *R v Harris* [1970] 3 All ER 746, [1970] 1 WLR 1252; *Re Pergamon Press* [1970] 2 All ER 449, [1970] 1 WLR 1075, affd [1971] Ch 388, [1970] 3 All ER 535.
16 *Maxwell v Department of Trade and Industry* [1974] QB 523, [1974] 2 All ER 122.
17 Department of Trade, *Scotia Investments Ltd*, Report (1981) chap 9.
18 Cf L. Sealey [1974] Camb LJ 225.
19 CA 1985, s 441.

268 Chapter 13 Investigations and Inquiries

thus take the report into account in deciding whether to order a winding up. The respondent may of course bring evidence to challenge it.[20]

COMPANY INVESTIGATIONS INTO SHARE OWNERSHIP[1]

A public company may itself investigate interests in its own shares. The present government assumes that companies should themselves take the initiative in obtaining information about interests in shares with recourse to the Department of Trade or the courts being a last resort.

Accordingly, CA 1985, s 212 provides that a public company may by notice in writing require any person whom the company knows or has reasonable cause to believe to be, or, at any time during the three years immediately preceding the date on which the notice is issued to have been interested in shares comprised in the voting capital of the company, to confirm that fact or not, and if it be confirmed, to supply information about his interest. The notion of an interest in shares corresponds roughly to the notion employed for the purposes of disclosure of share interests. It thus includes family and corporate interests, and the mutual interests of members of a concert party,[2] and options to subscribe for shares.[3] The company's power to require information is not limited to discovering who actually controls or is interested in the affairs of the company, as is the power under s 442 of the CA 1985, nor is it restricted to requiring information of a member; it can make inquiries of any person whom it considers to have been or to be interested in the company's voting capital.

In order to protect the company against abuse by persons in control of it, CA 1985, s 214 enables members holding at the date of requisition not less than one-tenth of the paid up equity capital of the company to requisition an investigation into share ownership.[4] The company is bound to act upon a proper requisition.[5] Two

20 *Re St Piran Ltd* [1981] 3 All ER 270, [1981] 1 WLR 1300; note, however, that because such a report contains only opinion and hearsay it is inadmissible in any other proceedings; *Savings and Investment Bank Ltd v Gasco Investments (Netherlands) BV* [1984] 1 All ER 296, [1984] 1 WLR 271.
1 For a detailed account of these provisions, see L. H. Leigh and H. C. Edey, *The Companies Act 1981*, paras 320–331.
2 CA 1985, s 212(5).
3 Ibid, s 212(6), but the limitations to s 209 (disregarded interests) do not apply. On disclosure generally, see Chap 12, ante.
4 CA 1985, s 214.
5 Ibid, s 212(4).

safeguards are provided against dilatory investigations. Where the investigation has not been completed within a period of three months, the company is under a duty to prepare an interim report, and a further interim report must be prepared at successive intervals of three months.[6] In addition, members could request the Department of Trade to appoint inspectors or to investigate under ss 442–444 of the CA 1985.

An investigation is to be regarded as concluded when the company has made all such inquiries as are necessary or expedient for the purposes of the requisition and, in the case of each such inquiry, either a response has been received by the company or the time allowed for such a response has elapsed.[7]

Where a person who has been required to furnish information about his interest in shares fails to do so, and he is or was in fact so interested (and not merely reasonably believed to be interested in particular shares), the company may apply to a court for an order that the shares be subject to the restrictions imposed by ss 454–457 of the CA 1985.[8] This formulation has the curious consequence that shares in which a person is merely believed to be interested cannot be restricted. This must detract from the utility of the investigation machinery. The power to restrict also depends upon there being shares which can be identified as prima facie the subject of investigation, and in which the person required to provide information may reasonably be thought to be interested.

The courts have only begun to construe these provisions. They have held that a restriction order may be made notwithstanding that the person required to disclose has declined to do so on the ground that he is the nominee or ultimate nominee of a person to whom he is bound by an undertaking to hold the information in confidence.[9] This is so even though the nominee's principal is a foreign corporation, itself holding for another, and would, if disclosure were made, be in breach of the criminal law of its jurisdiction of incorporation. As the court points out, it is not the English nominee which will be affected, but the ultimate principal and he, of course, could disclose his own interest without adverse criminal consequences.[10]

Where restrictions are imposed under these provisions, they may only be lifted by the court which may thus maintain or lift restrictions on shares or order their sale. The company or person

---

6 Ibid, s 215.
7 Ibid, s 215(6).
8 Ibid, s 216.
9 *House of Fraser Petitioner* 1983 SLT 500n.
10 *Re F H Lloyd Holdings plc* [1985] BCLC 293.

aggrieved may apply to the court for an order lifting the restrictions.[11] Obviously, the principal reason for doing so will be that the information requested has now been furnished. A court might however require an applicant to show that he did not obtain an unfair advantage as a result of non-disclosure, or might force the sale of shares as a condition of liberating them. The legislation does not, however, indicate with any particularity how the court's powers might be exercised.

---

11 Ibid, s 456.

Chapter 14

Meetings and Proceedings

The articles usually confer on the directors general authority to carry on the company's business.[1] Ultimate control over the company's business is vested in the shareholders in general meeting.[2] The articles will provide for the calling each year of an annual general meeting and for extraordinary meetings to be called when necessary.[3] All general meetings other than the annual general meetings are called extraordinary general meetings.[4]

A single shareholder cannot, as a general rule,[5] constitute a meeting. Where, therefore, one member proposed a resolution but was at that time the only member present, there was no longer a meeting at which a resolution could be passed.[6] This rule does not necessarily apply where a meeting at which the quorum required by the articles[7] was originally present subsequently falls below the number required. In such a case, the meeting may, depending upon the terms of the articles, still proceed to conduct business. In *Re Hartley Baird Ltd*[8] the articles provided that:

> No business shall be transacted at any general meeting unless a quorum is present when the meeting proceeds to business.

A quorum was present when the meeting began, but when the vote was taken on the resolution placed before the meeting the number

---

1 See Chap 8, ante.
2 *Barron v Potter* [1914] 1 Ch 895; *Bamford v Bamford* [1970] Ch 212, [1969] 1 All ER 969.
3 Table A, art 37.
4 Table A, art 36.
5 There are special powers under CA 1985, s 367 enabling the Department of Trade and the Court to call a meeting even though the membership of the company be reduced to one.
6 *Re London Flats Ltd* [1969] 2 All ER 744, [1969] 1 WLR 711.
7 See eg Table A, art 40; CA 1985, s 370(4).
8 [1955] Ch 143, [1954] 3 All ER 695.

was reduced below the quorum. One member who opposed the resolution had left the meeting. Wynn-Parry J held that the resolution was valid; on a construction of the articles it was sufficient for a quorum to be present when the meeting began.

The matter is, however, governed by the articles and, under the current form, art 41 of Table A to the CA 1985, the rule is that if a quorum ceases to be present, the meeting shall stand adjourned.

The general meeting of the company possess wide powers. There are, however, restrictions on its competence. For example, the general meeting may not exercise powers vested in the directors by the articles. Certain restraints are imposed by general legal principles. Thus, a general meeting could not alter the contractual rights of debenture holders and it cannot vary the contractual rights of shareholders by ordinary resolution.[9] The exercise of certain of its powers may subject the company to onerous consequences. While the general meeting can in theory always dismiss a director,[10] this power may be stultified by articles giving weighted voting rights.[11] And, even if this is not done, the company may in some cases be forced to compensate a dismissed director for breach of a collateral service contract.[12]

In spite of such limitations, the reserve functions of the general meeting have long been regarded as vital.[13] Accordingly, both statutory and common law rules have been devised in order to ensure that meetings will be called, that information sufficient adequately to inform the shareholders of the state of the company's affairs and the nature of the business to be conducted shall be given, and that shareholders shall have, if they so desire, an opportunity to be heard in respect of company management and policy. The law does not force shareholders to take an active part in the management of their company and most do not, in fact, do so. It can and does provide enabling machinery.

For certain purposes, a general meeting of a particular class of shareholders must be held.[14]

General meetings at which all members may attend and vote consist of the annual general meeting and extraordinary general meetings.

---

9 See Chap 7, ante.
10 CA 1985, s 303.
11 *Bushell v Faith* [1970] AC 1099, [1970] 1 All ER 53, HL.
12 CA 1985, s 303(5), and see *Shindler v Northern Raincoat Co Ltd* [1960] 2 All ER 239, [1960] 1 WLR 1038 and Chap 8, ante.
13 Report of the Company Law Committee Cmnd 1749 (1962) paras 100–107.
14 See, eg CA 1985, s 125.

THE ANNUAL GENERAL MEETING

An annual general meeting must be held in each calender year and not more than 15 months may elapse since the preceding annual general meeting. Notices calling the meeting must specify that it is the annual general meeting.[15] So long as the company holds its first annual general meeting within 18 months of incorporation it need not hold another meeting in the year of its incorporation or in the following year.[16] A company which makes default in holding an annual general meeting may be directed to do so by the Department of Trade acting on the application of any member. The Department of Trade has power to give such directions for the calling and conduct of the meeting as it thinks fit and may direct that one member of the company present in person or by proxy shall constitute a meeting.[17]

The Act does not specify in detail what business must be transacted at an annual general meeting, but the appointment of an auditor,[18] the adoption of the accounts,[19] the receipt of the directors' report[20] and the election and remuneration of directors are matters for the annual general meeting.[1]

EXTRAORDINARY GENERAL MEETINGS

An extraordinary general meeting may be convened by the directors if some business of special importance has arisen that justifies a meeting of members.[2] Such a meeting may also be convened on the requisition of members holding one-tenth of the voting power at a general meeting.[3] The requisition must state the objects of the meeting to be called, be signed by the requisitionists, and deposited

---

15 CA 1985, s 366, and see Table A, reg 38.
16 Ibid, s 366(2).
17 Ibid, s 367; failure to hold a meeting is punished by a default fine.
18 Strictly, the CA 1985, s 384 concerning the appointment of auditors refers back to s 227 thereof, and refers to a general meeting following the accounting reference period, but this will almost inevitably be the annual general meeting if the company is functioning normally.
19 CA 1985, s 241.
20 Ibid, s 235.
1 Table A, art 82 simply provides that directors' remuneration shall be determined by the general meeting.
2 Table A, art 37.
3 CA 1985, s 368; note that the obligation is to convene a meeting within 21 days of the resolution. It is not to hold a meeting within that period; *Re Windward Islands Enterprises (UK)* [1982] CLY 306.

at the registered office of the company. If the directors fail to proceed to convene a meeting within 21 days of the requisition, the persons making the requisition may do so. The expenses which they incur are payable by the company which is itself indemnified by withholding the sum from the directors' remuneration. Where an auditor has resigned, and his notice of resignation contains a statement that there are circumstances connected with his resignation which he considers should be brought to the attention of the members or creditors of the company, the auditor may require the directors to convene an extraordinary general meeting to receive and consider such explanation of those circumstances as the auditor may wish to place before it. The auditor is further entitled to require the company to circulate with the notice of the meeting a copy of any statement he wishes to make.[4]

In addition, the Court enjoys a reserve power on the motion of a director or a member to order a meeting to be held if it is impracticable to call a meeting in the normal way.[5] The normal way will of course be by requisition. *Re El Sombrero Ltd*[6] illustrates a situation in which the majority of the shares were held by X, and the two directors of the company held a minority interest. These three were the only shareholders and a quorum of two members was required for a meeting under the articles. The applicant, as majority shareholder, wished to submit resolutions to remove the directors. They declined to attend any such meeting, so preventing a quorum from being obtained. In granting the order, the Court held that its function was to determine whether on the facts, without the order, the desired meeting of the company could be conducted. Here, it could not. Similarly, the Court could order a meeting to be called of a two member company where one member had died.[7]

If the meeting is to function adequately as a check upon management, members must be apprised of the business to be conducted at it. Members must be given full notice both of the meeting and of the substance of the matters which the meeting is to consider. In the case of the annual general meeting of a limited company, at least 21 days' notice in writing must be given, and in the case of other meetings, at least 14 days' notice.[8] Where a resolution requires special notice, the company must be notified at least 28 days beforehand and the company must give its members notice of the

---

4   CA 1985, ss 390 and 391.
5   Ibid, s 371.
6   [1958] Ch 900. See also *Re H R Paul & Son* (1973) 118 Sol Jo 166.
7   *Jarvis Motors (Harrow) Ltd v Carabott* [1964] 3 All ER 89, [1964] 1 WLR 1101.
8   CA 1985, s 369.

resolution at the same time as it gives notice of the meeting.[9] Examples of resolutions requiring special notice are resolutions to appoint as auditor a person other than the retiring auditor or removing an auditor before the expiration of his term of office,[10] resolutions to remove a director[11] and resolutions to appoint a person over 75 years of age as a director.[12]

The leading case on what is meant by adequate notice of the business to be transacted is:

Baillie v Oriental Telephone and Electric Co Ltd [1915] 1 Ch 503.

The directors of the Oriental company used the majority voting power of that company in the subsidiary company to award themselves a substantial remuneration as directors of the subsidiary company. Later, on being advised that the scheme should have been approved by the Oriental company's shareholders, they called an extraordinary general meeting to approve the remuneration and to alter the articles in order to enable the directors receive payments for their services on the boards of subsidiary companies. The notice gave a grossly inaccurate picture of the amount of remuneration in relation to the profits of the company. In setting aside of the resolution, Cozens-Hardy MR stated that:
... special resolutions obtained by means of a notice which did not substantially put the shareholders in a position to know what they were voting about cannot be supported.

Similarly, in *Normandy v Ind Coope & Co Ltd*[13] a notice which failed to specify that resolutions to make certain pension and retirement payments to managing directors and to increase the emoluments and allowances of other directors was held to be invalid. And there are other examples.[14] Notice therefore must disclose facts upon which the member can exercise an informed business judgment.

---

9   Ibid, s 379. This section does not confer upon an individual member the right to compel the inclusion of a resolution in the agenda of a meeting (*Pedley v Inland Waterways Association Ltd* [1977] 1 All ER 209), although such a right is given by CA 1985, s 376 to members holding one-twentieth of the voting rights or to 100 members holding shares the average paid-up value of which is at least £100.
10 CA 1985, s 388(1).
11 Ibid, s 303(2).
12 Ibid, s 293.
13 [1908] 1 Ch 84.
14 Eg *Pacific Coast Coal Mines Ltd v Arbuthnot* [1917] AC 607, PC.

PROXIES

There is a problem in ensuring, so far as possible, that members may exercise their voting rights. Most shareholders of large companies do not attend the general meeting. In some cases, to find adequate physical accommodation for all the members if they desired to attend would be impossible. The solution is to enable voting members of the company to execute instruments called proxies in favour of another person, enabling that person to exercise the members' voting rights. Any member may appoint a proxy. A person who holds a proxy to vote at a specified meeting of the company is not deemed to have an interest in the share.[15] A proxy may both demand and vote upon a poll.[16] Furthermore, the company cannot by its articles exclude the right to demand a poll upon issues of policy.[17] The proxy holder can, if he so wishes, cast the members' votes as they desire; that is, he can vote some in favour and some against particular resolutions.[18] The sample form of proxy in Table A, for example, enables the member to indicate whether he wishes his votes to be exercised for or against any particular resolution or resolutions.[19] It is by no means certain whether the proxy holder is bound to cast his votes in the manner prescribed by the member, though the better view would seem to be that as he is the member's agent, he must abide by the instructions of the member. It would seem however that the chairman of the meeting need not inquire whether the proxy holder has followed the member's instructions.[20] It is unclear whether the company with whom proxies are filed can be required by a member to permit the member to inspect the proxies. There is Commonwealth authority which suggests that members have a right to inspect.[1] The authority given by a proxy is valid until it has been revoked in writing and notice of revocation given to the company.[2] Even where a proxy has been

---

15 CA 1985, Sch 13, Pt I, para 3.
16 Ibid, s 372. A proxy form authorising a proxy to vote at more than one meeting is liable to stamp duty and the chairman is entitled to reject votes cast by proxies in reliance on forms which ought to have been stamped and are not; but it is not *ultra vires* for the company to accept such proxies: *Marx v Estates and General Investments Ltd* [1975] 3 All ER 1064, [1976] 1 WLR 380.
17 Ibid, s 373(2).
18 Ibid, s 374.
19 Table A, art 60.
20 *Second Consolidated Trust Ltd v Ceylon Amalgamated Tea and Rubber Estates* [1943] 2 All ER 567; *Cousins v International Brick Co Ltd* [1931] 2 Ch 90; cf *Oliver v Dalgleish* [1963] 3 All ER 330, [1963] 1 WLR 1274.
1 *Armstrong v Landmark Corpn Ltd* (1967) 85 WN (Pt I) (NSW) 238.
2 Table A, art 63.

given and has not been revoked, the member may still appear and vote in person, in which case the proxy cannot be used. The reason for requiring written revocation is to protect the company or the chairman when acting on votes given by proxy. Such protection is not required where the member attends in person since the invalidity of the particular proxy is thus clearly manifested.[3]

Proxies are in fact normally solicited, either for or on behalf of management which wishes to affirm its policies, or on behalf of dissentient members seeking to oppose the management. In this respect, the management enjoys considerable power. In *Peel v London and North Western Rly Co*[4] the Court held that management was not entitled, but was bound, to send out circulars explaining their policy, was entitled to solicit votes in support of that policy, and could pay the necessary expenses from company funds. This power must be exercised bona fide, but it may well be difficult to prove lack of good faith. On the other hand, the company is required to give notice to members of properly moved resolutions by dissentients and is bound to circulate to members any statement not exceeding 1,000 words in support of the resolution. The expenses of so circularising the members are borne by the proposers in the first instances, though the company in general meeting may resolve that it shall bear them.[5] This places a considerable premium on success. Furthermore, the company or any other aggrieved person can apply to the Court for an order that the company shall not be bound to circulate any statement on the ground that the right to require the company to circulate the statement is being abused to secure needless publicity for defamatory matter.[6]

PROCEEDINGS AT MEETINGS

Section 370 of the Companies Act 1985, sets out a number of general rules which, in the absence of detailed provisions in the articles, apply to the calling and conduct of general meetings. In practice, whether or not Table A is adopted or a set of specially drafted articles is employed, detailed provision is made in the articles for the conduct of meetings.

Section 370 and Table A provide:

---

3 *Cousins v International Brick Co Ltd* [1931] 2 Ch 90.
4 [1907] 1 Ch 5.
5 CA 1985, s 376.
6 Ibid, s 377(3).

(1) Notices of meetings shall be served as provided in Table A. Table A regulates the periods of notice required[7] (21 days in the case of an annual general meeting and a meeting called for the purpose of passing a special resolution, and 14 days in any other case) and the manner in which notice may be given to members: either personally or by post to him or to his registered address or to the address if any within the United Kingdom supplied by him to the company for the giving of notice to him.[8]

(2) Two or more members holding not less than one-tenth of the issued capital, or, if the company does not have a share capital, not less than 5% of the members may call a meeting. If Table A articles are employed, however, the power to convene a general meeting is placed in the hands of the directors.[9] The directors' power to call a meeting is a fiduciary power to be exercised in the best interests of the company.[10]

(3) Adjournments, while not a subject dealt with in the Act, is dealt with in the articles. Under Table A, art 57 gives the chairman the power, with the consent of any meeting at which a quorum is present, to adjourn the meeting. No business is to be transacted at the adjourned meeting other than business left unfinished at the meeting from which the adjourned meeting took place. The articles may (and it has been said often will) provide for the immediate taking of a poll on the question of adjournment.[11] If the chairman improperly stops a meeting, the meeting can itself resolve to go on with the business for which it was convened and appoint a fresh chairman accordingly.[12] On the other hand where the articles provide (as does art 57) that the chairman may adjourn the meeting with the members' consent, he cannot be required by the members to adjourn.[13]

(4) Two members personally present shall be a quorum. Where the company's articles are in the form of Table A, a meeting is quorate if two members are present personally or by proxy.[14]

(5) Any member elected by the members present at a meeting

---

7 Table A, art 38 which reflects CA 1985, s 369. Articles providing for a shorter period of notice than that specified above are void: ibid, s 369(1).
8 Table A, art 111.
9 Table A, art 37.
10 *Pergamon Press v Maxwell* [1970] 2 All ER 809, [1970] 1 WLR 1167.
11 *Palmer's Company Law* (22nd edn, 1976) p 582.
12 *National Dwellings Society v Sykes* [1894] 3 Ch 159. In exceptional circumstances the chairman can adjourn the meeting *John v Rees* [1970] Ch 345, [1969] 2 All ER 274.
13 *Salisbury Gold Mining Co Ltd v Hathorn* [1897] AC 268.
14 CA 1985, s 370(4), Table A, art 40.

may be chairman thereof. Under Table A articles, in the case of a public company, the chairman of the board of directors is to act. The articles also make provision for the chairmanship when the chairman of the board is not available or will not act, and where no director is present or willing to act.[15]

(6) In the case of a company, originally having a share capital, every member shall have one vote in respect of each share or each £10 of stock held by him, and in every other case shall have one vote. Voting rights, however, are extensively dealt with under the articles.[16] As will be seen, the terms of issue may restrict the voting rights of shares. Such restrictions are imposed in the case of preference shares,[17] and, despite much disapproval, may be imposed so as to create non-voting equity shares as well.[18] If Table A articles are employed then, subject to restrictions contained in the terms of issue, each share will carry one vote.[19] A corporation which is a member of the company may appear and vote at the general meeting of the company by a representative.[20]

POLLS

Resolutions at meetings are normally passed orally or by a show of hands, but a poll may be demanded. Unless the articles otherwise provide, each member, even when he holds proxies, has one vote on a show of hands, but on a poll he has one vote for each share.[1] Polls may be demanded at a general meeting on any question other than the election of the chairman or the adjournment of the meeting. A poll may be demanded:

(1) by not less than five members (including proxies) having the right to vote at the meeting; or
(2) by a member or members (including proxies) representing not less than one-tenth of the total voting rights of all the members having the right to vote at the meeting; or
(3) by a member or members (including proxies) holding shares in the company conferring a right to vote at the meeting,

---

15 Table A, arts 42–43; CA 1985, s 370(5).
16 Ibid, arts 54–63.
17 See Chap 13, ante.
18 *Palmer's Company Law* (22nd edn, 1976) p 337.
19 Table A, art 54.
20 Ibid.
 1 CA 1985, s 370(6) and Table A, art 54.

being shares on which an aggregate sum has been paid up equal to not less than one-tenth of the total sum paid up on all the shares conferring that right.[2]

On a poll, a member need not cast all his votes in the same way.[3] A resolution adopted at a poll takes effect from the date when the result of the poll is ascertained.[4]

RESOLUTIONS

Where business of a special nature is to be transacted at a meeting, the directors may decide to circulate with the notice of the meeting an explanation of the business and their reasons for adopting their recommendation. It will be recalled that those who oppose what is proposed by the directors are now entitled to circulate their views to members.[5] Resolutions adopted by a company are of three kinds.

SPECIAL RESOLUTIONS

A special resolution must be passed by a majority of not less than three-quarters of those members who are entitled to vote and who do vote, either personally or by proxy, where proxies are allowed.[6] This resolution must be passed at a general meeting of which not less than 21 days' notice,[7] specifying the intention to propose the resolution as a special resolution, has been given. If a majority in number, holding not less than 95% in nominal value of the shares with voting rights, or, in the case of a company not having a share capital, the same percentage of members with voting rights, so agree, a special resolution may be passed although shorter notice has been given.[8]

---

2   Contrary provisions in the articles are void: s 373, see Table A, arts 59–67. Table A provides that a poll may be demanded by any two members: art 46. It is submitted that where a poll is demanded, the majority referred to in s 378(1) is the majority required by the Act, ie three-quarters in the case of special and extraordinary resolutions.
3   CA 1985, s 374.
4   *Holmes v Keyes* [1959] Ch 199, [1958] 2 All ER 129.
5   CA 1985, s 376.
6   Ibid, s 378(2).
7   Ibid, s 379(1) and Table A, art 38 as to the giving of notice. See also *Re Hector Whaling Ltd* [1936] Ch 208, [1935] All ER Rep 302, as to the 21 days' notice requirement.
8   Ibid, s 378(3) and see *Re Pearce, Duff & Co Ltd* [1960] 3 All ER 222, [1960] 1 WLR 1014, for discussion of the effect of this section.

The notice of intention to propose a special resolution must identify the intended resolution by specifying either the text or the entire substance of the resolution which it is intended to propose. The resolution, if it is to be validly passed, must be the same resolution as that identified in the preceding notice, so an amendment to the previously circulated text of a special resolution can be put to and voted on at a meeting only if the amendment involves no departure from the substance of the circulated text.[9]

Special resolutions are necessary, inter alia, to alter the objects clause of the memorandum, with the approval of the Court to alter the articles, and to reduce the capital of the company with the approval of the Court.

EXTRAORDINARY RESOLUTIONS

An extraordinary resolution must be passed by the majority required for a special resolution, at a general meeting of which notice specifying the intention to propose the resolution as an extraordinary resolution has been given.[10] The period of notice required may be specified in the articles, but it must not be less than 14 days. An extraordinary resolution may be passed to wind up the company under IA 1986, s 84(1)(c).

In computing the majority on a poll on an extraordinary or special resolution, the number of votes actually cast for and against the resolution must be counted. The votes exercised, not voting rights possessed, are relevant here.

ORDINARY RESOLUTIONS

These resolutions are passed by a majority of those present and voting at a general meeting. Special notice of some resolutions, eg a resolution to appoint as auditor a person other than the retiring auditor, or to remove a director under CA 1985, s 303, must be given to the company. Under s 379, not less than 28 clear days' notice of intention to move the resolution must be given to the company. The company must give members not less than 14 clear days' notice of the proposed resolution. It will be noted that in the case of resolutions of which special notice is required, it is notice *to* the company, not *by* the company that is called for by the Act.

A difficult question for the chairman of a meeting to decide is

---

9 *Re Moorgate Mercantile Holdings Ltd* [1980] 1 All ER 40, [1980] 1 WLR 227.
10 CA 1985, s 378.

whether he should accept an amendment of a resolution the text of which has been circulated. Possibly, any amendment of a special or extraordinary resolution should not be accepted, but it is submitted that any amendment which so changes the nature of the resolutions circulated to members as to make it business of which they have not had notice must not be accepted.[11]

Resolutions passed at an adjourned meeting take effect from the date on which they were passed.[12]

Unless a poll is demanded, the declaration of the chairman that a special or extraordinary resolution has been passed shall be conclusive evidence of this fact.[13] Where the declaration of the chairman shows on its face that it is invalid, the resolution is not protected by this section; in other cases the declaration is conclusive.[14]

REGISTRATION OF RESOLUTIONS

As a general rule, business transacted at a meeting of a company is a matter of indoor management and of concern to members of the company only. But because certain resolutions are likely to affect third parties, copies of them must be registered. Once registered, persons dealing with the company have constructive notice of them. Further, if a copy of a resolution of the kind enumerated below has not been registered, those dealing with the company are not entitled to assume that it has been passed.[15]

A copy of the following resolutions must be registered within 15 days of their adoption:[16]

(1) special resolutions;
(2) extraordinary resolutions;
(3) resolutions agreed to by all members but which would otherwise have been ineffective for their purposes unless they have been passed as special resolutions or as extraordinary resolutions;

---

11 See *MacConnell v E Prill & Co Ltd* [1916] 2 Ch 57, but it would be preferable for the notice to state that the business of the meeting is to consider and pass, with or without modification, the resolution in question.
12 CA 1985, s 381.
13 Ibid, Table A art 47.
14 *Re Hadleigh Castle Gold Mines Ltd* [1900] 2 Ch 419, and *Re Caratal (New) Mines Ltd* [1902] 2 Ch 498.
15 See Chap 8, ante, where the rules of indoor management and the doctrine of constructive notice are discussed.
16 CA 1985, s 380(1) and (2).

(4) resolutions or agreements agreed to by all the members of some class of shareholders, but which would otherwise have been ineffective for their purpose unless they had been passed by some particular majority or otherwise in some particular manner, and all resolutions or agreements which effectively bind all the members of any class of shareholders though not agreed to by all those members;
(5) resolutions requiring a company to be wound up voluntarily, passed under IA 1986, s 84(1)(a)–(c);
(6) resolutions by the directors of the company
   (a) that an old public company should be re-registered as a public company, passed under s 2 of the Consequential Provisions Act 1985; and
   (b) that the company's memorandum be altered, so that a public company may apply for re-registration as a private company, passed under CA 1985, s 146(2).

Where articles are registered, a copy of every such resolution for the time being in force must be attached to copies of the articles issued after the passing of the resolution.

MINUTES

Every company is required to keep minutes both of general meetings and of directors' meetings.[17] Any such minute purporting to be signed by the chairman of the meeting at which such proceedings took place or by the chairman of the next succeeding meetings are prima facie evidence of those proceedings.[18] They are not necessarily the only admissible evidence of what transpired at the meeting, either as between the company, or as between the company and third parties.[19]

UNANIMOUS ACQUIESCENCE

Where a company adopts articles in the form of Table A, a resolution in writing signed by all the members for the time being entitled to receive notice of and to attend and vote at meetings is as valid and

---

17 CA 1985, s 382.
18 Ibid, s 722.
19 *Kerr v Mottram* [1940] Ch 657, [1940] 2 All ER 629.

effective as if the resolution had been passed at a duly convened general meeting.[20]

Even if the company's articles are not in this or a similar form, in some cases the courts will treat the unanimous agreement or tacit acquiescence by the members to a course of conduct as equivalent to the approval of the members in a properly convened general meeting. This is because it is a basic principle of company law that all of the corporators acting together can do anything which is *intra vires* the company.[1] If it can be shown that all the shareholders with the right to attend and vote at a general meeting had assented to some matter which a general meeting of the company could carry into effect, the assent is as binding as a resolution in general meeting.[2] This principle is of practical importance in the case of closely held private companies. In *Re Express Engineering Works Ltd*[3] five persons formed a private company of which they were the only directors and shareholders. They sold property to the company and at a directors' meeting issued debentures to themselves in payment. The articles of the company provided that no directors should vote in respect of any contract in which he might be interested. It was held that, as the matter was *intra vires* and there was no fraud, it could be ratified by the unanimous agreement of the members. The shareholder could waive the rules relating to notice, etc and unanimously pass the resolution to issue debentures. The assents required may be obtained at an informal meeting or individually from the members without a meeting being held at all.[4]

The case of *Re Bailey Hay Co Ltd*[5] demonstrates how the corporators may act together for the purposes of this principle, although only some of them give express consent, whilst the remainder silently acquiesce. Five persons, of whom four were directors, held all the issued shares in the company. An extraordinary general meeting was convened for the purposes of considering resolutions for the voluntary winding up of the company and the appointment

---

20 Table A, art 53.
1 *Cane v Jones* [1981] 1 All ER 533, [1980] 1 WLR 1451.
2 *EBM v Dominion Banks* [1937] 3 All ER 555, PC qualifying *Re George Newman & Co Ltd* [1895] 1 Ch 674; this practice has, however, been disapproved of in respect of resolutions reducing capital; *Re Barry Artists Ltd* [1985] 1 WLR 1305, [1985] BCLC 283.
3 [1920] 1 Ch 466. The judgments make it appear that the general meeting had a residual power to allot the debentures. Under modern articles, at least under Table A to the CA 1948, the power is better considered as one to ratify the issue. See *Bamford v Bamford* [1970] Ch 212, [1969] 1 All ER 969.
4 *Re Duomatic Ltd* [1969] 2 Ch 365, [1969] 1 All ER 161.
5 [1971] 3 All ER 693, [1971] 1 WLR 1357.

of a liquidator. Two shareholders, who together held one-half of the issued shares, voted in favour of the resolutions but the other shareholders (one of whom attended by proxy) abstained. Shortly after the meeting, one of the abstaining shareholders discovered that the meeting had been convened upon insufficient notice, but the abstaining shareholders did not, for a period of approximately four years, attempt to claim that the resolutions should be set aside, or otherwise to halt the liquidation. It was held that all the shareholders should be treated as having assented to the resolution, because the abstaining shareholders had allowed the resolutions to be passed with knowledge of their powers to stop them. Furthermore, their conduct in permitting all concerned to act for some years on the basis that the resolutions were properly passed, also led to the conclusion that they assented to the resolutions.

There are, however, limits to what may be done by the corporators acting together. In particular, even if acting unanimously, they cannot ratify or make binding on the company a transaction which is *ultra vires*.[6] However, this rule is subject to one qualification, namely that payments of remuneration or gratuities cannot be attacked to the extent that when they were made the company had reserves on its profit and loss account capable of being distributed by way of dividend.[7]

---

6 *Cane v Jones* (supra); *Rolled Steel Products (Holdings) Ltd v British Steel Corpn* [1982] 3 WLR 715; *Re Halt Garage Ltd* 1978 (unreported) May 25 cited in [1982] 3 WLR at p 726 (but quoted *in extenso* in the *Rolled Steel Products Case*.)
7 *Re Halt Garage* (supra), see *Rolled Steel Products (Holdings) Ltd v British Steel Corpn* (supra) at p 744.

Chapter 15

Shares

NATURE OF SHARES

A person may invest in a company in either of two ways. He may contribute to the capital of the company by taking shares and thus become a member of the company, or he may lend money to the company and take security for that loan, eg a debenture. As the result of recent decisions, the distinction between the rights of a lender of money under a debenture and the rights of a preference shareholder has been blurred, but there remain essential points of difference. The debenture holder is not a member of the company; in no circumstances can he vote at a general meeting of the company unless he also has shares carrying voting rights.

The classic statement of the characteristics of a share was made by Farwell J in *Borland's Trustee v Steel Bros & Co Ltd* [1901] 1 Ch 279, 288. The learned Judge explained the twofold character of a share in these words:

> A share is the interest of a shareholder in the company measured by a sum of money, for the purpose of liability in the first place, and of interest in the second, but also consisting of a series of mutual covenants entered into by all the shareholders *inter se*.

A shareholder has an interest in the company which is defined by the terms on which the shares are issued. A debenture holder's rights are defined in the debenture itself. A shareholder has obligations to the company as well as rights. Thus, he is liable as a contributory in a winding up.

ISSUE OF SHARES

The power to issue shares may be vested in the directors either by the articles of the company or by the company in a general meeting.

Unless the directors are so authorised they may not allot shares.[1] Such an authority may be given for a particular exercise of the power or may be a power to allot shares generally and may be conditional or unconditional.[2] Such an authority must state the maximum amount of securities that may be allotted thereunder and the date on which the authority will expire.[3] Where the authority is contained in the articles of the company at the time of original incorporation, the authority expires five years from the date of incorporation.[4] In any other case the authority expires five years from the date of the enabling resolution.[5] Any such authority may be previously varied or revoked by the company in general meeting.[6] It may also be renewed by the company in general meeting for a further maximum period of five years. The resolution must again be specific as to the amount of securities which may be allotted thereunder and must specify the date on which the renewed authority will expire.[7] These provisions do not apply to shares shown in the memorandum to have been taken by the subscribers thereto or to shares allotted in pursuance of an employees' share scheme nor to rights to subscribe for or convert into shares any security granted pursuant to such schemes.[8]

There are provisions enabling the directors to allot shares notwithstanding the expiration of their authority to do so provided that the offer or agreement to do so was entered into at a time when the directors had authority.[9] There are transitional provisions relating to the issue of shares in old public companies.[10]

While a breach of the provisions relating to allotment is a criminal offence, the validity of any issue of shares is not affected by such a contravention; in other words the allottee is fully protected from the consequences of breach by the directors of the provisions relating to allotment.[11] As will be seen this is not necessarily true of a breach of directors' fiduciary duties relating to share allotments.[12]

The Companies Act 1985 also contains a provision which, prima

---

1 CA 1985, s 80(1).
2 Ibid, s 80(3).
3 Ibid, s 80(4).
4 Ibid.
5 Ibid.
6 Ibid, s 80(5).
7 Ibid, s 80(4).
8 Ibid, s 80(2)(a).
9 Ibid, s 80(7).
10 Ibid, s 80(11).
11 Ibid, s 80(10).
12 Pp 289–291, post.

facie, requires a company allotting shares to confer pre-emption rights upon existing shareholders. This provision is, however, heavily qualified.

Applicable to both public and private companies in respect of shares allotted for cash[13] s 89(1) of the Companies Act 1985 provides that a company proposing to allot equity securities shall not allot any of those securities on any terms to any person unless it has made an offer to each holder of the shares to allot to him on the same or more favourable terms a proportion of those shares *pro rata* to his existing holding, and unless the period for acceptance of the offer has expired.[14] Broadly, 'equity security' means shares in a company other than preference shares which carry a right to participate only up to a specified amount in a distribution and shares held or to be held pursuant to an employees' share scheme.[15]

The qualifications to the above provisions are the following. They are modified in relation to pre-emptive rights provisions which are commonly contained in the articles of private companies and which, by restricting transfer to outsiders, help to perpetuate close control.[16] The provisions of s 89(1) and certain ancillary subsections may be excluded in relation to a private company by a provision in its memorandum and articles. A requirement or authority contained in the articles of a private company which is inconsistent with the provisions of ss 89(1), 90(1) to (5) or s 90(6) has effect as a provision excluding them.[17] Where a company's memorandum or articles contain a provision requiring it, when proposing to allot equity securities, to allot those shares rateably to existing shareholders, the company may allot shares on acceptance by the member entitled to accept, or on acceptance by any person to whom the member has renounced his right.[18]

The operation of s 89 may also be excluded by the articles of a company or by a special resolution. The power granted to the directors may exclude the section generally or provide that it shall apply to the allotment with modifications. Such modifications may be determined by the directors or by the terms of a special resolution.[19] A power so given expires when the authority to allot shares

---

13   CA 1985, s 89(4).
14   Ibid, s 89(a) and (b). In relation to s 89(1) and (3), 'holder' of shares includes any person holding shares on any day within the period of 28 days ending with the day immediately preceding the offer: s 94(7).
15   Ibid, s 94.
16   Considered from this point of view at Chap 16, post.
17   CA 1985, s 91(1) and (2).
18   Ibid, s 89(2).
19   Ibid, s 95(1) and (2).

expires. It may be renewed for a period co-extensive with the period for which the power of allotment is renewed.[20] The directors may allot shares in accordance with its terms even though the authority has expired, provided that the transaction was agreed upon during its period of vitality.[1]

A special resolution to exclude the operation of s 89 may not be proposed unless it is recommended by the directors and a written statement by the directors is circulated with the notice of the meeting. The statement must set out the directors' reasons for making the recommendation, the amount to be paid to the company in respect of the equity securities to be allotted and their justification of that amount.[2] It is a serious offence knowingly or recklessly to permit the inclusion in such a statement of material which is misleading, false or deceptive in a material particular.[3]

Transitional provisions exist saving allotments made without regard to s 89 in the case of a company which is registered or re-registered as a public company and is obliged by the memorandum or articles or otherwise to make an offer to allot in a manner which is inconsistent with s 89(1).[4] The requirement must have been imposed before the relevant date (in 1982), or the time when the company applied to be registered or re-registered as a public company.[5]

A requirement on a private company to offer shares on a pre-emptive basis when it is not contained in the memorandum and articles has effect as though it were contained in those documents so long as the company remains a private company.[6]

It seems improbable that the above provisions will have much or any effect on British corporate practice. Rights issues made pursuant to the statute are renounceable and their characteristics are not therefore different from formerly. It is probable that shareholders will agree to reasonable management representations that the provisions of s 89 be excluded in any particular case; indeed, one would expect the articles or any special resolution conferring powers of allotment on the directors to exclude the section in order to preserve maximum flexibility.

Directors' powers are governed by fiduciary considerations. An

---

20 Ibid, s 95(3).
1 Ibid, s 95(4).
2 Ibid, s 95(3).
3 Ibid, s 95(6), the offence carries a maximum of two years' imprisonment if tried on indictment.
4 Ibid, s 96(1) and (2).
5 Ibid, s 96(3).
6 Ibid, s 96(3).

exercise of a power of allotment, though formally valid, may be attacked on the ground that it was not exercised for the purpose for which it was granted. The usual purpose for which the power is exercised is to raise funds for the company, but the power is not limited to this purpose alone. The applicable principles were discussed by the Privy Council in

Howard Smith Ltd v Ampol Petroleum Ltd [1974] 1 All ER 1126.

This was an action to set aside an allotment of shares in M Ltd. Ampol and Bulkships who owned a majority of shares in M Ltd made a takeover bid for the remaining shares which the M Ltd directors advised against. Howard Smith Ltd (S) intimated that it would make an offer. Ampol and Bulkships intimated that they would use their majority power to prevent its success. M's directors after consultation with those of S determined to allot and allotted shares to S sufficient to enable S to buy out the minority and secure control. The M directors purported to allot to secure working capital, but the trial judge found that although M needed capital, this was not the primary purpose of the allotment which was intended to enable minority shareholders to sell at advantageous terms. It was further found (a) that the M directors acted honestly throughout, and (b) that there was no element of oppression of the minority by Ampol and Bulkships. Lord Wilberforce held that it would be too narrow to argue that shares may only be issued to raise capital for the immediate financial needs of the company. An allotment of shares may be proper where it is made to ensure the financial stability of a company even though it defeats an attempt by a person to secure control by buying up shares. However, an exercise of power is not valid simply because the directors act honestly. Allotments which are not made for the benefit of the company as a whole will be invalid. The common example of an allotment for improper motives is one which is self-interested, eg made to perpetuate the directors' control. But self-interest is only an example of improper motive. Here the directors' purpose was to dilute control in order to enable shareholders to sell advantageously. But the power of allotment cannot be used simply to alter control; the right to sell at a given price is an individual matter to be decided upon individually and in respect of which the majority, in the absence of oppression, is entitled to prevail.

It is clear from this and from preceding cases that the directors are not restricted to taking only the short-term interests of the company into account. Equally, this and earlier cases establish that an issue of shares is not invalid simply because it deprives shareholders of control which they have or expect to have as a result of a take-over offer which they are making.[7] But directors are not entitled to issue

---

7 *Ashburton Oil No Liability v Alpha Minerals No Liability* (1971) 45 ALJR 162.

shares to prevent a take-over because they fear that putative controllers will conduct the operations of the company in a way which they consider disadvantageous to members or employees,[8] nor simply in order to eliminate an existing majority.

MEMBERS

A person may become a member[9] of a company either by:

(1) subscribing to the memorandum, or
(2) agreeing to become a member. This includes,
    (a) those who apply for an allotment of shares; and
    (b) those who take a transfer of shares;[10] and
    (c) a director who is required to take qualification shares but who is not a subscriber.

The subscribers to the memorandum, who must take at least one share, are deemed to have agreed to become members and, on registration of the memorandum, must be entered in the register of members.[11] Persons, other than the subscribers, do not become members until their names are entered in the register.[12]

A subscriber to the memorandum must take his shares from the company and pay for them. His obligation to pay may be discharged by his providing the money or in the case of a private company, with the consent of the company, money's worth.[13] If a subscriber is entitled to have shares allotted to him as fully or partly paid up otherwise than in cash under a contract with the company under which property has been transferred or services rendered, he need not pay for the shares subscribed for in cash.[14] A subscriber's liability to pay arises on registration of the memorandum; to make him a member, allotment and entry in the register are unnecessary.

Persons other than subscribers who have agreed to become members do not become members until entered in the register. The

---

8 *Hogg v Cramphorn Ltd* [1967] Ch 254, [1966] 3 All ER 420.
9 A person may be a member of, but not a shareholder in, a company, eg those which have no share capital.
10 Including those who take on the death or bankruptcy of a member.
11 CA 1985, s 22.
12 Ibid, s 22(2).
13 *Re Baglan Hall Colliery Co* (1870) 5 Ch App 346. See CA 1985, s 106.
14 But the contract or particulars thereof must be filed in terms of CA 1985, s 88(2)(b); and note the provisions concerning performance of undertaking and valuations in ss 101–103.

applicable section makes entry in the register an essential condition of membership.[15] Thus a person who has agreed to *place* shares, but not to *take* shares, does not become a member.[16]

A company may become a member of another company if it is authorised to do so by its memorandum. It may attend meetings by a representative appointed by its board of directors.[17] Section 23 of the Companies Act 1985 does, however, restrict the powers of a subsidiary company to become a member of its holding company. It can (except for interests subsisting before the Act came into force) only hold such shares as personal representative or trustee and neither the holding nor the subsidiary company can have any interest in the trust.

A minor[18] may become a member of a company unless the articles forbid it, but the directors may, if the articles so provide, refuse to accept a minor as a member. By s 1 of the Family Law Reform Act 1969 the age of majority is reduced from 21 to 18 years of age. A minor member may:

(1) repudiate his liability as a member during minority or within a reasonable time of attaining majority. Unless he repudiates his liability within this period, a minor will be liable to pay any calls made on his shares. In general he will be unable to recover the moneys paid in respect of his shares, since only if there has been a total failure of consideration will recovery be possible;[19]
(2) refuse to pay calls, but if he does he cannot retain the shares;
(3) enter into a contract for the sale of the shares, but such a contract is voidable.

If shares are transferred to a minor whose name is placed on the register in ignorance of the fact of minority, rectification by the Court may be sought by the company. The transferor's name may be ordered to be put back in the register.[20]

A person ceases to be a member:

---

15 Ibid, s 22(2), and see *Re Florence Land and Public Works Co* (1885) 29 ChD 421.
16 *Re Monarch Insurance Co* (1873) 8 Ch App 507.
17 CA 1985, s 375. By this section a foreign corporation may appoint such a representative. Cf *Blair Open Hearth Furnace Co Ltd v Reigart* (1913) 108 LT 665.
18 *Re Asiatic Banking Corpn, Symons Case* (1870) 5 Ch App 298.
19 *Steinberg v Scala (Leeds) Ltd* [1923] 2 Ch 452.
20 *Re Asiatic Banking Corpn, Symons Case* (1870) 5 Ch App 298, and see CA 1985, s 359.

(1) on the transfer of his shares, but he remains liable as a contributory if winding up commences within one year;[1]
(2) on the forfeiture of the shares;
(3) when the company has been wound up;
(4) on sale by the company under its lien;
(5) on death, but his estate continues to be liable;
(6) on the rescission of his contract to take the shares;[2]
(7) on the repayment of the capital represented by his shares.

Shares must be paid for in cash unless there is an express agreement to the contrary with the company. Subject to restrictions placed on public companies, a company may agree to accept some other form of payment and fully paid shares may be issued in consideration of property transferred or services rendered to the company.[3] In such cases the Court will not inquire into the adequacy of the consideration unless fraud[4] or an *ultra vires* or illegal issue of shares at a discount[5] is alleged. If a vendor of property purchased by the company later agrees to accept shares in satisfaction or partial satisfaction of the debt, this is treated as equivalent to a payment in cash.[6]

CLASSES OF SHARES

A company may have by virtue of its articles or may take by later alteration of its articles[7] power to issue different classes of shares. There is a presumption of equality as between shareholders, ie that all shares confer equal rights and equal liability.[8] But that presumption can be rebutted and usually is rebutted by the terms of issue which may by clear language give special rights to one class of shareholders. Preference shares and the rights attaching to them are an example. The terms of issue may make a distinction as

---

1 IA 1986, s 74.
2 See pp 59–62, ante, where rescission is discussed.
3 CA 1985, s 88, ss 101–103.
4 *Re Wragg* [1897] 1 Ch 796.
5 See CA 1985, ss 103, 108 on valuation of assets for which shares are to be allotted in case of public companies, and *Osborne v Steel Barrel Co Ltd* [1942] 1 All ER 634, at p 638. See further *Hong Kong and China Gas Co Ltd v Glen* [1914] 1 Ch 527; *Re White Star Line* [1938] Ch 458, [1938] 1 All ER 607.
6 *Larocque v Beauchemin* [1897] AC 358, at 365; *Harmony and Montague Tin and Copper Mining Co, Re Spargo's Case* (1873) 8 Ch App 407.
7 *Andrews v Gas Meter Co* [1897] 1 Ch 361.
8 *Birch v Cropper* (1889) 14 App Cas 525.

between classes of shareholders as to rights to dividend, to return of capital or to voting at meetings of the company.[9]

Where a company which does not have a share capital creates a class of members with rights which are not stated in the memorandum or articles or in a registrable resolution, the company must, within one month from the date of creation of the class deliver a statement containing particulars of the rights attached to that class.[10] A similar period applies to variations of such rights,[11] and to the assignment of a new name or designation to any class of members.[12]

Share capital may be divided into:
(1) preference shares, including redeemable preference shares;
(2) ordinary shares;
(3) deferred or founders' shares;
(4) shares with restricted or no voting rights;[13]
(5) stock;
(6) reserve capital.

PREFERENCE SHARES[14]

These shares ordinarily entitle the holder to payment of dividends in priority to other classes, or to a preference in repayment of capital or both. But the rights of the holders of this class of share may vary considerably from company to company; in all cases it is necessary to examine carefully the terms of issue to determine the precise nature of the preference conferred. It is impossible to state even a general rule because of 'the infinite number of combinations and permutations that company draftsmen are capable of using in what are called their *capital clauses* in ... memoranda or articles'.[15]

The terms of issue may confer on preference shareholders a

---

9   See M. A. Pickering, 'The Problem of the Preference Share' (1963) 26 Mod LR 499.
10 CA 1985, s 129(1).
11 Ibid, s 129(2).
12 Ibid, s 129(3).
13 Sometimes deferred shares do not carry voting rights. Some of the problems of non-voting shares are discussed in the Jenkins Report, Cmnd 1749 (1962) paras 123–140.
14 The present discussion of the rights of preference shares is related to the alteration of their rights.
15 *Re Walter Symons Ltd* [1934] Ch 308, 311–312 per Maugham J. The right may also be defined in the resolution authorising the issue of preference shares. To avoid the use of the expressions 'memorandum', 'articles' or 'resolution', the phrase 'terms of issue' will be adopted to refer to the instrument defining the rights given.

preference as to dividend at the rate of, say, 6%. In such cases, the preference shareholders will receive that dividend before the other shareholders receive any payment, but, if the preference is so limited, they will receive only that dividend no matter how successful the operations of the company may have been. In some cases[16] the terms of issue will give the preference shareholders not only the right to a preferential dividend, but also the right to participate with the ordinary shareholders in the distribution of the balance of the funds available for dividend.

The entitlement to a preferential dividend may be expressed as cumulative or non-cumulative. Only if they are cumulative preference shares will the holders be entitled to have deficiencies made up out of the profits of later years. Under a rule of construction adopted by the courts, a preferential dividend is prima facie cumulative and arrears are to be made up from the profits of subsequent years before anything is distributed to other shareholders.[17] Only if the terms of issue clearly deny this right to preference shareholders are their shares treated as non-cumulative. If their shares are non-cumulative, preference shareholders are not entitled to have deficiencies made up from subsequent profits.

In a winding up, difficult questions of construction are likely to arise. In almost every case, preference shares will carry the right to a preferential dividend while the company is a going concern and the right to repayment of capital (but not necessarily in priority to other shareholders) if there are sufficient assets available in the winding up. Other questions sometimes arise. Thus it may be necessary to decide:

(1) whether the preference shareholders are entitled to be paid 'arrears of dividend'[18] before any capital is repaid to shareholders? This involves two further questions: is it necessary that dividends should have been declared, and is the fund from which arrears are payable limited to the amount of undistributed profits?;
(2) whether the preference shareholders are entitled to have their capital repaid before the other shareholders;

---

16 Eg in the articles examined by the Court in *Re Isle of Thanet Electricity Supply Co Ltd* [1950] Ch 161, [1949] 2 All ER 1060.
17 *Webb v Earle* (1875) LR 20 Eq 556; *Foster v Coles and Foster* (1906) 22 TLR 555; *Staples v Eastman Photographic Materials Co* [1896] 2 Ch 303.
18 This phrase, which is commonly adopted, is inaccurate; it will be used to denote deficiencies in dividend; see *Re Wakley, Wakley v Vachell* [1920] 2 Ch 205.

(3) whether the preference shareholders are entitled to participate in the distribution of any assets remaining after all debts have been paid and all capital returned to shareholders.

It is possible in an introductory text of this kind to give only a short treatment of these different problems. Because the rights of preference shareholders depend on the terms of issue, the instrument defining the preference must be carefully examined to determine the rights attaching to the shares. The capital clause or terms of issue can be regarded as part of the contract on the basis of which the shares were taken. Whether the rights to be discussed attach to the preference shares is essentially a question of construction of the terms on which the shares were issued.

ARREARS OF DIVIDEND

Only if the company is solvent does the question of payment of arrears arise. Under IA 1986, s 74(2)(b), a sum due to a member by way of dividend is not deemed to be a debt of the company in a case of competition between a creditor and a member; the arrears are to be taken into account only for the purpose of final adjustment of rights of contributors, *inter se*. If there is not sufficient to pay all creditors, there will be no assets from which arrears of dividends could be paid.

Prima facie dividends (and arrears) are payable only while the company is a going concern and are, therefore, no longer payable once winding up has commenced.[19] But that presumption can be rebutted and will be rebutted if the preference shareholders can prove either:[20]

(1) that the right to be paid arrears of dividend is conferred by express words or by implication; or

---

19 *Re W Foster & Son Ltd* [1942] 1 All ER 314, 315–316; *Re Catalinas Warehouses and Mole Co Ltd* [1947] 1 All ER 51, 54. The power to declare a dividend is terminated on winding up.
20 *Re Walter Symons Ltd* [1934] Ch 308, [1933] All ER Rep 163 (arrears payable); *Re Wood, Skinner & Co Ltd* [1944] Ch 323 (arrears not payable); *Re F de Jong & Co Ltd* [1946] Ch 211, [1946] 1 All ER 556 (arrears payable); *Re E W Savory Ltd* [1951] 2 All ER 1036 (arrears payable). The last-mentioned case was decided after the decisions had been given in *Scottish Insurance Corpn Ltd v Wilsons and Clyde Coal Co Ltd* and *Re Isle of Thanet Electricity Supply Co Ltd* and was influenced by the construction placed on the capital clauses in those cases.

(2) that the words of the terms of issue define the dividend right in such a way that the right to the dividend includes the right to arrears.

The difficulties encountered in construing capital clauses are demonstrated by several cases where the clauses in issue were substantially the same. Whether only those dividends that have been declared are payable and whether the sum available for distribution in payment of arrears is the whole of the remaining assets or is limited to the amounts of undistributed profits depends on the terms of issue.[1]

In *Re E. W. Savory Ltd* [1951] 2 All ER 1036, the articles provided that: 'The preference shares in the present capital shall confer on the holders the right to a fixed cumulative preferential dividend at the rate of £6% per annum on the capital paid up thereon and shall rank both as regards dividends and capital in priority to all other shares, both present and future.' It was held that the preference shareholders were entitled to be paid arrears of dividend in priority to any repayment of capital to the other shareholders.

In *Re Wharfedale Brewery Co Ltd* [1952] Ch 913, [1952] 2 All ER 635, it was held that the assets from which the arrears of preferential dividends might be paid were not limited to the amount of undistributed profits, but included the whole of the divisible funds. In every case, the capital clause must be construed to ascertain the rights of the preference shareholders.

PREFERENCE IN REPAYMENT OF CAPITAL

By the terms of issue, preference shareholders may be given the right to have their capital repaid to them in priority to other shareholders. If this right is conferred, the assets in the hands of the liquidator can, if necessary, be exhausted in repayment of preferential capital. Only if there remains a balance will the other shareholders receive repayment of their capital. The provision giving the preference must be clear, otherwise all shareholders are entitled to participate in the property of the company on terms of equality.[2]

---

1 *Re Catalinas Warehouses and Mole Co Ltd* [1947] 1 All ER 51.
2 *Birch v Cropper* (1889) 14 App Cas 525, 543, per Lord Macnaghten; *Re National Telephone Co* [1914] 1 Ch 755, 774; per Sargant J. It will be noted that neither IA 1986, s 149 nor s 152 assists in determining the manner of distribution of assets. In all cases, it depends on the terms of issue.

298 Chapter 15 Shares

PARTICIPATION IN SURPLUS ASSETS[3]

The question may also arise as to whether the preferential shareholders are entitled to share in the distribution of surplus assets, after all debts have been paid and all capital has been returned to shareholders. Whether preferential shareholders have any further rights, apart from their preference as to dividends and return capital, depends upon the interpretation of the terms of issue. The decision of the Court of Appeal in *Re William Metcalf & Sons Ltd* [1933] Ch 142, which enabled preference shareholders who were not expressly excluded by the articles to share in any surplus after repayment of capital, was overruled by the House of Lords in:

Scottish Insurance Corporation Ltd v Wilsons and Clyde Coal Co Ltd [1949] AC 462, [1949] 1 All ER 1068.

In this case the question of the rights of preference shareholders to share in the surplus assets after the return of paid-up capital arose in relation to the compensation payable under s 25 of the Coal Industry Nationalisation Act 1946. Lord Simonds said at p 488:

Reading the relevant articles, as a whole, I come to the conclusion that arts 159 and 160 are exhaustive of the rights of the preference stockholders in a winding up.

The ordinary shareholders were held to be entitled to the surplus assets.

This decision was followed in:

Re Isle of Thanet Electricity Supply Co Ltd [1950] Ch 161, [1949] 2 All ER 1060.

After certain arrears of preference dividend were paid and the capital on the preference stock (£282,000) and on the ordinary stock (£15,000) had been repaid to the shareholders, there remained a substantial surplus in the distribution of which the preference stockholders claimed a share. Wynn-Parry J stated at p 167 [1062] that the effect of the decision in the *Scottish Insurance Corporation* case was:

---

3 By 'surplus assets' is meant the amount remaining after all debts have been paid and capital repaid. 'Excess assets' is perhaps a more accurate term; see *Re New Transvaal Co* [1896] 2 Ch 750, 754, per Vaughan Williams J; *Re Ramel Syndicate Ltd* [1911] 1 Ch 749, and especially *Re National Telephone Co* [1914] 1 Ch 755, 772, per Sargant J. There is some confusion of terms in the judgment of Wynn-Parry J in the *Isle of Thanet* case. At p 167 [1062] he refers to 'surplus assets', where it appears that the term is used in two different senses in the one extract.

... not merely to remove the onus in cases such as this from the holders of ordinary shares, but to throw the onus upon the holders of preference shares; and it is for the holders of preference shares to satisfy the Court that, on the true construction of the particular document, they are entitled to share in the surplus assets ...

The onus of proof, therefore, lay on the preference shareholders to show that they were entitled to share in the surplus assets because, as Wynn-Parry J stated at p 171 [1065]:

... where the article sets out the rights attached to a class of shares to participate in profits while the company is a going concern or to share in the property of the company in liquidation, prima facie, the rights so set out are in each case exhaustive.

The preference shareholders, having failed to establish that the articles entitled them to share in surplus assets, were denied this right.

The modern decisions therefore suggest that:

(1) if there is no provision whatever as to the distribution of assets in a winding up (eg if the only preference given is as to dividends) the rule in *Birch v Cropper*, supra, that each class shares equally, will apply;
(2) if there is any provision as to rights in a winding up, such provision is prima facie exhaustive of the rights of that class. Thus, if the articles give an explicit right to preference shareholders to share rateably in surplus assets with ordinary shares after prior repayment of capital and dividend, preference shareholders will share in the surplus.[4] If the articles give preference shareholders the right to prior repayment of capital and accumulated dividends the preference shareholders will have no further right to participate.[5]

The effect of these decisions is to place the holders of preference shares, and especially redeemable preference shares, in very much the same position as debenture holders. If a preference shareholder has no voting rights in general meetings and is entitled under the terms of issue only to a fixed cumulative dividend and to repayment of capital in a winding up, he is to all intents and purposes a debenture holder. An important difference, and that to the disadvantage of the preference shareholder, is that, having loaned moneys to the company, debenture holders are paid off before any

---

4 *Dimbula Valley (Ceylon) Tea Co Ltd v Laurie* [1961] Ch 353, [1961] 1 All ER 769.
5 *Re Saltdean Estate Co Ltd* [1968] 3 All ER 829, [1968] 1 WLR 1844.

shareholder receives any payment, whether in respect of arrears of dividend or of capital.[6]

REDEEMABLE SHARES

Formerly, companies had the right to issue redeemable preference shares.[7] The CA 1985 now gives both private and public companies the right to issue redeemable shares of any class, including preference and equity shares, and to deal in their own shares subject to safeguards in the interests of capital maintenance. These provisions are an exception to the general rule, discussed below in connection with the maintenance of capital, that companies may not deal in their own shares. The advantages of a power to issue such shares are these; first, it is helpful to a close held company which wishes to retain family control; it provides a means by which a shareholder or the estate of a deceased shareholder may find a purchaser for shares in an unlisted company; and it is particularly useful in relation to employee share schemes in enabling shares acquired by employees to be repurchased on their leaving the company's employ. These advantages apply in particular to private companies; the advantages to public companies are less obvious, but it is helpful to be able to buy out small shareholdings which are costly to service. The legislation applies both to private and to public companies, with greater safeguards in the latter case. Only in the case of private companies may shares be redeemed out of capital.

A company limited by shares or by guarantee and having a share capital has the right to issue shares which are to be redeemed or which are liable to be redeemed at the option of the company or of the shareholder.[8] The company must be authorised by its articles to redeem such shares. Redemption is to be effected on terms specified by the articles. No redeemable shares may be issued at any time when there are no shares issued which are not redeemable.[9] Curiously, given that this safeguard is intended to prevent a situation arising in which there would be no members left, there does not seem to be a requirement that such non-redeemable shares be equity shares, or shares with voting rights, at all times.

Redeemable shares may not be redeemed unless they are fully

---

6 See further M. A. Pickering, 'The Problem of the Preference Share' (1963) 26 Mod LR 499.
7 The Purchase by a Company of its own Shares, 1981, Cmnd 7944.
8 CA 1985, s 159.
9 Ibid, s 159(2).

Classes of Shares 301

paid, and the terms of redemption must provide for payment on redemption.[10]

Subject to the exceptions noted below, redeemable shares may only be redeemed out of the distributable profits of the company or out of the proceeds of a fresh issue of shares made for the purpose of redemption.[11] Any premium payable on redemption must be paid out of the distributable profits of the company.[12]

Shares so redeemed are deemed to be cancelled on redemption. The amount of the company's issued share capital is diminished by the nominal value of those shares accordingly, but the redemption of shares under the section is not treated as reducing the amount of the company's authorised share capital.[13]

A company which is authorised to do so by its articles may purchase its own shares, including any redeemable shares. The safeguards applicable to redemption also apply to 'own share purchases' with the exception that the terms and manner of purchase need not be determined by the articles. Public companies may purchase their shares only out of distributable profits or the proceeds of a fresh share issue. Shares are treated as cancelled on acquisition in order to prevent trafficking.[14]

There are additional requirements depending upon whether the company desires to purchase its shares in or off the stock market. The criteria are more stringent in the latter case.

Where off market purchases are concerned[15] the purchase and the terms of purchase must be authorised by special resolution of the company.[16] Such an authority must specify an expiry date which can be extended by special resolution.[17] It may also be varied or revoked in the same way.[18]

A member who holds shares to which the resolution relates may not so vote them as to secure its passage; if he does so the resolution will not be effective unless it would have been passed without his vote.[19] He may, however, vote other shares on a poll in respect of

---

10 Ibid, s 159(3).
11 Ibid, s 160(1)(a).
12 Ibid, s 160(1)(b).
13 Ibid, s 160(4).
14 Ibid, s 160(4).
15 'Off-market' purchase is defined by CA 1985, s 163(2) as a purchase of shares off the Stock Exchange or, as a purchase of shares on the Exchange which are not subject to a marketing arrangement on the Exchange.
16 CA 1985, s 164(2); on publicity for the resulting contract, see s (6) and (7).
17 Ibid, s 164(4).
18 Ibid, s 164(3) and (4).
19 Ibid, s 164(5).

the resolution. He may thus still be able to exercise considerable influence in respect of the transaction.

Similar provisions apply to contingent purchase contracts, that is, contracts under which a company becomes obliged or entitled (subject to any conditions) to buy its own shares.[20] A company can only acquire such rights for a consideration if this is paid out of distributable profits.[1]

Certain safeguards apply to market purchases. Prior authorisation by a general meeting is required.[2] Such an authority may be general, or restricted to the purchase of shares of a particular class or description. It may be conditional or unconditional. It must specify the maximum number of shares to be acquired and the maximum and minimum prices to be paid.

Rights of a company acquired under contracts approved or authorised under the provisions relating to on and 'off-market' purchases cannot be assigned and there are restrictions on releases from rights.[3] Maintenance of capital on redemption or purchase of shares otherwise than out of capital or the proceeds of a new issue is protected by the capital redemption reserve, and this aspect of the topic is dealt with below in relation to that reserve.

Private companies may redeem or purchase shares out of capital where the articles so provide. It would seem that such redemption or purchase may be made wholly out of capital where the company has no available profits.[4] A payment out of capital for the redemption or purchase of shares must be approved by special resolution.[5] The directors must make a statutory resolution specifying the permissible capital payment and stating their opinion that the company will be solvent immediately after the date of payment, and that it will be financially able to carry on its business as a going concern in the next financial year.[6] This must be supported by an auditors' report.[7] As with off-market purchases, a member may not vote shares to which the special resolution related.

Members and creditors who object to any such purchase or redemption out of capital may apply to the court for cancellation of

---

20 Ibid, s 165.
1 Ibid, s 168.
2 Ibid, s 166.
3 Ibid, s 164.
4 Ibid, s 171.
5 Ibid, s 173(1) and (2).
6 Ibid.
7 Ibid, s 173; for provisions concerning publicity, see ibid, s 175.

the resolution.[8] The court may adjourn the application so that a purchase of the shares of dissentient members may be arranged, or for the protection of dissentient creditors. It may make an order on such terms as it sees fit, confirming or cancelling the resolution. It may provide for the purchase of shares of any member of the company, and may make consequential changes to the company's memorandum and articles.[9]

The CA 1985 also contains provisions for the personal liability of directors who signed the statutory declaration, and of shareholders from whom shares were redeemed or purchased (wrongly) out of capital.[10]

Holders of redeemable shares or shares which the company has agreed to purchase under the above sections are placed in an invidious position. In respect of share issues or agreements to purchase made after the coming into force after 15 June 1982, the company is not to be made liable for damages for any breach of contract for failure to redeem or purchase, nor may it be subjected to an order for specific performance where it shows that it cannot meet the cost of redemption or purchase out of distributable profits.[11] The terms of a contract for redemption or purchase may be enforced against the company on winding up, but this is subject to significant exceptions. Where the terms of the contract provide for either redemption or purchase on a date after the commencement of winding up, or at an earlier date after which the company could not lawfully have made a distribution equal to the price of redemption, then the terms of redemption or purchase cannot be enforced against the company on a winding up. Furthermore, the claims of such holders of shares are postponed to the claims of creditors and shareholders with prior rights.[12] Redeemable shares may still, however, be issued on preferential terms.

ORDINARY SHARES

Ordinary shareholders are those holding shares to which no special rights are attached. They receive a dividend after any preferential shareholders entitled to a preferential dividend have been paid. Ordinary share capital is sometimes referred to as 'equity' share

---

[8] Ibid, s 176; the objection must be made within five weeks of the passing of the resolution.
[9] Ibid, s 177.
[10] IA 1986, s 76.
[11] CA 1985, s 59.
[12] Ibid, s 178(4) and (5).

capital, an expression which emphasises that ordinary shareholders are the proprietors of the company entitled to the residuary profits. The dividend paid to ordinary shareholders will vary with the fortunes of the company. Frequently, only the ordinary shares carry voting rights.

DEFERRED OR FOUNDERS' SHARES

These shares normally carry a dividend fixed in relation to the profits available after dividends have been declared on the preference and ordinary shares. The articles usually provide that any profits remaining undistributed after the preferential and ordinary shareholders have received dividends at fixed rates will be divided between the ordinary and deferred shareholders. As these shares are often held by the promoters and directors of the company, such persons will then have a very direct interest in the success of the company; the greater the profits of the company the higher their dividends will be. These shares were commonly issued to professional promoters, but they are now exceptional.

STOCK

Shares that are fully paid-up may be converted into stock[13] which may be either registered stock, in which case the holder appears on the register and the ordinary rules as to transfers apply, or unregistered stock, where share warrants are issued to the holder. Share warrants may be transferred by delivery in the same manner as negotiable instruments. Such stock may be in any multiple decided by the company, eg 100 £1 shares may be converted into five stock certificates for £20. The relationship between shares and stock was discussed by Lord Cairns in *Morrice v Aylmer* (1874) 10 Ch App 148, 154. He said:

> The use of the term 'stock' ... [merely denotes] that the company has recognised the fact of the complete payment of the shares, and that the time has come when those shares may be assigned in fragments, which for obvious reasons could not be permitted before, but that stock shall still be the qualification ... and that the meetings shall be of persons entitled to this stock, who shall meet as shareholders, and vote as shareholders, in the proportion of shares which would entitle them to vote before the consolidation into stock.

---

13 Ibid, ss 121 and 122.

The only advantage in having fully paid shares converted into stock is that the holder is not required to dispose of the stock in the denominations formerly represented by the shares he held. A person holding stock retains his membership in the company and is able to exercise all the rights of membership.

It is competent for a company to issue stock warrants to bearer.[14] The practice is now in abeyance.[15]

VARIATION OF CLASS RIGHTS

The variation of class rights is usually dealt with in the articles. If it is not, then the rules concerning the availability of and procedure for variation are contained in the Companies Act 1985.

If rights are attached to a class of shares in the company by the memorandum and the memorandum and articles do not provide for the variation of rights, those rights may be varied if all the members of the company (not simply all the members of the class) agree to the variation.[16] The same result could also be achieved by a scheme of arrangement.[17] It is not possible to circumvent the problem by first inserting a variation of rights clause in the articles and then exercising it.[18]

This conclusion derives from the provisions of ss 125(3)(a) and (b) and 125(7) of the Companies Act 1985. The former deal with the case where rights are attached to a class of shares in the company by memorandum or otherwise. Where rights are attached otherwise than by the memorandum, they may be varied by a provision in the articles notwithstanding that such provision was added later. Where rights are attached by the memorandum, the power of variation must have been included in the company's articles on incorporation. If the variation is not connected either with the giving, variation, revocation or renewal of an authority for the purposes of allotment of securities[19] or with a reduction of share capital[20] rights may only be varied in accordance with the articles.

---

14 *Pilkingtons v United Railways of the Havana and Regla Warehouses Ltd* [1930] 2 Ch 108.
15 Exchange Control Act 1947, s 10, formerly inhibited the practice.
16 CA 1985, s 125(2); this presumably is to be read literally and is certainly inhibiting, but the problem seldom arises.
17 Under CA 1985, s 425.
18 Such a course may have been possible at common law; see *Re National Dwellings Society* (1898) 78 LT 144.
19 CA 1985, s 125(3)(c) referring to s 80, ibid.
20 The reference is to CA 1985, s 135.

Where on the other hand rights are attached to shares as aforesaid, and the memorandum or articles do contain provision for variation, and variation is connected with the matters noted above, there can be no variation unless either the holders of three-quarters of the issued shares of that class consent in writing to the variation or an extraordinary resolution passed at a separate general meeting of the class sanctions the variation, and any further requirement of the variation of rights provisions of the memorandum or articles is complied with.[1]

Where rights are attached otherwise than by the memorandum and there is no provision in the articles concerning the variation of rights, the same procedure concerning written consents or an extraordinary resolution apply, and the company must further comply with any additional requirement concerning variation. however imposed.[2]

There can thus in any event be no variation unless the statutory criteria are satisfied and, where a power is found in the articles, any additional requirements therein contained. Furthermore, any alteration of a variation of rights provision in the articles, or for inserting such a provision in the company's articles, itself is treated as a variation of rights and subject to the same stringent safeguards as a variation itself.[3]

The general provisions of the Companies Act and the provisions of the articles relating to general meetings apply so far as applicable to meetings of members to consider the variation of class rights. The necessary quorum is two persons at least holding or representing by proxy one-third of the issued shares of the class in question and at an adjourned meeting, one person holding shares of the class in question.[4]

If at a class meeting a resolution is duly passed varying class rights, the holders of not less in aggregate than 15% of the issued shares of that class may, provided that they did not consent or vote for the variation, apply to the Court to have the variation cancelled. Once such an application is made, the variation is not to take effect unless and until it is confirmed by the Court.[5] An application must be made within 21 days after the date on which the consent was given or the resolution passed.[6] On hearing the application the

---

1 Ibid, s 125(3).
2 Ibid, s 125(2).
3 Ibid, s 125(7).
4 Ibid, s 125(6).
5 Ibid, s 127(1) and (2).
6 Ibid, s 127(3).

Court may, if it is satisfied having regard to all the circumstances of the case that the variation would unfairly prejudice the stockholders of the class represented by the applicant, disallow the variation. Otherwise, it shall allow it.[7]

On the question of what constitutes a variation of class rights, the courts have been very formal in their reasoning. A distinction has been drawn between the rights attaching to each share, and the conditions necessary for the full enjoyment of those rights. A changing of the conditions necessary for the full enjoyment of class rights is not treated as a variation of class rights so as to entitle the holder to protection. Thus an increase in capitalisation which by increasing the number of both preference and ordinary shares would dilute the control of existing preference shareholders was held not to be a variation. Lord Evershed MR thus remarked, in *White v Bristol Aeroplane Co Ltd*.[8]

> It is no doubt true that the employment of, and the capacity to make effective, those rights is in a measure affected; for ... the existing preference stockholders will be in a less advantageous position on such occasions as entitle them to register their votes, whether at general meetings of the company or at separate meetings of their own class. But there is to my mind a distinction, and a sensible distinction, between an affecting of the rights and an affecting of the enjoyment of the rights, or of the stockholders' capacity to turn them to account; ...

Similarly, in *Re John Smith's Tadcaster Brewery*[9] a proposal to increase the number of ordinary shares by a bonus issue could have had the effect of defeating the voting control of preference shareholders which was exercisable in certain contingencies such as the introduction of proposals for a reduction of capital on a winding up, or where preference dividends were in arrears. None the less, because the voting rights attaching to each share were unaffected, in the sense that they were not being 'modified, dealt with or abrogated', there was held to be no variation.[10] This principle has been taken so far that a rateable reduction of capital which affected the dividend rights of preference shareholders because it reduced the number of shares on which dividends might be paid was held not to be a variation of class rights since the proposal did not affect the rate of preference dividend to be paid on each share.[11]

---

7   Ibid, s 127(4).
8   [1953] Ch 65, [1953] 1 All ER 40.
9   [1953] Ch 308, [1953] 1 All ER 518.
10 The significance of the words used in the article was stressed by Jenkins LJ.
11 *Re Mackenzie & Co Ltd* [1916] 2 Ch 450.

308 *Chapter 15 Shares*

These cases have been much critised as detracting unduly from the protection which ought to be afforded to class rights.[12] On the other hand, a contrary rule which could treat any change in conditions required for enjoyment of class rights would put a considerable blocking power in the hands of a class thereby, perhaps, disabling the directors and the general body of shareholders from taking decisions required for the good of the company as a whole.[13]

CALLS

It should be noted that class rights can also be altered on a reduction of capital or a scheme of arrangement.[14]

CALLS

The articles usually confer on the directors the power to make calls on members in respect of moneys unpaid on their shares.[15] If shares are issued on the basis that 20% shall be payable on application, 10% on allotment, and a further 10% within a specified period of allotment, a call is made only in respect of the remaining 60% unpaid on the shares.[16] The debt due on calls is a specialty debt.

The call must be made strictly in terms of the articles, otherwise it will be held to be invalid. While mere irregularities will not invalidate the call,[17] the resolution making it must be properly passed. The amount of the call, to whom it is payable, and the time and place of payment must be specified.[18] The directors, as in all cases where they are exercising their powers, must make calls bona fide and for the benefit of the company as a whole.

---

12 *Gower's Principles of Modern Company Law* (4th edn, 1979) chap 23, has a full discussion.
13 It is to be noted that not only shareholders but also debenture-holders may vote to protect their own interests, restrained only by notions of fraud. See, in respect of debenture-holders, *British America Nickel Corpn v O'Brien* [1927] AC 369; *Re Hellenic and General Trust Ltd* [1975] 3 All ER 382, [1976] 1 WLR 123.
14 See Chaps 15 and 18 respectively.
15 Table A, arts 12–22.
16 But see Table A, art 16 which provides that for the purposes of forfeiture, sums payable on allotment or at a fixed period thereafter are deemed to be calls.
17 *Dawson v African Consolidated Land and Trading Co* [1898] 1 Ch 6.
18 See further, *Palmer's Company Law* (22nd edn, 1976) pp 369–374.

Alexander v Automatic Telephone Co [1900] 2 Ch 56.

The directors of the company resolved that shares be allotted to some of their number on which nothing would be paid on application and allotment, although the other members were required to pay 3 s on each share on application and allotment. Lindley MR stated at pp 66–67:

> The Court of Chancery has always exacted from directors the observance of good faith towards their shareholders and towards those who take shares from the company and become co-adventurers with themselves and others who may join them. The maxim *'caveat emptor'* has no application to such cases, and directors who so use their powers as to obtain benefits for themselves at the expense of the shareholders, without informing them of the fact, cannot retain those benefits and must account for them to the company, so that all the shareholders may participate in them.

> Similarly the directors could not make a call on the shares held by the ordinary members and not on their own.

Calls may not be made until the company becomes entitled to commence business. The articles may provide that interest shall accrue on calls not paid.[19] Calls must be paid in cash. The directors may be authorised by the articles to make calls so that there is a difference between the holders in the amount of calls to be paid or in times of payment.[20] A shareholder defending an action for calls on the ground of misrepresentation must prove not only that he has repudiated the shares, but also that he has taken steps to have his name removed from the register.[1]

---

19 Table A, art 15.
20 Ibid, art 17.
1   *First National Re-Insurance Co v Greenfield* [1921] 2 KB 260.

Chapter 16

Registration, Transfer and Transmission of Shares

REGISTER OF MEMBERS

Every company must keep a register of members in which are entered their names, addresses and descriptions. In general, the register should be kept at the registered office of the company.[1] Companies having a share capital must also show in the register the number of shares held by each member and the amounts paid or agreed to be treated as paid on those shares. The date at which each member was entered in the register and the date he ceased to be a member must also be included. Where the shares have been converted into stock the register must show the amount of stock held by each member. If the number of members exceeds 50 and the register is not arranged alphabetically an index must be kept.[2] The register and index are normally kept at the registered office of the company where they and any unregistered transfers are to be made available for inspection by any person, including non-members.[3]

On the issue of share warrants, the company must strike out the name of the member to whom the warrant is issued and enter details of the warrant in the register.[4] The bearer of a share warrant is entitled, subject to the articles, to be entered on the register on the surrender of the warrant for cancellation. The holder of a share warrant is entitled, subject to the Act and the articles, to the ordinary rights and privileges of membership.

The statutory obligation on the company to keep registers of directors disclosing their interests and those of their families in

---

1 CA 1985, s 352; it must distinguish each share by its number and class. It must specify the species of share held by each member where there is more than one species; *Re Performing Right Society Ltd, Lyttleton v Performing Right Society Ltd* [1978] 2 All ER 712.
2 Ibid, s 354.
3 Ibid, s 356.
4 Ibid, s 355.

shares and debentures of the company or group have already been dealt with in Chapter 9.

The Court has power under CA 1985, s 359 to rectify the register of members if:

(1) the name of any person is, without sufficient cause, entered in or omitted from the register; or
(2) default is made or unnecessary delay takes place in entering on the register the fact that a person has ceased to be a member.

These grounds are not exhaustive and the Court may order rectification in other cases.[5] The jurisdiction of the Court extends to all cases where a name stands on the register without sufficient cause. Thus, even where the registered holder executed a transfer in favour of another and the transfer was registered, the transferor successfully applied for the transferee to be struck off and the register rectified upon it appearing that the transfer was obtained by deception and that the transferor was led to believe that it would not be used against her.[6] The Court has power to refuse rectification or to order rectification and the payment of damages to the injured party. It may also determine questions of title to shares and other questions incidental to rectification. It may be rectified in respect of some part only of a member's shareholding. Where shares were never validly issued, rectification does not involve a reduction of capital.[7] An allottee who has been induced to take shares by fraudulent statements or misrepresentations in the prospectus must rescind before winding up commences; otherwise he loses his right to rectification. He must not only rescind, but secure rectification of the register.[8]

CA 1985, s 360 provides that no notice of any trust, expressed, implied or constructive, shall be entered on the register or be receivable by the Registrar. The company will not be liable for ignoring an equitable interest of which it has notice, unless a stop notice has been filed. Thus in:

---

5 See, eg *Burns v Siemens Bros Dynamo Works* [1919] 1 Ch 225.
6 *Re Imperial Chemical Industries Ltd* [1936] 2 All ER 463.
7 *Re Transatlantic Life Assurance Co Ltd* [1979] 3 All ER 352, [1980] 1 WLR 79.
8 *Oakes v Turquand and Harding* (1867) LR 2 HL 325; *Gibbs v General Mortgage Corpn Ltd* [1932] NZLR 584, 622.

Simpson v Molson's Bank [1895] AC 270, PC.

> The bank registered a transfer of its shares, executed by trustees and executors to one of the residuary legatees, in contravention of the provisions of the will. The bank held a copy of the will and its president was an executor under the will. The legatee disposed of the shares to a third person. The questions for the Court to decide were whether the bank had notice of the trust and whether, if it had notice, it should have refused to register the transfer. The statute establishing the bank had a provision in it similar in terms to s 360. Lord Shand stated at p 279.
>
> This language is general and comprehensive. The provisions seem to be directly applicable to trusts of which the bank had knowledge or notice; and in regard to these the bank, it is declared, are not to be bound to see to their execution.

It has been suggested that directors who allow a shareholder to transfer shares in breach of a trust of which they have actual notice are personally liable to the beneficiary.[9] This suggestion, though attractive, would seem to detract from any principle of finality attaching to the register and it has been said that no such liability may be imposed short of fraud on the part of the directors.[10]

As the bank did not have notice that the transaction was in breach of trust the transfer was valid.

The purpose of s 360 is to facilitate transfers, because the company and the transferee do not need to inquire if the transfer is in breach of trust. If it is desired to assert a non-registrable equitable interest, the claimant may file and serve on the company a document known as a stop notice.[11] Such a notice precludes the company from permitting the shares to be transferred by the registered holder without first giving notice to the claimant.[12]

The register is only prima facie evidence of the matters inserted therein[13] and evidence may be adduced to disprove statements contained in the register.[14]

Companies may keep branch registers in any part of Her Majesty's dominions, but notice must be given to the Registrar of their location, changes therein and discontinuance.[15]

---

9 *Société Générale de Paris v Tramways Union Co* (1884) 14 QBD 424, CA per Cotton LJ.
10 Ibid, at pp 453–454 per Lindley LJ.
11 RSC 1965, O 50, rr 11–14.
12 *Société Générale de Paris v Tramways Union Co* (1884) 14 QBD 424.
13 CA 1985, s 361.
14 *Re Briton Medical and General Life Association* (1888) 39 ChD 61.
15 CA 1985, s 362 and Sch 14.

SHARE CERTIFICATES

Section 185 of the Companies Act 1985 provides that unless the conditions of issue provide otherwise, a company must complete and have ready for delivery within two months of allotment or transfer a certificate of shares, debentures or debenture stock. Companies are exempted from this obligation if the securities are held by a Stock Exchange nominee. The nominee must be designated by order of the Secretary of State.[16] A company may have for use in sealing certificates relating to shares and debentures a fascimile common seal.[17] This can be used for authentication of certificates of the type described. The company may keep a register of members or debenture holders in computerised form.[18] The purpose of this machinery is to facilitate the introduction by the Stock Exchange of a computerised settlement and stock transfer system. The great advantage of these systems is that stock and share transfers between beneficial owners of securities which are held by the pool as nominee are carried out by book entries or computer. Instruments of transfer are only required for the transfer to and from the pool.[19]

The certificate is prima facie evidence of the title of the member to the shares.[20] A shareholder, by producing his share certificate, is able to show his title thereto, and the company is estopped from denying, as against a bona fide purchaser of the shares, that a member is entitled to the shares specified and that they are paid-up to the extent stated therein. A company that issues a share certificate makes a representation to the person named in the certificate and to persons with whom he may be expected to deal that the person named therein is entitled to the shares at the date of the certificate. The representation made in the certificate may be incorrect by reason of innocent mistakes, negligence or fraud. What remedies are available to persons misled by the certificate? A person may become liable for false representation in three ways.

First, the person making the statement may be a party to a contract in which he undertakes that the statement is true. Persons misled by a share certificate have no claim on this ground. A company which issues a share certificate does not thereby make a contract with anyone as to the truth of the representations in the

---

16 CA 1985, s 185(4).
17 Ibid, ss 40 and 186.
18 Ibid, s 723.
19 See remarks in [1976] JBL 106.
20 CA 1985, s 186.

certificate. A certificate under the common seal of the company, specifying the shares held by a member, is only prima facie evidence of the title of the member to the shares. Being only prima facie evidence the certificate is not conclusive, and merely shifts the burden of proof. It is still open to the company to show, if it can, that the person named in the certificate is not entitled to the shares. The company is not bound by any contract with the person named in the certificate to pay him damages if the statement is not correct. Nor is the company liable contractually to a purchaser of shares.[1] The share certificate is neither a warranty of title nor a negotiable instrument.

Secondly, a person may be liable for a misrepresentation. If the company, acting under the authority of a direction from the directors, issues a share certificate containing a material misrepresentation it will be liable to pay damages to the persons damnified. But the company is not liable for certificates issued fraudulently by the secretary for his own benefit by means of forgery: *Ruben v Great Fingall Consolidated*.[2] A share certificate may be a forgery although it bears the company's seal and in the genuine signature of the persons who, by the company's articles, are to sign its share certificates. In *South London Greyhound Racecourses Ltd v Wake*[3] the company's articles provided that the seal should not be affixed to any document except by authority of a resolution of the board of directors and in the presence of at least one director and the secretary. Without the authority of the board, a director and the secretary affixed the seal to a share certificate, signed and issued. It was held that the certificate was a forgery and not binding on the company. This decision, if correct, places a person dealing with a company in an almost intolerable position. It is submitted that this decision is wrong. The person relying on the certificate was entitled to assume that matters of indoor management—eg the holding of a board meeting—were complied with. He should therefore be entitled to rely on the document even though it is a forgery.

Thirdly, a person who has made a false representation may incur liability through the operation of the principle of estoppel. When an estoppel is pleaded, the statement that has been made to him by the defendant is asserted by the plaintiff as if it were true, and the defendant, by the operation of estoppel, is not allowed to prove that in fact it is untrue. No cause of action arises upon an estoppel in

---

1 *Re Ottos Kopje Diamond Mines Ltd* [1893] 1 Ch 618.
2 [1906] AC 439.
3 [1931] 1 Ch 496.

itself and the cause of action must be sought elsewhere. In the case of share certificates the cause of action may be either:

(1) that the company has removed the name of the plaintiff from the register, or
(2) that the company has refused to accept a transfer and to place the name of the transferee on the register.

Estoppel will not give any person a legal title to shares belonging to another person, but may enable him to recover damages from the company for loss caused by an act which the company could not lawfully have performed if he had been entitled to the shares.

CLAIM BY TRANSFEREE RELYING ON ESTOPPEL

This liability was first established in:

Re Bahia and San Francisco Rly Co (1886) LR 3 QB 584.

> The company registered a transfer of shares from the registered shareholder T to S and G, and issued a new certificate to S and G, certifying that they were the registered holders of the shares. S and G sold the shares to A, and a transfer was duly registered. It was then discovered that the transfer from T to S and G was a forgery, and the company had to restore the name of T to the register as the holder of these shares. A, who had brought the shares in reliance on the certificate issued by the company to S and G, took action against the company. It was held that the giving of the certificate amounted to a statement by the company, intended by the company to be acted on by purchasers of shares in the market, that S and G were entitled to the shares; and that as A had acted on that statement the company was estopped from denying its truth. A was therefore held to be entitled to recover from the company as damages for the loss of the shares the value of the shares at the time the company refused to recognise him as shareholder, with interest. The transfer to A had been registered, but the company would have been under the same liability even if it had not registered the transfer.

CLAIM BY REGISTERED SHAREHOLDER RELYING ON ESTOPPEL

A person named in the share certificate who merely receives his certificate and does nothing further will have no claim against the company in the event of his name being removed from the register unless he can show that he has suffered loss as the result of having relied on the certificate. He must prove, for example, that he had entered into a binding contract to sell the shares,[4] or that through relying on the certificate he has lost a remedy he previously had against the person from whom he purchased the shares.[5]

ESTOPPEL AS TO AMOUNT PAID UP

When an estoppel is raised against the company it relates to all the facts asserted in the certificate. This includes not only the assertion as to title, but also the assertion as to the amount paid up on the shares. In general such an estoppel will only avail a transferee since in general an allottee is aware of the footing on which he takes shares.[6]

Bloomenthal v Ford [1897] AC 156.

> A loan was to be made to a company by B, who took as security 10,000 fully paid shares. The share certificates issued to the lender (B) stated: 'On each of the shares the full amount has been paid up.' When the loan fell due for repayment it was renewed for a further period on the same security. The shares were in fact new shares on which nothing had been paid, and when the company went into liquidation the lender was placed on the list of contributories for the full nominal value of the shares. It was held by the House of Lords that the company was estopped from denying that the shares were fully paid, as it had obtained the loan and the renewal on the faith of the representation, and that the name of the lender must be removed from the list of contributories.

Where the estoppel operates, the defendant will be able to resist an action by the company or the liquidator to enforce payments by him in respect of his shares. To displace the estoppel the company (or the liquidator) must prove that the shareholder had notice of the fact that the shares were not fully paid up.[7]

This rule of estoppel is applicable not only in favour of transferees but even in favour of original allottees. Usually an original allottee will have notice of the true facts and will know whether the shares are really fully paid. But as in *Re Building Estates Brickfields Co, Parbury's Case*[8] and in *Bloomenthal v Ford* the circumstances

---

4 *Balkis Consolidated Co Ltd v Tomkinson* [1893] AC 396.
5 *Dixon v Kennaway* [1900] 1 Ch 833. See also *Re Exchange Securities and Commodities Ltd* [1987] 2 WLR 893.
6 For an exceptional case where he was not, see *The Penang Foundry Co Ltd v Gardiner* 1913 SC 1203.
7 *Burkinshaw v Nicholls* (1878) 3 App Cas 1004.
8 [1896] 1 Ch 100.

may be such that the original allottee is not aware that the shares are not fully paid as stated on the certificate.

The company is not estopped from showing that, in spite of the certificate, the shares are not fully paid up, if the shares were so issued under an arrangement which was known to the allottee and turns out to be *ultra vires*.[9]

It is a general rule applicable to all cases in which estoppel is alleged that no estoppel arises if the person to whom the erroneous statement was made knew the true facts, or was put upon inquiry (eg by special endorsement on the share certificate) and failed to ascertain the true position.

CERTIFICATE BASED ON FORGED TRANSFER

If a company issues a share certificate based on a forged transfer the company is not estopped by the certificate as against the person who requested the company to register the transfer, whether or not that person was aware of the forgery.

Simm v Anglo-American Telegraph Co (1879) 5 QBD 188.

> Coates was a stockholder in the telegraph company. His clerk forged a transfer from Coates to Spurling, who was ignorant of the forgery. Spurling transferred the stock to Simm. The telegraph company registered both transfers and issued a certificate to Simm. The forgery was then discovered, and the company refused to recognise the title of Simm and withheld payment of dividends. Simm had relied on the validity of the certificate which had been issued to him, and would normally have had a good claim against the company on the basis of estoppel. But as it happened, the transfer from Spurling to Simm had been merely as security for a loan, and the loan had been repaid before the forgery was discovered. On repayment of the loan the stock would normally have been re-transferred to Spurling, but as the company refused to recognise Simm's title as valid, Spurling endeavoured to recover damages from the company by means of estoppel. It was held, however, that he had acted on the faith of the forged transfer and had not relied on any act of the company. As he had himself equal means of knowledge of the true facts, and had induced the company to issue the certificate by sending the forged transfer to the company for registration, no action would lie for the company's refusal to recognise the title of the person named in the certificate.

---

9 *Re Eddystone Marine Insurance Co* [1893] 3 Ch 9.

318 *Chapter 16 Registration, Transfer and Transmission of Shares*

The case firmly established the rule that where a forged transfer is registered the transferee cannot compel the company to acknowledge him as the holder of the shares.

RIGHTS OF THE TRUE OWNER

If the name of the true owner has been wrongfully removed from the register he can compel the company to restore his name and to pay him any dividends he has missed, with interest. To minimise the risk of registering forged transfers many companies make a practice of sending a letter to the registered holder whose shares are comprised in the transfer, informing him that unless the company hears to the contrary it will proceed to register the transfer. This practice affords no protection to the company if it receives no reply, since the shareholder is not estopped from later proving that the transfer was a forgery and demanding to be restored to the register.[10]

THE COMPANY'S RIGHT TO AN INDEMNITY

The person who produced a transfer for registration does not represent to the company that the transferor is entitled to the shares (that being a matter which the company's own records should show) but he does represent that the transfer is a genuine document duly executed by the transferor. If the company accedes to the request for registration of the transfer, the person who presented the transfer for registration is deemed to have entered into an implied contract with the company whereby he warrants that the transfer is genuine. If it is a forgery, and the company, having issued a new share certificate, is compelled to make good the loss sustained by a person who has acted on the certificate, the company will be entitled to be indemnified, under this implied contract, in respect of its liability. Although the person who lodged the transfer may have been entirely ignorant of the forgery he will still be liable to indemnify the company.

Sheffield Corporation v Barclay [1905] AC 392.

> A banker in good faith sent to a corporation a transfer of corporation stock which purported to be executed by T and H, the registered holders, with a request to register the stock in the name of the banker as transferee. The corporation in good faith acted on the request and

---

10 *Barton v London and North Western Rly Co* (1889) 24 QBD 77.

issued a fresh certificate to the banker. He transferred the stock to third parties, and they became registered as the holders. Afterwards it was discovered that T had forged H's signature, and H recovered judgment against the corporation, whereby they were compelled to buy equivalent stock and register it in H's name and to pay him the missing dividends with interest. It was held that both parties having acted bona fide and without negligence, the banker, who produced the transfer for registration, was bound to indemnify the corporation against the liability to H, upon an implied contract that the transfer was genuine.

SHARE WARRANTS

A company limited by shares may, if authorised by its articles, issue share warrants in respect of fully paid-up shares.[11] Share warrants are negotiable instruments.[12] The shareholder receives instead of a share certificate a document stating that the bearer is entitled to the shares or stock included in the warrant. The bearer of the warrant is entitled to all the rights of a shareholder unless the articles provide otherwise. His name does not, however, appear on the register of members. Dividends are paid by coupons or otherwise to the holder of the warrant. Shares included in a share warrant are not a qualification for a director required by the articles to hold qualification shares.[13]

TRANSFER

Shares are personal property transferable in the manner provided by the articles.[14] A company may provide in its articles that the directors shall have a discretion in the acceptance of transfers for registration.[15] Private companies frequently in their articles restrict the rights of members to transfer their shares.[16] Unless, however, the directors are given a discretion to refuse to register a transfer, both the transferee and the transferor have a right to require it to be registered.[17] A shareholder has a property in his shares which he is

---

11 CA 1985, s 188.
12 *Bechuanaland Exploration Co v London Trading Bank Ltd* [1898] 2 QB 658.
13 CA 1985, s 291(2).
14 CA 1985, s 182(1).
15 *Re Smith, Knight & Co, Weston's Case* (1868) 4 Ch App 20.
16 See p 328, n 13.
17 *Re Cawley & Co* (1889) 42 ChD 209, 231 per Chitty J; *Re Stockton, Malleable Iron Co* (1875) 2 ChD 101.

at liberty to dispose of subject only to such express restrictions as are found in the articles.[18] This principle applies to both public and private companies,[19] but it is of course clear that the express restrictions on transfer found in the articles of private companies are rightly of an onerous character.[20]

Whether, therefore, shares are subject to restrictions and if so of what character, depends upon the articles. If Table A articles are employed, the directors may decline to register the transfer of a share (not being a fully paid share) to a person of whom they do not approve. They may also decline to register the transfer of any share on which the company has a lien.[1] There is also provision for refusal to register if the instrument of transfer is not accompanied by the certificate of transfer and such other evidence as the directors may require, is not lodged at the proper office, or if the instrument of transfer refers to more than one class of share.[2]

Where the articles give the directors the right to refuse a transfer unless certain restrictions are observed, a registration made without due observance of the articles is invalid. It may even be impeached by the transferor in a motion for rectification provided that he has not estopped himself from doing so. In *Hunter v Hunter*[3] a transferor who warned his transferee that a transfer would, in the light of a prohibition in the articles, prove ineffectual, was held entitled to move for rectification.

Where, as in Table A, the directors are given a right to refuse to register a transfer because they do not approve of the transferee, the directors must act on grounds personal to the transferee. They cannot refuse to register a transfer simply because to do so would enure to the advantage of some other faction within the company. On the other hand, if their approval of a transferee is obtained by fraud or concealment, the registration may be set aside.[4] Similarly, if the power of restrictions exists to protect a lien, the Court will not uphold a refusal to register based upon some other ground.[5] These points are but illustrations of the general principle that the directors' discretion to refuse to register transfers is bounded by the terms of the articles.[6]

18 *Re Bede Steam Shipping Co Ltd* [1917] 1 Ch 123.
19 *Re Copal Varnish Co Ltd* [1917] 2 Ch 349.
20 *Re Smith and Fawcett Ltd* [1942] Ch 304, CA.
1 Table A, art 24.
2 Ibid.
3 [1936] AC 222.
4 *Re Bede Steam Shipping Co* [1917] 1 Ch 123.
5 *Re Stockton Malleable Iron Co* (1875) 2 ChD 101.
6 *Re Smith and Fawcett Ltd* [1942] Ch 304, CA.

If it can be shown that a refusal to register a transfer was actuated by improper motives, the Court will make an order for rectification in the transferee's favour. The Court presumes, however, that the directors have acted properly. Where the articles enable the directors to refuse to register without assigning reasons therefor, the person challenging their conduct will have to prove that the directors exercised their powers improperly.[7] This may prove difficult. For example, whether interrogatories can be addressed to the directors inquiring into their conduct will depend upon the terms of the articles. If the articles provide that the directors cannot be made to specify the reasons for their action, but only the grounds, eg the head of the article under which they acted, interrogatories will only be allowed as to the grounds.[8] Where, seemingly, the directors need specify neither reasons nor grounds, interrogatories will not be available. If, however, the directors, though not obliged to assign a reason, give one which appears to be wrong, the Court is at liberty to consider whether their reasons are valid.[9]

These matters are even more important in the case of private companies. Article 24 of the current Table A does not give the directors an entirely unfettered discretion; they may refuse to register a transfer in favour of a person of whom they do not approve. None the less, it may well be difficult to raise the issue whether their motovation was impeachable. If Table A articles in their original form in CA 1948 were employed, the directors are given an absolute discretion to refuse to register a transfer of any shares without assigning any reason therefor. In such cases, the directors' obligation is to exercise their power in what they consider—not what a Court may consider—is in the interests of the company and not for any collateral purpose. The element of control thus accorded to directors, which is very strict, has been upheld as frequently necessary in the case of private companies. These are often structurally analogous to partnerships and good faith and confidence between the members may be of considerable importance.[10] Proof that the directors acted for improper motives may, as noted above, be very difficult to obtain.

Where a company refuses to register a transfer, it must send notice of the refusal and return the transfer to the transferee within

---

7 *Re Bede Steam Shipping Co* (supra); *Re Coalport China Co* [1895] 2 Ch 404, CA.
8 *Berry and Stewart v Tottenham Hotspur Football and Athletic Co Ltd* [1935] 1 Ch 718; *Sutherland (Duke) v British Dominions Land Settlement Corpn* [1926] Ch 746.
9 *Tett v Phoenix Property and Investment Co Ltd* [1984] BCLC 599.
10 *Re Smith and Fawcett Ltd* (supra).

two months of the presentation of the transfer for registration.[11] The right to disapprove of a transfer is vested in the board as such, and not in any individual director. Thus a mere failure to approve a transfer, caused by a deadlock on the board, is not a formal active exercise of the right to refuse and the transferee can maintain a motion for rectification.[12] Similarly, a motion for rectification will succeed where one director, by refusing to attend, prevented a directors' meeting from being held to consider the registration.[13] The directors are not entitled to delay consideration of an application to register a transfer indefinitely. The powers vested in directors to refuse to register a transfer must be exercised within a reasonable time. In *Re Swaledale Cleaners Ltd*[14] it was held that a delay of more than four months was unreasonable, that the directors had lost their power to refuse, and a later refusal was accordingly invalid.

PRE-EMPTIVE RIGHTS

Pre-emptive rights are often provided for. These may impose restrictions on transfer, or they may provide for the compulsory disposition of shares. An example of the latter type is the agreement sometimes entered into between a company's employee or officer and the company that, on leaving the company, he will sell and transfer his shares to the company's controllers at a price to be fixed by a suitable formula.[15] The former type, a relatively common restriction on transfers, is a clause in the articles giving pre-emptive rights to other members to acquire the shares of a member who desires to sell all or part of his holdings. Such restrictions are perfectly lawful.[16] Indeed, such a clause has been upheld where only one member remained to purchase the shares.[17] The courts will apply such provisions in strict conformity with their terms. A leading case is:

---

11 CA 1985, s 183(5).
12 *Moodie v W & J Shepherd (Bookbinders) Ltd* [1949] 2 All ER 1044, HL.
13 *Re Copal Varnish Co Ltd* [1917] 2 Ch 349.
14 [1968] 3 All ER 619, [1968] 1 WLR 1710, CA.
15 For an example see *Langen and Wind Ltd v Bell* [1972] Ch 685, [1972] 1 All ER 296. The Court there was concerned to safeguard the unpaid vendor's lien on the shares.
16 *Borland's Trustee v Steel Bros & Co Ltd* [1901] 1 Ch 279.
17 *Jarvis Motors (Harrow) Ltd v Carabott* [1964] 3 All ER 89, [1964] 1 WLR 1101.

Lyle and Scott v Scott's Trustees and British Investment Trust Ltd [1959] AC 763, [1959] 2 All ER 661.

A company's articles provided that every shareholder desirous of selling his shares should inform the secretary and that other shareholders were to have the right to purchase the shares at a price to be fixed by the auditor. The registered holders of certain shares entered into an agreement with another for consideration binding themselves to put him as fully in control of the company as they could without registering a transfer of the shares. The company sought a declaration that the shareholders were bound to implement the article and a decree ordering them forthwith to do so. The House of Lords held:

(1) the shareholders were persons desirous of transferring their shares so that the article applied. Transfer here could mean parting with an equitable interest in the shares, and
(2) that the shareholders could therefore be required to follow the procedure contained in the article, but
(3) they could escape this consequence by annulling their bargain with the third party.

However, the *Lyle and Scott* case is not authority for the proposition that, under an article of the sort considered in that case, a member who is in a position in which, by operation of law, he holds shares registered in his name as bare trustee for a non-member, is deemed to be a person desirous of transferring the shares, even though the beneficiaries disclaim any desire to exercise their right to compel a transfer to them:

Safeguard Industrial Investments Ltd v National Westminster Bank Ltd [1980] 3 All ER 849, affd [1982] 1 All ER 449.

The articles of W Ltd contained pre-emptive provisions in favour of members similar to those considered in the *Lyle and Scott* case, and required a proposing transferor to give notice of transfer. On the death of P, a member of W, the Bank as his personal representative became entitled to and was registered as holder of P's shares. At the time of the trial, the Bank held the shares on trust for G and M. G and M did not wish the shares to be transferred to them and the Bank did not propose to transfer unless directed by G and M to do so. S, a member of W, sought determination of the question whether the Bank, having completed the administration of P's estate, was bound to give notice of transfer.

It was held the Bank need not give notice because:

(1) the Bank was not a proposing transferor as it had not proposed and did not propose to transfer the shares and the *Lyle and Scott* case did not hold that, where the legal position is that a person other than the member can require a transfer to himself, the member becomes a proposed transferor, but was concerned merely with voluntary acts of disposition by the member;
(2) the term 'transfer' in the articles referred only to a transfer of legal interests and did not apply to a transfer of beneficial interests;
(3) the desire of P to transfer his shares as expressed in his will could not be attributed to the Bank.

Generally speaking, a sale to a third person in violation of the articles gives to that person no right to be entered on the register as a member. Such a sale is not, however, wholly devoid of effect. At least where the sale is made to other members, the failure to follow the procedure in a pre-emptive clause in the articles does not so vitiate the transaction as to give rise to a total failure of consideration. Instead, the sale operates to pass a beneficial interest in the shares to the purchaser.[18] This is a curious result which it is difficult to justify since in some cases it may deprive other members of the right to purchase. It is difficult to reconcile with the statement in *Hunter v Hunter*[19] that the articles provide the only means by which a member of a company can form an agreement for the sale of the shares.

It has been held that in cases involving the enforcement of pre-emptive rights a member may enforce the articles directly against another member who is obliged by them to purchase his shares.[20] The member need not, apparently, join the company in the action.[1]

One of the principal difficulties associated with pre-emptive clauses lies in the problem of the value to be attached to the shares. The articles frequently provide for sale at a fair value to be determined by the auditor. In such cases the auditor's valuation can only be challenged by showing that he made a mistake of a substantial character or materially misdirected himself in the course of his valuation, as by committing a serious arithmetical error. The

---

18 *Hawks v McArthur* [1951] 1 All ER 22; *Tett v Phoenix Property and Investment Co Ltd* [1984] BCLC 599.
19 [1936] AC 222, per Lord Atkin; in *Tett v Phoenix Property and Investment Co Ltd*, supra, Vinelott J distinguished *Hunter v Hunter* on the footing that there the articles created the company the sole agent for sale thus preventing a valid contract from being formed, presumably. But that, surely, should prevent an equitable interest from arising and *Hawks v McArthur*, on which the court relied, would, on that reasoning, have been wrongly decided.
20 *Rayfield v Hands* [1960] Ch 1, [1958] 2 All ER 194.
1 Cf *dicta* in *Welton v Saffery* [1897] AC 299.

Courts further distinguish between a speaking valuation (where the valuer states the basis for valuation) and a non-speaking one, holding that where no reasons are disclosed, the valuation cannot be impeached, though equitable relief may be granted where the transaction is not concluded. If, however, a speaking valuation is provided, it may be impugned where it appears to have been made on a fundamentally erroneous basis. The result is anomalous, but it is well entrenched.[2]

Where the company is in a perilous condition the auditor may rightly value the shares having regard to the break-up value of the company. Furthermore, even though the shares concerned constitute a controlling block, the valuation need not include a value on control at least where there is no reason to assume that the shares will be purchased *en bloc*.[3]

FORM OF TRANSFER

The transfer must, by CA 1985, s 183(1), be a proper instrument in writing notwithstanding anything in the articles to the contrary or be exempt under the Stock Transfer Act 1983. Thus, an article providing that on the death of a director his shares were to be deemed to have passed to his wife if she survived him and requiring her to be registered as the holder of the shares was held to be invalid.[4] On the other hand, an instrument of transfer need not necessarily be signed in accordance with or in the form required by the article. Mere irregularities are not fatal to its validity. In *Re Paradise Motor Co Ltd*[5] a transfer which, though signed by the transferor, did not comply with the articles because it was not signed by the transferee was, none the less, held to be valid.

Company articles, in general, required transfers to be executed by both transferor and transferee, in the presence of witnesses. This is decidedly cumbersome. As a result, the Stock Transfer Act 1963 makes provision for a new common form of transfer for use with fully paid shares and debentures.[6] The transferor alone need sign

---

2   *Burgess v Purchase & Sons (Farms) Ltd* [1983] Ch 216, [1983] 2 All ER 4.
3   *Dean v Prince* [1954] Ch 409, [1954] 1 All ER 749, CA considered in *Jones (M) v Jones (R.R.)* [1971] 2 All ER 676, [1971] 1 WLR 840. The entire problem of valuation is a difficult one. See *Holt v IRC* [1953] 2 All ER 1499 per Danckwerts J; *Lynall v IRC* [1970] Ch 138, [1969] 3 All ER 984; *Arenson v Casson, Beckman Rutley & Co* [1977] AC 405, [1975] 3 All ER 901; *Leigh v English Property Corpn Ltd* [1976] 2 Lloyd's Rep 298.
4   *Re Greene* [1949] Ch 333.
5   [1968] 2 All ER 625, [1968] 1 WLR 1125.
6   Stock Transfer Act 1963, Sch 1.

and no witnesses are required. If the transaction is a stock exchange transaction in which each of the parties is a member or acts through the agency of a member of a stock exchange, the transferee's name and address can be set out in a Brokers' Transfer Form[7] prepared later. This simplified procedure is helpful.

Until registration the purchaser has only an equitable interest which the company is entitled to ignore.[8] The legal interest passes on registration. As between persons having equitable rights, the first in time will prevail. A transferee entitled to an equitable interest in shares under an unregistered transfer will lose his rights if a subsequent transfer to a bona fide purchaser of the same share is registered, or at all events such purchaser complied with all the requisite formalities leaving only some ministerial act to be performed by the company.[9] The remedy is, as we have noted, for the person having an equitable interest to file and serve a stop notice under O 50, RSC 1965, in which case he must be notified before the company registers the transfer.[10]

Unless the contract provides otherwise, it is not part of the transferor's obligations to secure registration of the transfer. His duties are completed when he executes a valid transfer of the shares and hands it to the transferee with the share certificate.[11] If the directors, in the exercise of their discretion, refuse to register the transfer, the transferee cannot recover the purchase price, but the transferor will hold the shares as trustee for the purchaser. Presumably the transferee is liable to indemnify the transferor against claims made by the company on him as the registered holder.

GIFTS OF SHARES

The problems associated with the non-registration of shares could be particularly acute in the case of gifts of shares in private companies. A gift of shares may be made by the registered holder delivering to the donee an instrument of transfer in the form required by the articles, together with the share certificate, or by sending the certificate contemperaneously to the company. The transferee presents these documents to the company in order to register the transfer. On registration, the donee's name is entered

---

7   Ibid, Sch 2.
8   See the discussion at pp 311–312, supra.
9   *Moore v North Western Bank* [1891] 2 Ch 599, 602; *Peat v Clayton* [1906] 1 Ch 659.
10 See p 312, supra.
11 Under CA 1985, s 183(4) the transferor may apply for registration of a transfer.

on the books of the company as a shareholder. Such a gift may be made either to the donee absolutely or to the donee to be held on trust for him for the purposes of a settlement. The donee is of course at liberty to disclaim the gift.[12]

In order to make a valid gift of shares, the donor must do all that lies in his power to perfect it. Otherwise, the gift will fail for there is no equity to perfect an imperfect gift. The leading case is:

Milroy v Lord (1862) 4 De GF & J 264, [1861–73] All ER Rep 783.

> Medley, by deed poll signed by him and Lord, and in consideration of natural love and affection conveyed 50 shares in the Bank of Louisiana and the certificates and the dividends and profits to Lord to be held, on a marriage settlement, to the benefit of his niece Eleanor Rainey (later Milroy). Medley gave Lord certificates for 162 bank shares of which some 50 were those described in the settlement, and a power of attorney to receive the dividends accruing under the shares. Lord already held a power of attorney from Medley authorising him to transfer the stock of any incorporated company which might be standing in his name. The shares were, by the articles of the bank, transferable in the books of the company. No transfer was ever made. Lord remitted the dividends to Mrs Milroy sometimes himself and sometimes through the settlor. Out of these dividends, shares in another company were purchased at, at the instance of the plaintiff, put in Medley's name. On Medley's death, Lord delivered the certificates for the 50 bank shares and the further 13 shares to Medley's legal executor. The plaintiff brought action to recover the shares and to appoint new trustees of the settlement. The Court held that the 13 further shares had been purchased from moneys given by Medley to the plaintiff and that these were therefore to be treated as held on trust for her. The Court held further, however, that no gift of the original 50 shares had ever been perfected. Medley had not made any transfer of the shares so as to confer legal proprietorship on any other person. In order to render a voluntary settlement valid and effectual the settlor must have done everything which, according to the nature of the property comprised in the settlement, was necessary to be done in order to transfer the property and render the settlement binding upon himself. Here, he had not transferred the property to the donee, nor transferred it to a trustee for the purposes of the settlement, nor declared that he himself held the property on trust for the settlement. The Court would not protect an imperfect gift. Nor would it hold the intended transfer to operate as a declaration of trust, 'for then every imperfect instrument would be made effectual by being converted into a perfect trust'.

---

[12] *Re Paradise Motor Co Ltd* [1968] 2 All ER 625, [1968] 1 WLR 1125.

The shares were, of course, freely transferable on the books of the company. The settlor could readily have perfected the gift either by registering the transfer himself, or directing Lord, who held a power of attorney, to do this for him. But he did not. The power of attorney was not specifically conferred on Lord for this purpose. He held it as Medley's agent and without specific instructions from Medley would not have been justified in registering a transfer.

This seems not unreasonable. The Court, had it held that it could perfect the gift, might have adopted a course at variance with the intent of the donor who had ample opportunity to perfect it himself.

The principle in *Milroy v Lord* has been qualified in cases dealing with the transfer of shares in private companies, the articles of which, frequently, give the directors the power, in their discretion, to refuse transfers.[13] It can therefore happen that a transferee whose transferor has done all that he can to divest himself of his legal and beneficial interest in the shares may ultimately fail to secure registration because of a decision of the directors about which he and the transferor can do nothing. In such cases the courts hold that the gift is complete. *Milroy v Lord* and similar cases,[14] have been distinguished as cases in which the settlor failed to do all that he could, having regard to the nature of the property, to perfect the gift.[15]

Where the company refuses to register the transfer, equitable obligations will be imposed on the transferor in order to give, as against him, full effect to the gift. Thus where in such circumstances dividends are paid to the transferor, the transferor wil be treated as holding them for the transferee.[16] The gift plainly passes property to the full extent of the transferor's power to do so.[17] The gift is treated as made on the date when the instruments of transfer and share

---

12 *Re Paradise Motor Co Ltd* [1968] 2 All ER 625, [1968] 1 WLR 1125.
13 Because formerly such restrictions were compulsory for private companies: see CA 1948, s 28 (repealed CA 1980, Sch 4).
14 Principally *Re Fry* [1946] Ch 312, [1946] 2 All ER 106.
15 *Re Rose, Midland Bank Executor and Trustee Co v Rose* [1949] Ch 78, [1948] 2 All ER 971; *Re Rose, Rose v IRC* [1952] Ch 499, [1952] 1 All ER 1217, esp per Jenkins LJ; *Re Vandervell's Trusts (No 2), White v Vandervell Trustees Ltd* [1974] 3 All ER 205, at 212–13 per Lord Denning MR. For a criticism see L. MacKay, 'Share Transfers and the Complete and Perfect Rule' (1976) 40 Conv 139 where the argument is put that the accepted rule creates the possibility that the donor will be saddled indefinitely with the unwanted obligations of a trustee. This is no doubt true, but the very nature of the problem militates against any neat solution.
16 *Re Rose, Rose v IRC* [1952] Ch 499, [1952] 1 All ER 1217, per Lord Evershed MR.
17 See cases cited above and *Fitch Lovell Ltd v IRC* [1962] 1 WLR 1325 at 1328.

certificates were executed and delivered to the transferee. At that point, the transferor is treated as having irrevocably divested himself of the property in favour of the transferee.[18]

Although in these cases the Court treats an unregistered transfer as giving rise to equitable obligations on the transferor's part, there is no necessary inconsistency with *Milroy v Lord*.[19] The Courts will not perfect imperfect transfers. They will recognise 'the consequences of a transfer being complete without extraneous formalities having been complied with, which is the real point in the share transfer cases'.[20]

Where the directors refuse to register a transfer the transferee will be in a relatively secure position, if he has in his possession the transfer and share certificates. He can in any event protect his interests against the transferor and persons claiming under him by filing a stop notice.[1] But he will not be registered as a member, nor will a purchaser from him be certain that registration will be approved unless the directors have been sounded first. Presumably he may require the transferor to vote the shares as he directs. The transferor could be in an invidious position. He cannot compel the company to register the transfer and remains, therefore, subject to equitable obligations which he never wished to assume. He will hold dividends for the transferee. Prima facie he will be liable for any calls, though no doubt having a right to indemnity against the transferee. This sort of situation is, fortunately, likely to be rare. None the less, he is made subject to obligations which, *ex hypothesi*, he never wished to assume. The rights and obligations of the transferor and transferee in such circumstances have not been fully developed by the Courts.

Similar infirmities could affect an equitable mortgage of shares. In such a case the borrower remains on the register. If he sold to a bona fide purchaser for value without notice, the claim of the lender could be defeated.[2] The remedy presumably is to file a stop notice.[3] A legal mortgage which involves a transfer of the shares to the lender followed by a registration of transfer is not subject to these problems.[4]

---

18 *Re Rose, Rose v IRC* [1952] Ch 409, [1952] 1 All ER 1217.
19 The remainder of this section owes a debt to the suggested treatment of the topic by Mr J. D. Davies in [1968] ASCL 413–414.
20 Davies, loc cit, at p 414.
1 See p 312, ante.
2 See *Société Générale de Paris v Walker* (1885) 11 App Cas 20.
3 CA 1985, s 360.
4 See further, Palmer's *Company Law* (22nd edn, 1976) p 412.

CERTIFICATION OF TRANSFERS

Where a transfer affects only some of the shares comprised in a certificate, eg where the share certificate is for 300 shares and only 100 are being transferred, the transferor will not wish to hand to the transferee his share certificate. He will prefer to produce his certificate to the company which may then 'certify' the transfer for the 100 shares that the share certificate has been lodged with the company.[5]

CA 1985, s 184 provides that the certification by a company of a transfer of shares in or debentures of a company shall be taken as a representation by the company to any person acting on the faith of the certification that there have been produced to the company such documents as on the face of them show a prima facie title to the shares or debentures in the transferor named in the transfer. But the certification is not a representation that the transferor has any title to the shares or debentures. Where any person acts on the faith of a false certification by a company made negligently, the company is under the same liability to him as if the certification has been made fraudulently. A person who relied on the certification and suffered loss as a result can recover damages from the company.

The circumstances in which the certification of a transfer is deemed to be made by the company are set out in s 184(3). Under that sub-section, if:

(1) the person issuing the transfer is a person authorised to issue certificated transfers on the company's behalf; and
(2) the certification is signed by a person authorised to certificate transfers on the company's behalf or by any officer or servant either of the company or of a body corporate so authorised;

the company is deemed to have made the certification.

TRANSMISSION

Subject to the articles,[6] where the registered holder of shares dies, or becomes bankrupt, his shares vest in his personal representatives. The company is bound to accept the probate of the will or letters of administration as sufficient evidence of the grant, notwithstanding anything in its articles.[7] The personal representatives are

---

5 The need for certification is not affected by the Stock Transfer Act 1963. A space for certification is included in the forms set out in Sch 1 and 2.
6 Table A, arts 29–31.
7 CA 1985, s 187.

entitled, on evidence of their appointment, to enjoy the rights and privileges of the member.[8] A transfer, executed by the personal representatives of the deceased is as valid as if executed by the member.[9]

The personal representatives of a deceased member may transfer his shares without being included in the register of members. They may, however, ask to be registered as shareholders. In such case no particular form is required by statute. It is enough that there be a distinct and intelligible request to that effect.[10] But if they are put on the register under their own names, they become personally liable on the shares: *Buchan's Case*.[11] Similarly, if they take new shares in their own names, they will, of course, have a right of indemnity against the estate to the extent of the assets therein.

---

[8] See *Morgan v Gray* [1953] Ch 83, [1953] 1 All ER 213, and *Re H L Bolton Engineering Co Ltd* [1956] Ch 577, [1956] 1 All ER 799.
[9] CA 1985, s 183(3).
[10] *Re Jermyn Street Turkish Baths Ltd* [1970] 3 All ER 57, [1970] 1 WLR 1194.
[11] (1879) 4 App Cas 549.

Chapter 17

Capital

The primary emphasis of the EEC Second Directive concerns the safeguarding of the company's capital. Accordingly, the Companies Act 1985 contains extensive capital maintenance provisions.

The word 'capital' when employed in company law is used in different senses. It is customary to distinguish between:[1]

(1) the nominal (or authorised) capital. Every company limited by shares or limited by guarantee and having a share capital must state a nominal capital divided into shares of a fixed amount in the memorandum of association.[2]

(2) Issued capital. This is that portion of the nominal capital which has been issued to the members. A company is not obliged to issue all its nominal capital at once. It may have an unallotted residuum to be allotted in the future as and when the company needs further capital.

(3) Paid-up capital. This is the amount of issued capital that has been paid up, either in cash or for other valuable consideration. If shares are only partly paid up, the company may resolve to make all calls upon the shares up to the par value of the shares.[3]

(4) Reserve capital. A company may, by special resolution, resolve that the whole or part of its uncalled capital shall not be called up except in the event of a winding up.[4] The amount which the company resolves not to call up save in an event is called the reserve capital, or reserve liability.

In addition, the Companies Act requires the constitution of two accounts, funds attributed to which, though strictly speaking not

---

1 For further details, see Palmer's *Company Law* (22nd edn, 1976) pp 309–312.
2 CA 1985, s 2(5)(a).
3 Uncalled capital is not generally considered to be an asset of the company until a call is made (*Page v International Agency and Industrial Trust Ltd* (1893) 62 LJ Ch 610); but a company may mortgage its uncalled capital (*Re Pyle Works* (1890) 44 ChD 534).
4 CA 1985, s 120.

part of the company's capital, cannot, subject to the exception discussed below in relation to the share premium account, be distributed to the members without the leave of the Court. These are the share premium account[5] and the capital redemption reserve.[6]

English law now prescribes a minimum capital for public companies but not for private companies. The authorised minimum is £50,000 or such other sum as the Secretary of State may specify by Statutory Instrument.[7] The Secretary of State may by order require public companies whose share capital falls below the authorised minimum to re-register as a private company and make consequential provisions relating thereto.[8]

A private company may be formed with minimal capital. Such a practice, it has been said 'makes nonsense of the whole concept of a share capital and of limited liability'.[9] In such circumstances there is a risk that the business will fail due to undercapitalisation, and the fraudulent trading section of the Insolvency Act 1986, as we will see, does not afford as strong a protection against this sort of event as one might wish.[10]

The Companies Act 1985 not only prescribes a minimum capital for public companies but contains a series of provisions directed towards the protection of the capital. These are in addition to the existing provision which requires that the prospectus state the minimum amount of capital which the directors consider is required to enable the company to commence business.

PAYMENT FOR SHARE CAPITAL

The provisions concerning payment for share capital apply primarily to public companies including private companies which have resolved to re-register, old public companies and joint stock companies which have proposed to re-register as public.[11] There are transitional provisions which save certain allotments entered into

---

5 CA 1985, s 130.
6 Ibid, s 170.
7 Ibid, s 118.
8 Ibid.
9 Financial Report of the Commission of Inquiry Into the Working and Administration of the present Company Law of Ghana (1961) p 45.
10 See Chap 21.
11 CA 1985, s 116 and Companies Consolidation (Consequential Provisions) Act 1985, s 9.

by companies which were initially registered as other than public companies.[12]

The payment provisions enable payment to be made in money or money's worth, subject to restrictions on what a public company may accept. Extensive provisions are made for the valuation of assets for which it is proposed to allot shares. Extensive liabilities are imposed upon allottees in certain circumstances. These safeguards are, however, applicable generally to public companies only.

Shares allotted by any company may be paid for in money or money's worth including goodwill and know-how.[13] Shares issued to a subscriber to the memorandum in virtue of an undertaking in the memorandum and any premium on the shares must be paid in cash.[14]

In respect of a public company there are five categories of unlawful share allotments. In each case contravention renders the company and any responsible officer guilty of an offence.[15] It places the allottee under an obligation to make immediate payment of the value or part of the value to the company, and it places a subsequent holder of the shares under a joint and several obligation with the allottee towards the company unless the holder took for value without notice or, whatever his state of mind, took from a holder who took for value and without notice.[16] Thus a blameless holder is fully protected in his title to shares and may alienate them without placing his transferee under onerous obligations.

The five cases are:

(1) A public company may not accept in payment for its shares or any premium on them an undertaking that he should do work or perform services for the company or any other person.[17]
(2) The effect of transitional provisions apart, a company may no longer issue shares at a discount. An allottee of shares which are so issued is treated as holding paid-up shares of the company, but is liable to pay to the company the amount of the discount.[18]

---

12 Ibid.
13 CA 1985, s 99(1).
14 Ibid, s 106.
15 Ibid, s 114, and note the saving provisions where a cheque has been received. Ibid, s 115.
16 Ibid, s 112.
17 Ibid, s 99(2).
18 Ibid, s 106.

(3) Shares allotted under an employees' share scheme apart, a public company may not allot a share to any person unless not less than one-quarter of the nominal value of the share, together with the whole of any premium, has been received.[19]

(4) If a company allots bonus shares, on a fully paid up basis, but it has not applied funds to one-quarter of the nominal value of the share together with the whole of the premium on them, the allottee is liable to pay the minimum amount which should have been designated for payment, to the company, unless the allottee took in ignorance of the company's failure to do so.[20]

(5) A public company may allot shares as fully or partly paid up by an undertaking to transfer a non-cash asset to it or to a person nominated by it. Any undertaking must be performed or performable within five years from the date of the allotment.[1] The contract cannot be varied in such a way as to contravene the section.[2] Apart from the liability of the allottee to pay for the shares, where there is an issue in contravention of the section, he will also become liable to pay the company the value of any shares which he took if the contract is not duly performed.[3]

Again with respect to a public company, the Companies Act 1985 requires that assets or undertakings to be transferred to the company in exchange for an allotment of shares shall be valued in accordance with the Act, and a report made to the company with a copy to the allottee, within six months immediately preceding the allotment of the shares.[4] These provisions do not, however, apply to allotments by a company in connection with a take-over arrangement providing for the allotment of shares in the offeror company in exchange for shares in the target company or cancellation of all or some of the target company's shares or a proposed merger of that company with another company.[5]

In general, the valuation and report is to be made by an independent person who was qualified to act as an auditor of the

[19] Ibid, s 101(2).
[20] Ibid, s 22(4).
[1] Ibid, s 102(1).
[2] Ibid, s 102(3).
[3] Ibid, s 102(5) and (6).
[4] Ibid, ss 103(1) and 112 re payments in part for shares; these considerations do not however apply where shares are issued in the context of a general share-for-share offer in a takeover, or a cancellation in the same context, or a proposed merger; ibid, sub-s (5) and (6).
[5] Ibid, s 103(3) and (4).

company, save that he may, where it appears reasonable to do so, accept the valuation of another independent person who appears to have the necessary expertise for such a valuation.[6] The report must disclose the nominal value of and premium, if any, paid on those shares, the description of the consideration, the method used to value it and the date of the valuation, the extent to which the nominal value of the shares and any premium thereon are to be treated as fully paid up on allotment by the consideration, and the amount of any cash paid or to be paid for the shares on allotment.[7] The report of the independent person must also state that the method of valuation was reasonable in the circumstances, that it is up-to-date, and that on the basis of the valuation, the consideration plus any cash to be paid on allotment is not less than the total value payable on the allotment together with any premium payable on them.[8]

Again, in the event of contravention, onerous liabilities are placed on the allottee. If the company accepts consideration in contravention of the section and the allottee either has not received a report under the section or there has been some other contravention of which the allottee either knew or ought to have known, he will be liable to pay the company an amount equal to the nominal value of the shares together with the whole of the premium or, if the case so requires, such proportion of the amount as is treated as paid up by means of the consideration, plus interest.[9] Once again, a holder for value and without notice takes good title to the shares and does not come under any obligation to the company.

PAYMENT FOR ASSETS FROM SUBSCRIBERS

Restrictions are imposed upon the ability of a public company to acquire non-cash assets from certain categories of persons within a specified time. The restrictions do not apply to an old public company which re-registered as a public company.[10] They do apply to a joint-stock company which registered or re-registered as a public company and to a private company which re-registered as a public company and which was a public company before it was a private company.[11] Section 104 of the Companies Act 1985 provides that a

6 Ibid, s 108(1).
7 Ibid, s 108(4).
8 Ibid, s 108(6).
9 Ibid, s 24(6).
10 Ibid, s 104(1).
11 Ibid, s 104(3).

public company shall not, within two years of the time when it obtains a certificate to do business or within two years of the time when it re-registered as a public company, enter into an agreement with a person who was a subscriber or who was a member of the joint-stock company or private company when it re-registered for the transfer by him of non-cash assets to the company or another for a consideration to be given by the company equal in value at the time of the agreement to at least one-tenth of the company's share capital issued at the time unless the consideration is properly valued.[12]

The differences between this provision and those of s 103 are, first, that s 104 applies to the giving of any consideration by the company and not just an issue of shares, and secondly, that the terms of the agreement must have been approved by an ordinary resolution of the company. Copies of the valuer's report must have been sent to the members at the latest at the time when notice of the meeting was sent, and must have been sent to the vendor.[13]

In the event of contravention, the vendor, if he has not received a report or knew or ought to have known of some other contravention of the section or of s 103 concerning the qualifications of the valuer and the contents of his report, becomes liable to repay to the company any consideration given by the company or any amount equivalent to its value at the time of the agreement, and the agreement so far as it has not been carried out is void.[14]

In respect both of valuations under this section and s 103 the valuer is entitled to require such information as he thinks necessary to make his report.[15] It is an offence knowingly or recklessly to make a statement, oral or written, which is misleading, false or deceptive in a material particular to any person carrying out a valuation or making a report under either section.[16]

RELIEF FROM LIABILITY

The Court may relieve from liability any person who is liable to the company under the foregoing provisions (save those which relate to the consequences of an issue of shares at a discount) in relation to

---

[12] The valuation provisions are similar to those of s 103.
[13] Ibid, s 104(4).
[14] Ibid, s 105.
[15] Ibid, s 110.
[16] Ibid, s 110(2) and (3).

any payment or undertaking in relation to shares. The power is exercisable on general just and equitable grounds.

The Court may, on application relating to liabilities for shares, exempt the applicant from liability if, and to the extent that it appears to the Court just and equitable to do so having regard to the matters capitulated in the section, namely, whether he is liable to pay any amount in respect of any other liability relating to those shares or any other liability in relation to any undertaking given in connection with payment for those shares; whether any person other than the applicant has paid or is likely to pay any such amount whether by order of the Court or otherwise; and whether the applicant or any other person has or is likely to perform the undertaking in whole or in part or has done or is likely to do any other thing in payment or part payment for the shares.[17]

The Court has a general power on just and equitable grounds to exempt such a person in respect of any interest which he is obliged to pay the company in respect of those sections.[18] It has a similar broad power to exempt from liabilities incurred by subscribers etc, in relation to assets sold to the company otherwise than in payment for an allotment of shares.

The Court has a power, again restricted to certain capitulations, to exempt an applicant from liability by virtue of any undertaking given to the company in respect of payment for shares. The Court is to have regard to whether the applicant has paid or is likely to pay any amount arising out of an undertaking to do work, or to transfer a non-cash asset, or to liability arising from a contravention of the provisions relating to the purchase of assets without receipt of a valuer's report in circumstances of irregularity, and whether any other person has paid or is likely to pay any such amount, whether by order of a Court or otherwise.[19]

The Court is to have regard to certain overriding principles, briefly that a company which has allotted shares should receive value to the aggregate of the nominal value of shares and any premium thereon, and that where, if the company, but for a grant of exemption, would have more than one remedy against the person concerned, the choice of remedy is for the company. In other words, the company should have the right to elect which remedy it wishes to pursue.[20] There is also a provision which enables a Court to grant relief to a person against whom proceedings are brought for

---

17 Ibid, s 113(2)(a).
18 Ibid, s 113(2)(b).
19 Ibid, s 113(4).
20 Ibid, s 113(5).

a contribution by another person liable to the company.[1] The Court may, on just and equitable grounds, exempt such a person from liability in whole or in part or order him to make a larger contribution than he would otherwise be liable to make.

MAINTENANCE OF CAPITAL

The Companies Act 1985 places the rule that a company cannot deal in its own shares on a statutory footing, and it has inserted further protections intended to mark the nature of the capital as a reserve fund.

Section 142 of the Act requires the directors of a public company to convene an extraordinary general meeting of the company where the net assets of the company are half or less of the amount of the company's called up share-capital. The meeting must be called within 28 days of the date on which the fact is known to a director, and must be convened within 56 days from that date for the purpose of considering whether any measures should be taken to deal with the situation.[2]

The integrity of the capital as a reserve fund is further emphasised by the statutory rule that no company limited by shares or limited by guarantee and having a share capital may acquire its own shares for valuable consideration, whether by purchase, subscription or otherwise.[3] Contravention of this provision is an offence. A company may accept a gift of its shares from a member.[4] The rule against acquisition applies to all companies having a share capital, whether public or private. It is buttressed by a provision which not only renders a person who takes the company's shares on its behalf as its nominee civilly liable for calls for paying up shares or any premium thereon, but also (in some circumstances) his fellow subscribers to the memorandum or the directors of the company at the time of acquisition.[5] The Court has power to relieve from liablity where the subscriber or director has acted honestly and reasonably, and such relief may be granted either in proceedings already commenced or where proceedings are apprehended.[6]

---

1 Ibid, s 113(6) and (7).
2 Ibid, s 142; failure to convene such a meeting is an offence.
3 Ibid, s 143.
4 At common law a company could hold shares under a will by a trustee because it had not given consideration. See *Re Castiglione's Will Trusts, Hunter v Mackenzie* [1958] Ch 549, [1958] 1 All ER 480; *Kirby v Wilkins* [1929] 2 Ch 444.
5 CA 1985, s 144(1) and (2).
6 Ibid, s 144(3).

These provisions are not entirely rigid. A company may, as we have seen, issue redeemable preference shares subject to safeguards, or purchase shares, pursuant to an order of the Court, where a public company converts to a private company, or alters its objects, or as an alternative to a winding up order in cases of oppression.[7] The company may also forfeit shares or accept a surrender of shares in lieu, pursuant to the articles, for failure to pay any sum payable in respect of those shares.[8]

FORFEITURE AND SURRENDER

Forfeitures and surrenders of shares are proper and provision to this end is commonly made in the articles.[9] The procedure is, however, regulated by statute in the case of a public company.[10] In brief, unless the shares once forfeited or surrendered are disposed of within three years, the company must cancel them and diminish the amount of share capital by their nominal value.[11] Where the effect of cancellation is to bring the nominal value below that of the authorised minimum, the company must apply for re-registration as a private company.[12] The directors need not seek a special resolution for and order confirming reduction of share capital.[13] A company which fails to re-register is treated as a public company save in the vital respect that it may not offer its shares to the public.[14]

Seemingly, if the company decided to sell forfeited shares, it could sell them at a discount since the prohibitions against discounting shares apply only to allotment.[15] The purchaser of forfeited shares is liable to pay amounts unpaid on forfeiture, however, and is usually not entitled to vote until arrears are paid.

The power of forfeiture must be exercised by the directors bona fide for the benefit of the company. If the directors decide to forfeit their own shares in order to avoid liablity on them, the forfeiture is

---

7 Ibid, s 143(3).
8 Ibid, s 143(3)(d).
9 Because forfeiture or surrender was held only to affect the nominal value of the shares so far as unpaid, the procedure was permitted at common law; see *Trevor v Whitworth* (1887) 12 App Cas 409.
10 CA 1985, s 146; the provision also applies to a private company which forfeits shares and then, within three years, converts to a public company.
11 Ibid, s 146(2); note that neither the company nor a nominee for it may exercise voting rights in the shares, as to which see s 146(4).
12 Ibid, s 146(2)(b).
13 Ibid, the operation of ss 135–136 of the CA 1985 is thus excluded.
14 Ibid, s 149.
15 Cf ibid, s 100.

void and their liability remains.[16] The Court may grant relief to a shareholder whose shares have been forfeited if the forfeiture has been irregular.[17]

The surrender of shares may be accepted only when forfeiture is justified. Even if the surrender of shares not fully paid-up is made for the benefit of the company, it will be void unless forfeiture was justified. In one case the directors surrendered their shares to offset a loss made by the company; the surrender was void.[18] At common law a company could accept a surrender of fully paid shares where this did not involve a reduction of capital, and this seems still to apply.[19]

LIEN

A public company may not take a lien or charge on its own shares, and any such charge is void.[20] To this rule there are exceptions. Under the articles the company is usually given a lien on every share not fully paid-up for all moneys called or payable to the company.[1] Power is usually taken to enforce the payment of moneys secured by the lien by sale of the shares. If there is a surplus on sale, this must be paid to the member. This facility is preserved by statute.[2] Liens taken by private companies before re-registration as public companies remain valid as do liens by old public companies which did not apply to be re-registered as public companies within the transitional period.[3] Similarly, a company whose ordinary business includes the lending of money or consists of the provision of credit may take a lien in respect of its ordinary business transactions.[4]

Questions of priority as between the company by virtue of its lien and persons lending money to a shareholder on the security of his

---

16 *Re Esparto Trading Co* (1879) 12 ChD 191.
17 *Garden Gully United Quartz Mining Co v McLister* (1875) 1 App Cas 39.
18 *Bellerby v Rowland and Marwood's SS Co Ltd* [1902] 2 Ch 14.
19 Ibid, ss 143 and 146. For the authorities at common law see the *Bellerby* case, supra, and *Eichbaum v City of Chicago Grain Elevators Ltd* [1891] 3 Ch 459; *Rowell v John Rowell & Sons Ltd* [1912] 2 Ch 609, esp p 621; and *Moore v Northwood* (1960) 22 DLR (2d) 698.
20 Ibid, s 150(1).
1   CA 1985, Table A, arts 8–11. Under art 8, the lien extends to dividends payable on such shares.
2   CA 1985, s 150.
3   Ibid, s 150(4) and Companies Consolidation (Consequential Provisions) Act 1985, s 6.
4   CA 1985, s 150(3).

shares can arise. It is clear that if the person to whom shares are mortgaged gives notice of his mortgage before the member becomes indebted to the company, the mortgage has priority.[5]

Bradford Banking Co Ltd v Briggs, Son & Co (1886) 12 App Cas 29.

> Under the articles the company has a first and paramount lien. The member borrowed money from a bank on the security of his shares. The bank gave notice of their charge to the company before the member became indebted to the company. It was held that the bank had priority.

As between the company and transferee of shares to which a lien attaches, the transferee takes subject to any claims the company could enforce under its lien against the transferor. Claims arising against the transferor subsequent to the registration of the transfer cannot, however, be enforced against the transferee.

VARIATION OF CAPITAL

Under s 121 a company limited by shares[6] may, in general meeting if so authorised by its articles[7], alter the conditions of its memorandum in order to:

(1) increase its share capital by new shares of such amount as it thinks expedient;
(2) consolidate and divide all or any of its share capital into shares of larger amount than its existing shares;
(3) convert all or any part of its paid-up shares into stock, and reconvert that stock into paid-up shares of any denomination;
(4) subdivide its shares, or any of them, into shares of smaller amount than is fixed by the memorandum;[8]
(5) cancel shares which, at the date of the passing of the resolution in that behalf, have not been taken or agreed to be taken

---

5 The decisions dealing with priority as between the company and a mortgagee of shares are not easy to reconcile. Differences in the wording of the articles conferring a lien may be a partial explanation of the apparent conflict.
6 This will include a company limited by guarantee, but having a share capital.
7 See, eg Table A, art 32.
8 CA 1985, s 121(2)(d). Note that the proportion between the amount paid and the amount unpaid on each share must remain the same after commission.

by any person, and diminish the amount of its share capital by the amount of the shares so cancelled. A cancellation of shares under this provision is not a reduction of share capital.[9]

An unlimited company having a share capital which converts to a company limited by shares in its resolution to convert may increase the nominal amount of its share capital by increasing the nominal amount of each of its shares but subject to the conditions that no part of the increased capital shall be called up except in the event and for the purposes of the company being wound up.[10] It may also make provisions for reserve share capital.[11]

Variations of capital of this sort do not require the approval of the Court, nor, unless the articles so provide, need the resolution be passed by a special majority. Where the company increases its share capital beyond the registered capital it must notify the Registrar of this within 15 days.[12]

Variations which increase capital are normally made either with a view to the raising of further moneys for the company, or in order to bring the nominal capital into close relation with asset values. In the latter case a bonus issue may be made. Funds which could otherwise be used for the payment of dividends are used to pay for bonus shares which are issued to members as fully paid shares.

ISSUE OF SHARES AT A PREMIUM

Although a company may not issue shares at a discount, there is nothing to prevent it issuing shares above par, ie at a price in excess of their nominal value, if it chooses to do so. In fact, if shares stand at a premium, the directors should attempt to secure it for the company. Formerly, share premiums, being an accretion to capital, could be distributed as a profit, but the Companies Act 1985 requires that premiums be paid to a share premium account so that, subject to the exception discussed below, this account cannot be distributed.[13]

CA 1985, s 130 requires a company that issues shares at a

---

9 Ibid, s 121(2)(e).
10 Ibid, s 124(a).
11 Ibid, s 124(b).
12 Ibid, s 123(1).
13 *Hilder v Dexter* [1902] AC 474.

premium to transfer to a share premium account an amount equal to the aggregate amount of premiums on those share.

It is not the purpose of the share premium account to create a fund of ready money equal to the amount received by way of premium. The share premium account is an account rather than a fund. Share premiums can be charged to secure the company's indebtedness. The matter was explained in a Commonwealth case:

South Australian Barytes Ltd v Wood (1975) 12 SASR 527.

Per Sangster J. The answer to the question what is the purpose of the share premium account:

'... is that no book entry may be made by the company debiting its share premium account with any unauthorised item and, in consequence, no other account in the company's books may be credited *and no expenditure may be made* by the company which, if made, would have to be debited against the share premium account. This would, for example, prevent a company debiting against its share premium account a dividend other than one satisfied by the issue of shares to members of the company. On the other hand, the existence of an account in credit in the books of the company against which an item may properly be debited does not necessarily mean that the company has ready money equal to that credit.'

The account may be used:

(1) in paying up unissued shares to be issued to members as fully paid bonus shares, and
(2) in writing off the preliminary expenses, or the commission paid, or discount allowed, on shares or debentures issued by the company, and
(3) in providing for the premium payable on redemption of any debentures.

Re Duff's Settlement Trusts [1951] Ch 923, [1951] 2 All ER 534.

The court was asked to determine whether moneys distributed by a company from its share premium account constituted capital assets or income when paid to a trustee. Jenkins LJ stated at pp 928–929:

It is true that the section does not in terms convert the share premium account into paid-up share capital, but merely makes the provisions of the Act relating to the reduction of share capital apply as if the share premium account was paid-up share capital. But the provisions thus made applicable are the essential provisions on which the distinction between share capital and divisible profit depends, and on which the implied prohibition against the distribution of paid-up share capital otherwise than in pursuance of a duly authorised reduction of capital is based. It is thus clear at all events that s 56 does take the share premium account out of the category of divisible profit and prevents it from being distributed by way of dividend... Moreover, the terms of the section seem to us to show that where (as in the present case) the transaction in question is a distribution amongst shareholders of the share premium account, or part thereof, that transaction is to be treated as if the company was reducing its capital by paying off paid-up share capital... The company being thus by force of the section deemed to have paid off notionally paid-up capital, the sum distributed must, we think, clearly be deemed to have left the company as paid-up share capital returned to the members and not as distributable profit divided amongst the members by way of dividend.

Moneys received by the trustee were, therefore, capital assets.

Henry Head & Co Ltd v Ropner Holdings Ltd [1952] Ch 124, [1951] 2 All ER 994.[14]

RH Ltd, a holding company, acquired, for the purposes of amalgamation, the whole of the issued capital of two companies. The authorised capital of RH Ltd, £1,759,606, was equal to the aggregate of the issued nominal capital of two companies. £1 shares in RH Ltd were issued to the shareholders of the two companies on the basis of one £1 share for each £1 share in the old companies. It was held that the difference between the value of the assets of the two companies and the share capital of £1,759,606–£5,606,506—must be transferred to the share premium account, because this sum was in fact the premium on the new shares.

A company may not adopt measures intended to circumvent the general principal that shares may not be issued at a discount, eg a company may not issue debentures at a discount (which in itself is valid) on the understanding that the debenture holders may surrender £1 worth of debentures for paid-up £1 shares.

One question which used to cause some puzzlement was what share premium account had to be established when a company

---

14 See also *Shearer v Bercain Ltd* [1980] 3 All ER 295, [1980] STC 359, the effect of which has been drastically curtailed by CA 1985, ss 130–134.

acquired shares in another company in exchange for an issue of its own shares.

It is now quite clearly established that, if a company acquires shares in another company in exchange wholly or partly for an issue of its own shares, it must establish a share premium account equal to the difference (if any) between

(i) the nominal value of the shares which it issued, and
(ii) the market value of the shares which it acquired.[15]

Thus if Company A issued 100 £1 shares in exchange for shares in Company B worth £1,000, Company A should establish a share premium account of £900 in respect of that transaction.

The establishment of this share premium account had one particular restrictive effect which was not always appreciated. If Company A acquired all the issued shares in Company B in exchange for an issue of its own shares, and then a dividend was paid by Company B to Company A out of profits (generally known as pre-acquisition profits) earned by Company B *before* it was taken over by Company A, that dividend could not be distributed by Company A unless it went through the procedure for a reduction of share capital. The dividend could not be distributed because its distribution fell to be treated as a distribution of the share premium account.

It was widely felt that this restriction on the ability to distribute the share premium account, including in particular pre-acquisition profits, was unhelpful to business and accordingly the Companies Act 1985 provides some relief from the restriction.[16]

The relief is given in three ways.

First, because there was puzzlement about the position for many years (so that some companies had inadvertently made illegal distributions of pre-acquisition profits) s 12 of the Companies Consolidation (Consequential Provisions) Act 1985 gives relief for take overs which occurred before 4 February 1981.[17]

Thus where, before 4 February 1981,

(1) a company issues shares as the consideration for its acquisition of shares or for the cancellation of shares in another company which was to become, as a result of the transaction

---

15 *Henry Head & Co Ltd v Ropner Holdings Ltd* [1952] Ch 124, [1951] 2 All ER 994; *Shearer v Bercain Ltd* [1980] 3 All ER 295, [1980] STC 359.
16 See ss 130–134.
17 See Companies Consolidation (Consequential Provisions) Act 1985, s 12.

in question, a subsidiary of the company issuing the shares or of its holding company; and
(2) the shares acquired or cancelled were worth more than the nominal value of the shares issued, so that the company issuing the shares should have established a share premium account; but
(3) the issuing company failed to create such an account, the amount which should have been (but which was not) transferred to share premium account is now free from the restrictions on distribution imposed by s 130 of the Companies Act 1985 and is treated as always having been free of those restrictions.

The second relief is given in relation to share-for-share exchanges within a group of companies. This relief is given by s 132 of the Companies Act 1985.[18]

For this relief to apply, the company which issues the shares must be a wholly owned subsidiary of another company and must allot shares to its holding company or to another wholly owned subsidiary of the holding company in consideration for the transfer to it of shares in another subsidiary (which does not have to be wholly owned) of the holding company.

Where this relief applies, it operates by reducing the amount which has to be carried to a share premium account: in this case only 'the minimum premium value' has to be shown as share premium.

The minimum premium value is the difference between

(i) the nominal value of the shares issued by the issuing company, and
(ii) the lower of (a) the cost to the transferor company of the shares being transferred and (b) the amount at which those shares are shown in the transferor company's accounting records immediately before the transfer.

Any excess premium above the minimum premium value can, if not transferred to a share premium account, be distributed without the restrictions attaching to distributions of share premium accounts.

An example may help to explain this relief.

Company A owns all the shares in Company B and Company C. Company C owns all the shares in Company D, which cost it £100

---

18 CA 1985, s 132, and for transitional provisions, s 132(7).

but which have been written down in its accounting records to £50. The shares in Company D are worth £1000.

Company C transfers the shares in Company D to Company B in return for an issue of 10 £1 shares in Company B.

In the ordinary way Company B would have to establish a share premium account of £990 and all of the amount would be subject to the restrictions on distribution imposed by the share premium account rules.

However as the relief given by s 132 applies, the only amount which Company B need bring into a share premium account is £40 (the difference between the nominal value of the shares issued by it and the amount at which the shares in Company D are stated in Company C's accounting records).

Thus, if Company B were now to receive a dividend of £100 from Company D, it could distribute £60 of that dividend without infringing the rules about share premium accounts.

The last and most important relief is that given by s 131 of the Companies Act 1985.

Again, this relief only applies to transactions occurring after 4 February 1981,[19] and it is to be noted that it does not apply to cases where the 'group relief' just described applies.

This relief applies where three conditions are fulfilled. The three conditions are:

(1) The issuing company must issue shares which are comprised in its equity share capital.
(2) The issuing company must make that issue as consideration for the issue or transfer to it of shares in a company or as consideration for the cancellation of shares in a company which it does not own.
(3) As a result of the arrangement for 1 and 2 above to occur, the issuing company must own (either directly of through subsidiaries) 90% of the other company's equity share capital.[20]

Where this relief applies then, even though the shares in the issuing company have been issued at a premium, the issuing company can deal with that share premium account without being subject to the restrictions imposed by s 130 of the Companies Act 1985.

---

19 CA 1985, s 131(8).
20 If the acquired company has more than one class of equity share capital, 20% of each class must be owned. Ibid, s 131(5).

The Secretary of State has power to make regulations by statutory instrument changing the relief applying to share premium accounts.[1]

REDUCTION OF CAPITAL

Because of the rule forbidding a company to deal in its own shares, a company can only reduce its share capital pursuant to a power in the articles and subject to a special resolution and the approval of the Court.[2] If the articles do not authorise a reduction, then the articles must be altered by special resolution before a resolution for reduction may be passed.[3] Any scheme which amounts to the distribution by a company of part of its subscribed capital among its shareholders is a reduction of capital requiring a special resolution and the sanction of the Court.[4] The forfeiture, cancellation or surrender of shares thus does not amount to a reduction, nor does the surrender of fully paid shares in exchange for new fully paid shares.[5]

CA 1985, s 135 confers power to alter the memorandum by reducing share capital in any way, and in particular a company may:

(1) extinguish or reduce the liability on any of its shares in respect of share capital not paid up; or
(2) cancel any paid-up share capital which is lost or unrepresented by available assets; or
(3) pay off any paid-up share capital which is in excess of the wants of the company.

A reduction of capital requires the passing of a special resolution at a general meeting. While the Courts have given effect to an expression of the unanimous will of the members which did not take this form, it has been intimated that this will not be done in future and that the proper forms must be adhered to.[6]

After the special resolution for reducing share capital has been passed, application must be made to the Court for confirmation. Where the reduction involves either dimunition of liability in

---

1 Ibid, s 134.
2 Ibid, s 135.
3 *Re Patent Invert Sugar Co* (1885) 31 ChD 166.
4 *Bellerby v Rowland and Marwood's SS Co Ltd* [1902] 2 Ch 14.
5 *Rowell v John Rowell & Sons Ltd* [1912] 2 Ch 609; but cf *Re St James' Court Estate Ltd* [1944] Ch 6.
6 *Re Barry Artists Ltd* [1985] 1 WLR 1305, [1985] BCLC 283.

respect of unpaid share capital or the payment to a shareholder of paid-up share capital, and in any other case where the Court so directs, the rights of the creditors must be fully protected.[7] As the capital structure of the company is being altered in such a way as to reduce the capacity of the company to pay its debts, the following procedure is adopted in order to safeguard creditors:

(1) Every creditor who would be entitled to prove in a winding up may object to the reduction.
(2) The Court settles a list of such creditors and may publish notices fixing a date by which creditors not appearing on the list must claim or be excluded from the right to object.
(3) The Court may dispense with the consent of any ceditor who has not been paid if the company secures payment of his debt.

The Court, if satisfied that every creditor entitled to object has consented, or has had his debt discharged or secured, may confirm the reduction on such terms and conditions as it thinks fit.[8]

The function of the Court is relatively limited. Prima facie, the question whether to reduce capital is a matter to be decided by the company itself. The Court determines whether the proper steps have been taken by the company to reduce, that proper notices have been given, meetings held and resolutions passed. It also regards its functions as those of protecting the interests of creditors and shareholders.

Creditors are, it is true, well protected. It has been held repeatedly that no order for confirmation may be made unless the Court is satisfied either that all the creditors entitled to object to reduction have either consented or been paid up or secured.[9]

The interests of shareholders are also protected, albeit imperfectly. Where a proposed reduction is not in accordance with the class rights of preference shareholders the Court will require the company to show that the proposed reduction is fair. One way in

---

7 CA 1985, s 136.
8 CA 1985, s 137. The Court may order that the words 'and reduced' be added to the name of the company and the reasons for reduction published. The abolition of this provision has been recommended. Report of the Company Law Committee Cmnd 1749 (1962) para 187(b).
9 *Poole v National Bank of China* [1907] AC 229; *Re Thomas de la Rue Co Ltd* [1911] 2 Ch 361.

which this may be done is to show that it is supported by a majority of preference shareholders. Where, however, a majority of the class votes in its individual interests and not in the interests of the class as a whole, it fails to satisfy the test that the reduction must be for the benefit of the class as a whole and not merely individual owners within the class.[10]

Where a reduction is based on the ground of capital having been lost or unrepresented by available assets, the Courts insist upon evidence of the fact and that the loss is permanent. 'Permanent' means permanent so far as it is presently forseeable. If that condition cannot be met, a reduction cannot be put forward on that ground. In such case the Court must bear in mind that a reduction may prejudice members or creditors' rights. There is a danger that the resolution to reduce capital might have been passed as a result of a mistake or misrepresentation. It might be unfair to shareholders to confirm the reduction without evidence of loss.[11] If, however, their rights can be otherwise secured, the Court may still sanction a reduction. In *Re Grosvenor Press plc*[12] the court approved a reduction on the footing that any moneys received on the sale of certain assets would be placed to reserve and treated as undistributable, and a similar condition was required in *Re Jupiter House Investments (Cambridge) Ltd*.[13] The Court's power to confirm a reduction is, however, a general one. It can, and has, sanctioned a reduction where shareholders are not being treated in accordance with their rights. Where the reduction involves treating one part of a class of equity shareholders differently from another part of the same class, it is preferable to employ a scheme of arrangement under CA 1985, s 425 because the minority is better protected thereby. The Court will more readily confirm a scheme of reduction effected by cancelling part of the preference shares. The considerations are different because the maximum entitlement of the preference shares is known.[14]

In general, where a reduction involves a variation or reduction of class rights, the Court will require that the procedure contained in the variation of rights clause in the articles be complied with. Where the Court is satisfied that a reduction involving such a variation or abrogation is fair, it may none the less confirm it.

10 *Re Holders Investment Trust Ltd* [1971] 2 All ER 289, [1971] 1 WLR 583.
11 *Caldwell & Co v Caldwell* 1916 SC (HL) 120.
12 [1985] 1 WLR 980, [1985] BCLC 286.
13 [1985] 1 WLR 975, [1985] BCLC 222.
14 *Re Robert Stephen Holdings Ltd* [1968] 1 All ER 195n, [1968] 1 WLR 522.

Re William Jones & Sons Ltd [1969] 1 All ER 913

> The memorandum provided that in the event of the company being wound up and there being more than enough to repay the capital of the preference shares and the ordinary shares, the preference shareholders would be entitled to participate in surplus assets rateably until they received another 25s per share. The company passed a resolution proposing to reduce its authorised capital by returning the capital paid on the preference shares at par, without any premium, and cancelling them. At this time the preference shares stood at less then par and there was no prospect of the company being wound up. The Court held that in the circumstances the reduction was fair and should be confirmed, notwithstanding that the preference shareholders' rights to share in any surplus were being abrogated.

In any event, class rights are, as has been seen, narrowly defined. It will be recalled that the House of Lords has held that unless the terms of issue explicitly so provide, preference shareholders will have no right to share in excess assets in a winding up.[15] Furthermore, the cases, as we have seen, distinguish between class rights and the conditions necessary for the enjoyment of those rights.[16]

All this is of considerable importance because it is not clear whether the Courts will refuse to confirm a reduction on the ground of unfairness where there had been no interference with class rights. The Court's right to do so was asserted by Cozens-Hardy J in *Re Barrow Haematite Steel Co*.[17] The principal ground for refusing to confirm a reduction (and the sole ground adopted by the Court of Appeal) was, however, that the petition was founded upon an alleged loss of capital which had not been proved. In *Re Old Silkstone Collieries Ltd*[18] unfairness seems to have been one of the two grounds relied on in refusing to confirm a reduction. The other (and perhaps principal) ground was, however, that as the proposal involved a modification of rights, separate meetings of preference

---

15 *Prudential Assurance Co Ltd v Chatterley Whitfield Collieries Ltd* [1949] AC 512, [1949] 1 All ER 1094; *Scottish Insurance Corpn Ltd v Wilsons and Clyde Coal Co Ltd* [1949] AC 462, [1949] 1 All ER 1068.
16 *White v Bristol Aeroplane Co Ltd* [1953] Ch 65, [1953] 1 All ER 40; *Re John Smith's Tadcaster Brewery Co Ltd* [1953] Ch 308, [1953] 1 All ER 518.
17 [1900] 2 Ch 846, affd [1901] 2 Ch 746, CA, but without discussion of this point. In *Re Holders Investment Trust Ltd* [1971] 2 All ER 289, [1971] 1 WLR 583, Megarry J treated as axiomatic that he could dismiss a petition for a reduction of share capital, which was not in accordance with the class rights of preference shareholders, on the ground of unfairness. Furthermore, he did not distinguish this case from cases where there is no interference with class rights.
18 [1954] Ch 169, [1954] 1 All ER 68.

stockholders should have been convened to approve the scheme. And in general this seems to be the one English decision which has refused a reduction on these wider grounds.[19]

It should be further noted that the Court, in determining whether to sanction a reduction, is not concerned with wide questions concerning whether the reduction is in public interest. In *Re Westburn Sugar Refineries Ltd*[20] the object of reduction was to place some of the company's assets outside the reach of nationalisation, and to avoid profits tax.[1] The House of Lords held that provided that the reduction was not objectionable as being prejudicial to creditors or shareholders, it would not refuse to confirm it in the light of wider considerations of public policy.

The company is required to produce to the Registrar a copy of the order of the Court and a minute approved by the Court showing the new capital structure of the company. The order does not take effect until registration.[2]

The liability of members in reduced shares is limited to the difference, if any, between the amount of the share as fixed by the minute and the amount paid, or the reduced amount deemed to have been paid on the share. However, if the company is unable to pay the claim of any creditor entitled to object who was ignorant of the proceedings for reduction or of their nature and effect, and who was not entered on the list of creditors, every member at the date of registration of the order for reduction will remain liable to contribute to the assets of the company as if the company had been wound up on the day preceding the date of registration of the order.[3]

DISTRIBUTION OF PROFITS AND ASSETS

The rules relating to distributions at common law were defective in several important respects. They have been largely supplanted by legislation, but it contains some vexing obscurities. The legislation imposes negative restrictions concerning the circumstances under which distributions may not be made. Provided that these do not operate in any given case, the decision whether dividends should be

---

19 For a Commonwealth example where a reduction was refused as prima facie unfair in that it did not follow the priorities on a winding up, see *Re Fowlers Vacola Manufacturing Co Ltd* [1966] VR 97.
20 [1951] AC 625, [1951] 1 All ER 881.
1   The purpose is explained by Gower (1951) 14 Mod LR p 330.
2   CA 1985, s 138.
3   Ibid, s 140.

paid and if so in what amount is a decision for the directors.[4] The members can move a reduction, but not an increase. In the case of a closely-held private company repeated refusals to pay dividends, reserving profits for directors' remuneration could, depending on the original understandings between the members, constitute oppression and a ground for relief under s 459 of the Companies Act 1985 or s 122(1)(g) of the Insolvency Act 1986.

A company is forbidden to make a distribution except out of profits available for the purpose.[5] Distribution is widely defined to include every description of distribution of a company's assets to members of the company, whether in cash or otherwise, but it does not include the issue of fully paid bonus shares, the redemption of preference shares, the reduction of share capital by extinguishing or reducing members' liability on partly-paid shares, or by paying off paid-up share capital, and the distribution of assets on winding up.[6]

The Companies Act 1985 provides that (subject to special provisions relating to investment companies) a company's profits available for distribution are its accumulated, realised profits so far as not previously utilised (whether by distribution, capitalisation or otherwise) less its accumulated, realised losses so far as not previously written off,[7] in a reduction or reorganisation of capital.[8]

In certain circumstances, an unrealised profit may be treated as a realised profit. Where, on the revaluation of a fixed asset, a profit is shown to have been made, and on or after that revaluation a sum is written off or retained for depreciation of that asset, then the surplus value over and above the sum which would have been written off or retained for depreciation of that asset may be treated as a realised profit and so available for distribution.[9]

In some circumstances a loss arising on a partial revaluation of assets need not be considered as a realised loss for the purpose of determining the amount of distributable profit. The situation is one in which the directors, having revalued some assets, and having considered the values of the remaining assets, are satisfied that in

---

4 See *Scott v Scott* [1943] 1 All ER 582.
5 CA 1985, s 263(1).
6 Ibid, s 263(2).
7 Ibid, s 263(3); this would include a realised capital profit and it would follow that an unrealised increase in the value of paid assets could not be used to pay cash dividend. As to the meaning of 'realised profits', see s 742 and Sch 4, para 91.
8 Where development costs are shown as an asset in a company's accounts, any amount shown in respect of those costs shall be treated as a realised loss, or in the case of investment companies (see CA 1985, s 268, post) as realised revenue loss; CA 1985, s 269.
9 Ibid, s 275.

aggregate, the value of the latter is not less than their existing book value.[10]

Distributions of a non-cash asset in kind may be made out of unrealised profits to the extent that the unrealised amount forms part of the book value of the asset distributed.[11] This implies that the asset has been revalued and a profit on revaluation has been credited to the revaluation reserve.[12] The purpose of this provision is to facilitate distributions in a demerger.

Companies authorised by their articles before the coming into force of the Act to apply unrealised profits in paying up in full or in part unissued shares to be allotted to members as bonus shares, may continue to do so. The general meeting may also capitalise certain reserves on the recommendation of directors if Table A articles are used.[13]

Special provisions apply to fixed assets. The term is not closely defined by the Companies Act. For the purposes of Sch 4 accounts, assets of a company are to be taken as fixed assets if they are intended for use on a continuing basis in the company's activities, and any assets not intended for such use are to be treated as current assets.[14] All assets must thus be allocated to one or other category. Investments, especially in associated companies which are not intended as short-term liquid assets, would appear to be fixed assets.

Any provision in the accounts, other than one in respect of any diminution in value of a fixed asset appearing on a revaluation of the fixed assets of the company, is to be treated as a realised loss. Thus provision of depreciation, if made, must be set off against profit before dividends are payable.[15] If an unrealised profit is made on the revaluation of a fixed asset, and on or after the revaluation a sum is written off or retained for depreciation of that asset over a period, then an amount equal to the amount by which that sum

---

10 Ibid; see further, L. H. Leigh and H. C. Edey, *The Companies Act 1981*, paras 390–1. The drafting of these provisions is convoluted and they do not yield their meaning readily.
11 Ibid, s 276.
12 Ibid, Sch 4, paras 31 and 34(1).
13 Ibid, s 281; see Table A, art 110.
14 Ibid, Sch 4, para 77.
15 It would seem that the effect of s 221 of the Companies Act 1985 is to require a company to maintain a proper depreciation account since otherwise the accounts would not give a true and fair view of the company's state of affairs. Thus the doubts whether under earlier legislation provision had to be made for depreciation would seem by implication at least to have been resolved. See further *Lee v Neuchatel Asphalte Co* (1889) 41 ChD 1 and *Report of the Company Law Committee*, Cmnd 1749, paras 349 and 350.

exceeds the sum which would have been written off or retained for depreciation of the asset over that period if it had not been revalued may be of an asset which cannot be determined, the value shown in the earliest available record of its value made on or after its acquisition by the company is taken.[16] Where directors after making all reasonable inquiries cannot determine whether a profit or loss is realised or unrealised, they may treat the profit as realised and the loss as unrealised.[17]

Special provisions relate to investment companies.[18] An investment company is defined as a public company (whose shares must be listed on a recognised stock exchange) and whose business consists of investing funds in securities, land or other assets with the aim of spreading investment risk and giving members of the company the benefit of the results of the management of its funds.[19]

An investment company may only make a distribution out of its accumulated, realised revenue profits so far as these have not been previously utilised, whether by distribution or capitalisation. Its accumulated revenue losses whether realised or unrealised must be deducted so far as these have not previously been written off in a reduction or reorganisation of capital.[20] Its capital profits are not available for distribution. Furthermore, an investment company may not apply an unrealised revenue profit, or any species of capital profit in writing off revenue losses (realised or unrealised) or in paying up debentures or any amounts unpaid on any of its issued shares.[1]

Even though there are profits from which dividends could otherwise be paid, a public company may only make a distribution at any time if the amount of its net assets is not less than the aggregate of its called-up share capital and its undistributable reserves, and if and to the extent that the distribution does not reduce the amount of those assets to less than the aggregate.[2] An investment company may only make a distribution if, at the time of so doing, the amount of its assets is at least equal to one-and-a-half times the aggregate of its liabilities and if to the extent that the distribution does not alter the picture.[3]

16 CA 1985, s 275(3).
17 Ibid, s 263(5).
18 Ibid, s 265; note that special provisions apply also to insurance companies in respect of realised profits, as to which see s 268.
19 Ibid, s 266.
20 Ibid, s 265(1).
1 Ibid, s 265(6).
2 Ibid, s 264.
3 Ibid, s 265(1)(a) and (b).

Distribution of Profits and Assets 357

The undistributable reserves of a company are (subject to the exception discussed above) the share premium account, the capital redemption reserve, the amount by which the company's accumulated, unrealised profits so far as not previously utilised exceed its accumulated, unrealised losses, so far as not written off in a reduction or reorganisation of capital, and any other reserve which the company is prohibited from distributing by any other enactment or by its memorandum and articles, or any other constitutive document.[4] A public company may not include any uncalled share capital as an asset in accounts relevant for the purposes of determining whether conditions permitting a distribution exist.[5]

The question whether in respect of any company there is a profit available for distribution and, if so, whether in the case of a public company the capital maintenance requirements are met, must be determined by reference to the accounts of the company.[6] Prima facie the appropriate accounts are the last annual accounts laid.[7] To this rule there are two exceptions. If a distribution would be found to contravene the Act if reference were made only to the annual accounts, interim accounts may be used.[8] If a distribution is proposed during the company's first accounting reference period, initial accounts may be employed.[9] There are extensive provisions directed towards ensuring the integrity of the accounts. In particular the auditors of the company must have made a report in respect of the accounts, and if the accounts are qualified, the auditors must certify that the qualification is not material to the question of a distribution.[10] A copy of any such statement must have been laid before the the company in general meeting.[11]

The consequence to a member in receipt of an unlawful distribution depends upon whether at the time of receipt he either knew or had reasonable grounds for believing that it was made in contravention. If he had the requisite state of mind he is liable to make restitution to the company. If the distribution is made otherwise than in the case he is obliged to pay the company a sum equal to the value of the distribution at that time.[12]

---

4 Ibid, s 264(3).
5 Ibid, s 264(4).
6 Ibid, s 270.
7 Ibid, s 270(3).
8 Ibid, s 270(4)(a).
9 Ibid, s 270(4)(b).
10 Ibid, s 271(3).
11 Ibid, s 271.
12 Ibid, s 277.

Chapter 17 Capital

This latter provision is without prejudice to any obligation imposed, apart from the section on a member of a company, to repay a distribution unlawfully made to him.[13]

LIABILITY OF DIRECTORS

Where a dividend is paid out of capital, the directors who distributed the moneys are liable, jointly and severally, to the company for the full amount.[14] Because such a payment is *ultra vires* if not illegal, an individual shareholder can sue to have a proposed payment of dividend out of capital restrained. If, however, the member received a dividend knowing it to have been improperly paid out of capital, he cannot maintain a derivative action to enforce the company's right to compensation against the directors until he repays to the company the sum which he has received.[15]

---

13 Ibid, s 277(2).
14 *Re Sharpe* [1892] 1 Ch 154; *Re Exchange Banking Co Flitcroft's Case* (1882) 21 ChD 519.
15 *Towers v African Tug Co* [1904] 1 Ch 558.

Chapter 18

Borrowing Powers

PROVISIONS OF MEMORANDUM

A company derives its powers from statute, its memorandum,[1] and to a limited extent from its articles.[2] Unless the company is a trading company,[3] which has an implied power to borrow money in the furtherance of its objects, the power to borrow money must be conferred by the memorandum.[4] The memorandum may impose restrictions on the power of the company to borrow money. It is more usual, however, to include such provisions in the articles, eg the directors may be given power to borrow money up to a stated amount, the approval of a general meeting being necessary for any loans in excess of that sum. Alternatively, such a power may simply fall within the general power of the directors to manage. If a company has power to borrow money, it has the implied power to charge its property to secure repayment of money borrowed. This implied power will, of course, be subject to any express restrictions imposed by the memorandum or articles.

If a company exceeds the borrowing powers conferred by its memorandum, the borrowing is *ultra vires*. Where the borrowing is *ultra vires*, the lender cannot sue the company on the contract to

---

1 Questions of interpretation include the question whether a clause entitling the company to charge its property entitle it to charge its uncalled capital. The problem is usually dealt with by an express provision, see *Bank of South Australia v Abrahams* (1875) LR 6 PC 265. A company has the right to mortgage the premium on shares which a shareholder has agreed to pay; see *South Australian Barytes Ltd v Wood* (1975) 12 SASR 527 in which the English authorities are extensively discussed.
2 See Chap 7.
3 *General Auction Estate and Monetary Co v Smith* [1891] 3 Ch 432, and *Re Badger, Mansell v Cobham* [1905] 1 Ch 568.
4 Because lenders prefer not to rely on an implied power, express power to borrow is usually given in the memorandum. See CA 1948, Table A, art 79 for the form most commonly found.

recover the funds advanced. He has, however, certain remedies. He may:

(1) in some cases sue the directors on a warranty of authority.[5] Where the directors have expressly or impliedly warranted their authority to borrow, they may be sued on such representation;
(2) assert a claim to 'subrogation';
(3) assert a claim in quasi-contract for recovery of the moneys;
(4) assert a proprietary tracing remedy, and an injunction to restrain the company from parting with the money or property.[6]

Where the borrowing is outside the powers of the company, the third party will be fully protected provided that the provisions of s 35 of the CA 1985 are met; viz, that the matter has been decided upon by the board. Borrowing *ultra vires* the directors, but within the powers conferred by the memorandum, is voidable only and may be ratified by the company. If the borrowing is ratified, the company becomes liable to repay the moneys. The rule in *Royal British Bank v Turquand* (1856) 6 E & B 327, as explained in recent decisions will apply here to validate acts of directors within their ostensible authority.[7]

Under the doctrine of constructive notice a lender is deemed to have notice of the limitations imposed by the memorandum and articles on the borrowing powers of the company. Except where the CA 1985 applies to save the transaction, and where it does the borrower is not affected by constructive notice, the operation of that doctrine would enable the company to avoid liability on the ground that borrowing was known or was deemed to be known to be *ultra vires*. As we have explained, however, a lender who lends money to a company which has power to borrow is entitled to assume that the money will be expended on the proper objects of

---

5 *Weeks v Propert* (1873) LR 8 CP 427. It is probable that the remedy may be asserted in any case where directors impliedly warrant an authority to cause the company to borrow. See, however, *Chapleo v Brunswick Permanent Benefit Building Society* (1881) 6 QBD 696, 715 per Brett LJ; *Firbanks Executors v Humphreys* (1886) 18 QBD 54. There is no reason why the doctrine of constructive notice should bar a claim against the directors. Its office is rather to protect the company from being bound by representations of authority which the company could not authorise, or at any rate could not authorise without making public disclosure.
6 See pp 88–89, ante.
7 Chap 8, ante.

the company.[8] If of course the lender knows of the purpose for which the money is being borrowed and that purpose is *ultra vires*, and the transaction is not saved by the 1985 Act, the lending contract will be void, whether or not the lender knew of the provisions of the memorandum.

CHARGES

A company, if expressly or impliedly empowered to do so by its memorandum, may create a charge over its property to secure the repayment of moneys borrowed. It may charge its undertaking and its uncalled capital if the memorandum confers this power: *Re Russian Spratts Patent Ltd*.[9] Moneys borrowed may be secured by:

(1) a legal mortgage of any part of its undertaking;
(2) an equitable charge, which involves depositing the title deeds;
(3) a floating charge on the whole undertaking;
(4) promissory notes;
(5) debentures or debenture stock.[10]

REGISTRATION OF CHARGES

A copy of all charges created by a company and falling within CA 1985, s 395 must be registered with the Registrar. The copy must be accompanied by a statutory declaration as to execution of the charge and verifying it as a true copy. A copy of the following charges must be registered:

(1) a charge securing any issue of debentures;
(2) a charge on uncalled share capital;
(3) a charge created or evidenced by an instrument which, if executed by an individual, would require registration as a bill of sale;[11]

---

8 See *Re David Payne & Co Ltd* [1904] 2 Ch 608; *Charterbridge Corpn Ltd v Lloyds Bank Ltd* [1970] Ch 62, [1969] 2 All ER 1185.
9 [1898] 2 Ch 149. See also *Newton v Debenture Holders of Anglo-Australian Investment Co* [1895] AC 244, as to the meaning of 'on any security'.
10 Debentures of limited companies need not be registered as bills of sale, even if they include chattels. See Bills of Sale (Amendment) Act 1882, s 17; *Re Standard Manufacturing Co* [1891] 1 Ch 627.
11 See *Stoneleigh Finance Ltd v Phillips* [1965] 2 QB 537, [1965] 1 All ER 513.

(4) a floating charge on the undertaking or property of the company;
(5) a charge on land, wherever situate, or any interest therein,[12] but not including a charge for any rent or other periodical sum issuing out of land;
(6) a charge on book debts;[13]
(7) a charge on calls made but not paid;
(8) a charge on a ship or any share in a ship;
(9) a charge on goodwill, on a patent or a licence under a patent, on a trade mark, or on a copyright or a licence under a copyright.

Particulars of the charge together with the instrument creating the charge must be delivered to the Registrar for registration within 21 days after its creation.[14] These periods may be extended by the Court.[15]

Where a series of debentures ranking *pari passu* (ie with equal rights) is issued, it is sufficient compliance with the Act if there are registered the following particulars:

(1) the total amount secured by the series; and
(2) the dates of the resolutions authorising the issue of the series and the date of the covering deed, by which the security is created or defined; and
(3) a general description of the property charged; and
(4) the names of the trustees, if any, for the debenture holders,

together with a copy of the deed containing the charge, or, if there is no such deed, a copy of one of the debentures of the series, accompanied by a statutory declaration as to execution and verifying the copy as a true copy. Where there is more than one issue of debentures in the series, particulars of the date and amount of each issue must be sent to the Registrar, but omission to do so will not invalidate the debentures issued. If any commission, allowance, or

---

12 See CA 1985, s 396(1)(d). Formerly, charges on land needed only to be registered at the Companies Registry under s 395: *Property Discount Corpn Ltd v Lyon Group Ltd* [1981] 1 All ER 379, [1981] 1 WLR 300. Now, by virtue of the Land Charges Act 1972, s 3, they must also in the case of unregistered land be registered at the Land Charges Registry.
13 Ibid, s 396(1)(e) and *Ashby, Warner & Co Ltd v Simmonds* [1936] 2 All ER 697.
14 The period is somewhat extended where the charge is created outside the United Kingdom on property outside the United Kingdom. Ibid, s 398.
15 Ibid, s 404.

discount has been paid by the company in consideration of a person subscribing or agreeing to subscribe for debentures or agreeing to procure subscriptions for them, details of these payments must be sent to the Registrar with the above particulars.

EFFECT OF NON-REGISTRATION

If a copy of the charge is not registered as required by s 395, it is void as against any liquidator and any creditor of the company, but this does not prejudice the obligation to repay, and when the charge becomes void the moneys become payable immediately.[16] The effect of this section is to accord priority to the holder of a registered charge who knew of the existence of a void unregistered charge when his charge was created: *Re Monolothic Building Co.*[17]

Where a creditor stipulates for a first legal charge he is taken to have abandoned any claim to a pre-existing lien which might have ranked in priority to any later charge. Thus, where the charge is void because unregistered, priority cannot be asserted under the abandoned lien.[18]

Section 395 merely renders an unregistered charge void against the liquidator and creditors; it is valid against the company. An unregistered chargeholder retains any right he had to appoint a receiver.[19] Where an equitable mortgage or charge is created by deposit of title deeds, but the mortgage or charge is avoided for non-registration, everything ancillary to it is avoided too. Thus no separate legal or common law lien can be asserted by the borrower against the documents.[20]

When a company acquires property already subject to a charge which, if created by the company, would require registration, it must register a copy of the instrument creating the charge.[1] The company must also deliver to the Registrar a statutory declaration as to the date of acquisition of the property and certifying the copy as a true copy. These documents must be delivered to the Registrar within 21 days after the date on which the acquisition was completed.

---

16 *Capital Finance Co Ltd v Stokes* [1969] 1 Ch 261, [1968] 3 All ER 625.
17 [1915] 1 Ch 643.
18 *Burston Finance Ltd v Speirway* [1974] 3 All ER 735.
19 This course was adopted in *Capital Finance Co Ltd v Stokes* (supra). See also *Re Row Dal Constructions Pty Ltd* [1966] VR 249, and a note in (1966) 40 ALJ 238.
20 *Re Molton Finance Ltd* [1968] Ch 325, CA; *Wallis and Simmonds (Builders) Ltd* [1974] 1 All ER 561, [1974] 1 WLR 391.
1   CA 1985, s 400.

REGISTER OF CHARGES

The Registrar must keep a register of charges with respect to each company which must have entered in it the following particulars:[2]

(1) in the case of a series of debentures such particulars as are required on registration of a series of debentures;[3]
(2) in other cases,
   (a) if the charge is a charge created by the company, the date of its creation, and if the charge was a charge existing on property acquired by the company, the date of the acquisition of the property; and
   (b) the amount secured by the charge; and
   (c) short particulars of the property charged; and
   (d) the persons entitled to the charge.

On registration of a charge and the payment of the fee, the Registrar must give a certificate that the charge has been registered and stating the amount secured by it; this certificate is conclusive evidence that the requirements of the Act as to registration have been complied with. Thus, the certificate will be conclusive even though incomplete or partially incorrect particulars have been delivered to the Registrar,[4] or if errors, even perhaps errors made with intent to defraud, are made in the particulars provided.[5] The leading case is:

Re C. L. Nye Ltd [1970] 3 WLR 158, CA.

> The company was granted loan and overdraft facilities by a bank against the security, inter alia, of business premises. The charge was stamped, but was later mislaid in the office of the bank's solicitor. Some months later (in June 1964), a date of 18 June 1964 was inserted as the date of creation and the charge was lodged for registration on 3 July. Meanwhile before 18 June, the bank had honoured cheques on the faith of the charge. The company went into liquidation and the liquidator asked for a declaration that the charge in favour of the bank was void as against the

---

2 Ibid, s 401.
3 See ibid, s 397. The information includes the total amount secured by the whole series, and a general description of the property charged, and the names of the trustees, if any, for the debenture holders, the section applies to charges on English property by all overseas companies, and see *N V Slavenburg's Bank v Intercontinental Natural Resources Ltd* [1980] 1 All ER 955, [1980] 1 WLR 1076.
4 *Re Mechanisations (Eaglescliffe) Ltd* [1966] Ch 20, [1964] 3 All ER 840.
5 *Re Eric Holmes (Property) Ltd* [1965] Ch 1052, [1965] 2 All ER 333.

liquidator and creditors of the company. The Registrar had given a certificate under s 98(2) of the CA 1948 (now CA 1985, s 401(2)) showing that the Act had been complied with; viz that the charge had been registered within 21 days of its creation. The Court held:

(1) that the security was in fact created earlier (in March 1964), but
(2) that the certificate was conclusive both as to the date of creation of the charge and the correctness of the certificate's content. The Court would not allow the liquidator or a creditor to go behind the certificate. If it were possible to do so, no person could safely lend on the security of the charge;
(3) the bank did not rely on its own wrong since there was no evidence that any outside creditor advanced money to the company between the date of creation and the date of registration of the charge.[6]

A copy of the certificate must be endorsed on all debentures subsequently issued by the company.[7] The register is open for inspection on payment of a fee. The Registrar is required to enter on the register a memorandum of satisfaction or release from the charge, on production of evidence that the debt has been satisfied or property released therefrom.[8] When a person has been appointed a receiver or manager under a charge, particulars of the appointment must be notified to the Registrar within seven days and included in the register.[9] This provision enables persons dealing with the company to acquaint themselves with the fact that a security is being enforced.

EXTENSION OF TIME FOR REGISTRATION

The Court has power, on proof that omission to register or that an omission or mis-statement in a registered charge was accidental, or due to inadvertence, or some other sufficient cause, or is not of a nature to prejudice creditors, or that on other grounds it is just and equitable to grant relief, to extend, on such terms as it thinks just and expedient, the period of registration or the rectification of the omission or mis-statement.[10] The evidence filed in support of the application should disclose the circumstances which gave rise to the failure to register in time. It should not merely state that the failure

---

6 The Court cannot rectify the register (under s 404) in such case, because this would involve expunging the entry and this the section does not authorise.
7 CA 1985, s 402.
8 Ibid, s 403.
9 Ibid, s 405.
10 Ibid, s 404.

was attributable to inadvertence. The order for extending time should contain a form of words to protect persons who have accrued rights in the assets of the company. Such words do not, however, extend to protect the inchoate or other rights of unsecured creditors as such.[11]

The power of the court to extend time is discretionary. The imminence of liquidation is a factor to be taken into account.[12] So too is culpable delay in registration.[13] While the court has power to extend time for registration even after the commencement of winding up, it will only rarely, if at all, make an order in such a case.[14]

The rules are technical; an order extending the time for registration is made subject to the usual condition that such extension is without prejudice to the rights of any parties acquired prior to the time of registration. In order for rights to accrue they must have arisen after the 21 day period allowed for the registration of the first incumbrance and before the order allowing late registration. Thus a first debenture which was not registered within the time allowed took priority when ultimately registered over a second debenture which was registered in time but which the company had granted virtually contemporaneously with the first debenture; the second document did not confer rights acquired during a period in which the first charge was void for want of registration.[15]

The Companies Act 1985 makes provision for the giving of floating charges in Scotland and for their registration.[16] The holder of a floating charge may apply for the appointment of a receiver on grounds identical to those which appear in instruments creating floating charges in the case of English companies, for example an unsatisfied demand for payment of the principal sum due (21 days being allowed), the expiry of a period of two months during which the whole of the interest due under the charge has been in arrears, the making of an order or a resolution to wind up the company, or

---

11 *Re Kris Cruisers Ltd* [1949] Ch 138, [1948] 2 All ER 1105. On the commencement of the winding up, unsecured creditors acquire rights against the assets of the company. *Re Ehrmann Bros Ltd* [1906] 2 Ch 697.
12 *Re R M Arnold & Co Ltd* [1984] BCLC 535.
13 *Re Ashpurton Estates Ltd* [1983] Ch 110 [1982] 3 All ER 665.
14 *Re R M Arnold & Co Ltd,* supra: *Re Ashpurton Estates Ltd* supra; cf *Re Resinoid and Mica Products Ltd* [1983] Ch 132, [1982] 3 All ER 677 where the court thought that no such order could be made after winding up, but it is probable, given the absence of apt words of limitation in s 404, that the rule can only be one of practice.
15 *Watson v Duff Morgan and Vermont (Holdings) Ltd* [1974] 1 All ER 794, [1974] 1 WLR 450.
16 CA 1985, s 462.

the appointment of a receiver by virtue of any other floating charge created by the company.[17] The powers of the receiver are fully capitulated in the statute.[18]

In addition to the register of charges kept by the Registrar, every limited company must keep at its registered office a register of charges, and all companies must keep a copy of every instrument creating a charge requiring registration.[19] The company's register of charges must have entered in it details of all specific and floating charges, a description of the property charged, the amount secured, and, except in the case of a bearer securities, the names of the persons entitled. The register and copies of charges must be made available for inspection.[20]

The certificate of registration of a charge cannot be challenged by judicial review.[1]

DEBENTURES

Debenture is defined in CA 1985, s 744 as including debenture stock,[2] bonds, and any other securities of a company, whether constituting a charge on the assets of the company or not.[3] Debentures, and especially floating charges, form a convenient means of securing moneys borrowed by a company. A single debenture may be issued, or a number of debentures for small amounts, each ranking *pari passu* with the others in the series, may be found more convenient. Bowen LJ in *English and Scottish Mercantile Investment Trust Ltd v Brunton* stated that there were the following three usual forms of debentures, but he did not suggest that these were exhaustive.[4]

17 IA 1986, s 52.
18 Ibid, s 55.
19 CA 1985, ss 406–407.
20 Ibid, s 408.
1 *R v Registrar of Companies, ex p Central Bank of India* [1986] QB 1114, [1985] 1 All ER 105.
2 'Debenture Stock' can be compared with 'stock'. Each borrower instead of receiving a debenture is issued with a debenture stock certificate. The principal advantage of debenture stock is that the holder can transfer portions of the security and does not need to find a buyer for the whole security as he would in the case of a debenture.
3 *Knightsbridge Estates Trust Ltd v Byrne* [1940] AC 613, 621, 628. Most debentures are a charge on the assets of the company. If not so charged, the lender merely has an action against the company to secure payment of his debt and has no right of recourse, by virtue of his debenture, to its assets.
4 [1892] 2 QB 700, 712.

The first is a simple acknowledgement, under seal, of the debt; the second, an instrument acknowledging the debt, and charging the property of the company with repayment; and the third, an instrument acknowledging the debt, charging the property of the company with repayment, and further restricting the company from giving any prior charge.

If the debenture is one of a series ranking *pari passu*,[5] and there are insufficient assets to pay all the debenture holders in full, the amount is distributed in proportion to the amounts owing to each of them, and arrears of interest payable to some of the debenture holders will not first be paid so as to equalise interest payments: *Re Midland Express Ltd*.[6] Where a series of debentures are issued which do not state that they rank *pari passu*, they are repayable according to date of issue, or if they are all issued on the same date, they are repayable according to the number allotted to each. If the holder of a debenture in a series ranking *pari passu* enforces the security he must do so on behalf of all the holders of debentures in that series.

CLASSIFICATION OF DEBENTURES

Debentures may be classified according to the person entitled thereto as

(1) debentures payable to registered holder,[7] or
(2) debentures payable to bearer, or,

according to the nature of the security, as

(1) debentures over a specific property, or
(2) debentures operating as a floating charge.

Debentures payable to registered holder state that the moneys secured and interest are payable to the person named therein or the registered holder for the time being. They are transferable in the

---

5 If there are insufficient assets to pay all debenture holders in full, they abate in proportion. As to the power of a company to issue fresh debentures ranking *pari passu* with an existing issue, see *Gartside v Silkstone and Dodworth Coal and Iron Co* (1882) 21 ChD 762.
6 [1914] 1 Ch 41.
7 Every such debenture holder (and any other person) is entitled to inspect the register of debentures and to have a copy of the trust deed; CA 1985, s 191.

manner prescribed in the debenture; a company may not register a transfer unless a proper instrument is delivered to the company.[8] If the company refuses to register the transfer, it must advise the transferee and return the transfer to him within two months.[9] A transferee normally takes subject to equities enforceable against the transferor, but the company may preclude itself from enforcing equities.[10]

Debentures payable to bearer are payable to the holder for the time being; interest is generally paid on production of coupons attached to the debentures. These debentures are negotiable instruments.[11] They are, therefore, transferable by delivery, and a transferee in due course gets a title free from defects in the title of the transferor, or equities enforceable against the transferor, and notice of the transfer need not be given to the company.[12]

FLOATING CHARGES

Where a company charges the whole or part of its property, present and future, with the repayment of a debt, and the property is of such a nature that it will constantly be changing in the course of the company's operations, a floating charge is created. Romer LJ in *Re Yorkshire Woolcombers' Association Ltd* stated:[13]

> ... I certainly think that if a charge has the three characteristics that I am about to mention it is a floating charge.
> (1) If it is a charge on a class of assets of a company present and future;
> (2) if that class is one which, in the ordinary course of the business of the company, would be changing from time to time; and
> (3) if you find that by the charge it is contemplated that, until some future step is taken by or on behalf of those interested in the charge, the company may carry on its business in the ordinary way as far as concerns the particular class of assets I am dealing with.[14]

---

8 Ibid, s 183.
9 Ibid.
10 *Re Goy & Co Ltd* [1900] 2 Ch 149.
11 *Bechuanaland Exploration Co v London Trading Bank Ltd* [1898] 2 QB 658.
12 Formerly, by s 10 of the Exchange Control Act 1947 no bearer certificate or coupon could be issued without the consent of the Treasury.
13 [1903] 2 Ch 284, 295.
14 See also *Government Stock and Other Securities Investment Co Ltd v Manila Rly Co Ltd* [1897] AC 81, 86 per Lord Macnaghten; and R. R. Pennington, 'The Genesis of the Floating Charge' (1960) 23 Mod LR 630.

A floating charge crystallises, ie attaches to specific assets, when the debenture holder takes steps to enforce his security, eg by appointing a receiver, when the company ceases business, or when a liquidator is appointed.[15]

There is substantial doubt whether a floating charge can also be said to crystallise, when the debenture is expressed to crystallise merely on the breach of a condition in it, even though the creditor takes no steps to intervene. The problem with recognising such provisions as valid is that they enable the debenture to take priority over, eg an execution creditor, even though the debt which the latter represents occurred after the so-called crystallising event and at a time when the debenture holder was allowing the company to carry on business.

The authorities conflict hopelessly. On one view the matter is merely one of construction; does the instrument creating the floating charge stipulate for crystallisation occurring automatically on the occurrence of an event of which the world may be unaware, for example, a failure to pay interest monthly. A contrary view asserts that the happening of such an event merely affords an opportunity for the debenture holder to take steps to protect himself as by appointing a receiver. In the *Manila Rly* case both views are expressed.[16] Lord Halsbury LC treated the matter as one merely of construction, as did Lord Davey. Lord MacNaghten and Lord Shand (who did not believe the instrument to be self-crystallising) treated the happening of the specified event as affording merely a right to intervene. In *Evans v Rival Granite Quarries Ltd*[17] the latter view was strongly expressed in the Court of Appeal; in order to change the character of the security from a floating charge to a specific security by crystallisation, the debenture holder must act. In the most recent case, *Re Woodroffe's (Musical Instruments) Ltd*[18] the Court took the tentative view that automatic crystallisation is undesirable. Thus the appointment of a receiver in respect of a prior floating charge would not crystallise a later such charge. Crystallisation would however occur on the company ceasing to do business, a conclusion which Nourse J found to be supported on the authorities

---

15 Until this date, the company is entitled as against the charge holder to deal with its goods and creditors; *Re Florence Land and Public Works Co* (1878) 10 ChD 530, 541 per Jessel MR; *Re Borax Co* [1901] 1 Ch 326, CA.
16 *Government Stock and Other Securities Investment Co Ltd v Manila Rly Co Ltd* [1897] AC 81.
17 [1910] 2 KB 979. See also *Re Valletort Sanitary Steam Laundry Co Ltd* [1903] 2 Ch 654; *Wallace v Evershed* [1899] 1 Ch 891.
18 [1986] Ch 366, [1985] BCLC 227. See also *Re Brightlife Ltd* [1986] 3 All ER 673, [1986] BCLC 418.

and consistent with the basic purpose of the floating charge. At the same time, the learned judge supported the practice of conferring a power on a debenture creating a floating charge to give notice to the company converting the charge into a fixed charge as regards assets specified in the notice. This has been criticised as a device which is open to abuse, in the absence of any system of registering such notices of crystallisation.[19] There are, however, a number of cases to the contrary, and the matter cannot be said to be settled.[20] Happily, modern precedents are not, it would seem, cast in the self crystallising form and therefore the problem does not arise in practice.[1]

Questions of priority frequently arise, as between those claiming under a floating charge and those claiming under a subsequent specific charge. As a floating charge does not attach to specific property until it crystallises, a later specific charge will have priority. Even if the prior floating charge contained a convenant by the company that it would not create a subsequent charge ranking in priority to or *pari passu* with it, the holder of a subsequent charge who took without knowledge of the covenant will have priority.[2]

Until a floating charge crystallises, the holders thereof will be postponed to the claims of the following:[3]

(1) the holders of a subsequent specific charge. The holders of a subsequent floating charge will not secure priority;
(2) a landlord who has distrained for rent;[4]

---

19 A. J. Boyle (1985) 6 Co Lawyer 277.
20 *Re Horne and Hellard* (1885) 29 ChD 736 at 743 is the strongest authority. Most of the English precedents are discussed, most helpfully, by J. H. Farrar, 'The Crystallisation of a Floating Charge' (1976) 40 Conv 397. Of the Commonwealth authorities, *Mackay v Larocque* [1926] 3 DLR 864, affd *sub nom Gordon Mackay & Co Ltd v Capital Trust Co Ltd* [1927] SCR 374 is against self-crystallisation, while *Re Manurewa Transport Ltd (In receivership)* [1971] NZLR 909 is to the contrary effect.
1 See Palmer's *Company Precedents* (16th edn) Vol III, p 58.
2 A person who takes a later legal mortgage for value and without notice of the floating charge obtains priority by virtue of the legal estate. *English and Scottish Mercantile Investment Trust v Brunton* [1892] 2 QB 700. Similarly, an equitable mortgagee who takes without notice of the debentures obtains priority. *Re Castell and Brown Ltd* [1898] 1 Ch 315. See also *Re Valletort Sanitary Steam Laundry Co Ltd* [1903] 2 Ch 654; on the question of the operation of a floating charge on after-acquired assets see D. Milman, 'The Floating Charge And After-Acquired Assets' [1979] Conv 138.
3 It is assumed that the charges have been registered, otherwise the principle in *Re Monolithic Building Co* [1915] 1 Ch 643 applies.
4 *Re Roundwood Colliery Co* [1897] 1 Ch 373.

(3) a creditor who has secured a garnishee order absolute;[5]
(4) an execution creditor who has seized and sold goods under a distress warrant;[6]
(5) those who would be the preferential creditors on winding up.[7] These claims must be paid by the receiver on appointment;[8]
(6) a vendor under a hire-purchase agreement.

Debentures are usually issued in accordance with a resolution of the directors. Unlike shares which may not be issued at a discount, debentures, because they are not part of the capital of the company, may be issued at a discount.

The power to issue debentures ends on winding up, but a company may allot debentures that have already been issued. In *Re Hubbard & Co Ltd*[9] it was held that a company might allot to its solicitor as security for his costs debentures that had been issued, although the debenture holders had commenced an action for the appointment of a receiver. Had the receiver been appointed, the allotment would have been invalid.

Where a series of debentures is issued, trustees are usually appointed for the debenture holders by a trust deed. This has many advantages, perhaps the most important being that the trustees have power to act to enforce the security on default without waiting for an individual debenture holder to take the initiative. Subject to the provisions of CA 1985, s 192, provisions in a trust deed exempting a trustee from, or indemnifying him against, liability for a breach of trust are void.

By the Banking Act 1979 companies are forbidden to advertise for deposits except with the approval of the Bank of England. Before such approval is granted, the company must comply with certain accounting requirements, and while it continues to advertise, must deliver audited accounts to the Bank of England. The Act exempts from its terms debentures and secured transactions.[10]

Debentures may be perpetual, ie provide that they shall be irredeemable, or redeemable only on the happening of a remote contingency, or on the expiration of a long period.[11] This section

---

5 *Robson v Smith* [1895] 2 Ch 118, but not an order *nisi*. *Norton v Yates* [1906] 1 KB 112.
6 *Davey & Co v Williamson & Sons* [1898] 2 QB 194.
7 CA 1985, s 196; see on priorities, A. J. Boyle, n 19, supra.
8 *Westminster City Council v Haste* [1950] Ch 442, [1950] 2 All ER 65.
9 [1898] WN 158.
10 Banking Act 1979, ss 1(4)(b) and 34.
11 CA 1985, s 193.

excludes the application of the equitable rule under which a provision clogging the right of a mortgagor to redeem his property is void: *Kreglinger v New Patagonia Meat and Cold Storage Co Ltd*.[12] It was held in *Knightsbridge Estates Trust Ltd v Byrne*[13] that a mortgage by a company of land fell within the definition of debenture and could therefore be made irredeemable under this provision.

A company may reissue debentures that have been redeemed unless contrary provision is made in the articles, or in any contract made by the company, or unless the company has, by resolution or otherwise, evidenced its intention to cancel the debentures.[14] If debentures are reissued, the holders are entitled to the same priorities as if they had not been redeemed. Particulars of debentures that may be reissued must be shown in the balance sheet.[15]

Specific performance of a contract to take up and pay for debentures may be enforced by the Court.[16] Ordinarily, a borrower cannot secure specific performance of a contract to lend money.

REMEDIES OF DEBENTURE HOLDERS

If the debenture is one of a series ranking *pari passu* and trustees for the debenture holders have been appointed by trust deed, the remedies of the debenture holders are enforced by the trustees. It is preferable to have trustees appointed for the debenture holders for there is then a small body of persons who can watch the interests of a large number of investors who may be widely dispersed. If trustees have not been appointed, any debenture holder may take action on behalf of himself and the other debenture holders. Where there is a single debenture, the holder may take action to enforce his remedies. The remedies available to debenture holders are:

(1) he may sell the property subject to the debenture if the debenture gives him or the trustees a power of sale;[17]
(2) he may sue the company for arrears of interest and principal if the date of repayment has passed and he may levy execution to secure payment;

12 [1914] AC 25.
13 [1940] AC 613, [1940] 2 All ER 401.
14 CA 1985, s 194.
15 Ibid, Sch 4, para 41(2).
16 Ibid, s 85.
17 By s 103 of the Law of Property Act 1925 mortgagees have an implied power of sale.

(3) he may appoint a receiver or manager if the debenture confers this power; if no power is given he may apply to the Court for an appointment;
(4) he may present a petition for the winding up of the company,[18] and prove his debt as a creditor;
(5) if the debenture covers personal property, he may foreclose.[19] All the debenture holders together with the company must be joined in the foreclosure action.[20]

RECEIVERS AND MANAGERS

The debenture holders or the trustees for the debenture holders may appoint a receiver or manager if the debenture or trust deed empowers them to do so. If they lack the power,[1] or prefer the appointment to be made by the Court, they may apply to the Court for an appointment. In either case, notice of appointment must be given to the Registrar within seven days and he must make an entry in the register of charges.[2] Persons dealing with the company are then able to ascertain that the debenture holders have taken action to enforce their security.

The purpose in appointing a receiver or having him appointed by the Court is to protect the rights of the debenture holders to the assets included in the debenture. If it is desired that the business of the company be continued a manager must be appointed. There are advantages in having the Court appoint a receiver. The receiver is not then the agent for the debenture holders and, as he is an officer of the Court, interference with him in the performance of his duties may be contempt of Court.

An administrative receiver must be an insolvency practitioner and a body corporate is disqualified from acting as an insolvency practitioner.[3] Except where appointed by the Court, an undischarged bankrupt is similarly disqualified and the Official

---

18 Insolvency Act 1986, s 124.
19 *Sadler v Worley* [1894] 2 Ch 170. The statutory provisions as to receivers and managers are contained for the most part in Part III of the Insolvency Act 1986. The following is a brief summary of the law. A receiver or manager of the whole or virtually the whole of a company's property appointed by or on behalf of holders of debentures secured by a charge created as a floating charge is called an 'administrative receiver': IA 1986, s 29(2). An administrative receiver is thus a 'receiver'.
20 *Elias v Continental Oxygen Co* [1897] 1 Ch 511.
1 Usually the power to appoint a receiver arises when the debenture becomes enforceable, eg if interest is in arrears for six months, but debenture holders may wish the Court to make an appointment when they lack the power to do so.
2 CA 1985, s 405.
3 IA 1986, ss 388 and 390(1).

Receiver may be appointed receiver if the company is being wound up by the Court.[4] The fact that a receiver or manager has been appointed must be notified on every invoice, order for goods, or business letter issued by the company.[5]

The appointment of a receiver or manager must be distinguished from the appointment of a liquidator in a winding up. Winding up may follow the appointment of a receiver or manager, but this need not occur. The receiver or manager is appointed to protect the debenture holders and if the whole of the company's assets are charged, there will be little for a liquidator to do if winding up takes place. If the receiver has been appointed by the Court and a winding up order is made at a later date, the Court may remove the receiver and make the liquidator the receiver.[6] If the company is being wound up by the Court and the debenture holders subsequently appoint a receiver, the latter cannot interfere with the assets in the hands of the liquidator without the leave of the Court.[7] If, however, the debenture holders have appointed a receiver prior to winding up, the Court will not in general, interfere with that appointment.

While winding up deprives the receiver under a debenture of the power to bind the company personally by acting as its agent, it does not affect his powers to hold and dispose of the company's property comprised in the debenture including his power to use the company's name for that purpose for such powers are given by the disposition of the company's property which it made (in equity) by the debenture itself.[8]

STATUS OF RECEIVER OR MANAGER

A receiver or manager appointed by the Court is personally liable on his contracts, but he is entitled to an indemnity out of the assets. An administrative receiver appointed by the debenture holders is made personally liable on his contracts unless the contract provides otherwise.[9] Where he is personally liable, he has a right of indemnity out of the company's assets. An administrative receiver may apply to the Court for directions as to the exercise of his powers.

4 Ibid, ss 31 and 32.
5 Ibid, s 39.
6 See *Re Joshua Stubbs Ltd* [1891] 1 Ch 475 and *Strong v Carlyle Press Ltd* [1893] 1 Ch 268.
7 *Re Pound, Son and Hutchins* (1889) 42 ChD 40.
8 IA 1986, s 44(1) and *Sowman v David Samuel Trust Ltd* [1978] 1 All ER 616, [1978] 1 WLR 22; in particular IA 1986, s 127 does not avoid a sale by the receiver.
9 Ibid, s 37(1), (3).

Chapter 18 Borrowing Powers

APPOINTMENT BY COURT

A receiver may be appointed by the Court in a debenture holders' action if:

(1) the principal moneys secured by the debenture have become payable; or
(2) the company is being wound up; or [10]
(3) if the debenture holders' security is in jeopardy, eg if the company has ceased operations and is insolvent.[11]

A receiver appointed by the Court displaces a receiver appointed by the debenture holders. The Court fixes the remuneration of a receiver or a manager appointed by it and has power to fix the remuneration of a receiver or manager appointed by the debenture holders.[12]

POWERS OF RECEIVER

Ordinarily the function of the receiver is limited to the collection and distribution of assets subject to the debenture,[13] but the Court may, if it is obviously to the advantage of the company and the creditors, authorise the receiver to borrow money for use in the business. The Court must be satisfied that there is an urgent need for the expenditure, eg in effecting repairs.[14] If borrowing is authorised, the lenders will have priority over the claims of other creditors, including the debenture holders. The receiver cannot be compelled to perform existing contracts entered into by the company. He cannot be restrained by injunction from repudiating such a contract unless repudiation will operate to the detriment of the company.[15]

A receiver does not, however, enjoy powers of management to the exclusion of the board of directors. He may, for example, bring an action in the name of the company in respect of realising on the company's assets. However, the directors may themselves bring an

---

10 *Re Victoria Steamboats Ltd* [1897] 1 Ch 158.
11 *McMahon v North Kent Iron Works Co* [1891] 2 Ch 148.
12 IA 1986, s 36.
13 Where the debenture is secured over the uncalled capital of the company, the receiver cannot make calls on members unless the articles give the directors power to delegate this power to a receiver or the Court orders that the receiver may make calls: *Re Phoenix Bessemer Steel Co* (1875) 44 LJ Ch 683.
14 *Greenwood v Algeciras (Gibraltar) Co* [1894] 2 Ch 205.
15 *Airlines Airspares v Handley Page* [1970] Ch 193, [1970] 1 All ER 29.

action to recover assets or to pursue a claim on behalf of the company provided that this does not impinge prejudicially upon the position of the debenture holders by threatening or imperilling the assets which are subject to the charge. If such a claim results in judgment for the company the receiver may share in it for debenture holders if they have not been paid previously.[16]

The power to appoint a manager is commonly exercised when it is proposed to carry on the business of the company with a view to disposing of it as a going concern. The Court will probably approve the appointment of a manager if the nature of the business is such that its value would depreciate rapidly if it were not continued, eg the running of ferries.

An administrative receiver's powers are deemed to include (except so far as inconsistent with the debenture under which he was appointed) the powers set out in Schedule I to IA 1986.[17] These include the power to manage the business.

APPLICATION OF ASSETS

The receiver appointed on behalf of debenture holders entitled to a floating charge[18] must pay the creditors entitled to a preferential claim on winding up in priority to any claim of the debenture holders for principal or interest.[19] Assets received by a receiver or manager must be applied by him in the following order:

(1) the costs of realisation;
(2) the costs, including remuneration, of the receiver;
(3) the costs, charges and expenses of the debenture trust deed, including the trustees' remuneration;
(4) the plaintiff's costs;
(5) the preferential creditors,[20]
(6) the debenture holders.[1] Any surplus would be paid to the company for the unsecured creditors.

---

16   *Newhart Developments Ltd v Co-operative Commercial Bank Ltd* [1978] QB 814, [1978] 2 All ER 896.
17   IA 1986, s 42. These powers are very wide. NB also the power with leave of the Court to dispose of property charged to third parties: ibid, s 43.
18   *Re Victoria Steamboats Ltd* [1897] 1 Ch 158.
19   CA 1985, s 196 as substituted by IA 1986, s 439(c), Sch 13, Pt I. This provision does not extend to fixed charges.
20   CA 1985, s 196 and IA 1986, ss 40 and 386.
 1   *Re Glyncorrwg Colliery Co Ltd* [1926] Ch 951.

A receiver who pays out moneys without regard for any preferential claim of which he has notice is personally liable to the preferential creditor therefor.[2]

A receiver is in a fiduciary position vis-à-vis the debenture holders who appoint him under the debenture.[3] He probably owes the debenture holders a duty of care.[4] Furthermore, the duty of care almost certainly extends to the company over whose assets the receiver is appointed.[5] The receiver also owes a duty to the general creditors of the company, that is creditors other than those who appoint him or preferential creditors, to obtain the best price he can.[6]

REPORTS

Where an administrative receiver has been appointed, he must send notice of his appointment to the company.[7] The administrative receiver must by notice require some or all of the company's officers or employees[8] within 21 days of the receipt of the notice, to submit to him a statement as the affairs of the company setting out the particulars in prescribed form and verified by affidavit.[9] The administrative receiver must send to the Registrar, the trustees for the debenture holders and to all debenture holders reports showing his receipts and payments.[10]

In all other cases, the receiver or manager must deliver to the Registrar every six months an abstract of his receipts and payments.[11] The duty of the receiver or manager to make these returns may be enforced by order of the Court.[12]

---

2 *IRC v Goldblatt* [1972] Ch 498, [1972] 2 All ER 202.
3 *Re B Johnson & Co (Builders) Ltd* [1955] Ch 634, [1955] 2 All ER 775.
4 *R v Board of Trade, ex p St Martin's Preserving Co Ltd* [1965] 1 QB 603, [1964] 2 All ER 561.
5 *Expo International Pty Ltd v Chant* (1979) 4 ACLR 679.
6 *Standard Chartered Bank v Walker* [1982] 3 All ER 938, [1982] 1 WLR 1410; cf *Latchford v Beirne* [1981] 3 All ER 705.
7 IA 1986, s 39.
8 Or others: see ibid, s 47(3).
9 Ibid, s 47.
10 Ibid, s 48.
11 Ibid, s 38.
12 Ibid, s 41.

Chapter 19

The Taxation of Companies

Armed with a trust and a company the well-advised taxpayer was, until the late 1930s, able to minimise, if not to avoid, his liability to tax. Legislation has whittled away the advantages of the company as a tax-saving device, and today forming a company may have serious tax disadvantages.

This chapter outlines[1] the main provisions of corporation tax on profits and chargeable gains of a company, income tax on company distributions, and the incidence of capital gains tax and inheritance tax on company assets, and explains some of the factors which should influence the decision to incorporate.

CORPORATION TAX

Before 1965 companies were charged to income tax at the standard rate[2] and profits tax. Profits tax[3] was a tax purely on the company, but the income tax had an element of duality, in that, when the company paid a dividend to its shareholders, it could deduct and retain income tax from that dividend. Income tax was therefore paid only once on income which was distributed to shareholders by way of dividend, and the old system of company taxation thus did not make a rigid distinction between the company and its

---

1 This chapter is only an outline of company taxation. For more detailed treatment readers are referred to the standard works on the subject: *Simon's Taxes; British Tax Encyclopedia*; Bramwell: *Taxation of Companies*; Whiteman and Wheatcroft: *Capital Gains Tax; Dymond's Capital Transfer Tax*; Pinson: *Revenue Law*.
2 Companies, not being individuals, did not pay surtax, and could not obtain personal reliefs.
3 The top rate of profits tax was 15%. There was a sliding scale so that some companies paid a lower rate.

380 Chapter 19 The Taxation of Companies

shareholders. On this view, the company's income is no more than the aggregate income of the individual members.[4]

The Finance Act 1965[5] introduced what was then a new tax, corporation tax, which is charged on *all* the profits of a United Kingdom resident company, whether they are income profits[6] or capital gains,[7] wherever they arise[8] at such rate as Parliament shall fix.[9]

Corporation tax draws a distinction between the company and its shareholders, for whilst the company itself pays only mainstream or advance corporation tax, its shareholders are charged to income tax on distributions received from the company.[10]

Since 1965, then, the shareholders and the company pay different taxes, whilst under the old system of company taxation they paid largely the same tax—income tax.

Individual recipients of distributions were liable to surtax, and most companies were liable to profits tax, but income tax formed the main burden.

ACCOUNTING PERIODS

Corporation tax is assessed on companies by reference to 'accounting periods'.[11] Generally, an accounting period is the period for which a company draws up its accounts, if those accounts cover a

---

4   Royal Commission on Taxation of Profits and Income (Cmnd 9474) para 27.
5   FA 1965, s 46, now TA 1970, s 238(1).
6   Charged by TA 1970, s 238(1), (4)(a).
7   Charged to corporation tax by ibid, s 238(3), (4)(a).
8   Ibid, s 243(1).
9   The current rate is 35%, but there are lower rates for small companies which, if they have no 'associated companies' and have profits of less than £100,000 per annum pay corporation tax at only 27%. The rate slides between 27% and 35% where the company's profits are between £100,000 and £500,000 so that it is only when a company's profits are more than £500,000 that the ordinary 35% rate applies—see generally FA 1972, s 95(1), (2); Finance Act 1987. Special rules, limiting these reliefs, apply where a company has associated companies, as defined in FA 1972, s 95(4)—see ibid, s 95(3), (4).
10 Distributions are dealt with on p 389, post, where the significance of the terms mainstream and advance corporation tax is considered. It is to be noted that the system of corporation tax now in force was created only in 1972. This system, as will be seen later, creates some mixing of the taxes paid by the company and its shareholders where dividends are concerned. The original system of corporation tax, in force from 1965 to 1972, admitted no such mixing and produced a situation which many considered to be double taxation—see The Royal Commission on Taxation of Profits and Income (op cit) para 544, though see the dissent paras 90, 91.
11 TA 1970, ss 243(3), 247(1).

period of 12 months or less.[12] If the accounts are drawn for a period of longer than 12 months, then only the first 12 months of the account form an accounting period for corporation tax purposes.[13] A new accounting period will then begin,[14] which will end on the company's accounting date[15] or the expiration of 12 months if sooner. Thus if a company draws its accounts for an 18 month period, say 1 January 1987 to 30 June 1988, for corporation tax its first accounting period will end on 31 December 1987 (12 months from the commencement of an account) and its second accounting period will end on 30 June 1988 (an accounting date).

The primary rule, therefore, for an existing company is that a new accounting period will begin at the end of an accounting period.[16] But an accounting period may also begin when a company comes within the charge to corporation tax[17]—as for example, when it is first formed, or when, having been resident abroad, it becomes resident in the United Kingdom.

There are other occasions which bring about the termination of an accounting period besides the expiration of 12 months from the beginning of the accounting period and the accounting date of the company. These are:[18]

(1) the ending of a period for which the company does not make up accounts;
(2) the company beginning or ceasing to trade, or to be in respect of the trade or (if more than one) of all the trades carried on by it within the charge to corporation tax;
(3) the company beginning or ceasing to be resident in the United Kingdom;
(4) the company ceasing to be within the charge to corporation tax altogether.

Overriding all these provisions is one which provides that when a company is wound up an accounting period shall end, and a new one shall begin which is to end, subject to one minor exception, only on the termination of 12 months from the date of commencement.[19]

12 Ibid, s 247(2), (3).
13 Ibid, s 247(3)(a).
14 Ibid, s 247(2)(b).
15 Ibid, s 247(3)(b).
16 Ibid, s 247(2)(b).
17 Ibid, s 247(2)(a).
18 Ibid, s 247(3), as amended by FA 1972, s 107(1), (4).
19 Ibid, s 247(7). The exception is in ibid, s 245(6). It relates to the period from the end of an accounting period to final dissolution of the company.

Where a company draws its accounts for a longer period than an accounting period for corporation tax the profits shown in the company's accounts are to be apportioned to the accounting periods on a time basis, unless some better basis of apportioning profits to the period can be found, when the better basis of apportionment is adopted.[20]

One other point may be made. Corporation tax is charged *on* profits arising in an accounting period,[1] but it is levied *for* financial years. Thus if an accounting period crosses the boundaries of the financial year[2] (31 March to 1 April) the profits must be apportioned to the financial years[3] which the accounting period covers. Generally there is no practical need for an apportionment unless the rates of corporation tax are changed.

COMPUTATION

The income profits of a company are to be computed in accordance with income tax principles.[4]

In particular this means that income of a company is charged to tax under the well-known Schedules of the Income Tax Acts.

A company is none the less a company, and those parts of income tax law which apply to individuals[5] *qua* individuals, for example personal reliefs, certain reliefs for payments of interest, and higher rate income tax are excluded and do not apply for corporation tax. A company is not, and never has been, eligible for personal reliefs and is not liable to pay higher rate income tax.

In computing the chargeable gains and allowable losses of a company the principles of capital gains tax are applied.[6] As for income tax, those provisions of capital gains tax which relate specifically to individuals, for example the exemption from capital gains tax for the first £6,600 of gains in each year, are excluded.[7]

A company is not charged to tax on all its receipts—only on its profits. On a cash basis, one can look at all the receipts of the

---

20 Ibid, s 129, and see *Marshall Hus & Partners Ltd v Bolton* [1981] STC 18.
1 Ibid, s 247(1).
2 An accounting period running from 1 January 1983 to 31 December 1983 falls into two financial years: up to 31 March it is in the financial year 1982, from 1 April it is in the financial year 1983; see TA 1970, s 527(1).
3 TA 1970, s 243(3).
4 Ibid, s 250(1), (3).
5 Ibid, s 250(2), (6).
6 Ibid, s 265(2).
7 Ibid, s 265(3)(c).

company, deduct all the outgoings, and call the difference 'the profit' or the 'loss'. This is, however, a crude test of profit: the Revenue require a more sophisticated test, and only certain deductions are permitted from income, and certain deductions from capital. Those deductions which could be made in computing income for income tax purposes and capital gains for capital gains tax purposes may be made in the computation of income and of chargeable gains for corporation tax.

A company carrying on a trade may deduct from the income of that trade those disbursements or expenses which have been 'wholly and exclusively' laid out or expended for the purposes of that trade.[8] One of the most important deductions which may be made under this provision is the deduction for directors' fees. In all cases it is a question of fact whether or not disbursements are laid out wholly and exclusively for the purposes of the trade. Whilst, therefore, the Revenue cannot interfere with a payment of directors' fees simply on the ground that it is too large, it can do so if it can show that there was an element of duality in the payment, as for example if it is really to pay for the housekeeping and not for the benefit of the trade.[9] The size of the payment may, of course, be evidence of duality. Amongst the other deductions which are permitted are deductions for bad debts, rent paid for office premises, the cost of repairs to premises, the cost of replacing assets,[10] the incidental cost of raising loan finance, certain expenditure incurred before trading begins and extra large redundancy payments made by traders going out of business.[11] Capital expenditure[12] and sums which are charged to capital[13] are not allowed as deductions from income receipts.

Those items of expenditure which may be deducted from the consideration received or deemed to be received on a disposal of a capital asset by a company are:[14]

(1) the consideration given for the acquisition of the asset;
(2) any expenditure wholly and exclusively incurred on the asset

---

8   Ibid, s 130(a). Other deductions are permitted but the 'wholly and exclusively' test is the most important.
9   *Copeman v Flood* [1941] 1 KB 202.
10 TA 1970, s 130.
11 FA 1980, ss 38, 39 and 41. These provisions are interesting because they are examples of tax legislation aimed at achieving specific economic or social objectives.
12 TA 1970, s 130(f), (g).
13 *Coltness Iron Co v Black* (1881) 6 App Cas 315.
14 CGTA 1979, s 32.

by the company enhancing the value of the asset, which is reflected in the state or nature of the asset on the disposal, and any costs incurred by it in establishing or defending its title to the asset;

(3) the incidental costs of the disposal (eg legal fees, surveyors' fees).

A company which is an investment company, that is a company whose business consists wholly or mainly in the making of investments, and the principal part of whose income is derived therefrom[15] may deduct management expenses from both its income and its capital receipts.[16] It is, however, unlikely that large claims for management expenses will be allowed, by the Revenue[17] or by the courts.

After having computed the profits from all sources, including chargeable gains, and having made such deductions from each individual source as are permissible a company may then deduct such 'charges on income' as it actually pays from its total profits. If a company carries on several businesses, for example it trades in manufacturing doors, it invests in shares, and in one year sells a capital asset, and buys a new one (eg its factory) in drawing its accounts for corporation tax it includes all the receipts of its manufacturing trade and deducts from those receipts, payments made wholly and exclusively for the purposes of that trade (eg purchases of raw materials) and so finds the profits of its trade. Then it works out the profits of its investment business and on the sale of its factory, deducting losses from gains, and also deducting a figure for management expenses. It adds these three figures together to find its total profits, and from that it may deduct its charges on income.

Charges on income are defined as[18] (a) any yearly interest, annuity or other annual payment and any patent royalty or mining rent or royalty, which must usually be paid to a United Kingdom resident,[19] and (b) any other interest payable on an advance from a bank carrying on business in the United Kingdom, or on a loan from a member of the stock exchange or a discount house.

The most common charge on income is a payment of interest, but no payment is to qualify as a charge on income if:

---

15 TA 1970, s 304(1).
16 Ibid, s 304(1).
17 *L. G. Berry Ltd v Attwooll* [1964] 2 All ER 126, [1964] 1 WLR 693.
18 TA 1970, s 248(3).
19 A payment made to a non-resident may, in certain cases, be a charge on income: ibid, ss 248(4), 249.

(1) the payment is deductible from a particular source,[20] or if
(2) the payment (not being interest) is charged to capital or (whether interest or some other type of payment) is not ultimately borne by the company,[1] or if
(3) the payment is not made under a liability incurred for valuable consideration—but this does not prevent a covenanted donation to charity qualifying as a charge on income, if it satisfies the other requirements.[2]

If the payment passes all three of the above tests it has to pass at least one of the following further tests if it is a payment of interest:

(1) the payment must be made by a company which exists wholly or mainly for the purposes of carrying on a trade,[3] or
(2) the payment of interest must be wholly and exclusively laid out or expended for the purposes of a trade carried on by the company,[4] or
(3) the payment must be made by an investment company,[5] or
(4) that the payment, if not otherwise qualifying as a charge on income, would on certain assumptions be eligible for relief if paid by an individual on a loan for the purchase of land.[6]

It should also be noted that, since the enactment of FA 1976, s 38 no relief may be given for a payment of interest if the sole or main benefit derived from the payment is a reduction in tax liability and, since the enactment of FA 1977, s 48, no relief may, except in some very limited circumstances, be given for an annual payment where the liability to make the payment was incurred for a consideration which is not brought into account in computing the payer's income. Relief may however be given for interest which passes all the tests listed above but which is charged to capital in the company's accounts.

LOSSES

When a trading company incurs a loss in its trade in an accounting

20 Ibid, s 248(2), eg if it is a payment incurred 'wholly and exclusively' for the purposes of trade.
1 Ibid, s 248(5)(a) as amended by FA 1981, s 38(2), (4).
2 Ibid, s 248(5)(b).
3 Ibid, s 248(6)(a).
4 Ibid, s 248(6)(b).
5 Ibid, s 248(6)(c).
6 Ibid, s 248(6). The assumptions mentioned above are set out in s 248(6).

period, it may claim to set the loss off against profits of other accounting periods, and profits from other sources.

A company may first claim to set the loss off against its total profits (including chargeable gains) for the accounting period in which the loss occurs,[7] and on such a claim it may also claim to carry back the loss against total profits of earlier accounting periods,[8] but only if, in the earlier periods, it was carrying on the trade in which the loss occurred, and only for the same length of time backwards from the commencement of the accounting period in which the loss occurs as that accounting period stretches forwards from that date.[9] Thus if the accounting period in which the loss occurs is a 12 month accounting period, the carry back can only be for 12 months. If the 12 month carry back covers only part of an accounting period, there has to be an apportionment of profits on a time basis to the part of the period covered.[10]

Thus, if a company had accounted for two periods of nine months (period 1 and period 2) and had then accounted for 12 months in which it had a loss, the company could carry back the loss for the whole of period 2 and three months of period 1. One-third (3/9) of the profits of period 1 are apportioned to that period and are available for set off.

A company carrying on a trade, other than one carried on in the exercise of functions conferred by an Act of Parliament, can only carry back losses or set them off against current profits of another business if it shows that, for the period in which the loss occurred, the trade was carried on, on a commercial basis with a reasonable expectation of gain in the trade, or in any larger undertaking of which the trade formed part.[11]

If the company does not wish to set off the loss against total profits of the period in which the loss occurred, or to carry it back, or if the company has no profits against which to set off the loss, it may claim to carry forward the loss to future years in succession, until the loss is exhausted, but it may carry forward only against profits of the same trade in which the loss occurred.[12]

Where the loss exceeds the total profits of an accounting period,

---

7 Ibid, s 177(2).
8 Ibid.
9 Ibid, s 177(3). Note, however, that if the loss is derived from a first year capital allowance it may be carried back for three years—see ibid, s 177(3A) as inserted by FA 1971, Sch 8, para 16(6).
10 Ibid, s 177(3).
11 Ibid, s 177(4), (5).
12 Ibid, s 177(1).

there are provisions for artificially increasing the trade income by treating certain payments made under deduction of tax as trading income so as to enable the loss to be used up.[13]

Trading losses are to be computed in the same way as trading income,[14] but where a company has paid charges on income, which include payments made wholly and exclusively for the purposes of a trade, and those charges exceed the profits from which they were deductible, the charges are treated as trading losses to the extent of that excess or those payments and may be carried forward.[15]

Capital losses may be carried forward and set against capital gains according to ordinary capital gains tax rules.[16]

TERMINAL LOSSES

A company which ceases to carry on a trade may claim to carry back losses incurred in the last 12 months of that trade before the cessation and set them against profits of that trade for the three years preceding the final 12 months.[17] Such a claim may only be made where the losses are not eligible for any other form of relief.[18]

Where the last 12 months of a trade does not fall entirely within one or more accounting periods of a company, so that part only of an accounting period is within the 12 month period, there is to be an apportionment of losses occurring in the accounting period to that part of the period within the last 12 months, on a time apportionment basis.[19] A similar apportionment of income has to be made where accounting periods do not fall wholly within the three years to which the losses may be carried back.

---

13 Ibid, s 177(7).
14 Ibid, s 177(6).
15 Ibid, s 177(8).
16 CGTA 1979, ss 4(1)(a), 29.
17 TA 1970, s 178(1).
18 Ibid, s 178(1) proviso, eg under ibid, s 177(1), (2).
19 TA 1970, s 178(2). Example: a company commences to trade on 1 January 1987 and draws up its account for the nine months to 30 September 1987 and thereafter for the 12 months 1 October to 30 September, until 30 September 1990 and ceases to trade on 30 June 1991, so that its last accounting period is only nine months. That company may carry back the losses for the whole of the last nine month accounting period and ¼ of the losses occurring in the preceding accounting period, which was a 12 month period, only three months of which fell within the last 12 months of trade—so it can use losses referable to the period July 1990 to 30 June 1991—the terminal loss. It can carry those losses back against the income of accounting periods falling within the three years from July 1990, ie to 30 June 1987. One goes back to the beginning of the accounting period in which 1 July 1990 falls, ie to 1 October 1989. That was a 12 month

LOSS COMPANIES

It might be thought that a company with losses was of little or no advantage to anyone. On the contrary, however, a company with a trading loss is of use to a person who buys the company and can make profits from the same trade that was formerly making a loss. The loss can be set-off against future profits of the trade[20] and thereby tax can be minimised. But losses can only be set-off against future profits whilst the same trade continues. It was and is often difficult to tell from the case law when a trade is continuing, and when it has ceased and a new one commenced.[1] Statutory rules have now been enacted[2] which prevent losses from being set-off against future profits where there has been a change of ownership of the company and within three years before the change or within three years after the change there has been a 'major change in the nature or conduct of a trade carried on by the company',[3] or where 'at any time after the activities in a trade carried on by a company have become small or negligible, and before any considerable revival of the trade, there is a change in the ownership of the company'.[4]

A change in ownership occurs, very broadly, when one or more persons acquire on their own, or together, control of a company, by purchase of that company's share capital.[5]

SPECIAL TYPES OF LOSS AND OTHER RELIEFS

In the usual case a company's trading loss is ascertained solely by drawing up a trading account and discovering the loss in accordance with ordinary principles of commercial accountancy. However, it should be noted that the purchase of certain capital assets to be used in a trade (such as plant and machinery or industrial buildings) may

---

period. From 1 October 1990 to 1 July 1991 is nine months. Nine-twelfths of the income of that period is therefore available for set-off against the terminal loss. The accounting periods ending 30 September 1990 and 30 September 1988 cross no boundaries and all their income is available for set-off. One then goes back from 30 September 1988 to 30 June 1988—three months. That period is within a nine month accounting period so three months of the income of that period are available for set-off.

20 See p 385 et seq, supra.
1 See, for example, *F. G. Ingram & Son v Callaghan* [1969] 1 All ER 433, [1969] 1 WLR 456.
2 TA 1970, ss 483, 484.
3 Ibid, s 483(1)(a).
4 Ibid, s 483(1)(b).
5 Ibid, s 484(1).

entitle the purchaser to capital allowances which, depending upon their amount, may produce a loss.[6] Furthermore, a company is entitled to capital allowances when it buys a factory or other industrial building which it lets to a trader.[7] Relief is also given to an investment company which realises an allowable loss or an investment in unquoted shares of a trading company. In such a case the investment company may claim to have the loss treated as a revenue loss and set it against its income accordingly.[8]

RESTRICTIONS ON USING LOSSES

As a result, inter alia, of the recent proliferation of tax avoidance schemes there is now much anti-avoidance legislation which prevents certain types of losses from qualifying for relief. This legislation is elaborate and a knowledge of it is not necessary to an understanding of the scheme of corporation tax. Accordingly this legislation is not discussed here, the relevant provisions being referred to in the footnote to this sentence.[9]

INCOME TAX

DISTRIBUTIONS

All dividends and 'other distributions' paid by a company resident in the United Kingdom are taxed as income of the recipient under Sch F.[10]

When a company makes a qualifying distribution[11] it must pay an amount of corporation tax to the Revenue which is known as advance corporation tax ('ACT').[12] The amount of ACT which the company has to pay is a fraction of the amount or value of the distribution which it makes to its shareholders, the fraction currently being twenty-seven-seventy-thirds.[13] Although the company will have paid ACT when it paid its dividends it must still pay corporation tax in the oridnary way on its profits. This ordinary

---

6 See FA 1971, ss 40 to 50 and CAA 1968, ss 1 to 17.
7 See generally CAA 1968, ss 1 to 17, 73 and 74.
8 See FA 1981, s 36.
9 See TA 1970, s 180; FA 1973, ss 30, 31; F(No 2) A 1975, s 43(1); FA 1978, s 31.
10 TA 1970, s 232.
11 As defined in FA 1972, s 84(4).
12 See ibid, s 84. In certain cases involving groups of companies the paying company does not have to pay ACT—see TA 1970, s 256.
13 See FA 1986, s 17.

390 *Chapter 19 The Taxation of Companies*

corporation tax is called 'mainstream corporation tax'. However, subject to certain restrictions,[14] a company which has paid ACT may set that ACT against its liability to pay mainstream corporation tax for the period in which the dividend is paid: and if the ACT which it has paid exceeds its liability to pay mainstream corporation tax for that period it may carry back the ACT against mainstream corporation tax for up to six years or surrender the surplus ACT to its subsidiaries which can set it against their own liability to pay mainstream corporation tax.[15]

An individual UK resident who receives a dividend is treated as receiving a dividend of a gross amount equal to the dividend which he actually receives plus, in effect, the amount of ACT which the company paid when it made the distribution.[16] Such an individual is liable to pay income tax on the gross amount of the dividend, but he obtains a tax credit, in effect, equal to the amount of ACT paid by the company in respect of his dividend. This tax credit will be equal to tax at the basic rate on the dividend, so that the individual will, in terms of the cash that he has to find out of his own pocket, only be liable to pay higher rate income tax on the dividend and if, for some reason, he has to pay less income tax than the amount of the tax credit he may claim back an appropriate part of the tax credit.

An example will help to explain these principles. Suppose for a given accounting period a company with only one beneficial shareholder who is an individual resident in the United Kingdom has a profit of £500,000 and pays a dividend of £350,000. It must pay ACT of £129,452 (twenty-seven-seventy-thirds of £350,000) which it can set against its liability to pay mainstream corporation tax of £175,000 (35% of £500,000)[17] so that it only has to pay £45,548 mainstream corporation tax. The shareholder is treated as receiving a gross dividend of £479,452 (£350,000 actually paid to him plus £129,452 ACT) on which he will be liable to pay income tax of, say, £287,671. However, he receives a tax credit of £129,452 (which is equal to tax at the basic rate of 27% on a dividend of £479,452) so that he only has to pay a further £158,219 in tax.

A company resident in the United Kingdom which receives a dividend from another such company also obtains a tax credit.[18] In certain very limited circumstances (for example where the company

---

14 See FA 1972, s 85(2).
15 See ibid, s 92; FA 1984, s 52.
16 See TA 1970, s 232; FA 1972, s 86.
17 Small companies relief is ignored for the purposes of this example.
18 See FA 1972, s 86.

is exempt from tax) it may claim this tax credit back.[19] In other cases it may, in effect, use the tax credit to 'frank' its own dividends so that putting the matter very broadly, when it pays dividends, it does not have to pay ACT up to the amount of the tax credit.[20]

Similar principles apply where the recipient of the dividend is non-resident, although there are some differences in the detailed treatment in the recipient's hands (notably that such a recipient does not get a tax credit and does not have his dividend grossed up by reference to any tax credit) and reference will need to be made to any relevant Double Tax Treaty.[1]

No distribution is deductible from the profits of the company when they are being calculated for corporation tax and such distributions are not, *qua* distributions, chargeable to corporation tax.[2] In a way, therefore, company profits are charged to tax twice—once to corporation tax in the company, and then such part of the profits as are distributed are charged again to income tax although there is not now an element of complete double taxation because of the machinery of the tax credit, which means that the recipient of the dividend does get credit for some part of the tax paid by the company.

It is therefore very important to know what a distribution is. The most important category of distributions is that of dividends, which includes capital dividends.[3]

Any distributions made to shareholders in respect of their shares out of assets of the company are (subject to two very important exceptions considered below) taxable as distributions, as are payments made out of assets of the company,[4] to certain[5] security holders in respect of their securities.[6] This includes distributions of assets *in specie*. Accordingly payments of interest to holders of

---

19 Ibid, s 86(3).
20 Ibid, ss 88 to 90.
1 Ibid, ss 87(5), 86(1).
2 TA 1970, s 248(2), s 251(2).
3 Ibid, s 233(2)(a). A capital dividend from an English company although treated as income (see *IRC v Reid's Trustees* [1949] AC 361, [1949] 1 All ER 354), was not taxable before 1965 because the old s 184, ITA 1952 did not authorise deductions of tax from it, and there was no other charging provision. Capital dividends are now undoubtedly distributions and taxable as such.
4 TA 1970, s 233(2)(b).
5 Broadly, these securities are those which closely resemble, or which can be converted into shares.
6 TA 1970, s 233(2)(d). In order for payments which fall within this head to be distributions they must now generally be payments which represent more than a reasonable commercial return on the security in question; see FA 1982, s 60(2).

certain specified securities can be distributions.[7] If 'new consideration' is given to the company by the recipient of the distribution, then the amount of the new consideration given is deducted from the amount of the taxable distribution. Therefore if full value is given by the recipient there is no taxable distribution.[8] Consideration, to be new, must be given by the recipient. A company cannot use, even indirectly, undistributed profits or gains to pay for the distribution.[9]

If the company issues redeemable share capital,[10] or *any* security, that is a distribution[11] unless 'new consideration' as defined above is given for the issue. In particular, in this case, a company cannot by using undistributed profits or gains, provide new consideration.[12]

A company can make a bonus issue of irredeemable shares without that being a distribution.[13] Furthermore if a company makes a payment which is wholly or partly a repayment of share capital, or a repayment of the principal secured by a security, to the extent that it is so, it is not a distribution.[14]

If, however, a company first makes a repayment of share capital and subsequently issues bonus shares, that issue of bonus shares is treated as a distribution to the extent that the bonus shares are paid up by the company, but only so far as the amount paid up by the company on the bonus shares is not greater than the amount repaid on the share capital. To the extent, therefore, that bonus shares are issued to a value greater than the value of the share capital earlier repaid there is no distribution.[15]

If the repayment of share capital is a repayment of preference shares which were issued as fully paid prior to 6 April 1965,[16] or were, after that date, issued for new consideration,[17] the subsequent issue of bonus shares will not be a distribution.[18]

---

7 Ibid.
8 Ibid, s 233(2)(b), (c).
9 Ibid, s 237(1) and see FA 1972, Sch 22, para 8.
10 Companies Act 1985, s 159. Note that an unlimited company's shares are always redeemable, so that problems can arise under this head of distribution if an unlimited company makes a bonus issue of shares.
11 TA 1970, s 233(2)(c).
12 Ibid, s 237(1).
13 A bonus issue can only be paid-up out of a reserve fund which appears on the debit side of the accounts. After a bonus issue that fund is transferred to share capital, still on the debit side. There is, therefore, no distribution.
14 TA 1970, s 233(2)(b), (d).
15 Ibid, s 234(1).
16 Ibid, s 234(2)(a).
17 Ibid, s 234(2)(b).
18 Ibid, s 234(2).

Similarly, where a company issues bonus shares, and subsequently makes a repayment of capital, that repayment of capital is treated as a distribution to the extent that the amount of the repayment is not greater than the amount of the bonus issue.[19]

What these provisions achieved was a position in which, generally, the repayment of the share capital which was originally subscribed was not a distribution. Thus, if a man had subscribed £100 for 100 shares, those 100 shares could be repaid at £100 without there being a distribution. However, if those shares had become worth £1000, their repayment at £1000 would have involved a distribution of £900.

It was generally considered that this tax treatment could 'lock' shareholders into a company in such a way as to cause harm to a business and provisions have now been enacted to give relief from the charge to tax on distributions where a company repurchases its own shares (for example under the power given by s 162 of the Companies Act 1985).

The relieving provisions are, as usual, elaborate and closely circumscribed. In general, however, the repurchase by a company of its shares will not now involve a distribution if:

(1) the company is an unquoted trading company, or the holding company of a trading group,
(2) the repurchase is effected for the benefit of a trade; and
(3) the shareholder who is being bought out is resident in the United Kingdom, has owned his shares for five years, and substantially reduces his interest in the company.

In such cases, the repayment of share capital will not be a distribution even if it involves the repayment of more than the capital originally subscribed.[20]

It should, however, be borne in mind that, even though a repayment of share capital may not be a distribution, it will often involve the shareholder in a liability to capital gains tax.[1]

Overriding all those provisions which provide that certain payments made in respect of shares are to be distributions is one which provides that no distribution made in a winding up of a company to shareholders in respect of their shares is to be treated as a distribution for tax purposes.[2] One other fairly minor matter is treated as a

---

19 Ibid, s 235.
20 FA 1982, ss 53, 54 & Sch 9.
1 CGTA 1979, s 72.
2 TA 1970, s 233(1).

distribution. Where an asset or liability is transferred by a company to a member, or by a member to a company, such a transfer is treated as a distribution to the extent that any benefit to the member from that transfer exceeds any new consideration given by the member for the transfer.[3] That case covers, most obviously, a transfer of property by a company to a shareholder at an undervalue, the shareholder paying the under-value price. The difference between the true value and the price paid is a distribution.

It is also worth noting that in certain now fairly rare cases (the most common being the case in which a shareholder is given an option to take shares instead of a dividend, and the other case being the issue of bonus shares in respect of shares which carry a right to bonus shares), the issue of shares by a company otherwise than for new consideration may give rise to an income tax liability, even though the issue is not a distribution.[4]

FRANKED INVESTMENT INCOME

'Franked investment income' is that income of a company which is a distribution of another company paid to the first company.[5]

Franked investment income is not brought into the computation for corporation tax of the profits of the recipient.[6] The reason for this is that income is paid from profits of the payer company which have already borne corporation tax. To charge it to corporation tax in the hands of another company would be to charge it to the *same* tax twice.

The company has, however, in its hands, a distribution of another company which has borne, or is deemed to have borne, ACT. Since companies are not liable to pay corporation tax on dividends some relief ought, in principle, to be given to them against the payment of that tax, which has reduced their receipts. An individual who has suffered tax that he is not liable to pay may reclaim it, but a company is specifically prohibited from reclaiming the ACT suffered on a distribution received by it except in certain very limited circumstances.[7]

A company may obtain relief against tax suffered on franked investment income in one or all of three ways.

The first method—which has been briefly discussed previously—

---

3 Ibid, s 233(3).
4 F(No 2) A 1975, s 34.
5 FA 1972, s 88.
6 TA 1970, s 239.
7 FA 1972, s 86(3).

is that the company may set the ACT suffered on its receipts of franked investment income in one accounting period against its own distributions made in the same period.[8] A company doing this is said to 'frank' its own distributions.

The practical effect of these provisions is that the company may pay out as distributions the same amount as it has *actually* received as distributions, without incurring any liability to pay ACT. It may set tax paid against tax due to be paid. In theory this effect is achieved by the company 'grossing up' the distributions received by it, and then declaring a gross distribution itself. In so far as its own distribution is within the amount of the distribution received it does not have to pay ACT on that distribution.[9] If the amount of the company's gross distribution is greater than the amount of its gross receipts of franked investment income, it will, of course, have to pay ACT on the excess.

If a company has a gross amount of franked investment income for any one year, which is larger than the gross amount which it pays out by way of distribution, it may carry forward to subsequent years the amount of the excess of the franked investment income over its distributions and 'frank' future distributions with the excess.[10]

The second method is that a company may treat its trading income as increased by an amount equal to its current unused franked investment income. It may then set certain specified current year deductions[11] against the increase in its trading income. The tax credit in respect of the franked investment income so used is then repayable, but the amount of franked investment income so used is, of course, not available for any other form of relief.[12]

The third method is, broadly, that a company which has carried forward trading losses, or which has terminal trading losses may claim to set those losses off against such surplus amounts of franked investment income available to it as would have been treated as

---

8 FA 1972, ss 88 to 90.
9 Ibid, s 89.
10 Ibid, s 89(3).
11 TA 1970, s 254(2). The specified deductions are:
   (a) setting of trading losses against total profits under ibid, s 177(2);
   (b) of charges on income from total profits under ibid, s 248;
   (c) of expenses of management under ibid, ss 304, 306;
   (d) the setting of certain capital allowances against total profits under Capital Allowances Act 1968, s 74(3);
   (e) the setting of losses against income under FA 1981, s 36(2).
12 TA 1970, s 254(1).

trading income in its hands, had they not been received under deduction of tax.[13]

SET-OFF OF INCOME TAX AGAINST CORPORATION TAX

A company which receives payments under deduction of income tax (eg annual payments) has to gross those payments up and include the grossed-up amount in its return of total profits for corporation tax, but it may obtain relief from the income tax paid in one of two ways.

First, it may credit the income tax deducted against corporation tax payable by it on its profits,[14] or secondly, it may credit the income tax deducted against income tax which it is due to pay to the Revenue[15] (eg when it makes an annual payment).[16]

CLOSE COMPANIES

Very broadly, a close company is a United Kingdom resident company controlled by five or fewer 'participators' or by any number of directors who are participators.[17]

A 'participator' is a person who has or may obtain a share or interest in the capital or income of the company.[18] Obviously, a shareholder is a participator. Less obviously loan creditors, other than ordinary trade creditors, are participators.

In deciding whether a company is controlled by five or fewer participators, a participator and his 'associates' are treated as one person.[19] An 'associate' is a relative[20] or partner of the participator, or the trustee of any settlement created by the participator or a relative of his, or a person interested in any shares or obligations of the company subject to any trust or estate of which the participator and that person are both beneficiaries.[1] 'Control' of a company

---

13 TA 1970, s 255. The sort of income in question here is dividends and interest received by, for example, a dealer in shares.
14 Ibid, s 240(5).
15 FA 1972, Sch 20, para 5.
16 Under TA 1970, s 53 procedure.
17 Ibid, s 282(1).
18 Ibid, s 303(1).
19 Ibid, s 302(6).
20 A relative is a husband or wife, parent or remoter forbear, child or remoter issue or brother or sister: ibid, s 303(4).
1 Ibid, s 303(3), as amended by FA 1987.

means basically what it says—control[2]—but a person is treated as having control if he can acquire control, or the means of obtaining control although he does not already have it.

A company which has 35% or more of its shares quoted and dealt in on a recognised stock exchange and held by members of the public[3] is not a close company.[4]

It is most unlikely that any private company will be an 'open' company, although it is not impossible.

CONSEQUENCES OF CLOSE COMPANY STATUS

Until 1969 the most severe consequence of close company status was that directors' fees above a certain limit were not deductible from profits of a company brought into charge to corporation tax,[5] but these provisions have now been repealed,[6] and only the general restrictions may prevent the deduction of directors' fees from the profits of a close company.

There are now three main disadvantages to close company status.

The first is that benefits in kind, paid to or provided for a participator are treated and taxed as distributions, unless either they are provided for a director or employee who is chargeable to tax on them under the benefit in kind provisions of the Finance Act 1976 or unless the benefit is a pension or gratuity or similar benefit given to the spouse, children or dependants of an employee on his death or retirement.[7]

The second disadvantage is that, when a close company, other than a money-lending company, makes a loan to,[8] or leaves a debt (other than an ordinary trade debt) outstanding from,[9] a participator, the company is assessable to advance corporation tax on the amount of the loan or debt.[10] If the loan is repaid, or the debt paid off, the amount of tax paid on it is repayable.[11]

If such a loan or debt is subsequently written off by the company,

2 Ibid, s 302(2).
3 As defined in TA 1970, s 283(3).
4 Ibid, s 283.
5 FA 1965, s 74.
6 FA 1969, s 28.
7 TA 1970, s 284, esp sub-s (2).
8 Ibid, s 286(1). There are provisions which extend the cases in which a close company is treated as making a loan to a participator—see ibid, ss 286(7), 287A. These provisions were all enacted to stop tax avoidance schemes.
9 Ibid, s 286(2).
10 Ibid, s 286(1). Certain loans to directors or employees are exempted from this provision: ibid, s 286(3).
11 Ibid, s 286(5).

the recipient then becomes assessable to surtax on the grossed-up amount.[12]

The third and most important disadvantage is that a close company is encouraged to make distributions. If it does not, then its income (or a part thereof) is apportioned and it is assessed to ACT as if it had made a distribution, on the difference between the amount which it has actually distributed and the amount it ought to have distributed—called its relevant income.[13]

The relevant income that has to be distributed is part of a company's distributable income,[14] the part being dependent upon the type of company and the type of income.

A company's distributable income is the amount of its income on which corporation tax is paid less the amount of that tax plus the amount of franked investment income received by the company, which is not relieved from tax under TA 1970, ss 254, 255 and plus any group income received by the company.[15] Chargeable gains are not part of the distributable income.[16]

The distributable investment income of a company is its investment income reduced by £1,000 (£3,000 in the case of a trading company) or 10% of its estate or trading income whichever is the less.[17] Trading income is income from a trade. Estate income is income from land (which includes income from buildings).[18]

A trading company's relevant income is not to exceed its distributable investment income.[19] The relevant income of the company, including investment income, may be further reduced for a trading company if the company shows it could not distribute the full amount of its relevant income without prejudicing its current business,[20] and/or its future development.[1] If the company in

12 Ibid, s 287.
13 FA 1972, Sch 16, para 1.
14 Ibid, paras 8, 10(2).
15 Ibid, para 10(2).
16 Ibid.
17 Ibid, para 10(3).
18 Ibid, para 10(4).
19 Ibid, paras 8 and 9, as amended by FA 1980. The relevant income of a trading company may also be reduced when its estate or trading income is below certain specified amounts; see ibid, para 9(2), (3) (as amended). Similar rules apply to a company which is a member of a trading group.
20 Ibid, para 8.
1   Ibid. In some cases the purchase of a business or a controlling interest in a company may be treated as a matter which may reduce a trading company's relevant income—though in a lot of cases the purchase of the company's first business may still not be taken into account in determining the requirements of the company's business—see ibid, paras 8(3), (4), 5, 12, 12A. See also *Wilson and Garden Ltd v IRC* [1982] 3 All ER 219, [1982] STC 597.

question is an investment company its relevant income consists of all its distributable investment income plus 50% of its estate or trading income and it may only seek to reduce the part of its estate and trading income which forms part of its relevant income on the ground that to distribute that income would harm the business which produces the estate or trading income in question.[2] When a close company of any type ceases business, or a resolution is passed for the winding up of the company, it must distribute all its relevant income.[3]

A company may set any surplus of franked investment income available to it in the year in which it fails to distribute its relevant income against its liability to pay ACT on the shortfall, as it can if it actually makes a distribution.[4]

The corollary of the apportionment provisions is that the amount of the company's income which is apportioned is divided between the participators[5] in proportion to their interests in the company.[6] The participators are then charged to higher rate tax on the amounts so apportioned to them.[7]

Annual payments,[8] which would not have been deductible in computing an individual's total income, covenanted payments to charity[9] and payments of interest by investment companies (whose main income does not consist of interest from trading subsidiaries or estate income),[10] other than payments of interest on certain loans for the purchase and improvement of land or interests in certain types of companies or in partnerships,[11] are also to be apportioned amongst the participators.

Generally a company must have failed to distribute its relevant income before there can be an apportionment of its income but there may be an apportionment of the whole of the relevant income of a non-trading company, even though it has distributed all its relevant income.[12]

2 Ibid, para 8 (as amended by FA 1980).
3 FA 1972, Sch 16, para 13 (as amended by FA 1980).
4 Ibid, para 7 (as amended by FA 1980).
5 Ibid, para 1.
6 Ibid, para 4.
7 Ibid, para 5.
8 Ibid, para 3.
9 It should be noted that the apportionment of such payments does not generally give rise to any higher rate tax charge for individuals—see ibid, para 5(5A).
10 Ibid, para 3A.
11 Ibid, para 3A(3).
12 Ibid, para 2. This will apply primarily to companies which have *only* franked investment income.

There are elaborate provisions as to whom the income of a non-trading company may be apportioned where various devices have been placed between the company and the true participators.[13]

CAPITAL GAINS TAX

A company does not pay capital gains tax. It pays corporation tax on its chargeable gains. A company can, however, in the organisation of its affairs bring about a liability to capital gains tax in its shareholders. Similarly where a sole trader incorporates his business he can take advantage of provisions postponing a liability to capital gains tax.

TRANSFER OF BUSINESS TO A COMPANY

Where an individual transfers his business as a going concern, together with all its assets, other than cash, to a company, wholly or partly for shares in the company, he may deduct from the cost of the shares, which he purchased by the transfer of the assets, a proportion of the amount of the gains on the assets so transferred. When all the consideration he received for the business consists of shares he may deduct all the gains from the cost of his shares. Such gains are thus transferred to the shares and do not appear in taxable form until there is a disposal of those shares.

Such gains as are not deductible from the cost of the shares are immediately taxable in the transferor's hands.[14]

If not all the assets of the business are transferred there is an immediate liability to capital gains tax unless the relief given by the Capital Gains Tax Act 1979, s 126 applies. Broadly, this relief will apply where a business asset is transferred to a company which is controlled by the transferor for an actual consideration less than the cost of the asset. The liability to capital gains tax which will arise if the s 126 relief does not apply and not all the assets are transferred cannot be avoided by transferring the assets to the company at an undervalue, unless the sole trader gives up control of his business. A company and the person who controls it are 'connected persons' for capital gains.[15] Transactions between 'connected persons' are deemed to be at market value,[16] so the true value is substituted for

---

13 Ibid, para 4.
14 CGTA 1979, s 123. If there are no gains, but losses instead, such losses are allowable on this transaction, if not artificial.
15 CGTA 1979, s 63.
16 Ibid, ss 29A, 62.

the undervalue, and the market value is deducted from the cost of the shares. It is not, therefore, possible to reduce the gain on the assets, and the potential gain on the shares, by transferring the assets for less than market value. This is equally the case when business assets are transferred to an existing company by the person who has control of that company.

RE-ORGANISATION OF CAPITAL AND MERGERS

Very briefly if a company changes its share structure so that the original holders of shares own a greater number of and different types of shares after the re-organisation, that 'new holding' is treated as having cost the shareholder what his original shareholding cost him. The shareholder pays no capital gains tax or tax on the re-organisation, but when he disposes of the new holding he pays tax on the gain over the cost to him of his original holding.[17]

If companies amalgamate and part of the purchase consideration is an issue of shares or debentures of the purchasing company in exchange for shares or debentures of the acquired company, this is treated as a new holding and given the same base value to the shareholder as his original holding.[18]

Relief from capital gains tax is also given where companies carry out a reconstruction under the Companies Act 1985, s 582, so long as certain conditions are satisfied, the most important being that the company which is reconstructed does not receive any consideration in the course of the reconstruction except the take over of liabilities of its business.[19]

LIQUIDATIONS AND WINDING UP

If during a liquidation or winding up the company makes a distribution of assets, there are two consequences for capital gains tax, but usually no consequence for income tax.[20]

First, if the company distributes an asset in specie, it is treated as disposing of it at market value, and the shareholder is treated as acquiring it for the same value.[1]

---

17 CGTA 1979, ss 77 to 88. There are certain restrictions on the application of these reliefs in cases where a tax avoidance scheme has been carried out.
18 Ibid.
19 TA 1970, s 267.
20 Page 393, supra.
1 CGTA 1979, s 19(3)(a).

Secondly, when a company makes any distribution, including one of cash, the shareholder is treated as making a part disposal of his shares,[2] and his gain is computed accordingly.[3]

TRANSFER OF BUSINESS ON RETIREMENT

An individual who is a whole time working director of a family trading company is entitled to relief from capital gains tax on his disposal of shares in the company or in a holding company of that company,[4] if he is over 60 years of age when he makes the disposal.

If a company is to qualify as a family company, the individual must be able to exercise at least 25% of the voting rights, or his family must be able to exercise more than 50% of the voting rights, of which the individual must be able to exercise 5%.[5]

If on the disposal of his shares the individual has gains accruing to him, relief is given against these gains, but such relief may have to be reduced to prevent relief being given against non-chargeable assets, and assets not used in the trade, other than cash. This is done by multiplying the gain by a fraction, the numerator of which is the total value of the chargeable business assets plus the cash held by the company, and the denominator of which is the total value of the company's assets. The remainder of the gain is taxable on normal capital gains tax principles.[6]

A chargeable asset is an asset on which a capital gain chargeable to corporation tax arises or would arise on its disposal.[7]

The gain thus found may be reduced by up to £12,500 for each year that certain relevant qualifying conditions are fulfilled (basically that the company is the disposor's family company) up to a maximum of £125,000, and only the gain thus reduced is taxable. The £12,500 for each year is spread over each year day by day. Furthermore, in order for retirement relief to be available relevant conditions must have been fulfilled for at least one year.[9]

---

2 Ibid, s 12.
3 Ibid, s 35.
4 FA 1985, s 69 and Sch 20.
5 Ibid, Sch 20, para 1(2).
6 Ibid, para 7. See also paras 6, and 8 to 71.
7 Ibid.
8 Ibid, para 13, as amended by FA 1987.
9 FA 1985, s 69(5).

GROUPS[10]

The company tax system is designed so that it makes no difference whether the corporate structure of a business is unified or separated in subsidiaries. Three sets of provisions are designed to ensure that this is so.

GROUP INCOME

A company which is a member of a group[11] may pay and receive dividends (other than those treated as trading receipts) to and from other members of that group gross without ACT being payable[12] if both payer and payee concur. If the right to pay 'gross' is claimed, no ACT is paid by any of the companies until there is a distribution to a shareholder or to a person or a company outside the group.

GROUP RELIEF

Where companies are members of a group[13] and one company has a trading loss and another a profit (of whatever kind), it is possible to transfer the loss to the company with the profits and that company may use the loss as a set-off against its profits.[14] It is also possible to transfer certain capital allowances and management expenses from a company which cannot use those allowances, because of an insufficiency of profits, to a company which can use them.[15]

---

10 The various group reliefs are also available for members of consortia for receipts from a trading or holding company owned by the consortium. For these purposes such a company is owned by a consortium when three-quarters or more of its ordinary share capital is owned by UK resident companies none of which owns less than 5% of that capital: TA 1970, s 256(1)(b), s 256(6)(c), s 258(8).
11 For these purposes, a company is a member of a group if it is at least a 51% subsidiary of another. All companies which are 51% subsidiaries of the same company are within the group: TA 1970, s 256.
12 Ibid, ss 256, 257.
13 In order to be a member of a group for these purposes, a company must be at least a 75% subsidiary of another, and all other companies which are 75% subsidiary of the same company are (subject to the point next made in this note) within the group: TA 1970, s 258(5). However, again because many tax avoidance schemes took advantage of these provisions, a company will now only be a member of a group if it does not fall foul of an elaborate set of provisions contained in FA 1973, ss 28 to 32 and Sch 12 which is broadly designed to ensure that companies may only have the benefit of the group relief provisions when they are in every way members of a group.
14 Ibid, ss 258, 259, 260, 261, 262.
15 Ibid.

GROUPS OF COMPANIES AND CAPITAL GAINS TAX

It is provided that where companies are members of a group[16] they can transfer assets between themselves without incurring liability to capital gains tax. The acquiring company acquires the asset with the disposing company's base cost and no tax is payable until the asset is disposed of outside the group[17] or until a company within a group receives a trading asset of the transferor company and appropriates it to capital account (or vice-versa).[18]

INHERITANCE TAX

The inheritance tax legislation[19] is surprisingly silent about companies: and it is only necessary to make four points about this tax.

First, the gift of shares in a company by an individual may (if made within seven years of his death) attract a liability to inheritance tax, as will the ownership of shares by an individual at his death.[20]

Secondly, there are provisions designed to ensure that a shareholder cannot artificially devalue his shares by splitting them up between himself and his wife or charitable trusts or certain national or political bodies. In such cases, account is taken of the shares owned by the spouse or the trusts in valuing the tax payer's shares.[1]

Thirdly, in some cases business relief will be available when the size of the transfer of value resulting from a gift of shares or the death of a shareholder owning shares comes to be determined.[2]

Fourthly, a company is not itself directly liable to pay inheritance tax, but where a close company (or a company which would be close if resident here) makes a gift, the gift is apportioned amongst its participators who may themselves be treated as making the gift and become liable to inheritance tax accordingly.[3] If the participators

---

16 A company is a member of a group for these purposes if it is a 75% subsidiary of another. A company which is a member of a group as being a 75% subsidiary and has its own 75% subsidiaries brings those subsidiaries into the group with it: ibid, s 272.
17 Ibid, s 273.
18 Ibid, s 274. There are special provisions which apply when a company ceases to be a member of a group: ibid, ss 278, 278A.
19 Which is basically contained in IHTA 1984.
20 IHTA 1984, s 3A, 4.
1 Ibid, s 161.
2 Ibid, ss 103 et seq.
3 Ibid, ss 94 to 98.

fail to pay the tax it may be collected from the company.[4] There are also provisions designed to ensure that inheritance tax will be payable on any reduction in the value of shares caused by a variation of share rights and to ensure that transfers of assets within a group do not give rise to inheritance tax liabilities.[5]

FACTORS INFLUENCING THE DECISION WHETHER OR NOT TO INCORPORATE

In very many cases non-fiscal considerations will dictate incorporation. Large businesses need the flexibility that a corporate structure alone can provide—more flexible than a trust and with room for a larger number of participators than a partnership.[6] Limited liability is, undoubtedly, a large advantage which incorporation alone can give in a satisfactory form.

But very often commercial factors will not require incorporation. What, then, are the fiscal advantages or disadvantages of incorporation?

Most obviously a company pays a higher basic rate of tax than an individual—35% instead of 27%, subject, of course, to the relief for small companies described earlier. If a company makes distributions, the money distributed will, assuming that no small company relief is available, bear ACT and mainstream corporation tax of 35% and the recipient will be liable to higher rate tax on his dividend—and the combined rates of tax on the profits may well be higher than an individual would pay if he earned the profit directly.

However, in the case of trading or land owning companies which may be able to retain a part of their profits, and claim small company relief from the rate of corporation tax, it may very well be possible to accumulate income within the companies which may bear tax at rates lower than those which would have applied if the shareholders had received the income directly. It is, for example, quite possible that a company would only bear tax at 27% on income which, if received directly by the shareholders, would have borne tax at 60%. In such a case the company will be left with 73 out of every 100 that it receives and even allowing for the fact that 21.9 out of that 73 will be payable in capital gains tax if that money is ever distributed to the shareholders in a winding up, they may still be slightly better off than if they had received the profit directly.

---

4 Ibid, s 202.
5 Ibid, ss 97, 98.
6 Companies Act 1985, s 716.

It will be readily seen that it may well be advantageous to incorporate a trade or a land-owning business, so that the company will have trading or estate income. On the other hand investment companies are not so well treated.

An investment company has to distribute all its investment income, so that there can be no tax savings by retaining income in the company.

There is a further disadvantage in incorporating any business which has capital growth assets, though this will, of course, apply primarily to investment companies. Although a company pays tax on chargeable gains at about the same rate as an individual, the capital gain inherent in the company's assets will swell the value of the shares *pro tanto*, and that gain will be realised on the disposal of those shares, and will again bear tax, that time at 30%. Accordingly, the effective rate of capital gains tax on gains made by a company is, if the tax payable on an ultimate disposal of the shares is taken into account, around 51%, instead of the 30% which an individual pays on a gain which he makes.

There is only one major advantage to an investment company—the deductibility of management expenses which rank as earned income of the recipient. These are likely to be small.

From the capital gains tax point of view it is disadvantageous to have a capital growth asset in a company.

It is always important to weigh up, from the point of view of the individuals concerned, whether there is a tax advantage in incorporating a business. These days, with a general reduction in the rates of tax payable by individuals, there may, very often, not be any tax advantage in incorporating—and the decision to do so may need to be taken solely by reference to commercial factors.

Chapter 20

Company Reconstruction and Mergers

Economic factors may often determine that a company should alter the manner in which it is capitalised. Thus it may seek to reduce its share capital,[1] and by doing so make its accounts accord with reality. A reduction of capital may also enable a company to release profits for the payment of dividends and may be used to obtain taxation advantages.[2] Such a reduction affects only the rights and liabilities of the members, but a company may also alter its capitalisation more drastically by a scheme of arrangement,[3] which may affect the rights and liabilities of both members and creditors. Finally a company may seek to increase its size and obtain the advantages of economics of scale by taking over or merging with another company. Another advantage to be gained from merging with or taking over another company is the reduction of competition between like businesses.[4]

SCHEMES OF COMPROMISE OR ARRANGEMENT

A company[5] may enter into a scheme of compromise or arrangement with its creditors or a class of them, or its members or a class of them,[6] which may, with the sanction of the Court be made binding upon even dissentient members and creditors.

The word 'arrangement' in s 425(1) of the CA 1985 is interpreted widely and appears to extend to any scheme which affects the contractual relationship between the company and its creditors (or

---

1 Under CA 1985, ss 135–141 or ss 425–427.
2 Chap 17, ante.
3 CA 1985, ss 425–427.
4 But the policy of the law is against the creation of monopolies: see Fair Trading Act 1973, s 64ff.
5 For the purposes of CA 1985, s 425 a company is defined by s 425(6) as 'any company liable to be wound up under this Act'.
6 Ibid, s 425(1).

any class of them) or between the company and its members (or any class of them).[7] However, there are limits to what can be considered to be an 'arrangement' for these purposes. In the case of a commercial company the Court will refuse to sanction schemes which provide for the extinction of shareholders' rights without compensation. Confiscation is not an arrangement. 'A member whose rights are expropriated without any compensating advantage is not ... having his rights rearranged in any legitimate sense of that term.'[8] Whether the same principle should apply in the case of non-profit-making concerns is more questionable, but it has certainly been so applied.[9]

Furthermore, the wording of s 425(1) presupposes consent to the scheme by the company as a legal personality separate from its members. Accordingly if the company does not assent to the scheme, either through its board or by a resolution duly passed in general meeting, the Court cannot sanction the scheme under s 425.[10]

It is, of course, open to any company to come to practically any agreement with its creditors, if they all agree—the usual form being a moratorium whereby each creditor accepts a lesser sum than the amount of his debt.[11] Generally it will be to the advantage of the creditors to join in a moratorium so that these provisions are infrequently used where only creditors are involved.[12]

CA 1985, s 425 is mainly used to facilitate a merger between two companies, when it is to their mutual advantage to merge. There are three main ways in which mergers under these provisions may be carried out.

First, one company (the transferor company) may become a subsidiary of another (the transferee company). To do this the companies will propose a scheme whereby the transferor company cancels all its shares, the transferee company issues its shares to the

---

7 *Re Savoy Hotel Ltd* [1981] Ch 351, [1981] 3 All ER 646.
8 *Re National Farmers' Union Development Trust Ltd* [1972] 1 WLR 1548 at 1555 per Brightman J.
9 See [1972] ASCL at p 522.
10 *Re Savoy Hotel Ltd* (supra).
11 Section 425 applies also where the company is in liquidation, and where an administration order has been made in relation to it: s 425(1). A company has extra powers to compromise claims with creditors when in liquidation: see IA 1986, ss 165, 166, 167 and Sch 4, para 2. See also ibid, ss 1–7.
12 For an example of such a scheme see *Re Empire Mining Co* (1890) 44 ChD 402 where debentures were cancelled and ordinary shares issued in their place. Such a scheme would be unusual today because of taxation considerations.

shareholders of the transferor company, and the transferor company, using the reserves created by the original cancellation of capital pays up shares which it issues to the transferee company. The original shareholders of the transferor company have thus become shareholders in the transferee company and that company owns all the shares in the transferor company.[13]

Secondly, the transferor company may transfer its business or part of it to the transferee company and the transferee company can issue shares directly to the shareholders in the transferor company, which may, if it has no assets left, then be dissolved.[14]

Thirdly, two companies may transfer their businesses to a third company (which may be specially formed to take over the companies). Generally each company will cancel its shares, the third company will issue new shares to their shareholders and the original companies will issue new shares as fully paid up to the third company.[15]

This third method is the classic form of merger, the other two being much more like take-overs, but it may have taxation disadvantages for the shareholders.[16]

Although a company may reduce capital within the framework of a section 425 scheme, if it does so it must comply with the provisions of CA 1985, ss 135–141.[17] Furthermore, the Court has no power to approve a scheme which is *ultra vires* the company,[18] or which is contrary to the general law.[19]

It may be seen that, in substance, s 425 may be used to assist in a take-over of a company, where that company (or rather its directors) is not unwilling to be taken over and its directors are prepared to propose a scheme to its shareholders. In this situation s 425 may have several advantages over the usual take-over bid which is assisted by the provisions for compulsory purchase of dissentient members' shares in ss 428–430.[20]

A section 425 scheme needs the consent of three-quarters 'in

---

13 See Weinberg and Blank, *Take-overs and Amalgamations* (4th edn, 1979) paras 620–630.
14 See Weinberg and Blank, op cit, paras 642–647.
15 See Weinberg and Blank, op cit, paras 707–711.
16 It was for this reason that the proposed merger between GEC and EEC finally took the form of a take-over of the latter company by the former.
17 See *Re St James' Court Estate Ltd* [1944] Ch 6.
18 *Re Oceanic Steam Navigation Co* [1939] Ch 41, [1938] 3 All ER 740.
19 *Re St James' Court Estate Ltd* [1944] Ch 6. In that case it was the proposed conversion of issued shares into redeemable preference shares which was contrary to the general law as it then stood.
20 For the other advantages over ss 428–430 see Weinberg and Blank, op cit, paras 621–625.

410 Chapter 20 Company Reconstruction and Mergers

value of the creditors or class of creditors or members or class of members ... present and voting either in person or by proxy at the meeting' before the Court can, by sanctioning the scheme, make it binding on dissentient creditors and members.[1] There can be different classes within the same class; thus equity shareholders who form a minority, the majority being held by a part allied in interest to the proposers, form a separate class. The test for determining whether a group of shareholders constitute a class is whether they are united by an interest definable and different from other shareholders holding the same type of shares. In general, where a subsidiary is owned as to more than 50% of its shares by another company, it can be assumed to have a community of interest with the parent and one which, for the purposes of the section, is distinct from that of the shareholders.[2] If there is the necessary 75% vote the Court can sanction a scheme under this section even though it provides for the compulsory purchase of dissentients' shares, and even though, by contrast, the provisions of ss 428–430 require there to be a 90% vote in favour of a scheme within that section.[3]

Once a scheme has been proposed the procedure is for application to be made to the Court by the company or its liquidator (or, where an administration order is in force in relation to the company, by the liquidator or administrator) or any of its creditors or members. The Court may then order meetings of the creditors or classes of creditors, and of members or classes of members.[4] The Court has a discretion whether to order such meetings and may refuse to do so where, for example, the circumstances of the case show that the board of the company refuses its approval for the scheme, and is unlikely to reconsider the matter or approve the scheme, and the scheme makes no provision for the sanction of the general meeting.[5]

---

1 CA 1985, s 425(2).
2 *Re Hellenic and General Trust Ltd* [1975] 3 All ER 382, [1976] 1 WLR 123.
3 *Re National Bank* [1966] 1 All ER 1006, [1966] 1 WLR 819. But cf *British America Nickel Corpn v M J O'Brien* [1927] AC 369; *Re Hellenic and General Trust Ltd,* supra.
4 CA 1985, s 425(1). It is easy to tell different classes of members apart, but perhaps not so easy to distinguish between different classes of creditors. Plainly, secured and unsecured creditors belong to different classes, as do creditors whose rights have matured and creditors whose rights are still in futurity: *Sovereign Life Assurance Co v Dodd* [1892] 2 QB 573. It is for the applicant to decide whether creditors are of a different class: *Practice Note* [1934] WN 142. As to the pitfalls, see *Re Hellenic and General Trust Ltd* [1975] 3 All ER 382, [1976] 1 WLR 123.
5 *Re Savoy Hotel Ltd* [1981] Ch 351, [1981] 3 All ER 646.

Notices summoning the meetings ordered by the Court are then to be sent out to the creditors and members. Such notices must contain a statement explaining the scheme and 'in particular stating any material interests of the directors of the company' and of the trustees for the debenture holders,[6] 'whether as directors or as members or as creditors of the company or otherwise, and the effect thereon of the compromise or arrangement in so far as it is different from the effect on the like interests of other persons.'[7]

These requirements of disclosure are an important protection for the ordinary member and creditor, since they prevent the directors, who usually propose the scheme, from obtaining any secret advantage from its terms. Further the provisions of CA 1985, s 426 must be complied with, otherwise the scheme will not be approved.[8]

The meetings are then held and if there is the necessary majority of three-quarters in value of the creditors and members present and voting either in person or by proxy, the Court may approve the scheme.[9] The Court will, in deciding whether or not to approve a scheme, disregard the votes of a class of creditors or members who no longer have any financial interest in the company.[10]

A class of members or creditors which is not ordered to hold a meeting is not bound by the scheme.[11]

Even if the requisite majority of creditors and members approve of a scheme the Court is not bound to sanction it. The general attitude of the Courts was expressed in *Re English, Scottish and Australian Chartered Bank* by Lindley LJ:[12]

---

6 But only if the scheme affects the rights of debenture holders: CA 1985, s 426(4).
7 Ibid, s 426(2).
8 *City Property Investment Trusts Corpn Ltd*, 1951 SC 570, 1951 SLT 371; *Re Rankin and Blackmore Ltd*, 1950 SC 218, 1950 SLT 160; *Re Peter Scott & Co Ltd*, 1950 SC 507; *Re Coltness Iron Co Ltd*, 1951 SC 476, 1951 SLT 344; *Re Second Scottish Investment Trust Ltd*, 1962 SLT 392. If, after the circulation of the notice and statement under s 426, there is any material change in the director's interests, the members must be informed by a further circulation and in the absence of a further circulation the scheme will not be sanctioned unless the Court is persuaded that no reasonable shareholder would have altered his decision if there had been disclosure of the change: *Re Jessel Trust Ltd* [1985] BCLC 119; *Re Minster Assets plc* [1985] BCLC 200.
9 CA 1985, s 425(2).
10 *Re Tea Corpn Ltd* [1904] 1 Ch 12. In this case the dissentient votes of the ordinary shareholders were disregarded, because if the company's debts were to be paid there would be nothing left for the shareholders, so that they had no real financial interest in the company.
11 *Sovereign Life Assurance Co v Dodd* [1892] 2 QB 573.
12 [1893] 3 Ch 385 at 409.

> If the creditors are acting on sufficient information and with time to consider what they are about and are acting honestly, they are, I apprehend, much better judges of what is to their commercial advantage than the Court can be. I do not say it is conclusive because there might be some blot on a scheme which had passed that had been unobserved and which was pointed out later. If, however, there should be no such blot, then the Court ought to be slow to differ from (the creditors).

None the less, the Court will examine the scheme to ensure that it is:

> ... such that an intelligent and honest man, a member of the class concerned and acting in respect of his interest might reasonably approve.[13]

This does not mean that the member of the class is able to vote selfishly to promote his particular interests as a member of the class. The member is required to have regard to the interests of the class as a whole.

Thus in *Re Alabama, New Orleans, Texas and Pacific Junction Rly Co* Bowen LJ said:[14]

> I have no doubt at all that it would be improper for the Court to allow an arrangement to be forced on any class of creditors if the arrangement cannot reasonably be supposed by sensible business people to be for the benefit of that class as such.

In *Carruth v Imperial Chemical Industries Ltd*[15] Lord Maugham went so far as to say that:

> The Court will, in considering whether a scheme ought to be approved, disregard a majority vote in favour of it if it appears that the majority did not consider the matter with a view to the interests of the class to which they belong only.

Probably the clearest statement of principle is to be found in the judgment of the Privy Council in *British America Nickel Corpn v MJ O'Brien*.[16] In that case it was proposed to vary the rights of the debenture holders. The holder of a majority of the debentures was promised a block of shares in the company, but this was not apparent on the face of the scheme. Viscount Haldane said:[17]

---

13 *Re Dorman Long & Co* [1934] Ch 635 per Maugham J, p 657.
14 [1891] 1 Ch 213 at 243.
15 [1937] AC 707 at 769.
16 [1927] AC 369.
17 Ibid, pp 371, 372. See also *Re Holders Investment Trust Ltd* [1971] 2 All ER 289, [1971] 1 WLR 583.

The power to approve a scheme must be exercised for the purpose of benefiting the class as a whole and not merely individual members only. ... While usually a holder of shares or debentures may vote as his interest directs he is subject to the further principles that where his vote is conferred on him as a member of a class he must conform to the interest of the class itself when seeking to exercise the power conferred on him in his capacity of being a member.

This principle does not depend on misappropriation or fraud being proved. The duty is to look to the difficulties of the bondholders of a class and not to give any one of those bondholders a special personal advantage not forming part of the scheme to be voted for, in order to induce him to assent.[18]

The Court is astute to examine the voting and to look for evidence that the vote was not bona fide for the benefit of the class. In particular it will not permit, under the guise of a scheme of arrangement, what is in truth nothing other than an expropriation of the minority.[19] It is in this sense that the statement in *Re Hellenic and General Trusts Ltd*[20] that a shareholder is not obliged to vote against his best interests and in favour of those of the class is to be understood. The member's duty to have regard to the interests of others does not extend to requiring him to commit commercial suicide at the behest of a majority which is in truth endeavouring to perpetrate a scheme of expropriation.

The Court has refused to sanction schemes on grounds other than the general ground that the vote was not cast with a view to the benefit of the class as a whole. Thus the Court has refused to sanction schemes which did not provide for the costs of persons whose assistance was required in carrying out the scheme to be taxed in Court,[1] or which provided that, after the Court has ordered the class meetings those meetings should have power to approve the scheme without further reference to the Court.[2] Furthermore the

---

18 However, if the scheme openly provides for the person to vote selfishly then he may do so: *Goodfellow v Nelson Line (Liverpool) Ltd* [1912] 2 Ch 324. On the general principle see also: *Re Wedgwood Coal and Iron Co* (1877) 6 ChD 627; *Re New York Taxicab Co* [1913] 1 Ch 1, 9; *Re Consolidated South Rand Mines Deep Ltd* [1909] 1 Ch 491 (where the Court stopped the scheme and ordered the company to be compulsorily wound up); *Re Anglo-Continental Supply Co Ltd* [1922] 2 Ch 723.
19 *British America Nickel Corpn v M J O'Brien* [1927] AC 369 and see the cases referred to in note 17 above.
20 [1975] 3 All ER 382, [1975] 1 WLR 123.
1 *Re Mortgage Insurance Corpn* [1896] WN 4.
2 *Re Land Mortgage Bank of Florida* [1896] WN 48. Such a scheme is void as a delegation of the powers of the Court.

Court will not approve a scheme of compromise made by a company with its creditors if the effect is to prejudice a creditor whose rights would have been preferential in a winding up.[3]

An order of the Court sanctioning a scheme is of no effect until an office copy of the order has been registered with the Registrar of companies, and a copy of the order must be annexed to every copy of the memorandum issued after the order is made.[4] Once the Court has sanctioned the scheme, it may then make such ancillary orders as are necessary to secure that the reconstruction or amalgamation shall be fully and effectively carried out. These orders are made under CA 1985, s 427, which specifically provides for orders which:

(1) vest[5] the property, business and liabilities of the transferor company in the transferee company,
(2) provide for the allotment of shares and debentures,
(3) the continuation of any pending legal proceedings,
(4) the dissolution, without winding up, of any transferor company,
(5) the provision to be made for any persons who dissent from the scheme.[6]

The Court cannot, however, order the transfer of purely personal contracts from one company to another—the most obvious example of such contracts being contracts of service.[7]

Somewhat curiously the power to make orders under CA 1985, s 427 extends only to registered companies[8] although the power to approve schemes extends to all companies liable to be wound up under the Companies Acts.[9]

---

3   *Re Richards & Co* (1879) 11 Ch 676. In that case, a creditor had a judgment debt on which he could have levied execution. He did not do so on receiving a representation that the company would be wound up. Instead the company made a compromise with its creditors. It is thought that, apart from the misrepresentation, if the scheme were otherwise such as a sensible man of business would approve, the Court would give its sanction to the scheme. See also *Re Minster Assets plc* [1985] BCLC 200.
4   CA 1985, s 425(3).
5   Ibid, s 427(3).
6   Ibid, s 427(3)(e).
7   *Nokes v Doncaster Amalgamated Collieries Ltd* [1940] AC 1014, [1940] 3 All ER 549; *Re 'L' Hotel Co Ltd and Langham Hotel Co Ltd* [1946] 1 All ER 319; and see *Re Skinner* [1958] 3 All ER 273, [1958] 1 WLR 1043.
8   CA 1985, ss 427(6), 735(1).
9   Ibid, s 425(6).

RECONSTRUCTIONS IN A LIQUIDATION

It is possible for companies to merge or be taken over unhindered by any requirement that the Court must sanction the scheme.[10] A company may even be aided in carrying through its scheme by certain statutory provisions.[11] Of these IA 1986, ss 110–111 is the oldest.[12]

Under the provisions of these sections a company which is in a members' voluntary liquidation[13] may empower its liquidator by special resolution[14] to receive in compensation[15] for the transfer or sale of whole or part of its business or property to another company shares of that other company.[16]

The scheme may validly provide that the shares received as consideration for the sale are to be issued directly to the shareholders of the liquidating company,[17] or to its liquidator for subsequent distribution amongst the shareholders.[18] However, the scheme may only provide for the distribution of the shares amongst the shareholders in strict accordance with their rights to share in the assets in a winding up.[19]

A section 110 scheme does not require unanimity for approval; a three-quarters majority suffices.[20] Shareholders with one-quarter of the voting power may accordingly dissent from the scheme, and yet it may be approved and put into effect. To protect dissentients, who might otherwise be harshly treated by the scheme, it is enacted[1]

---

10 As under ibid, s 425 or, in a reduction of capital under ibid, ss 135–141.
11 Ibid, ss 428–430; IA 1986, ss 110–111.
12 Dating from the Companies Act 1862.
13 In a creditor's voluntary winding up the sanction of the liquidation committee or the Court must be obtained to the scheme: IA 1986, s 110(3)(b).
14 Such a resolution may validly be passed 'before or concurrently with a resolution for voluntary winding up or for appointing liquidators': ibid, s 110(6) but the special resolution must be sanctioned by the Court if it orders the company to be wound up within a year: ibid.
15 Or part compensation, ibid, s 110(1).
16 The liquidator may also be empowered to accept 'policies or other like interests' and to enter into profit-sharing agreements as consideration for the sale: ibid, s 110(2), (4).
17 *Re City and County Investment Co* (1879) 13 ChD 475.
18 CA 1985, s 110(2).
19 *Griffith v Paget* (1877) 5 ChD 894. As to the shareholders' rights in a winding up see Chap 21, post. One result of this decision is that preference shareholders may lose their right to preference when a s 110 scheme is proposed: *Griffith v Paget (No 2)* (1877) 6 ChD 511.
20 A section 110 scheme requires approval on a special resolution which requires a three-quarters majority to be passed: CA 1985, s 378.
1 Ibid, s 111(2).

that they might express their dissent to the liquidator[2] and require him either to abstain from carrying the scheme into effect or to purchase their interest at a price fixed by agreement[3] or by arbitration.[4]

The dissenting shareholders' position is not, however, a strong one. If they are unable to fix a price for the purchase of their interests by agreement they must go to arbitration, but they are unable, for that purpose, to examine the company's books,[5] or to examine the officers of the company.[6] If they wish to stop a scheme they can only do so by alleging either that it is *ultra vires* CA 1985, s 110[7] or by obtaining a compulsory winding up order if the scheme is manifestly unfair to them.[8] If such an order is made the effect is to prevent the scheme from going through unless it is sanctioned by the Court[9]—but this requirement gives the shareholders little added protection, for it seems that the Court will have regard to the wishes of the majority, and will not give the dissentients rights in addition to those which they have under s 110.[10] The dissentients[11] may also apply to the Court to stop the scheme under IA 1986, s 112, but it may be doubted if the Court would be willing to stop the scheme by making an order under that section if the scheme gives the dissentients all the protection to which they are entitled under s 110. The situation seems, in principle, to be no different from an application to sanction a scheme in a compulsory winding up.

---

2 Within seven days of the passing of the special resolution: ibid.
3 An agreement to be within the provisions of this section must be made between the shareholder and the liquidator (or possibly with the company in contemplation of a liquidation). It is not sufficient agreement if contained in the articles: *Baring Gould v Sharpington Combined Pick and Shovel Syndicate* [1899] 2 Ch 80.
4 Under the Companies Clauses Consolidation Act 1845 (see CA 1985, s 111(4)) and the Arbitration Act 1950, s 31.
5 *Re Glamorganshire Banking Co, Morgan's Case* (1884) 28 ChD 620.
6 Under IA 1986, ss 112 and 236: see *Re British Building Stone Co* [1908] 2 Ch 450.
7 Or *ultra vires* the company, since sometimes attempts were made to carry through what were, in effect, s 110 schemes under powers in the company's memorandum.
8 See *Re Consolidated South Rand Mines Deep Ltd* [1909] 1 Ch 491, esp p 499.
9 In a compulsory winding up the liquidator has power under IA 1986, s 167 and Sch 4, to propose a scheme which, but for the compulsory order, would be a s 110 scheme: see *Re Agra and Masterman's Bank* (1866) LR 12 Exch 56n.
10 Cf *Re Imperial Mercantile Credit Association* (1871) LR 12 Eq 504 esp p 515; *Re Cambrian Mining Co* (1882) 48 LT 114. These cases were both dealing with schemes proposed in winding up under supervision (a procedure since repealed)—but the principles are the same in a compulsory winding up.
11 The liquidator or any member of the company may apply to the Court to sanction the scheme under IA 1986, s 112.

Weak though the dissentients' statutory protection is, they cannot be deprived of it, whether the attempt to do so is made by providing in the articles that the shareholders cannot dissent from a section 110 scheme[12] or by including the sale of the company's whole undertaking and the division of the proceeds as an object in the memorandum.[13] The Court firmly struck down the then common attempts to deprive dissentients of their statutory protection by use of the memorandum in:

Bisgood v Henderson's Transvaal Estates [1908] 1 Ch 743.

The company had 1,770,386 fully paid-up shares of £1 each. It intended to wind up and sell its undertaking for shares to a new company. The new company was to issue a like number of £1 shares to be credited as only paid up to 17s 6d. The scheme provided that every member should accept one of the new shares for each one of the old shares owned by him. Any dissentients who did not take up the shares were, instead of having their interest in the company valued and purchased according to the terms of s 110, to receive the price received by the liquidator on a sale by him of the shares unapplied for. Held: the scheme was *ultra vires*. Buckley LJ said (at p 760):

It (s 110) is a section which enables the liquidator, instead of converting the assets into money, to exchange them for shares or like interests for the purposes of distribution among the members, but it safeguards the dissentient member by providing for the purchase of his interests at a price to be determined as mentioned in the Act.

And later he said:[14]

When the company is proposed to be wound up, or is in the course of being wound up (s 110) contains provisions which ... define rights in the members which cannot by any clauses in the memorandum and articles be excluded.

Other attempts were made to avoid the protective provisions of s 110 by framing schemes including clauses which provided that the shareholders must purchase shares in the new company and asking the Court to sanction it under CA 1985, s 425. The position in such cases was summarised by Astbury J in three propositions in *Re Anglo Continental Supply Co* [1922] 2 Ch 723, 734:

---

12 *Payne v Cork Co Ltd* [1900] 1 Ch 308. Such an article is *ultra vires*.
13 *Bisgood v Henderson's Transvaal Estates* [1908] 1 Ch 743, 761. Such a provision is not capable of being a corporate object.
14 Ibid, p 762.

418 *Chapter 20 Company Reconstruction and Mergers*

(1) When a so-called scheme is really and truly a sale etc under (s 110) *simpliciter* that section must be complied with and cannot be evaded by calling it a scheme of arrangement under (s 425).[15]
(2) Where a scheme cannot be carried through under (s 110) though it involves (inter alia) a sale to a company within that section . . . the Court can sanction it under (s 425) if it is fair and reasonable . . . and it may, but only if it thinks fit, insist as a term of its sanction, on the dissentient shareholders being protected in a manner similar to that provided for in (s 110).[16]
(3) Where a scheme of arrangement is one outside (s 110) entirely the Court can also and a fortiori act as in proposition 2, subject to the conditions therein mentioned.

The dissentient's protection comes to this: that he may not be put under any legal compulsion to participate in the scheme, or indeed to dissent from it.[17] If he neither approves not dissents he can obtain no consideration for his shares in the liquidating company and 'must lose them utterly'. Nor need the dissent or abstention of a great many of the shareholders necessarily be a hardship on the liquidating company for it may validly underwrite a section 110 scheme under CA 1985, ss 97–98.[18]

Furthermore a section 110 scheme may validly contain time limits within which application for the shares in the new company must be made.[19] Perhaps harshest of all, the consideration for the sale of the liquidating company's assets may be partly paid shares of the new company.[20] In effect, therefore, all the shareholders (but this is particularly unfair to dissentients) may be required to accept an increased liability, or must submit to having their interests purchased at valuation. In many cases a valuation, although done in accordance with the statutory provisions, may not accurately

---

15 It is not only that the Court will not sanction the scheme because it is unfair. It has no jurisdiction to give its sanction, *Re General Motor Cab Co Ltd* [1913] 1 Ch 377.
16 See *Re Sandwell Park Colliery Co Ltd* [1914] 1 Ch 589, and *Re Anglo-Continental Supply Co* itself.
17 *Re Bank of Hindustan, China and Japan Ltd, Higgs' Case* (1865) 2 Hem & M 657.
18 *Barrow v Paringa Mines (1909) Ltd* [1909] 2 Ch 658.
19 *Burdett-Coutts v True Blue (Hannan's) Gold Mine* [1899] 2 Ch 616; but if the Court is to sanction such a scheme it may require a modification to be in such a clause: ibid, p 623. If application is not made within the stipulated time the shareholder may not compel the new company to allot him shares.
20 *Mason v Motor Traction Co Ltd* [1905] 1 Ch 419; *Bisgood v Henderson's Transvaal Estates* [1908] 1 Ch 743, 760; note that the provisions relating to the valuation of non-cash assets in CA 1985, s 103(1) would not apply: ibid, s 103(3).

represent the true worth of the shares.[1] The shareholders cannot, however, be required to pay a premium for the shares in the new company,[2] but if they do pay a premium they cannot afterwards recover it.[3]

One further point on the position of the shareholders may be made. The section 110 scheme may validly provide for calls to be made, and the assets of the company including the amount called to be exchanged for shares,[4] but a provision that the assets of the company are to be sold in exchange for shares and that, if those assets are not of the expected value, calls will be made, is invalid.[5]

The creditors of the liquidating company may not interfere in a section 110 scheme. They must, of course, be paid their debts, for apart from the scheme, the liquidation must proceed as normal.[6] If the creditors are not paid they may obtain a compulsory winding up order.[7] If they do this within a year of the special resolution which passed the scheme, the scheme may not be put into effect without the sanction of the Court,[8] but this is their only remedy.[9] Further, it is only to the liquidating company that the creditors may look for payment of their debts, even if the new company gives the old company an indemnity, unless there is a novation[10] between the debtor, the liquidating company and the new company, or the liquidator misapplies the assets when they may claim against him personally.[11]

---

1 This will especially be so where a large part of the company's assets consists of goodwill, for, not only is that notoriously hard to value, but the valuation is done whilst the company is dying and its trade is being transferred.
2 *Imperial Bank of China, India and Japan v Bank of Hindustan, China and Japan* (1868) LR 6 Eq 91.
3 *Re Bank of Hindustan, China and Japan* (1873) 9 Ch App 1.
4 *New Zealand Gold Extraction Co (Newberry-Vautin Process) Ltd v Peacock* [1894] 1 QB 622.
5 *Clinch v Financial Corpn* (1868) 4 Ch App 117.
6 See Chap 21, post, for the normal procedure in a winding up.
7 IA 1986, ss 122, 123.
8 Ibid, s 110(6).
9 *Re City and County Investment Co* (1879) 13 ChD 475.
10 As to novations see: *Re Commercial Bank Corpn of India and the East* (1868) 18 LT 668; *Re Smith, Knight & Co, ex p Gibson* (1869) 4 Ch App 662; *Re Family Endowment Society* (1870) 5 Ch App 118; *Re Medical Invalid and General Life Assurance Society, Spencer's Case* (1871) 6 Ch App 362; *Re Medical Invalid and General Assurance Society, Griffith's Case* (1871) 6 Ch App 374; *Re International Life Assurance Society and Hercules Insurance Co, ex p Blood* (1870) LR 9 Eq 316; *Re Anchor Assurance Co* (1870) 5 Ch App 632.
11 *Pulsford v Devenish* [1903] 2 Ch 625.

420 Chapter 20 Company Reconstruction and Mergers

TAKE-OVER BIDS

Surrounded by commercial excitement and mystique, the most spectacular and the simplest method of obtaining control of a company is the take-over bid. Other methods[12] of merging companies require, at least, some measure of agreement from the boards of directors and the shareholders of the companies involved. The take-over bid requires the consent only of the shareholders in the company it is proposed to take over. It may, therefore, be used as the easiest way (because the least controlled) of merging companies where the boards and the shareholders are all agreed that the merger is to the mutual advantage of the companies involved, and the merger is of the simplest form, requiring no change of capital structure. Alternatively it may be used when a war situation exists—the one company desiring control, the other wishing to retain its independence. The one must then seek to woo the shareholders of the other to sell their shares, whilst the directors of the offeree company will seek to prevent the success of the offer.[13]

Stripped of its glamour, the take-over bid is nothing other than an offer to purchase the issued shares of a company made by another company.[14] The offer is usually stated to be open for acceptance for a fixed period[15] and made conditional upon acceptance by holders of a stated number of shares.[16] Once a shareholder has accepted, he is bound to sell his shares to the offeror, although the offeror is not bound to purchase the shares unless the conditions in the offer are fulfilled.[17]

---

12 See pp 407–414, supra.
13 As to directors' duties in a take-over situation see Chap 10, supra.
14 The offeror might be an individual, and an individual as well as a company can take advantage of the compulsory purchase provisions of CA 1985, s 429 as substituted by FSA 1986, Sch 12.
15 An offer ought to be kept open for acceptance for at least 21 days after the posting of the offer—see the City Code on Take-overs and Mergers (hereinafter referred to as the City Code) Rule 31. For other recommended time limits see rr 30–34. Where General Permission No 3 issued by the DTI under s 14(2) of the Prevention of Fraud (Investments) Act 1958 applies, the offer must remain open for 21 days: para 3(d).
16 The offer should, generally, be for all the shares of the company not already owned by the offeror, and should not be made conditional upon the offeror acquiring less than 50% of the shares. The City frowns upon offers not meeting these requirements: see the City Code, rr 9 and 10. Generally offers are made conditional upon acceptance by holders of 90% of the shares, since this allows the offeror to take advantage of the compulsory purchase provisions of CA 1985, ss 429–430F (post).
17 *Ridge Nominees Ltd v IRC* [1962] Ch 376, 382, 383.

The curious dichotomy between company, directors and shareholders might mean that the shareholders are in a weak position when evaluating the terms of an offer, for they are not always in possession of all the information about the company necessary to make a proper evaluation. Directors of a company which receives a take-over offer do, however, have a duty to act honestly towards their shareholders and not to mislead them.

Gething v Kilner [1972] 1 All ER 1166, [1972] 1 WLR 337.

The board of the target company agreed with that of the bidder to recommend an offer. Independent advice was sought which was that the offer was inadequate. None the less, the offer was communicated to shareholders, initially without reference to the adverse advice, later drawing attention to it but with a statement by the directors that they disagreed with it and recommended acceptance of the offer. An injunction was sought to restrain the offeror company from declaring the offer final. The injunction was refused on the facts. None the less, Brightman J stated that the directors of an offeree company have a duty towards their own shareholders to be honest and not to mislead them. A shareholder in an offeree company could be prejudiced if his fellow shareholders were misled into accepting an offer because the minority might be bound as a result by the compulsory purchase provisions of ss 428–430 of the CA. 'It seems to me that a minority could complain if they were being wrongfully subjected to that power of compulsory purchase as a result of breach of duty on the part of the board of the offeree company.'

Such legal and extra-legal controls as exist require that all relevant information should be given to the offeree company's shareholders.

The Department of Trade and Industry has issued a General Permission (No 3) under s 14(2) of the Prevention of Fraud (Investments) Act 1958 which applies to take-over offers where the terms are recommended by all of the directors of the offeree company.[18] Most offers are made through members of the Stock Exchange or through issuing houses, which are 'exempted' dealers[19] and do not have to comply with the permission which, for that reason and because it only applies in the case of agreed take-over offers, has little practical application.

---

18 The offer must be one for 'all the equity or preference share capital or all the debentures of a relevant company other than shares or debentures held by or on behalf of the offeror': General Permission 3, para 3.
19 As to who may apply for exemption see FSA 1986, ss 35, 42, 44.

The principal extra-legal control of take-over offers is that imposed by the City Code on Take-Overs and Mergers, which lays down standards of behaviour to be observed in matters relating to take-overs by those wishing to avail themselves of the facilities of UK securities markets. The Code,[20] which is administered by the Panel on Take-Overs and Mergers, contains a series of general principles and specific rules. It applies to all public companies, and to private companies which have filed a prospectus for the issue of equity share capital during the preceding 10 years.[1]

The principles are designed to secure that shareholders shall be 'given sufficient information and advice to enable them to reach a properly informed decision'[2] and that the directors of an offeree company should not do anything to frustrate a bona fide offer without the approval of a general meeting.[3] Naturally, the principles reject oppression[4] and require equal treatment of all shareholders.[5] A document or advertisement addressed to shareholders containing information from the offeror or board of the offeree must, as in the case of a prospectus 'be prepared with the highest standards of care and accuracy'.[6]

Shareholders are to be put into possession of all facts necessary to make an informed choice. Directors are required to advise shareholders according to their judgement as directors and without regard to personal or family interests. The board, whose recommendation may well carry decisive weight, must be prepared to explain its decisions, as between rival bids, to shareholders. Especial care is to be taken over profit forecasts.

Care is taken to ensure equal treatment of shareholders and to militate against insider dealing. The Rules are also directed against partial bids which might have the effect of locking in shareholders as a minority without effective recourse against controllers. Thus r 2 provides for absolute secrecy before the announcement of a bid and

---

20 April 1985 Revision: see *Palmers' Company Law* (28th edn) Vol III, para D–001. Take-over documents are also subject, in the case of a company listed on the Stock Exchange, to the requirements of the 'Admission of Securities to Listing' (The Yellow Book).
1 Or whose equity share capital dealings have been advertised in a newspaper regularly for a continuous six month period within those years: Introduction to City Code, paras 3 and 4.
2 City Code, General Principles, No 4; on the workings of the Code in general see B. Rider and E. Hew, 'The Role of the City Panel on Take-overs and Mergers in the Regulation of Insider Trading in Britain' (1978) 20 Mal LR 315.
3 City Code, General Principles, No 7.
4 Ibid, No 8.
5 Ibid, Nos 1 and 2.
6 Ibid, No 5. And see ibid, rr 23–27.

for the details of a proposed offer to be kept confidential. Rule 10 prohibits the making of an offer which would result in the offeror having voting control of the company unless it is on terms that it will be made unconditional only if the bidder acquires more than 50% of the votes attributable to equity share capital. Rule 36 provides that partial offers require the Panel's consent and that this consent will not normally be given where, as a result, the offeror would acquire over 30% but less than 100% of the voting capital of the company, if an offer for the whole of the equity share capital of the company has already been announced, or if the offeror or persons acting with it in concert have acquired selectively, or in significant numbers, shares in the offeree company during the 12 months preceding the application for consent. Rule 11 in effect requires that a bidder who buys more than 15% of a target company's shares for cash within a 12 month period prior to its commencement must either make an offer for cash or provide an alternative. The intent here is to stultify an avoidance technique which consisted of making an offer for shares in exchange for other securities, generally tainted with some unwanted aspect, and then purchasing shares which shareholders, unwilling to accept the offer, sold at reduced prices on the Stock Exchange. Rule 9 requires a cash or cash alternative offer to be made to other shareholders where a person acquires, over time, shares which carry 30% or more of the voting rights of the company, or where a person who controls 30% of the voting rights or more, but less than 50%, acquires, in any period of 12 months, additional shares increasing such percentage of voting rights by more than 2%. If during the offer period, the offeror company purchases shares in the market above the offer price, that higher price should be offered to all shareholders who had accepted that offer.

The Panel, in its introduction to the City Code, points out that the penalties which it can impose range from private reprimand or public censure, '... to further action designed to deprive the offender temporarily or permanently of his ability to enjoy the facilities of the securities markets.'[7] It may refer aspects of cases to the Department of Trade and Industry, the Stock Exchange, or other appropriate body. An Appeal Committee has also been set up which will hear appeals from persons against whom the Panel has

---

7 The 'further action' contemplated is reporting a licensed dealer to the DTI with a view to his licence being revoked and reporting a member of the Stock Exchange to the Council of the Stock Exchange, which can censure, suspend or expel a member. The result of revocation or expulsion is that the person involved can no longer practice in the field of take-overs and mergers.

recommended that disciplinary action should be taken. The major controls over take-over bids are thus extra-legal.

The Panel has stated that 'the City Code has not and does not seek to have the force of law'. That has now, however, prevented the courts from invoking the principles contained in it.

Dunford and Elliott Ltd v Johnson and Firth Brown Ltd [1977] 1 Lloyds Rep 505, CA.[8]

> Plaintiff, a steel firm, sustained severe losses and determined to raise capital by a rights issue. Its institutional shareholders who held 43% of the shares and who were acquainted with this and who feared that the public would not take up the offer formed a consortium to do so. The plaintiff gave certain financial information to the consortium in confidence. The directors had themselves used it when dealing in shares. The information was shown by them to the defendant whom they desired to join in the underwriting, but the plaintiffs were strongly opposed to the defendant's participation. The defendants declined to come in but instead announced that they were making a take-over offer to shareholders in the plaintiff company. The plaintiff claimed an injunction to enjoin the defendants from confidential information and to restrain the take-over bid due to be announced. The Court of Appeal held that an injunction should not have been issued. Their Lordships questioned whether confidential information which is not being made available to persons who are being invited to subscribe for shares should be given to underwriters. Lord Denning MR, invoking No 4 of the General Principles and r 19 questioned whether any substantial body of shareholders should be given confidential information which the others have not. In order for an injunction to be granted in respect of information it must have a quality of confidence about it, have been imparted in circumstances importing an obligation of confidence, and there must have been an unauthorised use of that information to the detriment of the party communicating it. Here the plaintiff's directors had made private use of the information. Its dissemination to the institutional shareholders, drove a hole in the blanket of confidence, a conclusion reinforced by the principles and rules of the City Code.

Very often the real intention of a take-over bid is to acquire complete control of an offeree company. If a small number of

---

8 Roskill LJ, in particular, also refers to a problem which arises with insider trading, that of the status and use of confidential information which for example financial institutions receive in more than one capacity. This case was not, however, akin to that of a merchant bank with two departments where it is desirable that one should not know what the other was doing. See also *R v Panel on Take-overs and Mergers* [1987] BCLC 104.

shareholders were not to accept the offer, they might successfully prevent the transaction even though the offer was accepted by the vast majority of shareholders. The Greene Committee (Cmnd 2657 of 1926) thought this was 'in effect an oppression of the majority by a minority'. Accordingly provisions were enacted to meet this situation by providing for the compulsory purchase of a minority shareholding, the present form of which are in CA 1985, ss 428–430F.[9]

The compulsory purchase provisions apply to a 'take-over offer' which is an offer to acquire all of the shares in a company[10] or all of a class of its shares (other than those held by the offeror or which he has contracted to buy[11]) where the terms of the offer are the same in relation to all the shares in which the offer relates or if the shares include shares of different classes in relation to the shares of each class.[12]

Where the take-over offer does not relate to shares of different classes, if the offeror[13] has acquired or contracted to acquire not less than nine-tenths in value of the shares to which the offer relates, he may give notice to the holder of any other such shares that he desires to acquire those shares.[14] Similar provisions apply in relation to each class of shares where the take-over offer is for shares of different classes.[15] The notice can only be given if the offeror acquires the necessary nine-tenths in value of the shares (or class of shares) within four months from the date of the offer and must be

9 As substituted by FSA 1986, Sch 12. References to these provisions are to the sections as substituted.
10 But only of a company registered under the Companies Act.
11 Or which are held by associates of the offeror: ibid, s 430E(1). 'Associate' includes nominees of the offeror, a holding company, subsidiary or fellow subsidiary of the offeror, a body corporate in which he has a substantial interest (as defined by ibid, s 430E(6)), any person who is (or is a nominee of) a party to an agreement with the offeror for the acquisition of the shares being an agreement mentioned in ibid, s 204(2)(a) or (if he is an individual) his spouse or any minor child or step-child of his: ibid, s 430E(4), (5) and (8).
12 CA 1985, s 428(1) and (5). The shares referred to are those allotted on the date of the offer but the offer can include those issued subsequently: ibid, s 428(2). Securities of the company convertible into shares are treated as shares for the purpose of these provisions: s 430F. A variation of the terms offered to shareholders is ignored if effectively required by the law of a country outside of the UK: ibid, s 428(3) and (4).
13 That is, the person making the offer, who may be a company or an individual: ibid, s 428(8). The offer may be made by two or more persons (ibid, s 430D(1)) in which case the rights and obligations of the 'offeror' are, in most cases, joint and several rights and obligations of the person making the offer: ibid, s 430D(2)–(7). See also ibid s 430E(2).
14 Ibid, s 429(1).
15 Ibid, s 429(2).

given within two months of his acquiring that proportion of the shares.[16]

A notice served under these provisions entitles and indeed requires the offeror to purchase the shares in respect of which the notice is given[17] subject to any application to court.[18] If the offer gives the holder of shares a choice of consideration—for example cash or shares—the person on whom the notice is served must be informed in the notice that he may select either choice within a period of six weeks or, if he does not, a specified consideration will be taken to be his choice.[19] The choice must be offered even if the time for making a choice under the offer has expired.[20]

At the end of the period of six weeks from the date of the offer, if the offeree has not accepted in the meantime, the offeror must send a copy of the notice to the company and pay or transfer the consideration for the shares to it.[1] Where the shares are registered, the notice must be accompanied by an instrument of transfer executed on behalf of the shareholder by a person appointed by the offeror, and when it receives the instrument the company must register the offeror as owner of the shares.[2] Any money or other consideration received by the company for the shares is held on trust for the former shareholder.[3]

There is also provision for a minority shareholder who has not accepted the offer to serve notice requiring the offeror to acquire his shares if before the period in which the offer can be accepted the

---

16 Ibid, s 429(3). The period of four months is a maximum period during which the event contemplated might occur and is not a fixed period during the whole of which the offer must remain open: *Re Western Manufacturing (Reading) Ltd* [1956] Ch 436, [1955] 3 All ER 733. The period runs from the date of the original offer and not from the date of an extension of the offer: *Musson v Howard Glasgow Associates Ltd* 1960 SC 371, 1961 SLT 87. A copy of the notice must be sent to the company together with a statutory declaration that the minimum share requirement has been met and there are criminal penalties for default: ibid, s 429(4)–(7). Note that acquisitions of shares otherwise than by acceptance of the offer are treated as acceptances of the offer if the consideration for which they are acquired does not exceed the offer price: ibid, s 429(8).
17 Ibid, s 430(1) and (2).
18 Ibid, s 430C(1). No order for costs may be made against the shareholder except in limited circumstances: ibid, s 430C(4).
19 Ibid, s 430(3).
20 Ibid, s 430(4).
1   Ibid, s 430(5).
2   Ibid, s 430(6). If the consideration is the allotment of shares, these must be allotted to the company: ibid, s 430(8).
3   Ibid, s 430(9). After 12 years, if after reasonable inquiry the former owner cannot be traced, or if the company is wound up, the money is paid into court: ibid, s 430(10)

offeror (and his associates[4]) has acquired shares or acceptances amounting to not less than nine-tenths in value of the shares in the company.[5] Similar provisions apply to any class of shares where the offer relates to any class or classes of shares.[6] The offeror must give notice to the shareholder of his rights in this regard within one month of the expiry of the offer period,[7] unless the offeror has already served notice under s 429.[8]

The shareholder's notice entitles and requires the offeror to acquire the shareholder's shares and in this case also the shareholder's choice of consideration is preserved if the offer gives the offeree shareholder a choice.[9] If the shareholder does serve a notice, the Court may, on any application by him or the offeror, order that the terms on which the shares are to be acquired are such as the Court thinks fit.[10]

Even if the offer has not been accepted to the extent necessary to entitle the offeror to give notice under s 429, the Court may authorise him to do so if:

(a) after reasonable inquiry he cannot trace one or more holders of the shares he seeks to acquire;
(b) the shares he has acquired or contracted to acquire together with the shares of the 'missing' shareholders amount to not less than nine-tenths in value of the shares to which the offer relates; and
(c) the consideration is fair and reasonable;

but the Court can only permit the offeror to do so if it is just and equitable to allow him to proceed under s 429 having particular regard to the shareholders who have been traced and not accepted the offer.[11]

As noted above, the Court has power, on an application by a dissentient, to order that the offeror shall not be entitled to exercise the statutory power of compulsory acquisition.[12]

---

4 Ibid, s 430E(3).
5 Ibid, s 430A(1).
6 Ibid, s 430A(2).
7 Ibid, s 430A(3) and (4). There are criminal penalties for default: ibid, s 430A(6) and (7).
8 Ibid, s 430A(5).
9 Ibid, s 430B.
10 Ibid, s 430C(3). The limitations on costs orders against the shareholder apply: ibid, s 430C(4).
11 Ibid, s 430C(5).
12 Ibid, s 430C(1).

The Court will only order otherwise where the scheme is unfair to the shareholders as a whole.[13] It is for the dissentients to show unfairness, and that is a heavy burden to discharge.[14]

In *Re Hoare & Co Ltd* (1933) 150 LT 374, Maugham J said:[15]

> Prima facie the Court ought to regard the scheme as a fair one inasmuch as it seems to be impossible to suppose that the Court, in the absence of very strong grounds, is to be entitled to set up its own view of the fairness of the scheme in opposition to so very large a majority of the shareholders who are concerned. Accordingly, without expressing a final opinion on the matter, because there may be special circumstances in special cases, I am unable to see that I have any right to order otherwise in such a case as I have before me unless it is affirmatively established that, notwithstanding the view of a very large majority of shareholders, the scheme is unfair.[16]

If the scheme is fair generally it cannot be attacked on the ground that a particular body of shareholders are put at a disadvantage.[17]

But subject to the provisions as to associates' shareholdings,[18] the shareholders who approve the scheme must be genuinely independent of the offeror. Thus in:

Re Bugle Press [1961] Ch 270, [1960] 3 All ER 791.

> Holders of 90% of the shares in a company incorporated a new company which made an offer for the shares of the first company. Needless to say, 90% of the shareholders accepted the offer and the new company served notice on the holder of the other 10% of the shares stating that it desired to purchase his shares.
>
> Held: In substance the new company was the same as the majority shareholders. Unless, therefore, good reasons in the interest of the company were shown making expropriation of the minority interest desirable the Court should not allow the compulsory purchase.

13 *Re Hoare & Co Ltd* (1933) 150 LT 374; *Re Press Caps Ltd* [1949] Ch 434, [1949] 1 All ER 1013; *Re Sussex Brick Co* [1961] Ch 289n, [1960] 1 All ER 722; *Re Grierson, Oldham and Adams Ltd* [1968] Ch 17, [1967] 3 All ER 192 and see Leigh (1967) 30 Mod LR 576.
14 The dissentient must show that 'he, being the only man in the regiment out of step, is the only man whose views ought to prevail': per Vaisey, J, *Re Sussex Brick Co* (supra).
15 Ibid, p 375.
16 The scheme must be 'obviously unfair, patently unfair, unfair to the meanest intelligence' before the Court will order otherwise: per Vaisey J, *Re Sussex Brick Co* [1961] Ch 289, [1960] 1 All ER 772.
17 *Re Grierson, Oldham and Adams Ltd* [1968] Ch 17, [1967] 1 All ER 192.
18 CA 1985, s 430E.

What the section is directed to is a case where there is a scheme or contract for the acquisition of a company, its amalgamation, re-organisation or the like, and where the offeror is independent of the shareholders in the transferor company, or at least independent of that part or fraction of them from which the 90% is to be derived.

It appears that expenses incurred by directors in resisting a take-over bid are incurred *intra vires* their powers provided that they are acting bona fide in the interests of the company's shareholders, both present and future.[19]

FINANCIAL ASSISTANCE IN SHARE ACQUISITIONS

In 1926 a company law committee reported that a practice had appeared which it considered to be highly improper:

A syndicate agrees to purchase from the existing shareholders sufficient shares to control a company, the purchase money is provided by a temporary loan from a bank for a day or two, the syndicate's nominees are appointed directors in place of the old board and immediately proceed to lend to the syndicate out of the company's funds (often without security) the money required to pay off the bank. Thus in effect the company provides money for the purchase of its own shares ... Such an arrangement appears to us to offend against the spirit if not the letter of the law which prohibits a company from trafficking in its own shares[20] and the practice is open to the gravest abuses.[1]

A later committee[2] reports that:

the cases in which the really scandalous malpractices have occurred have this feature in common, that an acquirer finds himself in control of a company with large liquid assets when he is under an obligation to pay for that control and has no respect of paying for it except out of the company's funds. The probable result is only too familiar: in one way or another the acquirer will use the company's funds to discharge his obligations and, when the facts are ultimately discovered the company's remedies against him will be worthless, either because he has disappeared, has disposed of his assets, or is insolvent, and minority shareholders and creditors will suffer accordingly.

19 *Peel v London and North Western Rly Co* [1907] 1 Ch 5 and cf *Morgan v Tate and Lyle* [1955] AC 21, [1954] 2 All ER 413.
20 But see 1962, Cmnd 1749, para 173.
1 Cmnd 2657, para 30. For a typical example of just this sort of thing being done see *Selangor United Rubber Estates Ltd v Cradock (No 3)* [1968] 2 All ER 1073, [1968] 1 WLR 1555.
2 Cmnd 1749 (1962) para 176.

CA 1985, ss 151–158 represent the most recent attempt to penalise only those modes and instances of giving financial assistance which lead to abuse.[3] They are undoubtedly complicated in character. The principal cases of honest transactions which the sections were drafted to validate were those, first, of setting the conditions under which financial institutions could safely lend where the schemes involved the giving of assistance by the company in connection with purchases of the company's shares, and secondly, and related to the above, schemes providing for the purchase, by managers in particular, of the interest of retiring controlling shareholders. It was thought particularly desirable to provide for this in the case of private companies, since managers often could not afford the full purchase price of the owners' interest themselves, and under existing legislation, banks and the ICFC were reluctant to lend for the purpose lest they engage in an illegal transaction with consequent risk to their security. The alternative to management purchase might be closure and that the government understandably sought to avoid.

The scheme provides for a basic prohibition against public companies giving financial assistance, but provides for a substantial relaxation in the case of private companies. Section 151 provides, subject to certain exempted cases in relation to public companies and to provisions in favour of private companies, that it shall not be lawful for a company or any of its subsidiaries to give financial assistance for the acquisition of its shares before or at the time such acquisition took place.[4] It is also unlawful for a company or its subsidiaries, directly or indirectly, to give financial assistance to reduce or discharge any liability incurred by a person in acquiring shares of the company.[5] A company is not prohibited, under these provisions, from giving financial assistance where its principal purpose is not to give assistance for the purpose of such acquisition, or the giving of assistance for that purpose is but an incidental part of some larger purpose of the company, and in either case the assistance is given in good faith in the interests of the company.[6] It is upon a defendant to prove these exceptions.

These are wide and obscure words; there is a danger that the section may be so interpreted as to conduce to abuse. Among the

---

3 On the former section, s 54 of the CA 1948, see Report of the Company Law Committee (Jenkins Report) 1962, Cmnd 1749, and on abuses associated with it, L. H. Leigh, *The Control of Commercial Fraud* (1982) pp 129–133.
4 CA 1985, s 151(1); 'financial assistance' is very widely defined in s 152(1).
5 Ibid, s 151(2).
6 Ibid, s 153(1), (2).

transactions which it would validate, however, not all of which are clearly proper, are the following:

> A is a director of company B. B sets up a pension scheme, by insurance, in favour of A, inter alia. The terms of the insurance scheme allow A to borrow on the security of the policy (or his expectation under the policy) for personal use. A buys shares in B with the loan proceeds. The loan to A will not reduce the net assets of B (although those net assets will presumably be reduced by the premiums on the whole scheme). Such an arrangement is presumably a 'larger purpose' than the aid to A and would be valid. If, however, it were used as part of a scheme to defraud B at the instance also of other directors of B and its controlling shareholder(s), it might well be impossible to get redress from anyone owing to the problems of proof which would arise.

> X Ltd, which owns 99% of the respective issued share capital of a number of other companies, agreed to sell the shares in those companies which it owns to Y Ltd. An incidental part of the agreement is that Y Ltd will allot 1000 shares in itself to X Ltd and the subscription price will be left outstanding. The deferment of the payment will constitute 'financial assistance' but, since it is part of a bona fide scheme in the interests of Y Ltd it would appear to fall within the exception of s 153(1).

The financial assistance provisions have to be interpreted in the light of ordinary commercial language, and so the commercial reality of each transaction must be examined to see whether or not it can properly be described as giving financial assistance. Receipt by a company of fair consideration—for example sale proceeds equivalent to the market value of an asset disposed of—may amount to financial assistance if the purpose is to put the company in funds to assist a share purchase.[7]

Section 153(3) contains a list of permitted transactions. Subsection 3(a) provides that any distribution of a company's assets by way of dividend lawfully made or any distribution made in the course of winding up cannot be attacked under s 151. The effect of this is to remove doubts about whether the payment of a dividend could amount to a forbidden assistance in the acquisition of shares.[8] Among the other permitted transactions are: the allotment of any bonus shares,[9] anything done pursuant to a court order in

---

7 *Charterhouse Investment Trust Ltd v Tempest Diesels Ltd* [1986] BCLC 1 (a case on CA 1948, s 54, but which appears equally applicable to CA 1985, s 151 as regards the general principles expressed).
8 See *Re Wellington Publishing Co Ltd* [1973] 1 NZLR 133 for a suggestion that this was possible under the old law.
9 CA 1985, s 153(3)(b).

connection with compromises or arrangements;[10] anything done under a binding arrangement between the company and its creditors under IA 1986, ss 1–7;[11] anything done under an arrangement pursuant to CA 1985, s 582;[12] any reduction of capital done under order of the court;[13] and a redemption or purchase of any shares made in accordance with ss 159–181 of CA 1985.[14]

Section 153 also specifies four categories of transactions which are permitted.[15] First, a company, part of whose ordinary business is the lending of money, may lend money in the ordinary course of its business. Secondly, a company may provide money for the acquisition of fully paid shares of the company in accordance with an employees' share scheme,[16] and thirdly, a company or any of its subsidiaries may give assistance for the purpose of enabling or facilitating transactions in shares in the company between and involving the acquisition of beneficial ownership of those shares by bona fide employees or former employees of that company or of another company in the same group or their spouses, widows or widowers or minor children or stepchildren.[17] Fourthly, money may be lent to employees, other than directors, to enable them to acquire shares in the company or its holding company. A public company may, however, only avail itself of the above permissions if the company has net assets which are not reduced as a result, or to the extent that those assets are reduced, if the financial assistance is provided out of distributable profits.[18] This is to ensure that the capital maintenance provisions of the CA 1985 are not subverted.

The above restrictions are relaxed in the case of private companies. In order that these may apply the company must be a private one, and if it is a member of a group or chain of companies, those others must also be private companies.[19] The giving of such assistance must be approved by special resolution of the company in general meeting, unless the company proposing to give the assistance is a wholly owned subsidiary.[20] In the latter case, a special

10   Ibid, s 153(3)(e).
11   Ibid, s 153(3)(g).
12   Ibid, s 153(3)(f).
13   Ibid, s 153(3)(c).
14   Ibid, s 153(3)(d).
15   Ibid, s 153(4) as amended by FSA 1986, s 196.
16   'Employees' share scheme' is defined in CA 1985, s 743, which also stipulates who may be beneficiaries under the scheme. Such a scheme need no longer involve trustees.
17   FSA 1986, s 196(1)–(3).
18   CA 1985, s 154.
19   Ibid, s 155(1) and (3).
20   Ibid, s 153(4).

resolution in general meeting must be passed by the holding company, and each intermediate holding company, except wholly owned subsidiaries.[1] The directors must make a statutory declaration giving particulars of the assistance to be provided, of the nature of the company's business, and of the person to whom assistance is to be given. It must also contain a declaration of future solvency.[2]

Shareholders or members of the company who did not consent to the resolution may apply to the court for an order cancelling it. Such a motion requires the support either of 10% of the company's members where the company is not limited by shares, or, where it is so limited, by the holders of at least 10% in nominal value of the company's issued share capital or any class thereof.[3] The application must be brought within 28 days of the passing of the resolution; the court may cancel or confirm the resolution, and may make such an order on any terms it sees fit, and it may adjourn proceedings in order that an arrangement may be reached for the purchase of the shares of dissentient members. The court may itself provide for the purchase by the company of the shares of any of its members, and for the reduction of the company's capital accordingly.

It is clear a transaction done in contravention of s 151 is void for illegality.[4] There is no reason to assume that the authorities under the former provision no longer apply, since the new sections contain the same basic prohibition, subject to wider exemptions and exceptions. The section was passed in order to protect the company against misuse of its assets by its controllers. The company is therefore not to be identified with the fault of its controllers, nor is it saddled with their knowledge when they act in breach of their duty to it.[5] It would follow that a security issued pursuant to an unlawful transaction will be invalid, even though it is given to an outside lender who is not aware of the unlawful character of the transaction.[6] However, a transaction which is collateral to a scheme

---

1 Ibid, s 153(5).
2 Ibid, ss 155(6) and 157; an auditors' report is required, s 156(4), and special time limits apply to the resolution in order to give an opportunity to dissentients to challenge it. See ss 157 and 158 for machinery.
3 Ibid, s 157(2).
4 *Belmont Finance Corpn Ltd v Williams Furniture Ltd* [1979] Ch 250, [1979] 1 All ER 118; *Selangor United Rubber Estates Ltd v Cradock (No 3)* [1968] 2 All ER 1073, [1968] 1 WLR 1555.
5 Ibid, and see also *Wallersteiner v Moir* [1974] 3 All ER 217, [1974] 1 WLR 991; *Steen v Law* [1964] AC 287, [1963] 3 All ER 770.
6 Cf *Victor Battery Co Ltd v Curry's Ltd* [1946] Ch 242, [1946] 1 All ER 519 which, however, depends upon the view that the company is not a statutory protégé and

which is in breach of s 151 is not avoided[7] nor is a whole agreement avoided because a part of it is in contravention of s 151[8]. It seems that a personal guarantee of a debt secured by a security rendered illegal by s 151 will be unenforceable, but that a contract of indemnity might be enforceable.[9] A guarantee only guarantees what is owed, and if the security is illegal, nothing is owed. A contract of indemnity is an insurance against loss.

Contravention of the section may impose civil liabilities upon guilty directors as well as a fine or imprisonment. It is not material that the directors were ignorant of the law. If they use their directorial powers to part with the company's assets in contravention of the section, they will be liable to make good any loss caused to the company by the breach, notwithstanding such ignorance.[10]

It is not only directors who may be liable for the consequences of a breach of the section. Action lies against an agent who assists his principal when that principal, being under fiduciary obligations towards the company, so conducts himself as to be liable to the company on the basis of constructive trust.[11] Liability under this head is most often imposed against lending institutions who have provided financial assistance for transactions forbidden by the section.

The mental element required for liability varies according to whether the defendant received funds, or assisted a fiduciary in the misapplication of funds. In the former case he is liable if he knew or ought to have known of the breach of trust.[12] In the latter he must have been fraudulent or at least have shut his eyes to the obvious.[13] Cases which suggest a strict rule of liability for negligence have been disapproved.[14]

In the United States the courts have gone some way to preventing serious losses to companies from the type of transaction intended to be prohibited by s 151 by holding controlling shareholders, who sell

    that the section was enacted exclusively for the protection of creditors, both of which propositions have since been disapproved. On the other hand, the proposition bears harshly upon the innocent lender.
7   *Spink (Bournemouth) Ltd v Spink* [1936] Ch 544, [1936] 1 All ER 597.
8   *South Western Mineral Water Co Ltd v Ashmore* [1967] 2 All ER 953, [1967] 1 WLR 1110.
9   *Heald v O'Connor* [1971] 2 All ER 1105, [1971] 1 WLR 497.
10 *Steen v Law* [1964] AC 287, [1963] 3 All ER 770.
11 *Selangor United Rubber Estates v Cradock (No 3)* [1968] 2 All ER 1073, [1968] 1 WLR 1555.
12 *Belmont Finance Corpn Ltd v Williams Furniture Ltd (No 2)* [1980] 1 All ER 393 at p 405 per Buckley J.
13 Ibid, at p 413 per Goff LJ.
14 Eg *Selangor United Rubber Estates v Cradock (No 3)* at footnote 11, supra.

control of the company to purchasers, whom they knew or ought to have known were going to use the company's assets to pay for the purchase, liable in damages for any loss resulting to the company from the sale of control.[15] It appears open to English courts to come to the same conclusion, at least where the controlling shareholder was a director and sold control in contemplation of the intended misfeasance by the new controllers.[16]

OTHER PROHIBITIONS ON SHARE DEALING

A company[17] cannot hold shares beneficially[18] in a company which is its holding company.[19] Any allotment of shares made by a holding company to its subsidiary is void. This provision was first introduced in 1948. Accordingly it is provided that if a subsidiary were a member of its holding company at the commencement of the 1948 Act it may continue as a member, but may not vote.[20]

This provision represents the philosophy that a company and its subsidiaries are in truth one, so that if a subsidiary could purchase shares in its holding company it would, in effect, be infringing the rule in CA 1985, s 143 against a company purchasing its own shares.[1]

COMPENSATION TO DIRECTORS FOR LOSS OF OFFICE

It is a not uncommon term of a take-over or merger transaction that the directors of the company which is being taken over should resign or retire.

There are provisions in the rules and regulations which control take-overs which provide for full disclosure of compensation payments being made to directors.

A company may not make a payment to a director in compensation for his loss of office or as consideration for his retirement

---

15 *Gerdes v Reynolds* 30 NY Supp 2d 755 (1941); *Insuranshares Corpn of Delaware v Northern Fiscal Corpn Ltd* 35 F Supp 22 (1940).
16 *Curtis's Furnishing Stores Ltd v Freedman* [1966] 1 WLR 1219 at 1224, and cf *Head v Gould* [1898] 2 Ch 250.
17 Or its nominee, CA 1985, s 23(3).
18 Ibid, s 23(4) and Sch 2.
19 Ibid, s 23(1). Broadly a holding company is one which has voting control of another, or can control the composition of that other board. A subsidiary company is one which is so controlled, ibid, ss 736, 744.
20 Ibid, s 23(2). The original provision was CA 1948, s 27.
1 It would seem that, because of CA 1985 s 23(3), the provisions of s 23 cannot be avoided by the trust device held legal in *Re Castiglione's Will Trusts* [1958] Ch 549, [1958] 1 All ER 480.

Chapter 20 Company Reconstruction and Mergers

from office without particulars being given to the members and the proposed payment being approved by the company.[2] Nor may such a payment be made to a director in connection with the transfer of the company's business and assets unless details of the payment have been disclosed to the members and approved by the company.[3] If such a payment is made to a director without the requisite disclosure and approval, he is deemed to hold the amount received in trust for the company.[4]

If it is one of the terms of a take-over offer to be effected by means of a purchase of shares[5] that a payment is to be made to a director as compensation for loss of office, or in consideration for his retirement from office, the director must take all reasonable steps to secure that particulars of the payment shall be given with the notice of offer sent to the shareholders.[6] If no such disclosure is made, or if the proposed payment is not approved by a meeting of shareholders, for whose shares the offer has been made,[7] before the transfer of their shares is effected, the director is deemed to hold any moneys received by him on account of the payment, in trust for the shareholders who sold their shares as a result of the offer.[8]

If in pursuance of any arrangement entered into as part of a take-over offer, or, within one year before, or within two years after a company has entered into a take-over transaction[9] a payment is made to a director, it shall be deemed to be one made in compensation for loss of office, so that he holds it on trust,[10] provided that

---

2 It seems that a payment of compensation made where there is no right to it under the director's contract of service or no breach of that contract is, in strict law, a gift. As to how far a company may validly make gifts see Chap 9, (supra), and cf the income tax case which allows such payments as deductions from profits: *Smith v Incorporated Council of Law Reporting* [1914] 3 KB 674.
3 CA 1985, s 313(1).
4 Ibid, s 313(2).
5 As defined in ibid, s 314(1). The definition includes an offer by an individual for only one-third of the voting power. A person can gain control if the directors are willing to resign and use their power to fill casual vacancies to appoint the individual's nominees to the board.
6 Ibid, s 314(1) and (2). If a director fails to take reasonable steps to secure disclosure he is guilty of a criminal offence, as is any person who, having been asked by the director to send out particulars of the proposed payment, fails to do so: ibid, s 314(3).
7 And of shareholders of the same class for whose shares no offer has been made: ibid, s 315(1)(b).
8 Ibid, s 315(1).
9 Whether the take-over is by purchase of the company's undertaking, or by purchase of its shares.
10 Either for the company, if the take-over is by purchase of the company's undertaking: CA 1985, s 313, or for the shareholders, if the take-over is by purchase of shares: ibid, s 315.

either the company or the offeror was privy to the arrangement.[11] Further, if a director who is to retire from office, or whose office is to be abolished, receives a higher price for his shares than the other shareholders could have obtained, or, indeed, receives any valuable consideration, the extra payment made to him is deemed to be paid as compensation for loss of office, so that, again he will hold it in trust.[12] However, a director is not deemed to hold any bona fide payment of damages for breach of contract or pension payments on trust and such payments do not have to be disclosed.[13]

The City Code requires disclosure of compensation payments to be made to directors, to be made in every take-over bid.[14]

These provisions protect shareholders against the directors of a company obtaining what are, in effect, secret profits in a take-over situation, under the guise of apparently lawful compensation payments. Such payments would not necessarily fall within the general equitable principles[15] which require directors to disgorge a secret profit, so that the statutory provisions are a necessary protection.

Sometimes a company, once it has taken over another company may wish to remove a director against his will, which it may do by ordinary resolution.[16] However, if the director has a contract with the company that provides that he shall be a director upon terms, none of which he has breached, his removal will be a breach of the contract and the company will be liable to him in damages.[17] A common question, then, is whether or not there is a contract, and, if there is, what its terms are.

It is now provided that a company must keep a copy of any directors' service contracts (if they are written) or a note of them (if they are not written) at an appropriate place,[18] unless within the next 12 months the company can terminate the contract on payment of compensation, or the contract requires the director to work mainly outside the United Kingdom.[19]

Mere appointment as a director does not import the existence of a contract of service. The clearest evidence that a contract exists is, of

---

11 Ibid, s 316(1), unless the director establishes the contrary.
12 Ibid, s 316(2), and see note 3 above.
13 Ibid, s 316(3).
14 City Code, Rule 25.
15 For a discussion of these principles see Chap 10, supra.
16 CA 1985, s 303.
17 The right to damages (if it exists) is expressly preserved by ibid, s 303(5); and see CA 1985, s 319.
18 CA 1985, s 318. Failure to comply with the section is an offence: s 318(8).
19 Ibid, s 318(5) and (11).

course, a written document setting out the terms of employment,[20] but a contract of service may be oral. In either case there is an express contract. If there is no such express contract the director will hold office on the terms set out in the articles.[1] The articles do not themselves form a contract between the company and the director *qua* director,[2] but 'from them you get the terms upon which the directors are serving'[3] unless there is evidence that these are not the terms.[4] The articles, then, are merely evidence of the terms upon which the parties are taken to contract. A problem which has often troubled the courts is the position of a managing director who, under a power in the articles, is appointed to hold that office for a fixed term.[5] The usual form of article provides that a director so appointed is not liable for re-election whilst he holds that office,[6] but his appointment is to terminate automatically if he ceases to be a director.[7] The question which arises is, if the company removes the director from office as a director, thus determining his appointment as managing director, before the fixed term has expired, is the company liable in damages for breach of contract.[8] It now seems clear that in such a case the company will be liable in damages[9] for the company impliedly contracts that it will 'do nothing of (its) own motion to put an end to that state of circumstances' (ie the continuance in office as a director of the managing director) 'under

---

20 By the Employment Protection (Consolidation) Act 1978 an employee (ie a person who has entered into or works under a contract with an employer) must be given a written contract of service. It seems every director who has a contract of service will be within this definition. As to when a director is generally an employee see *Lee v Lee's Air Farming Ltd* [1961] AC 12, [1960] 3 All ER 420.
1 See Table A especially arts 73–80 and generally arts 64–98.
2 Although they do between company and member *Hickman v Kent or Romney Marsh Sheep-Breeders' Association* [1915] 1 Ch 881.
3 *Swabey v Port Darwin Gold Mining Co* (1889) 1 Meg 385, and see also *Re City Equitable Fire Insurance Co* [1925] 1 Ch 407, 520; *Re T N Farrer Ltd* [1937] Ch 352, [1937] 2 All ER 505; *Re International Cable Co Ltd, ex p Official Liquidator* (1892) 66 LT 253; *Re Anglo-Austrian Printing and Publishing Union, Isaacs Case* [1892] 2 Ch 158; *Re New British Iron Co, ex p Beckwith* [1898] 1 Ch 324.
4 *Re T N Farrer Ltd* supra at 358.
5 See Table A, art 72.
6 An ordinary director is subject to retirement by rotation. Table A, arts 73–80.
7 As to when a director may be removed, see CA 1985, s 303 and Table A, art 81.
8 If the terms of art 81 are included in the managing director's contract, then, of course, he may be removed, without any breach of contract, in accordance with those terms.
9 *Southern Foundries (1926) Ltd v Shirlaw* [1940] AC 701, [1940] 2 All ER 445; *Shindler v Northern Raincoat Co Ltd* [1960] 2 All ER 239, [1960] 1 WLR 1038.

which alone the agreement can be operative'.[10] It should be noted in this context that a managing director will not be able to obtain an injunction to prevent a company altering its articles, although such an alteration may be a breach of his contract.[11] His remedy sounds only in damages.

TAXATION, RECONSTRUCTIONS, MERGERS AND TAKE-OVERS

Only infrequently will taxation considerations influence the decision to merge with or take over another company.[12] They may, however, be the sole reason for a reduction and repayment of share capital and simultaneous offer of debenture stock, for whilst dividends are a distribution[13] for income tax purposes and may not be deducted from profits,[14] debenture interest is an allowable deduction.[15]

Once a decision has been made commercial sense dictates that taxation considerations must influence the mode of take-over or merger;[16] and, especially the form of consideration for the acquisition of the company or its business. If the shareholders are investors (who would be liable for capital gains tax on a disposal of their shares), it will be better for the considerations paid to them to be

---

10 *Southern Foundries (1926) Ltd v Shirlaw* (supra) per Lord Atkin at p 717. The argument that the managing director's contract must include the term that it may be determined on the removal of the director from office, despite the fact that is for a fixed term, because that is what art 72 provides was accepted by Harman J in *Read v Astoria Garage (Streatham) Ltd* [1952] 2 All ER 292. He explained *Southern Foundries (1926) Ltd v Shirlaw* by saying that all it decided was that the company cannot take a power to remove its directors without being in breach of contract, by altering its articles, for in *Shirlaw* the articles were changed to give a power of removal. But see *Read v Astoria Garage (Streatham) Ltd* [1952] Ch 637, [1952] 2 All ER 292, CA where the case was decided on the ground that the contract was not for a fixed period anyway. The argument, accepted by Harman J, was expressly rejected by Diplock J in *Shindler v Northern Raincoat Co Ltd* [1960] 2 All ER 239, [1960] 1 WLR 1038.
11 *Southern Foundries (1926) Ltd v Shirlaw* (supra) esp per Lord Porter at pp 740–741. But see *British Murac Syndicate Ltd v Alperton Rubber Co Ltd* [1915] 2 Ch 186 where it was held that a company had no power to alter its articles for the purpose of committing a breach of contract; and see Chap 7, supra.
12 But see the comments on loss companies Chap 19, supra.
13 TA 1970, s 233(2)(a). A repayment of share capital is not a distribution: ibid, s 233(2)(b). As to distribution generally, see Chap 19, supra.
14 TA 1970, ss 248(2), 251(2).
15 Ibid, s 248(1).
16 Ie whether the take-over should be effected by a purchase of shares or of assets.

shares in the acquiring company, for they then obtain capital gains tax advantages.[17] If, however, the shareholders are trading in shares, they will be liable to income tax or corporation tax on any gain they obtain from the exchange of their shares, even though they do not immediately realise the gain.[18]

If at all possible, every scheme of reconstruction and merger should be so organised that it is possible to take advantage of the stamp duty relief which is available. Stamp duty is not chargeable where one company transfers the whole of its issued share capital to the acquiring company, provided that certain conditions are satisfied.[19] These are:

(1) the registered office of the acquiring company is in the UK;
(2) the transfer is part of an 'arrangement' by which the acquiring company acquires the whole of the other company's issued share capital;
(3) the acquisition is for bona fide commercial and not tax-saving reasons;
(4) the consideration for the issue is shares in the acquiring company;
(5) after the acquisition, each person who was a shareholder of the transferring company immediately before the acquisition is a shareholder in the acquiring company;
(6) after the acquisition, the shares in the acquiring company are of the same class as were the shares in the transferring company before the acquisition;
(7) after the acquisition, the number of shares of any class in the acquiring company bears to all the shares in that company the same proportion as the number of shares of that class in the transferring company bore to all the shares in that company before the acquisition was made; and
(8) after the acquisition, the proportion of any shares of any class in the acquiring company held by any particular shareholder is the same as the proportion of shares of that class held by him immediately before the acquisition was made.

Otherwise stamp duty is payable.[1]

---

17 See Chap 19, supra.
18 *Westminster Bank Ltd v Osler* [1933] AC 139.
19 FA 1986, s 77.
20 Ibid, s 77(3)(a)–(h).
 1 Stamp Act 1891, Sch 1; FA 1963, s 55; FA 1986, s 64(1) and (3).

Chapter 21

Winding up and Administration Orders

GENERAL

A company cannot die, but it can cease to exist by being dissolved and struck off the register of companies.[1] During the process leading up to dissolution, which is called winding up or liquidation, the company still exists.[2]

There are many and diverse reasons for a company to be wound up. For example, a company may have become insolvent, when the creditors, or the company itself, may seek to minimise the loss by closing down the business and selling all its assets. Or the company may be profitable, but taxation considerations might make it advantageous to the shareholders for the business to be run as a partnership.

A company may be wound up in one of two ways,[3] either:

(1) by the Court, or
(2) voluntarily (either by the members or by the creditors).

WINDING UP BY THE COURT

A company may be wound up by the Court[4] if:

(1) the company has by special resolution resolved that the company be wound up by the Court;

---

1 IA 1986, ss 201–205.
2 The continued existence of the company has some effect, eg a liquidator making a contract does so on behalf of the company. *Re Anglo-Moravian Hungarian Function Rly Co* (1875) 1 ChD 130.
3 IA 1986, s 73.
4 The Court means the High Court, or in certain cases where the Company's paid-up share capital does not exceed £120,000, the County Court: IA 1986, s 117. The County Court procedure is rarely used in practice.

442 Chapter 21 Winding up and Administration Orders

(2) the company was originally registered as a public company but has not been issued with a certificate under CA 1985, s 117, that it satisfies the minimum capital requirement, and more than a year has passed since its registration;

(3) it is an old public company within the meaning of Companies Consolidation (Consequential Provisions) Act 1985, s 1;

(4) the company does not commence its business within a year from its incorporation, or suspends its business for a whole year;

(5) the number of members is reduced below two;

(6) the company is unable to pay its debts;[5]

(7) the Court is of opinion that it is just and equitable that the company should be wound up.[6]

The Court does not choose to wind up a company of its own motion. It has to be petitioned. A petition may be presented by the company, or the directors, by any creditor (including any contingent or prospective creditor), by any contributory,[7] by a supervisor of a voluntary arrangement[8] or in some circumstances by a receiver. The

---

5 As to when a company is unable to pay its debts, see IA 1986, s 123 and *Cornhill Insurance plc v Improvement Services Ltd* [1986] 1 WLR 114, [1986] BCLC 26 and *Re a Company* [1986] BCLC 261. The winding up procedure is inappropriate where the debt is bona fide disputed by the company: *Stonegate Securities Ltd v Gregory* [1980] Ch 576, [1980] 1 All ER 241; *Re Claybridge Shipping Co, SA* [1981] Com LR 107, CA; *Re a Company* [1984] 3 All ER 78, [1984] 1 WLR 1090; *Re a Company* [1985] BCLC 37; and also where the debt is unascertained, has not been demanded and no opportunity for repayment has been given: *Re a Company* [1983] BCLC 492 (which also makes it clear that the creditor's motive is irrelevant if the petition is genuinely for the benefit of creditors as a class).

6 IA 1986, s 122(1). Special types of companies may be wound up under other provisions:
   The Bank of England can petition for the winding up of recognised banks and 'licensed institutions': Banking Act 1979, ss 18 and 50.
   Insurance companies may be wound up under the provisions of the Insurance Companies Act 1982, ss 53–59.

7 IA 1986, s 124. The term 'contributory' is considered below. A contributory may only petition if the number of members has fallen below two, or if his shares (or some of them) were originally allotted to him, or have been held by him for six out of the last 18 months before winding up (see *Re Gattopardo* [1969] 2 All ER 344, [1969] 1 WLR 619, CA) or if his shares have devolved on him because of a death. Ibid, s 124(2). A person who is a contributory solely under IA 1986, s 76, can only petition on grounds (6) and (7), but IA 1986, s 124(2) does not apply to him: ibid, s 124(3). A person whose name appears in the register of members has prima facie *locus standi* to present a petition: *Re Garage Door Associates Ltd* [1984] 1 All ER 434, [1984] 1 WLR 35; but see *Re Bambi Restaurants Ltd* [1965] 2 All ER 79, [1965] 1 WLR 750.

8 IA 1986, s 7(4)(b).

board of directors may present a petition on behalf of the company provided that their action is either authorised or ratified by a general meeting. The board can of course present such a petition if a special resolution to that effect has already been passed.[9] The practice of directors presenting a petition without the authority of shareholders is wrong.[10] An administrative receiver is not, as we have seen, appointed to wind up a company. None the less, he may have authority to present a petition depending on the memorandum and articles of the company and the powers conferred in the debenture. Where a winding up order will protect assets in the administrative receiver's hands from dissipation, he may be competent to present a petition which the Court will have a discretionary power to grant.[11] An allottee of shares has standing to present a petition even though he or she is not on the register; whereas a person claiming to be a shareholder must be shown on the register if he is not the original allottee, or if the shares have not devolved upon him by the death of a former holder, the law does not require registration in these latter cases.[12] A creditor or contributory may petition for a compulsory winding up, even though the company is already in voluntary liquidation, but the Court must be satisfied in the case of a contributory's application that the rights of the contributories will be prejudiced by a voluntary winding up.[13]

The Department of Trade and Industry may, in certain circumstances, petition for a winding up.[14] The Official Receiver is also

9 Ibid, s 122(1)(a).
10 *Re Emmadart Ltd* [1979] Ch 540, [1979] 1 All ER 599; an authority could be given by the shareholders even if no formal meeting is held: see Table A, reg 53.
11 Ibid, *Re Emmadart Ltd,* supra.
12 *Re JN2 Ltd* [1977] 3 All ER 1104, [1978] 1 WLR 183.
13 IA 1986, s 116, and see *Re Lowestoft Traffic Services Ltd* [1986] BCLC 81 and see *Re Palmer Marine Surveys Ltd* [1986] 1 WLR 573, [1986] BCLC 106. The liquidator in the voluntary winding up may give evidence at the hearing to assist the Court but must remain neutral towards the application: *Re Medisco Equipment Ltd* [1983] BCLC 305. As to the case where the company resolves to go into voluntary liquidation after the presentation of a petition for compulsory winding up, see *Re Surplus Properties (Huddersfield) Ltd* [1984] BCLC 89.
14 IA 1986, s 124(4) which refers to CA 1985, s 440 (referring in its turn to CA 1985, ss 437, 447 and 448 and FSA 1986, ss 94 and 105; see ibid, s 198) and ibid, s 72(1). The circumstances broadly are fraud or illegality in the running of the company's business or in its formation, or by its managers, or that it is run in a manner oppressive to any part of its members, or where it is just and equitable to wind it up or (in the case of s 72 of FSA 1986) the petition may be presented on the grounds of inability to pay debts. See also *Re Travel and Holiday Clubs Ltd* [1967] 2 All ER 606, [1967] 1 WLR 711; *Re SBA Properties Ltd* [1967] 2 All ER 615, [1967] 1 WLR 799; *Re ABC Coupler and Engineering Co Ltd* (No 2) [1962] 3 All ER 68, [1962] 1 WLR 1236; *Re Allied Produce Co Ltd* [1967] 3 All ER 399n, [1967] 1 WLR 1469.

empowered to petition for a winding up by the Court where a company is being wound up voluntarily or subject to the supervision of the Court.[15]

Every petition for winding up must be advertised not less than seven business days after service on the company and not less than seven business days before the day appointed for the hearing.[16]

The Court is permitted to wind up a company, but it does not, in every case, have to order a winding up. Different considerations apply depending upon who brings the petition, and the ground upon which it is brought.

A member's petition to wind up a company will only succeed if he is able to show that prima facie he has a tangible interest in a winding up. Whether he has such an interest is to be determined in relation to the size of his shareholding; the fact that his is a small minority shareholding does not deprive him of standing to bring a petition. Nor, provided that he has sufficient grounds, are his motives for bringing a petition relevant.[17] The notion of tangible interest includes but is not restricted to the case where there will be a surplus of assets available for distribution among shareholders after the creditors have been paid. The potential liability of a shareholder can constitute an interest for the purpose. The petitioner must show that he would derive some advantage or avoid or minimise some disadvantage which would accrue to him by virtue of his membership. An individual whose interest is in killing off the company of which he is a member for the sake of a competing business in which he has an interest would thus not disclose a

---

15 IA 1986, s 124(5). Under this provision, the Court is empowered to order winding up if the condition in s 124(5), ie that the voluntary winding up cannot be continued with due regard to the interest of the creditors, is satisfied, even if there is no other ground for making an order: *Re J Russell Electronics* [1968] 2 All ER 559, [1968] 1 WLR 1252.

16 Insolvency Rules 1986 (SI 1986/1925), r 4.11(2). If the petitioner is the company, the petition only has to be advertised not less than seven business days before the hearing. As to 'business day' see ibid, r 13.13(1). Different rules apply in the case of a contributories' petition: ibid, r 4.22. Where the petition is advertised prematurely, the petitioner may be held liable to pay the company's costs: *Re Signland Ltd* [1982] 2 All ER 609. Advertisement or publicising the petition prematurely may be restrained by injunction: *Re a Company* [1986] BCLC 127. As to the form of petitions see forms 4.2 and 4.414 of the Insolvency Rules 1986.

17 *Bryanston Finance Ltd v de Vries* (No 2) [1976] Ch 63, [1976] 1 All ER 25 dist *Charles Forte Investments Ltd v Amanda* [1964] Ch 240, [1963] 2 All ER 940 where no sufficient interest was shown. *Re a Company* [1983] 2 All ER 854, [1983] 1 WLR 927.

tangible interest of the sort required.[18] There is no need to show a prima facie surplus of assets where the petition is based on the ground that it would be just and equitable to wind up the company, based on its failure to supply accounts which precludes the petitioner from determining whether it is solvent or not.[19]

Furthermore, the Court will generally have regard to the wishes of all the shareholders and will not order a winding up if a majority do not wish it.[20] Nor will the Court order a winding up where there are few members and the company is solvent, for then the machinery of a voluntary winding up is adequate.[21]

A creditor, contributory, the Official Receiver or the Department of Trade and Industry may seek for a compulsory winding up even though the company is in voluntary liquidation. Where a petition by creditors is involved, the Court will usually give great weight to the views of the majority, but there may be circumstances, as for example where the majority of creditors come from the same group, where their views will not, as against creditors wishing a voluntary liquidation to continue, be decisive.[1] If the petition is brought by the Official Receiver the Court must be satisfied that the winding up cannot be continued with due regard to the interests of creditors and contributories. In respect of petitions by the Secretary of State the root question is whether it is just and equitable to make such an order. The attitude of creditors is a relevant consideration as are the conclusions of the Department of Trade and Industry. The Department's views are entitled to considerable weight since it acts in the public interest and not in the interest of any particular class. Where a Departmental inspection discloses evidence of fraudulent trading it is particularly desirable that a compulsory winding up order which imposes a duty to report to the Court on the Official Receiver should be made.[2]

On the other hand, a creditor who cannot obtain payment of his

---

18 *Re Chesterfield Catering Co Ltd* [1977] Ch 373, [1976] 3 All ER 294; a petition by one of two shareholders who is also a director is sufficient even though it merely recites that a surplus will be available for distribution, and see *Re W R Willcocks & Co Ltd* [1974] Ch 163, [1973] 2 All ER 93.
19 *Re Newman and Howard Ltd* [1962] Ch 257, [1961] 2 All ER 495.
20 IA 1986, s 195; *Re London Suburban Bank* (1871) 6 Ch App 641.
21 *Re Natal Co Ltd* (1863) 1 Hem & M 639; *Re Sea and River Marine Insurance Co* (1866) LR 2 Eq 545; *Re Great Munster Rly Co, ex p Inderwick* (1850) 3 De G & Sm 231.
1 *Re Southard & Co Ltd* [1979] 3 All ER 556, [1979] 1 WLR 1198, CA.
2 *Re Lubin, Rosen and Associates Ltd* [1975] 1 All ER 577, [1975] 1 WLR 122; note also the strong statement by Megarry J that the liquidator should not engage in one-sided representations to creditors to induce them to oppose a petition for compulsory winding up.

446   Chapter 21 Winding up and Administration Orders

debts is entitled to an order to wind up the company,[3] unless no advantage can accrue to the petitioner from the winding up,[4] or unless the petition is an attempt to enforce a disputed debt.[5]

A petitioner can only claim a winding up order on one of the seven grounds set out in IA 1986.[6] Six of these grounds are clear cut, requiring a precise state of affairs to exist;[7] but the seventh ground, that is should be 'just and equitable' to wind the company up,[8] is somewhat nebulous. The Courts have, however, granted winding up orders on this ground in nine types of situation:[9]

(1) Where the main object for which the company was formed has ceased to exist or is impossible; that is when the substratum has gone.[10] In each case it is a matter of construing the objects clause.[11]

(2) Where the company is a bubble—that is where there was no bona fide intention of carrying on business in a proper manner.[12]

(3) Where the company was formed for a fraudulent or illegal purpose.[13]

---

3 *Re London Suburban Bank* (1871) 6 Ch App 641, 643; *Re Western of Canada Oil Lands and Works Co* (1873) LR 17 Eq 1; *Re Camburn Petroleum Products Ltd* [1979] 3 All ER 297, [1980] 1 WLR 86.
4 *Re Krasnapolsky Restaurant and Winter Garden Co* [1892] 3 Ch 174; *Re Chapel House Colliery Co* (1883) 24 ChD 259.
5 *Holt Southey v Catnic Components Ltd* [1978] 2 All ER 276, [1978] 1 WLR 630; *Re Lympne Investments Ltd* [1972] 2 All ER 385, [1972] 1 WLR 523; *Re Bryant Investment Co Ltd* [1974] 2 All ER 683, [1974] 1 WLR 826; *Stonegate Securities Ltd v Gregory* [1980] Ch 576, [1980] 1 All ER 241.
6 IA 1986, s 122(1).
7 Ibid, s 122(1)(a)–(f).
8 Ibid, s 122(1)(g). This ground is primarily relied upon by contributories. In the case of a contributories' petition, the procedure differs somewhat from that followed in the case of a creditors' petition: cf the Insolvency Rules 1986, rr 4.7–4.21 and 4.22–4.24.
9 See also Chap 11.
10 *Re Haven Gold Mining Co* (1882) 20 ChD 151; *Re German Date Coffee Co* (1882) 20 ChD 169; *Re Red Rock Gold Mining Co Ltd* (1889) 61 LT 785; *Re Bleriot Manufacturing Aircraft Co Ltd* (1916) 32 TLR 253; *Re Baku Consolidated Oilfields Ltd* [1944] 1 All ER 24; *Re Amalgamated Syndicate* [1897] 2 Ch 600; *Re Suburban Hotel Co* (1867) 2 Ch App 737.
11 *Re Kitson & Co Ltd* [1946] 1 All ER 435, esp at 438; *Re Eastern Telegraph Co Ltd* [1947] 2 All ER 104, 111; *Re Thomas Edward Brinsmead & Sons* [1897] 1 Ch 45 on appeal 406.
12 *Re London and County Coal Co* (1866) LR 3 Eq 355; *Re Anglo-Greek Steam Co* (1866) LR 2 Eq 1, 6.
13 *Re Thomas Edward Brinsmead & Sons* [1897] 1 Ch 45 on appeal 406; *Re International Securities Corpn Ltd* (1908) 99 LT 581.

(4) Where a full and impartial investigation of the affairs of the company is needed. Such circumstances include: where the directors are allegedly tainted with fraud, where, in a case where fraud is suspected there has been a failure to keep books of account or to prepare accounting statements, or where, fraud being suspected, the company has a large amount of liquid funds on hand.[14]
(5) Where there is a deadlock in the management of the company.[15]
(6) Where the articles provide for winding up in the circumstances which occur.[16]
(7) Where the directors, having a majority of votes, omit to hold general meetings, submit accounts and recommend a dividend.[17]
(8) Where a member is unjustifiably excluded from the affairs of the company.[18] Generally this situation will only occur where the member is also a director.
(9) Where the company is in substance a partnership and there are grounds for winding up a partnership. It will be recalled that this principle applies where majority shareholders are in breach of agreements reached with other shareholders concerning the right to participate in management. The matter is more fully dealt with in connection with directors' duties.[19]

Formerly the Courts would not grant a winding up order on the just and equitable ground if there were some alternative remedy available to the petitioner. Now, however, it is specifically provided that, on a member's petition, if it is just and equitable for the company to be wound up, it shall be wound up, notwithstanding

---

14 *Re Peruvian Amazon Co Ltd* (1913) 29 TLR 384; *Re Armvent Ltd* [1975] 3 All ER 441, [1975] 1 WLR 1679.
15 *Re Yenidje Tobacco Co Ltd* [1916] 2 Ch 426; but see *Re Bambi Restaurants Ltd* [1965] 2 All ER 79, [1965] 1 WLR 750; *Re Expanded Plugs Ltd* [1966] 1 All ER 877, [1966] 1 WLR 514.
16 *Re American Pioneer Leather Co Ltd* [1918] 1 Ch 556.
17 *Loch v John Blackwood* [1924] AC 783.
18 *Re Lundie Bros Ltd* [1965] 2 All ER 692, [1965] 1 WLR 1051.
19 *Re Yenidje Tobacco Co* [1916] 2 Ch 426; *Re Davis and Collett Ltd* [1935] Ch 693; *Re National Drive-in Theatres Ltd* [1954] 2 DLR 55; *Re Cuthbert Cooper & Sons Ltd* [1937] Ch 392; *Re Expanded Plugs Ltd* [1966] 1 All ER 877, [1966] 1 WLR 514; *Re K/9 Meat Supplies (Guildford) Ltd* [1966] 3 All ER 320, [1966] 1 WLR 1112. See now *Ebrahimi v Westbourne Galleries Ltd* [1973] AC 360, [1972] 2 All ER 492; *Re A and BC Chewing Gum, Topps Chewing Gum Inc v Coakley* [1975] 1 All ER 1017, [1975] 1 WLR 579.

that an alternative remedy exists, unless the member who is acting unreasonably is not pursuing his other remedy.[20]

On the hearing of a winding up petition, the Court may dismiss it or adjourn the hearing, or make an interim order, or make any other order that it thinks fit, including, if the petition is presented on the ground of default in holding the statutory meeting, or delivering the statutory report, an order that the meeting be held, or the report be made.[1]

A petition will generally be supported by affidavit evidence. If the facts are unchallenged the Court may be prepared to make an order even though the affidavit rehearses hearsay. Similarly, the Court may be prepared to make an order, even on the just and equitable ground, where the report of an Inspector appointed by the DTI alleges fraud and this is unchallenged. Where the material filed in support of the petition is challenged the Court will require the petitioner to substantiate his claim, and this may require the attendance of witnesses and the production of documents.[2]

A winding up order must not be refused on the ground only that the assets of the company have been mortgaged to an amount equal to or in excess of those assets, or that the company has no assets.[3]

VOLUNTARY WINDING UP

A company may be wound up voluntarily when, by special resolution, it resolves to that effect, or if by extraordinary resolution it resolves that it cannot, by reason of its liabilities, continue its business and that it is advisable to wind up.[4]

The passing of such a resolution must be advertised in the London Gazette within 14 days after it is passed.[5]

20 IA 1986, s 125(2).
1   Ibid, s 125(1).
2   CA 1985, ss 440, 441; *Re Koscot Interplanetary (UK) Ltd* [1972] 3 All ER 829; *Re Armvent Ltd* [1975] 3 All ER 441, [1975] 1 WLR 1679.
3   IA 1986, s 125(1). It must, however, be remembered that a petitioning member must be able to show that he has an interest in the winding up.
4   Ibid, s 84(1)(b), (c). By s 84(1)(a) a company may also be voluntarily wound up when the period, if any, fixed for the duration of the company by its articles expires, or, on the occurrence of an event on the happening of which the articles provide for the company to be dissolved and the company has passed a resolution in general meeting requiring it to be wound up voluntarily. Such provisions are extremely rare.
5   Ibid, s 85(1). It is a criminal offence to default in complying with this section: s 85(2). A copy of the resolution must also be forwarded to the Registrar of Companies: ibid, s 84(3).

Voluntary Winding up

If the directors, after a full investigation, believe the company to be solvent, they may make a statutory declaration to that effect, stating that they believe the company will be able to pay its debts in full (together with interest at the rate prescribed by IA 1986, s 189(4)) within 12 months from the commencement of the winding up.[6] Provided that such a declaration is made within the five weeks immediately preceding the date of the passing of the resolution for winding up, or on that date but before the passing of that resolution, and embodies a statement of the company's assets and liabilities as at the latest practicable date before the making of the declaration, the winding up is then a 'members' voluntary winding up'.[7] Such a declaration must be delivered to the Registrar of Companies before the expiry of 15 days immediately following the date upon which the resolution is passed.[8]

If no declaration of solvency is made the winding up is a 'creditors' voluntary winding up'.

It is a criminal offence for a director to make a declaration of solvency unless he had reasonable grounds for his opinion that the company was solvent.[9]

In a creditors' voluntary winding up, the company must summon a meeting of its creditors for a day not later than the 14th day after the day on which the company meeting is held at which the resolution for voluntary winding up is to be proposed. Written notice of the creditors' meeting must be sent to creditors not less than seven days before the day of the meeting and the meeting must be advertised in the Gazette and two newspapers circulating in the area of the company's principal place of business.[10]

Where, in a creditors' voluntary winding up, a liquidator is nominated by the company, the liquidator cannot exercise his powers without leave of the Court before the creditors' meeting has been held.[11] There are limited exceptions to this rule. The

---

6 Ibid, ss 89(1), 251.
7 Ibid, ss 89(2) and 90.
8 Ibid, s 89(3). It is an offence to fail to deliver the declaration within the time required.
9 Ibid, s 89(4).
10 Ibid, ss 97(1) and 98(1). The notice must state the name and address of an insolvency practitioner who will furnish the creditors with information as to the company's affairs and a place where, on the two business days before the meeting, a list of creditors can be inspected: ibid, s 98(2) and (3). The company is guilty of a criminal offence if it fails without reasonable excuse to comply with s 98(1) or (2): ibid, s 98(6), and the liquidator must apply to the Court for directions as to how the default is to be remedied: ibid, s 166(5).
11 Ibid, s 166(2).

liquidator may exercise his powers to take into his custody or under his control property which belongs or appears to belong to the company; to dispose of perishable goods or goods the value of which is likely to diminish if they are not immediately disposed of; and to do anything else necessary to protect the company's assets.[12] The liquidator must attend the creditors' meeting and give a report on any exercise of his powers.[13] If he fails to comply with these provisions without reasonable excuse, the liquidator is liable to criminal sanctions.[14] These elaborate provisions are intended to deal with a fraud known as 'Centrebinding', the essence of which was that a liquidator could formerly have been appointed at an extraordinary general meeting of the company called at very short notice, and could dispose of assets before the meeting of creditors was held.[15]

The directors of a company must, in the case of a creditors' voluntary winding up, prepare a statement of affairs of the company (in prescribed form) which must be verified by affidavit.[16] The statement, which must include, inter alia, particulars of the company's assets, debts and liabilities, the names and addresses of the company's creditors, details of their securities and the date on which the securities were given, must be laid by the directors before the creditors' meeting.[17] The directors must appoint one of their number to preside at the creditors' meeting and it is the appointee's duty to attend and preside.[18]

In a voluntary winding up the property of the company is to be applied first in paying the preferential debts, then in satisfaction of its liabilities *pari passu* and lastly is to be distributed amongst the members according to their rights and interests in the company as determined by the articles.[19] Companies cannot contract out of this provision. The Court can refuse to give effect to provisions in contracts which achieve a distribution of property which runs counter to the scheme of the provision.[20]

---

12 Ibid, s 166(3).
13 Ibid, s 166(4).
14 Ibid, s 166(7).
15 The name derives from *Re Centrebind Ltd* [1966] 3 All ER 889; see further L. H. Leigh and H. C. Edey, op cit, paras 371–2.
16 Ibid, s 99(1)(a) and (2) and the Insolvency Rules, r 4.34.
17 Ibid, s 99(1)(b) and (2).
18 Ibid, s 99(1)(c).
19 Ibid, s 107.
20 *British Eagle International Airlines Ltd v Compagnie Nationale Air France* [1975] 2 All ER 390, [1975] 1 WLR 758, HL. Cf *Carreras Rothmans Ltd v Freeman Mathews Treasure Ltd* [1985] Ch 207, [1985] 1 All ER 155.

CONTRIBUTORIES

When a company is wound up, the then members and the past members[21] are liable to contribute towards the assets of the company to an amount sufficient to enable it to pay all its debts and liabilities.[1] A past member is only liable to contribute towards debts contracted before he ceased to be a member, and only if the present members cannot satisfy their contributions.[2] On their own these provisions would appear to destroy the purpose of limited liability. It is, however, expressly provided that no member of a company limited by shares is liable to contribute more than the amount unpaid on his shares.[3] Thus if a member holds shares which are fully paid up he is not liable to make any further contribution—and any provision in the memorandum or articles which provides that he shall be liable to contribute more than the amount of his shares is *ultra vires* the Companies Act and void.[4] There is an exception to this rule in the case of directors and managers whose liability under the memorandum is unlimited.[5] Such a director or manager may, if the Court deems it necessary,[6] have to contribute to the winding up

---

21 Ibid, s 74(1). Past members are persons who have been members of the company within the 12 months before the winding up, ibid, s 74(2)(a). Past members of companies which have re-registered as a public company under CA 1985, s 43 or as a limited company under ibid, s 51, are liable to contribute to the assets of the company in respect of debts and liabilities which were contracted by it before it re-registered if they were members at the time of re-registration and the winding up commences within three years of the registration: IA 1986, s 77. Conversely if a limited company re-registers as unlimited under CA 1985, s 49, persons who were past members at the time of re-registration, and have not since become members again are not liable to contribute more than they would have had to contribute if the company had not re-registered: IA 1986, ss 7, 8.

1 A member whose shares have been the subject of an invalid surrender or forfeiture may also be liable to contribute: *Bellerby v Rowland and Marwood's Steamship Co Ltd* [1902] 2 Ch 14.

2 IA 1986, s 74(2)(b), (c). Because past members may only be liable to contribute towards some of the company's debts, when the list of persons liable to contribute is drawn up it is divided into two parts—'A' and 'B', the A list including present members, the B list including past members. A past member is not liable to contribute if calls on his shares are met by the transferee. *Helbert v Banner* (1871) LR 5 HL 28.

3 Ibid, s 74(2)(d). There are equivalent provisions for companies limited by guarantee—no member is liable to pay more than the amount of his guarantee: s 74(3).

4 *Bisgood v Henderson's Transvaal Estates* [1908] 1 Ch 743, 759.

5 IA 1986, s 75(1). A director's or manager's liability may be unlimited under the memorandum, or CA 1985, ss 306 or 307.

6 IA 1986, s 75(2)(c).

452 Chapter 21 Winding up and Administration Orders

as if it were a winding up of an unlimited company even though his shares are fully paid up.[7]

Although neither past[8] nor present members, whose shares are fully paid up, are liable to make any further contributions, they, and members whose shares are not fully paid up, are subject to a disability in that they may not prove against the company in a winding up for debts due to them *qua* members.[9] Once the creditors have been paid such a debt is taken into account when distributing any surplus assets amongst the contributories.[10]

All the persons who are liable to contribute in the winding up (other than a person liable under IA 1986, ss 213 or 214 for fraudulent or wrongful trading) are contributories[11]—and this term includes holders of fully paid shares.[12] Once the winding up commences the shareholders become contributories, and their liability for the debts of the company as contributories is different from their liability as shareholders.[13] It arises '*ex lege* and not *ex contractu*'[14] and is governed by the provisions of the Insolvency Act.

In a winding up by the Court, the Court settles the list of contributories.[15] The liquidator has power to do so in any other winding up.[16]

THE LIQUIDATOR

When the winding up of the company commences the directors

---

7 Directors and managers who ceased to hold office more than one year before the commencement of the winding up are not liable to contribute—nor do they have to contribute towards debts contracted after they ceased to hold office: ibid, s 75(2)(a) and (b).
8 *Re Consolidated Goldfields of New Zealand Ltd* [1953] Ch 689, [1953] 1 All ER 791; *Re Phoenix Oil and Transport Co Ltd* [1958] Ch 560, [1957] 3 All ER 218.
9 Ibid, s 74(2)(f). A dividend is such a debt: see *Re L B Holliday & Co Ltd* [1986] 2 All ER 367, [1986] BCLC 227. Fees due to a director/member under the articles are not due to him *qua* member: *Re New British Iron Co, ex p Beckwith* [1898] 1 Ch 324. And see ibid, s 149.
10 Ibid, s 74(2)(f). See also ibid, ss 154 and Sch 4, Pts II and III.
11 Ibid, s 79. The liability of a contributory is a debt in the nature of a specialty: ibid, s 80. If a contributory dies or goes bankrupt his personal representatives or his trustee in bankruptcy stand in his shoes: see *Re Wolverhampton Steel and Iron Co Ltd* [1977] 1 All ER 417, [1977] 1 WLR 153 and ss 81, 82.
12 *Re Anglesea Colliery Co* (1866) 1 Ch App 555.
13 *Re Hull and County Bank, Burgess' Case* (1880) 15 ChD 507, 511.
14 *Hansraj Gupta v Asthana* (1932) LR 60 Ind App 1 per Lord Russell of Killowen at p 11.
15 IA 1986, s 148.
16 Ibid, s 165(4)(a).

cease to control its affairs[17] and the management of the company is then placed in the hands of a liquidator[18] who administers and takes custody or control of the company's business and assets.[19]

The manner of appointing a liquidator varies with the manner of the winding up:

(1) in a winding up by the Court the Official Receiver becomes the liquidator until such time (if any) as meetings of the creditors and contributories have been held and nominated a person to be liquidator. The liquidator is the person nominated by the creditors or, if they fail to make a nomination, the person nominated by the contributories. If different persons are nominated, the creditors' nominee is liquidator but any creditor or contributory may apply to Court to appoint the contributories' nominee as the liquidator or as joint liquidator with the creditors' nominee, or to appoint some other person to be liquidator;[20]

---

17 In a members' voluntary winding up the company in general meeting, or, in a creditors' winding up, the liquidation committee or the creditors, can sanction the directors' continued exercise of their powers. In a winding up by the Court the directors can be appointed special managers: IA 1985, s 235(3), and see *Re Mawcon* [1969] 1 All ER 188, [1969] 1 WLR 78 (directors acting as special managers must act within their powers, as restricted by undertakings given by them, to bind the company).

18 In a voluntary winding up, if no liquidator has been appointed or nominated by the company, the directors may not, subject to limited exceptions, exercise their powers before the appointment or nomination of the liquidator: IA1986, s 114.

19 IA 1986, ss 165–167, Sch 4. The business may only be carried on by the liquidator if it is beneficial to the company to carry it on: ibid, ss 87(1), 167 and Sch 4. If the business is carried on debts contracted after the winding up commenced have priority over debts contracted before the winding up began. *Re Great Eastern Electric Co* [1941] Ch 241, [1941] 1 All ER 409. The company's property does not vest in the liquidator unless the Court so orders: ibid, s 145. As to when the Court will so order, see *Re Fir View Furniture Co Ltd* (1971) Times, 9 February.

20 IA 1986, ss 136(1), (2) and 139. In certain circumstances, the DTI may appoint a liquidator: IA 1986, s 137. The liquidator is referred to as such and not by his own name: ibid, s 163. At any time after presentation of the winding up petition, the Court may appoint a provisional liquidator: see IA 1986, s 135, *McCabe v Andrew Middleton (Enterprises)* 1969 SLT (Sh Ct) 29 and *Re Exchange Securities and Commodities Ltd (No 2)* [1985] BCLC 392. Such an appointment is designed to protect the company's assets from jeopardy. The Official Receiver or any other fit and proper person may be appointed. The application may be made ex parte, but generally in such a case an undertaking in damages is required from the applicant unless the applicant is the Crown: *Re Highfield Commodities Ltd* [1984] 3 All ER 884, [1985] 1 WLR 149.

(2) in a members' voluntary winding up, the company, in general meeting, appoints the liquidator;[1]
(3) in a creditors' voluntary winding up, the creditors and the company at their respective meetings may nominate a liquidator but the liquidator is the person nominated by the creditors unless they have failed to make a nomination in which case the person nominated by the company is the liquidator.[2]

The liquidator must be an insolvency practitioner.[3] A company cannot be an insolvency practitioner.[4]

The ultimate object for which the liquidator aims is to distribute the company's assets, firstly to pay the costs of the winding up, then amongst its creditors to pay its debts and finally to distribute any surplus amongst the members.[5]

The liquidator is given various powers which assist him towards his objective and he is limited to the express powers conferred upon him by statute.[6] The main powers are to bring and defend actions in the name of the company, to pay the creditors, and, if necessary, to compromise their claims,[7] to sell and charge property of the company and generally to do all such other things as may be necessary for winding up the affairs of the company and distributing its assets. The company may ratify an act through the liquidator and can thus ratify the act of unauthorised persons who purported to commence an action on behalf of the company.[8]

---

1 IA 1986, s 91.
2 Ibid, s 100.
3 Ibid, s 389. Members of professional bodies recognised by the DTI and authorised persons may act as insolvency practitioners: ibid, ss 390(2), 391, 392. See generally ss 388–398.
4 Ibid, s 390(1).
5 *Ayerst v C and K (Construction) Ltd* [1976] AC 167 at 177 per Lord Diplock: ibid, ss 107 and 143(1).
6 Ibid, ss 165–167, Sch 4. The liquidator has power in a voluntary winding up to accept shares as consideration for sale of the company's property: ibid, s 110. This power is mainly of use in a reconstruction or amalgamation situation and is discussed in Chap 20.
7 But he may not seek to use his power of compromise to vary the creditors' rights. To do that a scheme under CA 1985, s 425 must be proposed: *Re Trix and Ewart Holdings Ltd* [1970] 3 All ER 397, [1970] 1 WLR 1421.
8 *Alexander Ward & Co Ltd v Samyang Navigation Co Ltd* [1975] 2 All ER 424, [1975] 1 WLR 673, HL. Only the liquidator can bring an action on behalf of the company once it is in liquidation. If he refuses to do so, a contributory may apply for an order compelling the liquidator to bring the action or authorising the contributory to proceed in the company's name: *Fargro Ltd v Godfroy* [1986] 3 All ER 279, [1986] 1 WLR 1134

The Liquidator 455

In a winding up by the Court the liquidator is subject to the control of the Court in the exercise of all his powers, and any creditor or contributory may apply to the Court for the liquidator to be controlled.[9] He may not exercise some of his powers except with the sanction of the Court or of any liquidation committee[10] (established under IA 1986, s 141).

A liquidator may exercise most of his powers in a voluntary winding up without any sanction,[11] but he requires the sanction of an extraordinary resolution of the company in a members' winding up or, in a creditors' winding up, of the Court or liquidation committee (established under IA 1986, s 101) or (if there is no such committee), of a meeting of creditors, to exercise some of them.[12] The liquidator is empowered to call general meetings of the company to obtain the necessary sanction, or for any purpose,[13] and to apply to the Court for the determination of any question arising out of the winding up.[14]

A liquidator may be paid.[15] This remuneration is fixed in accordance with the Insolvency Rules.[16]

In order to give the creditors some substantial degree of protection the liquidator is subject to statutory duties and to duties in equity. In particular the liquidator, in a winding up by the Court, is to have regard, in administering the company's assets, to any resolutions of meetings of the creditors and contributories[17] which he may call, and he must call such meetings if requested to do so by one-tenth in value of the creditors or contributories. A liquidator of

---

9 IA 1986, ss 167(3) and 168(4). For the circumstances when a Court will interfere with the liquidator's exercise of his powers see *Leon v York-O-Matic Ltd* [1966] 3 All ER 277, [1966] 1 WLR 1450.
10 Those listed in ibid, Sch 4, Pts I and II. The committee must be notified if the liquidator (other than the Official Receiver) disposes of property of the company to a person connected with it or engages a solicitor: ibid, s 167(2).
11 Ibid, s 165(3), Sch 4, Pts II, III.
12 Ibid, s 165(2). The powers the exercise of which require sanction are those contained in ibid, Sch 4, Pt I. As to control of the liquidator by the Court, see *Harold M Pitman v Top Business Systems (Nottingham) Ltd* [1984] BCLC 593.
13 Ibid, s 165(4).
14 Ibid, s 113. The Court has no power to authorise the liquidator to do any act which is *ultra vires* the company—*Re Salisbury Railway and Market House Co* [1969] 1 Ch 349, [1967] 1 All ER 813, 826.
15 Including the Official Receiver: see *Re Introductions Ltd (No 2)* [1969] 3 All ER 697n, [1969] 1 WLR 1359. The liquidator may use funds held in a suspense account to pay the costs of the winding up, albeit that the company was carrying on its entire business *ultra vires* and its assets are in the account: ibid.
16 Rr 4.127–4.131.
17 IA 1986, s 168(2). The Court may also have regard to the creditors' and contributories' wishes: ibid, s 195.

a company which is being wound up by the Court may be removed from office either by order of the Court or by a general meeting of creditors summoned specially for the purpose, but a provisional liquidator can only be removed by order of the Court.[18] A liquidator of a company being wound up by the Court may resign in certain circumstances by giving notice to the Court[19] and he or a provisional liquidator (other than the Official Receiver) must vacate office if he ceases to be qualified to act as an insolvency practitioner.[20] The Official Receiver is liquidator during any vacancy and may summon meetings of the creditors and contributories to chose a person to be liquidator in his place.[21]

A person who has ceased to be the liquidator or provisional liquidator of a company which is being wound up by the Court has his release from the specified time,[1] and the release discharges him from all liability in respect of his acts or omissions in the winding up and in relation to his conduct as liquidator or provisional liquidator.[2] The release does not prevent the exercise of the Court's powers against a liquidator against whom proceedings could otherwise be brought for misfeasance.[3]

In a voluntary winding up the liquidator must publish notice of his appointment in the manner specified.[4] His main duty is to call meetings, of the company in a members' winding up, and of the company and a separate meeting of its creditors, in a creditors' winding up, at the end of each year during which the winding up continues,[5] and, when the winding up is complete to call a final meeting of the company prior to its dissolution.[6]

If during a members' winding up the liquidator forms the opinion that the company will be unable to pay its debts in full (together with interest at the official rate) within the period specified in the directors' declaration of solvency, he must,

---

18 IA 1986, s 172(2). In certain cases the meeting must be requested by at least one-quarter in value of the company's creditors: s 172(3). A liquidator appointed by the DTI may be removed by it: s 172(4).
19 Ibid, s 172(6).
20 Ibid, s 172(5). The office must also be vacated after notice of holding of the final meeting under s 146 has been given to the Court and the Registrar of Companies: s 172(8).
21 Ibid, s 136(3) and (4).
1 Ibid, s 174(1)–(5).
2 Ibid, s 174(6).
3 Under ibid, s 212: see ibid, s 174(6).
4 Ibid, s 109.
5 Ibid, ss 93, 105.
6 Ibid, ss 94, 106.

(a) summon a creditors' meeting for a day not later than the 28th day after he formed the opinion;
(b) send notices of the meeting to the creditors not less than seven days before the meeting is due to be held;
(c) advertise the meeting in the Gazette and two newspapers in the locality, in which the company had its principal place of business;
(d) furnish the creditors with such information about the company's affairs as they may reasonably require;
(e) make out a statement of affairs of the company in prescribed form (containing inter alia particulars of the assets, debts and liabilities and details of its creditors and their securities) which must be laid before the creditors' meeting ; and
(f) attend and preside at the meeting.[7]

From the date of the creditors' meeting, the winding up becomes a creditors' voluntary winding up.[8]

A liquidator in a voluntary winding up may be removed by the Court on cause being shown[9] or, in the case of a members' voluntary winding up, by a general meeting of the company summoned specially for the purpose or in the case of a creditors' voluntary winding up by a general meeting of the creditors summoned specially for that purpose.[10] The liquidator may in certain circumstances resign by giving notice to the Registrar of Companies.[11] He must vacate office if he ceases to be qualified to act as an insolvency practitioner.[12]

A vacancy in the office of liquidator may be filled by the Court,[13] or if the liquidator was not appointed by the Court, by the creditors in a creditors' winding up.[14] Where the liquidator was appointed by the company it may, subject to any arrangement with its creditors, fill a vacancy caused by his ceasing to act.[15]

---

7   Ibid, s 95(1)–(4).
8   Ibid, s 96. See also s 102.
9   Ibid, s 108(2). See *Re London Flats Ltd* [1969] 2 All ER 744, [1969] 1 WLR 711.
10 Ibid, s 171(1) and (2). Where the liquidator was appointed by the Court, these meetings may only be summoned in restricted circumstances: ibid, s 171(3).
11 Ibid, s 171(5).
12 Ibid, s 171(4); or if a final meeting or meetings have been held; the liquidator has complied with ss 94(3) or 106(3) as appropriate and sent to the Registrar of Companies notice of the holding of the meeting(s) and of the decision(s) reached.
13 Ibid, s 108(1).
14 Ibid, s 104.
15 Ibid, s 92.

The liquidator owes duties of a fiduciary nature towards the company's creditors as a body.[16] It would appear, however, that he is not a trustee in the true sense, so that he is not liable for negligence but only for fraud.[17] However, if the liquidator misapplies the company's assets by admitting and paying an invalid claim without good cause[18] or by paying members before creditors, or creditors in the wrong order,[19] he is personally liable to the creditors, and a misfeasance summons may be issued against him.[1] The Court is empowered to set aside transactions between a liquidator and a person associated with him.[2]

THE LIQUIDATION COMMITTEE

Sometimes a liquidation committee may be appointed in a winding up by the Court or in a creditors' voluntary winding up to supervise the performance of the liquidator's duties, and in some cases the liquidator has to obtain its sanction before exercising certain of his powers.[3]

In a creditors' voluntary winding up, the creditors, at their meeting[4] held immediately after the passing by the company of the resolution for voluntary winding up, or at a later meeting, may appoint a liquidation committee consisting of not more than five persons. The company may also appoint up to five persons to the committee, but the creditors may object to those persons serving on the committee. If objection is taken, persons appointed by the company are disqualified unless the Court otherwise orders.[5] When the winding up is by the Court, the separate meetings of the contributories and creditors summoned either for the purpose of choosing

---

16   It is sometimes said that he is a trustee: *IRC v Olive Mill Ltd* [1963] 2 All ER 130, [1963] 1 WLR 712; *Re Oriental Inland Steam Co, ex p Scinde Rly Co* (1874) 9 Ch App 557; *Re General Rolling Stock Discount Co's Claim* (1872) 7 Ch App 646; *Re Paraguassu Steam Tramroad Co, Black & Co's Case* (1872) 8 Ch App 254, 262.
17   *Knowles v Scott* [1891] 1 Ch 717; *Re Hills Waterfall Estate and Gold Mining Co* [1896] 1 Ch 947.
18   *Re Windsor Steam Coal Co (1901) Ltd* [1929] 1 Ch 151.
19   *Pulsford v Devenish* [1903] 2 Ch 625.
1   IA 1986, s 212.
2   Insolvency Rules 1986, r 4.149.
3   IA 1986, s 167. See generally Insolvency Rules 1986, rr 4.151–4.172.
4   For the rules governing the conduct of meetings held by creditors and contributories during a winding up, see the Insolvency Rules 1986, rr 4.50–4.71.
5   Ibid, s 101.

a liquidator or by the liquidator [6] establish a liquidation committee.[7] No maximum number of committee members is prescribed but it is implicit that the committee will consist of both creditors and contributories. The committee must be established, even if only one of the meetings of creditors and contributories so decides, unless the Court otherwise orders.[8]

PROOF OF DEBTS

Once the winding up has commenced, either by order of the Court, or by resolution of the company, and a liquidator and a liquidation committee have been established, the next stage is for the creditors to prove their debts.[9] The liquidator then decides whether to admit or reject the proof of the debt. If he admits it, it becomes one of the debts the company has to pay unless a contributory appeals to the Court against its acceptance. If he rejects it, the creditor may accept that decision, or may appeal to the Court against the decision.[10]

The Insolvency Rules[11] make provision for the proof of debts in a winding up.[12] All debts and claims against the company whether present or future, certain or contingent, ascertained or sounding only in damages can be proved for. If the claim is not of a certain value, the liquidator makes an estimate of its value.[13] The liquidator is not, however, to admit a claim which would not be enforceable by action.[14]

Where there have prior to the liquidation been mutual credits or debts or other mutual dealings, an account is taken of what is due from and to the company and the creditor.[15] The creditor is only

---

6 The liquidator must summon a meeting for this purpose if so requested by one-tenth in value of the company's creditors: IA 1986, s 141(2).
7 Ibid, s 141.
8 Ibid, s 141(3).
9 Debts must be proved in the manner provided in the Insolvency Rules 1986, rr 4.73–4.85. Basically the debt is proved by a written claim in prescribed form sent to the liquidator: r 4.73.
10 Insolvency Rules 1986, r 4.83, confers the right to an appeal.
11 Rr 4.73–4.85.
12 Ibid, Sch 8, para 12.
13 Insolvency Rules, r 486 and see *Re Armstrong Whitworth Securities Co* [1947] Ch 673, [1947] 2 All ER 479; *Re House Property and Investment Co Ltd* [1954] Ch 576, [1953] 2 All ER 1525.
14 Eg debts barred by the Statutes of Limitations, see *Re Art Reproductions Co* [1952] Ch 89, [1951] 2 All ER 984, or claims for foreign taxes: see *Government of India v Taylor* [1955] AC 491, [1955] 1 All ER 292, HL.
15 Insolvency Rules 1986, r 4.90(1) and (2).

permitted to prove for the balance of the debt.[16] In certain cases, the creditor may prove for interest on his debt.[17]

A debt in a foreign currency must be proved in a liquidation according to the sterling value of the debt as at the date of the commencement of the winding up.[18] Even if the conversion as at that date results in the creditor suffering a shortfall in the sum owed to him, any surplus arising in the winding up is not available to meet the shortfall.[19] Special rules apply to secured creditors.[20]

ASSETS OF THE COMPANY

All the assets of the company are available for the payment of the company's debts—and the assets may be increased by the provisions for avoiding dispositions of property made before the winding up commenced.[1]

However, property which is held by the company on trust does not form part of its assets available to the creditors. It is important to note that property held on trust includes money lent for a specific purpose which fails, which is held on resulting trust on the failure of the purpose.[2]

ORDER OF PAYMENT OF DEBTS

At this stage in the winding up the liquidator has control of the assets and knows the extent of the company's liabilities. He will, throughout the winding up, take steps to bring money into the company, for example by continuing to run its business at a profit, or by realising its assets, to enable him to pay the company's debts. He is not, however, allowed to choose which debts he will pay at random. A strict order is laid down. The company's assets are to be

---

16 Ibid, r 4.90(3). As to the necessity to give credit for sums received from those jointly liable with the company, see *Re Amalgamated Investment and Property Co Ltd* [1985] Ch 349, [1984] 3 All ER 272.
17 Insolvency Rules 1986, r 4.93.
18 Ibid, r 4.91.
19 *Re Lines Bros Ltd* [1983] Ch 1, [1982] 2 All ER 183, CA.
20 Insolvency Rules 1986, rr 4.88 and 4.95–4.99.
1 See pp 469–470, post.
2 See *Barclays Bank v Quistclose Investments Ltd* [1970] AC 567, [1968] 3 All ER 651; *Carreras Rothmans Ltd v Freeman Mathews Treasure Ltd* [1985] Ch 207, [1985] 1 All ER 155.

applied first in paying all the costs, charges and expenses properly incurred in the winding up.[3]

After the expenses of winding up have been paid the preferential debts, which are statutory creatures,[4] must be paid. The debts which are preferential are many and are set out in full in IA 1986, Sch 6. The most important of these debts are payments due for taxes,[5] social security contributions and contributions to occupational pension schemes,[6] wages due to an employee[7] for services rendered within four months before the winding up and all accrued holiday pay due to him[8] and debts due to persons who advanced money to a company which was used to pay wages or holiday pay, to an employee, so reducing the amount for which the employee could claim in the winding up.[9]

If a landlord or other person has distrained on goods or effects of the company within three months before the date of a winding up order, the preferential debts are a first charge on the goods or effects so distrained on, or the proceeds of the sale thereof, to the extent that the company's assets are insufficient to pay them. If by virtue of the charge any person surrenders goods to the company or makes a payment to it, that person ranks as a preferential creditor to the extent of the proceeds of sale of the goods or the amount of the payment, except as against so much of the company's property as is available for the payment of preferential creditors by virtue of the surrender or payment.[10] These provisions apply only to a compulsory winding up, however, and not to a voluntary winding up.[11] In the latter case the distrainor may retain the proceeds subject only to the discretion of the Court to restrain a distress from proceeding further. The mere fact that a sale would place the distrainor in a

---

3 IA 1986, s 116 for a voluntary winding up. See also *Re Mesco Properties Ltd* [1980] 1 All ER 117, [1980] 1 WLR 96. There is no statutory provision to this effect for a winding up by the Court, but see Insolvency Rules 1986, r 4.218.
4 IA 1986, ss 175, 386.
5 Ibid, Sch 6, paras 1–5. The Crown has no right to priority except as provided by Sch 6, but see *Re Nadler Enterprises Ltd* [1980] 3 All ER 350, [1981] 1 WLR 23.
6 Ibid, paras 6–8.
7 Ibid, paras 9 and 13–15. The sum regarded as preferential under para 9 is subject to a prescribed maximum.
8 Ibid, para 10.
9 Ibid, para 11. Difficult questions arise where the advance is made from an already overdrawn current account: *Re Primrose (Builders) Ltd* [1950] 2 All ER 334; *Re E J Morel (1934) Ltd* [1962] Ch 21, [1961] 1 All ER 796; *Re James R Rutherford & Sons* [1964] 3 All ER 137, [1964] 1 WLR 1211; *Re Rampgill Mill Ltd* [1967] Ch 1138, [1967] 1 All ER 56.
10 Ibid, s 176.
11 Ibid, s 176(1).

better position in a voluntary rather than in a compulsory winding up is not a reason for staying a sale; the Court will not cure a statutory lacuna. In order for the Court to act there must be present elements of unfairness or negligence in the pursuit of his claim by the execution creditor.[12]

The preferential debts must be paid in full unless the assets are insufficient to meet them, when they abate rateably.[13]

Insofar as the assets of the company are insufficient to pay its general creditors, the preferential debts have priority over debts secured by a floating charge and are to be paid out of property subject to that charge.[14]

Once the preferential debts have been paid the ordinary creditors are paid.

There is, of course, no need, as a matter of law, to adhere to the order (set out above) in which assets are to be applied when winding up a solvent company, because, by definition, such a company will be able to pay all its debts. It is, none the less, by far the safest course for the liquidator to adopt the order, for then, should the company turn out to be insolvent at the end of the winding up, he will not be liable to the creditors, who could otherwise sue him for misapplication of the company's assets.[15]

Provision is made for interest to be payable on any debt proved in the winding up, even if part of the debt proved is interest on the original debt. After payment of the debts which have been proved, any surplus remaining is (before being used for any other purpose) applied in payment of interest for the period during which the debts have been outstanding since the company went into liquidation.[16] Interest ranks equally even if the debts do not and is paid at the rate payable on judgments at the date when the company went into liquidation or the rate applicable apart from the winding up, whichever is the greater.[17]

When all the debts have been paid, subject to the power of the

---

12 *Herbert Berry Associates Ltd v IRC* [1977] 3 All ER 729, [1977] 1 WLR 617, HL; *Re Bellaglade Ltd* [1977] 1 All ER 319.
13 Ibid, s 175(2)(a).
14 Ibid, s 175(2)(b). But if the charge has crystallised at the time of the winding up it has priority over the preferential debts: *Re Griffin Hotel Co Ltd* [1941] Ch 129, [1940] 4 All ER 324 (just as a fixed charge has: *Richards v Kidderminster Overseers* [1896] 2 Ch 212) and the assets comprised in the charge are no longer 'assets of the company' in the winding up for the purposes of s 176: *Re Christonette International Ltd* [1982] 3 All ER 225, [1982] 1 WLR 1245.
15 Page 475, post.
16 IA 1986, s 189(1), (2).
17 Ibid, s 189(3), (4).

Court to adjust such rights in a compulsory winding up, any surplus is distributed amongst the shareholders according to their rights under the memorandum and articles.[18] The memorandum or articles may deprive a shareholder altogether of his right to receive a share or surplus. For example, if the memorandum provides that, on a winding up, all of the surplus assets are to be transferred to a charitable institution, the shareholders are not entitled to distribution amongst themselves of surplus assets (even if the articles do not expressly disentitle them) and the transfer will be enforced in favour of the charitable institution.[19]

The Court may permit a distribution, notwithstanding the emergence of a last minute claim by a person claiming as creditor. The Court has a discretion in the matter. Whether a claimant was guilty of wilful default or lack of due diligence in not claiming earlier is a factor for consideration. The Court will be readier to permit a distribution to creditors than to members in such circumstances.[20]

The process of winding up is not completed at one time. The liquidator may take several years to administer the company's assets completely and bring its business to an end, and during this time he is obliged, where he has sufficient funds, to make interim payments to the creditors, without clearing the company's total liability to any one of them at one time.[1]

TRANSACTIONS AT AN UNDERVALUE AND PREFERENCES

In a winding up the liquidator may be able to avoid certain transactions entered into or payments made and securities given before the winding up commenced, and will thus be able to increase the assets of the company available to the general body of creditors.[2]

The liquidator may make an application to Court in any case where at the 'relevant time' the company has entered into a transaction with a person at an undervalue or given preference to any

---

18 IA 1986, ss 107, 154.
19 *Liverpool and District Hospital for Diseases of the Heart v A-G* [1981] Ch 193, [1981] 1 All ER 994, a case on a company formed for charitable purposes but the principle appears to be general.
20 Ibid, s 112 and see *Re R-R Realisations Ltd* [1980] 1 All ER 1019, [1980] 1 WLR 805.
1 Insolvency Rules 1986, r 4.180.
2 The provisions discussed in this section also apply where an administration order has been made in relation to the company (IA 1986, s 238(1)), when they can be enforced by the administrator rather than the liquidator.

person.³ Two types of transaction are treated as entered into with a person at an undervalue, that is to say,

(1) where the company makes a gift to that person or enters into any other transaction with him whereby it receives no consideration;
(2) where it enters into a transaction with him for a consideration the value of which (in money or money's worth) is significantly less than the consideration provided by it.⁴

The Court cannot make an order in respect of a transaction at an undervalue if it is satisfied that the company entered the transaction in good faith and for the purpose of carrying on its business and that at the time it did so there were reasonable grounds for believing the transaction would benefit it.⁵

A company gives a preference to a person if he is one of its creditors (or a surety or guarantor for any of its debts or liabilities) and the company does anything or allows anything to be done the effect of which is to put that person into a position which, in the event of the company going into insolvent liquidation, will be better than the position he would have been in had that thing not been done.⁶ The fact that something was done as a result of a Court order does not of itself prevent the doing or suffering of that thing from being a preference.⁷

The Court cannot make an order in respect of a preference unless the company was influenced, in deciding to give it, by a desire to put the person preferred in a better position in the event of the company going into insolvent liquidation than he would have been in had that thing not been done; but where the person preferred is connected with the company (otherwise than as employee) at the time the preference was given, the company is presumed to have had such a desire unless the contrary is proved.⁸

Ascertainment of 'the relevant time' is complex. The relevant time is,⁹

3   IA 1986, ss 238(2), 239(2).
4   Ibid, s 238(4). An example would be the sale of the company's Rolls-Royce motor car for 5p.
5   Ibid, s 238(5).
6   Ibid, s 239(4). An example would be the repayment by the company of an overdraft personally guaranteed by its managing director.
7   Ibid, s 239(7).
8   Ibid, s 239(5), (6). As to 'connected', see ibid, ss 249 and 435. The term covers, principally, directors and shadow directors of the company, their associates and associates of the company.
9   Ibid, s 240(1).

(1) in the case of a transaction at an undervalue, or of a preference which is given in relation to a person connected with the company (otherwise than as an employee), any time in the period of two years ending with the onset of insolvency;[10]
(2) in the case of a preference which is neither a transaction at an undervalue nor given to a person connected with the company, any time in the period of six months ending with the onset of insolvency;
(3) in either case, any time between the presentation of a petition for an administration order and the making of such an order on the petition.

In the case of a transaction at an undervalue, the liquidator can apply generally for an order; in the case of a preference, he can apply for an order to restore the position to what it would have been had the company not given the preference.[11] Although the Court may make such order as it sees fit, extensive specific powers are conferred upon it, particularly to order the restoration to the company of property transferred by it and to order the repayment to the liquidator of sums paid by the company.[12]

EXTORTIONATE CREDIT TRANSACTIONS

The liquidator may apply to Court where the company is or has been party to a transaction for or involving the provision of credit to the company if the transaction is or was extortionate and entered into in the period of three years ending on the day on which the company went into liquidation.[13]

The transaction is regarded as extortionate if, having regard to the risk accepted by the person giving the credit, the terms of it are or were such as to require grossly exorbitant payments to be made in respect of the credit or otherwise grossly contravened the principles of fair trading. A transaction is presumed to be extortionate

---

10   The date of commencement of the winding up except where the company goes into liquidation on the discharge of an administration order, in which case it is the date of presentation of the petition on which the administration order was made: ibid, s 240(3).
11   Ibid, ss 238(3); 239(3).
12   Ibid, s 241.
13   Ibid, s 244(1), (2). This provision also applies where an administration order has been made in relation to the company: ibid, s 244(1). The three year period ends in that case on the day when the order was made.

unless the contrary is proved.[14]

Wide powers are conferred on the Court to deal with extortionate credit transactions, including power to order repayment to the liquidator of sums received by the other party to the transaction from the company.[15]

FLOATING CHARGES

A floating charge created by a company is invalid except to the extent of the aggregate of,

(1) the value of so much of the consideration for its creation as either consists of money paid or goods and services supplied to the company at the same time as or subsequent to the creation of the charge, or of the discharge or reduction, at the same time as or after the creation of the charge, of any debt of the company;[16] and
(2) any interest payable under the agreement pursuant to which the money was paid, goods or services supplied or debt discharged or reduced.[17]

The charge is only invalid if created at 'the relevant time' which is, in the case of a charge created in favour of a person connected with the company, any time in the period of two years ending with the onset of insolvency[18] or in any other case the period of 12 months ending with the onset of insolvency.[19] However, in the latter case, the charge is not created at a relevant time unless the company is at that time unable to pay its debts[20] or becomes unable to do so in consequence of the transaction under which the charge is created.[1]

---

14 Ibid, s 244(3). An example would be the provision of credit at an interest rate of 1000% per annum.
15 Ibid, s 244(4).
16 The value of the goods or services is their reasonable value: ibid, s 245(6). See *Re Yeovil Glove Co Ltd* [1965] Ch 148, [1964] 2 All ER 849, CA and *Re G T Whyte & Co Ltd* [1983] BCLC 311. This provision prevents old debts being secured by a floating charge.
17 Ibid, s 245(1). This provision also applies where an administration order has been made in respect of the company.
18 Ibid, s 245(5).
19 Ibid, s 245(3). A change created between the date of presentation of a petition for an administration order and the making of the order is created at the 'relevant time'.
20 Within the meaning of ibid, s 123.
1 Ibid, s 245(4). Note however that the charge cannot be set aside if the debt which it secures is repaid before the commencement of the winding up: *Mace Builders (Glasgow) Ltd v Lunn* [1986] Ch 459, [1985] BCLC 154.

The costs of the winding up are to be paid before the creditors secured by the floating charge.[2]

DISCLAIMER OF ONEROUS PROPERTY

To enable the liquidator to carry out as quickly as possible his duties of administering the company's property he is given power by giving a prescribed notice, to disclaim onerous property belonging to the company,[3] which is defined as any unprofitable contract and any other property of the company which is unsaleable or not readily saleable, or such that it may give rise to a liability to pay money or perform any other onerous act.[4] The power of disclaimer may be exercised although the liquidator has taken possession of or attempted to sell the property or otherwise exercised rights of ownership in respect of it. There is no time limit for the exercise of the power except where a person interested in the property has applied in writing to the liquidator requiring him to decide whether or not to disclaim, in which case the notice must be given in 28 days or such longer period as the Court may allow.[5]

Disclaimer operates to determine the rights and liabilities of the company as from the date of disclaimer, but it does not, except so far as is necessary to release the company from liability, affect the rights of third parties.[6] Disclaimer of leasehold property is ineffective unless a copy of the disclaimer is served on every person claiming as underlessee or mortgagee and either no application is made to the Court or on such application the Court directs the disclaimer to take effect.[7]

The Court has power, on an application being made by an interested or potentially liable party, to vest the disclaimed property in any person who is either entitled to it (or a trustee for such a person) or in any person subject to a liability in respect of the property not discharged by the disclaimer (or a trustee for him).[8]

---

2 *Re Barleycorn Enterprises Ltd* [1970] Ch 465, [1970] 2 All ER 155.
3 Ibid, s 178.
4 Ibid, s 178(3). A lease is frequently 'onerous property'. Cf *Re Potters Oils Ltd* [1985] BCLC 203, which would presumably be decided differently under the new provisions.
5 Ibid, s 178(5).
6 Ibid, s 178(4).
7 Ibid, s 179.
8 Ibid, ss 181, 182.

Any person who suffers financial loss as a result of the disclaimer is entitled to prove the amount of his loss as a debt, as if he were a creditor.[9]

RIGHTS OF EXECUTION CREDITORS

A creditor who has issued execution against the goods or lands of a company, or has attached a debt due to it may not, unless the execution or attachment was complete[10] before the commencement[11] of the winding up, retain the benefit of it.[12] However, a purchaser in good faith from the Sheriff of goods sold under an execution acquires a good title as against the liquidator.[13]

Where goods of a company have been taken in execution, and before completion of the execution the Sheriff is given notice that a provisional liquidator has been appointed, that a winding up order has been made, or that a resolution for voluntary winding up has been passed, he must deliver the goods and any moneys received to the liquidator.[14] The rights of the liquidator may be set aside by the Court on such terms as it thinks fit.[15]

Executions and attachments commenced after a winding up by the Court are void for all purposes,[16] and in a voluntary winding up the liquidator may apply for a stay of proceedings.[17] A distress started before a winding up will be allowed to continue unless there are special circumstances in the nature of unfair dealing or fraud.

---

9 Ibid, s 178(6).
10 As to when execution is complete see ibid, s 183(3).
11 If the creditors had notice of a meeting called to pass a resolution for voluntary winding up, the execution or attachment must be complete before he received the notice: ibid, s 183(2)(a).
12 Ibid, s 183(1). *Roberts Petroleum Ltd v Bernard Kenny Ltd* [1983] 2 AC 192, [1983] BCLC 28.
13 Ibid, s 183(2)(b).
14 Ibid, s 184(1), (2). The costs of execution are a first charge on the goods or money. If execution was on a judgment debt exceeding £20, the costs may be deducted from the sale proceeds and the Sheriff must hold the balance for 14 days. If in that time he is given notice of a petition for winding up, or of a meeting to pass a resolution to wind up, he must pay the balance to the liquidator: s 184(3). The Sheriff is liable to pay the proceeds to the liquidator even though the notice he receives of a meeting to pass a resolution to wind up does not comply in all respects with the statutory requirements: *Engineering Industry Training Board v Samuel Talbot Engineering* [1969] 2 QB 270, [1969] 1 All ER 480.
15 Ibid, ss 183(2)(c), 184(5).
16 Ibid, s 128(1).
17 Ibid, ss 112, 126. See also *Re Aro Co Ltd* [1980] Ch 196, [1980] 1 All ER 1067.

As we have noted, s 183 does not affect the matter since it applies only to executions.[18]

DISPOSITIONS OF PROPERTY

After a winding up by the Court has commenced all the company's property is frozen. Any disposition of company property made by the company itself, or any transfer of its shares, is void, unless the Court orders otherwise.[19] The Court will not order the specific performance of a contract previously made for the sale of shares in the company, for to do so would be to force on the transferee a transfer which, although valid as between him and the transferor would be void as against the company.[20]

This is not the case in a voluntary winding up, for the liquidator has power to make dispositions.[1] However, a transfer of shares made after such a liquidation has commenced is void unless the liquidator gives it his sanction.[2]

The Court may make an order validating a disposition in advance of a winding up and it may do so on the petition of a creditor or the company. Where an application is made in the case of an allegedly insolvent company the Court must scrutinise the proposed transaction with care and must be satisfied that the proposed disposition would be beneficial to the company. Where the petition relates to a solvent company and is brought by the directors but relates to a transaction opposed by some part of the shareholders, the Court should, conformably with the general principles concerning the

---

18 *Re Memeco Engineering Ltd* [1985] Ch 86, [1985] BCLC 424; *Re Bellaglade Ltd* [1977] 1 All ER 319.
19 IA 1986, s 127. For circumstances when the Court will validate a disposition see *Re Clifton Place Garage Ltd* [1970] Ch 477, [1970] 1 All ER 353; *Re Operator Control Cabs* [1970] 3 All ER 657n. See *Re A I Levy Holdings Ltd* [1964] Ch 19, [1963] 2 All ER 556; *Re Gray's Inn Construction Co Ltd* [1980] 1 All ER 814, [1980] 1 WLR 711, CA. The Court has power under s 127 to validate a disposition to be made in the winding up before the winding up has begun. In order to present a petition the applicant must have a discernible interest in the matter; a shareholder has such an interest as the value of his shares may be affected by the transactions, *Re Argentum Reductions (UK) Ltd* [1975] 1 All ER 608, [1975] 1 WLR 186; *Re Burton and Deakin Ltd* [1977] 1 All ER 631, [1977] 1 WLR 390.
20 *Sullivan v Henderson* [1973] 1 All ER 48, [1973] 1 WLR 333.
1 IA 1986, ss 165, 166. In a winding up by the Court, the liquidator may make certain dispositions without a Court order: ibid, s 167(1)(b).
2 Ibid, s 88.

management of companies, give due weight to the directors' opinion that the transaction is beneficial to the company and should not refuse a validating order unless the opposing shareholders adduce compelling evidence proving that the disposition is in fact likely to injure the company.[3]

STAY OF ACTIONS

Once a winding up petition has been presented the Court has power to stay any proceedings pending against the company, even though no winding up order has been made.[4] The purpose of this power is to ensure the ultimate distribution of the assets of an insolvent company *pari passu* its creditors.[5] Furthermore, once a winding up order has been made no action may be begun or, if the writ has been issued, continued, against the company[6] without leave of the Court, although it is in the discretion of the Court whether or not leave will be granted.[7]

There is no automatic bar to actions in a voluntary winding up, but the liquidator can apply to the Court for a stay of proceedings,[8] although in this case the Court cannot order a stay unless it is first satisfied that the required exercise of the power would be 'just and beneficial' to the company's creditors.[9]

---

3 *Re Burton and Deakin Ltd* [1977] 1 All ER 631, [1977] 1 WLR 390; *Re J. Leslie Engineers Co Ltd (In Liquidation)* [1976] 2 All ER 85, [1976] 1 WLR 292.
4 IA 1986, s 126. In an English winding up, the Court may restrain proceedings commenced in Scotland and vice versa, *Re Dynamics Corpn of America* [1972] 3 All ER 1046, [1973] 1 WLR 63.
5 *Re J Burrows (Leeds) Ltd* [1982] 2 All ER 882 at 886.
6 Ibid, s 130(3). A set-off may be allowed against a claim by the company, but not a counterclaim: *Langley Constructions (Brixham) Ltd v Wells* [1969] 2 All ER 46, [1969] 1 WLR 503, CA. In the absence of special circumstances, the Court will however lean heavily in favour of granting leave to bring proceedings against a company in liquidation for damages in tort: *Re Berkeley Securities (Property) Ltd* [1980] 3 All ER 513, [1980] 1 WLR 1589.
7 *Re Aro Co Ltd* [1980] Ch 196, [1980] 1 All ER 1067; *Re Exchange Commodities and Securities Ltd* [1983] BCLC 186; *Re Coregrange Ltd* [1984] BCLC 453.
8 Ibid, s 112, *Re Calgary and Edmonton Land Co Ltd* [1975] 1 All ER 1046, [1975] 1 WLR 355.
9 *Re J Burrows (Leeds) Ltd* [1982] 2 All ER 882, [1982] 1 WLR 1177, where a stay was refused because inter alia the stay would have been beneficial only to the directors of the company but not to its creditors.

CRIMINAL OFFENCES

In a winding up whether it be voluntary or by the Court, the officers[10] of the company must assist the liquidator by disclosing to him all property, books of account and papers belonging to it, and by delivering up to the liquidator such property, books and papers which the officer has in his custody or control. The officers must make full and true statements of the affairs of the company. Failure to do any of these acts is a criminal offence.[11]

Penalties are provided for falsification of books[12] for frauds committed by officers[13] and for failure to keep proper books of account, even if these offences are committed before the winding up.[14] It is an offence to attempt to defraud creditors, whether by obtaining credit by false representations, or by obtaining the creditors' consent to an agreement with reference to the affairs of the company or to the winding up by misrepresentation.[15]

In the course of a winding up by the Court, the Court may direct the liquidator to refer the matter to the prosecuting authority[16] if it appears that any officer or member of the company has been guilty of an offence in relation to it.[17] In the course of a voluntary winding up, the liquidator is obliged to refer the matter to the authority together with all requisite information.[18]

FRAUDULENT AND WRONGFUL TRADING

Any person who has been party to the carrying on of the business of the company with intent to defraud its creditors or for any fraudulent purpose is liable, on the application of the liquidator, to make such contributions to the assets of the company as the Court thinks proper.[19] 'Carrying on business' includes collecting assets acquired

---

10 The term 'officer' is partially defined in CA 1985, s 744, and includes a director, manager or secretary.
11 IA 1986, ss 208, 210.
12 Ibid, s 209.
13 Ibid, s 207.
14 CA 1985, s 223.
15 IA 1986, s 211. The person against whom proceedings are taken must have been party to an act of carrying on the business: *Re Augustus Barnett & Son Ltd* [1986] BCLC 170.
16 In England, the Director of Public Prosecutions: ibid, s 218(2).
17 Ibid, s 218(1).
18 Ibid, s 218(4).
19 Ibid, s 213.

in the course of business and the distribution of assets in payment of creditors could constitute a carrying on of business for the purposes of the section.[20]

A single transaction can amount to a carrying on of business. Some of the principles are discussed in:

Re Cooper Chemicals Ltd [1978] 2 WLR 866.

The company while insolvent and unable to pay a loan from J Ltd, agreed to deliver goods to H Ltd which paid the purchase price in advance. H Ltd now claims a declaration that under s 213 of IA 1986 that J Ltd which secured payment of its loan from the company from the moneys advanced on the contract for goods by H Ltd was, with its directors, knowingly party to C Ltd carrying on business with intent to defraud creditors and therefore personally responsible without limitation for the moneys due from C Ltd to the applicants. The pleadings alleged that the directors of J Ltd knew that C Ltd could only repay its debts to J Ltd by using funds obtained for forward sales of goods which the company could not supply. On these facts it was conceded that J Ltd would become a constructive trustee for H Ltd of the moneys paid to it. On s 213 the Court holds (a) that a single transaction can amount to a carrying on of business and that the section applies where the person carrying it on, intends or realises that the consequence will be that creditors will be defrauded. The question is whether the company accepted moneys knowing that it could not meet the obligations of the contract. But a creditor who presses for payment is not a party to a fraud merely because he knows that no money will be available to pay him if the debtor remains honest; 'The honest debtor is free to be made bankrupt'. He is a party to fraudulent trading if he takes money which he knows has been wrongfully procured for the very purpose of making the payment to him.

Fraudulent purpose connotes actual dishonesty; the terms 'defraud' and 'fraudulent purpose' 'connote actual dishonesty involving, according to the current notions of fair trading amongst commercial men, real moral blame'. It has been said that an intent to defraud creditors may be inferred if the company continues to carry on business and incures debts when to the knowledge of the directors there is no reasonable prospect of those debts being

---

20 *Re Sarflax Ltd* [1979] 1 All ER 529. A person cannot be said to be a party to a fraudulent carrying on of business where his duties are ministerial and where his fault is that of failing to give proper advice to the company. *Re Maidstone Buildings Provisions Ltd* [1971] 3 All ER 363, [1971] 1 WLR 1085.

paid.[21] In *R v Grantham*[1] the judge directed the jury that the defendant was acting dishonestly and fraudulently if he realised at the time when debts were incurred that there was no reason for thinking that funds would become available to pay the debts when they became due or shortly thereafter. This direction was upheld by the Court of Appeal. However, in connection with the carrying on of business by distributing assets, a person cannot be said to be dishonest because he paid off one creditor in preference to another even though he knows that the assets of the company will not suffice to pay both. Apart from the insolvency laws, a person may pay off his creditors in whatever order he pleases.[2]

Quite apart from the civil consequences of fraudulent trading, it is an offence for persons to carry on or have carried on a company's business with intent to defraud creditors of the company or of any other person.[3]

Liability for fraudulent trading is notoriously difficult to prove. A further remedy available against present or former directors (including shadow directors[4]) of the company only, is the liability imposed for wrongful trading.[5] These provisions are only applicable where,

(1) the company has gone into insolvent liquidation;
(2) at some time before the commencement of the winding up, the director or former director knew or ought to have concluded that there was no reasonable prospect that the company would avoid going into insolvent liquidation (that is to say, its assets are insufficient to meet its debts, other liabilities and the expenses of winding up[6]); and
(3) he was a director at that time.[7]

In such a case, the Court on the application of the liquidator may order the director or former director to make such contribution (if any) to the company's assets as the Court sees fit, but cannot make

---

21 *Re Patrick and Lyon Ltd* [1933] Ch 786; *Re William C Leitch Bros Ltd* [1932] 2 Ch 71.
1 [1984] QB 675, [1984] 3 All ER 166, CA. See below as to criminal liability for fraudulent trading.
2 *Re Sarflax Ltd* [1979] Ch 592, [1979] 1 All ER 529.
3 CA 1985, s 458, which applies whether or not the company has been or is in the course of being wound up.
4 IA 1986, s 214(7).
5 Ibid, s 214.
6 Ibid, s 214(6).
7 Ibid, s 214(2).

an order against a person if, after he knew or realised that there was no reasonable prospect that the company would avoid going into insolvent liquidation, the director or former director took every step with a view to minimising the potential loss to the company's creditors that he ought to have taken.[8]

For the purpose of determining the facts which a director knew or ought to have realised and the steps which he should have taken, the Court has regard to the facts, conclusions and steps which a reasonably diligent person would have known or ascertained, reached or taken, if he had had both the general knowledge, skill and experience reasonably to be expected of a person carrying out the functions of a director of the company in question and the general knowledge, skill and experience which that director has.[9]

PUBLIC EXAMINATIONS

Where a winding up order is made by the Court, it is the duty of the Official Receiver to investigate the cause of the failure if the company has failed and generally the promotion, formation, business, dealings and affairs of the company. He makes such report to the Court as he sees fit.[10]

Furthermore, the Official Receiver may, in the case of a winding up by the Court, at any time before the dissolution of the company, apply to the Court for the public examination of any person who is or has been an officer of the company; who has acted as liquidator, administrator, receiver or manager of the company; or who has otherwise been concerned or taken part in the promotion, formation or management of the company.[11] The Official Receiver must make an application if so requested by one half in value of the company's creditors or three-quarters in value of its contributories.[12]

The Court may direct the public examination, and the person to whom the application relates must attend to be examined as to the promotion, formation or management of the company or as to the conduct of its business and affairs, or his dealings and conduct in relation to it.[13] Those who may attend and put questions include the

8 Ibid, s 214(1) and (3).
9 Ibid, s 214(4).
10 IA 1986, s 132. The report is prima facie evidence of the facts stated in it: ibid, s 132(2).
11 Ibid, s 133(1). Cf *Re Highgrade Traders Ltd* [1984] BCLC 151 (CA).
12 Ibid, s 133(2).
13 Ibid, s 133(3).

Official Receiver, the liquidator and any creditor or contributory of the company.[14] Failure to attend is contempt of Court and may be punished accordingly.[15]

A liquidator in a voluntary winding up may also apply to the Court for a public examination under these provisions.[16]

CIVIL REMEDIES

In addition to its powers in the case of fraudulent and wrongful trading, the Court may, on the application of the Official Receiver, liquidator or any creditor or contributory, investigate the conduct of any present or past officer of the company, any liquidator, administrator or administrative receiver of the company or any other person involved in the promotion, formation or management of the company.[17]

If the person investigated has misapplied, retained or become accountable for any money or property of the company or has been guilty of any misfeasance or breach of any breach of fiducary or other duty towards it, the Court can order repayment or restoration of the property or contribution to the company's assets of a sum by way of compensation.[18]

Section 212 creates no rights[19] but merely enables proceedings to be taken in summary form in appropriate cases.

COMMENCEMENT OF WINDING UP

It is often important to know when a winding up commenced.[20] It is provided that a voluntary winding up shall be deemed to commence at the time of the passing of the resolution to wind up.[1] A winding up by the Court is deemed to commence, not at the time of the order to wind up, but when the petition for winding up is presented.[2]

---

14 Ibid, s 133(4).
15 Ibid, s 134(1).
16 Ibid, s 112.
17 Ibid, s 212.
18 Ibid, s 212(1), (3).
19 *Re City Equitable Fire Insurance Co Ltd* [1925] Ch 407, CA.
20 Eg certain offences, to be actionable, must be committed with 12 months of the commencement of winding up.
1   IA 1986, s 86. This is so, even if there is a subsequent petition presented to the Court for a compulsory winding up: s 129(1).
2   Ibid, s 129(2).

DISSOLUTION

A company only ceases to exist when it is dissolved and not before, and a company may only be dissolved when its affairs have been completely wound up[3] so far as the liquidator is aware,[4] or if it is not carrying on a business.[5]

In a winding up by the Court, the liquidator sends notice of the final meeting of creditors and vacation of the office by him to the Registrar of Companies or (if appropriate) the Official Receiver notifies the Registrar that the winding up is complete.[6] The notice is registered and the company is dissolved at the end of the period of three months from the date of registration unless the DTI defers the date on the application of the Official Receiver or any interested party.[7]

On completion of a voluntary winding up the liquidator presents his final accounts[8] to meetings of the company's creditors and/or members. Within a week after that has been done the liquidator must send copies of the accounts and a return of the holding of the meetings to the Registrar of Companies.[9] The Registrar registers them, and three months from the registration the company is deemed to be dissolved, unless the Court orders otherwise on the application of the liquidator or any interested party.[10]

The Court has power on the application of the liquidator or any interested person at any time within 12 years of the dissolution to declare it void.[11]

---

3   Ibid, ss 94, 106, 201, 205.
4   *Re Cornish Manures Ltd* [1967] 2 All ER 875, [1967] 1 WLR 807.
5   CA 1985, ss 652, 653.
6   IA 1986, s 205(1).
7   Ibid, s 205(2), (3).
8   To the members in a members' winding up: ibid, s 94(1). To the creditors and members in separate meetings in a creditors' winding up: s 106(1).
9   Not to do so is an offence: ibid, ss 94(3), (4); 106(3), (4).
10 Ibid, s 201(1)–(3).
11 CA 1985, s 651. Relief is not automatically granted under s 651 and the matter is a discretionary one for the Court: *Re Thompson and Riches Ltd* [1981] 2 All ER 477, [1981] 1 WLR 682. For the circumstances when such an order might be made see *Re Boxco Ltd* [1970] Ch 442, [1970] 2 All ER 183n (where the company was solvent it was restored to the register); *Re Bayswater Trading Co Ltd* [1970] 1 All ER 608, [1970] 1 WLR 343 (undistributed money in the company's liquidation account. Company restored to register and ordered to be wound up to enable the money to be distributed); *Re B B H (Middletons) Ltd* (1970) 114 Sol Jo 431 (company restored to register to enable personal injuries claim to be pursued); *Re Thompson and Riches Ltd* (supra) (company restored to register to enable petitioner to continue with winding up proceedings); and

The Registrar of Companies may strike defunct companies off the register where he has reasonable cause to believe that a company is not carrying on business or in operation.[12] Before he does so, however, he must send the letters and publish the notices specified in the Act.[13]

The Registrar may also strike off a company that is being wound up if he has reasonable cause to believe either that no liquidator is acting, or that the affairs of the company have been completely wound up, and the returns required to be made by the liquidator have not been made for a period of six consecutive months.[14]

Any member or creditor[15] who feels aggrieved by the company being struck off may apply to the Court within 20 years of the dissolution for the restoration of the company to the register, and the Court may order it to be restored if it is of opinion that, at the time of the dissolution it was carrying on business or in operation, or that it would be just to do so.[16]

Where a company is struck off the register, in the manner described above, the liability to be sued, if any, of every officer and member of the company (but not of the company) continues as if the company had not been dissolved.[17] Every other form of dissolution puts any potential liability of the company, its officers and members into suspension.[18] If the dissolution is subsequently declared void[19] the liability revives.[20]

---

see *Re Servers of the Blind League* [1960] 2 All ER 298, [1960] 1 WLR 564; *Re Spottiswoode, Dixon and Hunting Ltd* [1912] 1 Ch 410.

12 CA 1985, s 652(1).
13 Ibid, s 652(1)–(3).
14 Ibid, s 652(4).
15 Only creditors and members at the time of the dissolution may apply under this provision: *Re New Timbiqui Gold Mines Ltd* [1961] Ch 319, [1961] 1 All ER 865; *Re Aga Estate Agencies Ltd* [1986] BCLC 346.
16 CA 1985, s 653(1), (2).
17 Ibid, s 652(6)(a).
18 *Coxon v Gorst* [1891] 2 Ch 73; *Re Westbourne Grove Drapery Co Ltd* (1878) 39 LT 30. Where a defunct company is struck off the register its liability, as opposed to the liability of its members and creditors, is suspended in the same manner.
19 Under CA 1985, s 651 or 653.
20 See *Re Spottiswoode, Dixon & Hunting Ltd* [1912] 1 Ch 410. However, proceedings which were taken whilst the company was in dissolution, which are therefore void, are not retrospectively validated by an avoidance of the dissolution: *Morris v Harris* [1927] AC 252. A claim established in such void proceedings may be re-established. See also *Re Lewis & Smart Ltd* [1954] 2 All ER 19, [1954] 1 WLR 755. It may be ordered that the time between a dissolution and its avoidance is not to count towards a limitation period for debt: *Re Donald Kenyon Ltd* [1956] 3 All ER 596, [1956] 1 WLR 1397.

478 *Chapter 21 Winding up and Administration Orders*

When a company is dissolved all of its property which has not been distributed passes as *bona vacantia* to the Crown.[1] The Treasury Solicitor on behalf of the Crown has power to disclaim any property so vesting.[2] When a dissolution is declared void the vesting of undistributed property in the Crown is also avoided, and the property revests in the company.[3]

ALTERNATIVES TO WINDING UP

A winding up of the company may be avoided if advantage is taken of provisions made by IA 1986 for Voluntary Arrangements or Administration Orders.[4]

VOLUNTARY ARRANGEMENTS

The general purpose of the provisions for voluntary arrangements contained in IA 1986, ss 1–7, is to enable a company to enter into binding arrangements with its creditors by means of a relatively straightforward procedure.

A proposal may be made to the company and to its creditors for a composition in satisfaction of its debts or a scheme of arrangement of its affairs,[5] but the proposal may only be made by the directors or (if an administration order is in force in relation to the company) by the administrator or (where the company is being wound up) by the liquidator.[6] The proposal must include provision for an insolvency practitioner[7] to act as trustee or otherwise supervise its implementation.[8]

If the person nominated as trustee or supervisor is not the liquidator or administrator of the company, the nominee must submit a

---

1 CA 1985, s 654. As to property of a dissolved foreign company see *Re Banque Industrielle de Moscou* [1952] Ch 919, [1952] 2 All ER 532.
2 Ibid, s 656. On the effects of such disclaimer see (1954) 70 LQR 25.
3 *Re C W Dixon Ltd* [1947] Ch 251, [1947] 1 All ER 279. It may be that in such a case the property never did, in fact, vest in the Crown.
4 IA 1986, ss 1–7 and 8–27. See also Final Report of the Review Committee on Insolvency Law and Practice (June 1982) (Cmnd 8558); White Paper: A Revised Framework for Insolvency Law (February 1984) (Cmnd 9175).
5 In the Act and hereinafter called in either case 'a voluntary arrangement'. The procedure is governed by the Insolvency Rules 1986, rr 1.2–1.29.
6 IA 1986, s 1(1) and (3).
7 See p 454.
8 Ibid, s 1(2).

report to the Court stating whether meetings of the company and of the creditors should be convened to consider the proposals and, if so, the date on which and time and place at which the meetings should be held.[9] The Court may direct a nominee who fails to submit a report to be replaced.[10]

A nominee who is a liquidator or administrator may summon the meetings of the company and of the creditors at any time but otherwise they must be summoned by the nominee at the time, date and place specified in the report to the Court.[11] Every creditor of the company whose name and address is known to the nominee must be summoned.[12]

The meetings summoned may approve the proposal with or without modifications,[13] but the modifications cannot cause the proposal to fall outside the ambit of s 1, affect the rights of a secured creditor to enforce his security (unless he agrees) or affect the priority or entitlement of a preferential creditor (unless he agrees).[14] The result of the meeting must be reported to the Court.[15]

The approval of the meetings may be challenged by application to the Court by any person entitled to vote at either meeting, or by the nominee, the liquidator or administrator on the grounds that the arrangement unfairly prejudices the interests of any creditor, member or contributory of the company or that there has been a material irregularity at or in relation to either of the meetings.[16] Except in the case of such an application, the approval is not invalidated by any irregularity at or in relation to the meetings.[17]

If satisfied as to the grounds of the complaint, the Court may revoke or suspend the approval of the meetings or of the meeting in relation to which the irregularity occurred or give directions for the summoning of meetings to consider a new proposal or reconsider the original proposals.[18]

Where the meetings of the company and of the creditors approve

9 Ibid, s 2. The report must be submitted within 28 days of notice of the proposal to the nominee (ibid, s 2(2)) who must be furnished with a copy of the proposal and of the company's statement of affairs (s 2(3)).
10 Ibid, s 2(4).
11 Ibid, s 3(1) and (2).
12 Ibid, s 3(3).
13 Ibid, s 4(1).
14 Ibid, s 4(2)–(4) and s 386.
15 Ibid, s 4(6).
16 Ibid, s 6(1), (2). There is a true limit within which the application must be made: ibid, s 6(3).
17 Ibid, s 6(7).
18 Ibid, s 6(4) and see s 6(5).

the proposed voluntary arrangement, it takes effect as if made by the company at the creditors' meetings and binds every creditor who had notice of and was entitled to attend the meeting, whether or not he was present or represented at it, as if he were party to the arrangement.[19] If the company is being wound up or an administration order is in force in relation to it, the Court can stay the winding up or discharge the administration order or give directions for facilitating the implementation of the voluntary arrangement.[20]

Any person dissatisfied with any act, omission or decision of the person implementing the scheme ('the supervisor')[1] may apply to the Court which may confirm, reverse or modify the act, omission or decision, give directions or make any order it sees fit.[2] The supervisor may also apply for directions to the Court[3] which has power to appoint an insolvency practitioner to fill a vacancy in the office of supervisor (or to increase the number of supervisors) if it is expedient to do so.[4]

ADMINISTRATION ORDERS

The purpose of IA 1986, ss 9–27 is to provide an alternative to the winding up procedure. The general object of these provisions is to give the company a 'breathing space' with a view to enabling it to survive and continue trading, or to enable its assets to be realised more advantageously for its creditors.

Accordingly, an administration order, which is an order directing that during the period for which the order is in force the affairs, business and property of the company shall be managed by an administrator appointed by the Court, may be made for the achievement of the following purposes:

(a) the survival of the company or of the whole or any part of its undertaking as a going concern;
(b) the approval of a voluntary arrangement under IA 1986, ss 1–7;
(c) the sanctioning of an arrangement under CA 1985, s 425;

---

19 Ibid, s 5(1) and (2).
20 Ibid, s 5(3) and (4). Note the compulsory delay of 28 days.
1 Ibid, s 7(2).
2 Ibid, s 7(3).
3 Ibid, s 7(4).
4 Ibid, s 7(5) and (6).

(d) a more advantageous realisation of the company's assets than would be effected on a winding up.[5]

There are two basic conditions for the making of an administration order:

(1) the Court must be satisfied that the company is or is likely to be unable to pay its debts within the meaning of IA 1986, s 123; and
(2) it considers that the making of an administration order would be likely to achieve one of the purposes for which the order may be made.[6]

The application may be made by the company, the directors or one or more creditors.[7] Notice of the application[8] must be given to any person (such as a secured creditor) who has appointed or is or may be entitled to appoint an administrative receiver.[9] The petition must be dismissed unless that person consents to it, or the security would be released, discharged, avoided or challengeable[10] if the order were made.[11] The Court may make an interim order restricting the exercise of the powers of the company or the directors.[12]

Once an administration order is made, certain consequences follow. These are:[13]

---

5 IA 1986, s 8(2) and (3). The order cannot be made where the company is in liquidation or if it is an insurance company, recognised bank or licensed institution: ibid, s 8(4).
6 Under ibid, s 8(3): ibid, s 8(1).
7 Ibid, s 9(1). The procedure is governed by the Insolvency Rules 1986, rr 2.1–2.10.
8 Which is by petition, which may not be withdrawn without leave: IA 1986, s 9(1) and (2)(b).
9 Ibid, s 9(2)(a). 'Administrative receiver' means a receiver or manager of the whole or substantially the whole of a company's property appointed by or on behalf of a holder of debentures of the company secured by a charge which is created as a floating charge: ibid, s 29(2).
10 Under ibid, ss 238–240, 242, 243 or 245.
11 Ibid, s 9(3)(b).
12 Ibid, s 9(5). During the period from the presentation of the petition until the order is made or the petition dismissed, no resolution may be passed or order made for the winding up of the company, no security over its property may be enforced except by leave of the Court and no other proceedings or execution may be begun or continued or distress levied against the company or its property except by leave of the Court: ibid, s 10.
13 Ibid, s 11(1)–(3). The company's documents such as business letters must show the administrator's name and a statement that he is managing its affairs: ibid, s 12.

(1) any petition for the winding up of the company must be dismissed;
(2) any administrative receiver of the company must vacate office;
(3) the receiver of any part of its property must vacate office if the administrator requires;
(4) whilst the order is in force:
   (a) no resolution may be passed or order made for the winding up of the company;
   (b) no administrative receiver of the company may be appointed;
   (c) no steps may be taken to enforce any security over the company's property or repossess goods in its possession under a hire purchase agreement except with consent of the administrator or leave of the Court; and
   (d) no other proceedings and no execution or other legal process may be commenced or continued, and no distress may be levied against the company or its property, except with consent of the administrator or leave of the Court.

The administrator[14] has power to do all such things as are necessary to manage the affairs, business and property of the company and, in addition, has the powers specified in IA 1986, Sch I, that is to say, he has thereunder the same powers as an administrative receiver.[15] He also has power to remove and appoint directors of the company and to call meetings of its members and creditors, and the company and its officers are prevented, without the administrator's consent, from exercising any of its or their powers in any way which interferes with the administrator's exercise of his powers.[16]

Furthermore, the administrator (who may apply to the Court for directions)[17] has power to dispose of any property subject to a security which, as created, was a floating charge and the Court may authorise him to exercise similar powers in the case of any other security.[18] The holder of a security created as a floating charge retains his priority as respects any property representing the

---

14 Who is appointed by the order: ibid, s 13(1) and may be removed by the Court or resign: ibid, s 19(1). The Court can fill any vacancy in the office: s 13(2) and (3). The administrator must on his appointment take into his custody or control all of the company's property: s 17(1).
15 Ibid, s 14(1).
16 Ibid, s 14(2) and (4).
17 Ibid, s 14(3).
18 Ibid, s 15(1)–(3).

property disposed of as he would have had in respect of the property disposed of; and the proceeds of sale of any property sold by authority of the Court are to be applied towards repayment of the secured creditor.[19]

When the administrator exercises his powers, he does so as agent of the company, but a person dealing with him in good faith and for value is not concerned to inquire whether the administrator is acting within his powers.[20]

The administrator is under a statutory duty to manage the affairs, business and property of the company in accordance with the directions of the Court before proposals have been approved under IA 1986, s 24, and, after such approval, in accordance with the proposals.[1] He is also obliged to summon a meeting of the company's creditors if requested to do so by one-tenth in value of the creditors or if directed by the Court.[2]

Once the administration order has been made, the administrator must notify the company and, within 28 days, its creditors of whose addresses he is aware.[3] He must then require a statement of the company's affairs (containing inter alia particulars of the company's assets, debts and liabilities, the names and addresses of its creditors and details of any securities held by them)[4] to be made by one or more of the company's present or past officers, persons who have taken part in the company's formation at any time within one year before the date of the order, its employees[5] (or those employed by the company within that year) who are, in the administrator's opinion, capable of giving the information required, or those who are or have been in that year officers or employed by a company which is or within the year was an officer of the company to which the order relates.[6] The statement must be submitted within the period of 21 days beginning with the date on which the administrator gives notice to the person required to submit the statement.[7]

---

19 Ibid, s 15(4) and (5). The Court has power to order further sums to be applied under s 15(5) in discharge of the debt. A copy of the order must be sent to the Registrar of Companies: ibid, s 15(7).
20 Ibid, s 14(5) and (6).
1 Ibid, s 17(2).
2 Ibid, s 17(3).
3 Ibid, s 21(1). A copy of the order must be sent to the Registrar of Companies and there are criminal penalties for breach of these provisions: s 21(2) and (3).
4 Ibid, s 22(4).
5 Employment includes employment under a contract for services: ibid, s 22(3).
6 Ibid, s 22(1)–(3).
7 Ibid, s 21(4). There are criminal penalties for failure to comply with the section: ibid, s 21(6), but the administrator can relax its requirements and the Court can exercise his power if he fails to do so: ibid, s 21(5).

Within three months of the order (or any longer period allowed by the Court) the administrator must send to the Registrar of Companies and all creditors of whose addresses he is aware a statement of his proposals for achieving the purpose or purpose specified in the order, and lay a copy of the statement before a creditors' meeting summoned for the purpose on not less than 14 days' notice.[8] A copy of the statement must within a similar period be sent to all of the company's members[9] of whose addresses the administrator is aware.

The creditors' meeting may approve the proposals and, if it does so subject to modifications, the administrator must approve them.[10] The result of the meeting must be reported to the Court and notified to the Registrar of Companies.[11]

If the meeting approves the proposals (with or without modifications) it may establish a committee which may, on not less than seven days' notice, require the administrator's attendance to furnish such information as it may reasonably require as to the carrying out of his functions.[12]

Furthermore, if the proposals have been approved (with or without modifications) and the administrator proposes to make substantial revisions to them, he must send to all creditors of the company (of whose addresses he is aware) a statement of his proposed revisions and lay a copy of the statement before a creditors' meeting called for the purpose on not less than 14 days' notice.[13] A copy of the statement must be sent to all members of the company of whose addresses the administrator is aware.[14]

The creditors may approve the revisions but if they do so with modifications the administrator must consent to each of them.[15] The Registrar of Companies must be notified of the result of the meeting.[16]

If after the administrator reports to the Court the creditors refuse

---

8 Ibid, s 23(1). Creditors' and company meetings are governed by the Insolvency Rules 1986, rr 2.18–2.31.
9 Ibid, s 23(2) but the administrator may, in lieu, publish a notice specifying an address to which members may apply for a free copy of the statement. Criminal sanctions apply in case of failure to observe these provisions: ibid, s 23(3).
10 Ibid, s 24(1)–(3).
11 Ibid, s 24(4).
12 Ibid, s 26.
13 Ibid, s 25(1), (2).
14 Ibid, s 25(3) or he can in lieu publish an address to which members may apply for a free copy.
15 Ibid, s 25(4).
16 Ibid, s 25(6).

to approve his proposals for achieving the purpose or purposes specified in the order, the Court may discharge the order or make any other order it sees fit.[17]

At any time when the administration order is in force, any creditor or member may apply to the Court for an order on the ground that the company's affairs, business and property are being or have been managed by the administrator in a manner unfairly prejudicial to the interests of its creditors or members generally or some part of them (including himself) or that any actual or proposed act or omission of the administrator would be prejudicial.[18]

The Court may make such order as it thinks fit for the giving of relief but its order may not prevent the implementation of a voluntary arrangement[19] or compromise[20] or if the application is more than 28 days after approval of any of the administrator's proposals or revised proposals, prevent the implementation thereof.[1] Otherwise the Court has a complete discretion and can, for example, regulate the future management by the administrator of the company's affairs, business and property or discharge the administration order.[2]

The administrator may apply at any time for the discharge of the administration order, or to vary it so as to include an additional purpose.[3] The application must be made if it appears to the administrator that the purpose or each of the purposes specified in the order has been achieved or is incapable of achievement or if he is required to do so by a creditors' meeting summoned for the purpose.[4] The Court may discharge or vary the order (and make such consequential orders as it sees fit) and, where it does so, a copy of the order must be sent by the administrator to the Registrar of Companies within 14 days.[5]

When the administration order is discharged, the administrator vacates office.[6] When he ceases to be administrator, his

---

17 Ibid, s 24(5). If the order is discharged, the administrator must send a copy of the discharging order to the Registrar of Companies within 14 days: ibid, s 24(6) and (7).
18 Ie, unfairly prejudicial. Ibid, s 27(1).
19 Approved under ibid, s 4.
20 Approved under CA 1985, s 425.
1   IA 1986, s 27(2) and (3).
2   Ibid, s 27(4). If the order is discharged, a copy of the discharging order must be sent to the Registrar of Companies: ibid, s 27(6).
3   Ibid, s 18(1).
4   Ibid, s 18(2).
5   Ibid, s 18(3) and (4). Criminal sanctions apply for breach of s 18(4): ibid, s 18(5).
6   Ibid, s 19(2)(b). The office must also be vacated if the administrator ceases to be an insolvency practitioner, ibid, s 19(2)(a).

remuneration and expenses are paid out of the company's property in his custody or control at the time in priority to secured creditors; and sums payable in respect of debts or liabilities incurred whilst he was administrator under contracts entered into or employment contracts adopted by him or any predecessor of his are likewise payable.[7]

The administrator has his release after ceasing to act as such when the Court determines (except in the case of death, when the release is from the time when the Court is notified of his death) whereupon he is discharged from liability for his acts or omissions in the administration and whilst acting as administrator.[8]

---

[7] Ibid, s 19(4) and (5) which apply whenever a person ceases to be administrator (for whatever cause): ibid, s 19(3). The administrator is not taken to have adopted a contract of employment by reason of anything done or not done within 14 days of his appointment: ibid, s 19(5). See generally the Insolvency Rules 1986, rr 2.47–2.55.
[8] IA 1986, s 20(1) and (2), subject to s 20(3).

Index

Accountant
  duties of, 145
Accounts
  abridged, 178
  accounting reference periods, corporation tax, for, 380–381
  provisions as to, 163–165
  alternative accounting rules, 168
  auditors' report on, 184–185
  balance sheet, 167, 177
  books of account, keeping of, 162
  consistency of, 167
  contents of, 166–167
  directors, disclosure of transactions involving, 172, 175, 179
  dormant companies, of, 178
  emoluments, disclosure of, 171, 172
  exemptions, 176–177
  form of, 166–167
  general rules, 167–169
  group, 165
  historical cost accounting rules, 168
  notes to, 169–173, 179
  profit and loss, 166, 168, 169
  publication of, 177
  records, keeping of, 162
  share details, etc, to be given with, 169
  types of, 162
Action
  minority, by, 221–232
  personal,
    ratification, whether defeated by, 233–236
    shareholders, by, 232–236
  stay of, in winding up, 470
Adjournment
  meeting, of, 278
Administration order
  administrator,
    agent of company, as, 483

Administration order—*continued*
  administrator—*continued*
    Court appointment, 480
    powers of, 482
    proposals for company, statement of, 484
    remuneration, 485–486
  alternative to winding up, as, 480
  application for, power to make, 481
  conditions for making, 481
  consequences of making, 482
  discharge of, application for, 485
  purposes of, 480–481
  unfair prejudice, application for order as to, 485
Administrative receiver
  administration order, effect of, 482
  authority and function, 443
  civil remedies against, 475
Advertisement
  deposits, for, 10, 372
  securities, offering, 47, 217
  unlisted securities, 45, 47
Agent
  director as,
    actual authority, with, 148
    apparent authority, with, 149, 150
    preliminary agreement, liability for, 34–36
    representation of authority, 150
    unauthorised transaction of, statutory protection from, 156
Agreement
  preliminary, 34–36
  underwriting, 43
Allotment
  acceptance of contract, as, 48
  conditional application, where, 50
  improper, by directors, 195
  irregular, effect of, 49–50
  letter of, 42

Allotment—*continued*
  restrictions on, 49–50, 287
  return of shares alloted, 57
  unlawful, 334–335
Annual general meeting, 273
Arrangement
  scheme of. *See* SCHEME OF ARRANGEMENT
  voluntary. *See* VOLUNTARY ARRANGEMENT
Articles of association
  alteration of,
    agreement with shareholders, by, 116, 117
    breach of contract after, 118–119, 438–439
    discriminatory, with, 112–117
    prevention of, 119, 120, 439
    procedure for, 110–112
    restrictions on, 111
  construction of, 103
  contents of, 102–105
  director, and contract with, 120, 438
  effect of,
    members *inter se*, on rights of, 109
    rights of membership, on 106
    rights other than membership, on, 107–109
  form of, 102–104
  generally, 101–102
  limitations of, in EEC directive, 93
  memorandum, conflicting with, 101
  registration of, 37
  Table A, application of, 103
  unlimited company, of, 103
  variation of rights clause, 305, 306
  winding up distribution rights of shareholders under, 463
Assets
  application of, on winding up, 377–378, 460–461
  availability for payment of debts, 460
  current, 168, 355
  distribution of, 353–357, 462–463
  fixed, 168, 169, 179, 355
  non-cash, transfer of, 208–209, 338
  sold to company, liability where, 338
  valuation of, 324, 325
Auditor
  appointment of, 181, 182, 183, 273
    disqualifications, 183–184
  compensation of, 182
  duties of, 145, 184, 185

Auditor—*continued*
  investigations by, 184–185
  liability of, 187
    relief from, 236
  qualifications for appointment, 183
  removal of, 182
  remuneration of, 169, 181
  report of, 178, 184, 302
  resignation of, 181, 182, 184
  standard of care of, 184–185
  unpublished price-sensitive information, knowing, 214

Balance sheet
  contents of, 167, 177
  documents annexed to, 166
Bankruptcy
  director as bankrupt, 123, 128
Banks
  loans to directors by, 138
  name suggesting connection with, 72
Board of directors
  chairman of, 278–279
  general meeting, not agents of, 146–147
  petition of winding up, 443
  powers of, 146, 147
  primary organs of company, 92
  quorum at meetings of, 145–146
  sole director as, 92
Bonus shares
  allotment of, financial assistance for, 431
  distribution, 211
  income tax on, 394
  issue of, 42, 335, 343, 393
  unissued shares as, 355
Borrowing
  memorandum, provisions of, 359
  receiver, by, 376
  restrictions on, 359–360
  sources of company's powers, 359
  ultra vires, 359–361
Breach of duty
  civil remedies, 475
  disqualification for, 128
Business
  certificate re doing, 38–40
  letters, registration information required on, 75
  transfer of,
    company, to, 400–401
    retirement, on, 402

Index 489

Calls
  power to make, 308
  provisions as to, 308–309
Capital
  allowances, 389
  equity share, 165, 288, 289, 300
  increase of, 342
  issued, meaning, 332
  maintenance of, statutory rule, 339
  memorandum, amount stated in, 96
  methods of raising, 41–42
  minimum, for public company, 10, 12, 15, 16, 37, 39, 333
  nominal, 39, 332
  paid-up, 332
  redemption of shares out of, 300, 302
  redemption reserve, 333
  reduction of,
    class rights, varying, 352
    confirmation by Court, 352–353
    liability of members, 353
    procedure for, 349–350, 353
    refusal to confirm, 353
    when permitted, 349
  re-organisation of, capital gains tax on, 401
  repayment of, to preference shareholders, 297
  reserve, 332
  transferred non-cash assets, 336–339
  share capital, 37, 333–336, 339
  variation of, 342–343
Capital gains tax
  disadvantages of incorporation, 406
  group of companies, where, 404
  liquidation or winding up, on, 401–402
  merger, on, 401
  re-organisation of capital, on, 401
  transfer of business,
    company, to, 400–401
    retirement, on, 402
Centrebinding
  fraud of, 450
Certificate re doing business
  conditions for issue of, 39
  importance of, 39–40
  requirement to hold, 38
Certificate of incorporation
  conditions for issue, 14
  function of, 38
Certification of transfer, 330–331
Chairman of company
  disclosure of emolument, 172

Chairman of members' meeting
  election of, 278–279
Charges
  chargeable asset, meaning, 402
  floating. *See* FLOATING CHARGE
  kinds of, 361
  non-registration, effect of, 363
  power of company to charge property, 359
  register of,
    company, kept by, 367
    Registrar, kept by, 364–365
  registration of,
    certificate of, 364, 367
    extension of time for, 365
    requirement, 361–363
Chartered companies, 1, 2
City code
  Take-overs and Mergers, on, 422–423, 437
Class rights
  meaning, 305
  variation of,
    alteration of, 306
    provision for, 305
    reduction of capital, 352
    what constitutes, 307
Close company
  consequences of status as, 397–399
  definition of, 396
  required standard of distributions by, 398–399
  shortfall assessment, 399
Cohen committee
  recommendations of, 76
Commission
  underwriting, 43–44
Company
  best interests of, director's duty to act in, 192, 193
  books and papers of, inspection of, 258–259, 262–263
  business letters, 75
  capital allowances, 389
  certificate re doing business, 38–40
  close. *See* CLOSE COMPANY
  defunct, struck off register, 477
  dormant, 178
  enemy character of, 21, 22
  exempt private, 11
  family, 402
  group, as member of, 404
  guarantee, 10, 300
  history of, 1–7

Company—*continued*
  incorporation of, 8, 9
  insider dealing, 211–219. *See also* IN-
    SIDER DEALING
  legal entity, as separate, 18–29
    exceptions to rule, 21–23
  limited by shares, 10, 18, 50, 300, 342
  loan by,
    director, to,
      disclosure in accounts, 172
      intra group transactions, 139, 140
      low value transactions, 139
      ordinary course of business, in, 138, 139
      prohibited transactions, 133, 134–136
        exceptions, 136–140
    purchase own shares, to, 432
  loss companies, 388–389
  maintenance of capital of, 339–340
  member of another company, as, 292
  membership, Department of Trade investigations as to, 261
  money-lending, 137, 432
  non-existent, 34
  order forms, 75
  private. *See* PRIVATE COMPANY
  public. *See* PUBLIC COMPANY
  purchase of own shares by, 300, 301, 302, 339–340, 393
  registration of, 36–40
  repurchase of its own shares by, 393
  residence of, 24
  subsidiary. *See* SUBSIDIARY COMPANY
  third party dealing with, statutory protection for, 156–158
  types of, 10–11
  unlimited. *See* UNLIMITED COMPANY
  unpublished price-sensitive information, individuals having, 212–219

Compensation
  director, to,
    dismissal, on, 126
    loss of office, for, 132, 133, 435–439
    loans transactions contravening s 330, for, 141
    untrue statement in prospectus, for, 57–58

Compromise
  scheme of. *See* SCHEME OF ARRANGEMENT

Compulsory purchase of shares
  application of provisions, 425

Compulsory purchase of shares
  —*continued*
  classes of shares, offers relating to, 427
  consideration, offer of choice of, 426, 427
  Court order as to terms of acquisition, 427
  notice served by non-accepting shareholder, 426–427
  notice to shareholder, 425, 427
  offeror's holdings, requirement, 425
  registered shares, instrument of transfer for, 426

Computerisation
  register of members or debenture holders, 313
  Stock Exchange Settlement and stock transfer system, 313

Concert parties
  disclosure of interests arising under, 255–257
  investigation into interests of, 268

Contract
  articles, as to non-alteration of, 118–119
  breach of, altered articles as defence, 118–119
  directors and company, involving. *See* DIRECTOR—contracts with company
  director's interest in, disclosure, 203–206
  infant, by, for sale of shares, 292
  preliminary agreement, 34–36
  rescission of, 52–56
  shares, to take, 48–49
  ultra vires, 85–88
  remedies for third parties, 88–89

Contributions
  political, disclosure of, 180

Contributories
  'A' and 'B' lists of, 451n.
  directors and managers as, 451
  liability of, 451–452
  past members as, 451
  winding up petition by, 442, 445

Corporation tax
  accounting periods, 380–382
  advance (ACT), 389, 390
  charges on income, 384
  computation of, 382–385
  deductions, permitted, 383

Corporation tax—*continued*
  generally, 379–380
  income tax set off against, 396
  investment company, relief for, 389
  loss companies, 388
  losses,
    set off or carry back, right to, 385–387
    terminal, 387
  mainstream, meaning of, 390
  qualifying distribution, payable when made, 389
Court
  liability as to transferred shares, powers to relieve, 338–339
  receiver, appointment of, 374
  reduction of capital, confirmation of, by, 349–353
  re-registration of companies, powers as to, 15–18, 366
  scheme of compromise or arrangement, approval of, 410–411
  winding up by the. *See* WINDING UP BY THE COURT
Credit card
  director, for, 135
Creditors
  accounts, particulars of amounts due to, in, 169
  defrauding, offence of, 471, 472–473
  execution creditors, 468–469
  meeting, 458
  proof of debts, 459
  reconstruction scheme, dissenting from, 418
  reduction of capital, on, protection for, 350
  scheme of compromise or arrangement with, 407–414
  voluntary winding up, 450
  winding up petition by, 442, 443, 445
Criminal liability
  company, of, 28, 29
  false statement by officer, 68, 69
  obtaining property by deception, 69
  officers of company, of, 29
  ultra vires crime, for, 89, 90
  untrue statement in prospectus, for, 47, 60
  winding up, offences on 471–474
Crown servant
  unpublished price sensitive information, knowing, 215n

Damages
  misrepresentation, for, 56–57
  untrue statement in prospectus, for, 57–58
Dealer
  insider, definition of, 211–212. *See also* INSIDER DEALING
  off-market,
    advertised securities, deals as to, 217–218
    definition of, 218
Death
  inheritance tax provisions, 404
Debenture holder
  receiver, appointment of, 374
  remedies of, 373–374
  rights of, 286, 299–300
  trustees for, 372, 373
Debentures
  classification of, 368
  debenture stock, 367n
  definition of, 367
  details of, in accounts, 169
  disclosure of interests. *See* SECURITIES—disclosure of interests in
  issue of, 372
  perpetual, 372–373
  private limited company, of, 10
  registration of, 362, 366
  reissue of, 373
  sale of, restrictions on, 59–60
  series of, 362, 368
  transfer of, 368–369
Debts
  foreign currency, in, 460
  order of payment of, 460–463
  preferential, 461
  proof of, 459–460
Deed of settlement company, 3, 4
Deferred shares, 304
Defunct company, 477
Department of Trade
  inspector, 249–250, 260–265. *See also* INSPECTORS
  investigation by,
    company,
      books and papers of, 258–260, 262–263
      membership, as to, 261, 264
      securities of, ownership of, 264–265
    criminal offence in voluntary winding up, 261
    directors, of, 262

Department of Trade—*continued*
 investigation by—*continued*
  expenses of, 263
  formal, 260–265
  fraud, as to, 261
  inspectors, appointment of, 249, 260–261
  powers as to, 258–265
  preliminary inspections, 258–260
  procedures, 265–267
  result of, 267–268
  share dealings, 261
  share ownership, 264
 power of,
  annual general meeting, to call, 273
  authorisation of advertisements, 47
  investigations, as to 249, 258–270
  petition for winding up, 250, 443
  prospectus, rules as to, 45

Deposits
 advertisement for, 10, 372
 business, 60

Director
 age limit for, 124
 allotment of shares by, 286–291
 alter ego of company, as, 159
 appointment of, 122
  defective, 130
  parent company, by, 165–166
 bank account, investigation of documents relating to, 262
 bankrupt, as undischarged, 123, 128
 Board of Directors. *See* BOARD OF DIRECTORS
 borrowing powers of company, 359
 calls, power to make, 308
 change of, notification of, 123
 compensation to,
  dismissal, on, 126
  loss of office, for, 132, 133, 436–437
 competing directorship, 201
 contracts with company,
  acquisition of non-cash assets, 208–211
  employment, 206–208
  service contract,
   breach, claim as to, 125, 159
   compensation for dismissal, 126–127
   copy, deposit of, 131, 205, 437
   types of contract, 206
 contributory, as, 451–452
 credit card for, 135
 definition of, 122

Director—*continued*
 disclosure of interests, 202–206
 dismissal of, 124–127
 disqualification,
  acting, from, 127
  acting after, 130–131
  appointment, from, 123
  duration of, 127, 129
  grounds for, 127–130
  indictable offence, where convicted of, 127
 duty of,
  act in best interests of company, to, 192–195
  care and skill, of, 189–190
  exercise powers for proper purposes, to, 195–196
  loyalty and good faith, of, 191–192
 emoluments of, disclosure of, 172
 employees, duties as to, 193–195
 expenditure incurred by, funds for, 136
 fiduciary position of, 191–201
 fraud, 224–225
 generally, 121–122
 health insurance for, 135
 individual, as agent. *See* AGENT
 insider dealing, 211–219. *See also* INSIDER DEALING
 interest of. *See* INTEREST
 investigation by Department of Trade of, 262
 knowingly connected with company, dealings where, 213
 liability of,
  acts of company, for, 159
  dividend out of capital, for payment of, 358
  financial assistance for shares acquisition, for, 433–434
  redeemable shares, as to, 303
  relief from, 236
  share transactions, regarding, 26, 39–40
  untrue statement in prospectus, for, 57–58
 loans in favour of,
  banks, by, 138
  connected persons, as to, 133–134
  contravention of s 330, in, 140–141
  credit transaction, definition of, 135
  disclosure of, in accounts, 172
  expenditure incurred by, for, 136
  home improvement, for, 137

Director—*continued*
  loans in favour of—*continued*
    home purchase, for, 137, 138
    intra group transactions, 140
    low value transactions, 139
    money-lending company, by, 137
    ordinary course of business, in, 138, 139
    prohibited transactions,
      exceptions, 136
      generally, 134–136
      rules as to, 134–135
    quasi, 134, 135, 137, 139, 140
  managing, 127, 158, 438, 439
  meaning of, in EEC directive, 92
  meetings, 145, 283
  negligence, proceedings by minority shareholders, 229
  nominee directors, 201
  permanent life directors, 125
  powers, exercise of, 195–196, 453
  qualification shares of, 123, 130
  re-election of, 124
  relationship to company of, 189
  removal of,
    company's right to, 243
    dismissal, by, 124–125
    take-over, following, 436–439
  remuneration of, 131–133, 177
  resignation of, 123–124
  retirement of, 124, 132, 133, 402, 437
  secret benefits, 206
  secret profits, 196, 200
  servant, as, 122, 133, 204
  shadow, 122, 133, 204
  sole, 93
  special manager, as, 453n
  substantial property transactions of, 208–211
  take-over offer, duty to act honestly, 421, 422
  ultra vires transactions, responsibilities as to, 91

Directors' report, 179–180

Disclaimer
  onerous property, of, by liquidator, 467

Disclosure
  accounts, in, 169–176
  compensation to director on loss of office, of, 436, 437
  directors' report, in, 180
  emoluments of directors, of, 172

Disclosure—*continued*
  exemptions for small and medium companies, 176
  interest in contract with company, of, 202–206
  price of limited liability, as, 7
  prospectus, in, 44–46
  protection from, under Department of Trade investigation, 259, 266
  scheme of arrangement, where, 196–200
  shares, notifiable interest in,
    concert parties, 255–257
    directors', 251
    obligations to disclose, 253–255
    person acquiring 5% interest, 253
    register of, 257
  Stock Exchange requirements, 44–48
  take-overs, in, 422, 436

Discount
  shares issued at, 334, 343

Dismissal of Director
  compensation, 126
  procedure, 124
  terms of contract, 126–127

Disqualification
  director, of,
    acting after, 130
    appointment, from, 123
    grounds for, 127–128
    duration of order, 128, 129
  liquidator, of, 128
  manager, of, 128
  officer, of, 128
  receiver, of, 128

Dissolution
  liability of members, 477
  procedure for, 476–478
  restoration of company to register, 477
  striking off the register, 477
  void, declared, 476

Distribution
  close company, by, 397, 398
  income tax on, 389–394
  profits and assets, of, 353–358
  what amounts to, 391

Dividends
  advance corporation tax paid on, 389–391
  arrears of,
    fixed cumulative, 169
    right to, 295–296
  income tax on, 390

Dividends—*continued*
  payment of,
    liability of directors, 358
    provisions as to, 353–354
  preferential, 295
Documents
  Department of Trade's powers of inspection, 258
  subsidiary company, powers of disclosure over, 23

Emoluments
  disclosure of, 172
  meaning of, 172
Employees
  directors' duties as to, 193–195
  emoluments, disclosure, 172
  share schemes, 300, 335, 432
Equity shares
  allocation, 288–289
  meaning, 165, 288
  right to issue, 300
Estoppel
  applicability of rule, 316–317
  displacement of, by company, 316
  false representation in share certificate, against, 313–315
  transferee, benefit available to, 316
European Economic Community
  capital maintenance provisions, 332
  harmonisation of company law, 6
  public company, effect on, 6, 7
  reform, effect on, 6
Examination
  public, on winding up, 474–475
Execution creditor
  rights of, 468
Exempt private company, 11
Expert
  statement in prospectus by, 47, 58
Extortionate credit transactions, 465–466
Extraordinary general meeting, 272, 273, 274–275
Extraordinary resolutions, 281

Family company, 402
Financial Services Act 1986, provisions of
  compensation for misleading particulars, 57
  disclosure, 44–50

Financial Services Act 1986, provisions of —*continued*
  irregular allotment, 49
  share-pushing, 59–60
  unlisted securities, 45
Floating charge
  crystallisation, 370
  priority of, 371–373
  registration of, 362, 366
  relevant time of creation, 466
  validity, extent of, 466–467
Foreign currency
  debt in, 460
Foreign stock exchanges, 218
Forfeiture of shares, 340–341
Forgery
  forged transfer,
    certificate based on, 317–319
    indemnity, right of company to, 318–319
    owner, rights of true, 318
  liability of company for, 156, 314
Foss v Harbottle
  rule in, 221
  exceptions to, 222–229
Founders shares, 304
Fraud
  centrebinding, 450
  civil liability for, on winding up, 475
  defrauding creditors, offence of, 471
  Department of Trade investigations as to, 261
  disqualification for, 128, 129
  fraud on the minority,
    alteration of articles as, 111
    establishment of, 228
    nature of action based on, 225
    proof, matters requiring, 225–226
  fraudulent purpose, company for, 22, 471, 472
  fraudulent trading, 473–474
  misrepresentation in prospectus, 56
Fraudulent trading, 473–474

Gift of shares
  registration, 326–328
  validity, 327
Group of companies
  accounts, 165
  capital gains tax, 404
  income, 403
  relief, 403
Guarantee, company limited by
  liability of members, 95

Guarantee, company limited by —*continued*
meaning, 10
redeemable shares, 300

History
companies, of, 1–7

Holding company
accounting exemptions as to, 176
accounts of, 170
directors' report, details in, 179
investigations of, 261
meaning of, 165
subsidiary. *See* SUBSIDIARY COMPANY

Income
franked investment, 391, 394–395, 399
group, 403

Income tax
advantages of incorporation, 406
bonus issue, whether payable on, 392
distributions,
credit for amount of ACT paid, 390
payable on, 389–394
what amounts to, 391–394
franked investment income, 391, 394–395, 399
set-off against corporation tax, 396

Incorporation
advantages of, 9, 405–406
certificate of, 14, 38
charter of, 2, 3
consequences of, 18–29
lifting the veil of, 20
private or public company, 10

Indemnity
company, for, on transfer of shares, 318–319
director or officer, for, 236

Indictable offence
disqualification of director where convicted of, 127

Inquiries
Department of Trade, by. *See* DEPARTMENT OF TRADE

Insider dealing
companies, prohibitions not applying to, 212
foreign stock exchanges, as to, 218
individuals,
knowingly connected with company, 213
prohibitions applying to, 212

Insider dealing—*continued*
individuals—*continued*
unpublished price sensitive information, having, 214–215
insider dealer, definition of, 211
off-market dealer, 217
penalties for, 219
securities,
foreign stock exchange, on, 218
investment exchange, through, 212
stock exchange, on, 212
take-over bids, as to, safeguards against, 215, 422–423
unpublished price sensitive information, 214–215
definition of, 211

Insolvency practitioner
liquidator to be, 454
voluntary arrangement, in, 478

Insolvency rules, 459

Inspectors
Department of Trade,
appointment of, 249, 260–261, 264
powers of, 262–263
reports by, 263–264

Insurance policies
equity linked, 60
private health, directors, for, 135

Interest
director, of,
contract with company, in, 203–206
directors' report, details in, 179
disclosure of, 131, 203–206, 251–255
register of, 131, 251, 310
what amounts to, 252
notifiable, acquisition of, 253
transferred shares, liability as to, 337–338
register of interests in shares, 257

Interest payments
deductible, 384–385
in winding up, 462

Investigations
application to Court for, 475
company, by, into its own share ownership, 268–270
Department of Trade, by. *See* DEPARTMENT OF TRADE

Investment company
distribution of profits and assets of, 356, 406,
tax relief on losses, 389

Investment exchange, 212

Investments
  details of, in accounts, 169
Jenkins committee
  recommendations by, 76
Joint stock company
  development of, 2, 3
  payment for,
    assets from subscribers, 336–337
    share capital, 333
  registration of, as public company, 14

Law reform
  EEC, effect of, on, 6, 7
  generally, 5–7
  ultra vires, doctrine of, 90
Lien
  shares, on, 341–342
'Limited'
  name, as part of, 70
  power to dispense with, 75
Limited company
  conversion to, 17, 343
  meaning of, 10
  redeemable shares, issue of, 300
Limited liability
  development of, 4
  disclosure as price of, 7
  memorandum, stated in, 95
Liquidation
  capital gains tax on, 401–402
  reconstructions in, 415–419. *See also* RECONSTRUCTION
Liquidation committee
  appointment, 458
  powers of, 453n, 455
Liquidator
  appointment,
    creditors' voluntary winding up, in, 454
    DTI, power of, 453n
    members' voluntary winding up, in, 454
    publication of, 456
  creditors' voluntary winding up, in, 449–450, 456
  criminal offences, duty to report, 471
  disclaimer of onerous property, 467
  disqualification, 128
  liability for fraud, 458
  meetings called by, 456–457
  members' voluntary winding up, duties in, 456–457

Liquidator—*continued*
  Official Receiver as, 453
  powers,
    securities, dealing in, 216
    voluntary winding up, in, 453, 455
    winding up by Court, in, 454
  provisional, Court appointment, 453n
  receiver, distinguished from, 375
  release from office, effect of, 456
  removal, grounds for, 456, 457
  remuneration, 455
  statutory duties, 456
  vacancy in office, 456, 457
Loans by company
  acquisition of company's shares, for, 169
  company's own shares, to purchase, 430, 432
  credit card, for director, 135
  credit transaction, meaning, 135
  director, in favour of,
    connected persons, meaning, 133–134
    contravention of provisions, 140–141
    disclosure of, in accounts, 172
    expenditure incurred, for, 136
    home improvement, for, 137
    house purchase, for, 137
    intra group transactions, 140
    low value transactions, 139
    ordinary course of business, in, 139
    prohibited transaction,
      exceptions, 136–138
      generally, 134–136
      statutory authority, 133–134
  quasi,
    definition of, 135
    director, to, 134–135, 139
    money-lending company, by, 137
    voidable transactions, 140–141
Loans to company
  interest information in accounts, 169
Losses
  computation of, for corporation tax, 385–387
  loss company, 388
  terminal, 387

Manager
  appointment of, 374
  contributory, as, 451
  disqualification of, 128

Manager—*continued*
meaning of, 141
status of, 375
Managing director
breach of contract, 438–439
during receivership, 127
status as to employment, 159
Meetings
adjournment of, 278
annual general, 273
board of directors, of, 145–146
business at, 274
call, power to, 272, 278
chairman, 278–279
circulation of statements supporting resolutions, 277
creditors', 449, 450, 457
creditors and members, of, where scheme of arrangement, 410
extraordinary general, 273–275, 284–285, 339
general,
funds for director's expenditure, provision of, 136
powers of, 273
liquidator's duty to call, 456
minutes of, 283
notice of, 274, 275, 278
polls, 276, 279–280
proceedings at, 277–279
proxies, 276–277
quorum, 271–272, 274, 278
requisition of, 273–274
resolutions, 280–283. *See also* RESOLUTIONS
take-over offer, to consider, 422
unanimous acquiescence at, 283–285
voluntary arrangement, in, 479
voting at, 279–280
Members
beneficiaries on death of, rights of, 107–108
ceasing to be, 292–293
company as, 292
contributories, as, 451–452
liability of, 95–96, 353
minors as, 292
past, as contributories, 451, 452
personal representatives, 238, 331
reduction of, 26, 96
register of, 291, 310–312
rectification of, 292, 411
scheme of compromise or arrangement with, 409–410

Members—*continued*
subscriber to memorandum as, 291
subsidiary company, as, 292
two, business having less than, 26, 96
voluntary winding up, 449
who can be, 291
Memorandum of association
alteration of,
private company re-registering as public, 11–12
procedure, 97–100
public company re-registering as private, 15–17
unlimited company converting to limited, 17–18
articles, conflicting with, 101
borrowing powers, provisions in, 359
capital stated in, 96
contents of, 70–97
effect of,
contractual, 105
members *inter se*, on rights of, 109–110
rights of membership, on, 106–107
other than membership, on, 107–109
generally, 70
liability of members, 95–96
name of company, 71–73
objects clause, 75–79
alteration of, 98
construction of, 77–79
registration of, 37
subscribers to, 291
ultra vires acts, 82
variation of class rights, 305–308
winding up distribution rights of shareholders under, 463
Merger
capital gains tax on, 401
City Code on Take-overs and Mergers, 422, 437
forms of, 408
Panel on Take-overs and Mergers, 262, 423
stamp duty on, 440
taxation considerations on, 439–440
Minor
member, as, 292
Minority shareholders
fraud on the minority, 111, 222–223, 225–232
oppression of, petition of winding up, where, 243–245

Minority shareholders—*continued*
   shareholding, compulsory purchase of, 425–429
   statutory protection for, 237–238
   unfair prejudice orders, where, 97, 244–245
Minutes, 283
Misfeasance proceedings, 475
Misrepresentation. *See also* MIS-STATEMENT
   compensation by directors or promoters, 57–58
   damages for, 56–57
   fraud, action for, 57
   negligent, action for, 58
   rescission of contract where, 52–56
   share certificate, in, 314
Mis-statement. *See also* MISREPRESENTATION
   criminal liability for, 60–61
   damages or compensation for, 57–58
   duty of care in actions concerning, 59
   negligence, action for, 58
   prospectus, in, remedies for, 51–59
   rescission of contract where, 52–56
Monarchy
   name suggesting connection with, 72
Mortgage
   creation of, 363
   shares, of, 329

Name of company
   abbreviations, 74
   business name, 72–73
   change of, 73, 74
   'Limited',
     dispensing with, 74
     part of name, as, 70
   publication of, 74–75
   registration of, 71
   unauthorised use, 72
   unsuitable names, 71, 72
   words and expressions for which approval is required, 72
Negligence
   directors, by, 190
   negligent misrepresentation, action for, 58–59
Notice
   constructive, doctrine of, 151, 360
   meetings, of, 274–275, 277
   resolutions, of, 280–281
   special, resolutions requiring, 274–275

Notice—*continued*
   stop, notice, 311–312, 326
   trust, of, 311–312

Objects of company
   alteration of, 97–98
   main, 77–78
   memorandum, clause in, 79–84
   ultra vires rule, 75
Off market dealings, 217, 218
Offences
   disqualification for conviction for, 125, 128
Offer
   securities, of, procedure as to, 41–42, 45
   take-over bid, in,
     acceptance period, 420n
     City Code, standards of behaviour in, 422
     compulsory purchase provisions, 425–426
     directors' recommendation of acceptance, 421
     'take-over offer', meaning, 425
Officer
   definition of, 141, 142
   director as, 158
   disqualification of, 128
   emoluments of, 172
   insider dealings, 213
   liability of, 236
     determination by contract, 142
     relief from, 236
     ultra vires contract, for, 89
   powers of, 142
Official receiver
   liquidator during vacancy, as, 456
   petition for winding up, 443–444
   public examination, application for, 474
Oppression
   minority, of, winding up petition, where, 243–245
Option dealings, 211
Order forms
   registration information required on, 75
Ordinary resolutions, 281–282
Ordinary shares, 281–282

Personal representatives
   dealings in securities, 216

Personal representatives—*continued*
  deceased member, of, 321
  in winding up, 238
Placing, 42
Polls, 276, 279–280
Pre-emptive rights
  existing shareholders, 287–288
  restrictions imposed, 322
Preference
  forms of, 464
  relevant time, ascertainment, 465
Preference shares
  arrears of dividend, right to, 295, 296–297
  cumulative, whether, 295
  disclosure in accounts, 171
  dividend on, preferential, 295
  generally, 294–295
  redeemable, 300, 303
  repayment of capital, preference in, 297
  shareholders, rights of, 294, 297, 300
  surplus assets, participation in, 298
Preferential debts, 461
Preliminary agreement
  agent, liability of, under, 34–36
  difficulty of, 34, 35
  enforcement of, 34–36
  incorporation, before, 34, 35
  legal effects of, 35
  ratification of, whether, 35
Premium, shares issued at
  distribution of premiums, 343
  share premium account, 343, 345–346
Private company
  advertising for deposits, 10
  directors, election and tenure of, 10
  financial assistance for share acquisitions, 430–432
  incorporation as, 10
  limited, 10
  meaning of, 36
  minimal capital requirement, 333
  payment for share capital, 333
  pre-emptive provisions of, 288
  public company,
    distinguished from 9–10
    re-registration as, 11–14
  redeemable shares, 300, 302. *See also* REDEEMABLE SHARES
  trading stamp schemes, 10
  transfer of shares of, 319–320, 321

Proceedings
  actions brought by company, 220
  proceedings at meetings, 277–279
Profit and loss account
  balance sheet, annexed to, 166
  commencement of, 164
  contents of, 167, 168, 169
  modified, 177
Profits
  computation of, corporation tax, for, 382–385
  distribution of,
    assets available for, 354, 357
    fixed assets, special provisions as to, 355
    investment company, of, 356
    profit available for, 357
    reserves unavailable for, 357
    unlawful, 357–358
  promoter, taken by, 31–33
  realised, 354
Promoter
  definition of, 30
  fiduciary duties of, 31–33
  functions of, 30
  liability of, for untrue statement in prospectus, 57
  profits taken by, 31–33
  remuneration of, 33
Proof of debts, 459–460
Property
  directors' substantial transactions, 208–211
  disclaimer of onerous, by liquidator, 467–468
  dispositions of, on winding up, 469–470
Prospectus
  disclosure of information in, 45–47
  expert's statement in, 47, 58
  issue of, 45–47
  misrepresentation in, 51–56, 58
  offer in, meaning, 45
  penalty for contravening statutory provisions, 60
  Stock Exchange requirements, 48
  unlisted securities, rules applying to, 45–46
  untrue statement in,
    compensation for, 46
    criminal liability for, 60
Proxies, 276–277

Public company
  certficate re doing business, 38–40
  conversion to, 11–18
  EEC legislation, effect of,
    effect of, 6, 7
  incorporation of, 10
  loans to directors, 131, 132
  minimum capital requirement,
    application to public company, 10
    failure to satisfy, 15
    memorandum, statement in, 37
    reduction below, 16
    Registrar, declaration to, 39
    statutory provisions, 13–14
  old,
    conversion to private company, 15–18
    meaning of, 36
    payment for share capital, 333
    public or private company status, 14, 15
  payment for,
    assets from subscribers, 336–337
    share capital, 333–336
  private company,
    distinguished from, 9–10
    re-registration as, 16, 17
    redeemable shares, 300. *See also* REDEEMABLE SHARES
  share capital statement in memorandum, 37
  unlawful share allotments, 334–336
Public examination, 474–475

Quorum
  Board of Directors, 145–146
  meetings of members,
    attendance falling below quorums, 271–272
    Court order regarding, 274
    minimum requirement, 278

Ratification
  borrowing *ultra vires*, where, 360
  personal action defeated by, whether, 233–236
  preliminary agreement, of, 35
  special resolution, matters requiring, 222
  ultra vires act, of, 222–223
Receiver
  administrative receiver, 443, 475, 482
  appointment of,
    Court, by the, 374, 376–377

Receiver—*continued*
  appointment of—*continued*
    managing director's service contract and, 127
  assets, application of, 377–378
  borrowing by, 376
  disqualification of, 128
  fiduciary position of, 378
  liquidator, distinguished from, 375
  petition for winding up, 442
  powers of, 376–377
  reports by, 378
  securities, dealing in, 216
  status of, 375
Reconstruction
  protection for,
    creditors, dissenting, 418
    shareholders, dissenting, 415–419
  stamp duty on, 440
  statutory provisions, 415–419
  taxation considerations on, 439–440
Rectification
  register of members, of, 59, 292, 311
Redeemable shares
  breach of contract as to, 303
  private companies, as to, 300, 302
  provisions as to issue of, 300
  public companies, as to, 300
  purchase of,
    contingent purchase contracts, 302
    off-market, 301
    own shares, company's dealings in, 300–303
    stock market, in, 301, 302
  redemption of, 300
  right to issue, 300
Re-election
  director, of, 124
Register
  charges, of,
    company, kept by, 367
    Registrar, kept by, 364
  directors, of, 131
  interests, of,
    directors' interests, 131, 251, 310
    interests in shares, 257
  members, of, 291, 310–312
    rectification of, 59, 292, 311
  restoration of company to, 477
  striking company off, 477
Registered office, 38
Registration
  charges, of, 361–367
  company, of, 36–38

Registration—*continued*
  debentures, of, 362
  extension of time for, 366
  re-registration under Companies Act 1985, 11–18
  resolutions, of, 282–283
Remedies
  debenture holders, for, 373–377
  mis-statement in prospectus, for, 51–59
Removal
  auditor, of, 182
  director, of, 124–127, 243, 437
Remuneration
  auditor, of, 169, 181
  director, of, 131–133, 177
  liquidator, of, 455
  promoter, of, 33
  receiver, of, 376
Report
  auditors', 178, 183–186, 302
  Department of Trade inspectors, by, 239–240, 263
  directors', 179–180
  receiver or manager, by, 378
Requisition
  investigation, of, 260
  meeting, of, 273, 274
Rescission of contract
  conditions for, 52–56, 311
  loss of right to rescind, 54
Reserve capital, 169, 332
Resignation
  auditor, of, 181–182, 274
  director, of, 123–124
Resolutions
  amendment of, 282
  circulation of, 277, 280
  extraordinary, 281
  notice of, 280–281
    special, 274–275
  ordinary, 281–282
  registration of, 282–283
  special. *See* SPECIAL RESOLUTION
  statement in support of, 277
Restrictions
  borrowing, on, 359
  sale of shares and debentures, on, 59–60
  transfer of shares, on, 319–320
Retirement of director
  provisions for, 124, 132–133
  take-over, on, 130, 436
  transfer of business on, 402

Return
  annual, documents annexed to, 162
Revaluations
  details of, in accounts, 169
Rights issue, 42
Royal British Bank v Turquand
  rule in, 151–152

Sale
  shares or debentures, of, restrictions on, 59–60
Scheme of arrangement
  Court, sanction of, 409, 410, 413–414
  matters pursuant to court order, financial assistance for, 431–432
  meaning of arrangement, 407–408
  mergers, for, 408
  orders of Court sanctioning, 414
  procedure for, 409–413
Scotland
  provisions as to floating charges, 366
Seal
  company, 74, 313
Secretary
  powers and duties of, 142–145
  unpublished price sensitive information, knowing, 213
Securities
  advertised, dealing in, 217
  advertisement offering, 53
  disclosure of interests in,
    certain family and corporate, 254–255
    concert parties, 255–257
    directors' interest in, 252
    person acquiring 5% interest, 253–255
  foreign stock exchanges, dealing on, 218
  insider dealing, as to, 211–219
  off-market dealer in, 217, 218
  ownership of, investigation as to, 264
  unpublished price sensitive information,
    definition of, 212
    individuals having, 212–219
Servant
  director as, 158
Share certificate
  estoppel, liability for false representation through, 314–316. *See also* ESTOPPEL
  facsimile common seal for, 313
  forged, 314

Share certificate—*continued*
forged transfer, based on, 317–319
misrepresentation in, 314
statutory requirements, 313
title, as evidence of, 313
Share dealings
prohibitions on, 339, 435
Shareholders. *See also* MEMBERS
alteration of company's articles by agreement between, 117
debenture holder, compared with, 286
minority. *See* MINORITY SHAREHOLDERS
personal action by, 232–236
Share premium account, 333, 344
'Share-pushing', 59–60
Shares
accounts, details to supplement, 169
allotment of. *See* ALLOTMENT
bonus, 42, 335, 343, 393
calls on, 292, 308–309
cancellation of, 342
class rights, variation of, 305–308
classes of, 293–294
compulsory purchase, 425–429
deferred, 304
Department of Trade investigations into, 261, 264,
directors' report, details in, 180
disclosure of interests in,
concert parties, 255–257
directors, 251–253
general requirements, 253–255
discount, issued at a, 334, 343
employees' share scheme, 335
forfeiture of, 340–341
founders', 304
gifts of, 326–330
issue of, 286–291
liability as to, powers of Court to relieve, 338
lien on, 341–342
loans for acquisition of, 169
mortgage of, 329
nature of, 286
ordinary, 303–304
ownership, investigation into company itself, by, 268–270
Department of Trade, by, 264
payment for, 291–293
preference. *See* PREFERENCE SHARES
premium, issued at. *See* PREMIUM, SHARES ISSED AT
private limited company, of, 10

Shares—*continued*
public issue of, 41, 42
purchase of,
loan by company for, 430–431
own shares, 300–303,
petitioner, from, 248, 329, 333, 334
qualification shares of director, 123, 130
redeemable. *See* REDEEMABLE SHARES
redeemable preference, 300
register of interests in, 257
repurchase of, by company, 393
restrictions during investigations, 269
rights issue, 42
sale of, restrictions on, 59–61
stock, conversion into, 304–305, 342
surrender of, 340–341
transfer of. *See* TRANSFER OF SHARES
transmission of, 330–331
valuation of, 249, 325, 335–336
Share warrant, 319
Sheriff
duty of, on winding up, 468
Special notice, 274
Special resolution
actions on matters calling for, 222–223
alteration of articles, for, 110–111
financial assistance for share acquisition, for, 432
private company re-registering, 11–13
procedural requirements, 280–281
public company re-registering, 15
redeemable shares, for purchase of, 302
reduction of capital, for, 349
unlimited company, for conversion of, 17–18
Stamp duty
reconstructions or mergers, on, 440
Stay of actions, 470
Stock
conversion into, 304–305, 342
debenture stock, 367n
Stock exchange
disclosure requirements of, 48
foreign, insider dealing as to, 218
insider dealing in securities, 211–219
listed securities, 44–45
listing rules, 44–45
redeemable shares, 300–303
unlisted securities, control of offers, 45
witness, compellable, 262

Subsidiary company
  accounts of, 165
  definition of, 165
  details of, in holding company's accounts, 170
  directors' report, details in, 179
  documents, powers of disclosure over, 23
  holding company, relationship with, 23–25
  investigation of, 261
  member of holding company, as, 292, 435
  powers of, 24
Surrender of shares, 340–341

Take-over bids
  acceptance of offer, recommendation of, 422
  agent, liability of, 434
  Appeal Committee, 423
  City Code on Take-overs and Mergers, 422, 437
  compulsory purchase provisions, 425–426
  director,
    compensation payments to, 133, 436
    duty to act honestly, 421, 422
    issue of shares, responsibilities as to, 290–291
    removal of, 437–439
  disclosure in, 422, 436
  financial assistance in share acquisitions, 429–435
  function of, 420
  insider dealing, safeguards against, 215, 422–423
  loan by company for purchase of own shares, 430–432
    exceptions to prohibition, 432–433
  meaning of, 420
  minority shareholding, compulsory acquisition of, 425
  offer. *See* OFFER—take over bid, in
  Panel on Take-overs and Mergers, 262, 422–424
  partial bids, 422–423
  scheme of arrangement for, 407
  secrecy, 422
  shareholders, equal treatment of, 422
  shares offered in exchange, 45
  taxation considerations on, 439–440
  void transactions, 433–434

Taxation
  accounts, details to supplement, 169
  advantages and disadvantages of incorporation, 405–406
  capital gains tax. *See* CAPITAL GAINS TAX
  close companies, 396
  company, of, prior to 1965, 379
  corporation tax. *See* CORPORATION TAX
  group of companies, of, 403
  income tax. *See* INCOME TAX
  inheritance tax legislation, 404
  reconstructions, mergers and take-overs, on, 439–440
  residence for tax purposes, 24
  stamp duty, 440
Tort
  company liability, 159
  ultra vires, 89, 90
Trading stamp schemes, 10
Transactions at an undervalue
  avoidance, 463
  relevant time, ascertainment, 464
  types of, 464
Transfer
  business, of,
    company, to, 400
    retirement, on, 402
  debentures, of, 368
Transfer of shares
  breach of trust, in, 314
  certification of, 330
  estoppel, claim by transferee relying on, 314–315
  forged certificate, 317–319
  form of, 325–326
  gift, by, 326–330
  pre-emptive rights, 288, 322–325
  private company, of, 319–320, 321
  refusal to register,
    directors, by, 320–321
    gift, where, 328
  restrictions on, 320
  stop notice, 311–312
  unregistered, 326
  valuation of, 335–336
  winding up, on, 469
Transmission
  death of bankruptcy, on, 330–331
Trust
  notice of, 311–312
  property held on, not assets, 460
  secret profit, where property acquired by, 200

Trustees
debenture holders, for, 372, 374
securities, dealing in, 215–216

Ultra vires
act, action in respect of, 90, 222
borrowing, 360
construction of objects clause, 75–79
contract, 85–88
    remedies for third party, 88–89
crime, in, 89–90
memorandum, acts *ultra vires*, 82
objects clause, 80–85
rule,
    amendment, basis for, 91
    purpose of, 75
    reform of, 90
tort, in, 89, 90

Underwriting
agreement, 43
commission, 43–44

Unfair prejudice
minority, of, 237, 245
petitioner for order, alleged by, 245–246
types of order to remedy, 247

Unlimited company
articles of, 103
conversion of, to limited company, 17, 343
generally, 10–11
liability of members of, 95, 451n
registration, as public company, 14

Unlisted securities
advertisement, 45
Financial Services Act 1986, regulated by, 45, 47
prospectus, requirements, 46

Variation of capital, 343

Variation of class rights
attached to class of shares, 305
cancellation of, application for, 306
class rights, meaning of, 307
procedure for, 306–307
reduction of capital, on, 351
what constitutes, 307

Voluntary arrangement
administrator as supervisor, 478
alternative to winding up, 478
meetings, requirement to summon, 479
procedure, 478–480
proposal, 478

Voluntary arrangement—*continued*
purpose of, 478
supervisor, insolvency practitioner as, 478

Voluntary winding up. *See also* WINDING UP
commencement of, 475
creditors', 449, 450, 457
criminal offence, investigation of, 261
declaration of solvency, 449
dissolution of company, 476–478
distribution of property, order of, 450
extraordinary general meeting, insufficient notice for, 285
liquidation committee, 458
liquidator, 284–285, 454–458
meeting of creditors, 450
members', 449, 454
resolution for, 449

Voting
members' meetings, at, 279
proxies, by, 276–277
restrictions on, voting rights, 279

Winding up
alternatives to, 478–486
assets of company, availability of, 460
capital gains tax on, 401–402
civil remedies, 475
commencement, 475
contributories, 451–452
Court, by the. *See* WINDING UP BY THE COURT
criminal offences, 471–474
disclaimer of onerous property, 467–468
dispositions of property, 469
execution creditors, rights of, 468
floating charges, 466
generally, 441
preference shareholders, rights of, in, 295–296
public examinations, 474
redeemable shares, 303
registration after commencement, 366
stay of actions, 470
transactions at an undervalue, 463
voluntary. *See* VOLUNTARY WINDING UP

Winding up by the court
commencement of, 475
dissolution of company, 476–478
grounds for, 441, 446–447

Winding up by the court—*continued*
   just and equitable, where, 239, 446–447
   liquidator, 453, 455, 456, 457
   orders made by Court, 447, 448
   petition for,
      administrative receiver, by, 443
      allottee of shares, by, 443
      board of directors, by, 443
      contributory, by, 442, 443, 445
      creditors, by, 442, 443, 445

Winding up by the court—*continued*
   petition for—*continued*
      Department of Trade, by, 250, 443, 445
      members, by, 444, 447–448
      receiver, by, 442
   proof of debts, 459–460
Witnesses
   Department of Trade's powers as to, 262